McQUEEN

ALSO BY CHRISTOPHER SANDFORD

FICTION
Feasting with Panthers
Arcadian
We Don't Do Dogs

SPORT
The Cornhill Centenary Test
Godfrey Evans
Tom Graveney

MUSIC
Mick Jagger
Eric Clapton
Kurt Cobain
David Bowie
Sting
Bruce Springsteen

CHRISTOPHER SANDFORD

McQUEEN

The Biography

HarperCollins*Entertainment*
An Imprint of HarperCollins*Publishers*

HarperCollins*Entertainment*
An Imprint of HarperCollins*Publishers*
77–85 Fulham Palace Road,
Hammersmith, London W6 8JB

www.**fire**and**water**.com

Published by HarperCollins*Entertainment* 2001
1 3 5 7 9 8 6 4 2

A catalogue record for this book
is available from the British Library

ISBN 0 00 257195 1

Set in Plantin by
Rowland Phototypesetting Limited,
Bury St Edmunds, Suffolk

Printed and bound in Great Britain by
Clays Ltd, St Ives plc

For Johnny Johnson, Al Meyersahm and
Godfrey Evans – the greats

Contents

LIST OF ILLUSTRATIONS

Steve McQueen and Dustin Hoffman in *Papillon*. © Aquarius Picture Library

Steve McQueen with Ali MacGraw on the set of *The Getaway*. © Aquarius Picture Library

Poster for *The Towering Inferno*. Author's collection

Steve McQueen in Ibsen's *Enemy of the People*. © Aquarius Picture Library

Steve McQueen and Barbara Minty. © Aquarius Picture Library

Steve McQueen in *The Hunter*. © Aquarius Picture Library

William Kelley. © William Kelley

Steve McQueen in 1979. © Aquarius Picture Library

ACKNOWLEDGEMENTS

First, Steve McQueen, who established some of his film characters as living beings. Brilliant actor, hard man. In writing his biography I came to have a quite genuine and deep sympathy, and respect, for him.

For recollections, input and advice I'm grateful to, institutionally: Academy of Motion Picture Arts and Sciences, Amazon.com, *Atlantic Monthly*, Book Mail, British Library, British Newspaper Library, City of Slater, City University, Columbia School District, Consulate of Mexico, County of Los Angeles, Elliott Bay Book Co., *Esquire*, FBI, Focus Fine Arts, Foyles, Gravelly Run, Hollywood Legends, Hollywood Magic, IDS, Indiana Birth and Death Records, Indiana Chamber of Commerce, *Life*, McQuotes, Maltese Falcon, the Margaret Herrick Library, Miller Management Services, Motion Picture Association, National Personnel Records Center, *New York Times*, Orearville School, *People*, Rainier Beach Library, *Rolling Stone*, *Saturday Evening Post*, Seattle *Post-Intelligencer*, Seattle Public Library, *Seattle Times*, *Slater Main Street News*, *Sports Illustrated*, State Bank of Slater, State of California, *Time*, US Consulate Juarez, US Department of Justice: Freedom of Information – Privacy Acts Sections, US Marine Corps, *Variety*, Ventura Missionary Church, the Western Channel.

Professionally: Tony Bill, Virginia Bowden, Linda Lee Caldwell, Charles Champlin, Caroline Chavasse, Angela Cheyne, Cliff Coleman, Gary Combs, Dale Crowe, Paul Darlow, Revd Leonard De Witt, Kathy Di Paolo, Leslie Dufresne, Charles Durning, Richard Dysart, Roger Ebert, Harold Eddy, Bud Ekins, Susan Ekins, Hillard Elkins,

Mike Fargo, Toni Gahl, John Gavin, Jim Geller, Don Gordon, the late Lew Grade, Revd Billy Graham, Gene Griffith, Katy Haber, Natalie Hawn, Bo Hopkins, Jim Hoven, Emily Hurt, Stan Jackson, Kent James, Loren Janes, Norman Jewison, Pat Johnson, Dean Jones, Sam Jones, Marvin Josephson, Dr William Kelley, John M. Kelso, Frank Knox, the late Ring Lardner Jr, Barbara Leigh, the late Jack Lemmon, Barbara Levy, John Little, Biff McGuire, Lucinda McNeile, Neile McQueen Toffel, Karl Malden, Sammy Mason, Lee Mattson, Don Modi, Darla More, Stirling Moss, Jules Mowrer, Don Murray, Gene Neff, Alan Nerob, Bob Newhart, Barry Norman, Hannah Pakula, Fess Parker, Nick Payne, Harold Pinter, the late Donald Pleasence, the late Dilys Powell, Howard Prouty, the late Anthony Quayle, Neil Rand, Robert Redford, Marian Reid, Robert Relyea, Wayne Rogers, Dee Dee Sadler, Jim Stanfield, Sally Struthers, Bud Summers, Marshall Terrill, Jack Valenti, Eli Wallach, Burt Ward, David Weddle, Bill Wilcott, Ken Wilson, Robert Wise, Dave Wolfe, Dora Yanni.

And socially: Pete Barnes, Jeanne and Ray Bates, Robert and Hilary Bruce, Chao Praya, Albert Clinton, *Cricketer International*, Deb K. Das, Monty Dennison, John and Marie Dowdall, Milan Drdoš, John Engstrom, Mary Evans, Malcolm Galfe, the Gay Hussar, Jeff Griffin, Patrice Haultcoeur, Marlys Higgins, Charles Hillman, Hollywood Roosevelt Hotel, Amy Hostetter, Jo Jacobius, Rick Keat, Reggie Kendall, Kinko's, the late George Lambert, Joan Lambert, Terry Lambert, Lon Landis, Belinda Lawson, Lazerquick, Vince Lorimer, Melinda Maxwell, the late Al Meyersahm, Jim Meyersahm, Michael's Toyota – Hamid Borjian, Sheila Mohn, Liz Morganroth, Chuck Ogmund, Robin Parish, Peter Perchard, Chris Pickrell, the Prins family, Keith Richards, Amanda Ripley, Debbie Saks, Delia Sandford, Karen Sandford, Sefton Sandford, Peter Scaramanga, Seattle CC, Sue Sims-Hilditch, Fred and Cindy Smith, Katie Spalding, Debbie Standish, the Stanleys, Ti-fa, Tucker, Ben and Mary Tyvand, Tony Vinter, Lisbeth Vogl, Von's, Victoria Willis Fleming, Zoopa. I owe a special debt to my son Nicholas. Northwest Airlines, Patricia Price and Sprint were no help at all.

Thanks, Tim Wilson.

C.S.
2001

'The soul of the thing is the thought;
the charm of the act is the actor;
The soul of the fact is its truth, and the
NOW is its principal factor'
Eugene Fitch Ware

'I'm a little screwed up, but I'm beautiful'
Steve McQueen

1

The American Dream

Steve McQueen was dead. It was a strange enough ending for a life that had scaled the heights of fame and plumbed the depths of depravity, laid out in a cold bare-walled room in a Mexican clinic. On this November morning a pale, watery sun came through the barred windows, sending chopped-up light onto the narrow bed. All the grief which marked the last year of McQueen's life seemed purged by death. His eyes which, oddly, had turned dark grey were blue once more. In his hands was a Bible, turned to McQueen's favourite verse, 'For God so loved the world, that he gave his only begotten Son, that whosoever believeth in him should not perish but have everlasting life.' A doctor and a nurse both noticed the look that came over him at the end. It was the quizzical half-grin he made his own, that frighteningly unamused smirk at once attractive and not quite welcoming. Steve McQueen was himself again.

The king of cool had died at fifty. If the cancer hadn't done for him, then a human agent had: according to McQueen's doctor, it is 'certain' that a person or persons injected him with a fatal coagulant late on 6 November 1980, his final night alive. His patient was, he says, executed as he lay drugged and immobilised in a hospital bed. But no one should feel pity for Steve McQueen. He was neither broken nor bitter. Sick as he was, the happiest chapter of his life may have been the last one, in the care of Barbara, his third wife, flying his antique planes and slipping anonymously into church. He'd been living first in an aircraft hangar and then in a ranch with a big

1

pot-bellied stove that filled half the room. Behind the house were fields and behind the fields were mountains. Here, in Santa Paula, California reminded Steve of the Missouri heartland he'd fled as a boy but never left. Here, the circle was complete.

A few other circles had been closed, too. McQueen's first ever appearance on the big screen was as a prowling, knife-wielding punk. For his minuscule role as Fidel in 1956's *Somebody Up There Likes Me* he earned $19 a day. Twenty-four years later, *The Hunter* ended on a poignantly downbeat note with McQueen spark out on a hospital floor. For that picture he made $3 million, plus 15 per cent of the gross. Running as a throughline in between, film audiences met one of the most arresting personalities in American art. Not too many others could hold a candle to McQueen's striking affirmation of individuality. Far, far from the usual Hollywood pieties, Steve spent his off-duty hours dirt-biking or squatting in the desert with Navajo Indians. As a man, few ever came close to him. As an actor, nobody did. At his worst, McQueen gave off a quietly passionate sense of love and loss, eyes reeling with meaning, which perhaps promised more than it delivered. On peak form, he gave substance to even the thinnest plot. Not since the salad days of Brando had the words 'movie' and 'star' been in such proximity. Above all, McQueen knew that performance wasn't a matter of right and wrong but of life and death – of the material. Jim Clavell, who worked up *The Great Escape*, would say that 'Steve played suffering perfectly,' since it chimed so well with his experience.

'*Lo hice* – I did it' were McQueen's last known words. Towards the end, according to an orderly who was there, he 'talked a lot about the early days, the farm, growing up and most of all reform school'. His nostalgia for the lost world of 1945 hid a grim truth: Steve had been committed by his own mother and her new husband. The squat bunker of Junior Boys Republic, the burr-cuts and bib overalls, the carbolic smell ground deep into the floor, the reek of the laundry – those were the stinking madeleines of his youth. And as McQueen lay dying, pressing ice cubes to his cheeks, doctors would hear him sob, 'Three-one-eight-eight,' over and over, his old school number of thirty-five years earlier echoing his fluttering heartbeat. Steve went out, if not with a whimper, then whey-faced for all the bewildered souls, not for his legendary groupies and least of all for Candyland, but for the 'real folks'. For those who like their types cast, it was a quite heroic death.

They took him to the mortuary in Juarez, bumping along dusty roads where paparazzi from across the border already cowered behind trees. The *Globe* and *Enquirer* stringers squealed like game-show contestants when the car pulled in to the Prado Funerales. On that frenetic morning reporters were attempting to bribe medical staff with $80,000 for a shot of the corpse. In the end it was *Paris Match* who located McQueen's body, calmly lifted the undertaker's sheet and got off a picture for their front page. An orderly took exception and wound up rolling around with the photographer on the morgue floor. Later that afternoon the cortege made its way to the frontier town of El Paso, Texas, where a private jet stood fuelled and ready for the flight to Santa Paula. The sight of more press on the runway even as the plane revved up set off a round of groans and denunciations among McQueen's friends. It was like the climactic scene from *Bullitt*. Two hours later they landed in California in thick fog. The plain Mexican coffin, flimsy for even his gaunt body, was loaded on a station wagon and taken to the Chapel of Rest in Ventura for cremation.

It was what McQueen had wanted. He'd always hated fires. He was nearly killed by one as a boy and in later years often had occasion to head-butt his demons. 'You lookin' at me?' or a tart 'Fuck you, candyass' defiantly masked his inner terrors. Steve once ran through hot smoke to rescue his wife and young baby from a brush fire in Laurel Canyon. Drink and dope were balanced, for him, not only by fast cars but by constantly testing how he felt about himself and nature; and McQueen experienced that sense of challenge again in 1966, when he helped fight a three-alarm blaze at the studio. Ironically, the two worlds of fact and fiction finally merged eight years later when, at a routine briefing with the technical adviser on *The Towering Inferno*, McQueen responded to a real-life emergency by suiting up to save yet another torched stage. On that occasion a fireman looked over his shoulder, started and blurted out, 'Holy crap! Steve! My wife won't believe this.' 'Neither will mine,' said McQueen calmly.

The body was burnt, and the ashes placed in a cheap urn. Steve had wanted 'nothing fancy' for himself, and he was famous for his spartan tastes – a can of Old Milwaukee was fine by him. Especially towards the end: by then, instead of goons and gofers, McQueen was keeping company with a distinctly rough-hewn crew of local barnstormers and pilots. Together they shared hobbies and traditions that were already old when Steve was born. They had an overriding love of keeping it simple, and many was the night they sat around the hangar, drinking and hugging themselves against the cold, whooping it up at Hollywood. This new McQueen was, above all, 'real folks', which is to say much the sort of person done on screen by the old McQueen. He favoured flying the flag in every school, early nights, and affirming the sanctity of marriage. That never ruled out a beer or a smoke. As for protocol, he didn't overdo it. McQueen's language was famously earthy. As far as acting went, he felt as if he'd pissed away about twenty years, wondering aloud what the fuck he'd been doing in half his films, although he always cashed the cheques. 'You know, guys,' Steve would say, squinting up at the snowy Rafaels, 'I only really feel horny when I'm flying.'

They took the urn up in McQueen's favourite antique Stearman, headed for the coast and scattered his ashes over the Pacific. That big bug. He'd loved it almost as much as he loved wheels. Fumes and altitude, the part of the American dream that went high and fast. Up there in the yellow biplane all the lines and wrinkles and what Steve called 'broken glass' were dissolved, blown away in the alpine air. They'd watched him, Sammy and Doug and Clete and the other flyboys, as he'd climbed sheer gradients, swooping with wild speed, and, just as fast, pulling back, rushing headlong towards the mountains, then levelling out at last towards the trails that went up into the hills and the clear sharpness of the peaks beyond. He would waggle his wings and it was exciting to him as though he were living, or at least exhaling, for the first time. That and the ranch and the silvered grey of the sagebrush, the quick, clear water of the Santa Clara and the missionary church were the sights and sounds he'd chosen for himself at the end. He'd always had a great imitative style, attitudes and poses associated with other people. But for the last year at least, Steve McQueen was playing himself.

That flight in the Stearman was a defining symbol of McQueen's real breakthrough: that worldly success, for which he'd fought the System like two ferrets in a sack, was yet more 'shit'. He was back to basics. Fire, air and sea were the true representation of Steve's own words echoing down his last year – 'Keep it elemental.' His friends said a prayer for him over the water and came back low across the channel to Ventura. On McQueen's orders, there was no grave or marker of any sort. His widow moved out of the ranch to a remote cabin in Idaho, and the plane and McQueen's other goods were mainly given away. That, too, chimed with the 'poor, sick, ragged kid' who was father to the man.

Even Steve's latter-day humility wasn't enough to protect his cherished privacy. They came from all parts looking for clues, fans and paparazzi alike, doorstepping the ranch and swarming round his figure – soon removed by curators – at Hollywood's wax museum. More than a few straggled back to the clinic, but none pierced the narcotic smog of medical debate, especially on the knotty subject of 'alternative' cancer treatment. Certainly nobody seriously floated the idea that McQueen had been murdered.

William Kelley, a one-time Texas dentist who apparently cured himself of cancer and went on to found the impressively styled International Health Institute, first treated a man posing as Don Schoonover in April 1980. 'I told Schoonover – who turned out to be Steve – what he had to do. Sure enough, he began to get better . . . Six months later McQueen was in the clinic in Juarez and wanted to have his dead tumours surgically removed. I advised him of the risk, but Steve, being Steve, insisted. "I'm going to blow the lid off of the American cancer-treatment scam," he told me. The medical establishment was freaked, shit scared of being exposed by a man like that. I was there the last night of his life, and I know what happened.'

A gutsy pioneer and whistleblower, or a demented nut? When Kelley started his institute, he had no surgical and little enough medical kudos. Even his orthodontist's licence had been suspended after people complained that he was more interested in treating other health problems than in straightening teeth. A court injunction then briefly stopped publication of his book, *One Answer to Cancer*. By 1976 Kelley was being investigated by more than a dozen government agencies. For several years he and his wife moved onto an organic farm in Washington state, fantasised as a place of old-fashioned ideals, perfect peace, happiness and wholeness, with good vibes for all. He sold vitamins.

At this stage Kelley expanded his mail-order business and began hawking a 'nonspecific metabolic therapy' programme to patients disillusioned, like him, with the American Medical Association. His staggeringly complex nutritional regimen had some striking successes. Nobody knows exactly how many people are alive today because of him. However, after co-leasing the clinic in Mexico, Kelley achieved a series of remissions and apparent cures in even terminal cancer cases, McQueen allegedly among them. Both nurses and surgeons agree that the tumours removed from McQueen's body were themselves already dead – 'like cotton candy', Kelley explains. 'Steve was cancer-free for the last six months of his life. He died, pure and simple, of an induced blood clot.' The accusation comes from a man, it has to be said, whose diet- and enema-based remedies landed him on the American Cancer Society's blacklist. Some of Kelley's deathbed scenario is also, like his therapy, nonspecific, but when his last doctor says 'Steve was done in,' you can be sure it's because he believes it and not because of some slick dash he's trying to cut. It would be astonishing if a freelance American celebrity like Kelley were vanity free, and he isn't. With his treatment of McQueen already on record, he makes sure that people know of his other accomplishments – that he's survived attacks by the FBI and the CIA, along with the 'enemy Jew-controlled establishment', for over thirty years. If Kelley's racism repels, there's still another strain in him that attracts as well. He talks fast, with a wheedling energy, but also with a wry humour and a string of wisecracks. Above all, he was there when Steve needed help, almost certainly prolonged his life, and was intimately involved in the events of 6–7 November 1980. Kelley may be a radical; he's no nut.

Why did McQueen turn to what his first wife, at least, calls the 'charlatans and exploiters'? The question still fascinates Hollywood's ruling class who, for the most part, stood in such awe of him. Possibly because he felt so marginal – he never met his father and barely knew his mother – McQueen had the lifelong need to feud, to 'twist people's melons', as he put it. Intrinsic to nearly everything he did was the sense of proving both himself and others. The truculence became part of this pattern, and any attempt to separate it from the gentler, mature Steve would split what's indivisible. Throughout his life he was a cynic sometimes made credulous by his urge – almost a pathological need – to wing it. And McQueen would have automatically been well disposed towards anyone who, like Kelley, was at war with the world.

Sam Peckinpah, a man whose wit outlived his liver, put it best: Steve was every guy you didn't fuck with. There are various mysteries about McQueen, shy kid and adult male equivalent of the Statue of Liberty, the chief one being that he seemed to be several different people. He was the insecure boy who didn't much like being famous. Mostly he liked being alone, driving a straight ribbon of blacktop through the canyon dirt and past the lemon groves and orchards down into the desert. He loved the open spaces. Animals he usually tolerated but didn't trust. People were 'bad shit'. If there was any fellow-feeling, it was towards those he saw as other loners. There was the pill-popping and grog-quaffing McQueen who worked out three hours daily in the gym. There was the loving husband who boasted of 'more pussy than Frank Sinatra' on the side. There was the dumb hick (his phrase) who fought the studio system to a draw. The charismatic man who brought oxygen into a room. The last true superstar. The great reactor.

McQueen was the character who revels in his rebelliousness, the larger-than-life stud and free spirit who was actually a martyr to self-hate. During the periods when he wasn't working Steve would get monumentally wasted, one of his typical pranks being when he stopped exercising and drank or snorted himself into oblivion. The pattern became a familiar one. While there was a suicidal component in some of these binges, McQueen didn't actually want to die – the need for revenge was still too powerful for that. But he depended for his survival on a small but fanatically loyal gang of old friends; and his rude health. When most of those went south, and he made a genuine if tardy conversion to God, it's not surprising McQueen pondered his options with Bill Kelley.

In the late 1960s, when Steve reached adulthood and suddenly realised he didn't want to be there, the inverted world of movies was a wonderfully soothing place. McQueen's personal myth, what he called his mud, ran to the bitter end. Many of the actual parts played were laughably weak, but McQueen was better than his scripts. Character counted with him, because in the end character was all there was. More than anyone, he knew that films exist in a kind of delicate balance with their moment. They can, sometimes mysteriously, either catch or miss their time. His own defining eloquence – a combination of the tough and the goofy – spoke directly to the embattled, mixed-up spirit of a war-torn republic. No one did the Sixties better than McQueen. He was, said Frank Sinatra, who would have known, 'absolutely the greatest zeitgeist guy. Ever.'

The designation was hard won. Obviously he wasn't someone, like a De Niro, who physically aped his characters. The question of full-scale possession remains. All the fear and doubt and past experience McQueen brought to bear only heightened the surface dazzle of his cool under-playing. He didn't call it a method: it was a policy, a life-plan of realism that was simply a part of him. It was also a good way for him to 'twist melons'.

Karl Malden remembers a scene he did with McQueen in *The Cincinnati Kid*. 'Steve came on, in character, to confront me about whether I was double-dealing cards. He sprang at me like an animal. McQueen was prowling around the room where we were shooting, and he was absolutely terrifying. His fiery blue eyes were covered with an electric glaze and he was whipping about like a loose power line. He was so tense, I felt like I was gonna see an actor blow up for real . . . I mean, I was in awe of him.' And this was a tough guy himself, who'd worked with Brando.

His aggression! People who knew and even loved Steve still marvel at it. It consumed him. The actor Biff McGuire remembers an odd and touching instance of it on *The Thomas Crown Affair*. This particular take called for McQueen to chip a golf ball out of a bunker, something that could have been done in a minute using a double or some other trick. 'Steve toiled away at the shot most of the day, trying to hit the ball – going off to rest after a while, but then drawn back to it, totally focused on the job. He'd swing over and over and the ball would dribble up just a few inches and roll back in the pit again. Sometimes the director and crew would encourage him, but mostly I remember him alone, with that blinkered "Don't fuck with me" expression of his, the club poised, then down, and the little shower of sand would spurt up. But everyone knew Steve would get the ball on the green, and in the end he did.'

He must have holed out just in time for his next – and best – picture, *Bullitt*. McQueen's long-time friend (and sidekick in the film) Don Gordon was on location with him in San Francisco. 'As well as kicking against the producers and suits generally, Steve applied his monster talent for competitiveness every night. First, he had both our motorbikes secretly shipped up from LA – secretly because the studio would've thrown a fit. He stowed them somewhere in a private lock-up. Around five every evening, just as the spring light was softening, Steve would yawn and announce he was turning in early. An hour later we'd meet at the garage and zip up into the hills, just the world's biggest movie star and me, Steve thrilled like a kid breaking curfew but his edge immediately taking over.' Gordon would good-naturedly watch McQueen put the throttle on and roar off into the dark. He 'took it hard and fast because he was damn good, but also because he was stoked by knowing someone else was right behind him. I mean, Steve had to win.'

When McQueen died, more than twenty years ago, there was still a mythical America; an individual could still wrap himself in that myth. A large part of the legend had already gone Hollywood – not least in the lens of a John Ford or Frank Capra – before McQueen, but he also created his own. Vulnerability, decency and a real sense of menace all combined to fix him as the 'new Bogie', although Steve's on-screen chemistry with women was the more toxic of the two. Some are put in mind of the 'torn shirt' school epitomised by Montgomery Clift and Brando, though McQueen's reputation was always based on rather more than a few grunts and stylised nasal tics. With rare exceptions, he kept upping the risk, enlarging the dimensions of his own performance both on screen and off. Each of Steve's roles was a grander and more precariously improvised adventure of the mind. His tragedy was that he could neither change the world nor ignore its creation of him. But it made for a life.

McQueen was able, out of his arrogance, to do something which was selfless. Of course he cashed the cheques, but in the best roles he created the walk, the look and the presence of the truly universal. Steve McQueen's is the story of our time.

2

War Lover

Many of Steve's first memories were of machines; they seemed to exert a pull on him from the start. They stood out, conspicuous against the human world, notable for their tireless, solid qualities, their efficiency, their resilience and power. They seemed responsive to his touch, and they were rational. He quickly found his place.

His time, early spring of 1930, was one of uneventful peace brooding over Europe. Britain grappled with its perennial labour and sterling crises and the worldwide trade slump, both cause and result of the Depression. The sovereign people of the US still lumped it under President Hoover, Advisory Boards on everything from Reconstruction Finance to Illiteracy marking the real beginning, three years pre-Roosevelt, of the New Deal. Yet, if lacking in surface drama, 1930 was still a turning-point, with two or three events of real long-term significance. In Germany the first Nazis took public office; on the sub-continent Gandhi began his civil disobedience campaign, with all the dislocation *that* entailed; and in the American rust-belt Steve McQueen was born.

It was a grim enough time, an icy 24 March, and a grim enough spot, the Indianapolis suburb of Beech Grove. He was delivered at ten that morning in the branch hospital, hard by the Conrail depot, where shabby passenger cars came to be fixed. Among the first sounds he would have heard were of engines. Everywhere more and more machinery was grinding: the city mills were still running at full bore and coal was being quarried in record weight. The factories blasted night and day; the clang of iron plates made a thought-annihilating thunder. The stockyards sent up a thick reek, wooden shacks standing beside animal swamps which bubbled and stank like stewing tripe. Dirty snow hillocks formed along the kerbs and sewage water ran raw and braided in the gutters. The inner slums, like Beech Grove, were already long since pauperised. Even the leprous hospital block was half-enveloped in weeds. This was the place, full of blood, stench and the sulphurous glare of the railyard, that fixed itself in the young boy's imagination.

It's often said that McQueen lived five lives, the juvenile and late years and one time around with each of his three wives. Like many people he used to wonder whether, in the last resort, those mewling early days weren't the happiest and best. 'I remember running in the hog yards ... My people had this big field. And I'd come lighting out from school and play [there] and I remember how buzzed I felt.' In later life Steve was skilled at softening hard memories with happy stories. His nostalgia for the 1930s and 1940s masked the grim truth that he was odds-on illegitimate, very probably abused and certainly unwanted. The experience left McQueen with the unshakable conviction that he was 'a dork', a friend explains. 'He always described himself exactly that way. Steve was very sold on his being damaged goods.'

His mother, Julia Ann Crawford, known as Julian, was a nineteen-year-old runaway and drunk. In 1927 she'd taken off from the family farm for the city. Julian was blonde and pert, an apparently stylish and independent woman, if not the model of sanity. On closer inspection her very face was demented. Julian's eyes, small and dark, suggested a substitute set of nostrils at the wrong end of her nose. At moments of excitement her head would loll wildly. She soon made a whole lifestyle out of being fractious. For a while it was only semi-prostitution, but before long Julian was dancing the hoochy-koochy and swigging 'tea', which she fortified from a silver flask in her handbag. Lipstick smudged across her pasty cheeks, face drawn, arms frail, black dress cinched round her thighs, stockings rolled down, she lurched from partner to partner, half gone but occasionally soaring into a shrill, manic high. The city authorities often called for her.

Long before bi-polarity had a name, Julian was screwing herself in and out of madness.

In June 1929 she met and bedded an ex-flyboy named Bill McQueen. Steve's mysterious father was one of those old-time rowdies who bent iron bars, pulled trains with their teeth or barnstormed at county fairs. All that's known of his early days is that he flew in the navy and later toured North America with an aerobatic circus. Aside from drink, his two major loves in life were of planes and gambling. On his twenty-first birthday Bill came into a windfall of $2000. He took the cash and opened an illegal casino called Wild Will's below a brothel on Indianapolis's Illinois Street. After the club folded he became a drifter and an alcoholic. Around 1928 he began to suffer so badly from liver attacks and heart trouble that his doctor had to dull the pain with morphine. That set up yet another vicious circle of addiction. By the time Bill met Julian Crawford he was a sick man, in his late twenties but prematurely aged, with death all over him. They lived for a while in a rooming house, riding the trolley down to Schnull's Block, the commercial zone, looking for work. None ever came. When Steve McQueen was born the following March, his parents had to apply for funds under the Poor Law. Julian took Bill's surname, though there is no evidence they ever married. The father took off one night six months later, leaving the mother and son in a dismal hotel downtown. Bill came back once, a few weeks later, asking to be forgiven. Julian kicked him out.

Bill headed for the hills.

Steve's claim that 'my life was screwed up before I was born' might be mawkish, but there's no denying the shadow cast by this earliest 'shit', as he called it. Right to the end, he often quoted *The Merchant of Venice*, 'The sins of the father are to be laid on the children', sometimes substituting 'of the mother'. The rich, famous and fulfilled man the world saw still considered himself a freak maimed for life by that early catastrophic shock.

In both manner and matter, McQueen was firmly tied to the fate of a bastard child of the 1930s. He rarely or never trusted anyone, and knew the value of a dollar as well as a crippling sense of doubt throughout years that were gritty and filled with struggle. It was a new world he grew up in, unique to the place, peculiar to the time;

and, his friend confirms, 'always, to Steve, something of a cross'. On the very morning he was born the weather broke in a filthy shawl of snow. Back in the rooming house the pipes had to be thawed with blow-torches while Bill brooded over his bottles. By day thick fog descended, leaving spectacular rime deposits on Market Street. At night the White river froze solid and the cold seemed to have the pygmy's power of shrinking skin. Even in early spring, few of the locals ventured beyond the narrow confines of the city canal. Trains would haul freight and animals east, but rarely people. Some did claim they liked to travel, but they meant to Chicago perhaps, 130 miles north, or that they once visited St Louis. Indianapolis had few illusions about ever becoming world class. It was the typical submerged existence of the poor; people accepted it, hardly realising that their destiny could ever have been different. In short, it was the kind of place that teaches a boy to be practical while it forces him to dream of other, headier realities.

The past slowly faded: Civil War veterans, though a few still held court in Military Park; Indians, first as names and then as faces; even the great Jazz Age of the twenties. Culture in the Midwest was a marginal enterprise. The news that March Monday in the *Hoosier Star* was of Hitler, Gandhi and Stalin, and closer to home of Indianapolis itself, where the talk was of unemployment, foreclosures and the Ku Klux Klan. On the 24th fiery crosses burned on Mars Hill and the downs around Beech Grove, and the Catholic cathedral was pipe-bombed. Thugs terrorised Jewish shopkeepers. That long winter's gloom wasn't just climatic; it acted on the streets and the houses, but also on character, mood and outlook. It was a powerful depressant.

Nineteen-thirty was also, on another level, a time of mass escapism. The old music halls had gone, but the dramatic heart of the nation started up again in the movies. Sixty million men, women and children paid at the box office weekly. Mummified 'flickers' were fast giving way to modern production values: widescreen action in general and the Grandeur process in particular were blazed in 1930's *The Big Trail*, starring John Wayne. The Depression would prove to be Hollywood's finest hour. *Disraeli*, *The Blue Angel* and *All Quiet on the Western Front* were all soon playing amid a relentless diet of Dracula and primitive adult and slasher films. That same March Al Jolson opened in *Mammy*, while Garbo's first talkie, *Anna Christie*, started out as an epic and soon mutated into something more, a picture Julian herself saw every night for a week. Between times, she would trudge with Steve to the downtown Roxy or sneak into the Crescent 'colored house', full of smoke, chrome and low-budget flickers which faded away to reveal the main visual drama – punch-ups and, in not a few cases, lynchings in the surrounding ghetto dealt out by the Klan. It was here that McQueen first made the acquaintance of sex and violence.

Meanwhile, more and more concerned women's groups said that children could not be trusted around a cinema.

And yet the Daughters of the American Revolution probably weren't unhappy. They had one cause of never-failing interest, and that was censorship. That same year Hoover established the Motion Picture Production Code, the so-called Hays Office, to police a grow-ing trend towards blasphemy or crude Scandinavian naturism. Later in 1930 Loew's on Meridian Street was actually raided during a live illustration of 'civic hygiene' involving two women, a tub and their silk smalls in a striking combination. According to the deadpan police report, 'The sexual parts, around which the pubic hairs seem[ed] to have been shaved off, [were] clearly visible and so imperfectly covered by the wash cloth, that the lips bulge[d] out to the left and right of the towel . . . The glands were uncovered.' Mae West's celebrated trial on a similar morals rap opened in New York. This early, seminal association of the lively arts with sex and rowdyism was one Steve became aware of early on and never forgot. Play-acting would give him the licence to be dirty, sweaty and lewd, the licence to get even, to make the real world vanish – and, eventually, to blow town. Once he started emulating the hoary two-reelers from Hollywood, it was only a matter of time for him and the rust-belt.

The pre-war decade was also a great flying era. Stunt pilots, barn-stormers and wing-walkers attracted crowds undreamed of in the 1920s. Air displays sold out. In the same three-month period Charles Lindbergh and his wife set a transcontinental speed record, Amy Johnson made the haul from London to Sydney and Francis Chich-ester brought off the first solo crossing by seaplane from New Zealand to Australia. Bill's intense devotion to this world reflected the same recklessness his son later experienced in drinking, drug-taking and dirt-biking. Like his father, Steve put himself on the line, on-screen and off; he dared all and he 'went for it' until self-destruction, or a sense of parody, kicked in. His whole career was the celluloid equivalent of the Barrell Roll. Long before he went aloft in his own vintage Stearman, McQueen had already flaunted his patronymic DNA – what Julian called the 'butch, brawling, ballsy' school of life. The winging it.

Born to poverty and bred to insecurity, Steve soon thrived on loneliness. He could never pinpoint how old he was when he first began to feel wretched in his own skin, but the critical scene haunted him the rest of his life. Running upstairs to the dive he shared with Julian, he suddenly heard her screaming, 'hollering and howling [like] she was bein' done in' but accompanied, curiously, by gales of mirth from the neighbours' stoop. His mother was in bed there with a sailor. 'We ragged him,' says a childhood friend, Toni Gahl. 'Steve was very sort of geeky in those days. He was dirt poor, wore britches and Julian was no more than a prize slut. The other kids were down on him.'

So, suddenly, life became bewildering, and before he could even read or write McQueen was a reformatory case. His fate to always be the outsider was blazed early on. He was old enough to know he was 'trash', and young enough to dream about being part of a fantasy world in the movies. An imaginative, hyperactive child who would always rather be elsewhere, doing something else, Steve came to hate his mother even more than his runaway father. Every night he wandered among the drunks and rat-infested garbage while Julian turned tricks in their bedroom.

McQueen's later binges were also a legacy of Bill's – and Julian's – world. What went into his movies was part of what went into his monumental craving for sex and drugs. The plethoric screwing, in particular, wasn't normally for fun or pleasure; nor, says a well-placed source, was it 'likely to thrill the girl. Steve was very much a wham, bam guy, not the kind to pour sap about love in your ear.' That, too, echoed his father (motto: 'They're all grey in the night'), whose mark was in the boy's marrow. His very names, Terrence Steven, were in honour of a figuratively legless, literally one-armed punter at

Wild Will's. The 'McQueen', from the Gaelic *suibhne*, meant 'son of the good or quiet man'. As a derivative it was strictly out of the ironic-name school, and in fact, two choicer words could hardly be used to describe Bill. His own father had been a soldier, from a family of soldiers or sailors, who had moved from Scotland around 1750. By the early nineteenth century the McQueens were living in North and South Carolina before fanning out west at the time of the Civil War. An Arian (the 'me' sign), Steve was by a neat twist, within a few weeks' age of both Sean Connery and Clint Eastwood, the three great ball-clanking icons of their era. The 24th of March was also celebrated in ancient Rome as the Day of Blood. Any child born that day was likely to be punished by an early death.

Julian's people were devout Catholics and tradesmen in Slater, Missouri, gently rolling farm country midway between Columbia and Kansas City. For most of the 1930s she and Steve would shuttle from Indianapolis to the heartland and back, boarding with her parents and fostering an arbitrary highway persona, equal parts brief, ad hoc arrangements and cyclical transience, which he never broke. Much of McQueen's on-screen insight came from the highly imaginative and disturbed five-year-old who once clutched his mother's hand in genuine perplexity:

'What's wrong with us?'

Julian remained mute.

'I'm starving, Ma.'

Julian was unaware of it at the time, but he was consumed with envy when he compared life even to that of the other slum kids in the city. Most of his peers were living in semi-comfort, while he had to content himself with cast-off clothes and meagre, wolfed-down meals. Toni Gahl remembers that Steve 'didn't say a lot. Basically he was pretty much of a clenched fist.'

Around mid-decade things, already apparently at their darkest, would turn black. Julian's father went broke in the slump and he and his wife moved in with the latter's brother Claude Thomson, a hog baron with a prodigious appetite for moonshine and also, with that spread, catnip to the ladies. The next time the bus pulled in from Indianapolis, Julian and Steve also joined the displaced family.

17

Claude lived on a 320-acre farm on, aptly, Thomson Lane, three miles out of Slater by Buck creek. It was as near to a fixed childhood home as Steve ever had. He spent eleven years there on and off, sometimes with his mother, more often not. A woman named Darla More once saw him, head down, tramping alongside the Chicago & Alton railway between Slater and Gilliam. 'Steve was just a poor, sad, fatherless, mixed-up kid. I don't think it's possible for a human being to look as absolutely beat as he did at that moment.' More sat down with him and learnt that Julian had left for Indianapolis, without bothering to tell her son, the night before. 'Steve slumped there on the tracks and wept his eyes out. It sounds corny, but I promptly went and picked a flower to cheer him up and gave it to him. I still remember the smile Steve flashed me back.' When alluding to the scene in later years, McQueen himself would sometimes choke and have to compose himself.

In all, Steve grew up in 'about twenty different shacks and dumps', he said, and his imagination seems to have provided more richly furnished accommodations. There were any number of lifelong connections from that era, but a handful beat a straight path to sado-masochism: watching Julian casually come and go, for example, her soft, fat lips, her assertion that fun was more important than family.

Neglected by both parents, he was raised in large part by a man who ran the farm with a mixture of shrewdness, opportunism and brute force. Husbandry in those days was an often violent business, and they did have gangsters in Missouri. In fact, the only mention of crime in the Slater paper for Christmas 1933 records a sorry fall from grace: on 24 December two men shot at a third after catching him interfering with a sow. Although Uncle Claude owned several guns, there was no suggestion that he was tied up in this scandal. He did, however, protect his own, worked all hours and drove a hard bargain. All through the Depression he made a good living, becoming one of Slater's richest men. Unfortunately, he was also an alcoholic whose great-nephew, for all the Catholic ritual and dogma his family tried to beat into him, grew up virtually wild.

Accordingly, Steve stood far closer to the moonshine than to any holy sacraments. By contrast, Julian's mother Lil was a religious nut and disciplinarian said by McQueen to habitually 'spit icicles in July'.

She fussed around the white stucco home (first in the county to get electricity), a rambling pile with sixty-five scalloped windows and endless corridors, all lined with bad paintings and an occasional life-size nude. What Claude Thomson had in cash, he lacked in class, the threadbare rugs and wooden pews (to give things a churchy feeling) contributing to a kind of mingy staleness. Despite all the glass, the farm had a dark, gothic feel, grimy paint and heavy mahogany mingling with a reek of dishwater, slops and Lil's speciality, garlic, oozing from the kitchen. Everybody muttered about private grievances and never shared. In an unresolved row over money, Claude soon evicted his sister and her husband, who moved into an unlit railway car put up on blocks in a neighbouring field. When Lil was later widowed, her brother promptly had her committed to the state hospital for the insane.

Slater itself, of 4000 souls and a single stop-light, was inhabited by cadaverously thin men in overalls working the land for soya beans, by the peculiar musty stench of the loam and salt deposits, by defecating hogs and ancient trucks beached in front yards, by fire-and-brimstone preachers and illicit stills and funereal hillbilly music drifting up out of tomb-dark shacks. Local politics were a depressing spectacle, most attitudes pre-Lincolnian, race relations fundamental. Tradition was all. The place boasted twenty-one Protestant and two Catholic churches. Behind these lay the wheatfields and the occasional plantation, like Claude's, in a grove of trees; obviously places of pretension at one time. The whole area was a throwback to a vanishing America. As for the people, they may have been, as Claude said, 'no Einsteins', but for the most part they possessed a certain earthy frankness. They were also capable, gruff, and kissed up to no one, including a new, 'dorky' arrival. Steve now knew what it was like to be shunned in two communities.

The trouble grew worse each year, especially after McQueen worked out the full truth of his parentage. From the start, though fully alive to the gossip, he'd been determined to ignore it, to 'shut [himself] down'. At first there were only whispered reports; the locals simply looked away when he walked by. Returning along the trail that led across the creek to town, deep in the green shade of the thickest part of the prairie-grass, Steve was regularly aware of the same group of boys sitting at a turn of the road, at a place just before it led up the hill to the railroad and the shops. They squatted between the cottonwoods, quietly talking. When he came up to them he'd keep his head down, and they always did the same, remained silent a moment until he'd gone by, then nudged each other and hooted out, 'Bastard!'

By the time Steve was six or seven, this already tense scene gradually gave way to violence, and verbal abuse degenerated into punch-ups. One local teen known only as Bud once spat at him as he walked by on Main Street. The response was dramatic. Quite suddenly, McQueen's indifference ended. Vaguely, Bud remembered one of the other boys screaming and then felt a cracking pain as he went down on the kerb. There was another blow, and blood began to spurt out all over his face. A wiry meatpacking arm began to flail downwards, and with one hook of his left fist, Steve split the much older boy's nose. Two passers-by, fearing he'd brain him, started yelling, 'You'll kill him, Mac! You'll kill him!' and dragged McQueen off. The police were called.

Steve would later attend a small, all-white school, where his aggression was matched by sullenness. For the most part his hobbies were solitary, his companions subhuman. So far as he ever let himself go, it was with a series of animals and household pets – his best friend was one of Claude's hogs – with whom he abandoned himself in a carefree display of emotion, an uninhibited effusion of irresponsibility, happiness and love. He also, says Gahl, 'dug anything with wheels'. Within those massive confines, it wasn't a bad childhood, merely a warped one. First Bill's and then Julian's defections were a blow that helped to shape, or did shape him, making him tense, hard-boiled and edgily single-minded. He had his code worked out. People were swine; performing for them was simply to rattle the swill bucket. The sense of parental love which nourished even a Bud was shut off totally. On the other hand, McQueen learnt the value of self-help early on, and in the one surviving contemporary photo of him, taken in the pig-pen, he's tricked out for the occasion in boots, bib overalls and a wide grin. Striking a pose that's at once studied and casual, he leans against a trough with his knees slightly bent, as if ready to spring into action the moment the shutter's released:

finishing his chores early would earn him a bonus from Uncle Claude, and a Saturday matinee ticket to Slater's Kiva cinema. 'I'm out of the midwest,' McQueen would say, from the far side of fame. 'It's a good place to come from. It gives you a sense of right or wrong and fairness, and I've never forgotten [it].'

He made his life within the cycles of manic depression, and they shaped him as much as the cycles of seasons and weather and fat and famine shaped the lives of other Slaterites. For the most part, Steve was happy enough to lose himself in Claude's farm and the hardware. But clearly there was a part of him, burning down inside, that wanted to get away as far and as fast as possible.

McQueen's morbid ambition was in large part revenge. Right down the middle of his psyche ran a mercenary core: the will to get even. Someone, he thought, was always trying to screw him; somebody else was having him on. All the world – but never he – was a con. Not exactly a prize sucker for the sell, Steve started off life 'thinking *everyone*, from [Julian] down, was after me', and went on from there to get paranoid. The bitchy litany became the sustained bark punctuated by the snarl and – when backed into a corner – outbreaks of hysterical frothing at the mouth. Even when McQueen got what he wanted, he combined the swagger of the aggressor with the cringe of the abused.

As Steve's suspiciousness increased, so did his solitude. At a 1900-era diner stranded on Slater's Front Street, the ex-owner remembers McQueen 'real well . . . he came in after school and spent an hour sitting alone there over a glass of water. He wasn't like other kids.' Robert Relyea, with whom Steve went into business in the 1960s, recalls him 'practising the famous baseball drill in *The Great Escape* for two days . . . I don't think he'd ever been much for team sports.' This key truth, more broadly unsociable than narrowly un-American, was echoed a few years later, when Relyea and his family were playing football with McQueen in a California park. 'It was touching that he was running around, laughing at a fumble, punching triumphantly with his fist in the air when he made a touchdown, smiling and nodding when one of the kids brought off a catch, having the time of his life . . . touching, but also sad that he'd never once played the game as a boy.' Little wonder McQueen hit the heights in offbeat roles in breakout films. In the process, the improbable wisdom of his moodiness would be fully vindicated.

His life was transformed – at least intensified – by the accumulated blows of 1930–44, to the point where the whole ordeal seemed to be a jail sentence. Not only was McQueen an orphan and condemned case, the Midwest itself was a haven of kidnapping and racketeering, stony-jawed icons like Bonnie and Clyde, Machine-Gun Kelly and the Barkers all plying their trade along the Route 44 corridor. The young Steve once saw John Dillinger being led into jail in Crown Point, Indiana. In later years he remembered how the killer had turned to him with his grinning, lopsided face, curling away from his two guards, and winked. Quite often, McQueen said, he couldn't go to sleep for replaying the scene in his mind.

Against this felonious backdrop, marches and violent pickets in Saline county reflected the feelings of most Americans in the face of the appalling and mysterious Depression. Fist fights, or worse, regularly broke out between labour organisers and the law. 'Most of my early memories', McQueen once told a reporter, 'are bloody.'

One morning in 1937 Steve was walking with Claude up Central Avenue in Slater when he saw several protesters holding banners turning the corner ahead of them. Soon there was shouting from around the bend. Armed police began to run towards the intersection. Steve looked up at Claude, who said quietly, 'Something's up.' They walked on to the general store on Lincoln Street and heard shots fired. When they got nearer the crowd, they saw one of Claude's own farmhands being dragged along the ground by three policemen. He was kicking. There was blood, Steve noticed, all over his face and shirt. 'We better not have anything to do with it,' Claude calmly told his great-nephew. 'Better stay way out of it.' The seven-year-old shook his head.

Steve's clash with formal education, later that same year, came as a mutual shock. Every morning he walked or biked the three miles down to Orearville, a small, segregated elementary school on Front Street. Stone steps led up under a canopy to the modest one-room box he later called the 'salt mine'. It was certainly Siberian. A coal stove in the vestibule there gave off as much heat as a 60-watt bulb and when it rained, which it did constantly most winters, water seeped through the roof. Like many shy boys, Steve relied on memorising to get by. (The rote student of Mark Twain would become an actor who hated to learn lines.) Parroting Huck Finn, for his peers, was enlivened by the 'deez, demz and doz' tones, plus stammer, in which he flayed the text. It was later discovered that he was suffering from a form of dyslexia. The muffled sniggers were yet another small snub, avenged by Steve with a quick, impersonal beating in the dirt bluff behind the schoolyard or, more often, playing truant. A Slater man named Sam Jones knew McQueen in 1937–8. 'We all heard stories about him, but the truth is he didn't show up much.'

By his ninth birthday he was firmly in the problem-child tradition, a pale, sandy-haired boy whose steely-blue eyes gave Jones the uncomfortable feeling of 'being x-rayed'. People called it a striking face, broad-nosed but narrow-chinned, so that the head as a whole was bullet-shaped rather than oval. Another Slaterite recalls 'that tense, hunted look he always had in a crowd'. Aside from the claustrophobia, McQueen owed his trademark quizzical squint to hearing loss. An undiagnosed mastoid infection in 1937 damaged his left ear for life, bringing him further untold grief in class and completing a caricature performance as small-town misfit. His remaining time there would be brief, violent and instructive.

As soon as he could drive Claude's truck or fire a rifle, Steve immediately entered into such active conflict with Slater that the local sheriff called at Thomson Lane to issue a caution, and he aroused the school's indignation by appearing, when he did so at all, reeking of pig dung. But he also deftly took to his relatives' world. He liked to hunt, for instance, and once, to Claude's eternal admiration, he took out two birds with a single shot. Steve often stalked deer or quail in the woods north of town, on the banks of the Missouri, at least once with a pureblood setter named Jim, the officially designated 'coon dog of the century'. (The animal could apparently understand elaborate human commands, and also predicted the winners of horse races and prize fights.) In short, he said, it was a 'schizo existence', in which the wilderness, bloodletting and the magic of the primal, male life jarred against the drudgery of school and church. Steve's great-uncle and grandparents didn't bring him up to be

23

violent – something beyond even their nightmares – but they showed him the world, and that was enough.

All this changed for the worse in 1939.

A flash of inspiration as can only be produced by a newlywed parent now caused Julian to send for her son from Indiana. Early that autumn, the same month that Britain went to war with Germany, Steve was taken out of school, packed a kit bag and sat, shrouded in his moth-eaten city clothes, cap pancaked down on his head, in the very back seat of the bus east. It was crowded with immigrant farmworkers going home to enlist. Many of them knew as much about the rest of America as they did about the Antarctic and sat staring or muttering over the noise of Steve's neighbour, a Negro with a mouth-harp, as they crossed the Mississippi at St Louis. The Greyhound wound through Illinois until, late at night, it came around a curve into town. On both sides a sudden, windswept ruin opened out, the bus ploughing down dark alleys and backstreets, hardly better than furrows between the slums with, Steve noticed, 'only a couple of pissing rats' as proof of life. Indianapolis.

McQueen himself looked unhappily through the back window taking in the acrid smell of the city. Those 400 miles were worlds exquisitely separated. Where once there'd been Claude's pigs, now there were pool halls, the Crescent and the Roxy. Racially, too, Indianapolis was segregated, black and white symbolically split by the railway – somewhere, downtown, men wore cheap Irontex suits and drove boatlike cars past hand-painted signs saying EATS. Local unemployment and, not incidentally, racketeering and Klan activity were all at their height and there was a curfew. It was raining. With two mismatched homes and no fewer than four warring role models (five, including his new stepfather), it's hardly surprising McQueen would return to the theme of self-reliance throughout his career, channelling it into his best work and telling one startled reporter, 'I'd rather wake up in the middle of nowhere than in any city on earth.'

The bus pulled in to the Meridian Street depot at midnight. Julian was more than an hour late meeting it, and Steve could smell the gin on her breath when she kissed him. He was introduced to her dour, clinically psychotic, it emerged, husband, and the three of them walked down dark streets, frequently challenged by police, to the boarding house. It was on the site of a former stockyard, and the old stink still haunted the place. Even through the shut window, the familiar depressing reek of meat, tallow, pulverised bones, hair and hides wafted up to Steve's cold room. Towards dawn, he could hear Julian's voice pleading and begging through the wall, and then the sound of her husband punching her. Finally, with daylight, the boy fell asleep. After all, he later told a close friend, it wasn't as if it were permanent. They already owed their landlord ten dollars.

Before long Steve's fourth-grade teacher in Indianapolis wanted nothing to do with him, and the contempt was mutual. Most mornings he went back to his earliest haunts, nowadays alone, slipping into the darkness of the Roxy, then begging some bones at the kitchen door of a diner. It wasn't unknown for him to scavenge from the dustbins outside the canal bars, and he became an underage, lifelong beer toper. One day Steve fell in with some older boys who showed him how to steal hubcaps and then redeem them for cash at a store downtown. It was his first glimpse beyond his own rebellion into a world of organised crime that he would find more intriguing than the weekly mass to which his grandmother had dragged him in Slater. Julian and her husband tried, too, packing him off to a delinquents' summer camp and Sunday school. But Steve acquired neither religion nor social graces. Soon, he was spending his nights running with a gang. He rarely, if ever, slept at home.

There was some building done during the late 1930s and early 1940s: hospitals, museums and parks all overlaying the great Lockefield Garden prank, a slum clearance scheme that provided housing for 7000 families. Several of these projects went broke and the Reconstruction Finance Corporation had to bail them out. By the time Steve arrived for the second time, the feds had assumed much of the local relief burden and a bewildering raft of agencies funnelled funds to help towns like Indianapolis to their own grass-roots 'solutions'. Soon enough, there was money and food available to the needy. The young McQueen doted on the pleasure it would bring to relieve the suits of their cash.

Steve not only legitimately applied for ration tickets. He began working a lucrative forgery scam with his street mob. Between them they printed bundles of the tatty coupons and sold them at a profit to their contact downtown, who was in turn reimbursed by Washington. It was a crude but highly effective form of pioneering welfare fraud. Steve might have been a flop at school, but his inner fire – the vitality that erupted whenever he got away with something – was uncanny for a so-called loser. From about 1940 onwards he was busy either as a petty hood or generally twisting the system – and people's melons – to his own ends. 'You had this sense he was getting back on folks,' says Toni Gahl. 'He just tried everything, like he was fighting for his life. I heard about his [welfare] thing. Son of a bitch! No one else was doing that then, I couldn't believe it.'

There was something almost confidence-inspiring in McQueen's later career. For the few who knew him and millions who didn't, his was the big magic that offset the clichés of the American film industry. Partly this was a result of his image, partly the result of his personality. Even in the 1940s a gap opened up between the angry thug and the shy boy wearing a pair of overalls hand-labelled *Huck* who was quiet, kind and fanatically loyal to friends. One was dark, one was sunny, but the two McQueens had this in common: both were warped by a sense of being alone in a 'shit' world. That long and hard childhood made him a master at walking a thin tightrope, buffeted by the warring rivalries of Julian, her husband and Slater, with church, school and his criminal interests to consider as well. It was a neat balancing act.

When her man left, as they all did, Julian made it a point of honour not to resort further to food stamps. Prostitution only ever supplemented her typing and waitressing but, after the day Steve caught her *in flagrante*, it took on a symbolic importance for him far outweighing its fiscal value. She hated doing it, obviously. No she didn't. She didn't hate it all that much. She was always fucking at it, he told Gahl. Sailors. Suits. Anyone, any time at all. From then on Steve spent his few evenings at home sitting on the stoop of their small downtown hotel while Julian was at work upstairs. She'd yell at him and throw a shoe at the door if he ever interrupted her, and he even had to fit his sleeping arrangements (by now he and his mother were sharing a bed) around hers. If Julian was entertaining late, Steve would make up a sort of bunk for himself, using his jacket and a few flattened boxes as blankets, on the ugly, geometric-patterned tile floor of the vestibule. One winter when she was unusually busy, he ate all his meals out there, crouching behind stairs or walls, or anywhere that was protected from the snow.

Indianapolis aged him, but arguably he never really grew up. Steve's family life was dire and, at times, outrageous. On Saturday mornings, after a week in which she'd been with four or five men, Julian would shout downstairs and ask him the time. The ritual gave Steve a rare link back to Slater, since his one valuable possession was a pocket watch he'd been given by Claude. He'd yell up in his high, reedy voice, breaking slightly but also militant, 'Nine o'clock, Ma.' This was the signal for one of those sudden reversals in behaviour that constituted the basic pattern of Julian's life. She'd come down in her high heels and dress, kiss him on the mouth and then hurry off with him to the Roxy. Steve already lived for the cinema. Even in the drenching rain which seeped through the brickwork, he could soak up the lushness and grace of the western landscapes he loved, the grandeur and ruggedness, the seductive combination of sex and violence. By his eleventh birthday, he was hooked.

It was a boom time for the movies. In the early war years Hollywood went from a half-shod outpost dealing in flickers to a culture factory employing the likes of Mann, Brecht and Faulkner. A large number of Broadway's classical stars were coming west as fast as they could make it. The very best pictures of the day – *Gone with the Wind*, *The Grapes of Wrath*, *Mrs Miniver* – created characters that weren't just some new aspect of stage acting, but new from the ground up. Bogart's *High Sierra*, above all, won Steve over. This far-fetched gangster yarn had its faults, even he would admit, but in the lonely, sardonic yet soulful leading man it boasted a recognisable role model – 'someone [whose] mud I dug'. More than thirty years later he was still mining the lode of that film, along with trace elements of *The Maltese Falcon* and *Casablanca*. 'I first saw Bogie on screen when I was a kid,' Steve said in 1972. 'He nailed me pronto, and I've admired him ever since. He was the master and always will be.'

There were better technical actors than McQueen, more classical or orthodox, but none who did a more brilliant take-off of his hero. He was more volatile than the actual Bogart, colder, more threatening, more thoroughly lost in the parts. He reprised and improved the famous sneer; he paid homage to Bogie and outdid him in the same breath. But Steve's emotional authenticity went far beyond getting off a decent impersonation. His smallest movements had the kinetic flow of an animal, something feral. Whether playing the loner, the loser or the lover, he drew on his own signature mix of ego and insecurity. There was, first up, the man himself. Steve McQueen looked like a movie star. A front page of him, whether tight-lipped and scowling or smirking archly, was usually worth thousands of extra copies. But there was more to his success than bright blue eyes and a fetching grin. McQueen was one of that rare breed of actors who didn't need to 'do' anything in order to shine. It was enough that he had, as Brando puts it, 'the mo', the properties of a bullet in flight.

Laser-like focus was key to the young Steve, always adapting to some new competition, some fresh conflict. When not brooding at home or prising off hubcaps, he would make for the downtown pool hall. He played the game like a war, often wagering his entire day's cash and immersing himself in the ritual, polishing shots and practising slang – picking up the protocol of the sport. Steve's technique was sound, his gamesmanship honed, the depth of concentration frightening. But what most struck people, says Gahl, was the way 'he got in part . . . Even broke, he'd show up with his own monogrammed stick and a bridge that was pure Minnesota Fats.' McQueen played with self-assured pride, gliding this kit around the baize and carefully stowing it at night in a leather travelling case. He took it with him everywhere and, in 1956, its third or fourth successor became the very first item of the 'stuff' (as he called his stage artefacts) he worked so brilliantly on screen. Persistence, panache, props: the three ingredients were already filling out Steve's street education, and he soon added a fourth. The fear he aroused in people was palpable, and he reinforced it more than once around town with that same pool-cue.

How much of the juvenile delinquent McQueen would be in his films? The answer is that the more you watch him, the more of him you recognise. It was precisely because he was real – working off his own reactions, not the director's – that he managed to create roles with mass appeal to high- and lowbrow alike. When he played a loner or a hustler, an emotional basket case, you could be sure it was coming from deep source material and not just a script. Those early years fell, Steve said, as 'ashes and muck' on adult life but as gold and fame on his career. In a rare cultural allusion, he sometimes compared his Indianapolis gang days to Fellini's *I Vitelloni*. 'That one . . . seemed to sum up the kind of kids we were at the time – whistling at chicks, breaking into bars, knocking off lock-up shops . . . a little arson.' That kind of thing. His early childhood was the 'baddest shit imaginable', McQueen later told his wife.

Then things took another turn for the worse.

Late in 1940 Julian, apparently unable to cope, sent him back to the farm in Slater. Steve spent the next two years there. Home again became the tall prairie-grass pastures around Thomson Lane, the hulking grain storage silos and the love-seat under the old elm close to the house where Claude would sit swinging on summer nights with his new maid and future wife (less than half his age), Eva. McQueen's room was a tiny attic under the eaves. Because of his obvious affection for his great-nephew, his tendency to josh him, and the enjoyment he took from his company as time went on, much would be made of Claude's influence on Steve. With such a father figure a boy could hardly be an orphan. 'The main script read like *Tom Sawyer*,' one McQueen biographer has written. But there was also a dark sub-plot from Tennessee Williams around the place.

A heavy drinker, Claude had a volcanic temper. His fiancée, an ex-burlesque dancer from St Louis, where she left an illegitimate daughter, wore fake diamond rings on every finger and drove a gold Cadillac. The money soon ran out and the farm resorted to raising fryer chickens to sell at Christmas. Steve's grandfather Vic was still living across the field in the disused sleeper, suffering from terminal cancer. His wife Lil went from being merely pious to fanatical, sometimes hobbling up Thomson Lane nude except for her crucifix and rosary in order to 'see God'. Most days she didn't recognise, or even acknowledge, her grandson. There were constant rows between husband and wife, brother and sister, plates flung, cops called. Julian, meanwhile, never once visited. All in all, it was no place for a chronically depressed twelve-year-old with an already fractured home life.

If Indianapolis seemed like Fellini, then Slater was a living embodiment of American Gothic, the starkly realistic painting of Midwestern
farm life unveiled, like Steve himself, in 1930. He ran away more
than once, loping down to the railroad tracks with his few belongings
in a knapsack, accompanied by a black-and-tan dog of uncertain
ancestry and his black cat Bogie. The brick depot at the far end of
Main Street made a viable overnight shelter from the madness of the
farm.

The central fact of Steve's childhood is that he was destroyed by
men and blamed a woman. He carped at his vanished father for the
rest of his life, but always with the key qualification, 'Julian!' He
caught the right note of bewilderment. Claude himself wasn't merely
cranky, he was a tough disciplinarian who used strap and rod on his
great-nephew; McQueen once called him 'a shouter, very vociferous
. . . He'd blow me out of the place, but I deserved it.' His first
stepfather, according to Gahl, 'sexually molested Steve. He told me
the two of them had been together one cold night while Julian was
downtown, and how [McQueen] could always remember the beads
of ice dripping from the ceiling like the sweat on the old geek's lips
. . . and that he, Steve, had tried to focus on the sound of the water
and the wind flapping the hotel sign around outside the door to avoid
thinking about what was going on.' This was the same man who
casually – and quite frequently – beat up his wife. That long winter
of ritual abuse, physical and emotional, can only have been a trial to
Steve's mother as well, tied as she was to a perverted bully she
couldn't acknowledge as such. Steve, for his part, would always hold
Julian responsible for the misery of his early years. 'Don't talk to me
about love,' she used to say. 'I feel the same way before, when and
after I fuck somebody – like shit.'

In mid 1942 Julian, now divorced and remarried to a man called
Berri (Steve could never remember his first name), sent for her son
to join them in California. Various circumstances had led to the move
west, earlier that spring, among them another landlord-related crisis
in Indiana. The specific reason that brought her to Los Angeles was
that Berri was offered steady manual work on the fringes of the film
trade. They took an apartment together on a drab, half-paved road
of cheap motels between Elysian Park and the Silver Lake district,

a mile or two north of downtown. Though there were sweeping views and a few modernist piles nearby, it was practically a genetic rule of thumb that Julian would end up in a slum. If the change was as good as a rest, its effect was to shatter her already primitive concept of family.

Day one she broke out the peroxide, nestled into a deck chair and whooped, 'California!'

In fact neither the address nor the building itself could have been much worse. The Berris counted rats, raccoons, snakes, wild dogs and prairie-wolves in three or four varieties amongst their neighbours. Coyotes, the most feared, regularly came prowling down from the Verdugo hills. It was all a long way, figuratively, from Hollywood, let alone either Indianapolis or the farm. Steve arrived in LA, he told Gahl, feeling like he'd 'crash-landed on Mars', a pale, sulky refugee who now barely recognised his mother. Her first words when she met him at the depot were to tell him to behave around his stepfather, whose name they now took.

One night in his tiny back bedroom, with the vermin grazing outside, Steve lay down to write a letter to Slater. It wasn't the usual perfunctory note home of a young teenager and it turned into a long one, as there was real hell as well as news involved. His new stepfather, he told Uncle Claude, was a thug who regularly beat him up. Steve was torn between his desire to run and a strong, but not yet overpowering, urge to fight back. Surely his family would rescue him. Is that what they were? Yes, he decided, those were his loved ones back in Slater. 'Tonite after supper', the letter continued, '[Berri] came to my room when he was ripped and lit off on stuff that he yells at Ma and me about and which he's crazy over. That is, me and Ma finding jobs. Says he will likely toss us out if we dont start work.' Steve went on like this for three pages, all of them covered in his spidery, retarded scrawl, sloppy, verbose and misspelt, though with sudden and surprising jolts of insight. The very last word over the signature, and the keynote of his whole year in LA, read 'Help'.

The letter never made it to Slater. Berri, now lacerated by ulcers as well as by failure, got up in the night and noticed the light from under Steve's door. Grabbing the letter, he read the first line or two before tearing it in half. When Steve bent over to pick it up, he was kicked or at least swatted hard on the rear. Berri followed this up by threatening to brain him. Unscrewing the dim bulb overhead, he then left Steve alone in the dark, whimpering in long, shuddering sobs and vowing revenge.

'Berri used his fists on me,' McQueen said later. 'He worked me over pretty good – and my mother didn't lift a hand. She was weak . . . I had a lot of contempt for her. *Lot* of contempt.' Unsurprisingly, he was soon back running with a gang of toughs and shoplifters who worked the area around the bottom end of Sunset Boulevard. On Christmas Eve Steve was booked for stealing hubcaps from cars parked in Lincoln Heights. Truancy officers from the Los Angeles school board also called. At this dire pass, Julian wrote Uncle Claude a letter of her own, telling him how bad the boy was, and that they were considering sending him to the reformatory. A month later Claude wired money for the bus fare back to Missouri.

It had changed in Steve's absence. Now the trains hauled troops as well as cattle, and a local factory converted from shoe manufacturing blasted out parts for the B-29 bomber. On the farm, too, began a painful induction into the world of peers and rivals. Claude's wife Eva had sent for her own child, Jackie, from St Louis. The teenage girl was a year older than Steve and, it seemed to him, was spared chores around the house as compensation for having been dumped. Though he began innocently dating another relative of Eva's, Ginny Bowden, Jackie's would duly be the 'first cooze I ever saw', ogled through the crack in her bedroom door. There was also a suspicion that the seventy-year-old Claude was more interested than was proper in his stepdaughter. It was now, too, that Steve's widowed grandmother was hauled off to State Hospital One, as the local asylum was called. The last sight he ever had of her was of her being dragged, kicking and screaming, out of her room. They used a straitjacket on her; an experimental model, it dislocated one of Lil's painfully thin shoulders. Steve stood in open-mouthed horror as the old woman whirled free, yelling in agony and biblical righteousness, before being muzzled and hauled off like a mad dog. Once in the ambulance, she became a muffled shade and disappeared.

Steve, for his part, enjoyed his freedom to go drinking, hunting, or cruising off on his red bike with the black-and-tan or his pet mouse. For an inquisitive boy, he did remarkably little reading; the business of showing up for eighth grade was so tedious and time-consuming that he never made more than a few stabs at it. He was a dab hand at story-telling, but that was his one and only accomplishment back at Orearville. Formal learning never mattered much to Steve, aka Buddy Berri. At the end of the summer term, after calmly informing his schoolmistress of his dream of becoming a movie idol, he ran down the seven steps onto Front Street, laid out his cap on the ground in front of him and began doing Bogart and Cagney impersonations. When the afternoon was over he'd collected a total of two dollars. Thrilled at his success, Steve rode his bike home to Thomson Lane, where he repeated his career plans to Claude and Eva. His great-uncle's response was to let rip with a contemptuous belch from behind a gin bottle.

One evening Claude tore a strip off him after the law called yet again at the Thomson farm, this time in response to complaints that Steve had shot out a café window with his BB gun. After the shouting had died down, the fourteen-year-old took off into the night. By way of a travelling circus he grubbed his way back west, eventually reaching California. Steve never set foot in Slater again. For the rest of his short but active life he carefully avoided it. McQueen had mixed views about the place. On one level he clearly loathed it, running it down as a 'sewer' where he'd felt his welcome to be, at best, sketchy. On the other hand it was precisely in his retreat into the world of guns, engines and play-acting that he found his way in life. Keenly aware of his role as Hollywood's misfit, he played the part with a flair that gave his performance that touch of genius. He made a whole career out of his rich source memory.

Most of his best films were attractive reflections of his own personality. Long before his fifteenth birthday, Steve knew what it was like to be dyslexic, deaf, illegitimate, backward, beaten, abused, deserted and raised Catholic in a Protestant heartland. He was the fatherless boy who was a hick in the city and a greaser back on the farm. Not surprisingly, nobody would do outcast roles better than he did. And to the bitter end: it was one of the weird paradoxes of McQueen's cv that while everything got better, he experienced it as having worsened. Only a true depressive could complain as he did, while earning $12 million a film, of being 'screwed blind'. After the Dickensian time he'd had of it, no one would ever blame McQueen for bitterly anticipating more 'shit' even as life, materially, turned up roses. They merely got used to it. Most sympathised with what Cagney would tartly call McQueen's 'clutching at the bars of his sanity' in an 'Alcatraz of self-loathing'. As a superstar, he maintained his old ways. At heart, Steve always saw himself as last in life's queue, with few real options – or, in psychiatrists' jargon, a touch of moral masochism – given the odds stacked up against him. A measure of his despair in 1944 was that, after quitting the circus, he soon thumbed his way back to his mother and stepfather in Los Angeles.

McQueen the film star would be a man alone – just as he'd once been a boy alone, hoboing his way across America or stealing out the window of the Berris' shack to duck another beating. If, in the end, he was a loner by choice, nature and circumstance did their worst to set him on the path. 'He once told me he'd wanted to murder his folks,' says Toni Gahl. 'He'd actually stood in their doorway with a butcher knife, it was that close. And you know he could have done it. You *know* it.'

According to her, 'Steve always said Berri ran that family like his own Stalag Luft III. Living with him was like being a POW, only most POWs don't get the crap kicked out of them every day for no good reason, and they also ate better.' As the quietest and one of the smallest, wearing rags and usually sporting a thick lip, Steve knew what it was like to be given hell at school, too. He solved the problem by rarely turning up there. Most days he was out on the verminous streets around Silver Lake, up by the reservoir, resuming his old trade in hubcaps and food stamps. In January 1945 he was brought in front of a judge after being involved in a violent street brawl. Steve's age saved him from the lockup that time.

The next morning he awoke to a flash of white light, followed by shooting pain across his whole face. He crawled out of bed half blinded. Coming home late to a tearful wife, Berri had belted him unconscious while he slept. Largely out of laudable respect for Julian, Steve had never fought back before. Now he finally went berserk. That dark new year's morning he flew at Berri, knocking him across the room and out the door. Before long the two of them fell down a flight of concrete steps onto the street. Steve's parting comment, hissed through broken teeth, was, 'You lay your stinkin' hands on me again, I'll kill you.' Then he began shambling up Glendale towards Griffith Park, where a city gardener, Dale Crowe, found him coiled in the foetal position and sobbing under a tree. It wasn't a pleasant sight. Nor, however, was it Crowe's problem. 'I asked Steve if he needed help, and he told me to go fuck myself,' he says. 'I took that as a no.'

As early as 1940 Steve had narrowly escaped a stretch in the Indiana Junior Reformatory, alma mater of his friend Dillinger. The one night he did spend in custody, in a prison ward after another fight, the clang of the door behind him – which a guard then locked, banging him up with the criminally mad confined there – was the 'second worst shit' of its kind he ever experienced. Rock bottom came on 6 February 1945, when his mother and stepfather signed a court order confirming the fourteen-year-old to be incorrigible. That same evening Steve arrived at Junior Boys Republic in Chino, one of LA's far eastern suburbs in the foothills of the Santa Anas. But even this craggy fastness wasn't secure enough for him to serve out the sentence worthy of his crimes. After an immediate bolt and recapture, Steve achieved his recurrent lifelong fate – he was put in solitary.

Steve was never to forget the hell of those first hours. He slumped there in the dark, breathing in the sharp tang of rag mats, cabbage and stewing tripe. Suffocating. Other boys' voices could be heard mumbling or sobbing through a shut metal door. McQueen lay awake all night, alone in the cooler, his bedroom a moth-eaten mattress on the floor. The word 'murder' soon came to mind too enthusiastically for anyone's liking but his own.

In fairness, though no 'candyass scam', as he later put it, Chino wasn't the borstal sometimes portrayed. The 200-acre campus was encircled not by bars and fences, but by open fields, and the regime stressed hard work, not punishment. None of the 'trusted', as opposed to solitary, inmates was ever physically locked up. But if the security was lax, the story was sturdy, and duly found its way into the early McQueen fiction. 'Ex-con' was the fell phrase used in one biography. The reality of Boys Republic was more like a boarding school, with an elaborate system of rewards and fines. Its house motto was 'Nothing

Without Labor' (almost too perfectly, though unconsciously, Himmlerian), the prime trade the manufacture of fancy Christmas wreaths for sale around the world. There was an emphasis on practical discipline. For the first time in his life Steve made his own bed. He learned to lay and clear a table. Most afternoons he was at work in the laundry, whose close, chemically scented walls still haunted him years later; McQueen would vividly recall that reek on his deathbed. The next time he ran away, over Gary Avenue and through Chino's southern outskirts towards the mountains, the Republic's principal gave him twenty-four hours before he called the law. They found Steve hiding out in a nearby stable. It was the second of five escape attempts, which appear to have been concerned less with actually absconding – he never made off by more than a mile or two – than with proving he could. The bolstering idea was rebellion.

Boys Republic would only be one part of McQueen's breakout theme, first switched on with such voltage when he ran downtown to the bright lights of the Roxy. After Chino, he would jump ship and go AWOL from the Marines. He bailed out of literally scores of affairs – 'fuck-flings', he called them – as well as two marriages. Right to the end Steve would quite seriously talk of 'getting away from it all' on a sheep farm in Australia. Commercially, *The Great Escape* was in a long line with *The Great St Louis Bank Robbery*, *Nevada Smith*, *The Thomas Crown Affair*, *The Getaway*, *Papillon* and *Tom Horn* as variants of this – to him – magnificent obsession. Short of beating off Harrison Ford to *The Fugitive*, it's hard to see what more McQueen could have done to make the point. When they hauled Steve back to the Republic for the fifth and final time, he actually knuckled down for a few weeks and was elected to the Boys Council. That last stretch of his year-plus there was always the one he later referred to nostalgically. But this seems to have been a ceasefire, not a real truce in the war between Steve and the powers that be. 'I didn't hang around with no crowd that dug suits,' he confirmed.

Steve would spend fourteen unremittingly grim months at Boys Republic. His mother never once came to visit him. One Saturday morning, not long after Berri himself left her, Julian rang Chino to say she wanted to take her son out for the weekend. Steve spent the whole day, from breakfast until supper, sitting on a chair by the front door. Towards evening he began to whimper quietly, raking his hands up and down his dust-caked overalls. The visit was finally cancelled hours late, and Steve sent back to the dormitory with a brusqueness that turned mere disappointment into mad fury. 'I remember what I did that night,' he'd say – namely went on the rampage: the steel door with its sliding panel, the walls, bed, table and windows were all beaten and spat on. To face, on his own, not only incarceration but now rank betrayal was a formative experience. When Julian did at last send for him to join her, at her new lair in New York, he left Chino at a clip, a bone-thin teenager in blue denim and an institutional haircut, with the general aspect of a 'whipped cur'.

After a week-long bus journey Steve arrived at the Port Authority depot in Manhattan on 22 April 1946. It was another catacomb. There was the familiar brief, stilted reunion with Julian, now technically a widow (Berri had died just before the divorce went through) and living with a man, also on the fringes of the film trade, named Lukens. The three of them walked in the rain down Seventh Avenue to Barrow Street. As usual, Julian's new apartment had no pretension to elegance. An iron gate gave on to foul-smelling steps, the stone worn to the thinness of paper, leading down to a sort of crypt. This subterranean pit was divided from its neighbour by a narrow barred window, or squint; through the iron grille two men could be seen lying on a bed in each other's arms. Lukens mumbled, 'Here's your place,' and pushed the boy forward. Steve peered through onto this scene and, a moment later, started to cry again. At the same time he began to shake his head, apparently in violent refusal, but was prevented by the bars from making the gesture at all adequately. It was another captive moment. McQueen's final response to these dire living arrangements was theatrical: he threw up. Then he took to his heels and ran up Seventh, round a bend and effectively out of his mother's life for ever.

When Julian died nearly twenty years later, Steve McQueen was a rich and famous movie star. The triumph of perseverance and reconstruction that had, almost incredibly, led to this coup had begun in 1933, when she first took him to the Roxy in Indianapolis. He owed her, in one sense, everything. But she almost destroyed him, too, and was single-handedly responsible for most of the 'shit' of his early life. The emotionally stunted boy duly grew up into a man clear-eyed about the precariousness of love, as 'tight as a hog's ass in fly season' towards women, says one of the Thomsons. There was a vampiric duality to McQueen's sex life. By day, he was the picture of reasonableness – usually or always courteous to the ladies. By night, though, Steve sluiced new blood into his dark self through a series of fuck-flings. Promiscuously, quite often cruelly. Once or twice violently. 'He treated females badly,' notes Gahl.

McQueen's ambivalence on the subject was legendary. Whatever he thought about them as 'chicks', he distrusted them as people, and his suspicious mind frequently crossed over into that less attractive realm, paranoia. Some of this equivocal mood was on show at Julian's funeral in October 1965. Steve, acting as officiant, variously ranted, raved, knelt, implored and suddenly wept, before looking down and weakly muttering the word 'Why?' into the open grave. In later years he always spoke of her in the same bewildered tone. McQueen's mother could never lie in peace; she could be dug up precipitously, her praises might be sung – but more often, her old sins would be remembered.

With nowhere particular to go Steve took in all New York had to offer, and he liked it. He won a few dollars in pool tournaments, bought a used Vespa and befriended the streetwalkers and other people of the night. He already knew something about sex. One plausible but unproven theory is that, long before that dungeon in Greenwich Village, he'd been in his share of deviant physical dramas, even that he was homosexually raped at Chino. As McQueen later recalled it in his dramatic hint, 'I lost it *big-time* when I was [living] in California,' thus leaving all his biographers to speculate on the identity of the other party – a boy? an older woman? – who initiated one of the twentieth century's red-hot lovers.

According to a New Yorker named Jules Mowrer, who still lives in the city, 'I met Steve McQueen in the summer of '46 and wound up, when they were out, at my parents' brownstone uptown. "Nice place," he'd say. I always got the feeling Steve knew life could be better for him. He yearned for something more.'

Something more, at that moment, turned out to be sex. 'Steve had a broken heart. That was the reason for all the attitude. And I think it made him hard – what I mean is, I think it gave him that edge. For a fifteen-year-old [sic], he knew exactly what he was about . . . I remember Steve took all my clothes off and casually looked me up and down. He *posed* me, and it was made clear that I was only one of his harem.' (The voyeur routine resurfaced when McQueen's later partners were told to 'sit for me' and his wives' bodies were subjected to minute inspection.) 'Steve was a dear, even if he rushed things a bit in bed, sweet and with a dozy smile like a little boy who'd just woken up. Naughtiness and innocence – *that* was my Mac.' McQueen told Mowrer that he'd lost his virginity to another teenage girl 'in an alley someplace' behind one of the Silver Lake night spots. Moreover, anyone who had regularly hitched his way along Sunset into Hollywood was unlikely to be a stranger to 'straight' prostitution.

Mowrer remembers Steve 'hunched up, no money, no food', leaving the brownstone for the last time to 'go do the world'. In a bar in Little Italy he duly fell in with two comic-opera chancers, Ford and Tinker, who stood him several drinks before asking him to sign a scrap of paper. After the hangover died down, McQueen found himself in the merchant marine. He shipped out, bound for Trinidad, on board the SS *Alpha*, and jumped it a week later in Santo Domingo. There Steve lived in a bordello for three months. It was a heady scene: a thick vine jungle lay between his room and the ocean. The cathouse itself, made of palm fronds and tin scraps, provided viable winter digs in return for odd jobs and physically extracting the customers' dues. Something similar happened after Steve worked his way back to the Texas panhandle. His burgeoning career as a towel-boy in the Port Arthur brothel was, in turn, cut short by a police raid. Next he signed on as a 'grunt' labourer in the oilfields around Waco. He sold pen-and-pencil sets in a medicine show. January 1947 found him starting out as a lumberjack in Ontario, Canada. There, with a partial reversion to his original name, he emerged as 'Stevie McQueen'. Several other such stints followed, including prizefighting and petty crime. If he never thought about acting, that must have been the one job he failed to tackle, though McQueen's permanent audition for the role of Jack Kerouac hints otherwise. 'I got around,' he understated.

While spending an Easter break in Myrtle Beach, South Carolina, on 7 April 1947, Steve wandered into a bar and saw a recruitment poster advertising the US Marines. This appealed to his sense of adventure, not to say of the ridiculous. Exactly three weeks later, after one final binge in New York, he became Cadet McQueen, serial number 649015, rising to Private First Class and training as a tank-driver. It wasn't so much the breadth as the speed of Steve's apprenticeship that struck friends. As he quite accurately put it, 'I was an old man by the time I was seventeen.'

After boot camp, McQueen was sent to Camp Lejeune in North Carolina. Here he carried out basic training, as well as such extra duties as lugging beds, bedding and clothes baskets for the officers when they moved to new quarters. It was the 'same old shit' as Chino, he griped. After three frustrating and uneventful months as a private soldier, Steve was ready to desert. The sole surviving photo of him in khaki shows a teenager with a face so taut his garrison cap is sliding down it; scowling, thick through the shoulders and chest but cinched at the waist, Steve looked like a welterweight boxer with submerged psychopathic tendencies. Colleagues remember his legs were constantly restless and his feet 'gave nervous jerks'. Below, shuffling energy; above, coolness and poise, a certain menacing hand- someness. His best friend in the corps recalls how 'that look of Steve's bothered you until you got to know him, and then it bothered you some more . . . There was nobody better in the world to have on your side, and nobody worse to cross, than McQueen.'

Speaking of this era to the writer William Nolan, Steve described his technique for dealing with a platoon bully:

> His name was Joey, and he was always with this tough-looking buddy of his. Real big dude. These two were like *glued* together, and I knew I couldn't handle both of 'em at once. So I played it smart. I hid inside the head until Joey came in alone to take a piss. I said, 'Hello, pal,' and when he turned around with his fly unzipped, I punched him in the chops.

After that, harassment never visited Private McQueen.

Another marine walked into the barrack hut one day and found McQueen alone on his bunk, writing a letter to Julian. What struck the other man, whom Steve called over to help with his grammar, was the opening statement, scrawled in an ink that looked uncommonly like blood – 'IM MY OWN MAN now, fuggit!' – and which went on from there to get angry. There would never be a more accurate or succinct description of McQueen's three-year hitch in uniform. Those first four words, in particular, expressed the whole throughline of his career. His own man. Fuggit. While most of the grunts tore about the camp in quick-moving, impetuous gangs, seeing almost nothing, Steve was watchful, curious, even as the rawest recruit, about the way people behaved. The military, as a rule, humiliates the individual, but never so McQueen. His rebellion turned on the familiar devices of sarcasm, cunning and obliging charm – Why didn't he wash everyone's jeeps? 'I'll make 'em glow!' – again and again.

A note of satire, needless to say, lurked just below the smile. 'Steve was always on the side of Steve,' is one ex-marine's fond memory. Yet another contemporary account of Camp Lejeune has McQueen 'marching up and down, mumbling obscenities and doing hilarious impersonations of the officers under his breath'. He was a gifted mimic, and now military ritual was feeding his inborn talent as fast as he could hone it. Not surprisingly, Steve got involved in his unit's biannual revue, and in later years he always felt that his time in the service had made it natural for him to 'hang with show types', and even to join them.

Gambling, whether for high stakes or laughs, played a large part in 2nd Recruit Battalion life. McQueen played too, but only when there was cash on hand instead of chips. Poker was a key factor in Steve's judgement of his friends; he was said to form an opinion of a new recruit's 'mud' – his basic code – only after he'd played cards with him. McQueen was one of these games' fiercest competitors and one of their most engaging personalities. He was highly disciplined at the table, as well as a natural bluff – cool-headed, daring and independent. His only interest was in winning, but his best friend at Camp Lejeune insists that 'Steve would frequently, and on the QT, slip back what he'd taken off you ... The key factor was always whether or not you'd had the balls to "see" him instead of folding. That kind of style counted for a lot with McQueen.'

Besides the fighting and gambling, Steve's only other long-term legacy from the military was his cancer. The exact illness that led him to Dr Kelley was mesothelioma, an acute form of asbestos poisoning. In those days the stuff was everywhere, including in the tanks he drove at Camp Lejeune. It was also used for such insulation as there was in his barracks. In one sorry incident (part of a punishment for his exploding a can of baked beans) McQueen was ordered to strip and refit a troop ship's boiler room. Most of the pipes there were lagged with asbestos. The air was so heavy with it, Steve would say, 'You could actually *see* the shit as you breathed it.'

Ample evidence, including his own, documents that McQueen's visceral mistrust of 'suits' continued to harden in the Marines. Free, fast-living, for him all discipline offended. Specifically, Steve wanted no such austere figure as his CO interfering in the schedule he meant to set himself. Long experience had taught that with any brass restraint, even 'shit', was inevitable. As McQueen encountered more authority, the bones of a deeply individualistic, anarchic view of life emerged more clearly. He was no ideologue. Rather, Steve was romantically attached to certain personal principles which weren't necessarily owned by the left or right. One army buddy recalls him 'reading his rights', as he put it: the right to drink, to get laid, to race bikes and to tool around in his souped-up jeep. With that agenda a clash with authority was ordained, and duly came. From then on, Steve's insubordination became proverbial. The one moral or intellectual datum it brought with it was a programmed response – one of his crisp variants of 'Fuck you' – to being cooped up. McQueen hated fences.

Leave soon came around.

'I'll be hootin' and hollerin',' Steve said with glee. 'I'll be boozing! Fucking and fighting! Do you hear me?'

'Just watch it,' they told him.

But after extending a two-day pass into a two-week holiday with a girlfriend, Steve spent forty-one days in the Camp Lejeune brig. (This stint in the stockade, suitably dramatised, would provide much of the source material for *The Great Escape*.) Following a second AWOL episode – this one involving a punch-up with the Shore Patrol – he was busted down to private, the first of seven straight demotions. Not long after that, Steve was posted to the military arsenal in Quantico, Virginia, before graduating to the Gun Factory in Washington, DC. His best marine friend – who asked to follow him there – recalls the scene in the barracks when McQueen burst in after yet another report: 'I remember he flung his cap into a corner and shouted, "Well, pal! Busted!" And I said, "What are your plans now, Steve? Somehow I can't see you as officer material." And with that he gave me that cool, drop-dead squint of his. "As far as I can see," Steve said, "I got two choices. I could go on stage, or I could go to jail." Most people's money would have been on the latter.'

McQueen may have been a full-time morale problem for the uniformed class. His beefs about military life in general, and the lack of women and good food in particular, became lore. When his unit pulled a midwinter tour of Lake Melville (then 30 degrees below zero), it seemed to his friend that 'all the ingredients were there for Steve to go ape. A lot of guys, better adjusted than he was, snap in those conditions.' The first few days in Canada, spent in various cold-water amphibious exercises, were bad enough. McQueen complained ever more bitterly about his rations. Frozen bully-beef – '*Shit*,' he growled as he crunched his. One early morning, when a transport carrying tanks and jeeps set off for Goose Bay, the divisional brass sensed there might be further trouble with McQueen. He was standing on the bank, hunched double against the snow, while waiting for the boat to pick him up. The few other men around him could hear him curse, over and over, moving from his cold and hunger to his lieutenant, to whom he offered certain medical advice as blunt as it was impractical: 'rich stuff', according to one witness, even for the Marines. In short, everything looked set fair for a confrontation.

And then, before anyone quite realised what was happening – before the officers could shout warnings – the transport floundered on a spit. Several vehicles and their drivers slid off the deck into the arctic water. Because of its speed, the ship itself capsized and began going down within seconds.

People watched.

McQueen sprang from his crouch and began snapping out orders, grabbing two or three soldiers (striking one of them as being 'almost inhumanly calm') and launching a small flatboat towards the sandbar.

Inside a minute he was at the scene of the wreck, ducking down into the ice to rescue survivors – he personally pulled five men to safety – while keeping up a flow of commands, echoing crisply over the water, so as to avoid a second sinking. (Another boat that set out to help did keel over, with the loss of three lives.) Back on shore, he then saw to it that warm clothes and blankets were broken out before accepting any help for himself. Even his commanding officer seemed disarmed. After the shock had worn off, and before his own court-martial, there was a seizure of gushing thanks – a notable reversal for a hip-hup type who had long promised to 'break' his company misfit. 'Steve, you amazed me,' he admitted. According to the hand-written citation, 'Pfc McQueen's initiative in immediately setting a rescue in motion was the key to what followed afterwards . . . Had Pfc McQueen not acted promptly in that direction, more loss of life would have ensued.'

Once again, the bloody-minded loner had been redeemed by his instinctively gutsy, dogged alter ego: this was McQueen's track record in the forces. His mutinous streak, his overall volatility and neon changes of mood would provide most of the copy for biographers mining his early years. But the artful, organised side deserves attention, too; no one personified grace under pressure like he did. 'Watching him take charge that morning,' his friend now says, 'was the most revealing experience I had in the military.'

From Newfoundland, McQueen worked his way into a plum job by displaying a new instinct for keeping his head down. According to friends, by 1949–50 he had almost obsessive hopes of an honourable discharge, ones that would have been far-fetched a year or two earlier. But as at Chino he wanted to go out on his terms, for once having 'done something' for his country. His own boats were only half burned. Enlistment was an ordeal before him as well as behind. In time McQueen's patriotism duly found expression when he became a member of the guard manning Harry Truman's yacht, the *Sequoia*; he may have spoken to the president for a moment or two, as he would to four of his successors. Around 1950 Steve also began, or formalised, his lifelong exercise regime, and never quite forgot the bends and squats he learned in the marine gym. Aside from that and the poker, he had few other interests. The internal combustion engine, and driving it too fast, wasn't strictly speaking a hobby. It was more what McQueen did.

Having joined the corps as a private in April 1947, McQueen left it exactly three years later with the same rank. From Camp Lejeune he hitched his way down the Pee Dee river to South Carolina. There was some talk of him moving in with – even marrying – his girl there, neither of which ever happened. Steve always preferred tearless exits, women knew, and he didn't disappoint his Myrtle Beach connection that summer. In the early hours of 22 August 1950, his mustering-out pay gone, McQueen jumped a train to Washington, DC, where he eventually became a taxi driver. His parting note to his fiancée said he was sorry, he'd tried, but, as far as loving someone went – 'I cant remember the drill.'

But then, Steve had a lot to forget.

The next year was a relatively happy one for McQueen, even though his income wasn't large or his jobs very promising. He moved back to New York, to a $19 a month cold-water flat in Greenwich Village. Having thrown over a good living as a cabbie, he worked as a builder's mate, did a paper round, repaired TV sets, trained as a cobbler, boxed, played stud, recapped tyres in a garage and ran numbers for a local bookie. On his own cheerful admission, he 'got wasted a lot'. By now, pot, wine and beer had become his constant companions, his most dependable friends. Sometimes, late at night, Steve would take his bottles and bags down from the shelf, count them and fondle them as, other nights, he was known to do to his guests: there were literally dozens of women. It's significant that he recognised the ways in which his cynical but childish twenty-year-old self kindled emotions associated with a much younger boy. Even teenagers wanted to mother him.

Nor did McQueen get about much. If he ever needed male company, his card-playing or dirt-biking crew would come round. Two ex-marines once paid him a visit at the apartment. Steve generously urged them, along with his current girl, to go out on the afternoon of her day off while he made dinner. They returned and found no trace of food or of McQueen. He was discovered in the kitchen reading the paper and drinking beer. Supper was ready: it consisted of meat loaf, potato salad and pie, all scrounged from the local diner. Steve was inordinately proud of this achievement and boasted of it for years later. Aside from a few tins and paper plates, his only personal effects around the place were a stolen NO PARKING sign he used as barbells and the 1946 Indian Chief motorcycle he kept by his bed. Dora Yanni, who knew McQueen in late 1950, remembers the look of 'almost sexual awe' that came over him whenever he gazed at the bike – quite unlike the 'perfunctory stuff' he went through with the women whom, she shrewdly guessed, 'Steve needed but didn't like'. Julian, for one, never called.

Though, naturally enough, he didn't realise it at the time, McQueen had lived through the most pivotal years of his life. Although still technically a minor, he had the raw material to harness his own adult personality. Already a pattern had emerged: thoughts of disgust upon waking in the morning. Feelings of depression for most of the day. Dreams of manic elation and triumph on a great tide of sexual encounters after dark. During the night itself, he often lay awake reviewing things, and they often made him sick.

In the five years since he left Boys Republic, McQueen had variously worked as a deck ape, card-sharp, gigolo, huckster and runner in a brothel. His mind went in dolorous circles around the dim past – furnished slums, he always remembered, with gaslight laid on and find your own heating. Steve's self-dramatising impulse, so crucial to his acting genius, grew out of a need to escape. He was a serial runaway, a Leatherneck and a boxer, an expert at pool and motorbikes. Not surprisingly he had a temper. Yanni's recollection of him gripping the stationary Indian Chief, swaying back and forth on the seat as if it were a rocking horse, is chilling enough; but the self-destructive fits, not often encountered in the life of the publicised McQueen, were 'worse – the pits'. Drinking for fun was out, but drinking to induce coma was a way of coping with life, specifically with 'chicks'. The thought of sex while sober was like a doom before him.

Nor were career prospects that rosy. For most of the winter of 1950–51 Steve's odds-on fate was a swift exit into jail, if not an undignified grave. Hundreds or thousands of men like him fell every year in New York, first in the gutter and then down the drain. What separated him from them was, oddly enough, both a strength and a weakness – his insecurity. Steve was, as he saw it, in a death struggle with the world, and he successfully passed off his dark streak as a sign of necessary moral fibre. Tenacity was what life was about. He was going to 'grab the brass ring', he told Yanni, who remembers visiting Steve one wet evening that March, carrying beer and cake 'to celebrate, for once'. But by the time she got inside McQueen was already on the Indian Chief, rocking to and fro and repeating, like a machine, 'Bad . . . Very bad,' while gazing straight ahead of him with a glazed expression 'like a man scoping hell'. Some of the 'madness and fire' that drove McQueen was there that night in the apartment, as Yanni watched him slowly nodding, then lurching with furious speed, kicking at the wheels of the bike, falling at last into an exhausted slump and sobbing with dreadful, ever-increasing momentum, panting and miserably trying to blink out the dampness in his eyes.

He was twenty-one.

'Should I lay bathrooms, or should I perform?'

McQueen's mother never visited him in New York, even though she was living a few blocks away. In a sad twist on Steve's life, Julian, too, drank fanatically and slept from bed to bed, the great masculine prop of her thirties, Lukens, casually admitting to keeping a wife and family at home in Florida. After he left, Julian drifted around the Village, where she eventually ran into McQueen one night in a bar. From her crouch on a stool, he remembered this 'zonked out lady', now plump and with matted hair, piped up, 'Tell me you don't know me, Steven.' His reply was curt: 'Drop dead.' But the reunion wasn't over yet. 'For God's sake,' she sobbed, 'at least give me your hand and help me out of here.' A moment later Steve was walking her outside, where they awkwardly exchanged phone numbers. There was the faintest suspicion of a reel as mother turned one way up Broadway and son the other. Apart from that barely visible lurch, Julian's slow departure wasn't without dignity. For years afterwards Steve would remember her 'shuffling off home alone', and if he had his regrets on other fronts, they were as nothing compared to how he felt about Julian. That 'narcotic whiff' of mother loss, says Yanni, would be the first source of his genius as an actor.

A few years later McQueen hit the heights with more than his share of personal 'shit'; but this almost always fed his career. For one thing, as the 1950s prove, he was an uncommonly driven man in his need for greatness, achievement, recognition; the sort of drives that come from doubt rather than, in the Freudian sense, being his mother's darling. As he so often did later, when creating his best characters, McQueen sought to mitigate despair through toughness. His grubby twenties were largely spent trawling Manhattan in the years before being 'different' enjoyed much status there. In those days you sensed you were illegitimate or off the farm based on who picked fights with you in bars. A year after separating from the Marines, McQueen was back weight-training again. By now the thin, pockmarked teen had bulked into a stud, small and compact but with the sinewy mark of his boxing days. Steve's face was a similar case of taking the rough with the smooth. According to Yanni, he 'was like a crude sketch for one of Rodin's hulks' – rough-hewn and finely chiselled in equal measure. McQueen seemed to be hungry or tired at least half the time. What mattered more was that he always looked dangerous.

Steve's great achievement was to make a living without ever finding much of a job. That spring alone, he sold encyclopaedias and laid tiles; arranged flowers and trained as a bartender; applied for a long-shoreman's card; and was known to roll both dice and sleeping drunks. On a whim, he drove the Indian chief to Miami and back. Money, even during periods of relative fat, was always tight. When things were going badly, as they often did, Steve wasn't above cadging 'loans' as well as collecting welfare. He took to haunting the kitchen door of Louie's, his neighbourhood diner, where he earned the half-cowed, half-affectionate nickname Desperado. Between times, McQueen took up with another woman, this one a resting actress, who, largely on the basis that 'you've already conned your way round the world – you're a natural', nagged him to audition. Occasionally, Steve's voice would soar into a girlish treble. Now it broke. When the laughter had died down, he casually rang his mother to tell her he was thinking of enrolling in drama class. 'Be sure to call me back when you flunk,' she said.

'I won't flunk.'

'Oh my God.' Julian sloshed some more gin into a mug and hung up.

McQueen smashed his own glass against the wall. For him, too, the idea of acting – *his* acting – was no less unlikely. Clowning around in tights, Steve's own phrase, jarred badly against the Levi-and-leather biker image he was already buffing. Yet in one sense it was a sane, logical move. McQueen, the unhappy outsider, had been posing all his life. Putting on a front to get what he needed, or to make the household reality vanish, was one of the few lessons he'd learned at Julian's knee. His own term for this charade was scamming, and it was an art he made his own. The sheer hell of being natural deepened his gall and also his repertoire, so even his performances at home, in New York, swung from glum to tragic, which was the true reflection of his state of mind. Tortuous and immanent, much of Steve's play-acting was a puerile need, near pathological, to bolt. What's more, performing restored the Bogart, and other boyhood connections in McQueen's life. Both Berri and Lukens, incomparably vile as father figures, had exposed him to some of the tools, cameras and the like, of their trade. There was the fact that he was a gifted mime. Finally, and this pulled heavily with Steve, 'There were more chicks in the acting profession who did it.' He was with one of them now.

McQueen signed up.

On 25 June 1951 Steve took the subway to Sandy Meisner's dark, ivy-covered studio, the Neighborhood Playhouse. Meisner instantly grasped what film audiences would learn later. 'He was an original, both tough and childlike – as if he'd been through the wars but preserved a certain basic innocence. I accepted him at once.' A combination of the GI Bill and poker paid McQueen's tuition.

It was Steve's long-standing conviction that if you did your best in life, held your 'mud' always, then whatever happened you at least knew it wasn't for lack of trying. But he was also a great believer in fence-sitting. His friend Bob Relyea remembers how 'Steve had to be talked into almost all his best films.' Some of the same ambivalence was there that first term at the Playhouse. Steve startled one group reading by declaring the day's text (*Hamlet*) to be 'candyass'. Even years later, when scripts were unfurled for him like rolls of silk before an emir, and McQueen's accountant suffered a nervous collapse from hauling so many bags of money to the bank, he quite seriously told a reporter, 'I'm not sure acting is something for a grown man to be doing.'

This sort of wavering, suspended between worlds, was Steve's hallmark. Throughout that autumn and winter he commuted from squalid Christopher Street to the smooth Meisner, from all-night stud and truck-driving to parsing Chekhov. He quickly emerged as one of the Playhouse's true characters, a man who lolled in, milk-pale and with a hunchback's slouch, mumbling, unlit cigarette dangling at the perfect angle. His eyes caught the melancholy of his life. McQueen's smile, according to Meisner, was 'warm but always conditional'. For Yanni, watching Steve's attempt at seduction 'was as cosy as having a pit-bull lick your hand . . . You waited for him to snap.' McQueen's unabated desire to chop and change – almost a morbid addiction – proved that neither work nor women had cured the deep vulnerability inside the alcoholic's boy from the farm. Insecurity was his watchword. When not electrifying the class, Steve seriously pondered a return to tile-laying at $3.50 an hour. He asked a friend called Mark Rydell, 'Should I lay bathrooms, or should I perform?' Rydell would remember, 'I think he got into acting because he didn't want to bust his ass.'

McQueen's greatest skill was his ability to radiate. Picking up women, many of them as broke as he was, he switched on what Yanni calls 'several million volts of synthetic charm', and Steve himself termed his 'shaggy-dog look' when sponging money. It was rarely refused. But McQueen always went further than the mere touch. He believed that he had to shore up people's confidence as well as trawl their purses. Years later one of his overnight guests recalled how she had hesitated when Steve asked her to take classes at the Playhouse in addition to her work as a secretary. Seeing her pause, he 'half closed those eyes of his' and asked: 'Did you know any more about typing or filing when you started that?'

She shook her head, and he smiled. 'You picked it up, didn't you? Well, you can pick this up too.' Then he leant over, kissed her, and said simply, 'I'm with you.'

She enrolled at the Playhouse, 'and because Steve was there I had the time of my life. My God! What an operator, and what a beautiful man.'

51

Largely thanks to the missionary work of Brando and Montgomery Clift, by 1951 a mainstream acting generation was still – just – running the show. A Method-acting generation was coming up behind, fast. Those who belonged to the new, so-called 'torn shirt' school, or were linked with some other group opposed to established convention in the arts, were already the critics' darlings. Meisner's class drew in a small but distinguished house. Talent scouts and even a few directors would come to the Playhouse's annual revue, a combined graduation and gala night. This new cult of anti-hero duly attracted an agent named Peter Witt to the Christmas production of *Truckline Café*. Witt 'loved the kid in the sailor suit', whose near-actionable Brando parody both cribbed and surpassed the original. Peers like Rydell also began to talk up the novice who upstaged nearly every other actor in the intensity department. To them McQueen had an 'air of wild rage', even if, to others, it was really more Method with an animal glaze. Voice, movement, technique. Steve quickly made a whole system out of his childhood. He did anger so convincingly that, for the first but not last time in his career, he made people's flesh creep. McQueen had few duties in handling such a slight role on such a small stage, chief of which was to look animated, and to make the other actors shine. He proved incapable of doing either, but otherwise used the play well. 'Steve was spellbinding,' says Yanni.

Meisner saw quite another thing in McQueen:

'Professionalism, always the professionalism. Dog tired, he'd put his feet in a bucket of ice water to jerk himself awake while he learnt lines.' There were plays and scripts to be read. Steve threw himself into it all with an energy born of ambition. He'd set out to become, he announced, a great American actor.

His commercial debut followed that spring of 1952, in a Jewish repertory production on Second Avenue. The very first words McQueen uttered on stage, in Yiddish, were direly prophetic: 'Nothing will help.' After the fourth night he was fired.

That same season on 25 May 1952, Steve transferred to the Hagen-Berghof drama school. He celebrated by buying his first racing bike, a used K-model Harley. On that note, and clutching a few wadded dollars, he again took off for Miami while classes were out for the spring. One moment that should have lived but hasn't, not least because in an increasingly photogenic career no one yet had a camera on him, was Steve tearing up Highway 1, bare-chested and laughing, under the swaying royal palms. Once on the beach, he soon found the saloon that would become his home from home during the New York 'shit season', a dark cave with a bar where the owner remembers McQueen for his 'bleached hair, bronzed body and faintly bad smell'. He ate with a burger in one hand and a slab of pie in the other, gulping down his beer at breakneck speed. Much the same intensity characterised his policy on women. Steve was rarely without an aspiring model or college co-ed in tow, and within a week he enjoyed the local handle, before it was ever a retail cliché, of 'Big Mac'.

McQueen often went diving in Florida with an old marine buddy named Red. Early in June, about three miles out in Biscayne Bay, Steve spotted a small shark which, characteristically, he chased to the ocean floor. After failing to bring it up on a gaff so that Red could net it, McQueen surfaced dangerously fast and punctured his already bad left eardrum. That evening the two men returned to Miami to get a doctor to test Steve's hearing. It was further seriously damaged, and even though he laughed it off himself, his voice coach in New York was furious with McQueen for his carelessness.

Soon after getting home he was cast in no fewer than three provincial shows. Though none rang bells in the far universe, McQueen made both a small name and a thin living for himself on the road. During the last, *Time Out for Ginger*, he was able to put down $450 for a red MG roadster.* Steve needed a replacement because he had just wrecked his previous car, a hearse, racing it zigzag across Columbus Circle, actually flipping it upside down, the long black roof shedding sparks at the point of impact, McQueen himself walking away. That incident cost him financially, but it did wonders for his reputation. Thanks in part to his poker money, Steve was flush enough to give up non-theatrical work and now focus full-time on acting. He did a verbal deal for Witt to represent him. As McQueen said, it was 'grooving together'. He'd made 'people talk' about him. It was all, at least locally, paying off. Bloody-mindedly, he'd pay

---

* The play dispensed with his services when McQueen aggressively demanded a pay rise specifically to cover its running costs.

Julian back in a way that would brook no more 'shit' or sarcasm.

He would become a legend.

With at least a first whiff of success Steve worked, if possible, even harder. 'Busting my ass to read,' he said, let alone memorise the texts. Line by dismal line – a triumph of will over semi-literacy. But he allowed himself to unwind, too. Behind his volcanic rage he was capable of something approaching real charm. The perfectly timed smile, the easy, apt jokes and above all the brilliant send-ups, not least of himself, all testify to the fact that Big Mac was tempered by his sweeter kid brother, Little Steve.

The two rubbed along together during those next five years of graft. Fame, for McQueen, wouldn't suddenly come calling after one audition; he had to ring the bell, pound on the door and finally smash on through. Witt, though aquiver for new talent, never quite turned creative vision into commercial triumph. Until 1958 nothing could avail against that hard truth. That Steve did, in the end, make it was due, in roughly equal part, to talent, luck and others' unshakeable faith in him; that and an underlying self-confidence that he wasn't only in the right place, but there at the right time. 'I found a little kindness,' as he later said. 'A joint where people talked out their problems instead of punching you.'

There wasn't a city in the world where an alert twenty-two-year-old could have had a better day-to-day sense of *possibility* than New York in the early 1950s. The place was awash with actors, especially those who trod in Brando's huge, 'slabby' (as McQueen put it) shadow. The rehearsal group known as the Actors Studio had opened in 1947 in a semi-converted church, apt digs for what now became, under Lee Strasberg, a bully-pulpit for teaching Stanislavski's Method. It was a wide-open enterprise still, more than living up to its fame. After *A Streetcar Named Desire* threw off the yoke of what a star was meant to look and sound like, diners like Louie's and the dives around Sheridan Square pulsed with men in biker gear who drank and fought and then slouched their way to the school on 44th Street where, during the summer rush, a Ben Gazzara or a Marilyn Monroe took turns at the switchboard. When McQueen was eventually accepted in 1955, he was as busy and happy – if broke – as he'd ever been. Irrespective of the value of what it actually produced, the benevolent originality of the Studio would reverberate for the rest of his life. Steve bought a leather jacket. He had his glossies taken. At an informal reading he stood toe to toe with James Dean and took turns to recite 'Sailing to Byzantium'.

Eli Wallach, who, 'like the great McQueen', trained at both the Playhouse and the Studio, believes 'Steve already had the raw skill. But what he learnt to do [in New York] was what separates the true artist from the ham – to watch and, above all, to listen.' In an impressively short time 'McQueen was the best *re*actor of his generation.' Peerlessly, he arrived.

A few brief years later various agents and loon-panted studio heads would fall over themselves to claim him as theirs, an accolade that, for Steve, had a lack of fascination all its own. He flattered but never fawned over his real mentor; he seems to have recognised that success was a more lasting and effective plug than obsequiousness. McQueen did what he could to notice those who had noticed him. 'I had that gift in me,' he said, 'but [Strasberg] had the key to unlock it . . . Nobody gives you talent. You either have it or you don't. What Lee gave me was definition.'

He did. But someone less attuned than he was to 'being' and more to theatrical elegance could never have kept in character, as Steve did, for a quarter of a century. And the character he kept in was both riveting and surprisingly versatile. Unlike some of the lesser lights at the Studio he was never just brazenly 'acting', an exclamation without a point. At worst, McQueen beamed what Meisner called his 'exquisite innocence'. In top gear, he had the rare gift of understatement, and even wizened hacks would come to admire how his each look adapted to the scene, how subtly and lightly he angled for the shot, every line dropping like a fly on the course. The brute realism was there, too: McQueen followed Bogart and Garfield and narrowly preceded the likes of De Niro in showing what it was like to actually live a life, how to elicit respect, how to bear up under misfortune. In what seemed like a flash and was only a few months, those qualities would mark him for a star.

Plausibility was Strasberg's business. And in Steve he had an actor who was all too blazingly real, human – and male. His love scenes, like his love life, soon became gladiatorial. According to the school's

Patricia Bosworth, McQueen and his actress girlfriend once improvised a scene in bed at the Studio. 'They were really rolling around – we actually thought they were screwing and everybody wanted to take this girl's place . . . I just kept staring at him. Finally Steve came over and said, "Do you want me to take you out?" I said, "Yes." He said, "OK. I'll take you out." I hopped on his motorbike and off we went.'

His key moral notion remained that actresses 'did it'.

McQueen, of all those who rose from the assembly line, was the most famously well slept. Here, too, versatility was the keynote of all his couplings, whether taking his women singly or in pairs, together with a lifelong fondness for the phrase 'I'll call you'. Some around New York thought Steve's eclecticism even swung to his own sex. There was, for one thing, the way he looked. For an alpha male, McQueen was disturbingly epicene: like something made by a jeweller's art, body perfectly honed, facial planes expertly turned, his china-blue eyes ornamented by long lashes. From his beauty spot up to the sandy hair he had artfully pouffed each week at a Chelsea salon, Steve was exquisite designer crumpet. His narrow head accentuated the sallowness of his skin. Like his acting, he had a wide expressive range – 'a Botticelli angel crossed with a chimp', in one critic's arch review. For several years McQueen alternated his *Wild One* leathers with a pair of Bermuda shorts, almost a specific, around the Village, against being 'straight'. Then there was the whole begged question of his name. More than one of his stage-school friends would blithely drop the prefix 'Mc', while McQueen, when once using the Studio bathroom (the one Strasberg labelled 'Romeo'), was shocked to see his surname daubed on the wall, with the last letter twisted into an 'r'.

Steve at times liked to play the caricature of a luvvie in class, insisting that he had the right, as well as the duty, to stretch. But outside 44th Street this tendency to see himself as both Steve the tease and McQueen the stud wasn't necessarily a good move. As one ex-friend puts it, 'He forgot that some folks didn't make the distinction.' It was no doubt this role-playing that led to the buzz that Steve was bisexual; bent. The photographer Bill Claxton, for one, speaks of being taken by McQueen on a voyage around his old New York haunts. 'He would show me where he'd lived . . . places he worked as a hustler. He had some pretty wild stories.' A persistent Studio rumour that McQueen dabbled in cross-dressing (frocks particularly) was a vile slur, but expressed a view some people had of him.

Both the book *Laid Bare* and a California radio DJ similarly offer, even today, any number of plausible 'McQueer' scenarios, if few real details. There may not be any. It is certain, though, that he idolised James Dean – whose act he shamelessly filched in *The Blob* – and that a friend of Dean's, Paul Darlow, was firmly under the impression that 'Jimmy and Steve were swishes'.

Those scenes in Dean's room at the Iroquois Hotel didn't create the gossip, but they did nonetheless colour it. Darlow and several other men were present one night in 1954 after a drinking binge uptown at Jerry's Bar. 'Like to do my hair?' Dean asked McQueen, helpfully drawing it back from his forehead as if clearing his mind, and producing a brush. Steve sat down behind him and patiently back-combed the famous quiff, thick and shiny as a mink's, breathing or perhaps lightly chuckling down the back of Dean's neck. Darlow then witnessed the following:

'Would you do mine?' Steve asked.

'Drop dead.'

'Come on, JD. Don't you dig my fur?'

'No,' Jimmy replied, 'it always looks so dago to me.'

Dean treated McQueen gingerly, once inviting him backstage at a performance of *The Immoralist* but then dropping him. Less than eighteen months later he was dead.

For the rest of his own life an undercurrent of all McQueen's relationships, marriages and affairs alike, was the nagging threat of homosexuality. He was legendarily touchy on the subject. According to the Londoner who first offered Steve 'a fag', he promptly 'threw a fit, prodding his fingers at me and yelling, "Fuck you! I'm Steve McQueen! Kiss my ass."' (It was his girlfriend who explained that in England they came twenty to a packet.) Six years later, in January 1968, Steve took a phone call at home in California. The anonymous party told him, 'There's a new book coming out that lists all the celebrities who are queer. I thought you'd like to know your name is in it.' He hung up. According to his ex-wife, Steve became phobic

– 'possessed' is the word she uses – from that day on, greatly accelerating his paranoia and, not incidentally, her own exit. On the set of *The Getaway* in 1972 McQueen was 'seriously freaked' at shooting a nude scene with 'real cons who happened to be gay', says Katy Haber, who worked on the film. And two years later, when Paul Newman broached the idea of his taking a homosexual role, McQueen told him, 'I could never play a fag.' It was an expression of disgust and also, so it seemed, of fear.

Mostly, though, Steve shrugged all that off. Publicly he bore most of his hangups in silence.

Back in the fifties there was something almost defiant about the flaming heterosexual whose line of active bachelorhood would fix two words on the New York stage scene, just as it had on the Florida beach. Big Mac: the serial seducer who dazzled his women with a neat mix of the goofy and the gothic. It was the end of December 1954 when several Playhouse students met in an automat off Times Square. Steve was there when they arrived. He startled one actress, Emily Hurt, by 'jumping to his feet and rolling his eyes while sticking his tongue out, like a mad kid'. McQueen's meal, she says, was 'hoovered down – he ate as though he was on fire, then calmly reached over and speared the meat from my plate'. There was also beer. 'Steve was sort of writhing around in his seat. He'd go into a slump and then suddenly toss off one-liners in a screwy way that reminded me of his acting.' One of them was in the form of a question: 'Why not come back for some New Year grog at my dump?' Steve appears, from the accounts of this dinner, to have behaved like a badly neglected child, because he now asked, according to Hurt, 'Want to see how a farm boy eats chicken?' Whether or not anyone took up the offer, he 'grabbed a drumstick and began ramming it in and out of his mouth, sucking it ostentatiously'.

The party broke up. 'Steve was kind of slouched there alone. His face was grim and set, and by now his shoulders were hunched. I held back, too, and I remember that he looked up and said something that shook me.

'"How would *you* treat a suicidal nut? Just the same as any other guy, or make an exception?"'

On that note the two of them walked arm-in-arm down Seventh

Avenue to Sheridan Square. Once inside Steve's bleak apartment, 'he again became the hyperactive kid, bouncing off walls and pleading with me to feed, by which he meant breastfeed, him'.* Broadly, according to Hurt, 'Steve loved anything with wheels or tits, probably in that order . . . All in all, a very torn-up guy. We became lovers. God knows, he shouldn't have added up to much, but that came from his sweet, klutzy side and the charm he could turn on like a switch. Nobody played the hurt puppy like Steve did.'

It was doubtless these same mood swings that led to the New York rumours he was bisexual, as well as bi-polar. McQueen's Bermuda shorts made for a particular talking point around the Studio. To others, the mumbling actor was but a lisp away from the drama queen. The truth is, at bottom Steve was an old-fashioned (and deeply unfashionable) man who wanted his partners, as most confirm, barefoot if not pregnant. While they 'took the precautions', says Hurt, McQueen wore a condom over his heart. Feeling himself let down by the first woman he knew, he never again let go with a woman.

Somehow, alone or with a mate, Steve managed an ever more wild pace. Whether tearing up Broadway on the Harley or wolfing his food and drink, he seemed to be an actor in a race with life. A twitchy figure in black, McQueen hustled along at a bouncy clip, with his toes cocked out at an angle, his very shoes – scuffed trainers – of a piece with a man on the move. Even his music was right: Steve listened nonstop to 'Fidgety Feet' and the jump-jive of a Louis Jordan. Aside from an ancient gramophone, the bike and the car, his few possessions were athletic: sweat pants, a punching bag, the barbells. When not actually working out, McQueen did most of his weightlifting with a fork and mug. The otherwise spartan flat was always well stocked with junk food. His only kitchen appliance was a blender, in which he mixed up an unholy brew of eggs, mouldy yogurt and coffee every morning. According to one visitor, 'Steve got up dead, but after the second hit of that crap he was like a dog off the leash. People had to run just to keep up with him.'

* The same mammiferous yen would be combined years later with a motoring one, when McQueen calmly asked another party to 'flash [her] headlights' for him. Emotionally, the woman says, 'Steve was naïf.'

As an actor, McQueen was emerging almost fully formed. He was poised; he was go-getting. He was also – and always – spoiling for a fight. In his wordless way, a clear plan of attack grew out of his five-year apprenticeship.

By his twenty-fifth birthday Steve had been in three plays far off Broadway, and had a reputation for being both talented and difficult. The money from these productions was long since gone. Early that winter he was forced to trade down to a fifth-floor slum on East 10th Street with a tin bathtub in the kitchen. His previous place, he now decided, was 'fucking near the Plaza' by comparison. McQueen sold the MG and took part-time work as a mechanic in an Upper West Side garage, where he once suffered the indignity of having to service James Dean's Harley. Something about the flush to his face when he handed back the keys suggested, to a mutual friend, that 'Steve was jealous of Jimmy, and was busy figuring out how to deal with it'. Aside from a brief encounter at Jerry's, that was the last time the two actors ever met.

Steve did, however, reluctantly put in several man-hours of hard work with Julian. They eventually got back in touch. Whatever his normal code on women, these tedious and often trying interventions were much to McQueen's credit. Two or three times that winter his mother called him to discharge her from hospital, where she was being treated for acute alcoholism. He always went, walking her home from Bellevue through Gramercy Park and down Irving to East 18th, where Julian liked to stop in for a beer at Pete's Tavern. By any account there was something heroic about Steve's self-control: he was able to rally round Julian while never again daring to trust, let alone to love her. As Dora Yanni quite rightly says, 'That woman put the iron into Steve's soul.' Iron, she adds, that ran deeper than blood. Without Julian he would never have been a great tragedian, as opposed to another pantomime punk figure. Yanni happened to see McQueen hurrying into the hospital one evening, his white gym shoes snapping against the polished floor. 'She's frothing,' he told her.

Implacably, Julian's influence was everywhere.

Meanwhile Steve continued, as Yanni herself knew, to 'root himself stupid' around New York. For other actors the most seductive aspect of Big Mac may not have been his innocence, but the startling, pre-emptive willingness to do literally anything to make it. When McQueen auditioned for Strasberg, he was one of only five actors out of 2000 applicants to be accepted that season. He also lobbied Witt nonstop for work. Later that spring of 1955 he landed a spot in an hour-long dramatic NBC anthology series, the Goodyear Playhouse. Both ten ratings points lower and twenty IQ points higher than current TV fare like *I Love Lucy*, *The Chivington Raid*, broadcast on 27 March, was McQueen's screen debut.

He followed it by launching himself, as Yanni says anachronistically, 'like a Scud missile' at a play called *Two Fingers of Pride*. This pro-labour harangue, set in the New York docks and broadly in the mould of *On the Waterfront*, was being cast by its writer Jim Longhi and the director Jack Garfein. Steve read for the second lead, having assured them that he, like his character, was Italian-American and twenty-two years old. Neither was true, but otherwise McQueen fitted the part well. He then borrowed $35 (never repaid) to buy his first Actors Equity card. Even though the show never transferred from summer stock in Ogunquit, Maine, Steve's 'original, primitive' portrayal of Nino the longshoreman was noted warmly by the *New York Post* and without insult in the *News*. Garfein managed to get McQueen an appointment with the talent agency MCA. Steve arrived for his interview at the glass-and-marble office on Madison Avenue by riding his Harley through the lobby, into the lift, and up to the eleventh floor. MCA accepted him.

Later that winter the director Robert Wise was in New York casting his biopic *Somebody Up There Likes Me*, set in the roasted light of Hell's Kitchen and the prize ring. Wise remembers an audition when 'this kid came in, cocky, wearing a sport jacket and a beanie cap, and told me: "I'm your man."' There were dozens of other actors in immaculate black denim up for the bit part of Fidel (often wrongly given as Fido), the blade-wielding punk. Wise had never heard of McQueen. He did, however, recognise the potential of the 'lean, tense boy you felt could slug you as fast as smile' whom MCA brought him. Steve got the job. For $19 per diem (rising to $50 on the few days he had any lines) he got to play out scenes from his own adolescence.

Somebody was a remarkable case study of the transaction between life and art, at its core dramatising the career of the boxer Rocky Graziano. McQueen came on as a greaser, whose sudden eruptions of energy – 'You lookin' at *me*?' – lent, with their De Niro-like emphasis, a touch of added menace to the proceedings. His safari down the back alleys of New York was freighted with three obsessions – hubcaps, pool and mob violence – as well as a touch of mimicry, specifically a disgruntled Brando mushmouth. It was the first, though not the last instance of Steve's knack for projecting his own life's path on screen. *Somebody* was good, hard-bitten stuff.

As a member of Graziano's street gang Steve offered his usual concentration, quickness and stern, appraising gaze. Appearing in only the first fifteen minutes of the film, he cut a slick dash as well as a tone that was satirical and vicious to the outside world, yet warm and accepting of friends – the distinctive McQueen tone, in his first fully confident role. Following the style of the movie as a whole, Steve's movements were crisp and taut, his voice gruff, his type now cast as a threatening hardnut, yet whose performance was never sacrificed to the action. Mostly, of course, the critics still ignored him. McQueen's role was uncredited, and thus somewhat below a *Variety*'s radar. His few notices in the trades were good enough, but what struck Steve more, if possible, was the wallop he had on Hollywood. Men like Wise and MCA's John Foreman now sat up for the 'kid' whose talent for engaging menace was complemented nicely by a slit mouth and the shaggy-pup eyes.

The man who played top dog to Steve's Fido was a thirty-year-old actor in only his own second role. From then on, Paul Newman's career became a kind of pace car for McQueen's. Steve's first director is only the most compelling witness to the fact that it was 'undeclared war' between them, two physical types whose commonplace, yet heroic qualities inspired, on one level, several PhD theses and, striking a lower note on the academic scale, Erica Jong's orgasm in *Esquire*. 'Who has the bluest eyes? Newman or McQueen? It's difficult to say, but McQueen's twinkle more. He makes me think of all those leathery-necked cowboys at remote truck stops in Nevada. Does he wear pointy boots? And does he take them off when he screws?' The most charitable reading of this rivalry is that it neatly relit the torch once carried by Steve for James Dean (originally slated for the Graziano role) before the latter died in September 1955. It reached its shining apogee, or leaden nadir, when the two stars came to debate their billing, eighteen years later, in *The Towering Inferno*. A compromise was eventually reached whereby McQueen's name would be on the left, and Newman's a shade higher, exactly a foot to the right, on the marquee. Steve knew very well the direction in which people read. That twelve-inch gap was supremacy superbly controlled.

Mutual ambivalence, meanwhile, bordered on open war. Only this can explain the bile which seeped out of McQueen's private assessment of Newman like an oil leak. 'Fuckwit', he dubbed him at moments of stress.

Frank Knox, an extra on *Somebody*, remembers Steve as the 'sweetest guy' off the set and a 'bear in rutting season' on it. One night after work the two of them went out for a beer at Pete's. When the time came for McQueen to talk about acting, according to Knox, he 'outlined his positive accomplishments to date, noted that more needed to be done, and promised that it would be'. Steve ended the evening by pledging to 'pull [his] shit together', to 'grab the brass ring' and, all in all, to 'get some sugar out of this business – to be a big star' by his thirtieth birthday.

Fighting words, but for Steve McQueen, who believed in doing rather than talking, they raised a flag. There was no way, says Knox, McQueen would ever settle for the sad fate of most struggling actors' careers. 'You got the impression, with him, it really *was* Hollywood or bust. He'd either go under or hammer a few million bucks out of the system. Even then, Steve was always ten per cent more rabid than the rest.'

Work, in Tinseltown, bringing more work, McQueen appeared on TV again early in 1956. He walked through the 'US Steel Hour' drama unobtrusively, wearing a shapeless grey suit that somehow on him looked suave, draping him like folded wings. Steve was quiet, small and slightly stooped, but the wooden appearance was deceptive: there was a nervy concentration about him, his half-hooded glance murderous and sharp. Aptly enough for McQueen, that particular episode was entitled 'Bring Me a Dream'. Soon after it aired, he was badgering Strasberg, MCA and both the director and writer for a part in the watermark play *A Hatful of Rain*, a stark depiction of the misery, though occasionally blissful mundanity of drug addiction. After weeks of brutal jockeying the role of Johnny Pope, the doomed greaser lead, went to type in the form of the Studio graduate, McQueen's rival Ben Gazzara. By then, Gazzara also had a contract for the film *The Strange One*. He soon left New York for an oddly unfulfilled career in Hollywood. Without him, the play's future was uncertain.

McQueen wanted *Hatful*, but he was trouble. What with the pay demands and the firings he had, over the last four years, cost producers plenty – 'a lot of freight', as they say in the business, to carry for an actor many thought unemployable at worst and a long shot at best. But he was persistent. McQueen always had a hawk eye for where real power lay, how to scam a casting. He kept up a nonstop flow of notes and cards, not only to the suits but to their wives: 'Roses, always roses,' says one of the latter. That spring McQueen spent time amongst real junkies in Hell's Kitchen. He read, rehearsed and understudied. He offered to defer his modest salary in exchange for a percentage of profits. 'Short of some shtick involving a horse's head,' says Frank Knox, 'it's hard to think what more Steve could have done.' In a bravura ploy beyond his own means he even had his few trade notices photocopied, professionally bound and sent round.

It was a full-time siege, and it worked. Stockholm syndrome, the obscure love that flowers between ransomer and captive, paralysed the producers' will. By midsummer Steve had the job.

The critics weren't happy. McQueen threw himself into the role, never missing a cue, much less a trick, and even dying his hair black. And yet, with all his intensity and his million-toothed smile, his performance was oddly earthbound: it came down to inexperience, earning Steve the backstage name Cornflake. He never settled into a rhythm or pitch that brought out the best in his speeches.

With Gazzara, at least, the character had existed in the round. Steve never combined the same sense of insight into personality and condition with that seemingly easier thing, a good voice. Whereas the loudest noises in the house had once been the shocked gasps of the crowd, for McQueen audience vocalisation tended to be in the form of sniggering as lines like 'Watch my back!' broke into falsetto. Physically, his Pope thrummed with a wildness that was all the more dramatic for being contained and controlled; but when Steve let go vocally, he squeaked. Only six weeks into his run he was fired from *Hatful*, though he briefly returned to it on tour. By then, of course, accepting rejection had long since become a part of McQueen's résumé, under the bold heading of 'Skills'. But 1956, the year he flopped on Broadway and first discovered film, was a true turning-point. Steve never worked in the theatre again.

What made McQueen still run? His pride, obviously, but also the fact that he was slowly carving out a name on two coasts. Even fucking up in lights, as he put it, was *something*. He knew the significant prestige of failure. Among a loyal if obscurely positioned cult, meanwhile, Steve was a man to watch. Their patronage may not have pulled much with the critics, but it meant a lot to McQueen. MCA's support was also critical in allowing his idiosyncratic and highly individual talent to flourish. All he had to be now was strong enough to survive the wait. The truly charismatic, he knew, are never long delayed by the paroxysms of the second-rate.

His first night in *Hatful*, a middle-aged fan had rushed the stage, flinging at McQueen a pair of red silk panties.

From the beginning, Steve wasn't only worshipped by a group of T-shirted male admirers, barrio types, he was a virtual religion among women. Tooling around on his bike, the blender and a bottle permanently clamped under his arm, McQueen skilfully exploited the first free-love generation, the main source of his 'juice', says Emily Hurt, being his shrewd understanding that 'the smiley-tough look would get those undies down'. Aspiring actresses loved him. Back in East 10th Street he always seemed to understand what they were driving at, believed that it was the right thing, and enthusiastically did what he could to help. He invariably told them he thought they were talented and wanted to hear them read. Many of these ad hoc auditions lasted to all hours. According to Hurt, 'Back in those days, Steve was virtually a sex machine. You were either sleeping with him, or you knew someone who was.' His partners knew he could be foul-mouthed – snapping at a lame suggestion, cursing his luck with producers – and deeply bored by subjects that didn't personally move him. But that wasn't the Steve McQueen of their common experience. On countless nights a woman like Dora Yanni had seen him charm a guest by 'a quiet tear or that billion dollar grin'. It was the same for Hurt. 'Steve already knew how to moisturise his audience. He may not have made it on Broadway, but he was a true superstar in the Village.'

More and more, words like 'fucker' echoed around when either sex spoke of him.

The horizontal skirmishes were legendary, and followed broadly down the maternal line. 'Steve was addicted to being thrown off-balance,' says Hurt. 'Because Julian had been crazy, he expected that from his mate.' That autumn of 1956 McQueen took a pale, flapper-thin girl named Mimi Benning to a movie or two and then made her cry in a taxi. Numerous others went out on variants of the same 'yo-yo date', as she puts it. Consummation would come almost immediately after these trips to Loew's or the Quad, and was guaranteed by the sort of groping that was mandatory in the back row. One casual partner remembers being fed blueberry pie and beer by Steve in 10th Street after a showing of *Giant*, and being told, 'I'll never make it – as a man or an actor.' Yet within a few weeks McQueen was in and out of lights on Broadway; and he fell in love.

Her name was Neile Adams, and when he met her she was already starring in her second musical, *The Pajama Game*. This lucky and talented showgirl, then just twenty-three and with a pixieish vigour, had, like him, never known her father. Neile was brought up by her mother in the Philippines, and eventually spent three years there in a Japanese concentration camp. After that, the teenager was sent to a convent in Hong Kong and boarding school in Connecticut. As if not already exotic enough, after seeing *The King and I* Neile then announced her intention of becoming a dancer. Against all odds, she made it. With her dark hair cut short, gamine-style, dressed in a silk shirt, scarf and toreador trousers, Neile was a frail, classic beauty with a surprisingly loud, throaty laugh. They met at Downey's restaurant – where McQueen made his move over a bowl of spaghetti – and the fascination was mutual. As an admiring friend says, they might have won the Nobel Prize for chemistry. There was also the old saw of opposites attracting. Whereas Steve lacked the ability to make light of misfortune, Neile presented a more straightforward type: the outgoing young ingénue who 'dug people'. Her inner life, while rebellious, found its outlet on stage.

Later that same night there was a knock at Neile's apartment door. It was Steve. She said, 'I'm going to crash.' Then he said, 'Yeah, I am too.' He couldn't learn to clean and would sooner starve than cook but he did, nonetheless, light up that small, cluttered bedroom.

'Boy,' says Neile, 'was I happy.'

He was disguised, veiled, going through social motions; she was enjoying herself, displaying what she was, opening herself up to immediate experience. One was playing for time, the other was full of life for the moment. A koala and a leopard, they somehow found themselves on the same limb of the tree. Sure enough, Neile joined the long list of lovers, though for once Steve, radically for him, was on turf well beyond what Benning calls 'Olympic screwing'. After exactly a week he moved into Neile's digs at 69 West 55th Street. McQueen arrived carrying a battered suitcase full of old clothes, his crash helmet and the barbells. As Neile says, 'The man was obviously used to travelling light.'

That September, once fired from *Hatful*, Steve took off on his new BSA through Florida and, from there, to Cuba. The ominous signs of revolution were already brewing when McQueen got himself arrested for selling *yanqui* cigarettes in a bar. On 3 October 1956 Neile was handed a telegram at her hotel in Hollywood, where she was then testing for Bob Wise's film *This Could Be the Night*:

I LOVE YOU HONEY SEND ME MONEY LET ME KNOW WHATS HAPPENING IN CARE OF WESTERN UNION CON AMOR

ESTEBAN

The central theme of all McQueen's adult relationships – that contempt for those who caved to him had its parallel respect for those who didn't – was quickly brought home when Neile turned him down. Steve limped back to West 55th, having sold most of his clothes and cannibalised the BSA for bail, with the words: 'It's all right, baby. I admire your spunk.' Then he sought out a jeweller friend in the Village and talked him into designing a twisted molten gold ring for $25 down and eight further quarterly instalments. Two years later Neile herself finally paid off the balance.

Steve, who had an instinct for reality, would remember the shabbier details of the next month all his life: the 'dark pit' when Neile returned to California to film *This Could Be the Night*, the two or three now suddenly tacky 'honkings' behind her back, the constant trickling rain of New York, the flow of reverse-charge calls to the coast; and finally, the guilty sale of Uncle Claude's watch to raise funds. McQueen himself arrived in California on the morning of 2 November 1956. Bob Wise recalls 'the kid from *Somebody* suddenly holed up with Neile in the hotel. Fair enough, but when he also hung around the lot, I had him barred.' As Wise saw it, despite her own rough knocks, 'the girl in my movie was young and impressionable', and McQueen, a hard man to resist, had definitely hustled her. Her manager Hillard Elkins remembers 'Neile asking my advice, and me telling her she was being a shmuck. In those days, I didn't know McQueen as an actor. What I did know was that he screwed anything with a pulse, and I thought he was wrong for her.' On the other hand, Neile and Steve had a peculiarly dire family past in common. They'd already bonded with each other's mothers in New York. Carmen Adams took to him as one orphaned, deprived, too thin (if sadly lacking in manners) and fed him on nourishing Spanish dishes. McQueen had also introduced his fiancée to Julian, whom she liked. 'Whatever she'd done or hadn't done for Steve, as a woman I empathised,' Neile says today. 'When she had him, she'd only been a kid herself, trying to find her way in the world.' The Adamses, too, had had troubles at home. 'It was two damaged birds flocking together,' says Neile. 'Plus, I really loved the man.'

That same Friday night Steve and Neile climbed into a rented Ford Thunderbird, waved to the film crew and headed for the border. The two lapsed Catholics decided on a whim to marry in the mission at San Juan Capistrano, twenty miles south of LA. When that was vetoed by the nuns on the unanswerable grounds that no banns had been published, McQueen exploded. For a while back there, courting Neile, he'd been fine. His truncated vocabulary and make-do syntax had both risen to the occasion. But now he had a schedule to keep. Fuck the banns. Nor were anxieties about the 'young people's' piety misplaced. 'Open a vein,' McQueen snarled, and took off again in a crunch of gravel. A few miles further down the coast the now fugitive couple were stopped by the police for speeding. What followed was a scene at the very edge of a Chaplin skit as the law, once briefed by Steve, hurriedly escorted them to a local Lutheran minister. The McQueens were duly married, just before midnight, in a small chapel in San Clemente. The legal witnesses were the highway patrolmen who had pulled them over an hour earlier. 'It was far out,' Steve recalled. 'Here we were getting hitched, and these two big cops with their belted pistols an' all. Felt like a shotgun wedding.' By now he'd known his wife for just over three months.

The man Neile Adams married was as gritty as a half-completed road. McQueen wasn't yet the popular notion of the alpha male – the ape who gets to have sex with all the females and swagger past the competition – but he was getting there, fast. Neile remembers that he rarely or never had any money, gobbled down his food and had a fondness for both Old Milwaukee beer and pot. Steve was ill-read, indeed semi-literate (his next wife famously complained that he couldn't spell the word 'blue'). As for social graces, he didn't overdo them. When Elkins invited him to lunch in the Polo Lounge, McQueen gazed dolefully at the French menu before finally asking if he might be allowed a burger and a shake. He did, however, Neile saw, have that much rarer thing – instinct. 'Steve could always tell the very few good guys from the phony.' As the nuns had rightly feared, he wasn't religious. Besides Neile, McQueen's sustaining love was of machines, and for him happiness – its possibility and reality, its attainment and capture – came out of a finely tuned call-and-response with the internal combustion engine, the channelling of some great unknown, copulating force that called for the perfect alignment of man and motor. 'A good set of wheels gets me *hard*,' he'd say. In a race, Steve always felt that his own car, like a woman, was personally challenging him.

His competitiveness! No one who knew McQueen ever forgot it. The actor Dean Jones saw the classic, turbo version of it around the late 1960s. 'Steve and I used to go biking, and he couldn't stand – I mean he pathologically hated – being second. The reason McQueen got in so many wrecks is that, good as he was, he overcooked it.' A charger, in race lingo. No piss-ant limits, he always said, for *him*. Stirling Moss, one of the few men Steve deferred to on four wheels, encountered the same thing whether on the track at Sebring or driving the canyon roads of Bel Air. 'McQueen was fast, but he was also undisciplined. My God, the *fearlessness* of the man. But that was his whole life.' Sure enough, Steve offered continual homages to 'mud' both on and off the screen. He'd already lived too long with the rules and restrictions which pettily obstructed his happiness. Far too fucking long. McQueen 'constantly had to be proving himself', notes Neile. It was the same whether at poker, pinball, sex, fighting or acting. 'You didn't win, *he* did.' No doubt it was this 'madness and fire' that led men like the director Buzz Kulik to portray the Steve of 1956 as a 'little shit'. A perceptive friend noticed that he 'was never difficult with people he didn't like, the people he didn't take seriously. He was the world's most charming guy to waiters. On the other hand, he fell out at one time or another with almost all his cronies.' To Dean Jones, 'Steve's film career made a virtue out of his flaws as a man. For me, he had the edge and frenzy of genius.'

The newlyweds' honeymoon in San Diego and Ensenada was a balmy bit of upward assimilation, but soon enough they came down to earth again with a bump. Only two days later the McQueens drove back to Neile's Culver City hotel. After twenty-four hours of continuous drinking and drag-racing the Ford, Steve promptly fell asleep over the soup course of their welcome-home supper. Various members of the film crew picked him up and put him on a couch. McQueen apparently slumbered for a few minutes, suddenly waking up again to telephone an order for two cases of Old Milwaukee, together with a fleet of taxis to take the entire *Night* cast out to a club. Bob Wise, who still had his doubts about Steve's acting, was impressed with the pair's mutual spark and kept an image of them as romantic lovers. He felt protective of the woman. There was something 'young-boyish', too, about the nearly middle-aged man. At weekends Steve and Neile started on a search that continued for some years for his lost father Bill, then thought to be living in California. Most other days, while Neile worked on *This Could Be the Night,* her spouse mooched around the Ballona Creek bars, tearing off into the Baldwin Hills on the 650 BSA or in the couple's new VW (traded in, with Neile's next pay cheque, for a Corvette, then a second red MG). Passers-by couldn't help but notice that McQueen liked to ride the bike bare-chested and that he carried a bullwhip over the back wheel.

California had opened Steve's eyes, but it hadn't made him much money. He wound his way back to New York at Christmas. Between filming, guesting on *The Walter Winchell Show* and starring in a Vegas revue, Neile was now among the most prolific and commercially hot women on the stage. Creativity like that is usually part discipline and part indiscipline. Hers was all discipline. Steve constantly demanded Neile's attention, particularly now that he – the 'guy who [couldn't] get arrested', as he put it on honeymoon – paled, professionally, next to her. The cycle that emerged was explosive. One night, rushing to the theatre, she served him up a quickie TV dinner. McQueen said nothing, merely acted. In a single swoop, turkey bits, reconstituted peas, diced carrots, instant mash and the plastic sauce cup splattered the far wall. *Frozen shit.* According to their next-door neighbour, it was a 1950s role-reversal, the man 'always flopping around the apartment' while the woman, saintly in just about every account, 'did everything, everywhere, all the time'. More to the point, Neile, though 'ambitious and hyperactive – a mini Audrey Hepburn', was also fanatically loyal to her husband's cause. She introduced him, for instance, to Hilly Elkins and her agents at William Morris. Between them, they got him a role in a TV drama called *The Defenders*, opposite Bill Shatner of later *Star Trek* fame. Steve used to read for the part, alone or with his wife, in that cramped flat with the strong reek of damp and Lucky Strike cigarettes, honing his gift to affect any identity at the drop of a hat – to become, in a split second, according to the demands of his public, a hick, a thug, a greaser, a romantic hero, while remaining at bottom a world-weary child. As they walked around a New York which has since disappeared – open drains that stank, and horsemeat burgers he devoured as if they were famine relief – she encouraged him to see everyday life as a form of rehearsal. Steve's mind would latch mathematically onto the number of steps he took between lights, or the exact beat of each foot, and then how he could fit his stage lines to the rhythm. It was Neile who gave him the great advice to show more of his 'wonderful smile' and childlike wit on screen. She told him frankly that he'd 'stunk – done a bad Brando' in *Somebody Up There Likes Me*. Neile's support helped him sidestep many of the struggling actor's other occupational hazards. Steve had always hated having to wash dishes or do anything too low to make ends meet. Nowadays he no longer had to. In the first year of their marriage McQueen and his wife earned $4000 and $50,000 respectively, which they pooled evenly.

Then he began to catch up.

If *Somebody*'s Fidel had to a large extent been an imaginative manipulation of Steve's own life, the killer role in *The Defenders* was almost pure invention. 'McQueen was brilliant,' says Hilly Elkins. 'Everyone knew the material was lame – there was a certain amount of shtick involved – but looking at Steve's face, seething with passion, even the most gnarled cynic melted. What struck me most were those eyes. God, but he had presence.' The other thing McQueen had was a voice. Perfect pitch. Diction: dramatically improved. Gone for ever was Johnny Pope's castrato croak, replaced by a rich, full-toned instrument which Steve lowered pointedly when he was most threatening, and raised when irony called. After that broadcast of 4 March 1957 the CBS switchboard took dozens of calls from fans praising his performance.

It was the last year of Steve's long education. While Neile signed on for a revue in Vegas he took another job for CBS and severed his final ties with the Actors Studio. From now on, the 'mad Hungarian' Pete Witt, still clinging doggedly to his protégé, Elkins and the William Morris agency, suddenly all dancing crisply executed gavottes around their 'kid', would work together day and night to 'break' him. Three more television spots quickly followed. McQueen would later blame 'a lot of [his] early marital shit' on the fact that he awoke each day 'knowing that either the wife or I would be out grooving away' on location. On many of those days Steve would have to go for an audition, shoot a test or do a reading. In retrospect it was astonishing that he could combine such stress with a relentlessly full social life. Somehow, he always found time for play. When not shuttling between coasts, he was still busy around the bars and fleshpots of Greenwich Village. Once Neile was gone Esteban quickly became Desperado again, haunting the back room at Louie's, where women in tight skirts loitered round the pool table. Commitment was fine, he said. He'd never abuse it. It was just hussies he wanted, the little sluts.

One night Steve showed up at Louie's on his BSA, brandishing the bullwhip. By his own account, he drank 'about a vat' of Old Milwaukee. Much later on, some sort of ruckus broke out with another actor, a young Disney star who, in his own wry homage, carried a white rodent named Mickey in his breast pocket. There was a brief fraternal punch-up over the green baize, the pet mouse carefully avoided. Then Steve announced he was buying everyone a drink, to keep him company while 'the old lady' was out of town. Two women, encouraged, followed him up to the bar. Discouraged, one of them called him a shit. Towards dawn the other one accompanied Steve to 55th Street.

Many of those TV spots, not least the one called *Four Hours in White*, were *tours de force*, as McQueen first found and then glossed what Emily Hurt calls his 'smiley-tough combination'. In that particular soap he appeared as cool and detached as a Strand cigarette advertisement. Even in the grainy, low-budget production values of early television, men like Elkins recognised a remarkable face and presence that could, with a year or two's more work, trump even a Bogie or Walter Brennan. Thanks to Elkins, McQueen's seismic break would follow in the summer of 1958. Seven years to the month after he first applied to stage school, he finally had a hit. From then on McQueen was a seller's market for twenty-two years, the terms increasingly in his favour, right through to the end.

Professionally as well as sexually speaking, Steve was often told he was a shit in those years, and he didn't disagree. Even Bogart, as McQueen was always reminding people, had had to claw his way to the top. As he also never tired of saying around Louie's, 'When I believe in something I fight like hell for it . . . All the nice guys are in the unemployment line.' Even – or perhaps especially – at this first rip of his career, Steve was continually pushing for more 'face time' and wasn't above throwing a fit, or walking off, if denied. He was a virtuoso self-promoter. Sometimes it worked, as when he told a TV director, 'You're photographing me, not some fucking rocks,' and then had him swap a lavish, colour supplement shot of Monument Valley for extra close-ups of himself. Sometimes it didn't. A friend remembers a scene in 1959 when the producer of McQueen's series tore a strip off him for 'bullying' some of the crew.

Puzzled, Steve asked what he meant.

The suit replied that he meant McQueen was being a shit, that's what.

Unbelieving, Steve replied that he only wanted what was best for the show, and besides, 'I don't need your stinking $750 a week – I've got bread in the bank.'

The mogul calmly pressed the button on his office speaker and said, 'Find out how much money McQueen has in the bank.' Five minutes later the machine spoke back: 'Two hundred dollars.'

McQueen never fully understood acting, or he chose not to, which made him carve away at it all the more. For all the voice lessons and facial drills in front of the West 55th mirror, there was something more innate than Methodic in the way he rubbed grit into even the blandest lines. By the end of 1958 Steve was being touted as a TV star, but always wanted to work on the big screen; the transformation was so successful that he virtually invented the crossover, fully five years and ten pictures before Clint Eastwood. His new style, which he discovered almost immediately, was bluff and laconic – he hid behind silence as behind a bomb-proof door – and yet, like Steve himself, it had an unmistakable elegance and wit. It was perfect cool with a flash of menace.

McQueen's second film was five star gobbledegook. The role itself was less scanty, if not much better than the first. Largely through Peter Witt, he landed the part of a young Jewish lawyer in *Never Love a Stranger*, Harold Robbins's latest effort to fillet the sex from a thin, not to say gaunt plot. This queasily melodramatic tale of the Naked City wasn't released for nearly two years, and then tanked. As a story, it was reminiscent of a bad episode of *The Untouchables*.

There was no pretence at range. The whole thing seemed to shrink down to a stage play and then simply to have forgotten to tell the cameraman to stay home. *Stranger* was located along a narrow strip of the Hudson river, which served as a central metaphor for the soggy, meandering plot. Most of the acting conveyed the shrill, one-note dramatics of Ed Wood on a much lower budget. For once McQueen's damnation of an out-and-out bomb, and his own part in it, was underdone. Dick Bright, best known as the omnipresent Mob crony in *The Godfather* trilogy, thought Steve 'shit' in *Stranger*, yet sagely guessed he was still 'working on a formula'. In that eventual blueprint, the voice, the sense of mood and action would be so well crafted that it would – and did – take pages to even review the underlying sense of danger, the hidden motivations McQueen could pack into a few tart lines of dialogue. Before long, he would play it tight and hard in even the most asinine soap opera. At this stage, Steve was still more concerned with merely acting than he was with pace or narrative drive, but his Cabell was a heroic failure. A star wasn't born.

The reviews shook him – McQueen a ham? Back to grunt work, weekly handouts from his wife? – as if he'd been slapped from a trance. After that, Steve rehearsed twice as hard as before. Not the least of the lessons from *Stranger* was that if he dominated the rest of the cast backstage, he could handle them on screen, too. Especially the women.

That cramped little crew hotel.* Steve made a start towards super-stardom by following the lead of young actors who became notorious for their behaviour. The leading man John Drew Barrymore, for one, had already run afoul of the law and his own temper, landing himself first an arrest sheet and then a year-long suspension by Actors Equity. Barrymore spent most of his evenings in the unbuttoned privacy of the 'sin bin' or crew lounge, convivially doling out what were probably cigarettes. Some of these, along with Barrymore himself, would in turn make their way to the junior actresses' room known as 'the dorm'. McQueen, failing to heed the film's title, soon began an affair with his co-star Lita Milan. This, too, had some of the properties of a St Trinian's romp. The couple signalled each other excitedly at night with torches from their adjacent suites, and at one point Steve climbed into an empty maid's room to eavesdrop on a call between Milan and a girlfriend immediately below, repeating the intimate conversation to her in bed. There was an abandon and fun, even frivolity, about the place, though Robbins and the movie itself were a lurking presence. Most nights, Steve would stop off for an Old Milwaukee in the lounge, dine on a burger, and then join Milan in the room with the red neon light from the Chinese restaurant

---

* Eccentrically, half of *Never Love a Stranger*, a film with an almost cartographic obsession with New York, was shot in Hollywood and elsewhere in California.

flickering outside. At weekends he drove back to Neile in Las Vegas.

Emily Hurt saw McQueen becoming a star before her eyes. They still ran into each other around the Village, and he told her about Lita Milan. On the other hand, he had a marriage, and 'Steve was intent on having most of its vows kept', specifically the one about the woman obeying the man. He told Hurt that Neile gave him the royal treatment, and asked only that he 'be careful' – discreet, in other words – with the overcaffeinated young starlets who filled his time between one take and the next. Neile was well aware of the casual screwing that went on throughout their marriage. She tolerated it. When McQueen coined the admiring phrase, 'Slopes are different' he was talking about several characteristics peculiar to Eastern women – but mainly the way they give men a long leash, even if all the leashes ultimately are held in female hands. He usually confessed to his wife straight away. 'Oh, Steve,' she would murmur as he started in, silently pour them both a drink, and say no more until a quiet 'Why?' or 'It's all right, baby,' as he finished.

As Neile writes, 'My combination Oriental and Latin upbringing had taught me that men separated love and marriage from their feckless romps in the hay . . . So, OK, I thought. I can handle it – I have to – as long as he doesn't flaunt it.' And McQueen didn't, says Hurt. 'He wasn't stupid. Steve nearly always told Neile before someone else did.' Sex, fear, guilt. 'Scared shitless. What am I gonna do about the fuck-flings?' he'd ask Hurt, one of the flung. Worse, 'What will the wife do? I can't live without her.' Luckily for him, McQueen had chosen an exceptionally stoical mate. It was only when Neile cast back over their lives fifteen years later that the carefully preserved biodome cracked, under the twin stresses of drugs and madness, with shattering results.

Somebody and *Stranger* may not have been much, but between them they formed a hyphen linking the Cornflake to the king of cool. In the late fifties Steve was still inclined to bad Brando and Dean parodies, but as he got older he began to prefer acting that was formed out of the actor's own 'mud', simple and to the bone. He was fond of a remark by Hitchcock, who held that true drama involved 'doing nothing well'. Steve rightly liked to say that he'd lived, and it showed in his work. The strong jaw and X-ray stare gave him a knocked-about look. McQueen seemed much more grown up than most of Hollywood's new crop of pretty boys. His range as an actor may not have been wide, but it was profoundly deep. He was the self-sufficient male animal, the kind of Hemingway hero who combines complexity with reserve to portray a tortuous emotional life. In film after film he carried himself like a regular guy, fissile but superbly taut, and Steve could no more slither into histrionics than he could enjoy a night out in women's clothing. The sheer intensity of his second twenty-five years was certainly deepened by the horrors of the first. As Hurt rightly says, 'Steve McQueen could have been a character in a Steve McQueen movie.'

He served up some other fare in 1958–9 and did well, using the same skills he'd honed in *The Defenders* and adding touches brought by Neile. She urged him, for example, to finally drop 'Steven' for the more freewheeling Steve. 'When I met [McQueen] he'd no name or stage presence – that came later – but he did have a great head on his shoulders and he learnt fast.' She wasn't the first woman to groom a star, some would sniff jealously; but Neile was, nonetheless, stunningly successful at converting the B-film hack into a potent Hollywood player. Now more than ever, she hammered his case with Elkins and Stan Kamen of William Morris. Thanks in turn to their all-hours agentry, Steve won the lead in *The Great St Louis Bank Robbery*, his first ever above-the-title billing – a modest caper directed by Charles Guggenheim and funded by family money. The idea behind this vanity picture was to show, in excruciating detail, how an actual heist might be planned, intercut with doomed efforts to convey 'character'. McQueen played the getaway driver. His whole-heartedness offset what, on the most charitable view, were the gang's familiar cardboard types: the muttering hophead, the rough diamond, the gentle weakling and the voice of reason – the hero's girlfriend, played by one Molly McCarthy. Against this cut-out backdrop, Steve did his best, at once glamorous and tragic, but *St Louis* soon tipped into farce. Real indignity befell the climax, with McQueen sobbing, 'I'm not with them!' as the cuffs went on. By then the script seemed to have lost all interest in suspense, either in this particular rip or within the larger saga; although the Guggenheims talked about a sequel, their services as film moguls weren't to be required again.

Steve auditioned every chance he could, on his way to being one of the envied stars in a town full of them; Neile and Elkins and Kamen pounded on every door they could, bulk-mailing his glossy to scouts and producers. With talent and support like that he was picking up speed like a competition-tuned Ferrari, bigger and more menacing every time anyone glanced in their mirror.

Along the way McQueen also took some desperately lame roles, simply in order to have somewhere to go in the mornings. At least one of his self-coined 'fuck films' would make *St Louis* look like Sophocles. This was *The Blob*, his last ever 'something or anything' picture, done, according to Elkins, 'pure and simple to get Steve seen'. The three-week shoot with a threadbare air to it in Downingtown, Pennsylvania, cost a total of $220,000. For his part as Steve Andrews, the local high schooler, twenty-eight-year-old McQueen was offered $3000 or 10 per cent of the film's gross. He opted for the cash. To date, close to $20 million has rained down for *The Blob*, a figure as over the top as most of the acting. Steve fumed about this miscalculation for the rest of his life.

Mixed-up kids, authority figures and the definitive, gelatinous red menace. With all the stock types and plot cued by contemporary culture, *The Blob* actually had its moments. The story, daringly for its day, unfolded in very nearly real time. Between them, director and producer pulled two masterstrokes. First, *The Blob* conformed to – in some ways defined – the late fifties morality tale about the small town that refuses to listen to its teenagers. Then, instead of the usually confident, not to say cocky lead, they cast McQueen as a bolshie but well-meaning mug without the faintest idea how to cope. The loner and anti-hero legend effectively started here. As Bob Relyea, Steve's later business partner, says, 'Oddly enough, most of the famous looks and grunts were present and correct in *The Blob*. The way McQueen plays off the other kids, I always think, gives a hint of the Don Gordon relationship in *Bullitt*.' Finally, the whole film was a minor miracle of stretching a little a long way. In particular, the miniatures and special effects, shot in the basement of a Lutheran church, gave at least some gloss to the deathless 'Omigod, it's alive!' rhetoric of the budget sci-fi romp. But that was about all you could say for *The Blob*. Every day McQueen would drive in from Philadel-

phia to be directed by that same church's vicar in scenes opposite a
man-eating Jello. Then every night he would drive back to the hotel
and 'vent', as she put it, to Neile.

The real star, as Steve used to complain, may have been the
amorphous slime oozing down those Pennsylvania streets. But he
did for it in the end. The simplicity of the part's trajectory – rebellious
dope to town hero – mirrored at least some of his own story. In
the movie's satirically duff climax, the Blob, seen a minute earlier
steamrollering entire houses, beats a quivering retreat from McQueen
and a lone fire-extinguisher. Wooden acting and a smoochy theme
by Burt Bacharach added up to a film equally wobbly, with even
basic drama unaccountably glossed over. From there the credits
worked their way to 'The End', only to have the letters swirl into an
ominous, sequel-begging question mark. Long before then, *The Blob*
had lapsed into truly ham-fisted efforts to convey danger, as in the
epic scene between McQueen and his date Aneta Corseaut:

SM: You sure you wanna go with me?
AC: Yes.
SM: I wouldn't give much for our chances . . . you know, wan-
    dering around in the middle of the night trying to find
    something that if we found it, it might kill us.
AC: If we could only find a couple of people to help us.
SM: Who?
AC: Why, your friends – Tony, Mooch and Al.
SM: [*Excitedly*] Hey! You know, that's worth a try.

In time, *The Blob* became that then rarity – a cult that gave tangible
as well as critical meaning to the word 'gross'. After Paramount
bought the rights and pumped in $300,000-worth of PR, it earned
an initial $2 million, the first wedge of what, for them, became a
stipend. McQueen would soon and long regret having taken his flat
fee. In chronological order, the film became first a fad, then a full-
blown hit, latterly a video staple, made the producer Jack Harris a
rich man, spawned both a sequel and a remake, warped into one of
those camp classics loved precisely for being bad and finally found
its true home on TV – *The Blob* is on somewhere most Friday nights,
and features in virtually every trivia quiz show. Its entry in the

reference books invariably includes the footnote, off by two years, of being 'Steve McQueen's first film'.*

Around William Morris they were soon celebrating, and the PR office began concocting what was the prototype of so many puff pieces: 'Young people today want a new hero to relate to, someone whose success isn't for himself but for his fans everywhere. Their enjoyment [of the film] is his best reward of all.' But Steve's true feelings hardly amounted to pride. He reacted to *The Blob* with a mixture of hilarity and embarrassment. After fame finally struck, he tended to shrug it off – suggesting they hang a poster of it in his executive john – when not quite seriously denying any knowledge of it. Near the end of his life McQueen told his minister Leonard De Witt that he'd always rued not having taken the points on *The Blob*, 'but at the time he did it he was flat broke – being evicted'. The man with the by then legendary clout around town 'just laughed at the whole mess'. But that was later. In 1958, according to Neile, 'Steve was shocked – it was like, "Jesus Christ! I'm in one of *those* things." Total horror. On the other hand, that's when he knew he was on the way.'

Ambition, money, sex: whatever else you said of him, McQueen didn't skirt the big issues in life. Many Hollywood producers, with their penchant for docile idiots, hated him on sight. But he was hard-working and talented, and with others that nearly cancelled out his quirks about 'face time' and close-ups.

A man like Jack Harris saw McQueen as taut and tightly strung, physically as well as in type. 'Steve had a reputation for being trouble,' he'd say. 'He was always hard to handle.' Another actor remembers that McQueen 'walked tense, and when he walked he'd really strut out. *Bang, bang, bang.* Onto the set. I mean, he didn't have a leisurely, graceful walk.' On stage or in the hotel, Harris and the rest watched him act or sulk or argue aggressively in an obvious and deliberate effort to overcome his basic shyness, to win the very approval his intensity often prevented. 'I don't think he ever had an ounce of self-confidence.' To others, though, the effort was all too convincing.

---

* A similar bit of confusion broke out in *M*A*S*H*, a series otherwise unique in staying so close to an unpopular war, where *The Blob* often got a name check. The American 'police action' in Korea actually ended in July 1953, five years before the film was even a twinkle in Paramount's eye.

'Steve had an almost animal streak about him,' says Hurt, 'which was why some people gave him a pass. He could be wild.' And violent: one morning in New York McQueen and his wife were out walking in the park when a man wolf-whistled at Neile from a passing convertible. Steve immediately ran after the car, caught up with it at a light, dragged the man from his seat and forcibly extracted an apology. The alternative to this solution had been 'a pop in the chops'.

McQueen's flip side, in contrast, was a childlike insistence that life was supposed to be fun. He had the great capacity to take things solemnly but not seriously, and a part of him remained firmly rooted in 1938, the shy but self-contained boy on the hog farm. (Soon after Steve married Neile, he took her to meet Uncle Claude – carefully bypassing Slater itself.) Although he was a realist at heart, he never quite lost Claude's own conviction that life not only should but *could* be enjoyed, and in the right mood, says Hurt, 'McQueen had a great sense of humour – always provided the joke was in the proper context.' Friends remember his helpless laughing jags when Steve simply abandoned himself. A roar with a giggle in it, and quite often hysterics. 'Knock knock' gags sent him into fits. Not quite Oscar Wilde then, this man-child, but warm and witty enough to offset at least some of the darker side.

That first year or so after Neile met him, McQueen 'virtually invented a new way to live': gunning the bike down New York alleys, adopting the ugliest pets – mutts in the street always seemed to follow him home – jogging into the apartment, hot and fetid (if not an accomplished athlete, a spirited one), then running downtown, unchanged, for beer and burgers and yet more belly-laughs in Downey's. In other words, Steve was the consummate mood swinger – Hollywood's swinger. 'When something bugged him, he let you know it,' says Hurt. 'But, otherwise – God, what a smoothie.'

Above all, Steve doted on Neile and, eventually, even came to trust her. He may have avoided being 'head-over-heels in love', but, he asked, who wouldn't? The accident of being worked over by a woman was one thing. Courting such grief was another, and if a charge of aggressive intent were lodged against McQueen he answered it with a plea of self-defence. 'I try to get along, and I'll continue to get along. In fact, I plan on doing as much getting along, with as many folks, as possible. I will get along until I drop. How 'bout that?' He seldom bad-mouthed a woman or a colleague in public, rarely displayed his obvious first-strike potential and never jilted a friend. Or not yet. Everything else, as he often said, was 'just business'.

Within only a year or two McQueen was one of the few stars who could 'open' a picture, a man apparently with his finger on the pulse of the mass audience. Strangely enough, he was never 'one of the people' himself. Steve essentially went from zero to eighty without feeling the need to level off at forty or so en route. Late in 1957, cheered on by wife, manager and agent, he duly made the full-time move west. He had never spent more than a few weeks, at least at large, in California, and his prospects there were as unpredictable as the country. But Elkins, particularly, was all for it. He and Stan Kamen went to work on Steve, still the sweatshirted hipster, getting him first into chinos and suede jackets and then on to a plane. Kamen took him aside and talked out his reasoning: 'Kid, you can be one of the chorus line in New York or you can make for Tinseltown . . . I know it's a risk to take. Do you want to fold your cards, maybe, or raise the ante?'

Go for it.

He and Neile arrived deep that midwinter and rented their first house, admittedly not much more than a shack, beside an auto shop and a Mexican cantina on Klump Avenue in Studio City. At the time he moved in, McQueen owned his clothes, a bike and a car, and one Indian quilt. He loved the place. Klump may have been no Beverly Hills, but it was, nonetheless, Hollywood, and Steve would never forget riding his BSA up into the canyon trails, cruising under winter skies streaked with red and purple. His whole life now went from *noir* to Technicolor. By the end of a new year that had begun in 55th Street, he was a sunny fixture in a town gaudily decorated in 1920s Moorish, fêted if not always loved, rich, famous, and a serial collector of unpaid tickets in his fancy Porsche Super Speedster. He would never again go back to live in New York.

Steve settled in California at Christmas, and got his break by Easter. He still had no real reputation except the one Neile gave him by her support and flattery, but because she yielded so freely, he began to grow in confidence. McQueen now regularly met their mutual manager for planning sessions: and like others Elkins came to love his private lack of pretension, his habit of breaking into fits, telling little stories, making irreverent jokes about *The Blob*, his uncanny impressions of famous actors. Klump soon became the unlikely command post for Steve's next offensive. It started with the familiar combination of talent and good luck.

Elkins happened to also represent one Bob Culp, then starring in the weekly CBS series *Trackdown*. 'The producers, Four Star, hit on the then novel idea of a companion piece. The spinoff was about a bounty hunter in the old West. I immediately knew that McQueen, playing this quasi-heavy lead, wouldn't only be perfect for the part – he'd use it as a launch pad for stardom . . . I made my pitch to Steve and to Four Star. He did the pilot, then made *The Blob* while the jury was still out. The Western was a smash and the rest is history.' Instead of doing more B-films, McQueen suddenly found himself being rung up and chauffeured to the Four Star offices. The first of the four he met there was David Niven, who, like Elkins, soon also grasped the fact that 'Steve had "it", and that "it" – whatever it was – was the future'. One of the great Hollywood icons of the then recent past, merely by launching McQueen, thus illustrated that legends of their day would inevitably become prey for those who followed them.

The only way Steve himself could avoid this fate was to establish a character for the long haul.

An actress friend was invited to dinner at Klump one night that summer. She remembers that McQueen 'actually put down his knife and fork to take an enormous script from his coat pocket to bounce ideas off everyone'. For the remainder of the meal Steve chewed over the text as much as his food. Later that same evening, he was still up 'trying out voices, practising quick draws, doing funny little moves, going over scenes where he needed a reaction'. It's doubtful that McQueen's guests did any serious advising. By then Steve was an uncontrollable ball of energy, his voice sometimes soaring back to *Hatful* register and the peak of blond hair rising on his head, his hands flapping and his feet in biker boots stamping up and down.

His rehearsal was a gala performance in which he sang and played all the parts.

McQueen's *Trackdown* slot aired on 7 March 1958. CBS and Four Star both liked what they saw and bought the series. *Wanted Dead or Alive*, as it now was, made its prime-time debut that September. Virtually overnight Steve became the first though not the last TV cowboy to shoot his way towards the big screen. But where Richard Boone, Chuck Connors and the other fauna of the half-hour 'oater' barely made it onto film, McQueen would leapfrog the entire Hollywood pack. The breakthrough was stunningly achieved. In 117 straight episodes, whether riding into the sunset or daringly allowing his character to be human, Steve staked out a claim bordered by Bogie's eruptive cool and Gary Cooper's suave languor. Though McQueen soon had company on that turf, he drew more from it than most. He became a star. Men like Niven and his partner Dick Powell now related to him as a virtuoso peer, as well as a self-dramatist. Trade reporters who had barely heard of McQueen in 1957 now began to speak in his voice and wrinkle up their noses at things that had a bad smell for him. A few fans doorstepped him at Klump. Steve's relationship with Neile also changed. She remained his friend and gatekeeper as well as his wife, but he was no longer her project. Steve himself affirmed this when, the same week *Wanted* went on the air, he asked her whether it wasn't time to settle down and have a baby. By mid September of that year Neile was pregnant.

Then, for fifteen years, she stopped working.

McQueen, meanwhile, never resolved his feelings towards the paired universe of his own childhood, the lonely son of the absent father and the mother who was a nervous wreck. This legacy gave rise to the ruthless demands he made on himself and others. When *Wanted* first went in front of the cameras, Steve was twenty-eight and pretty much fully formed. He was intense, grim (except when he collapsed in giggles), insecure, prickly and exceptionally focused – a flinty product of fly-by-night adventurism and naïveté, hardened by reform school and the Marines. It took all his combined experience, ambition and sheer nous to lift *Wanted* out of the mire of competing horse operas. *Cheyenne*, *Wyatt Earp*, *Wagon Train*, *Gunsmoke*, *Maverick* and Zane Grey were only the upmarket end of a genre tethered by the likes of *Rifleman* and *Wells Fargo*. McQueen's series went out in the cut-throat 8.30 p.m. slot on Saturday nights, after an hour of Perry Mason and directly opposite Perry Como. Steve declared a private ratings war on the famously smooth, cardigan-wearing crooner. Como's weekly guests – an assortment of 'real folks' such as construction workers, on hand to make requests – never looked half as real as McQueen himself, sporting dirty boots and a sawn-off Winchester shotgun dubbed the 'Mare's Laig'. More than forty years later, rerun episodes of *Wanted* are still saddled with a Violence rating.

Steve very soon changed and then embodied most people's stereotype of a cowboy. Rugged, wan and bow-legged like a prairie John Wayne, self-contained, cool, he also liberated the postmodern, ironic school which sprang up in the years ahead. In an equivalent move, thousands of female fans – many of them defecting from Como's jacuzzi – duly responded to the all-action hero who had the nerve to, as he put it, both 'fight and think'. Men simply wanted to be like him.

Elsewhere, however, it was another story. Behind the scenes, among at least some of *Wanted*'s crew and cast, it's fair to say that McQueen wasn't just not liked, he was disliked. For one, there was his relationship with the show's primary advertiser, Viceroy cigarettes. Steve's contract called for him to be wheeled out, in character as the star Josh Randall, to make his periodic pitch ('It's good entertainment for the whole family . . . yessir . . . and that's what'll sell any product') for both sponsor and series. Somehow, the way he did it was always thought to be lacking in warmth. One ex-Viceroy mogul, Nick Payne, recalls McQueen working the company's convention, 'cruising the room like a zombie . . . He'd stare at you with that squinty, butch look, offer a "Howdy, mac" and move on, his arm outstretched to his next mark. What I remember him telling us was that he'd sold millions of cigarettes for us, for a few bucks' return,' says Payne. 'Been there, done that. It was extremely flip.' McQueen's tone was cool, his grip cold and clammy. Nor did he exactly endear himself to the Viceroy suits by ostentatiously smoking one of their rivals' brands. 'It was obvious to most of us that Steve was a so-so salesman, and that the product he was really plugging was himself.'

McQueen became a star, but he didn't immediately decide who Josh Randall was. It was an important question, quite apart from its personal stake for him, because it involved the whole business of anti-heroic acting. Steve began his invention of the future by going back to the past, specifically to the hoary Western star Randolph Scott and his 1954 *The Bounty Hunter*. He worked out characteristic poses, moves, both by constant rehearsal and by studying the masters. But McQueen was always much more than a clever copyist. For one thing, he was small for a leading man, giving Randall the advantage of the underdog. *Trackdown*'s producer Vince Fennelly would remember that 'I needed a kind of "little guy" who looks tough enough to get the job done, but with a kind of boyish appeal . . . He had to be *vulnerable*, so the audience would root for him against the bad guys. McQueen was just what I had in mind. I knew he was my man the minute he walked through the door.' When the character got in a fight, he'd do exactly what his alter ego did to his old marine buddy Joey – wait until the odds were even, and then deliver a quick beating. There was nothing particularly macho about Josh Randall. When two or three men came at him at once, he either high-tailed it out of town or, at a pinch, pulled the Mare's Laig – his whole weight leaning into the gun, levelling it as easily as if it were a pistol. It was an extension of McQueen's nervous system. Steve's control of both his props and his body was always masterful, with no energy wasted. Finally, for authenticity's sake, he got rid of the designer jeans and starchy shirts and wandered around in what looked like Scott's old duds and a scuffed hat. It was the reverse of the classic Hollywood makeover, and it worked.

Much as McQueen had superb control of his body, he was also (as Viceroy now dubbed him) the thinking man's cowboy. In 1979 he startled an old guest star on *Wanted* by recalling how 'something in my look had once moved him during a take, and instead of punching me out, as we'd rehearsed, he'd just gently helped me up onto my horse. That's the way we shot it, and I kept thinking Steve had obviously gone nuts and that it was now a lousy scene. Then when I saw it on TV, I couldn't believe what came across. McQueen made it deeper and subtler, less bad cop and more Jimmy Stewart, and he did it all, I finally learnt, on the fly.' Steve would never talk much

about that dread word 'motivation'. But he revealed clearly enough
to men like Elkins the churning McQueen interior that so drove his
work, and so embedded another actor's scared look in twenty years'
memories of pity. His character, he once rightly said, was a 'contradictory dude'. He was talking about Randall, but it was a self-sketch
if ever there was one.

Besides the audience, Steve's only other long-term relationship on
Wanted was with trouble. He yelled at directors, writers, wardrobe
men – particularly the last if their gear wasn't pilgrim enough, namely
too clean. Everything had to be perfect. If it wasn't, you fixed it. 'He
was a shit' comes *Wanted*'s echo of him again and again. Always,
everywhere. McQueen even fought with Ronald Reagan over a script
for the latter's 'General Electric Theater'. He wasn't doing any stinking guest spot, he announced. Compared to Steve, Reagan ambled
along as loose and haphazard as a tumbleweed.

Two men got closer to him than most. One was Dave Foster, his
publicist and later co-producer of *The Gateway*. Foster was to play
a major part in the unfolding drama of McQueen's career and, particularly, his morbid distrust of the press. He also met his stunt
double of twenty-two years, Loren Janes. Janes got the job only after
Steve had fired three other stuntmen – two because they had the
wrong look, the third because he ribbed McQueen about his name
– on the very first day of shooting. To colleagues like Janes, the
pattern was jagged but constant. They generally accepted Steve with
affection and respect for his sincerity, talent and total absorption in
the part. They smiled a bit over his petulance, particularly towards
those above him on the food-chain. 'McQueen raged nonstop at the
suits,' says one of the *Wanted* crew. Contrarily, and particularly to
those below him on the food-chain, he developed a reputation for
being, on a whim, 'either a prince or a royal pain in the ass'. Mostly,
they felt that he tried too hard and had too much front, and they
were uncomfortable with his obsessive concern with future glory,
which he couldn't resist airing from time to time.

He had no close friends.

The same colleagues were divided on whether McQueen was a
shit or merely too serious: pathologically nasty or exercising a due
quality control. But the results were clear enough. In the three years

it was on air, *Wanted* became a proving ground for several noted directors of the near future, including Dick Donner of *Superman* and *Lethal Weapon* fame. Steve gave Donner 'utter crap' when he first appeared on set, blaming him for every conceivable hassle from the script to the quality of the canteen lunch. Donner was driven home that night quite literally in tears. When McQueen decided to bare fang like that, there *was* a touch of the bad cop. Not Jimmy Stewart. It was a side of him that alienated many co-workers and 'didn't allow him to be accepted as much as he might have been'. Things were hardly less ugly further down the evolutionary ladder, with Josh Randall's horse. This jet-black bronco, named Ringo, was once called upon to stand patiently behind McQueen as he rehearsed a scene with another actor. Instead, startled by the noise and lights, the animal first head-butted and then reared up and stamped on Steve's back. As McQueen spun round, his mount at once made ready to bite him. Steve cocked back his fist, popping it in the 'chops', then hurled his script into the air and, as Ringo snapped its halter, ran for his life. After that particular chase petered out, McQueen and his horse got along famously together.

Wanted took a season to find its audience, but Steve became an instant cult. Suddenly, he was an early middle-aged golden boy who had views on everyone in town. Hollywood, in turn, sat up and noticed McQueen for one reason or another; he didn't inspire many lukewarm feelings. The airwaves and hoardings were dominated by pictures of him in character, posing on the prairie in chaps, boots and Stetson, and brandishing his long gun. He was making a steady $750 a week, plus endorsements. Out of his new earnings McQueen bought his first Porsche and an underslung, production model XK-SS Jaguar – the 'green rat'. A replica Winchester was bolted to the hood, the snub nose tilted against the sky like a live cannon. Steve collected so many unpaid tickets in these two machines that, within a year, his driver's licence would be torn up. He also, much less publicly, embarked on a gradual self-improvement course at the Amelia Earhart branch of the LA library, immediately around the corner from his house. Steve's autodidactism sprang out of genuine simplicity and humility, as well as the familiar, nagging doubts about his long-term security as an actor. 'I don't want to grow old living in a street called Klump,' he explained to Julian.

His wife stayed home now, barefoot and pregnant, allowing Steve to indulge his quite unmodified, pre-Aids lifestyle. Nor, in that bygone era, was sexual equality ever much of an issue. 'All I can say is, that so far as I'm concerned, a woman should be a woman. By day she should be busy making and keeping a home for the man she loves. At night she should be sleeping with him.' To this stark ideology Neile would add that '[Steve was] the quintessential male chauvinist pig.' The flesh, meanwhile, kept coming, whether on set or in the room McQueen sometimes kept downtown, described by one guest as 'conceding nothing to romance ... the brown walls were peeling, the wooden bed creaking and the three greasy windows covered with yellow tar paper'. Another colleague from *Wanted* happened to see Steve setting out from this establishment late one afternoon in 1958. The short journey west down Sunset towards Laurel Canyon amounted to a one-man demolition of the Highway Code. It was driving Le Mans-style, foot hard on the gas, stamping on the brake, lurching, squealing, once swerving away from a pedestrian and mounting the pavement.

'I didn't know where he'd been or where he was going, but I can see him now in that hopped-up rat, doing about eighty, scattering people left and right. A real man on the move ... Then that same week, I was watching TV and there was a trade show where they praised Steve to the sky for having the right stuff, and saying that with a few other things in place, he was bound to get better still and become a worthy successor to the John Waynes and Gary Coopers, and even to be – I'm quoting – the baddest star in Dodge.'

4

Candyland

McQueen never really enjoyed being a TV star. He had a riff, which he gave to anybody who would listen, entitled 'The Factory'. Every trade reporter Dave Foster brought him heard it, to the extent that it induced affectionate eye-rolling when it came up. 'The Factory' was based on Steve's dislike of having to get up at five in the morning in order to report on set for a full day's filming. 'They just want it slam-bang, one take and onto the next. Assembly-line stuff. I didn't bust my ass all those years in New York just to end up acting in some factory.' Behind McQueen's self-pity lay a broad streak of professionalism, even perfectionism. He wanted every shot and every show to count and he wanted to grow as an actor. When not berating a Donner, Steve would often stand at his director's shoulder, asking about camera angles and lighting. McQueen 'had only to be exposed or shown, and he never forgot . . . He absorbed knowledge of any kind like a blotter.' Across that nightmare first season, and into its second, Steve became *Wanted*'s player-manager, suggesting scenes and set-ups, quite complicated shots like 'Let's track fast to the gun, then pull back in a smooth flow – tension and release' or, 'Dolly-out on the silhouette, Dick', – advice that could raise hackles as well as the show's quality. In a format where time was tight, most directors had no higher ambition than staying in focus and nobody bothered much about motivation, it was inevitable that people would talk about the new kid in town who wanted everything done right, or, failing that, his way.

They did talk. Men like Janes saw how 'Steve was fixated on the part. He wanted to make it unusual, and also to [break into] films . . . So he'd get furious . . . he was so focused on what he was doing,' crashing back and forth between set and trailer, a brute even by Hollywood TV standards. To many who watched him work, McQueen – with his tendency to kill a weak scene with a curt *Shit* – still did a fair impression of a 'royal pain in the ass', however apposite and penetrating his remarks. According to Nick Payne, 'he was combative rather than conciliatory,' but then contradictorily would take the entire *Wanted* crew and their wives out to dinner. Another colleague remembers that 'McQueen usually arrived on set looking like thunder.' But this soon broke and followed a familiar pattern. 'He'd be a turd and the director would snap,' he says. 'Then they'd make up.'

Steve's arrival on his motorbike for the day's shoot, at least early on, was the signal for muted groans, the respect accorded an admittedly gifted but temperamental child. The first cameraman on *Wanted* claimed he could tell his boss's mood by the clothes he showed up in. All-black leathers evidenced a storm – trouble ahead. A denim rig with a loud shirt was the sign of good humour – a day when he was approachable and nearly an entire episode could be shot. A neutral outfit with dark glasses signalled the unpredictable. This last look was the most common.

Despite or because of the tension, *Wanted* soon began to improve. As a rule, the scripts had no pretensions to subtlety. In a typical plot Randall would chase and get his man (first act), be foiled (second act), then resolve the crisis in a mild twist (third act). Justice was done, loose ends tied up, and there was never a dull moment, a scene that unfolded merely for its own sake. But within a dozen episodes, and thanks largely to McQueen, *Wanted* was breaking new ground. Then, it had been a formulaic channelling of John Wayne. Now, it toyed with the familiar genre of half-hour Westerns while skilfully distancing itself from almost all cliché. Daringly, Steve played the role with an ethical centre closer to Bogie's in *High Sierra*. But he went vastly further than that onto what had hitherto been the stage's traditional turf: his hero wasn't a shoot-'em-up hard man with no time for metaphysical asides, but instead the critical study of a morally aware adult willing to do anything reasonable, but no more, to get his bounty back to town. Once or twice Randall even let his man go.

Sympathetic, low-key, physically active; there was both charity and cruelty in this radical hybrid of McQueen's.

Wanted barely troubled the Nielsen ratings for its first six months. But by late March 1959 it had moved into the charmed circle of the Top Ten, with a 30.6 share – 15 million viewers. Everything now went overboard. Week after week, Steve's picture appeared in the trade press and the Hollywood fanzines, some thirty hits in all. As well as Foster's 'awareness campaign', there were hand-outs, potted biographies, glossies and souvenirs, all coupled with a strategic year-long blitz by CBS that would lead to stories in *Variety* and *Photoplay*. People who would never go near Broadway now knew the name and, above all, the face of Steve McQueen.

The camera loved him. To Four Star and the network he was blue chip – even in black and white, a glossy shot of him, tanned, trim and hardy, with a thatch of fair hair, big eyes and a quizzical grin was enough to bring the sponsors running. Not that Steve just stood in front of the lens and allowed himself to be photographed. He had certain tricks and impenetrable mannerisms like the 'squinty, butch look' (at least partly a response to deafness) and the lopsided, crinkly smile; but the forging of a direct personal link to the audience, a vector of just-you-and-me was something they didn't, and couldn't, teach him at stage school. One obvious form of it was that McQueen always looked another actor dead in the eye when he spoke or, more typically, listened. It was the instant way of establishing that he was missing nothing, and that he knew what to do about it. Steve was never an all-out action hero in the sense of a Stallone or Schwarz-enegger. At the same time he was a man who gave the impression, rightly or wrongly, that he would stop at nothing. If he decided to kill you, he'd kill you; if he thought it sufficient to walk away, he would. What's more, he patently had a wry, deep awareness of the inherent failings of human nature; the ultimate slipperiness of all relationships. Steve's internal gyroscope – his 'bullshit detector' – never stopped turning. On screen, as in life, precious little got by him. Wayne Rogers, who guested with McQueen on *Wanted*, particularly remembers his 'taciturn, Gary Cooper quality that made one feel he was always thinking a lot more than he was saying'. Nick Payne also cites the 'less-is-more vibe' that made McQueen the sharply prejudiced, brilliant observer he was. 'It's the obvious analogy of the killer iceberg – most of him was submerged.' Even in those prehistoric days Steve was proving his key theory that what the actor omitted was as vital as what he did. Neile, for her part, remembers his heroes as four men – Cooper, Bogart, Cagney and Walter Brennan – not exactly known for their hamming.

To some people in 1959, McQueen wasn't so much an actor who knew how to cope as a man consumed with violence. The controversy simmered throughout the series' first season, at which point it boiled into a crisis. According to a *Variety* report published in mid-run, *Wanted* was a 'brutal, hard-boiled actioner [some] feel single-handedly responsible for the big business pickup in the sale of pistols and shotguns'. The complaint duly made its way to the FBI, who opened a file on both show and star that 12 November. Meanwhile, *The Great St Louis Bank Robbery* was finally released to an indifferent audience and critics who also used it as a weapon to beat the man who seemed to be 'blasting at the rest of the world . . . a loner . . . obviously the hard type'. While partisan, the description reflected much of what Steve's closest colleagues felt as well.

At the same time, money was nudging McQueen out of his dark haze. The couple moved upmarket in 1959, buying their first home together in Laurel Canyon's Skyline Drive, a semi-private street hidden by thick ivy and bougainvillaea. A sign read 'Patrolled by Armed Security'. Number 8842 with its high window and skylight was, however, fully visible from the road. Standing on a neatly mani-cured plot landscaped with a trellis and bushes, the back of the house enjoyed a view over Hollywood. Pharaohs like Marlon Brando lived nearby on Mulholland Drive. Steve liked to gun his cars up and down the steep access road, duly collecting more tickets; after he appeared in Long Beach District traffic court that spring, Neile became his designated driver for several months. When not actually working or on the trail, McQueen spent whole days at the Union 76 station on the corner of Laurel Canyon and Ventura, where he oscillated between being a regular guy – talking shop with the mech-anics – and that old 'royal pain in the ass'. He wanted his Porsche hand-waxed for free whenever he bought gas, he announced once. The help scoffed at this. No, it would be good PR for them, Steve insisted, thereby demonstrating the yawning gulf between Hollywood and real life. He also loved to browse at the nearby flea market, where he's fondly remembered for once having 'chiselled the price of a Johnny Mathis LP from fifty cents down to something like a dime'.

It was a rare day when McQueen didn't have at least one row about money. He under-tipped, his cheques bounced. Steve seemed to get tighter as he got richer, and the general theory was that he feared he could lose it as quickly as he'd made it.

Even while he banked $750 a week on *Wanted*, McQueen used to talk to Neile and a few others about quitting and 'emigrating to a sheep farm in Sydney'.* To Julian, whom he never saw but wrote to intermittently, he soon began to send curt, moody, often despondent accounts of life, pouring out the frustration and discouragement he felt over the reviews and 'The Factory' generally. Steve was never to talk openly about how near he came to chucking Hollywood. Twenty years later, he did recall his misery in a conversation with a flying friend in Santa Paula. 'I was as confused and down as anyone at one time or another,' he said. 'But acting still had all the other jive beat.' McQueen invariably met such jive by desolation, despair and the threat to quit, quickly followed by a grim if still uncertain determination. By mid 1959 he had begun to cultivate a few key contacts in the industry, like the gossip queen Hedda Hopper. Hopper adored him. She noted affectionately how Steve used what she imagined was his 'formal' vocabulary whenever he did interviews. But around the house, or on set, he adopted the lingo of the mudlark he once was: words like 'bread', 'juice', 'pork', 'jive' and 'gas' would come around like pit-stops on a race track. 'He was insecure,' Hopper shrewdly observed. It was a measure of Steve's depth and strength, though, that 'he could talk to me about stagecraft, then go out and basically be a grease-monkey for the rest of the day'.

According to the actor Dean Jones, Steve was 'an odd mixture of ego and immaturity' when they worked together in 1959. McQueen 'would always bring his Mare's Laig with him wherever, and show

* The same line runs as a kind of theme in 1972's *Junior Bonner*.

the rest of us how he could handle it. *Look guys.* By then he was really fast on the draw. Impressive and endearing as it was, with Steve there was also that sense of a sleeve being tugged for attention.'

A year or so later, Jones was shooting a TV series on the next-door lot to McQueen's. 'I remember seeing Steve once going down the cafeteria line at lunch, except, being Steve, he was actually behind the counter, helping himself from over the cooks' shoulders. I ribbed him about it and he turned on me: "When your show's a big hit, *you* can come back here, Jones."' But it was a sign of McQueen's complexity that while still enveloped in his own ego trip he could, and did, reach out to others. Jones also remembers that during one discussion McQueen made a crack about a mutual girlfriend. 'I turned on my heel, walked out of his dressing room and started up the street. Steve must have sensed my feelings, because he ran after me calling "Dean! Dean!" and apologised with tears in his eyes.' Genuinely stirred and charmed, Jones realised that 'McQueen's fear of being rejected and outdone was what motivated his outer behaviour. When and if he ever relaxed, he was capable of radiant kindness.'

Then, for hours, he was the best company in the world.

The gesture to Jones remained private, though there were similar acts of warmth his fellow actors saw more openly. Sometimes with his director, more often alone, McQueen would spend long afternoons entertaining in the children's ward of Midway hospital. He befriended the very old and the very young as few others, and later, throughout his life, quietly gave tens of thousands of dollars to medical charities. Nurses who watched him at Midway recall vividly how he listened intently to each child, how, with his already asbestos-worn lungs, he grunted and staggered as he carried them piggy-back, how gently he set them down again, then stayed until nightfall telling stories and laughing with his thrilled fans. Wayne Rogers saw a similar sensibility after he and McQueen did an episode of *Wanted*. Steve was typically tense and focused during the shoot, but still went out of his way to help the lesser cast shine. Once actors have made it, it's assumed, without being a given, that most of them will be supportive enough of their peers. They're all in the same designer padded cell. Even in this context, McQueen stood out as unusually loyal. 'Steve was an incredibly [sincere] person and helpful to many people.' Jones, sick children, Hopper and Rogers – the brooding, uptight TV star showed them much the same empathy and tenderness his wife and a few close colleagues saw in him, the 'real Steve' that was somehow tragically warped by the orphan he'd been and the legend he became.

He never met his natural father. Ironically, by 1959 Steve was living less than ten miles away from Bill McQueen in Los Angeles. Ever since marrying Neile, and becoming an expectant parent, he'd grown more inquisitive, if no less resentful, about his own upbringing. His feelings on the subject were fast-moving, tiered, and sometimes nostalgic. Bewilderingly changeable, because the bedrock truth was that he didn't know what he'd do if he found Bill. Following a tip-off, Steve began to methodically comb the Echo Park neighbourhood, close to where he'd lived so miserably with Julian and Berri in 1942. His persistence paid off. One night a woman called, identifying herself as Bill's common-law wife, and inviting Steve to visit. He arrived at the rundown apartment block only to be told that his father had died of heart failure three months earlier. The woman added that Bill had always watched *Wanted* on Saturday nights and wondered whether the star wasn't, in fact, his son. She gave McQueen his father's photo and an engraved Zippo lighter which, Steve told a friend, 'I slung down the gutter . . . Then I went out to a bar. And that was the end of me and the old man.' Even though the friend, Bud Ekins, 'believed Steve implicitly', it was a lie. McQueen kept the photo and left the lighter to his own daughter. After he died, Bill assumed a more prominent and warmly human role in Steve's life than Julian ever could. A wary affection showed through whenever he talked about either his father or Uncle Claude, who also died that winter. Steve heightened the poignancy of the Indianapolis and Slater years by often drawing attention to the timing of this double blow. As a dedicated actor, he understood and rued the 'motivating shit' he saw in both men's lives. He no doubt regretted it as much as the shit in his own.

The losses killed whatever hopes there might have been that Steve would square his past. Like the Jaguar fish-tailing down the canyon lane, he began to accelerate now.

One late afternoon in May 1959 Steve and a heavily pregnant

Neile went shopping for baby clothes on Rodeo Drive. It was a moment of real crisis for them, since one of McQueen's flings had recently taken to phoning the house and Steve evidently felt the need to confess. According to Neile, 'For the next few days he brought me flowers and presents and cards. For a while I was so hurt that I refused to speak to him, but eventually we again became a happy couple.' On this particular hot spring evening Neile began to blanch as she stood at the sweater counter. She fainted away in Steve's arms just as a young fan approached, her own face wreathed in goofy goodwill:

'I know it's a bad time, Mr McQueen. But could I please have your autograph?'

As Steve recalled it, he went 'fucking nuts', raving at the girl while simultaneously helping to revive his wife. Neile soon recovered, but McQueen never willingly signed his name for anyone again. It was, for him, the first of several hopeless gestures to privacy.

The McQueens' daughter, Terry Leslie, was born in Los Angeles that 5 June. With the actor's instinct for detail, Steve made notes on his first child that night: 'Oh God, looks like me. Isnt she smart, though – just perfect.' A boy, Chadwick Steven, followed on 28 December 1960. Steve's son inherited his mother's looks and soon settled into his father's lifestyle. 'Always smells like hot brakes,' McQueen would say of Chad approvingly. It was a neat simile. The amount of engineering in Steve's conversation was impressive. Cars and parts were always apt to have a symbolic importance. Being 'full of juice' was as high a tribute as he ever paid to man or machine. Like many of his fictional heroes, McQueen, too, sensed an affinity between happiness and hardware.

But Steve in the flesh kept rather less to the straight and narrow than one of his famous Porsches. Weeks after Terry's birth, he was keeping company again in the hotel room downtown. He also began entering sports car heats around LA – he won his first ever event, held at Santa Barbara airport – despite promising Neile he'd stop as soon as their first child was born. Instead, semi-professional racing became a sub-plot of Steve's career; whenever he got behind a wheel he suddenly realised he no longer had to defer to any 'fucking suit' – he had what he called the 'big jolt', the thrilling alchemist's gift of turning an inert object into something else. And racing provided a sort of equaliser, particularly for a man with McQueen's nagging sense of guilt that his day job was 'candyass'. 'It gave me a fresh identity,' he said. 'I was no longer just an actor, I was a guy competing. And it was real important to me – to have this separate identity.' The other thing both racing and fatherhood gave Steve was insomnia. Already having trouble unwinding at night, Neile recalls how he snapped when 'a work crew put up a big new street light which shone right into our bedroom'. When the City refused to move the light, McQueen solved the problem by promptly shooting it out.

One lunchtime that same summer Steve rode his Bonneville into Bud Ekins's motorcycle shop on Ventura Boulevard. Ekins, both as a dealer and an all-round biker, was the very best of the breed – a triple-A rider who was gruff, cool and toadied up to no one, including McQueen. 'I knew Steve from *Wanted* and thought he was a pest. He used to hang around the shop.' Gradually, however, Ekins began to warm to the man he describes as 'totally paranoid . . . Not only didn't Steve trust people, he kept them separate from each other. You'd never meet his other friends.' A complicated man, McQueen – even then, an embarrassment of paradoxes. 'Basically, Steve couldn't ever make up his mind whether he was a big star or a little kid made good. I always remember how he'd put on a fake beard and shades in order not to be hassled, then get pissed when no one recognised him. Other times, when they *did* come up for autographs, he'd flip.'

Gradually, this serene middle-aged outlaw began to notice key differences between his new buddy McQueen and the other groupies who passed their time on Ventura Boulevard. There was, first of all, his natural flair. The two started going desert-riding together, and Ekins found that 'Steve was good – great reflexes and fast, even if reckless. He'd hit everything en route.' Two additional traits grew out of and complemented that talent: an intense curiosity and a slow but profound ability to bond. McQueen wanted to know all that he could about motorcycle history, and he'd 'try to get a rise' from people until he narrowed the field down to a few trusted cronies. Ekins evidently passed the test, because he and Steve were close for the next twenty-one years.

Then there was Don Gordon, a thirty-year-old actor living near McQueen in the Hollywood hills. 'Steve would literally go by the front door on his way to work and sort of announce himself. It happened over two weeks, in four phases. First, he'd just drive by and stare; not a word. Then he'd drive by and wave. Next he'd drive by more slowly and smile. Finally, he actually stopped and said, "Hey, I've seen you on TV." I said the same, and that's how we got tight.' Soon enough, bolstered by the power of his ratings, McQueen offered Gordon a guest spot on *Wanted*. 'In those days Steve was still groping his way through the maze, discovering what did and didn't work for him. For instance, that smile and a particular kind of walk were in. Surplus dialogue was out.' Yet when he talked to Gordon about bikes, the mouth that chewed fastidiously on lines like bits of gristle suddenly relaxed and grinned, 'Beat you to the top, man.'

Once you got used to him, you found he was a very nice person.

McQueen's perfectionism and his undying paranoia did for him with at least some of his peers. But, for others, the over-intense actor was but a '*Cut*' away from the passionate friend. 'I loved the man,' says Gordon. 'Many was the night he'd come by late, I'd grab my leathers and we'd literally ride off into the hills. Great times.' As for how Steve in turn treated his friends, nine years later Gordon was invited out of the blue to read for a film being shot at Warners. The title was *Bullitt*. When Gordon tried to thank McQueen for getting him the job, 'Steve looked me in the eye and said, "I had nothing to do with it." That was typical of the guy. It was endearing, and it was also total crap. Steve didn't want me to feel beholden to him.'

That same summer of 1959 MGM put together a budget for *Never So Few*, the screen version of Tom Chamales's World War II novel set in Burma. It was a solid melodrama starring Frank Sinatra and, as was his wont, a few of his clan, including Sammy Davis Jr. After Davis talked himself out of the job, Stan Kamen at William Morris rang his own friend the director John Sturges. Kamen not only had a replacement for Davis in mind. He told Sturges that he could get him Hollywood's 'next Bogie' for ten weeks at just $2500 per week.

McQueen then had to report to Sinatra, who laid it on the line.

'Steve, baby,' he said, 'here's how it's gonna be. I turn up, I say the lines, I fuck off back to the hotel. They got any light left, I'll tell 'em to focus on you. Dig it?'

McQueen dug it.

Perhaps the most winning quality of *Never So Few* lay not in its deadpan, pre-ironic swashbuckling, nor in the jungle locations (largely faked in Hollywood and Hawaii), nor even in Sinatra himself, but in the gum-chewing Ringa, the renegade army driver played by McQueen. He was brilliant. More than a year in front of the camera had taught Steve how to react. But his first appearance, leaping down from the jeep with a feline grace and giving his signature crinkly grin, was so naturally deft, and the impact so sudden, that if Gene Kelly had done it audiences couldn't have been more impressed. At the New York premiere Sturges heard people actually gasp at the scene. McQueen photographed like a god, yet basically carried and conducted himself like a regular guy. Somewhat taut, watchful, but with a touch of shyness, he was never more human. Steve was so cool and lithe, with his muscle shirt specially cut for him by Neile, that gnarled, goateed Sinatra never really got to grips with being the picture's star. *I'll tell 'em to focus on you.* Sturges and MGM also picked up on McQueen instantly, the studio signing him to a non-exclusive contract. Finally, Steve made a friend of the assistant director Bob Relyea, who worked closely with him throughout the sixties. After twelve years of puzzled study and a further thirty since they split, Relyea gives his wry assessment of McQueen's career. 'Steve in some respects – the way he was always on his toes – was the same offstage and on. But he did more than just hold his character. For all the defensiveness and deadly mood swings, McQueen had the best instincts I've ever known for what he could and couldn't get away with. His choice of scripts was masterly. The man was a genius at planning his next move.'

Mood swings a problem? Some would say they were Steve's meal ticket. Critics loved the gregarious loner, the anti-heroic McQueen; his family and few friends were proud of the 'regular guy' who liked nothing more than to swig beer and talk mechanics. No one, however, ever responded more enthusiastically to Steve's taste for low comedy than Sinatra did. It matched his own – no small accolade.

If a staccato, comradely bond characterised the two men's relationship in *Never*, then the same quality regularly surfaced off screen. McQueen and Sinatra were 'both children emotionally', as Steve put it. One afternoon on location McQueen was diligently reading his script when Sinatra crept up behind him and slipped a lit firecracker into his belt. After the explosion had died down, Steve levelled his prop tommy gun and let off a full clip at Sinatra's chest. At that range the paper wadding from the blanks actually bruised him; the director 'heard Frank gasp out'. After that there was a long silence, finally broken by Sinatra's admiring laughter. 'You got stones, kid,' he said. From then on the two of them could be seen zipping off to one bar or another, a surfeit of Y chromosomes rasping along in a liberated jeep.

Every account of the *Never* shoot depicts it as a summer of frathouse antics, dissipation and frequent practical japes, usually involving fireworks. It was the summer in which Steve, in a fit of beery hi-jinks, detonated an 'entire fourth of July show' inside Sinatra's dressing room. In some versions, Sinatra was tickled by this display; in others, he emerged singed and ranting, like Hitler after the generals' plot of 1944, and began demanding blood. It was the summer in which the stars nearly killed Loren Janes by blowing up his trailer, dragged another crew member to the edge of a cliff, promising to push him off, and threatened to dunk Charles Bronson, claiming there was no danger since, like his acting, he was 'all wood'. It was the summer in which McQueen, banned by MGM from riding his motorbike on set, asked if he could borrow Dean Jones's Triumph – and Jones said yes, only to have Sturges appear later and tell him, 'McQueen's just driven through a fence; now you're both banned.' Above all it was the summer in which Sinatra's first words on screen to Steve – 'You interest me, Ringa' – echoed real life. He'd found a protégé who was tough, playful and bad-assed; and that was certainly part of the truth.

In the end, salty performances kept *Never So Few* from sinking in its own melodramatic plot. One reviewer called it a 'schizoid war romancer that, when it comes to split personalities, is up there with Sinatra himself'. Sadly, he was wrong: *Never So Few* had precious little personality to split. McQueen's own sense of humour and spirit, at least, was well done. There was a steadiness there which carried him through. All his war films would manage the rare feat of combining rebellion and charm in equal parts. Cocky, unfeasibly bronzed and swaggering, McQueen's Ringa announced the arrival of a major talent.

The comer.

Sinatra, says Bob Relyea, 'encouraged Steve to be the next officially tolerated bad boy in town'. The two men and their families were inseparable that year. Sinatra and the McQueens spent a week together in New York, where they ate at Louie's and took innocent pleasure in demonstrating how far each had come. One evening McQueen stood at the window of his hotel suite, pointed a finger down Fifth Avenue and said, 'It's a lot longer from Barrow Street to here than you think.' That Saturday night the McQueens went backstage at Sinatra's homecoming concert in Atlantic City. Steve was mistaken for one of the band and mobbed. '*That's it!*' Sinatra remembered him yelling. '*That's* what I want.' Feverishly excited, Steve and Neile then flew to a preview of *Never So Few* in Hollywood. As the final credits rolled, Sinatra turned to McQueen, slapped him on the back and said, 'It's all yours, kid.' Neile recalls running across the parking lot, two figures whose doll-like smallness gave them the air of kids breaking curfew 'beside ourselves with glee. "The pope's just blessed you," I told Steve, and then we hit Cyrano's to celebrate.' Thanks to luck, talent and timing, McQueen's dues-paying years were over. Hollywood's idea of a hero was ruthlessly tumbling forward, and Steve triumphantly captured the moment. After *Never So Few* he became the consensus superstar-in-waiting. 'I remember going to a party where all the A-list flocked around Steve,' says Neile. 'Jennifer Jones and Rita Hayworth were both jostling to get a look at the "next big thing".'

They weren't alone. Over the coming few months an unlikely friendship developed between the sixty-nine-year-old Hedda Hopper and the 'young gun', as she dotingly called him. At eleven in the morning, as soon as Hopper awoke, she began her day by phoning Steve on the *Wanted* set. The venerable columnist and one-time vamp followed down a line from Powell and Niven as stars of an earlier era for whom McQueen now became a kind of mascot. 'He excites,' she said. 'I knew he had a past after one look at that hardened face.' Evidently, he also had an effortless kind of glamour from the rear – 'such an *arrogant* back', Hopper added. As well as promoting McQueen nonstop in print, she cannily advised him to turn down Sinatra's *Execution of Private Slovik* and *Ocean's Eleven* by posing the stark question, 'Do you want to be a Rat Pack flunky, or say no to Frank?'

Say no to Frank.

Steve returned the favour by, allegedly, taking Hopper to bed. He always referred to her around town as a 'great lady', often dropping a syllable amongst friends. After her death in 1966 lavish, black-bordered tributes to Hopper appeared in all the trade press. The mourner was anonymous. But Hopper's staff, by dint of detective work, tracked him down. It was McQueen.

In the autumn of 1959 Steve reluctantly went back to *Wanted* and the small tube. It's difficult today to imagine the power and the precise chemistry he and Josh Randall had together – and how receptive pre-Vietnam America was to the adage 'A man's gotta do what a man's gotta do'. The initially sparse audience for McQueen's frontier show had first made it a cult and then a phenomenon. By the end of its second season *Wanted* was firmly atop the ratings and sponsors were beating a trail to CBS's door.

Steve responded with a new frenzy of bickering with the series' producers. For him, there was no inherent contradiction between titanic personal ambition and a genuine commitment to getting it right. Although he asked for, and won, a pay rise – now $100,000 a year from all sources – his real leverage went towards upping the quality of the show. The quickest annoyance duly came with the arrival, on set, of a suit. McQueen often seemed to conflate all his authority figures into a vast anti-Steve conspiracy. 'This is jive,' he'd tell Dick Powell. Or: 'You're twisting my melon, man – screwing me.' Once, on being told an episode was behind schedule, McQueen carefully counted off ten pages of script, ripped them out and snarled, '*Now* we're on track.' The pages never went back in. He ranted when CBS talked about changing *Wanted*'s transmission time, then ranted when they didn't and a rival network scheduled *Leave It to Beaver* in the same slot, inviting viewers to choose between Steve and one of America's pet sitcoms. Most of all, he ranted about Josh Randall not being 'real'. Often he would break off and snarl at the malevolent figures behind the lights:

'Bull*shit*!'

As McQueen told one of the show's writers, Bill Nolan, 'I wanted to play [Randall] . . . as a guy trying to do a dangerous, unglamorous job with a minimum of fuss. But the Four Star dudes kept trying to turn him into a jaw-busting, sure-shot hero. I had some bad times with them over this.' Steve's manager Hilly Elkins confirms that 'McQueen's wars weren't about bigger trailers or more lines – usually they were about less, but better lines.' The view that Steve simply tried too hard was a common one amongst detractors. 'McQueen always wanted it to be *Hamlet*,' a well-known *Wanted* guest star says. 'That was his strength, but at a certain point it became a weakness. It was only a cowboy show, for God's sake.'

'The Factory', with its 5 a.m. calls and work-sheets, was McQueen's great theme, but there were rewards too. With his combined big- and small-screen earnings, Steve had bought land and blue-chip stock in Dow Chemical, as well as a new Lotus Mark XI. Early in 1960 he formed his own production company and began to talk of developing a racing film with the title *Le Mans*. This particular obsession would tick steadily away for the next ten years, at which point it promptly exploded. 'Steve was so *up* around then,' says an ex-family friend; 'he was twenty-nine, tanned, rich and had that manic zip. The guy was fresh goods.'

There were also some darkly revelatory moments around the house on Skyline Drive, frequently after McQueen had overdone his beloved Old Milwaukee or Peruvian flake. He never forgot a slight, real or imagined, wrote off anyone who crossed him and, as Neile says, 'trusted exactly one soul in the world – me'. Steve's paranoia could be as heated as his affection. 'If anybody hurts my family, I'm gonna put them down in a little black book.'

One balmy evening in late 1960 Steve, his young daughter and their dog went for a walk up the canyon road. Far below them in the valley the jumble of downtown LA and Century City were strung with Christmas lights. In the spirit of the season, McQueen knocked on the door of a neighbour, one Edmund George, to make peace.

Recently, there had been complaints about Steve 'partying' and 'scaring the shit out of the street' by gunning the Lotus on his midnight rounds to and from Hollywood. When the neighbour came out and his attitude wasn't satisfactory, McQueen socked him in the mouth to make it so. Out of sheer shock and frustration, George allegedly retaliated by punching not Steve but his own wife. Meanwhile, the dog went berserk. McQueen then strolled the few yards back to his house where, sure enough, he was promptly hit with a lawsuit. (It was thrown out of court several months later.) A tangled contradiction for a man who continually wanted his TV series to be 'less violent'.

Why did *Wanted* succeed?

'Impact,' says Don Gordon. 'A fresh approach. Steve wasn't a worn-out ham. The very few great screen actors know to break through that veil between them and the camera. They just do. It was McQueen's greatest strength and his greatest hassle – he busted his ass. He worked. That's what people forget when they talk about a big star.' Among the 'business' Steve would perfect was his trademark, swivel-fire technique with the Mare's Laig and various other quick-draw stunts he practised hours on end. He researched countless books on the correct 1890s-era wardrobe. There were his other finely-tuned mannerisms, like the way he walked or mounted a horse. McQueen would give certain scenes an hour or two while he pondered a move. Cast and crew got used to hanging restlessly on until the spirit moved him, at which point he would emerge at a run, once skidding at top speed into a prop cactus as he bawled excitedly:

'*Roll 'em.*'

Once an idea was lodged in McQueen's mind, he was raring to go and, as soon as the sets were ready, plunged in with his 'manic zip'. Beneath it all was a hard unsaid truth. He was manic, he was depressive. The imitative, or impressionable, in Steve was there too. He was still given to his cherished Brando and Dean impersonations. Often it came through off set, as in his hi-jinks with Sinatra. And yet, by 1960, one look at the hardened glint in those shaggy-dog eyes told you there was something there rather deeper than mere mimicry. McQueen had unbeatable film sense. As Eli Wallach, who worked with him that year, says, 'Steve's great skill – the word genius comes to mind – lay in being observant. He could always find what it had been in an earlier scene that led, logically, to what he was doing just then. Nobody quite grasped the poetry in the flow of film like him.' McQueen's latter-day refusal to truck with decorative flourishes, but simply to wire back the facts, was also what struck Gordon. 'Jimmy Cagney said it best: "Walk into the scene, hit your marks, look the other guy in the eye and tell the truth." Steve did that in spades.'

McQueen made it big that year, his thirtieth, presiding over the birth of modern cool. Before there was Clint Eastwood or Jack Nicholson or Robert De Niro or Bruce Willis, before Sean Connery first suited up as Bond or Gene Hackman perfected his common touch in *The French Connection*, Steve cast his eye over the house and determined that both men and women would go for a 'type': someone who, if he got any more virile, could have joined the World Sumo Federation, yet who also had a heart. One half of the audience saw the icy surface and thought they could melt it. The other half merely applauded. As the critic Barry Norman says, 'It was a clever unisex appeal. Males wanted to be him – the females wanted to bed him, which a fair number duly did.' The character 'Steve McQueen' was a definite artefact of the mass market.

McQueen was up for three films that year, *Ocean's Eleven*, *Pocketful of Miracles* and *Breakfast at Tiffany's*, all of which he walked on or vetoed. His *Wanted* contract allowed him only the vague option to take outside work at 'mutually convenient times' for Four Star and CBS. Then Steve heard that John Sturges was applying the model of a Josh Randall type to the big screen in a version of Akira Kurosawa's film *The Seven Samurai*. Sturges's model was Westernised, starring seven gunslingers hired by a Mexican border town to halt periodic forays on the pueblo by bandits. By the time McQueen first got wind of it, the project already had a long and chequered history. The producer Walter Mirisch had been developing the story with his old friend Yul Brynner for six years when, between takes on *The Guns of Navarone*, Anthony Quinn filed suit alleging that he, not they, owned the rights to the 1954 screenplay. Mirisch and Brynner then had their own falling out about money. On several occasions the Mexican government came close to torpedoing the whole project on the grounds that 'bad things', such as torture and buggery, were done in Sturges's original adaptation. Clearly, *The Magnificent Seven* wasn't destined to be a standard oater. McQueen saw his character Vin as more sombre and internal than Josh Randall, at least as envisaged by Four Star. He quickly signed up.

Four Star acknowledged the news, then hit Steve with a hammer-blow. They refused to release him from his *Wanted* shooting schedule. Dick Powell waved away the very idea that a successful movie star could impress himself on the series and the ratings. It seemed as though McQueen's first real shot at the 'brass ring' would be lost. Before he had time to get the snarl off his face, he was already doing the mental arithmetic. He was a few weeks shy of thirty, the age by which he'd promised to 'get some sugar out of the business', and he was stuck there, in 'The Factory', atop Ringo and greased up like Tom Mix; playing cowboy 'for fucking seven-fifty a week' when Candyland lay just over the horizon; wondering whether he should, after all, book three tickets for Australia. 'For me and my ol' lady and my kid,' he told David Niven. 'I'm tired of the whole scam.'

'He really meant it,' says Hilly Elkins. Elkins appealed to Niven and Powell, who referred him back to Four Star's manager Tom McDermott. The two men had known each other for years in New York. 'I met with McDermott and told him, "Steve has a real opportunity and it'll bring only good PR to the series. Give him a couple of weeks' leeway."' That was cut off with an angry chop of McDermott's hand. He reddened, glared at Elkins and delivered the blow.

'Fuck you. McQueen's paid for.'

As Elkins caught his breath, McDermott rushed on, trying to convince himself as much as Elkins that 'We own McQueen. We made him and we can break him.' A long pause greeted this remark, broken by Elkins saying, 'Tom, you may want to think it over. I hate to hear you say that, because Steve's so emotionally set on the film. You don't want an unhappy actor.'

'What in the name of fucking shit does that mean?'

Elkins groaned.

'Be reasonable, Tom. All I said was, You don't want McQueen unhappy.'

'Well, fuck you.'

Then, according to Elkins, 'McDermott went completely out of control, prodding his fingers towards my face, yelling, "Don't try those fucking Mafia tactics with me," and "I'll take you and your client out and kick both your asses." He told me to put my coat on and leave. As an afterthought, I asked him if he really proposed to kick Steve McQueen's ass. And that was the end of the interview.'

Elkins drove back to his office, picked up the phone to McQueen, who happened to be visiting Boston with Neile, and told him, 'Have an accident.'

'Steve, being Steve, promptly rammed his rental car into the side of a bank, narrowly missing a cop on the way. It made the press. McQueen – who was completely unhurt – came back to LA in a neck brace, and I dutifully told Four Star that their golden boy was laid up and unable to work. Next thing, McDermott was back on the line screaming, "I know this is a fake, motherfucker, but you've got your film."' Whatever McDermott thought, Elkins was playing tough, so tough that he renegotiated Steve's contract. He had Four Star double his salary as well as his stock in the company. After the yelling had died down, he rang the Mirisch brothers and upped McQueen's fee for *The Magnificent Seven*. 'I told 'em, "This is a guy who's going to be huge and I'll let you have an eighteen-month option on him." They went for it. Steve did the film and the rest is history.'

Shooting began early that spring in and around Cuernavaca, fifty miles outside Mexico City. McQueen headed south, Harry Mirisch recalled, 'like a bat out of hell bound for glory'. He arrived at the Hotel Jacaranda alone on a Monday evening, his wife remaining behind to nurse Terry and hear more of McDermott's convulsions. By Tuesday morning he was in bed with one of the Indian extras. McQueen loved Mexico: after his honeymoon there, he'd often driven back and he once offhandedly spoke of settling down to 'live, die and be buried' there. In Cuernavaca the streets were lined with strolling mariachi players and locals eager to entertain the famous star.

At the same time, McQueen was preparing for what he rightly knew could be his breakthrough, constantly lobbying Sturges for more 'juice'. He had exactly seven lines, but they, too, were magnificent, including 'Never rode shotgun on a hearse before,' and 'We deal in lead, friend.' Steve's tantrums on location were both logical and unnervingly dislocated. A full litany followed on his character, Vin, written, he complained, as 'a kind of ass-wipe to Yul'. But McQueen was shrewd enough to play on Sturges's vanity, and the director soon became his knowing patsy. With Brynner partly footing the bill, *The Magnificent Seven*, Sturges promised, would 'give Steve the camera'.

McQueen's relentless preoccupation with McQueen took various forms on set. While others cheerfully improvised, Steve took the attitude that the stage was a laboratory for precisely calibrating each setup. He spent hours correcting and editing his own lines in a maze of inserts, arrows, zigzags and fussy, infinitesimal revisions. That was for starters. McQueen liked every shot to be a completely rehearsed and blocked routine where each step and nuance was perfected down to the last detail. Eli Wallach, playing the heavy, remembers pulling his pistol on McQueen during a run-through. 'Hold it exactly at that angle, not an inch left or right in the take,' Steve told him.

'But it's an action sequence.'

'Try your best.'

Onstage, McQueen was the most fiercely competitive of an overadrenalised cast, constantly 'catching flies', as Sturges put it, waving his white hat or rattling his bullet-casings around behind Brynner's head. Offstage, he earned the half-fond, half-cagey nicknames Supie (for superstar) and Tricky Dick. 'Most of the Seven, including Yul, would at least play cards together,' says Bob Relyea. 'Steve, by contrast, seemed typically self-contained.' Another of Sturges's crew notes that 'McQueen tended to be standoffish – when he wasn't screwing for America – which is what a star needs to be.' Actors have always indulged themselves in dewy-eyed rhapsodies about their fellow luvvies. But, as Olivier once asked, 'Why should the film set be treated any differently from the office?' And why should entertainers be expected to get along any better than, say, a firm of suits? Steve never found rivalry, or a degree of insulation, unseemly. 'Not my favourite part of a movie,' he once muttered, as the cast gathered for a team dinner in the Jacaranda.

Film-making, McQueen maintained, was a state of war. For him the hostilities were made bearable by the money, a pretty wife who visited at weekends, and plenty of Mexican pot. Even so, he saw himself as the underdog.

With McQueen getting tetchier by the day, 'a bust-up was inevitable', says Eli Wallach. 'He probably respected Yul the actor. But Yul, don't forget, was also very much the shah of Brynner. He had his whole court, with someone taking his coat and someone else lighting his cigarette for him. Big movie star treatment. Steve, I'm sure, thought, "I'm not gonna buy that crap" . . . And he didn't.' McQueen not only trawled for scenes – the taunting ironic practicality of scooping up water in his hat while fording a river – he actively played Ahab to Brynner's great white whale. He taught him, for instance, to draw his pistol so slowly, 'I got three shots off before he even had his gun out of his holster.' Another time, Elkins remembers, 'Yul built himself a mound of dirt to stand on in one of his scenes with Steve. McQueen, during the shot, began accidentally-on-purpose kicking away at the pile, so Yul began looking shorter and shorter. By the end of the take, Brynner was disappearing down a hole.' Sturges, for his part, wasn't afraid to go it alone against the Mirisch brothers or the cast. What he was loath to do was side openly with one highly touted star against another, especially McQueen and Brynner, reflex foes who ruffled easily at real or imagined snubs. 'Total mutual paranoia,' says Wallach. However loose the two hung on stage, their private feud was rock solid, especially after a scoop about 'creative differences' appeared in the trades. When Brynner confronted McQueen about the story by grabbing his shoulder, his reply, hissed an inch from his co-star's face, spun heads the length of the hotel:

'Get your stinking hands off me, or I'm taking you down to the pavement.'

For the next twenty years, if you brought up Brynner around McQueen's house, you wouldn't be invited back. 'He was one uptight dude,' Steve informed the press. 'He didn't ride very well, and he didn't know anything about quick draws and all of that stuff. I knew horses. I knew guns. I was in my element and he wasn't.'

The Magnificent Seven opened worldwide, amidst an $800,000 publicity blitz, on 23 October 1960. While the critics' thumbs twisted up or down, the consensus was that Sturges had created a splashy yet lucid morality yarn, in which character mattered as much as action and both combined to make the most of an unwieldy script. Part of the fun of the film lay in seeing several actors, notably James

Coburn, launch their careers. Moreover, as the story was played out, the audience watched the spectacle of a superstar being born. Long after the last Panavision shot of the range, and the climactic chord of Elmer Bernstein's score, there was the physicality and intelligence that made you appreciate Vin's strength and humour, not to mention that hunter's eye. Steve's character was as sly and quick on the uptake as he was on the draw. Even more than the epic low-lying photography, those scenes stolen from behind Brynner's back were the greatest of *Seven*'s many pleasures. Vin outdid himself as a virtuoso among equals, stretched tauter than the rest, with a temper fused as short as he was. Witty, lewd, allusive and violent, Steve played fast and loose with stereotypes, earning himself some of the critical yappings and shin-bitings that invariably greet true originals, while the public promptly sat up and bayed for him. In terms of buzz and hard cash, he now duly got his first real juice out of the business. McQueen missed his self-imposed deadline for fame by exactly seven months.

To the surprise of the few people who got to know Steve at home, he didn't look the slightest bit driven, twisted, crazed, gnarled or bitter. He looked tired, though. On 3 May 1960 Four Star told him they were exercising their option to do another season of *Wanted*. That same week McQueen signed a contract for a thirty-minute TV drama called *Masquerade Party*, to be filmed live in New York. Three days later he shot yet another promo for Viceroy's parent firm, Brown & Williamson. Add his responsibilities to his wife and young family and a taste for beer and late-night dirt-riding, and it's easy to see how the strain could begin to tell.

McQueen, whose favourite outpost remained the racing circuit, was a man who was driven incessantly, the manic type who can achieve wonders but occasionally has to be hospitalised for his own good. He could also put unbearable pressure on others. Coburn, who quite plausibly insists 'I loved him dearly,' also admits, 'There was kind of an evil streak to him.' Tales were told of his self-obsession, the hours he spent each day muttering about his childhood and plotting revenge. Nobody denied Steve his refuge in the world of make-believe, or his chance at personal success and redemption. The unrelenting gloom of his upbringing made even a Brando's or a Dean's seem like *Happy Days*. But it grated to hear McQueen speak of 'us' or the 'gang', when a study of his actions behind the scenes shows that his first and overpowering loyalty was to himself. The only time he liked making a film, he quipped, was on payday.

In what seemed like a moment, Steve had made a breakthrough, cordoned off from his old life; leapt from sci-fi flummery in *The Blob* into a stylistic and original world of his own. He quickly picked up the pace. Nowadays, most mornings McQueen could be seen stalking the studio halls, hunched and scowling with the burden of his latest character. He needed people to follow. Those who did found him outrageous at times but often stimulating, a tonic, and generous in his loyalty as well as his rewards. He could even countenance inefficiency if enough talent came with it, as with Sam Peckinpah. To others, though, Tricky Dick was perhaps all too cleverly named for his own good.

A year later McQueen locked horns with the director of his eighth film *Hell is for Heroes*, who, like Sturges before him, saw it as an ensemble piece rather than a star vehicle. The director was fired. Something similar happened on *The Great Escape*, whose writer would call Steve 'an impossible bastard'. The stamp-feet-and-sulk factor bulked large in both *The Sand Pebbles* and *Thomas Crown*. Meanwhile, McQueen's friend Mark Rydell, who worked with him in *The Reivers*, remembers that 'He was hard and he could be mean . . . He wanted to feel that nothing could happen without him.' *Him first, everybody else nowhere*, people remember. Sturges himself walked away from McQueen's next film, terminating their friendship. When Steve came down with flu – or a very early intimation of cancer – on 1972's *The Getaway*, the exasperated crew put it to a vote (70 for, 49 against) whether or not to buy him a get-well card. There were more run-ins with the screenwriter of *The Towering Inferno* and the original director of *Tom Horn*. The list isn't exhaustive. For twenty years McQueen was in and out of production meetings in black leather, pondering budgets and scripts. His rudeness Sturges believed to be part of his idea of thrift, a need to eliminate all time-wasting. Steve expected immediate answers to hard questions. *Don't think. Do it.* The legendary profanities tumbled out in a verbal pile-up. *Christalmighty, whad-*

dyamean, goddammit. McQueen's intensity was compelling, he demanded complete attention. His chilly blue eyes under the thatchy hair bored in relentlessly as he enquired about a term or condition, and gave it the drama of an international crisis. One Hollywood producer would compare negotiating with him to 'dealing with a six-year-old who was carrying a nuclear bomb in his lunch-pail. Any meeting's greatest potential was for an explosion.'

The alternative idea of his trusting Hollywood was and always would be pathetic.

As soon as he banked his *Magnificent Seven* money, Steve moved both upmarket and uphill to 2419 Solar Drive in the city heights. The Continental-style house, costing $60,759.84, was one of the very best situated in town, craning over Hollywood like a hippie Berghof. From the terrace and back garden the view swept towards mountains in the west, the Mojave desert in the east and downtown below, the far side of Silver Lake. Here 'Supie' became plain Steve, or Esteban again, playfully wolf-whistling at the woman he now called Nellie. There were moments of genuine empathy between the couple – as when they hosted elaborate Thanksgiving dinners for local children or stray race drivers – and, in the proper mood, they could give stunning performances of husband and wife. 'A good woman can take a bum from the streets and turn him into a king,' he said. In January 1960 Alfred Hitchcock cast Steve, with Neile as his co-star, in two of his TV melodramas, including the famous *Man from the South* episode. (One man bets his new Cadillac against another man's little finger that he can't flick a cheap Bic lighter ten times in succession.) 'For kicks' they did a number of shows together after Terry's birth, including slots in the Bob Hope and, of all people, Perry Como revues. They made a good-looking couple, the bullet-headed tough, who could also be soft, and the small, stunningly svelte dancer. As Steve ascended, they might yet have become a hip version of Burton and Taylor, but it wasn't to be. Shortly after testing for the film of *West Side Story* that spring, Neile learned that she was pregnant again. The role she settled on was at once stranger and more ordinary than anything Hollywood could have scripted, that of 'plain Mrs Superstar'.

Meanwhile, the so-called 'tail' kept coming. McQueen pulled

women, as one of them puts it, 'like a magnet does iron filings'. Those with long memories made the connection to certain well-slept stars of the recent past: the Clark Gable, Errol Flynn type. He doted on Neile and the children, but he liked to mingle too. At parties Steve's beautifully groomed hair positively glowed. His lithe, pumped-up body fitted perfectly into Fashion District denim and patent leather boots. The girls crowded round him panting. They obviously wanted to touch the hem of his garment, and frequently more, and it was all McQueen could do to fight them off. He didn't always bother. A woman called Natalie Hawn remembers a scene where 'some bit sidled up to him. "I wore these for you, Stevie," she said, hand[ing] him a pair of panties. After she moved out of earshot . . . [McQueen] turned to me: "That's the kind of shit I have to put up with."' When Steve, in turn, wound up alone with Hawn, she found him 'a sweetheart' and says that, just as McQueen was the quickest draw in Hollywood, so something similar went on in bed. He told Hawn he'd hustled both men and women while down on his luck in New York, but was 'cured' by the time he met Jack Kennedy a few years later in Santa Monica. The then President apparent had taken Steve aside and asked him, 'Don't you find you get a headache if you don't have at least a poke a day?'

Around 1960 McQueen was nearing Kennedy's ideal. The tally was 'two or three hundred' a year.

There were rumours that he was manic depressive, and unburdened himself to his woman friends. Hawn also remembers him 'raving' about Julian and then, in answer to her questions, discussing his childhood – if a mumbled 'yep' or 'nope' could be elevated to the level of discussion. These were the times when he should have been with his family, when it might have been possible to scale down if not vanquish his furies and acquire much-needed perspective on the misery of his youth. But not for the son of Julian Crawford.

Hawn adds, 'Sometimes Steve would turn up, and sometimes he wouldn't. My instructions were that, if he was in town, I'd wait by the phone for him to contact me. We'd meet and then, as he put it, shtup. Towards the end I had to sit in all day, because I never knew when he'd call me. As it turned out, he never did. And I never found out where he went.'

His close male friends rhapsodised over McQueen, and with good cause. Don Gordon calls him a 'straight arrow – almost uniquely for [Hollywood], totally bullshit free'. His biking partner Bud Ekins talks of Steve's personality with perhaps more understanding than anyone. Ekins claims that this 'complicated guy' who 'basically trusted nobody' and 'did best one-on-one, and then only from amongst four or five people' was 'unknowable . . . It was almost impossible to pin him down. He was first and last an actor. But to a few people he was the best company, the most loyal guy on earth.' Steve always made it abundantly clear that, whereas he admired anyone who could 'hold his mud', he only really had time for a few dirty-faced peers prepared to pit themselves against one another. Most or all of the inner circle, like Ekins, Gordon and McQueen himself could handle themselves on wheels. In 1960, while on location in Cuernavaca, Steve was named Rookie of the Year by the American Sports Car Association. He let it be known that the award meant more to him than 'any fucking Oscar'.

Depressingly often, a brilliant early film is a cul-de-sac, not a road to greater things: in the industry quip, you've got a lifetime to make your first move and three months to make your second. So it went. As a further judgement-impairer, massive amounts of pot were now being smoked by both McQueen and his immediate circle. Early in 1961 Elkins signed Steve (after Cary Grant wisely passed) to star in MGM's *The Golden Fleecing*, later renamed *The Honeymoon Machine*. The hammy, more manic style and plumbing of comic depths only hinted at in *The Blob* was a disaster. (*The Honeymoon Machine* made that film look like *Othello*.) According to Neile, 'Steve was under contract to MGM when the part was offered and, on the grounds that it had more lines than stares, Hilly pushed him to do it.' Not surprisingly, McQueen himself always denied responsibility for the fiasco. 'I take full credit,' Elkins loyally agrees. 'Strangely enough, Steve *could* do comedy and it wasn't a bad script. Something just went wrong in the production and direction departments.' What began as a diverting romp ended in shoulder-hunching embarrassment.

The plot wasn't that bad, with a full arsenal of *Dr Strangelove*-era paranoia: bombs, spies and a naval computer jimmied to break the bank at a Venice casino. But McQueen still felt it necessary to take no chances and go for a glib, speeded-up performance that made it sound as if his palette was cleft. Neile recalls how Steve 'soon realised he was making a dog and just started doing anything, funny voices and all, for laughs'. From then on McQueen dabbled in increasingly mangled slabs of pidgin Italian. 'Grass-y,' he kept mumbling, like a schoolboy struggling to master a tricky noun. '*Servicio roomio, grassy*,' he said on the phone. '*Mucho grassy*,' he told someone else – before, emboldened by the progress he seemed to be making, he tried a premature and unwise stab at a full sentence. Steve fought his co-star Brigid Bazlen nonstop when not shtupping her, rowed with the director and hated the film, which the critics called 'fake, witless, unfelt . . . clumsy slapstick . . . a flop'. Ironically, probably the only person who avoided Steve's bile was the manager who signed him to the part in the first place. 'I don't remember any harsh words,' says Elkins. 'But then, McQueen handled failure much better than success.'

Since warning Neile off him five years earlier, Elkins had long since developed an affectionate respect for Steve, and he saw to it through eight films that the friendliness of their business dealings never impinged on the borders of that respect. By 1961 McQueen was a wealthy man; he needed to be, and never felt himself totally secure, but by the standards of most thirty-year-olds, even those in Candyland, he'd little to complain of. He was shrewd, well managed, tight with a buck, and usually got the best advice. In Hilly Elkins, Steve found the right guide for his interests and success, and Elkins played a starring role in the actor's early career. The result was a true and time-tested partnership. Yet, by 1960, Elkins's days were already numbered. As Steve scaled the evolutionary ladder to film stardom, he crabbed endlessly about his old relationships. Many of the relationships did the same. They couldn't decide whether they admired him or whether, as Elkins says, he was just a little crazy. They loved the great leap forward, and they knew that he was capable of anything. They noticed, in particular, how he was always checking his watch – clocks everywhere, with precision chronometers in all his cars. Fast work.

It had already been a couple of years. Ten since he'd become an actor. Given his peerless ability to skim a script and know instantly whether it worked, whereas others' track record in that area was spotty, it was inevitable that Steve would come to realise he could just as easily use Elkins's tactics without using Elkins. Moreover, their original joint venture, 'The Factory', was winding down. After a disastrous switch to Wednesday nights, *Wanted* was axed in the spring of 1961, a victim of what Elkins calls 'a mass migration away from TV cowboys'. That was certainly so, though it's true that in Steve's own case the cancellation was more abrupt since he was caught *in flagrante* with his pretty continuity girl, 'on set and in *company time*', as Dick Powell put it reproachfully. After 117 episodes, the series went off the air that March. With the exception of a few guest appearances (one of them, ironically, for Powell) and variety shows, McQueen's made-for-TV career was over.

As part of his push towards independence, Steve formed his own production company. Scuderia Condor Enterprises (after the Italian Scuderia car stable) was incorporated on 15 February 1960, with offices in Beverly Hills. As well as nominally retaining Elkins, McQueen's Maginot Line was rounded out by the Morris agency and a law firm with the strikingly Dickensian name of Mitchell, Silberberg & Knupp. A show of his new leverage came exactly a year later, in February 1961, when Steve signed a 'loan-out' agreement between Condor and Paramount which stumped up $100,000 for him to play Private Reese in *Hell is for Heroes*. And that was without the 'perks package' awarded to stars, covering everything from personal gyms, trailers and hotel suites to flights in the studio's jet. Under a separate deal with Condor of 20 December 1961, McQueen would pay himself a salary of $1,500 a week, or twenty times more than the average blue-collar worker.

Going with the Hollywood grain, there was also property. As well as the Solar house, McQueen spent $25,935.77 on a weekend home in Palm Springs. Both spreads were fairly modest in the movie-star hierarchy: each revolved around the garage, where Steve soon added a BMC sports car, a Land-Rover and yet more bikes. They weren't palaces in the classic sense, some would sneer, with their muddy carpets, their plain furnishings and their chaotic kitchens. But both places were, none the less, strikingly located. McQueen's new-found friend, the Formula One champion Stirling Moss, visited him at Solar Drive that summer. 'I'd already met Steve in that funny little dump [Klump Avenue] in Hollywood. Now here he was, a couple of years later, living in the proverbial mansion on the hill. I remember thinking, My God, if you get one thing right in America, you get it all right.' McQueen agreed with this rosy assessment. 'I got me an ol' lady who digs me, two healthy kids, and plenty of fruit and nuts on the table. The lean days are over – and the ride from here on leads straight to Candyland.'

The rest of the journey was made at speed. As Moss puts it, 'For a film star, Steve was fantastically fast – with luck, he could have raced internationally. He was reckless, but, Jesus Christ, he was good.'

Once behind a wheel, Moss adds, McQueen shot out like a plane from a catapult.

It was a passion that consumed him, a life of dirt tracks, of kidney-jolting heats that went on for hour after hour, of revving V6 engines with the requisite 'poke' to them, of slumping under a tree beside the finish line with a can of beer or a fat cigarette, the steam rising up off his leathers, asbestos-lined mask rolled down under his chin, the fibres slowly poisoning him; that and the pride of a professional result. It was the thrill of affirmation and instant gratification. 'All the racers I know aren't in it for the money. They race because it's something that's inside them . . . They're not courting death. They're courting being alive.'

In local club events McQueen would typically be placed third or fourth in a field of thirty, actually won a race in his Formula Cooper and impressed even Moss with his enthusiasm. Steve would sit in the bar and 'pour out technical talk to anybody who happened to be about. He laughed at his own jokes loudly and with quite unaffected enjoyment . . . McQueen was always at his best around race people.' Sports in general and driving in particular were ways for Steve to be one of the boys, something he'd always found hard. Furthermore, organised violent activity – two-wheeling especially – was pure fun for him. The greatest of fun, in fact, the one thing in his life he could throw himself completely into purely for its own sake. 'McQueen was a bat out of hell,' adds Bud Ekins. 'Let's just say he was always fast, if strictly over the short haul. No one was quicker than him out of the gate, but you wouldn't bet on him lasting the course. Steve seemed to have a lot of wrecks.'

McQueen was always a contender, Ekins maintains – an assessment Steve himself confirmed. He made a great point of telling everyone that he was the best first-lap man in town. A charger.

In the 1930s and early forties, when Steve was discovering the cinema, romantic figures in films were never casually introduced to their lovers. Writers racked their brains so that their characters could 'meet cute'. For example, the hero might, through a happy gaffe at the booking office, share the heroine's overnight sleeping compartment, or she might back her beat-up old Ford into his shiny new Futuramic convertible. However chastely they ended, Hollywood affairs always began with a bang.

McQueen had much the same melodramatic flair. A Los Angeles woman, long since married and now a grandmother, remembers how 'I was working on the lot in Television City when Steve, as Josh Randall, came riding into the foreground, over a fake hill, and right towards me.' Suddenly she felt a strong arm pulling her up into the saddle, and when McQueen turned round she found herself staring into a lean, bronzed face and two of the bluest eyes she'd ever seen. When their owner spoke – the classic frontier intro, 'Howdy, pardner' – she actually felt faint. 'What can you say when a man like that sweeps you off your feet?' They went round the corner together to a hayloft. A more surprising fact than the sex was that Ringo tagged along, grazing indifferently while the two made out, thus demonstrating that, whatever their early mishaps, Steve and his prize possessions weren't easily parted. The sawn-off shotgun, the woman couldn't help but notice, also accompanied him.

During the next week McQueen and the woman ate together, laughed together and 'shtupped endlessly', but her real joy lay in anticipating spending a weekend alone with him when Neile was out of town. Then, on the Friday evening in question, she got a sarcastic telegram from Steve saying that he was reading *The Magnificent Seven* – she assumed with a female cast member – but would try and make time for her on Sunday. That was the last she ever heard or saw of him.

Sex, booze, and the less vagarious world of male bonding. For anyone who still thought McQueen was gay, what could be more bracing than to see him reborn as a Hemingway hero, rewriting his past and reshaping his public image, snapping into his routine with that roast-beefy American muscle? The author himself committed suicide on 2 July 1961, just as Steve pondered *The Great Escape*. It was a chronological, in some ways logical, succession. Both were men who personified the ball-clanking, hard-living type, and yet time and again they both delivered the goods. The notion that Hemingway's touch of insurrection and macho swagger might have been handed down from Jazz Age studs to arch swingers like himself clearly tickled McQueen. There was even the totemic pot and Old Milwaukee in common. Like Hemingway, Steve clearly didn't care to be considered 'candyass'. When that misguided neighbour, for example, tested McQueen's mettle in front of his daughter, calling him a wimp, the result was a swift pop to the jaw. The incident made the 'People' column of *Variety*, while the *LA Times* headlined its story: ACTOR STEVE MCQUEEN BY K.O. IN BATTLE. He was fast becoming the 'heavyweight champ' of American film.

For his next role Steve played a Hemingwayesque lone wolf, Reese, the insubordinate GI whose death-wish spirals into a suicide mission in *Hell is for Heroes*. According to Neile, McQueen 'took the job because he had more than seven lines' (although he actually spoke fewer than 500 words over ninety minutes) and, presumably, to neutralise the damage done by *The Honeymoon Machine*. Steve first signed on for what was then called *Separation Hill* on 1 February 1961 at $10,000 a week for ten weeks. The writer Bob Pirosh, also set to direct, soon fell from grace when McQueen complained that the script, while fostering Reese's singular moral code, also dared to feature the sub-cast. 'Why can't they just do the picture about one guy – me?' he asked, and promptly left the set.

He had a good laugh at the suits who, in his assessment, 'went mental'; swarms of candyass little men, each with phone in his right hand, adding machine in left, and the fear of the sack like a maggot in his heart. Soon enough, a deputation came scurrying up to Solar.

'We've got a problem,' they told him.

'Oh yeah?'

He shrugged and they gritted their teeth. The adding machines came out.

Over the next week, Paramount executives learnt much about Steve's 'shit', and about conflict, dissent and creative differences between star and director, as McQueen insisted that Pirosh be fired, which he was. Peace was restored when the studio then hired Don Siegel, of *Invasion of the Body Snatchers* fame, who revamped both script and title. Steve, Siegel said 'walked around with the attitude that the burden of preserving the integrity of the picture was on *his* shoulders . . . I told him he bored me, that I was as interested in [*Hell*] being good as he was, and that when this fact sunk through his thick head we'd get along. I could see he was angry. I knew he was capable of violence, and I knew he could whip me. But I decided that if he stood up and came for me, I'd hit him first as hard as I could and hope for the best. Fortunately for me, he didn't stand up. Eventually, we grew to like each other.'

Next McQueen clashed with his co-star, the ex-teen idol Bobby Darin, wrote off a studio rental car, told Paramount they were 'fuckheads' when they queried the bill and confidentially assessed another actor as 'a pussy'. Overnight, the duck-suited goofball of *Honeymoon Machine* was converted back into an outlaw, thug and morale problem. Now Steve was ready to go to work again.

Principal shooting began in the woods around Redding, California, that spring. McQueen was his usual bundle of joy on set, his mouth a snarl of blacked-up teeth held in suspense by a steady diet of gum and cigarettes, perpetually frowning, occasionally flying off into stratospheric declamations about the studio's cheapness and the general shit of just about everything. The sitcom comedian Bob Newhart made his screen debut in *Hell*. According to him, 'Steve believed because of his character he should have as little contact with the cast as possible.' 'I can't claim we were ever really buddies,' adds another co-star, Fess Parker. 'I admired McQueen the performer. As a man . . . he was incredibly tense, generally wound up, always apart. At the first opportunity he'd hop onto a motorcycle and take off into the hills.' McQueen wrecked that bike and a total of three cars in the first two weeks of filming. Paramount kept supplying him with replacements, though Steve declined the offer of a driver.

In the movie, too, Siegel's characters would break down, fall apart and flay themselves and others. *Hell*'s locale was World War II Germany, where a group of seven American soldiers are left to protect a front and, ultimately, to destroy an enemy bunker. (The David and Goliath theme echoed *The Magnificent Seven* down to the digit.) The stark black-and-white footage and the slightly weary satire of military life didn't make for an easy mix. That was *Hell*'s charm, and the reason it never found a mass audience. Perversely, McQueen, the unit's sullen, word-at-a-time sociopath, provided the main spark and delivered the film's sharpest lines, if not its bluntest, largely consisting of 'Yep,' 'Nope,' 'Uh-huh,' 'Scram,' and 'You show up, I'll blow yer head off.' Throughout he's in permanent fuck-you mode, committed to self-definition through self-destruction by taking out the Nazi pillbox. It might be stretching it to say that Steve was playing himself, but the rest of the cast all made the connection; how, for instance, when Reese was called on to cry, although Siegel tried onions and, rashly, slapping his star in the face, McQueen simply couldn't manage it.

Neile also saw how Steve lost himself in the part. He'd come home to the hotel, she'd ask, 'What gave today?' and he'd say, 'Nothing.' Then Neile would look at the rushes, and there was McQueen turning his loaded rifle on a terrified Newhart or maniacally wielding a butcher's knife. *Hell* was perhaps the only genre film to date to seriously examine how a soldier's homicidal behaviour could turn heroic under battle conditions. Siegel brought off the trick of combining action with his own highly moral message about the futility of war. Even when the money ran out and Parker's climactic what's-it-all-about speech was cut in favour of a simple zoom-in on the bunker, it only underlined the rich irony of the title. No director was ever better served by a star. Reese's chiselled features were like an explosive period detail in themselves. The laconic, hair-triggered McQueen was perfectly cast and made the most of his hard-won opportunity to take control of his part – he'd rarely be cooler, smarter or nastier in his whole career.

Hell was premiered on 26 June 1962, and found even the first-night audience indifferent, when not busy being shocked by it. They gulped along with the rest of America when Steve's character, already mortally wounded, blew up both the pillbox and himself. 'Sickening' was the *Times*'s verdict. Long before then, McQueen had given due warning that the film was something other than all-round family entertainment. Apprised by posters starkly promising them 'guts' and 'futility', most people stayed away. The critics, too, had to be educated up to *Hell*, which many of them later touted as a classic, paving the way for the likes of *Platoon* and *Full Metal Jacket* (it was Stanley Kubrick's favourite war film). President Kennedy, as well as providing its spoken foreword, watched it, by his own reckoning, 'fifteen or twenty times' in the White House. McQueen himself kept up a private litany of insults and grievances whenever speaking about it, which he did rarely, and worked with only one of the cast again. Sixteen years later he auditioned Don Siegel to direct his penultimate film *Tom Horn*. Siegel quit after two weeks, telling his friend Lee Marvin, 'I just don't know where [McQueen's] coming from. Every meeting he was late. Every fucking meeting he'd freak out. Where does he get off treating people this way? But you know what's the greatest tragedy to me? That shit's a great actor.'

Marvin joined the consensus.

Steve had now made eight films in five years, plus three seasons of *Wanted*. He was no longer the comer but an A-list star, spoken of in the same breath as Newman and now Beatty. Fan mail was pouring in to Solar. His press relations were a journalistic homage. These were the days when McQueen was still doing interviews. Steered by Dave Foster, various grandees of the Hollywood media – Hopper, Louella Parsons, Sheilah Graham – would file into the hotel suite and flank the indifferent sovereign. Later, in their copy, they would individually swear allegiance to him like courtiers to a king – 'the Versailles shit', as McQueen called it. It jarred against the image, but then Steve was always playing one or other of the parts from his internal drama for all he was worth. His next filmed role, yet another World War II anti-hero, was the least of it. McQueen wanted, among other things, to be an actor, a racer, a superstar, a hard nut, a good guy, an opportunist, a man of honour, real folks; to be very rich, to be very poor, to have 'more pussy than Frank Sinatra', to love Neile faithfully, to be on the best of terms with all men, to 'twist melons'.

He used moodiness as a pesticide, and his runic good looks were a particularly disconcerting contrast to his sharp tongue. 'I like the feisty bastard,' cooed Hopper. 'He *excites*.'

What an operator, others said, trying to 'get' this artisan king. Was he playing himself? Was that the angle?

People had reason to be perplexed. It was Steve's expectation that they jump to his moods that caused trouble.

McQueen's behaviour on set was often obnoxious, though critics squabbled as to whether his tantrums were perfectionist or ego-bound: technically astute or peevishly negative. Those scenes on *Hell*, as Don Siegel sighed, 'made you weep', but more because of what they said about Steve's past than what they said about him. Truculence, for McQueen, was the continuation of his childhood shit by other means.

Indeed, his inner brat was endearing. He loved to clown – when McQueen read for producers he'd cross his eyes ferociously and try on manic voices. *Goon Show* situationism was fine by him. When Steve lunched daily at the Paramount commissary, he was able all week to maintain the gag that he had a stunt double, Jock, who also ate there. Each time the waitress tried to resume the conversation of the day before, McQueen would say, perplexed, 'You must have been talking to my stand-in, Jock.' The waitress would protest: 'But didn't you tell me yesterday you were buying a car – ?' 'No, no,' Steve would interrupt, po-faced. 'That was my man Jock.' The next day he became the double again. 'Are you sure you're not confusing me with that shit McQueen?' The waitress would reel away, leaving Steve and his table in gales of mirth. He never tired of practical jokes and laughed a lot, sometimes at himself.

As to sex, he didn't stint himself. A friend named Jim Hoven remembers 'see[ing] Steve in a Hollywood bar, swilling beer and daiquiris with a drop-dead brunette, who was doing a lot of bitching about small things such as there was too much light on the bar, the drinks were too cold, why couldn't they go someplace else, etc., while [McQueen] flipped around, sometimes laughing and sometimes not.' The brunette in question wasn't Neile. It was neither the first, nor by any stretch the last of his wife's many humiliations. Friends would wince when, a couple of years later, after seeing the film *Cat Ballou*,

Steve berated Neile because her 'ass wasn't shaped as good as Jane Fonda's'. Domestically, McQueen was a 'right 'un', says Hoven, more worthy of love and contempt than anyone outside his inner circle knew. After his fashion, Steve 'doted' on family – he 'really dug' his children.

Straight after wrapping *Hell*, Steve made his first and only film in Britain. It was a flop, alas, but at least he shone in it. Once Warren Beatty pulled out, McQueen starred as Buzz Rickson, a psycho variant of Reese though with added sex interest, in Phil Leacock's *The War Lover*. His fee was $75,000. For that, Steve spent four full months, from September 1961 to January '62, commuting between Bovingdon airfield, central London and Shepperton. According to Neile, 'He took and loved it because it gave him the chance to race – that's when Stirling Moss really came into his life.' (Neile herself admits to a crush on Moss, while, once in England, McQueen's co-star Robert Wagner fell for Joan Collins; Steve, for his part, had to make do with pursuing the actress Shirley Anne Field, alternately trying to 'fight with or fuck' her, though only achieving the former with unqualified mastery. 'You know why you should have been a man?' he asked Field one morning. 'You keep screwing the scene.' A volatile shoot, in other words.) McQueen moved out of the Savoy Hotel once the management, unimpressed with his habit of torching his curtains with the flame from a gas stove, hinted that his presence there be more sparingly required.

'Perhaps Sir might wish to consider his position.'

Sir might. Steve gave it a second, then told the Savoy to go fuck themselves.

Then there was the noise of slammed doors, and soon Hilly Elkins found himself sharing a penthouse with Steve in the Carlton Towers. 'He liked his room to be steaming hot and I liked mine to be cold. We had a neutral zone in between where we'd work on the script, which needed it.' When not 'running amok in a jeep through the English countryside', Steve raved for months afterwards about a costume ball he attended in Chester Square. The crowd numbered about three hundred, and there were many familiar faces in unfamiliar garb: McQueen went as Humphrey Bogart, complete with soiled Burberry and leer (in truth, the scowl was no stretch). He particularly enjoyed the fact that he got to 'feel up Queen Victoria'.

Those in the know said *Lover* presented an idealised view of American crews flying B-17 missions out of wartime East Anglia. It rang of truthfulness, though. It may not have been realistic, but it felt real and it felt right – if it wasn't what war was like, it was what audiences liked to *think* it was like. The film's generally stellar cast further promoted the illusion of grainy verisimilitude, though the bolted-on love triangle (McQueen's and Wagner's characters chasing Field's) soon palled, a crude manipulation that detracted from the jolt of the actual bombing runs. Steve was so good in it that you felt his presence even when he was offscreen. You hung not just on his every word but also on his frequent silences. Rickson had all the qualities fans and foes alike think of as the high-water mark of McQueen's acting: a huge chip on his shoulder, an exquisitely calibrated softer side and that engaging rebelliousness of the still-angry kid snarling, *Don't fuck with me.*

'Rules are for sergeants,' Steve would snap to one character. 'Drop dead,' to another, just before the scene where, alone and shot-up in his Fortress, he smirks, dips his wings, decides oh, well, what the shit, and flies into a cliff.

As Neile points out McQueen also indulged himself on the hallowed British car racing circuits. Elkins remembers him coming second in one heat to the UK's top female driver, Pat Cooper – 'total ignominy; believe me, he would have preferred a wreck'. Sure enough, a week later, McQueen skidded a souped-up Mini off a wet track at Brand's Hatch, slammed into a dirt bank and walked away with a fat lip. (Leacock improvised during the next day's shoot by having Rickson wear an oxygen mask.) That pile-up had two direct and long-term consequences for McQueen. First Columbia and then Hollywood studios generally began adding the so-called 'asphalt' rider to his contracts, warning him that if he ever crashed, and a picture was shut down, he would 'personally and without limitation' be sued for its full cost – something to which, Hoven recalls, 'Steve said, "Bullshit."' He also began to wear more and heavier flame-retardant materials while racing, including ever thicker asbestos padding. As he lay dying, McQueen would rue that decision as a 'kind of suicide [meant] to save my life'.

A final result of *The War Lover*, usually shrugged off as a 'creative

difference' or 'the vision thing', was a firing from McQueen's inner
court. According to Neile, 'Hilly Elkins, whom Steve respected but
never trusted, was like Napoleon . . . I remember [McQueen] ranting
that [Elkins] had had the goddamn nerve to go to Paris for a weekend
while keeping on his London hotel at his, Steve's, expense. He was
history.' Those eight films together evidently cured McQueen of the
need for full-time management. For the next few years he always
relied on the William Morris agency, with whom he signed a new
deal on 2 January 1962. Stan Kamen there would read the incoming
scripts, then sift five or six for Neile herself, who in turn gave the
best one or two to Steve. A film wouldn't get made unless husband
and wife both liked it.

Neither party was a sucker, though only one of them was obsessed,
if not half crazed, with consolidating success.

McQueen's price duly went up, not only in fees but in participation, the all-important 'points' of his films' profits. When he resigned with William Morris he acquired not just more cash but a
taste for all kinds of 'collectable shit' as well. Cherubs carved in
marble. Indian rugs and furniture, old rockers. A stable of motorbikes
and jalopies. He hated to spend small change but threw cheques
around, said Darin, 'like a sailor on shore leave'. Steve opened an
account with his local liquor wholesaler. When he was going strong,
really out there, between movies, a party could last two days, two
nights sometimes, without sleep, without a wake-up call and wardrobe and rehearsals, without the 'candyass day' slipping in and ruin-
ing everything. Other times he spent holed up alone in his den –
'whatever room Steve was in tended to be off-limits', says Neile –
gulping peyote and repeatedly totalling up his net worth on the back
of an envelope. Both activities calmed him down, he said.

On 1 March 1962 Condor Enterprises, in the legalese prose of the
deal 'loaned artist's services to [the producers] Mirisch-Alpha for
The Great Escape'. McQueen was paid $11,111.11 a week for a basic
nine weeks, though overtime would up his fee to $172,222. In return,
Condor were to

> agree . . . that Artist shall conduct himself with due regard to
> public convention and protocol . . . You also agree that Artist

shall not do or commit any act or thing that will degrade him or subject him to public hatred, contempt, scorn, ridicule, or disrepute, or shock or offend the community, or violate public ethics or decency, or prejudice his standing in the community . . .

The great rolling phrases, the legendary morals clause, so compelling in their gravity and simplicity, might be thought inadmissible for the most brute, the bolshiest, to shun, so fair, so obviously right in the circumstances, were their provisos, so reasonable – even to the point of charity – the manner in which the Mirisches drafted the principles of making the Artist world-famous. McQueen, it has to be said, didn't rise to the occasion. As usual he fought nonstop on location, leaving it more than once, and the tow-trucks of southern Germany broke down from hauling away his wrecked cars. But otherwise Steve used the time well. While stuck in Bavaria he began plotting his next move, a strange, sentimental comedy called *Soldier in the Rain*, directed by Blake Edwards (who soon dropped out) and 'sharing' – in the contract's word – Jackie Gleason. Sharing anything wasn't the way McQueen thought, and William Morris soon outdid themselves, telexing crisply phrased codicils to the producer: 'Gleason is to receive First Star billing in 100% of the size of type of the title and no one is to be on the same line except McQueen, who will be billed equally in all respects except that he will be in Second position.' Steve was again paid $100,000 for his time.*

That same summer McQueen's accountant calculated a 'nut projection' for his client, who was spending $3009.50 a month or $36,114 p.a. The ledger showed $66,500 in the bank, along with his 500 shares of Four Star, worth $11,000, various land, and a $30,000 stake in Jerry Lewis's restaurant. Aside from his two homes, Steve had fixed total assets of $172,000. The private cover letter added a shrewd and personal overview to the bottom-line. 'You are in great condition and considering the tempo of your career, are well on the way to building a comfortable fortune. Just keep your feet on the ground.'

---

* Following the success of *The Great Escape*, he renegotiated his fee upwards.

It was good advice, but it wasn't enough. McQueen needed far more than financial security. He always sought something to counteract his paralysing sense of inadequacy, to ward off an encroaching world he'd seen, and still saw, as mean and venal. When he got back from England in January 1962, a rich and now famous man, Steve laboured for a day and a night on a letter:

> With the completion of The War Lover it has been called to my attention that there are several items that have been checked out to me and so that I will not be charged for them, I should like to clarify the position regarding these said items:
>
>> One pair of RAF flight boots; one light blue crew-neck sweater and one dark blue crew-neck sweater which I am sorry to say I know nothing about . . . There was also the case of two teapots that where [sic] purchased for me so that I should be able to have tea early in the morning . . . It was never clarified whether these would be charged in my name or not . . . Unfortunately, one tea pot was stolen from my dressing room before it had even been taken out of the box & this I reported immediately I discovered there had been foul play. The other tea pot was confiscated by one of the Assistant Directors in making tea for the crew in the morning before they started production. This was quite alright by me, [but] as for the other teapot, again, I know absolutely nothing about it other than that it was quietly removed from my dressing room on or about December 12th, along with [the] miscellaneous cups, saucers & spoons . . .

and so on, over four pages, copied by McQueen to thirteen parties. As Don Gordon says, 'Any time Steve thought you were screwing him, even for a dime, he'd be at you like a rottweiler on your jugular vein.' The upshot was that Mitchell, Silberberg & Knupp, along with William Morris and the accountant, kept up a five-way correspondence with Columbia and RAF security police for most of 1962, eventually writing off the cost of the boots and sweaters, though the knotty problem of the teapots remained: McQueen would duly be

debited a total of $7.50, one ten-thousandth of his fee, and com-
plained about it, often bitterly, for the rest of his life.

The 'don't-fuck-with-me' moral was deadly earnest, and so, in
general, was the acting. If Steve's professional choices tended towards
the impassive, he still played it tough, sexy and above all vigilant.
He was ultra focused. McQueen's success lay, in large part, in his
unique understanding of the public. It wasn't always mutual – Hopper would call him a Chinese puzzle. 'The complexity of the man's
simplicity!' cooed *Cinema*. By 1962 the parallel track to McQueen's
dark side had long since emerged: his understated gift in front of the
camera, where he 'carried his own set of lights', in the Broadway
phrase. His best roles eclipsed those of other, earlier-day tough guys,
because Steve did something almost unheard of – he made audiences
care about him. His extraordinary awareness, along with his outbursts
of bristling hostility mingled with humour, made for a career built
on empathy, as well as on genius.

Part of the appeal was technical. That was the McQueen nobody
saw – the man who studied angles with trigonometrical precision,
who learnt about sound and lights and always conjured up the right
props. As an actor he tended to avoid self-conscious explication –
he was masterly at letting the bit players 'do' the plot. Yet he was a
superbly expressive performer. He had an undeniable gift for fixing
onto the character and shaping him into someone you felt you knew.
What he'd discovered in Strasberg's method, early in his career, was
the sense of overall composition in which each word, each look, was
as significant as any other, a composition in which nothing seemed
to happen, but one which, through certain repetitive tricks and
incremental gestures, moved forward to the climax. It was out of this
patient bricklaying technique that Steve became the 'picture perfect
image' (*Variety*) of the American male – a 'cocked weapon'.

And lethal with it. At one point in *The War Lover* the characters
played by McQueen and Field, in a terrifying shift, were suddenly
in the midst of some ugly private spat. He grabbed at her, ripping
her dress as she pulled away, then hurled her onto a couch. The
crew all applauded, but the violence was more than credible – it was
real. Steve would never do a simple 'side swipe' as in the Bond films.
When he hit other actors, they felt it. To paraphrase John Ford, he

put something up on screen that people, or most people, wanted to do or be. 'The loser who wins', Don Gordon calls it.

What Steve was best at, it turned out, was something that the Studio, his stage training and his whole life had been a preparation for: projection. There was a plausibility, a sense of physical presence, in all his major roles. The technician in McQueen knew it and cultivated it. He learnt lines at the last minute for spontaneity, and ate three doughnuts with coffee for the sugar rush. Harold Pinter, who came into Steve's orbit a few years later, calls his half-acquired, half-native talent 'dynamic . . . it was his athleticism, obviously, his sheer being and strength – his focus. Mainly, he was so *alive*.' 'A weird mixture of Cary Grant and the Lone Ranger' would be Strasberg's own assessment. According to this reading, Steve was the consummate outsider, someone society needs but who doesn't need society, who could win through personal fulfilment, even if that brought a touch of violence along the way: the thug with submerged hippie tendencies, a kind of post-Bogart who listened to *Sergeant Pepper*.

Critics had good reason to call him 'natural', or 'really like that', though few explained the terms. It went beyond lack of front, obviously, and consisted of someone inhabiting his own skin, effectively blurring the art/life divide. Acting, for McQueen, was believing. Acting wasn't acting. It wasn't putting on a face and dancing around in make-up. It was believing that you were that character and playing him as if it were a normal day in the life of that character. A Reese, for example, is just as everyone knows him to be, and that's enough. According to the *New Yorker*, 'The message the [McQueens] beam to us goes something like "This is, more or less, the sum of me, and you can take it or leave it." The offer is so generous that we tend to take it,' particularly if they're also the goods. In this context, Steve's friend Cliff Coleman calls him 'the real stuff. He was the same . . . [McQueen's] gift was the way he could flip from blue-eyed charm to that sense of menace. I saw it on screen and I saw it off.' Don Siegel perfectly captured a mood when he said, 'I think McQueen and Lee Marvin are both killers. I really do.'

And what was Steve like when he was home in Solar Drive, dressed in his jeans and cropped jacket, drinking cases of Old Milwaukee and smoking something like three packs of cigarettes daily? Generally, he was teasable and fun, feline, smart, good company, excited in the boyish sense. 'Neat, isn't she?' he'd say of his new car. This was the man-child who loved to read the comics and wolf down comfort food. A cook named Mildred worked all hours, along with a house-keeper and a valet – though Steve liked Neile herself to whip up his favourite steaks and burgers. Fun. Revenge. Those were McQueen's twin, frequently linked objectives as he clanked around wearing his beads and St Christopher medal, a cold butt end clamped in the corner of his mouth. He had very few close friends: aside from his wife, Don Gordon and Bud Ekins, there was a club-owner named Elmer Valentine, and Jay Sebring, who supplied him with wonderful haircuts and high-quality drugs. Sebring always remembered how, after a night of bar-hopping, 'at 6 a.m., Steve would be in the shower singing "Yankee Doodle" . . . He [had] an energy level that was off the chart.'

Conversely, McQueen's only outer show of 'shit' was when, rather than erupting, he calmed ominously – a ticking bomb, as Siegel once called him. Even Julian had always or usually sat up when Steve had one of his 'turns'. She'd paid more attention when he was quiet than when he was ranting. McQueen, who had a tendency to brood in later years, learnt the tactical value of petulance at his mother's knee. These were the times when he'd sit alone in his den, quaffing beer and smoking industrial-strength pot or gobbling peyote and LSD. Or he might indulge his rabid passion for burnt rubber and big engines. Sex and competitive racing, though not necessarily in that order, remained his two physical lusts. To them he devoted huge chunks of his time and energy; from them he drew a massive charge. In March 1962 Steve was placed third in the Four Aces Run, a semi-professional dirt bike endurance event. That same month he drove a Le Mans Healey in the twelve-hour international rally at Sebring, Florida. In his next two outings McQueen won in his new Cooper at Del Mar and Santa Barbara. Jim Hoven met him, mud-spattered and panting, a few minutes after the second race. Steve had no sooner towelled off than he began to talk to his mechanic about tyre pressure, trying to decide between 30 and 35 pounds apiece. When all this was settled, he asked Hoven to help him strip

132

down the engine. 'Talk about in his element ... [McQueen] had that little boy's fidgety energy, like a kid you prop up on a phone book at the dinner table. Loved to get his nails dirty.' Hardly the behaviour of a movie star merely out to entertain and impress. Nor, as his accountant noted ruefully, much of an investment.

A middle-aged fan once came up beside him at the finish line and barked: 'Give me your autograph.'

'Cost you ten bucks,' he said.

'Jesus!' She scuttled back into the crowd.

He'd meant it. In general, McQueen's attitude to money was that it was something to be hoarded, stashed in fireproof safes and counted regularly. However, he vacillated wildly on the subject. Whether through guilt or gratitude at his good luck, Steve adopted a markedly more charitable policy around 1962–3. Along with Valentine, he often drove the 600 miles to the Navajo reservation around Red Rock, Arizona, bringing the Indians medicine and blankets (and frequently exchanging them for more peyote). With marriage, success and now fatherhood, he seemed newly conscious of the possibility, or responsibility for giving something back. Sometimes friends wondered how McQueen could reconcile yelling at people, or worse, with his being the sweetest man in the world. After flying home from England that spring, he visited and set up a scholarship at Boys Republic, endowed his old acting school and even narrated a thirty-minute PR film for the Marines. Perhaps the most compelling old 'shit' of all, however, was with Julian. According to Neile, a 'kind of tenuous peace broke out, largely on account of Terry, Chad and me. The three of us would take the train up to San Francisco, where she'd now moved. We'd go to her place – whatever families do. The grandkids would crawl around the apartment, and we'd swap stories.' McQueen himself tolerated, but never once joined in these reunions.

The War Lover opened on 25 October 1962 to the usual mixed reviews. It did little in the home market but was popular abroad, notably in Britain. Rickson, perhaps even more than a Vin or a Ringa, was McQueen's international breakthrough. Here was a figure who could strike a responsive chord in the heart of every true fan, not to mention tap into the fad – where the premium was on image, not academic consistency – for Americana. 'Steve was really Mr Stars and Stripes,' says McQueen's friend Stirling Moss. 'He had all the qualities that people want an American man to have.'

He arrived.

That winter critics began explaining why there could be no question he was a landmark. 'An oddball who combines the cockiness of Cagney, the glower of Bogart and the rough-diamond glow of Garfield,' wrote *Life*. The public, for its part, knew that any McQueen performance lent itself to intensity – people wondered if he were acting at all, as he prowled around scowling and muttering from the side of his mouth. The contained rage on-screen was mirrored by real-life paranoia. When the family bought a new $225,000 mansion early in 1963, Neile excitedly showed off the sweeping ocean views, the garden and the giant oaks where the children would build their tree houses. A reporter then asked Steve what he most liked about the place. 'Security,' was the quick reply. 'It's got the biggest, strongest front gate you ever saw. Man, I don't wanna be bugged by anybody, OK?'

That cover story in *Life* would tell a somewhat different story. We see Steve presenting his scholarship at Boys Republic, hiking in the Sierra Madres, romping with Chad and lying in a tub with Neile, 'his glamorous wife of English, German, Spanish and Chinese descent', a bottle of wine propped nearby. 'I dig my old lady,' McQueen confirmed. Making whatever allowance one will, there was still something odd about the man who loved to unwind in Elmer Valentine's Whisky à Go Go and trawl the fleshpots of Sunset Strip insisting he 'seldom did parties or clubs'. The intended note of domesticity rang false. Moreover, that camping trip to the hills was 'all a put-on for *Life*', James Coburn told the author Marshall Terrill. The second the reporter's back was turned, McQueen would scuttle back to his jeep for a joint and one of the catered box-lunches he ordered from Musso & Frank's in Hollywood. Nor was his claim to 'give a shit' about clothes generally, and a tux specifically, quite accurate. McQueen wasn't sold down the *soigné* river, but he didn't hit on his style by accident. For instance, when Steve wanted to go shopping to buy jeans he'd insist that Jay Sebring accompany him and stay with him until he chose just the right cut, at which point he'd buy a dozen pairs. The same thing with shirts, coats, sunglasses. The idea McQueen had was to fastidiously capture the perfect 'casual' look, and he wanted a known style plate around while he did it. That particular cover story was the first most of the outside world had actually heard of Steve. It was a notable coup by Dave Foster, but the text was too generously seeded with wishful thinking. The most accurate part of it was the actual lead: PROBLEM KID BECOMES A STAR.

Even then, *Life* hadn't the faintest idea of how big he would soon become. And that wasn't surprising, because nobody else did either. The audience out there has always been a terrifying mystery to both press and talent alike. It seems clear that the public took to him because he was real, yet didn't reduce everything to its lowest common denominator. A strange, clenched everyman.

In fact, McQueen wasn't firing on all cylinders until August 1963, when *The Great Escape* began to lay full-time siege to posterity. Before then, he'd generally been better than his films. Only *The Magnificent Seven* had taken off globally, let alone risen to the level of a catchphrase, and that was an ensemble piece. Most of the rest had had their moments, but still tended either to knockabout farce or the grimly sentimental 'pity-of-it-all' epic. Their stock elements followed fairly predictably down a line from John Ford's *Long Voyage Home*, say, or Sam Fuller's *The Steel Helmet*. Brilliant as it was, much of McQueen's acting was uniform enough to guarantee a kind of inevitability, or sameness to it. Most of his roles weren't to be reckoned in movies at all. His genius was better judged by character, sometimes by lines, more often by gestures and moods, but never by titles. Strictly there was no such film as *Never So Few*. There was no such film as *Hell is for Heroes*. They were simply strips cut from the flowing and mixed entity called McQueen – any given length of which was bound to contain a high proportion of the right stuff.

Everyone now assumed he was there for the long haul, a man who traded on level terms with a Brynner and who airily informed the world he was Candyland-bound. So he was. But that wasn't good enough. Even now Steve still wanted to be the baddest star in Dodge, and soon, or else emigrate, if not turn pro as a race driver. When shooting *The War Lover* he told Julian and a few friends that he'd come as far as he could, journey's end, with nowhere to go. If the next one didn't 'crack it open', he was fucked if, at thirty-something years old, he'd keep playing 'Charge' like fucking John Wayne on his tin horn. The last scenes of the original Steve McQueen story were flickering out.

In the final fade, he put his reluctant lips to the bugle, and blew.

One afternoon in April 1962 Steve pulled into Bud Ekins's motor-cycle shop on Ventura Boulevard. It was a typical spring day in the Valley – dull and overcast in the morning, burnt off by ten, now clear and warm and blue. McQueen waved at his friend across the asphalt scorched with the spilt oil of a thousand bikes.

'Hey, man.' The voice projected to millions was, in private, a bullet-train mumble. 'Gonna do a movie. In Germany. Got some stuff in it. Called *The Great Escape*. Wanna come?'

'You kidding?'

'No expense spared.'

A month later Ekins duly found himself flying, tourist class, to Munich. It was yet another John Sturges ensemble piece, the true story of Allied POWs tunnelling their way out of Stalag Luft III, with McQueen predictably playing the lone wolf. (After *Escape*, he would soon tire of this particular world of male bonding followed by unbonding, and turned down such collectives as *Return of the Seven* and *A Bridge Too Far*.) While waiting for the flight to Europe, Steve, in particular, and even Ekins couldn't help but notice that the small matter of the film's plot – who actually said what, for instance – remained frustratingly on the hazy side. But what the fuck. Lacking the slightest vestige of a script, they tried to compensate with the rowdiest possible social life. By the time they left LA, both had tuned their bikes and their clubbing, at least, to fever pitch, and Steve (though already on full pay) was calling the whole thing a scam. Sturges was quietly offended, especially since he was working an average fourteen hours a day on the deal, now known within Mirisch-Alpha, not affectionately, as the 'Great Headache'.

It nearly didn't make it. The original script, nearer to Paul Brick-hill's book, was sufficiently downbeat, with none of the tacked-on heroics, to have caused the late Louis Mayer to say, 'Lemme see . . . Three hundred guys in a kraut POW camp, seventy-six bust out, two or three actually make it – and you want to call it *what*?' Not, he thought, the sort of thing likely to spawn a movie that grossed $30 million off the bat. Sturges eventually turned to United Artists, home of *The Magnificent Seven*. After two and a half years the promised sequel still hadn't materialised, but Sturges sold them on the idea that three of the 'old gang' – Steve, Coburn and Charles Bronson – were signed for *Escape*. The studio offer, even after haggling, was far below even the very moderate norm of a 1962 Panavision film budget. *The Great Escape* would be shot for $3,769,531.71, or roughly what an A-list star today makes in perks. But it was enough. By late spring an Anglo-American cast had been hired, locations scouted and a whole village in Bavaria decked out with a WELCOME ... FRIEND STEVE MCQUEEN banner splayed across the main street where, on 31 May, an oompah band duly escorted him to his chalet, from a balcony of which Steve threw red roses down to the crowd.

Now all that remained was the shoot, which did not go well.

Actually, it was genial enough at first, as Steve chose to socialise with his friends and employees – some of whom he'd known since he was playing a TV cowboy, or even before then, when he was scuffling for bit work – stick cans of beer into their hands and generally laugh it up at the suits and the studio and the whole scam. Such friends included Ekins, as well as sundry gaffers, grips and flunkies, with whom he always or usually got on well. Those particular men could never pose a threat.

'Might as well chill,' he told Sturges.

'Why not?'

Steve's eyes narrowed. The gloss flaked off him, leaving an insecure actor with no script. He didn't like his director agreeing with him.

The first real hint of ugliness came with the Brits, specifically Richard Attenborough, James Donald and Donald Pleasence, who all reported for work a week later. By then McQueen had had ample time to consider things, and them. Fucking candyass limeys, he spat. Steve's confrontation-loving style was immediately detectable in the way in which he always made sure that they, not he, were the ones on set waiting for a rehearsal. By all accounts, the subsequent take would present the disturbing spectacle of three well-heeled poodles attempting to interact with a pit-bull. 'What's the matter with

[McQueen]? Why does he act that way?' Attenborough asked James Coburn. (Coburn's one-word answer, 'Paranoia.') In later years Pleasence, at least, was conciliatory. 'As far as I'm concerned,' he would say, 'all the stories about Steve-the-shit are a joke. When he committed to a scene he was always punctual, disciplined and friendly. The problem was in getting him to commit in the first place.' In private, Pleasence complained that some of his best work with James Garner in *Escape* was cut, sacrificed on the altar of 'Steve's lovable need to deball the competition'.

McQueen's own loftiest contempt was reserved for the script – as usual in a Sturges film, still being frenziedly drafted as the cameras rolled. Steve thought that he was being shafted not so much by Attenborough and Pleasence as by Garner, playing an amiable spiv – much like his later stint in *The Rockford Files* – and wearing both a fluorescent smile and an eye-catching white sweater to McQueen's dun grey. When scenes weren't added for his character, Hilts, he walked off the picture – though actually 'walked' underestimates a saga Neile calls 'horrendous . . . when Steve saw the early rushes, he just tore off in a car by himself for the night – at least I'm assuming it was by himself. Stan Kamen from William Morris had to take the next flight from LA to Munich, calm Steve down, then fly home again. Everything was in turnaround.' It was 5000 miles to get from the Morris office to the set, the last fifty of which were the worst. McQueen met his agent on a vintage motorbike, and took off with Kamen bouncing up and down in the sidecar. They made the run in forty minutes.

Two days later Steve saw some more footage, and still didn't like it. Neile's heart sank.

Back in LA, Kamen heard his name being paged as he staggered through the airport terminal towards a taxi. He made the call, drank numerous cups of coffee and then he, too, found himself in turnaround. Kamen's return flight to Germany that night was his third Atlantic crossing in seventy-two hours.

'I don't want to waste your time,' he told Steve on arrival. Kamen tried to shout, but his voice husked on a combination of jet lag and frustration. 'Either haul ass back to work, or Sturges says you're toast. Got it?'

He got it. For McQueen, the inevitable result of so-called team work was always a needless loss of star quality both for himself and the film. The peculiar paradox of *Escape* was that he wanted to find an 'identity' – the very mantra, Bob Relyea remembers, of the whole shoot – yet not by saying or being anything he could actually name. In Garner's words, 'Steve wanted to be the hero, but he didn't want to do anything heroic.' The result was a role seemingly bolted on to the main feature, incongruously (though, it has to be said, brilliantly) using McQueen's love of machines to regulate his insecurity. Meanwhile, the veteran writer W. R. Burnett,* drafted in to add American interest to the plot, became the latest victim of Steve's mania for the 'right' script – which was the only script the public would ever know about. 'McQueen was an impossible bastard,' Burnett said. 'A third of the way through the picture he took charge. I had to rewrite his scenes and rearrange them. Ohhh, he drove you crazy.' McQueen told Burnett towards the end of filming that he was sorry for the way he'd treated him and wanted to apologise. Burnett, a mild man for an author, looked at him and said, 'It's too late for that.'

'Steve,' Sturges once told him, 'please don't blink.' This simple and not unreasonable request was pondered. As director and crew set up the shot, Burnett recalled, 'McQueen seemed on the point of imploding.' The silence was as brittle as ice. Suddenly, it was as though Sturges, the twenty or thirty technicians and the cast had lost him; his head fell, he stared into the dust of the prison yard, and his whole body sifted down. 'Anything was possible,' said Burnett. Promptly on the cue of '*Action!*' McQueen emerged from the abyss. Up came his chin, up came a smirk, and he seemed to swell before their eyes. For a splinter of a second he stood there, frozen, and even Burnett thought he was the 'loneliest guy' – loneliness had been the theme all along. Then Steve began to move, flowing into that feline prowl against a dramatically hushed background, and coolly caught the baseball tossed to him without even looking. By the time he got to the famous last scene back in his cell, the insecure kid was once again the Cooler King, 'reincarnated' or 'nearpossessed', according

---

* Author of both the novel and screenplay of McQueen's earliest love, Bogart's *High Sierra*.

to Sturges. 'It made me cry, because Steve had that kind of grief, and he had that ecstasy. I've never forgotten it. He worked like a surgeon for that shot.' McQueen, holding forth at a pitch of bolshiness and charm, was home at last.

Had a Louis Mayer had anything to do with it, *Escape* would have been shot entirely in the US, specifically California, doubling Big Bear Park for Germany. The Mojave desert would have stood in for Bavaria, with those prison interiors knocked up on the lot in Culver City. As it was, the location couldn't have been bettered, beauty as well as misery satisfying the need for wartime detail. By Burnett's calculation, *Escape* featured almost as many alpine backdrops as would *The Sound of Music*. As the peak count mounted, he started lists for lakes, fields and forests, but there were too many overlaps: water surrounded by steeply angled trees and pastures, and so on. Franconia was magnificently right for the film. It was gorgeous – even many of the PR stills as well. The actual camp was mocked up in a small town called Geiselgasteig. McQueen and his family lived twenty-five miles away in Deining, northern Bavaria, where he continued to be a local attraction. A crib was bought for Chad and the family settled down there for the summer. The neighbours' view of Steve honking in and out of town in his rented Mercedes was Deining's major talking point, though the morning he casually wandered around dressed as a Nazi (doubling for his adversaries in a bike scene) made a strong bid for second place. The house itself was transformed, like the Savoy before it, into the environment Steve found most relaxing – something that combined comfort with the semblance of a garage recently ransacked by Hell's Angels. When the family left they were billed for 'Rent, telephone and broken equipment' by one Rudolph Jugert, the local gauleiter.

This was minor compared to Steve's other debts. That twenty-minute drive between Deining and Geiselgasteig all too often became a convoy: McQueen in his Mercedes 300-SL at full revs, with the German police right behind him. He'd drive on down the line of the Danube, sometimes through deep pine timber, sometimes coming out into a clearing and smallholdings, shedding farm animals in his wake, and finally make an abrupt, lurching stop at the studio gate. That car was where he did his best thinking, Steve said. It was also where he collected thirty-seven speeding tickets in the course of the shoot: arriving in Germany on Memorial Day and departing in the last week of summer, McQueen ran up a fine roughly every three days and narrowly avoided jail when he failed to show his driver's licence, later discovered at home in Hollywood. The studio lawyers saved him on that occasion. But that wasn't the end of it. On 24 July Steve bounced the Mercedes off a tree. He was mildly shocked, though not hurt, and he sat for a moment while the car hissed and blew its horn spontaneously, and through a noise like a cherry bomb exploding in the engine.

McQueen gave it a second, then began to laugh wildly.

In contrast, various members of the Bavarian judicial system were extremely shaken. They didn't regard Steve's antics and increasingly manic behaviour as an illuminating commentary on the paradoxes of preserving the collective in the context of self-expression by a great and busy man. They saw it as, simply, *dümmlich*. That particular wreck would dog McQueen for more than a year to come, bringing him untold grief and eventually a repair bill of DM 7115. There was a final fine *in absentia*. And when Steve balked at that – and he talked about counter-suing – Mirisch-Alpha paid up; just stopped counting *Escape*'s receipts long enough to write out a cheque and send it off, docking him part of his pay.

McQueen complained at that, too.

As for the film: Sturges's camera was relaxed, moving with the characters, but still Steve, with his uncanny feel for expressing inner tension through a few underplayed looks, burst the frame with his vitality. Even by action-man standards, his dynamism stood out. His relentless search for Hilts's 'identity' conjured up some of *Escape*'s best scenes – the one where the US contingent brew up moonshine (filched from an old episode of *Wanted*, via *Never So Few*); the chase where he doubled for one of his own pursuers; and the Jump, the one the suits told him categorically not to do.

McQueen spoke two words to them and went on riding.

According to the original script, McQueen was supposed to escape (before, like almost everyone else, being recaptured) by train. And so they rehearsed it. Steve, whose passion for factual history tended to be exceeded by his interest in wheels, soon pitched a much better idea. 'I found myself suggesting I beat it on a motorbike. [Sturges] said he'd like me to give a demonstration, which I later did. He fell in with the gag – despite all the crap with the insurance honchos.'

Early that Sunday morning McQueen, Ekins, a stunt rider named Tim Gibbes and the second-unit director began digging. The four of them made up the advance party for the scene in which Hilts would make a mad lunge for freedom over the German–Swiss frontier. For several hours they scooped a ramp out of the valley where the grass was cropped green and smooth to the line of the pines, making it about nine or ten feet long, and then Steve hit it in third gear and promptly wrapped himself and his bike around the fence. 'I could have bust my melon,' he said. So Ekins began rehearsing the scene, practising his take-offs, so psyched that they could see his neck muscles bulge as he lifted his head, then landing, hard, on a natural rake, braking in a yellow mounting cloud of dust. The dust never settled, as Ekins tried more jumps, at ever increasing heights, and finally it hung like a yellow fog over the whole party. Sometimes McQueen and Gibbes would encourage him, 'but mostly I remember just doing it, over and over', his back bent like a half-open knife, 'narrowly clearing the wire, which was actually a string-and-rubber band prop . . . Early the next day I said to Sturges, 'Let's roll.'

Steve's voice rustled. 'Think you can handle it?'

'Positive.'

Ekins, now with hastily dyed hair, brought off the move in a single take. For gourmets of technical detail, he cleared the twelve-foot fence on a 1961 650cc Triumph (disguised as a side-valve wartime BMW) in fourth gear, at 65 m.p.h., and promptly throttled back into chosen obscurity. 'We all kind of kept it quiet that I'd done it, not Steve, but that always happens on a movie. Didn't faze me none.' Ekins's landmark stunt helped make *The Great Escape* a major hit in both Europe and America. He was paid his standard daily fee by Mirisch-Alpha, $100.*

By contrast, the jump that McQueen now made was into a perma-

---

* Some time later, it's only fair to point out, the producers paid Ekins a bonus which was between $500 and $1000.

nent and starring role as the King of Cool. Within a few weeks he
was the enthroned man's man of the Western world. Steve loved it.
Inevitably, there was some low-level debate in fan magazines and
newspaper columns about whether he was really 'as good as that'
and how much he 'actually did' (though no one dug up the story
behind the jump) in *Escape*. It's true that the film had a number of
charms beyond the simultaneous sang-froid and swagger of
McQueen. There was the stellar cast, with Garner and Attenborough
to the fore; Daniel Fapp's lavish photography; the taut, even brusque
score, owing motor energy and some of its harmonic tang to *The
Magnificent Seven*, another symphonic blockbuster strutted out by
Elmer Bernstein's orchestra. In *Escape*'s sheer sweep, too, size mattered. At nearly three hours it easily outdid other POW-genre fare
like *The Wooden Horse* and *Password is Courage*. Unlike theirs, its
stock continued to rise – if *Escape*'s plucky yarn looks obvious today,
that's mainly a tribute to its influence. And not even the most wizened
hack could seriously fault a performance that still, forty years on,
provides the best one-stop spectacle of what made McQueen great. As
Hilts he epitomised the cool myth at a time when his only rivals on that
turf were Clint Eastwood, still in the saddle in a fading TV series, and
Sean Connery, whose 007 was never quite the same archetype of the
Hemingway hero once self-parody began to blight the films.

McQueen became the vicarious realisation of people's dreams.

Soon he was everyone's – or every man's – best secret image of
himself: the self-sufficient rebel slicing clean through the system, the
survivor, the alpha wolf who finally chooses a glorious exit rather
than ignominious surrender. It was seductive, and it had the added
bonus of being mainly true. 'The Steve of *Great Escape* was the man
I knew for twenty years,' says Don Gordon. 'Like Hilts, he was cool,
together, abstracted from the group, his own guy.' The question
arose among the intelligentsia of whether anyone so viscerally alive
could also be *un homme sérieux*, or whether, in fact, he was a kind of
male equivalent of Brigitte Bardot. (The doubt was decided in Steve's
favour when he went on to give tart performances in distinctly non-
macho films, culminating in Ibsen's *Enemy of the People*.) *Escape* gave
rise to a spirited debate on its star's technique, in which McQueen
himself took no part.

The night of the press preview, Steve and Neile took a photographer named Bill Claxton and his wife along as their new friends. They came out after the screening, climbed into a rented Lincoln (McQueen insisting that the two women sit up front) and took off for a party. Claxton remembers Steve turning to them later that night and saying he was going to be – was – bigger than Paul Newman. A flicker of a smile appeared, like a breeze on a calm sea. Then Steve's lips moved, though just barely, and he added in a voice so soft the women had to strain to hear it from three feet away:

'Make that the biggest movie star in the world.'

They loved McQueen in Europe. This unequivocal conclusion can be gleaned from the fact that Paris, Rome and even Berlin experienced something like municipal breakdowns on the day of *Escape*'s premiere. In London brass bands paraded in front of the Strand Theatre while jets buzzed it overhead. On screen, Steve was a dour, pent-up and angry spirit, oozing menace, who never really 'did' anything until the final scenes. Yet there was enough of a spark in him, enough of the universal, to make people care. No one since John Wayne had given foreign audiences such a slab of American pie. McQueen posters began to appear in bedsitters and JCRs the length and breadth of Britain. Steve himself was quoted frequently, always with approval. A fan club was organised. *The Great Escape* played to overflow houses for weeks into the autumn and early winter. When they showed it in Brighton, rival gangs of Mods and Rockers would cheer and dance and fight in front of the screen. That jump of Ekins's cleared far more than twelve feet. It soon hit iconographic heights as McQueen's fans first applauded and, in not a few cases, mimicked it. One youth sailed off the breakwater at Brighton and broke a leg. It was the same in Glasgow and Leeds and Cardiff. Every time Hilts went anywhere near a motorbike, the roars and wolf-whistles would surge up from the stalls. McQueen was the first real international action hero, preceding Eastwood by three years.

But Steve's blitzkrieg on pop culture didn't stop there. The funhouse of hysteria now cut three ways. Ordinary people loved McQueen. The press, stroking their collective stubble over this latest mythologised hunk of beefcake, got behind him as for no other tough guy since Brando. From *Escape* on, the media chorus became a giant band playing but one tune. Meanwhile most of the industry came, if not quite to like, then to admire and fear him. On 18 December 1962 Mirisch-Alpha paid Steve $72,222.21 for overtime services rendered on *Escape*, the first instalment of what turned into a stipend. William Morris became the command post for McQueen's next offensive. The lights at 151 El Camino now blazed until the early hours of the morning, Stan Kamen's or Abe Lastfogel's relentless phoning and memo-writing keeping them burning on nights when they weren't actually huddled with Steve. Slowly, over the course of a year, a new McQueen began to emerge. When Jim Hoven visited him he felt 'real energy emanating from Steve for the first time'. Fame hadn't rushed to McQueen. He was thirty-three, with only seventeen more years to live, when Candyland called. A thousand twists of fate could have taken him elsewhere, yet his entire life seemed to have readied him for that moment, when he could take his leather satchel full of biker comics, his temper and fire and idealism and fearsome grin, his bottles and bags and his wife and two adored children – take them all with him out to a small town in Germany where he'd leapfrog the entire Hollywood pack and grab the brass ring.

The future looked perfect.

5

Solar Power

Fade in here: a sweet spring sky over Brentwood, one of the lushest hamlets in all Los Angeles, a knoll of Spanish villas and mock-Tudor follies with sweeping views over the Pacific Ocean. Pan down slowly, down past the TV antennae, down past the pink-walled school and the Mission church, down past the double rows of palms, down all the way into Oakmont Drive, where the luxury's of an unremembered, pre-neon kind, the tiled and white-washed houses almost obscenely brilliant with bougainvillaea. Down through the wrought-iron gates and the wild vines that hedge in the entrance lodges and the cobblestoned driveways, where the chopped-up light comes through the treetops. Down, finally, into number 27, an ivy-clad pile known as 'The Castle', equipped with its own cloisters, an Olympic-grade pool and a courtyard the size of a football field where a dozen cars are parked.

The McQueens moved there in 1963. Solar Drive, says Neile, 'was just too small, although with a great view'. Then, they could see clear to Silver Lake, where Steve was once bounced out the door by his stepfather Berri. Now, the family looked straight onto the sea and, to the east, the red smudge of Bel Air. It was canyon country, with hills that grew thick on the side of the mountains, cut by the valleys of several watercourses that sprang out of the Santa Monica range. Fingers of the forest came down onto the heads of some of the slopes and it was there, at the tree line, that Terry and Chad liked to watch for deer. Steve himself spent hours topside in his den, up the red-carpeted spiral staircase, gazing out to where the land flattened and fell away to reveal the main visual drama, the shine of the Hollywood reservoir. He got a laugh out of that. Almost as much as he did out of bugging his neighbour, a man McQueen could see was 'very neat around his place . . . Grass always cut. Flowers trimmed. No papers in the yard – that sort of thing. So, just to piss him, I started lobbing empty beer cans down the hill into his driveway. He'd have the drive all spic-'n'-span when he left the house, then go home to find all these empty cans . . . We had ourselves some good chuckles over how pissed he got.'

The neighbour was James Garner.

By the time of *The Great Escape* Steve had a full set of movie-star accessories: a stone mansion in a private road, a weekend home in Palm Springs and a business manager who told him to buy. As well as the two houses, McQueen splashed out on a gun collection, both antique and modern, two local office blocks, a Christmas supply firm and his own press agent. Then there was the fleet of muscle cars: along with his XK-SS, Steve owned a Porsche, a Land-Rover, a Cooper, a Lincoln, a Cobra, a Volkswagen, a pickup, a dune buggy, a red Ferrari and a half-tank, half-truck hybrid, complete with gunsight, which Neile bought him on his thirty-third birthday. The list isn't exhaustive. His possessions were a roll call of a rich man's playthings and investments. In similar vein, McQueen now converted Condor into Solar Inc., initially a tax shelter but soon a full-scale production company with an organisation, offices, a reporting structure and the like. Steve was already one of the best-recognised faces in the industry. Behind the scenes, he was becoming one of the most powerful. The mark of his hungry years was stamped all over Solar's mission statement and negotiating strategy, particularly in the late sixties. Nothing McQueen did was illegal or unprecedented in the strong-arm world of movie production, where everyday work habits would have raised eyebrows in a Mafia den. Yet he, more than anyone, became the artisan tycoon. Any conversation about Steve was bound to arrive, sooner or later, at the subject of his money, because his longstanding habit of squeezing out every last dime seemed, to some, to encapsulate Hollywood's unseemly chasing after the stuff. Being the first million-dollar star – in one legendary case, without even going to the hassle of actually making a picture – would become the easy shorthand for his whole career, and Steve dug it.

'*Show me the bread.*'

A purr like a car engine throbbed under his voice. The adding machines would appear – that thrilling *chuck chuck chuck*, and Steve would look up with a crooked smile. His big hand would reach out and they put the cheque in it. He bent over to read it. A metal box clicked open, clicked shut.

The suits would grin and start waxing about 'the property', and how, just out of courtesy's sake, they should once again stress that they didn't want any delays or shutdowns, no shit whatever, not for this sort of money. Nor, they warned him, did he want any once the cameras started rolling.

McQueen told them that personally he wasn't so sure.

He eventually banked $200,000 for *Soldier in the Rain*, plus points. Along with the cash, schizophrenia now set in. Steve was the hard-working pro who hated the candyass world of make-believe; the liberal whose politics lapsed, at worst, into a smorgasbord of anarchist-Nixonian drivel; the self-critic with a tongue as sharp as his suit in *The Honeymoon Machine*; the power-packed businessman who spoke of 'juice' and 'vibes'. Above all, McQueen was the man of deeply held irony. 'Maybe I have the reputation for getting into trouble because I'm in the public eye,' he told *Variety*. 'Actually I feel that I'm a home guy . . . I'm normal, I'm married and I don't run around' – a claim he illustrated, that night, by holding a closed-door audition in the Beverly Hills Hotel for an actress not his wife.

Or he'd ride out through the palms and dappled shadows to Chino and spend all day, alone, talking to the boys there.

Steve went back to Allied, home of *Never Love a Stranger*, for *Soldier in the Rain*. He drove up onto location in northern California, parked the Ferrari and tore into the first rehearsal. It was a bright, frosty morning, the ground covered with a sleet that had frozen so that it seemed as if all the bare trees, the bushes, the lights and the props and the production huts had been varnished with ice. The St Christopher medal jingled under his shirt, splayed open as if for heart surgery; McQueen pulled off his glove and felt for it. It also was cold. He threw a few personal possessions into his dressing room, the very one used by Gary Cooper. Coop had climbed up the three steep flights of stairs on a good many mornings during the fifties, often just to have somewhere to go, but never, he'd reflected with an obscure sort of pride, merely to 'catch flies'. He'd died of cancer in 1961.

Steve arrived at the sound stage; it had a grey, stone facade and a good deal of corrugated metal, like a factory, around the entrance marked with the letter S. A woman with brassy red hair who looked like a young Lucille Ball came out. Noticing that Steve was carrying a package under his arm, she held the door partially open for him. McQueen grunted and went in. It was a case of Old Milwaukee he'd brought to help him get through the morning's reading. He was inclined to be tetchy about run-throughs, the cast knew – at times he seemed to implode. But then Steve's anger would burst free and he'd take off like a drag racer in the Ferrari. Socially, nobody expected too much from him, and, except for that continuity girl, they weren't disappointed.

'It was my second film,' says Tony Bill. Bill had just played Frank Sinatra's kid brother in *Come Blow Your Horn*, and later went on to both produce and direct. 'I was pretty naïve, and I wasn't really ready for McQueen. He came in, sized us up and turned to Ralph Nelson, the director. "You're not going to do any masters, are you?" Steve said. He meant he didn't want to be fucked with any. Something about the way he said it made it clear that he, not Ralph, was going to be calling the shots. It would be Steve McQueen's picture.'

Nelson, indulgent towards this beer-swilling Pan as he'd never been to his TV stars, greeted Steve's screw-you air with a kind of mute fear that at least got them through rehearsals.

'Due respect, I found, was one of the ingredients for dealing with McQueen.'

Steve himself bore the two pre-production weeks with massive aid from his continually replenished supply of Old Milwaukee. A few suits came and went. No matter how hard they tried, they could never quite get used to him. In everything he did, McQueen was well aware of his power position on set and of what it meant, as he tended to remind people. Read-throughs, PR photography, approval of stills, tests and fittings – that was the kind of crap he had to put

149

up with. At the end of the fortnight, there were two distinct views of Steve. Most of the cast, including Bill, and certainly all the crew he befriended, thought he was troubled but well-meaning, technically brilliant. His co-star Jackie Gleason agreed about the trouble but doubted the brilliance. All of them could make out a reasonable case for their own slant on him. Everyone would remember different things; but it was almost always a striking affirmation of his willpower.

'I got along great with him,' says Bill. 'For Gleason, it was another matter. He, Jackie, found himself in the position from day one of having to hang around on set for Steve to appear. Gleason was forty-seven, a big star, and more to the point a consummate professional. McQueen was in the first flush of success . . . After a couple of days, Jackie went to the assistant director and said, "I'll be in my trailer, waiting, tomorrow morning. When McQueen deigns to appear, and only then, call me." Steve got wise to this and refused to play ball. It was stalemate. Neither one would show up until the other was already on set. We could all still be waiting there today if Ralph hadn't intervened.'

That was McQueen's power play. 'It was the first deal he packaged with Solar,' says Neile. 'He really got into that role – dug down for it. I'd say there was a bit of Walter Brennan there, but Steve covered the waterfront,' making himself by turns a GI, a spiv, a wag, a letch and a male bonder with Gleason's character. It was too much. And not enough: Nelson somehow managed to make the film more ordinary than Bill Goldman's novel, with none of the coded compassion, or homoeroticism of the original. As Sergeant Clay, McQueen seemed bent on creating sight-gags rather than understanding, his motor-mouth delivery, for once, having nothing to do with either communication or conversation; it was more like a boxing match: back and forth, jab, counter-jab, punch lines badly askew. Hamming and a heavy slug of melodrama both floored the comedy.

Steve's broad caricature did nothing for the critics, though he did, ultimately, win over the crew. 'I was quite famous for mooning,' he'd say, brushing modesty aside. 'This one time . . . I dropped 'em right as a VIP party came on set – dignitaries and honchos from the studio. Sensational. Gleason laughed so much he had to be taken to hospital.'

To reach this particular pass, Steve had deep-sixed Carl Foreman's

Victors and snubbed both John Sturges and Frank Capra. It was a curious decision of pacing to graze even lower on the comic food-chain than *The Honeymoon Machine*, just two years earlier. And yet not so curious. His friend and partner Bob Relyea remembers 'this deep perverse streak Steve had. He was an actor who, firstly, hardly ever wanted to act – he had to be talked into it. Then, once he did commit, he didn't want to be too comfortable. He had a perfect understanding of his limitations, what would and wouldn't work for him, perfect pitch for the audience, but a strong need to flog himself – to experiment. That's where you got the interesting career moves.' Among his twenty-eight films, McQueen was less stuck on such big-ticket hits as *Bullitt* than on his softer-edged, and usually commercially less golden stretches like *The Reivers*, *Junior Bonner* and *Tom Horn*. And he would have instinctively been drawn to a script, like *Soldier*, that, however badly it came off, dealt with the theme of sons and father-figures. It was 'heavy mud', McQueen said. As well as quite serious bread: he made 20.5 per cent of the net.

'The material was gimmicky,' says Tony Bill. 'But Steve still shone, with that weird genius of his.' The result was a strange mix of military satire and sub-Bilko screwball comedy, which aimed low but fell short.

McQueen working the corridors at William Morris was more of a performance. A whole team of lawyers and agents were employed reading scripts and parsing contracts for him. It wasn't unusual for Steve to call Kamen at 2 or 3 a.m. to ask him a question about something – say, whether his double was up to snuff or his rewrite man briefed, take notes, memorise them, then make the same points, with a few dramatic hammer-blows, later that morning in the studio. As far as the honchos knew, Kamen was Mr Outside, attending the meetings, reading the memos, but otherwise invisible. Steve was Mr Inside, micro-managing the deals, supervising scripts, frowning, prowling the lot with his black notebook. They listened warily whenever he complained of any shit on the set. What a combination, people thought. Fame, power, military grasp of detail; 'McQueen stalked around like Mussolini,' Jack Warner once said. He meant it as a compliment.

Stan Kamen never minded when people spoke of Steve's breadth. He himself denied all influence, though he and Neile were the true power behind the throne. Between them they began to work on the problem of what *Variety* called 'Steve's schizo side . . . [Was] he celebrating or satirising the rug-chested mysogynist?' In this context, Neile remembers 'Stan's helping [McQueen] to grow as an actor – specifically, getting him out of dirty clothes'. His schizo side, and much else, would be fully resolved by Kamen's next deal. The result, *Love with the Proper Stranger,** was pure genius precisely because it merged the twin hemispheres of Steve's brain: he became a romantic lead, the 'macho guy who dared to be vulnerable', in Neile's words. Having decided, and rightly, that the only writer and director really worth dealing with were himself and himself, McQueen gave a mesmerising performance. Rough and smooth were as one. His twelfth film demonstrated a magisterial lightness of touch and proved for all time that his appeal wasn't just deep but, now above all, broad.

Steve on set was a curious mix of personal calm and stellar rage. He'd turn to his secretary or wardrobe man and whisper something in their ear that made them shake with laughter, then suddenly yell, at no one in particular: 'Let's do it! Fuck, I'm dying here. *Roll* 'em!'

Like all movie sets, *Love*'s, in Brooklyn, was a whirl of chaotic inactivity. As well as the production managers, the designers and decorators, the stand-ins and extras and the passers-by who trilled Steve's name, there was his co-star Natalie Wood. 'She had a crush on him,' says Neile. 'Big time.' To this potential 'skin-flick within a flick' (*Cinema*) Neile herself soon added a new wrinkle. A source at Paramount who prefers anonymity recalls the triangular relationship between McQueen, his wife and Wood as 'perfect in the way each one acted a different role . . . Steve became the object of desire for Natalie, whom he may or may not have been boffing, and who Neile loved like a kid sister. Wood, meanwhile, was divorcing Bob Wagner, who was one of Steve's few close friends in the business and dating Warren Beatty, who was another. That kind of Woody Allen shtick can go either way. Here, it spelt box office.' Wood's sister Lana confirms that she, too, 'sensed a closeness between Natalie and Steve that went beyond the camera'. Not an unusual occurrence for McQueen, though not one he chose to exploit; nor a woman, to use

* No relation to the 1958 bomb.

one of his favourite expressions, he cared to nail. Bluntly, Natalie would but he wouldn't 'shtup', at least for another eight years. Steve still cared too much about his family, his film, his image, the preservation of both his marriage and the peace.

He cared even more about the preservation of people. McQueen began to spend more and more time at Boys Republic, where his monthly visits were regarded like the coming of the Magi. He went back even more often in 1963–4. Once, Steve ate lunch in the hall – shovelling down his ice cream with a fork, just as they'd taught him to – then wandered back into a dormitory. All the boys were there, plus the director and most of the staff. McQueen was introduced, and he spoke of dignity, of love and family. He said we must respect one another and honour one another. There were mostly adult grunts of agreement.

But as the speech continued it became more pointed. He asked the staff, 'Do you do enough to make sure these boys, right here, feel your love? Do you bring them each day your joy and caring?' Some of the faculty in the audience began to shift in their seats. And he continued, 'I feel the most important thing in the world is to have your identity. Be free,' he said, and then he told them why, in uncompromising terms. After that there was something like pandemonium among his younger listeners. Applause and wolf-whistling swept across the room. Steve didn't stop there, but went on to explain why 'chicks' were cool and why a lot of the 'so-called straight people' were more screwed up than anyone. Then he basked in the sort of rowdy whoops normally associated with a rock concert. He went out to the director's office and wrote him a fat cheque. 'Please see they enjoy it,' he said.

Steve, from now on, would associate himself only with quality work – he underwent a class upgrade. He became, in fact, the leading man of American film, comparable to Cagney and Bogart in their tough-and-tender forties heydays. Like Cooper at his early fifties peak, McQueen was transcendentally right on sight, someone audiences cheered with real expectancy. Just like that captive crowd at Chino, they howled in cinemas throughout the fall of 1963, for example, at the *Love* trailer, a typical romantic-movie capsule of dewy lips and Natalie Wood posing in her slip until the final frame, which was simply Steve, with a sly smile, winking directly at the camera. They loved him for that. And he loved *Love*. Once his arch rival, Newman, had passed in favour of some spy romp, McQueen fairly flew at Robert Mulligan's virile folk poem. He even agreed to do it for a mere 5 per cent of the net.

Why this untypical restraint? The most obvious explanation is that Steve, his antennae quivering, instinctively knew that *Love* was a hit; like him, both a conservative and a trendy phenomenon, dabbling in taboos like women's rights, sexual politics and abortion, yet reassuringly tethered to a simpler, white-bread-era plot: boy meets girl, gets girl in trouble, marries her. The whole thing, at times so lumbering it seemed in danger of stalling, harked back to the nonchalant mush of a *Marty* or early Billy Wilder, a genre McQueen now both toughened and softened. Toughened, by portraying his character Rocky as an authentically crass, Beatles-era swinger. Softened, by completely spurning the macho snake-handler role he perfected in *Hell is for Heroes*. There was, true, a more polished *Never So Few* texture, but *The Blob* now seemed as remote as a Chaplin comedy.

Kamen could only gaze at the man who commanded audience involvement as well as interest, the truly three-dimensional McQueen, and reflect in amazement how far he'd come.

Love itself, in the way it cleverly went both backwards and forwards, would duly corner a vast market. The main story expressed a male yarn as broad and simple as a lager commercial; its prophetic sub-plot (later enshrined as a woman's 'right to choose') creating a distant world far from what Steve lyrically called 'beer an' tits', yet drawing both sexes into it so subtly they ceased to notice the novelty. The pattern here was one better done by 1966's *Alfie*, though *Love* had the clear edge in casting. McQueen's ultimate decision to marry Wood may have been inevitable, but, as in all his best roles, it was his way of reaching the obvious that gave the script both its tension and its triumph.

Love was a smash both at home and in Europe, Australia, Japan and other far-flung parts whose sense of the universal in human relationships overcame the film's inconsistencies. On the plus side there was Steve himself, underplaying and physically ravishing, Tommy Crown foretold. Whereas he got all the good lines, and most of the close-ups, Wood was blithely convincing as the Nice Italian Girl. The director and producer, hot off *To Kill a Mockingbird*, again boldly went (then to rape, now abortion) where American film had rarely gone before.* There were Edith Head's costumes and Elmer Bernstein's score. On the downside much of the non-McQueen dialogue seemed vacuous and increasingly trite – as why wouldn't it be? It was a Hollywood ending, after all. Not that poor writing was entirely to blame: Arnold Schulman's completed screenplay contained nuanced, character-building scenes that never should have wound up on the cutting-room floor. Likewise, the chain of events that drove Steve's trumpet-tooting Rocky back towards Wood struck a bum note. It said volumes for McQueen's credibility that, when he appeared at her door waving a sign reading BETTER WED THAN DEAD people cheered rather than laughed.

Some of them sighed.

Once again, McQueen was the toast of the town, and deservedly so. This time he'd turned Hilts, the lone wolf with no known sexuality, into a walking valentine. With his hair lightened and layered by Sebring in the style of a young Grace Kelly, Steve looked fabulous; at least he seemed Italian, as he conspicuously hadn't in *A Hatful of Rain*. *Love* marked the first coming-together of the broader legend. It was now, numerically nearly midway through his film career, that he transcended the label of mere Supie and became, once and for all, *Steve McQueen*, the lead in a seventeen-year melodrama of star-crossed sex, wild speed and frequent dunks in the tabloid trough.

In a world that worked through ego and power, while touting an often candyass product, how could an earnest man, a public figure who was clinically paranoid, gratify his ambition and yet remain morally pure? If, like Steve, he happens to be a man of latent religious zeal, the stage is set for big trouble.

This was McQueen turf, through and through: the tense, the tortured, the pathologically weird – that impaling stare on which he skewered hypocrisy and bullshit – yet privately ecstatic that he'd

---

* Certain scenes in *Love* were rewritten or cut altogether out of respect to the Catholic Legion of Decency.

made it. All at top speed, competition tuned. Physical fitness was Steve's accompanying mania to the cars and bikes. Whenever he could, McQueen swam, played tennis, ran, pressed both weights and more or less reluctant friends into arm-wrestling. All his contracts now called for him to be furnished with a set of barbells (200 lb) and one of dumbbells (80 lb) in his dressing room. One day on location he heard of a sponsored thirty-mile walk from Manhattan to Greenwich. McQueen, who always had to test himself against everything, decided that he too would make the trek. To Wood and Herschel Bernardi, who had the bad luck to be with him, he said, 'You're comin', aren't you?' At six o'clock on Sunday morning the three joined the pack in Central Park. Their plan was to walk to, or towards, Connecticut. The thermometer stood at twenty degrees. After two miles Steve was alone of the *Love* contingent. On he doggedly went to the finish, blistered and numb, having made both his point and $4000 for charity. He was on set again at seven the next morning.

The charity in question was for homeless children.

Rocky's feathered cut and crinkly grin suggested that *Love*'s audiences were being lured into the land of schmalz, a perilous and often seriously tedious place to be. But McQueen managed to bring off both a sense of humour and a sense of suspense, as well as sheer presence. And violence: without the familiar Western or war props, he now hit the emotional battlefield. For Steve, in *Love*, language was the offensive weapon. Conversation was a type of combat, and even evasion was a form of skirmish. His flinty speech, tone and manner were all perfectly in synch. There was none of the amped-up hamming of *Soldier in the Rain*. This was McQueen's definitive performance as the caring but cynical soul who had DANGER tattooed on his forehead, and knew it.

Whipped up into Beatlemania-like frenzy by that trailer and sundry studio 'glamour' shots of Wood pouting in her lingerie, the holiday crowds flocked to *Love with the Proper Stranger* when it opened on Christmas Day. It was a perfectly well-made film. But it was really Stan Kamen's masterpiece. For two or three years now he'd known that something was missing. The movies had been agreeable in a dourly muscular way, but market research showed up a hard truth:

most women were unwilling to sit through two hours of motorbikes and men lobbing hand grenades at pillboxes, even with Steve to moon over. They wanted a proxy; someone to actually root for. What those Christmas crowds cheered was romance, or at least a fantasy of it fleshed out in the most durable of American sagas: that of the taut but warm-hearted rebel, who gets by with a worried conscience, a single syllable, a shrug of indifference, yet who tries to connect. The critics and the industry swooned. *Love* garnered five Oscar nominations, none of them, bizarrely, for Best Actor. But any doubt that McQueen could 'really act' was decided, for all time, in his favour by his third film of 1963. Almost immediately the box offices, from Beirut to Fargo, confirmed this fact in hard cash. Then the intellectuals sat up and took notice. Then the McQueen myth took over.

Steve once said that the only reason he did films was to hasten the time when he wouldn't have to. It was almost true, but not quite. He also enjoyed being famous and rich, had fun tormenting directors and was entertained by movie-set politics, sex and gossip. But, sooner or later, the gilt began to flake off the gingerbread. The bureaucratic part of Hollywood wasn't his forte. 'Fucking honchos', he often muttered. The rest of McQueen's career would be a desperate, daring and sometimes brilliant bid to beat the System – its typecasters, anyway – while periodically strapping on the holster or the seat-belt for one more blockbuster. Steve's next role wouldn't be one of these. Robert Mulligan's *The Traveling Lady*, later named *Baby, the Rain Must Fall*, was a classic case of what Bob Relyea calls 'McQueen's need to flog himself', a brooding black-and-white drama with a habit of mirroring his own childhood; hardly the stuff of which smashes are made. Already, so he thought, in a rut, McQueen had to kiss off his career or spurn the candyass for a few genuinely risky but potentially rewarding bold moves. He chose shock therapy.

Steve reported on location in Bay City, Texas, virtually the minute he left the farewell party for *Love*. To a sordidly commercial eye, *Baby* would be one of his worst films; dramatically, it was one of his very finest. He melted into the role of Henry Thomas so completely that, from the moment he first slouched on screen, he was vivid, whole and fully alive. The thrill lay in watching Thomas as he watched himself fall apart, hurt and baffled, with only his dignity keeping him company.

McQueen acted out whole reams of his Slater life without any comment.

There was a price to pay for this immersion, which was that Steve was limited by the clarity of his performance. Between takes, too, he was merely playing himself. The flight down to Houston had been nerve-racking, through clouds most of the way, with sudden terrifying jolts into pockets of burning sunlight. He wasn't afraid of flying. The actual uneasiness had begun, as it always did, when he'd committed to making the film in the first place. For those last few days at the Castle, McQueen had been a wreck. Each morning on waking, he'd smelled the freshly cut grass, heard the birds' familiar chirping in the bushes and said to himself that he couldn't be fucked. 'Steve customarily approached a movie like a man walking to the gallows,' says Relyea. His anxiety reached fever pitch on the day he left Los Angeles. Then, once in Texas, Steve promptly announced to the cast that he 'didn't really get' the script and that 'after this, I'll never work again'. That crippling sense of inadequacy came through brilliantly in the film, while, offstage, McQueen worked off his phobias either behind the wheel or in bed. It was an interesting shoot.

His co-star Don Murray remembers it as a tight-knit crew 'and an athletic one . . . There was a lot of football, tennis and golf played, which Steve, I noticed, never joined in. He struck me as all too sadly like the lonely kid not picked for the team, always standing there on the sidelines with a kind of tense expression . . . I noticed he did do a lot of weightlifting and shadow boxing, though.' One afternoon McQueen offered to drive Murray and two or three others from Houston to Wharton in a studio Ford. 'Steve, being Steve, took off like Stirling Moss and frightened the hell out of his passengers. After a minute or two of screeching around I told him, through gritted teeth, to take it down a notch. McQueen's response was to go completely ape, flooring it and driving the car through a field. At that stage the engine began to smoke . . . As we ran off, it actually caught fire. He totally gutted it.'

McQueen just laughed savagely.

Despite his various foibles as a husband, Steve had at least made his peace with monogamy on the set of *Love with the Proper Stranger*. For six or seven weeks he'd refused both Natalie Wood and several female extras. 'It ain't going to happen,' he'd told them. No such restraint was embraced with his new leading lady, the married Lee Remick. Feeling 'lonely and isolated from family and friends', he duly took her to bed in the cast's small 1930s-style hotel where, he told Sebring, he regained both his strength and his roots. But rejuvenation, for McQueen, had to be accompanied by confession. After the ten-week shoot he flew back to LA, drove to the Castle, and, without bothering to unpack first, came clean to his wife. As Neile says, 'There was no reason for me to find out except for his compulsion to tell me. Not to hurt me – just to make it all right. For him.' There seemed to be no end to the chain of betrayal, penance and forgiveness. Neile told herself that this constant pattern was a common enough misapplication of Steve's 'shit', but that didn't make it any easier.

Above all, she was the voice of reason. Calming him down, seeing him through the burnout. Wouldn't have made it without her, Steve said.

McQueen had now made thirteen films in seven years, eight of them in the last three. He went back to the Castle in January 1964 and pulled up the drawbridge. No one who knew Steve ever had any trouble understanding why he'd bought the place. It stood on one of the shaded private roads winding up from Sunset towards the Santa Monica mountains, but nobody ever went there for the sightseeing. After McQueen added yet more security it was impossible to get near the house without negotiating the massive oak gate under a stone arch, where a visitor would be asked to speak into a metal grille. After a suitably dramatic pause, the grille would speak back: 'Yep,' 'Nope,' or, in not a few cases, 'Fuck off, man.' Even if a guest was expected, he'd then have to trudge up a driveway through a rock garden where, alongside the cars and bikes, cameras – in which for domestic use Steve was something of an optical pioneer – panned and zoomed, while dogs sounded a kind of dire welcome as they bayed at the door. Not the kind of scene to encourage stray autograph hounds.

In the proper mood, under controlled conditions, Steve could be a genial host. That August he and Neile threw a star-studded party for the local glitterati. It was a characteristic Hollywood affair – large, loud, happy, with satiric toasts and heckling guests. As a gag McQueen hoisted Neile in a fireman's lift and ran up the spiral staircase with her into the bedroom while everybody cheered. Then he sat up talking with Jay Sebring and his girlfriend Sharon Tate till three in the morning. Later still Steve insisted on playing several frames with Kirk Douglas in the Castle's billiard room. McQueen's list of house rules was long – very long. The least of it was that Douglas bet against him using only hard cash. As dawn came up over the mountains, Steve was still at it, having taken 'several hundred bucks' off his opponent. Douglas, merely by playing, illustrated that the great stars of their moment would inevitably become fodder for McQueen's ego. Both parties marvelled over that particular scene for days.

Generally, like other movie stars, Steve tried to protect himself and his family from unwelcome attention. That oak door was nothing compared to the protective wall he threw up of reserve and mystery, topped by a razor-wire strand of total paranoia. He was a hard man to get to know. It wasn't just McQueen's corrosive spats and the fact that several good judges quite seriously thought him a warlock – he'd disappear alone into the night at Halloween and full moons – but that the private man seemed as distant as the public. 'We got quite close,' says Don Murray, 'and yet there was something about him, a sort of childishness, that could be very destructive. You never had the faintest idea of what he'd do next.'

For most audiences' tastes, praise didn't come any higher than that.

Hollywood badly needed such a figure. McQueen appeared just as the traditional star system seemed to be crumbling and fans were crying out for more 'characters'. His own appraisal of the actual benefits of rebelliousness was always pyrrhic, amounting to a theme of persecution. 'The public dig [me],' he told Sebring, 'but the honchos shit bricks when ol' Steve comes around.' Over the next decade there appeared to be no limit to the brick-shitting McQueen saw in Tinseltown. Almost every run-in with a director or producer could be traced to his unforgivable streak of bloody-mindedness. 'Now love, then hate. Then love, now hate. Then love,' he'd wryly tell his daughter exactly twenty years after that historic shoot of *The Magnificent Seven*. 'The reason people freaked out is that nobody could control me – not the press, not the suits, not the studio bigwigs . . . I did what I felt was right for the pictures, and when it worked, I was a threat.' His successive snubs by the Academy – 1964 began a pattern in which McQueen doled out and yet never received Oscars – were ever afterward to be a kind of revelation of the suits' reprisal as well as triumph, and so, too, a rationalisation of Steve's behaviour.

These same suits, of course, were happy to hire McQueen, pandering shamelessly to the hooting crowds for *The Great Escape* and the rest. By and large, they saw him as a necessary evil. The press, for its part, treated Steve like an exotic and potentially dangerous animal. True fans admired him for much the same reason. A few friends uncritically adored him. Reciprocally, McQueen's own preferred audience was one of strays, waifs, Navajo Indians, dropouts, dirt-bikers and mechanics. As Sebring said, 'That was something that really fuelled his soul . . . They didn't know who he was and didn't give a fuck, frankly. And Steve loved it. He loved it.' It wasn't only that he was schizo-paranoic. No one could be more fun than McQueen; no one more alive, with those bursts of joy, gloom, grit, aggression and vulnerability oddly intermingled in his vivid personality. He was the perfect Beatles-era film star, with, like the Fabs themselves, matching doses of irony and sincerity, frequently both flaunted at once. No wonder the studios freaked out. He was their worst nightmare, an 'uneducated boob' who was by turns lucid and lubricious, and famously awake at the wheel when it came to line-reading scripts and contracts. Steve did well in meetings, often displaying a quick wit. That also peeved some of the bigwigs. And most of the industry would reflexively be uptight around anyone who, like him, quite plainly wanted to 'get some sugar out of the business', then quit.

Fuck you, he'd finally say, and then off he'd dust. *Adios*.

An ability to look after himself was one of McQueen's many strong though threatening qualities, not one always shared by his highly touted peers. His old role model Walter Brennan comes immediately to mind. Steve was self-contained socially as well as professionally.

Off hours he stuck to certain tried and tested friends, none of them Hollywood novas, all of them the best at their jobs. They became part of a Mafia. Perhaps twice a month a group of them would take off on their bikes into the Mojave desert. They'd make camp and squat around a fire and, as Steve said, 'put about ten points on Old Milwaukee stock'. When the sun went down and the cool air from the river below with its sting of woodsmoke rose to the level of the camp, McQueen would stretch out on a blanket facing the western sky, and feel the dying sun's heat still strong underneath his body. It was one of the perks of the job, to just take off and watch the light changing in the valley below, when dusk and the smoke from the fire slowly blotted out the horizon. There always came a moment when all that was left was the faint smudge, dingy and grey, of Hollywood, a dull glow from the throb of distant TV transmitters that beat like hearts. The buildings themselves were no longer there, and eventually even the mountains went. That was when Steve might light one of his special fat cigarettes, stretch out and start telling stories about Slater. More especially, about Julian.

Then silence.

Then, suddenly, McQueen would be off and running again. He and Don Gordon or Sebring would race up to a club or, specifically, the Whisky à Go Go where, as Gordon says, 'we'd be waved in ahead of the queue to the permanently reserved booth'. There Steve might indulge his new-found taste for amplified rock music, the watusi and hallucinogenics. The platinum blonde starlet Mamie Van Doren met him at the Whisky one Friday night that summer. After a turn around the floor, McQueen soon proposed that they go on to her place. Once inside they stood on the balcony overlooking the city lights. 'There was the faint smell of sweat from our bodies,' she says, 'the result of our exertions on the dance floor. From the rate of Steve's breathing, I could tell he was looking forward to some further exertions in bed.' Two nights later they duly met again at Sebring's mansion.

This time, says Van Doren, McQueen suggested they take LSD prior to going to bed. 'There was a flash of red light, like a skyrocket across the room. Following that, there was another, and another. Soon the room was crisscrossed by tracings of coloured lines of light

... "It's the acid," [said] McQueen. "Don't worry. Just let yourself go."' The whole thing, alas, turned out badly for Van Doren, as it would for so many, because 'Steve was a married man who [was] unwilling to leave his wife'. Even when he did divorce, McQueen never totally abandoned that core conviction.

These frivolities over, Steve renewed his efforts to be taken seriously outside Hollywood. For ten months he didn't step in front of a camera, leading to ugly gossip and even a few 'Whatever happened to?' stories in the trades, for whom fame remained a state of reminder. McQueen, he said, didn't give a shit. Literally not a fuck. He rarely, if then, met with any Beautiful People except when actually working on a script or on set. As a result of this, there was plenty of scope for what Stan Kamen would call 'revisionist crap' to be propounded. Perhaps due to such revisionism, Steve came to be talked about not only as a great actor, but also as a pre-Elvis recluse, lolling slack-jawed in his own private Graceland while retainers ferried in comic books and cheeseburgers.

The truth, as usual with McQueen, was different. A close study of his actions behind the scenes in 1964 shows that he wasn't only plotting his next moves, but running a rule over his sub-career. Suddenly it would be after midnight, and all that grunting and banging around in the garage stood out against the hour.

'You move around as much as I do,' he said, 'you learn to love your wheels.'

Precise details of Steve's hobbyism varied – drag-racing, autocrossing, eventing – but the basic pattern was fixed. He craved speed. McQueen once said he only felt 'truly alive' when he was at home in the Castle, but, as Kamen saw it, 'Steve really wanted to be alive that way no more than a few hours a day.' For the rest of the time he was out on the asphalt or scrambling up the dunes of Mandeville canyon. Friends used to wonder how McQueen could sense everything when he was on wheels or a stage, and almost nothing, it seemed, when he wasn't.

Steve won five scrambling trophies in 1964, spent his weekends either dirt-riding or desert-racing, broke an arm and a foot, knocked out some teeth and snapped a rib. He didn't care. 'You're out there twisting the tiger's tail,' he said. 'You're groovin' . . . groovin'. I can't really explain it.' McQueen's motorial career revved to a new high that September, when he was selected as part of the US team for the international six-day motorcycle trials in East Germany. That was the last time he'd ever have to do the 'I'm a regular guy and I just like to hang out with bikers' speech. Steve was now competing, on level terms, with the very best in the world.

The actual race went well enough, though Bud Ekins broke a leg and McQueen himself swerved to avoid a spectator, putting his Triumph over the side of a hill and out of contention. The other three Americans all took home medals. One of them, Cliff Coleman, has fond memories of the 'Supie' otherwise known as Rider 278: 'Taking Bud Ekins as a ten, I'd say McQueen was a seven or eight as a bike-racer. That good, although I always felt he held back for fear of hurting his face, where he knew his fortune lay ... Steve could and did do wonderful things for his friends, but, God, the man was cheap. That particular trip, the five of us were renting a house in London on the way over to Erfurt ... The first day there, McQueen held a meeting to tell us, in no uncertain terms, we were splitting expenses evenly down the line. There I was dossing in the attic, while Steve's downstairs in the master suite ordering in champagne. What an operator. With the women, too. One afternoon we were tooling down the motorway in England in a rental car. Steve looks over, sees a pretty girl in the next lane and waves at her. She waves back. Without a word McQueen pulls over and so does the girl. He calmly got in her car and that was the last we saw of him for two days.'

In Paris, where Steve – now joined by Neile – put up at the Crillon, he was mobbed like all four of the Beatles. 'McQueen loved it when everyone chased him around town,' says Coleman. 'He loved being recognised, whereas a lot of stars don't and cherish their anonymity when they're travelling. Steve, on the other hand, cherished his privacy in other ways but dug being famous.' Neile agrees: 'He tried wandering around in a fake moustache and goatee, then got uptight when no one noticed him. Steve couldn't get back to the hotel fast enough to wash his face, grab me and go downtown to be gazed at.' Merely by walking through the door, McQueen caused riots at Maxim's and the other scene restaurants where *Paris Match* picked up the tab in exchange for a story. He was the biggest thing in France since Marlon Brando.*

Steve's passion for fame and money, in which he'd been a slow starter but an extremely fast study, got a new fillip from an offer by Filmways Limited in April 1964. Filmways was the production company behind the movie of Dick Jessup's novel *The Cincinnati Kid*. They now signed McQueen, via Solar, for $200,000. The original twelve-page draft contract would also give Steve 25 per cent of the net, $20,000 a week overtime and various rights, allowances and benefits. It wasn't enough. Mitchell, Silberberg & Knupp replied on 24 June with a five-page addendum of perks: Filmways to submit the script to Solar for McQueen's comments; Solar to furnish 'at least one-half of the creative elements for the picture, such as co-stars, music, cameraman, etc.'; the overtime fee to be £30,000 a week; Steve to have his own stuntman, secretary, assistant secretary, still photographer, stylist, trailer, dumbbells, first-class hotel suite, drinks, meals, limo, tax indemnity; and so on, down to six separate paragraphs of animated technical chat on the colour and typeface of McQueen's name in the advertising. Everything was strictly formulated, with no margin for error. If circumstances offered the opportunity for Steve to loot and pillage, he would; Filmways expected it, superstardom demanded it.

That was common knowledge. What may have been less well-known was the man who, along with Neile and Elmer Valentine, drove south from Paris, through the Pyrenees and into Spain, where McQueen would park and wander over the empty tableland of Catalonia. There was nothing up there but the birds and a few stray sheep that ran quick-legged across the road, heavy-bodied and cackling. Everything else was below in the valley: the towns, the gardens and the river winding east towards Barcelona. McQueen would sit on a point of rock far above and look down at the people walking in the alleys of Berga. It was only later that he went down and saw what

---

* A similar bit of horse-trading went on with the department store Le Printemps, which happened to be featuring a range called 'Le Ranch Steve McQueen' – jeans, cowboy boots and the like – that year. As well as helping himself to the actual merchandise Steve not unreasonably demanded a cut, some say as high as 20 per cent, of everything sold. The store paid up.

they were like. Over the next few days Valentine was a spellbound witness to Steve's affinity for 'real folks'. Watching him squat in the dust to befriend a child or help an old man change a tyre brought a revelation: he was good with people. It was just groups of them together he had his 'shit' with. McQueen awaited with dread the day when he'd have to get up at dawn and go on location to work. He had a few smokes and for a while he thought his mind was playing tricks on him and he was actually home already, right there among the farm animals and smiling rustics. But then he'd get yet another telegram from Filmways and snap out of it.

That 1 October he reported back to Hollywood.

The idea that Steve – in pop-Darwinism terms – was a gentle beta male who adopted alpha male behaviour wasn't, however, quite true either. He could, and did, violently cork off at people. Bawling out a writer or director was in its way a telling mark of the taut, pressured man Steve had become and was becoming at thirty-four. It silhouetted the fragile sense of self that lay near the surface of bloody-mindedness and sheer discipline, one that drove him both to his best work and to petty, sometimes brutal tantrums. Those fuck-you roles went well beyond mere plausibility; McQueen knew them in his soul.

Even now, he found it hard to deal with committees. As well as a bank, Solar was set up as a safeguard enterprise between Steve and what he called the 'flood of offers and deals . . . It was scary, the way everybody began hittin' on me.' Materially, he wasn't complaining. All those fruit and nuts. 'Life is good and I mean to take a big slice,' he informed the *New York Times*. It was just that people kept twisting his melon. A classic case came in August 1964, when President Johnson co-opted him into the Democratic fold at a party for his re-election campaign. McQueen went along with it, and got himself photographed dancing with Johnson's daughter, but he chafed when incumbent and challenger alike asked him to formally endorse them. Steve went 'fucking nutso' when both candidates then started referring to him on the stump. These false gods having slurred his good name, all he could do was head down the lonesome trail, hoping that by making enough films and giving enough interviews he could put his word over. It wasn't, strictly speaking, political but more the code of his whole life:

'I'm only a layman, but as an American, I think very strongly about my country. It's a wonderful country and I don't want to see it go down the drain . . . We need to revert to a hip kind of conservatism, man.'*

The problem, in old strategic arms terms, was too many emotional missiles and not enough guidance systems. *Baby, the Rain Must Fall* released in January 1965, was a moving ballad of failed relationships but without any very strong idea of its own goal.

In this downbeat drama McQueen ditched the fey sexuality of *Love with the Proper Stranger* for something closer to Tennessee Williams. Horton Foote's stark, morally alert adaptation of his own play didn't allow audiences to root too loudly for its hero. Steve's character was doomed, but, eerily like his own youth, he wilfully courted trouble, and McQueen made him dim, stolid as an introverted ox, scary and also pitiable. The basic nut was his inability to adapt to a wife and child, with Don Murray providing ballast as the good cop who tries to help. The cheesy, semi-documentary feel – it was Steve's last film in black-and-white – presenting bare, stubbly fields and dirt roads in all their authentic ugliness, didn't make for an easy mix. Nor did the flighty lurches of mood and atmosphere, running the gamut from the gothic to, of all things, the rockabilly, with touches of *Great Expectations* and *Psycho* along the way. *Baby* wasn't bad; Bob Mulligan laboured on it for nearly a year in the editing suite, but audiences turned away, either confused or embarrassed that such care had been taken with grim yet haphazard stuff that seemed all wrong for the cinema. The innocence of the piece was lost in dark and needlessly tortuous sub-plots, from which Foote's original play signalled wildly to be let out.

McQueen dredged up a masterful performance. His brilliantly spare portrayal drew, of course, on his own experience (Neile says she can 'barely stand to watch it' to this day), the tale of an animalistic and also vulnerable dud who degenerates into a world-hating, self-hating wreck, the Stan Kowalski of Texas, whose frenzy finally implodes at the point where there's nothing left to destroy but

---

* McQueen supported, for instance, the war in Vietnam.

himself. True, there were moments when the part curdled into bathos. The script called, for instance, for Steve (coached by an uncredited Glen Campbell) to sing the title song. The moment came, he opened his mouth and duly made a sound like a hollering, half-slaughtered hog. But such were the tribulations of a true artistic journey. McQueen had all the period melancholy of a Steinbeck hobo, Remick gave an understated, sharply articulated performance as his wife. They were an odd, wistful couple.

Baby, the Rain Must Fall flopped, but Steve McQueen again proved he could act. His ability to encompass a private world within a compressed role that stretched like a concertina gave the film an amazing pull – a paradoxical, low-key urgency. 'I admired him,' says Don Murray. 'Steve realised there was something more to life than just being a hard ass. Films like *Baby* may not have been commercially rewarding, but they brought their own kind of success. As far as I'm concerned, he came out of that picture a star.'

It'd probably be going too far to say that *Baby* was the role that linked the old, action dude Steve and the Ibsen lover yet to come – going too far, but not going in entirely the wrong direction. Apart from being worthy in himself (and the Academy could have done worse for an Oscar) his Henry Thomas was one of the three or four characters who helped shape what he felt 'real folks' should look like, not to mention what they should sound like, on screen. Since he grew up late himself, Steve, as Thomas, hit perfect notes of childish vulgarity and vulnerability, and turned what might otherwise have been an early Leonard Cohen video into, say, a Lou Reed one. It's the collision of these two extremes – McQueen as erotic thug, McQueen as lonely kid – which sustains the whole curious enterprise.

In the matter of persistent childhood, of Steve's embodiment of the dark side of Slater, his friends and enemies had different theories. Four streams mingled in these waters: sympathy, awe, fear and the carping resentment chucked at him by suits and a few peers. To most of the outside world he was the non-acting actor whose only serious rival as the King of Cool was, strangely enough, Dean Martin. Nowadays, McQueen's fans not only applauded him – thanks to Foster's genius they could read about him, too, in decidedly non-laddish slicks like *Harper's Bazaar*, *Life*, *Look* and *Woman*. Distance perhaps magnified his charms: he was the photogenic god, the trusty spouse and father, the man who raced in much the same way Hemingway had hunted – to stave off boredom and the nagging sense that his day job was candyass – who saved Judy Garland from a house fire, fought off a prowler at the Castle and calmly punched a tactless heckler in the chops. Whether on the screen or on news-stands, the McQueen legend swung to its zenith over the next two years, while the man himself, buttoned up in cropped denim and shades, swaggered down Sunset closely followed by an entourage of black-clad bikers in visual counterpoint to the blond Supie.

Steve's darker behaviour, whether boozing, brawling or snarling at 'Fuckwit', was worrying for two reasons: it was unusual, and it was usual. Van Doren, apparently, is the only one to remember him babbling about 'tracings of coloured lines of light' and getting himself seriously, falling down stoned. On the other hand, beery aggression was standard procedure for McQueen. According to Don Murray, there was an 'edge' to him, though he could be stranger and harsher than that, almost rabidly brutal.

The paradoxes of McQueen were a natural for the journalistic imagination. Few enough hacks got him right, but at least they hinted there were layers to peel back. As well as the mythic star and the gamin who didn't grow up, there was a side of Steve that could be sheer fun to be with. As Jim Hoven says, 'You could feel a kind of direct communication without the BS or whatever other people do.' And: 'He was much more alive than most people, let alone movie stars, because he was constantly absorbing, reacting, responding . . . And, of course, he was crazy. You had the feeling you were with someone who could go in any direction, and that anything could happen. He had a kind of lit-rocket quality to him.'

Don Gordon remembers, 'One day Steve called me: "Hey, man, we're going to the movies." This was in Palm Springs. He picked me up in his tank, drove it right across the desert, over the sand and over dunes, went to the show and then drove me home again, laughing all the way. You'd have to be dead not to love someone like that.'

McQueen, others thought, was the outlaw who could have been a sheriff: although he had his stable of Porsches, the vehicle he liked most was the one he used for his power trips, a contract. 'Steve swung back and forth between being a hippie and the Führer,' said Kamen. 'He was an injustice collector – I saw him make hard men weep when it came to deal time.' The demands were legendary: everything from the wallpaper in his trailer to the crease in the jeans he had the studio 'loan' him, ten pairs at a time. As James Coburn told the author Penina Spiegel, 'I don't know what Steve's IQ was, but the way he kept the producers and agents jumping around was marvellous to watch. He really made those moguls move. It was a pleasure to see.'

True enough, most encounters between McQueen and an MGM or Columbia played out like a rock hurled into a shallow pond. To his credit, he almost always picked on people his own size. It was as if one lobe of his brain wanted to be real folks, on good terms all round, while another waged trench war with the world. Early in 1965 Steve and the lawyers began hammering 20th Century-Fox over his participation in Bob Wise's film *The Sand Pebbles*. The basic nut was $300,000 in three instalments, points, and the usual perks involving hotels, limos, secretaries, make-up men, stylists and billing. Stan Kamen thought that it was 'Hollywood's Most Powerful' list, first published that year, that 'put McQueen into overdrive'. No matter what anybody thought of him and his acting, there was something about a public ranking that carried a potency all its own. Steve not only wanted to head the list, he cared about the exact order of the stars who came below him. It wasn't enough to succeed. Others had to fail.

Me first, everybody else nowhere.

It clearly delighted McQueen when the studios caved in, like MGM, and bolstered his fragile sense of himself. Yet he also kept up the fight later, whilst on location. *The Cincinnati Kid*, in particular, ran through nearly every possible production hassle (not all of them star-related) when it began shooting in late 1964. Sam Peckinpah, the director, evidently had a darker idea of this version of *The Hustler* in spades than the producers did. Aside from the actual poker, *Kid*'s second major plot strand concerned sex – specifically, Peckinpah's ad-libbed filming of a nude scene and the unbuttoned presence of Sharon Tate, of whom Neile remembers, 'Steve came home one night and said Sam was shooting her wearing a silk shirt with no bra, you could see her nipples . . . Ohh, that set was wild.' (A 'juiced-up *Satyricon*' was Peckinpah's own fond assessment.) In a move that did little to check the emotional voltage, Tate was replaced by Tuesday Weld, an actress whose own crackups and attempted suicides had become almost public property. McQueen's co-star Spencer Tracy, meanwhile, not caring for the role, quit in favour of Edward G. Robinson. Finally Peckinpah himself departed, axed by Filmways' Marty Ransohoff after one too many disputes over the 'vision thing'. The total cost of the shutdown that followed was $750,000.

Of that, the studio gave Steve $25,000 pocket money while they rooted around for another director. He blew some of it on women and pot but otherwise used the cash well, playing stud in Las Vegas. Largely on Kamen's recommendation, Filmways soon hired Norman Jewison, a young Canadian chiefly known for directing glittering Doris Day romps like *The Thrill of It All*. Jewison tore up the script by Paddy Chayefsky and Ring Lardner and commissioned one by Terry Southern. Southern cut out the sex and incorporated a fight scene for McQueen. But the biggest change of all was to Peckinpah's whimsical decision to shoot the film in black and white. 'As if we could,' says Jewison. 'It *was* all about cards, for God's sake.' Once the Metrocolor cameras were duly set up and waiting, Steve drove in across the desert from Vegas.

'I'm only thirty-eight,' Jewison told him at their first meeting. 'I can't be your father, but why not look on me as your big brother? I'll fight for you against [Ransohoff], and I'll make you wonderful in the film. You lose the card game, but you'll have the empathy of the audience.'

They shook hands on it. 'You could hear Steve purring at that point,' says Hoven.

But it wasn't quite enough. McQueen felt bombarded by too many unfamiliar factors, namely that here were a director and producer who actually liked him. He went back to Ransohoff, demanded and got a bonus for having been so patient.

More cash, and a full-size pool table.

After ten months away from the boards, it took McQueen three days to 'groove together' with the script. He never really did so with

171

Robinson. 'Remember, Eddie had Hollywood's finest art collection and spoke four languages,' says Jewison. 'Steve was at his happiest stripping down a car engine. Since they were adversaries in the film, I fed on that.' Jewison also recalls the day when, after two weeks on location in New Orleans, 'McQueen realised he wasn't being invited to view the rushes ... I told him not to worry, directors should direct, actors act, and besides I'd given him my word I'd look out for him.'

This time around, Steve baulked.

'How can I trust you if I don't see any rushes? You're twisting my melon, man. Twisting my melon.'

On that note, Jewison patched together a few minutes of film for Steve, who was thrilled. 'Things calmed down a lot once he relaxed ... McQueen, reciprocally, wasn't what you'd call a giving man. Frankly, he was a cheapskate. When Steve left the set at night he'd always hit up me or one of the crew for five bucks "gas money", which we never saw again ... Just as he was personally stingy, he was something similar as an actor. McQueen had this habit of looking down at the floor between setups, so no one could take their cue from him. Then, promptly on *Action*, he'd come up, shoulders rising, with that open-eyed animal expression – a readiness to please and also, if necessary, to maul you. Mesmerising ... when you looked through a camera at a Laurence Olivier you'd say, "He's magnificent, but he's acting." When you looked at Steve, he was *real*. I don't think the truth has ever been brought off in movies quite as well as he did it – with so little condescension, such lack of pretence. The man's honesty, in that sense, was frightening.'

When everything came together, McQueen would subjugate his ego and taste – just a little – to the pursuit of exquisite teamwork.

Steve edited his own work according to a couple of basic principles. Once in a while a line he struck was 'shit', but usually it was just 'unnecessary'. In all, he worked hard for his $10,000 a week. McQueen didn't give it away, professionally or personally, but that was the psychology of a poor boy who always feared that his cash could vanish just as fast as it had come. That sense of paranoia, or at least doubt, was one of the things that made up his full-bodied realism on screen, in which nothing was sacred but nothing was taken for granted, either – not wealth or power or happiness or freedom. Steve also had an uncanny understanding of the kind of narrative that made for a successful film. He was a genius at creating characters the audience could easily and instantly bond with, and he was expert when it came to the mechanics of movie-making. Egalitarian niceness wasn't a hallmark of McQueen's on-set persona. He didn't yearn to be a luvvie. But he knew exactly how to put his long experience, star power and undoubted professionalism to good use in the cause of raising not only audience interest but his own profile. On *Cincinnati Kid*, in particular, he wanted to 'get the look of the thing right', because 'that's what sucks people in'. He kept hammering the point to Norman Jewison.

Jewison remembers that 'Steve, to his delight, realised we both hated the front office, the dreaded suits represented by Marty Ransohoff. Whenever Ransohoff walked on the stage, I'd walk off. One time I ran round the corner and hid in a prop elevator we were using in this particular scene. It was a fake elevator. All it did was sit there. It didn't go up or down. I crouched inside for about ten minutes, holding my breath every time I heard Ransohoff's voice asking where I was. Then, after a while, everything went quiet. It was dark and silent, and I was there in this wooden box. Suddenly I heard a very light, furtive tapping on the door. "Norman? Norman, are you OK?" Steve whispered. "You can come out. The bad guys have gone now."'

Ransohoff left them to it, and between them they came up with a novel if not quite new film where the comforting conventions don't apply.

Jewison's rich production was about arrogance and competition and betrayal, but time and again it substituted psychiatry for the full theatricality of the opening rip, where McQueen, trapped by card-sharps, smashes a window and jumps across thirty-five sets of railway tracks to make his off. Conversely, the film itself never quite broke loose. In point of pacing and overall theme, *The Cincinnati Kid* was a transparent reworking of Paul Newman's *The Hustler*. At least it borrowed from a true original. Fuckwit's vehicle (co-starring Steve's other favourite actor, Jackie Gleason) was a good example of what Wagner called the *Gesamtkunstwerk*, the completely organic piece of art. *The Hustler*'s detractors, who accused it of pretentiousness, self-consciousness and static tableaux, weren't silenced by Jewison's adaptation, but were at least mollified by the intelligence, intensity and sweeping grandeur. Jewison lacked the will to make a totally new film, but did the next best thing: he took some of *The Hustler*'s characters and found what was universal in them.

Kid tells the story of a young stud poker player who works his way up to a showdown with Robinson's character, the Man. The game's dealer (Karl Malden in an extraordinary turn) tries to rig the odds. There are some meaningless side slabs of romance involving McQueen and both Ann-Margret and Tuesday Weld. Conventional Hollywood wisdom would have the hero win the pot and at least one of the girls; instead Jewison dared to let Steve lose it all to a one-in-a-million hand (actually dreamt up by Joe Schoenfeld of William Morris), accompanied by the classic riff:

DEALER: You still playing, Kid?

KID [*swallowing*]: No, I'm through.

DEALER: You raising tens on a lousy three-flush.

THE MAN: Gets down to what it's all about, doesn't it? [*Lights cigar*] Making the wrong move at the right time.

KID: Is that what it's all about?

THE MAN: Like life, I guess. You're good, Kid, but as long as I'm around, you're second best. You might as well learn to live with it.

It took nerve for Jewison and McQueen to go along with this pay-off, which the front office, specifically Ransohoff, hated.

Kid broke other rules, too. It departed from its handsome, exquisitely crafted 1930s-period locales throughout the movie, most notably in the scenes between Steve and the parts played by Malden and Rip Torn. The former was sacrificially thrown to McQueen, by then 'prowling around the room . . . absolutely terrifying . . . He was whipping about there like a loose power line.' (Malden's own expression in the scene was that of a surprised spud.) The film centred on such cleverly calculated tension, and moral ambivalence, of the kind which doesn't tend to thrill executives at major studios. Steve himself was brilliant throughout. His streamlined performance redeemed the movie's whole strategy. And its premise: as played by McQueen, the Kid had a faintly tragic air about him, and even the things he does best turn out badly; at the end, he trembles on the brink of winning, then implodes. It was a tribute to both director and star that, as Jewison promised, audiences everywhere rooted for the loser.

Commercially, *The Cincinnati Kid* was a major hit, grossing more than $10 million off the bat. Creatively, it was another stage in McQueen's education, as well as in Jewison's. The latter went on to shoot two sumptuous if only mildly successful musicals, *Fiddler on the Roof* and *Jesus Christ Superstar*, along with vintage fare like *In the Heat of the Night*, *Moonstruck* and, more recently, *The Hurricane*. Neile calls him 'one of the few that side [of the camera] Steve trusted, and the only one who also became a family friend'. (Sam Peckinpah, by contrast, would barely work again until he directed *The Wild Bunch* in 1969.) Jewison still remembers fondly how 'I was born, grew up and almost died doing [*Kid*] . . . If McQueen ever saw you were insecure or worried, he'd bore in and make it even worse for you. He could reduce people to tears, just be an angry, bewildered brat.' Jewison's voice sinks to a sigh. 'But he was so confident in front of a camera. That's the Steve I knew. The child, the genius.'

Finally, *Cincinnati Kid* was a kind of gangster-cowboy film with a major twist: here the gunfight was done with cards. In Jewison's world there were no quick draws or six-shooters. Instead, he took audiences into smoke-filled rooms and across the green baize to a menacing place where the greed was contagious and the only thing that wound up in the morgue was a man's good character. It was an exquisitely done, if derivative moral drama. As well as the director, credit went to the editor Hal Ashby and the cast generally, none more so than the leads. But where a man like Robinson performed, applying himself to the role with an intensity that suggested he was truly happiest when he was someone else, Steve preferred to evoke. One was full of stagecraft, while the other showed no sign of it – with only trace elements of any visible acting. As a result, the contained vacuum of professional poker, where a lifted eyebrow counts as frenzy, finally got the movie and the star it deserved.

Now McQueen could address himself to the fundamental problem of being the biggest star on the planet.

Bigger, as he liked to say, than Fuckwit. Bigger even than the Beatles.

The Cincinnati Kid was actually a relaunch for him. It was also the beginning of his great stretch, the first of five back-to-back smashes that made him a household name in Africa, the Soviet Union and other far-flung outposts where he became a kind of living embodiment of the Marlboro Man. He'd already lasted long enough to survive the low-radius cycle of trendiness that did for a Jim Garner. With Steve's fourteenth film – half the final total – the world first accepted, then discovered him as its favourite fantasy of the American male, staring down the opposition with his gunslinger's squint and wandering off with that precise lope of the cowboy's tread. Even Robinson was impressed. 'He comes out of the tradition of Gable, Bogie, Cagney and even me,' he told the press. 'He's a stunner.'

The movie's premiere, a glittering charity event, was scheduled for 15 October 1965 in New Orleans, the South's biggest such gala since *Gone with the Wind*. On the 14th, the family got a call from Mount Zion hospital in San Francisco. Steve's mother had suffered a cerebral haemorrhage and was in a coma. When McQueen reached her room there, it was the early hours of the following morning. He sat down in the near dark. As his eyes grew accustomed to her shape, he could see that Julian was now a plump woman of fifty-five, big but also light, with golden-brownish hair and glossy lipstick. He looked down at her, suddenly shaking slightly, remembering everything, right back to the Roxy, yet knowing nothing of her. He still knew nothing.

My mother, he said. Mine.

Steve touched her arm with his hand. Julian didn't respond. He leaned over and put his head on her chest. She was breathing hoarsely, and the smell of cheap scent and iodine from a scalp wound was almost overpowering. McQueen straightened and now silently mouthed the words *I love you*. There was a tiny groan from far within him. His mother also seemed to stir slightly, causing her heart monitor to flutter, but Julian's eyes remained shut blind. According to all available records, she never actually woke up.

★   ★   ★

During that last year or two Julian had lived as an elderly flower child in San Francisco, running a small boutique and cruising about in a Volkswagen beetle that Steve had bought her. He'd deliberately given her a used car instead of a new one, he told Neile, 'so she [wouldn't] get spoiled'. Mother and son never met again. Steve communicated through his wife and children, as well as by sending prints of his films and a regular cheque signed by his business manager. The day after Julian died, McQueen let Neile and himself into her North Beach apartment for the first time. On the mantelpiece he saw photos of himself as a boy, as well as movie fan magazines neatly displayed on the coffee table. Framed stills from *The Great Escape*. There was also a dress and a note for Terry that Julian had finished just before she collapsed.

'That's when he broke down and cried,' says Neile. 'Steve felt guilty for having treated her shabbily ... He was desperate to ask for Julian's forgiveness and when she didn't recover he carried that pain around with him for years.'

Julian was buried on 20 October in Forest Lawn memorial park, just across the Golden State freeway from Hollywood. From the shade of the cypress tree overlooking the plot Steve could, and did, stare down onto the grillework of Silver Lake, where the family had lived together in 1942. The grave was in the most secluded, expensive corner of the cemetery, marked by a brass plaque:

JULIAN CRAWFORD MCQUEEN

BERRI

1910   1965

LOVE BY YOUR SON STEVE

McQueen conducted the service himself, with no priest and only a few invited guests, all the while muttering and crying into the open grave. 'He just stood up there [and] rambled,' says Dave Foster. 'About his memories, his recollections, how it all went wrong ... It was very sad. He was talking about a woman he never really knew.' In lieu of flowers, Steve asked that donations be sent to his old school, Boys Republic.

★   ★   ★

177

By now Foster had joined the inner circle, a five- or six-man prae-
torian guard whose job was to remain glued to Steve's side, ensuring
that he had nothing but fun. The motorcycling detail among them
went with him to the Whisky, up to the hills, or out to the desert to
eat peyote. And when McQueen wanted to raise Cain at the Castle,
they'd turn up on their Triumphs and Harleys; tool through the
electric gate and up under the trees to the medieval Spanish courtyard. Once inside, they might flop around the fireplace or watch a
print of one of Steve's films, often complete with outtakes. The
projector would show as much as three or four hours of additional
footage, and McQueen used a pool cue for a pointer as he demonstrated the stupidity of a director or how a shot had been ruined by
'too much yapping'. They were afraid that, sooner or later, he'd stab
the cue through the screen. In summer, the situation might not
exclude a swim and dinner in the grounds: an odd medley of red
meat, spuds, organic vegetables and the seaweed pills Steve bought
in a healthfood store, accompanied by recreational dope, wine and
Old Milwaukee. Whether at home or in a restaurant, McQueen barely
spoke during meals, hoovering down the fare at wild speed.

'What if they run out?' he'd always say if people commented.

Yet the real shock of being his friend, which should have been
slightly less amusing than a hernia, was that Steve made you laugh.
Particularly when rasping up dirt trails on his bike. McQueen loved
the feel of grit under his wheels, and nobody was more endearingly
fun when he was out scrambling, mud-spattered and happy – 'the
true Steve', as Don Gordon says. McQueen's very presence was
exhilarating: 'he was the greatest company, so cool and so together
and so determined to wring every last minute . . . Of course, he'd
test people out. If you passed, he was your blood brother for life.'
Steve quite often told a Gordon or Sebring 'weird shit about himself'
just to see whether it would surface later in the *Hollywood Reporter*.
When it didn't, they found themselves being ferried across the desert
in a tank, wined and dined at the Whisky or Palm Springs' Stein
Room, entertained in the Castle or raced up the asphalt rollercoaster
that snaked along Beverly Glen into the mountains. For those who
failed the test, as many did, McQueen was an unrelenting enemy.
'The pendulum swung a lot wider for him than it did for most,'

er, Missouri, a town of
thousand souls and a
le stop-light, seen at
time McQueen grew
here in the 1930s
early 1940s.

Cadet 649015, who
joined the U.S. Marine
Corps in April 1947
and left it exactly three
ears later with the same
nk. McQueen was both
a morale problem and a
hero while in uniform.

Wanted Dead or Alive (1958–61) took a season to find its audience, but McQueen, as Josh Randall, became an instant cult.

Broke, *The Blob*'s star accepted a flat fee of $3000
ad of 10 per cent of the gross as offered. To date,
ilm has done close to $20 million-worth of business.

The magnificent seven. Back row (*left to right*): James Coburn, Brad Dexter. Front row: McQ, Yul Brynner, Horst Buchholz, Robert Vaughn, Charles Bronso

McQueen at about the time fame struck, with his first and most resilient wife Neile Adams.

2419 Solar Drive, craning over Hollywood like a hippie Berghof and providing the name of McQueen's long-running production company.

The one watchable thing in MGM's *The Honeymoon Machine* (1961).

McQueen's first and only film made in Britain, *The War Lover*.
Apart from his $75,000 fee, the shoot gave him the chance both
to race at Brand's Hatch and to 'feel up Queen Victoria'.

Although the famous fence-jumping scene was actually handled by a double, *The Great Escape* gave McQueen (*seen above with Neile*) a permanent starring role as the king of cool.

Sebring said. Underneath all the male bonding and the jokes there was that brooding loner. Don Gordon, Sebring thought, was at bottom 'a happy guy'; Steve McQueen 'a sad guy'.

And a powerful one. Behind Sebring's not always forceful admiration lay a genuinely forceful apprehension – that Steve 'could flip'; that he was a man driven by a conviction of greatness, a panache of genius, a certitude about talent. All of which vaulted gaps in quality and taste. It was important for friends to offer up due praise for even a *Blob*. To think that he took that shit seriously, at least in public . . . or maybe, Sebring figured, it was just embarrassment. There was always a little stiffness there, a certain defensive wariness.

You're proud of me, aren't you?

'Hell, yes,' they said.

McQueen's clear goal now was to reach the point where he was famous and rich enough to take the projects he wanted to do, as opposed to the ones William Morris told him to do. As he put it, 'Stardom equals freedom. It's the only equation that matters.' Already, by mid 1965, he was well on his way to carrying off his tainted gains and nailing his ambition. Steve had a company, an office, a full-time secretary named Betsy Cox and the power of veto over the scripts Neile and Stan Kamen brought him. He duly passed on *King Rat*, *The Ski Bum*, *The Kremlin Letter* and both *Return of the Seven* and *Triple Cross*, the last two starring his old friend Yul Brynner. McQueen did, however, sign up for his first Western since 1960. Neile remembers Kamen and Abe Lastfogel pitching the horse opera *Nevada Smith* to Steve one night in the Castle. McQueen, typically, wouldn't commit. 'Take it,' she told him later in private, and he did. Meanwhile, Bob Wise, the man who first cast the 'cocky kid in the cap' in *Somebody Up There Likes Me*, also made the pilgrimage to Brentwood – as he says, 'from a cheap dump to a mansion on the hill all in a decade' – to sell Steve on his adaptation of Richard McKenna's novel *The Sand Pebbles*. 'I'd actually wanted to do it for four or five years,' Wise says. 'The problem was the old one of convincing Fox both star and director were bankable. In 1962–3, evidently, we weren't . . . Finally, two little pictures called *The Great Escape* and *The Sound of Music* seemed to swing it.'

All these hassles with the studios, all these fucking errands.

179

Finally, McQueen himself began to lobby for a property variously called *Le Mans*, *The Cruel Sport* and *Day of the Champion*, essentially a *Cincinnati Kid* transferred behind the wheel of a Grand Prix car. John Sturges was to direct, Steve to star, and Stirling Moss to be production consultant. No film project was to bring McQueen as much pleasure, and ultimately as much grief as this would over the next five years.

A few numbers: McQueen made $300,000, plus overtime and points, for each of *Nevada Smith* and *The Sand Pebbles*. He had his investments, some cash sheltered from the IRS, and an account at Security Pacific National Bank. After paying monthly bills, his credit balance would come to $45,000 or $50,000, and the situation at Solar was golden. On 31 August 1966 McQueen's company signed a long-term production deal with Warner Brothers, which reaped an immediate mutual dividend in *Bullitt*. As for spending it, Steve had his hangups, especially when it came to notes and coins dredged from his own pocket. Paradoxically, he could be the most generous of men. The Neighborhood Playhouse, Boys Republic and dozens of schools and playgrounds, whether in LA or on location, would awake to find their leaky roofs repaired or their gyms stocked with expensive sporting goods. Happiness, to McQueen, was displaying such stray wisps of humanity, and having enough left over for his own titanic appetites. (Just as no meal was complete with less than three courses, so, said Sebring, 'some of Steve's nights were like a menu, with an entree, a meat dish and a dessert' in the form of a blonde, a brunette and a redhead.) Some of the contradictions were unattractive, but also oddly expressive. Like most of the characters McQueen played on film, he was, indisputably, a very human study.

Quick draws, Winchesters, Bowie knives, saloons, Indians, not to mention rugged California hills and Louisiana swamps: the stock stuff never stopped coming in *Nevada Smith*, the self-important but juicily entertaining prequel squeezed out of Harold Robbins's *Carpetbaggers*. It was basically a tale of revenge. The eponymous lead, played by McQueen, sets out to find and kill the sadistic murderers of his parents. Even in 1966 everyone knew what that meant. The clash between idealism and evil could be seen coming a mile off. When it did, alas, it was an anti-climax. The whole picture was mired in a sense of period convention, though most of the time it – and Steve himself – looked gorgeous. For at least some of the shoot, bowing to McQueen's wishes, willing to indulge his whims if simultaneously they'd serve the movie, the director Henry Hathaway agreed to give him 'less lines, more moments'. Other times the off-screen drama rivalled the scripted one. Throw in an unwieldy cast (sixty-eight speaking parts), arduous locations and several spats over the 'vision thing', and soon everybody wanted to kill somebody else. Steve would always call the sixty-seven-year-old Hathaway 'Sir' or, on more relaxed occasions, 'Dad'. Hathaway generally called Steve 'Mr McQueen'.

The director treated him formally, telling him he was certain two men of their undoubted professionalism could get along and that, if not, McQueen could go fuck himself.

'Why should I?'

'I'm nice to be nice to, pilgrim. I'm not nice not to be nice to.'

'Listen hard and you'll hear my teeth chattering.'

Hathaway grunted. He gave Steve a look and repeated his terms and conditions.

'Got it?'

'I –' McQueen began to say, then paused, recognising something in Hathaway's eye. 'I'm going for a ride.'

They all just about made it through location, on and near Lake Pontchartrain, where the actress Suzanne Pleshette caught typhoid, though Steve leavened the 'shit' by demanding an air-conditioned trailer where his private chef would serve him a buffet lunch, bone his salmon and chill his Old Milwaukee. (The crew ate a sandwich and an apple.) Gary Combs joined McQueen's friend Loren Janes to do stunts on the picture. 'The guy's energy level was off the wall. The second Hathaway yelled "Cut", Steve would rip off his shirt as though it were on fire, jump on his bike and take off into the woods . . . I remember him there doing wheelies through the trees and [Hathaway] yelling, "Get your ass back here," and a few choice words through a bullhorn. Incredible scenes . . . It never occurred to Steve that he was putting the whole shoot at risk. I mean, if he'd got hurt we all would have been sent home.'

McQueen trudged back grinning and licking the sweat off his lip.

'Miss me?' he asked.

Nevada Smith, though never aspiring to the mural-wall sweep of a *Seven*, towered over most Westerns of recent vintage – towered, in fact, over films like *Cat Ballou*, where Lee Marvin squandered his Maverick gifts on quick-turnover fare and won an Oscar. By now, the whole horse-opera culture had shifted, gone rhinestone, trading off its old moral fables for ready laugh-track ironies. *Nevada*, by contrast, dared to be square. The nobility of the story was matched by the purity and simplicity of the acting, not to say of Hathaway's direction. Many of the new-wave cinéastes, the critics living under the day-to-day strain of being hip, panned it for much the same reason old-wave audiences loved it: its yarn. Money rained down for *Nevada* at the box office, not least in Japan, the Far East and such virgin territory as India, Egypt and Latin America. (In Trinidad riot police were called in to quell crowds trying to break down a door to see it.) McQueen enhanced and extended his fame as the world's biggest star. He gave a ruthlessly accurate and thoughtfully convincing performance: doing the interviews, appearing on TV, imploding behind his castle wall but rarely, if ever, in public. The Supie role seemed right for him, and he played it to the hilt.

Steve was at the press preview of *Nevada Smith*, held on the Paramount lot in June 1966, when a fire broke out on the next-door sound stage. While most of the guests quickly filed away, McQueen stripped off his jacket and rushed in to help save property and, as far as he knew, lives. A gruelling hour later, as the media sidled back to their seats, Steve stood grinning and sweating in the moonlight.

'It was one of those moments you don't think . . . When you let up on the past for a while and don't worry about the future, you just sort of live. You're free.'

Bob Wise's epic of an American gunboat navigating between 1920s Chinese warlords, *The Sand Pebbles*, was an immediate hit. But one of its many sub-plots was the pitched battle fought to get it made in the first place. By November 1965 Fox had finally agreed a budget of $7 million, and Dick McKenna's best-selling novel been adapted, through seven or eight drafts, into a three-hour screenplay. Alongside McQueen, Wise cast Richard Crenna, the young Candice Bergen (fresh from her debut, playing an apparently deep-frozen lesbian in *The Group*) and Simon Oakland, later to surface in *Bullitt*. Eli Wallach auditioned for the sidekick role of Frenchy, which instead went, whimsically, to Richard Attenborough. As well as his fee, it was agreed that Steve was to get 25 per cent of the net. William Morris then wrote to Fox 'to make certain you and we both have a record of McQueen's requests', namely that the studio provide him a luxury home, a Condor camper, portable gym, Triumph TR6 bike and 'personal security whereby non-authorised persons cannot get to him' whilst on location. The entire 111-man crew left for Taiwan that Thanksgiving.

As the shoot unfolded, at least at first, the oriental hospitality flowed. It was a scene to make the sixties swing.

A suite at the Grand Hotel, Taipei, would be permanently reserved for Steve for the next five months, though when Neile and the children joined him the family moved to a large farmhouse with a cook, valet and nanny. Bob Wise would shrewdly come to guess that 'when things were going well at home, Steve was fine. When they weren't, he could be a grumpy bastard.' Just as on *Kid*, McQueen's insecurity soon came into full bloom. Often he insisted that a scene be shot two completely different ways, his and the director's, so that he could choose between them late at night when inspecting the rushes. 'The main thing with Steve was the mood swings,' says Wise. 'He'd be a pussycat or he'd be . . . let's say something else. I remember when we had a new consignment of uniforms coming in late one day. Earlier that same morning I was trying to line up quite a complicated shot over the side of the gunboat. There I was dangling off the railings, shouting instructions to the extras, when I felt a tap on my shoulder. It was McQueen, wanting to talk about his wardrobe. I'm afraid I blew up. "For Christ's sake, Steve, not *now*," were the exact words. He sort of slunk off with that hurt little boy's look and gave me the freeze for the next three days. Didn't speak a single word to me.' McQueen's good humour returned when 'he saw the new rushes and how great he looked . . . After that Steve never gave me a hard time again.'

McQueen was at his most intense, no small accolade, on *The Sand Pebbles*. He broke out with a fever blister on the first day of shooting and, as Neile says, 'generally act[ed] like a caged animal while he thought about and got a fix on his character'. Watching him become Jake Holman was to watch a series of finely tuned movements that would seem spontaneous, unrehearsed and even lazy on the screen. Nothing could be further from the truth: 'Steve worked like a navvy,' says Wise. 'The whole scene with the wardrobe flared up because he was so fussy about that sort of thing, always wanting the exact look and the precise props. Nobody did detail better than he did.'

The novelty of the location began to wear off. One month, two, three, he moaned. Steve squatted there amongst the muttering crew, of whom several jumped ship, chewing on his peanut-butter sandwiches rather than risk the local swill.

Four months, five.

In the shoot, too, everything turned out much as Wise had feared, only worse. First the Keelung river was too shallow for the gunboat. Then it rained in Taiwan for four straight weeks. There were problems with snakes, disease, drinking water, bribes and student riots. Steve, unlike Neile, had never seen this part of the world before. Like an exotic fish changing colour in the water his face went from light to dark, heralding a tirade:

'Roll 'em. For Chrissake, *roll 'em!*'

The McQueens lived in a house whose garden ended in a wilderness of plants and vines. Just beyond them a raw green mountain cut across the sky at a 45-degree angle, its slope plunging violently from the cloudy heights down into the valley where the river ran. Steve at least liked to walk along the water's edge towards the village, where, one evening, he found a Catholic orphanage for young girls. The squat stone building had only three complete walls. The fourth was dilapidated and part exposed. Branches of a lemon tree reached into a dormitory still palpably full of life and motion; almost all the children could be heard moaning with cold. As he stood there feeling the night wind roll over him, McQueen, too, began to shudder slightly. A day or two later he introduced himself to Edward Wojniak, the missionary priest who ran the institution. Wojniak would remember Steve 'talking with no hint of condescension' to him and his staff about their job and its many problems. McQueen's eyes were misty as he spoke of what it was

184

like to 'have no home in the world', to be 'beat and broke' but, above all, 'to fight . . . Even when you're down and out and being kicked around, you have to get up and come back. You can always do it. And when you feel you can't go on, you must do it. As long as you're alive, it's always worth fighting back . . . that's what makes us human.' Although he was ostensibly addressing the priest and his team, on a more profound level Steve was really talking to himself. Along with Wise he then wrote out a cheque for $20,000, and would help sustain the place, equally quietly and generously, for the next ten years.

Nobody in Hollywood ever heard about it.

Back on set, everyone who knew anything at all about Steve knew that he was mad. They didn't mean it as an insult, or even in any judgemental sense, but as a clear statement of fact. The way he inhabited a role was more like possession than play-acting. Nothing else seemed real to him. 'McQueen was the last true under-your-skin star,' says Don Murray. 'He established a character on screen that worked for him, and he for it. An authentic persona. Beneath the sex symbol lay the heart of a savvy, incredibly hard-working professional. I did *Bus Stop* with Monroe, and it was the same thing. Those were the two who managed to be legends and have something serious to say about the way we live our lives.' To a jaundiced few, Steve appeared so devoted to keeping up his fictive appearance that he disappeared. 'You've got to realise that a McQueen performance lends itself to monotony,' was Robert Mitchum's cutting verdict. Yet, for millions of others he invoked what shrinks call the 'cute response', a pre-conditioned reflex also triggered by the likes of koalas and pandas, though in McQueen's case one with uniquely sharp claws. On a certain level, Steve the blue-eyed Supie with the trailer and the personal stylist could be made to seem like a character from the pages of a Nathanael West novel. Yet he worked harder, longer and above all smarter than most. According to Norman Jewison, 'Steve often said if you're going to do a part, you've got to excel at everything. That meant learning the character, his back story, his habits, mannerisms – the works – from the ground up.' Not only was McQueen a master at finding a prop, or some physical piece of business, whether it was a particular shirt or a type of gun, to extend his character; he had that much rarer quality – believability. Other actors played; Steve knew.

It was when the cameras switched off that he felt alone and naked to the world.

When McQueen made a film he brought his whole heart and soul to it. Whether on a stage or location, the actual shoot followed down drawn lines. He liked to have everything meticulously blocked and acted out for him in rehearsal, then to do the scene itself in one or two takes. There was no wasted energy or emotion. Everything was channelled towards the maximum impact with the minimum apparent effort. McQueen had a talent for thinking ahead, not just to the next setup but to the next week or month. He had antennae which could pick up on a minute character trait and then develop it into a soul-baring performance. Above all, Steve had infallible instinct. 'He wasn't the greatest actor in the world,' says Bob Wise, 'but he knew exactly what worked for him . . . Two or three times a day, he'd loom up with a script and say, "I think I can get this across better without a line, with just an expression" . . . The first couple of times I kept thinking, He's not giving me anything. He's killing the scene. Then when I saw the rushes, I was knocked out. Steve was right. It was something the naked eye couldn't see, but the camera could. McQueen worked brilliantly well within his limitations.'

Like a Cooper or Bogart, Steve contributed, through sheer horse sense, far more to the roles than any number of well-buffed speeches. That quizzical, plausible presence was better – and infinitely more commercial – than the slickest dialogue. And while McQueen had competition at the box office, his only serious rival as a behavioural male superstar was the man who'd once enjoyed top billing while he, Steve, scrounged $19 a day – Newman. Both were all-American phenomena, both blue-eyed icons who liked beer and low-slung cars. There comparison ended. In fact, it became a running joke among press and producers alike to be either 'pro Steve' or 'pro Paul'. Pop psychologists would eventually write entire theses about how the two men represented the yin and yang of American culture. Only the public, it seemed, could hold in its head simultaneously the ideas that McQueen was playing variations on a basic type who was both recognisable, yet flexible and attractive; that Newman was an intelligent hunk with the good luck to appear in a high percentage of superior films; and that they seemed to hail from opposite sides of the tracks. The overall contrast was like something out of Hogarth's etchings of the idle and industrious apprentices. Newman, for all his hard knocks, was seen as intrinsically smooth; McQueen, despite his flair, as a scrapper who brought steely-eyed conviction to the flimsiest role. It seemed to Steve, too, that Newman had had all the breaks; he was well-educated, verbal, powerfully connected in Hollywood. For all his own success, McQueen still – as ever – felt he was getting the fuzzy end of the lollipop. Half his best scripts, including *Sand Pebbles*, reached him only 'after Fuckwit says no'. According to Jim Hoven, 'It seemed to Steve that Paul was always, tantalisingly, just a bit ahead. Consequently, he targeted him. The goal was to be bigger than Newman.'

McQueen didn't pretend otherwise.

Steve response to success was perverse but sadly in keeping with the man. Frank enjoyment was out. Relaxation eluded him. McQueen couldn't forget old slights and his gratitude always had an edge of rebuke. As for professional peers: mere actors were fine, even friends, but fellow stars were strafed with a mixture of ambition, fear, scorn and resentment. Neile to this day insists, 'Steve saw himself in a kind of race with [Newman], one I believe finally wore him down.' McQueen could feel and express professional respect for a film like *The Hustler*, but the general message he had for rivals, whether seen in his windscreen or his rear-view mirror, was *eat dust*. People who knew and even liked him marvelled at his competitiveness. It devoured him. It was sad and it was sometimes funny. (In all seriousness McQueen used to tell mutual friends like Faye Dunaway, 'You know, two Paul Newman autographs buys you one Steve McQueen autograph.') The very night before Steve and Neile left for Taiwan, the Newmans came by the Castle to wish them *bon voyage*. 'See ya in nine weeks,' Paul chuckled as he drove out the gate. In dark moments McQueen always used to claim that 'that fucker wasn't smiling – he was sneering' as he said it. Thanks to successive drought and flood, the McQueens would straggle home seven months later.

The Sand Pebbles was now about halfway finished, and the day-to-day saga of the shoot had become a full-time news beat. In mid March the crew moved to Hong Kong, where first boredom and then the flu set in. A camera operator was nearly killed when, in a fight scene, he took a flaming torch to the chest. It rained yet again. Filming was then closed down for several days by an earthquake. 'The whole thing was tense,' says Wise. 'You try dropping Americans into a completely foreign country, add interminable delays and budget overruns, and see what happens.' For his part, Steve took to spending more and more time with his stuntman Loren Janes and some of the rougher-hewn extras. 'Hard drinking, hard fighting . . . as time ticked by, McQueen and his gang grew increasingly restless and often spent nights on the prowl, roaming the city, drinking, heckling, picking fights and pummelling,' in Candy Bergen's words. The superficial camaraderie of the actual movie did nothing to dispel the frustration of the long months stranded on location. 'All hell's going to bust loose,' predicted one of the film's publicists.

All hell already had.

One wet night in Hong Kong McQueen and some of his cronies wandered out of the rain into a nightclub. Two local men approached their table. One, Steve remembered, 'was big – Sumo size'. The other was small and, as it turned out, passive. After a long, silent appraisal, the glandular type went from fawning on McQueen to taunting him when he refused to arm-wrestle, using words like 'fairy' and several others unlikely to endear him to a man famously uptight about that side of his craft. In a virtual replay of his latrine encounter with Joey, the platoon bully, Steve invited the man into the bathroom, where he dropped into a karate crouch and promptly rendered him unconscious in a matter of seconds.

'Fuck you,' he added.

Next, at the same brisk clip, McQueen came chugging back to the bar, straightening his shirt and craning his neck to locate his worried friends. 'Fucking heavy,' he kept babbling. '*Fucking* heavy.' They quickly finished their drinks. Then he and one of his stuntmen tore off down the street and made an abrupt, lurching stop in front of a passing cab. That was the last that particular club ever saw of McQueen. According to a source present, 'Steve freaked out not because he'd hit the guy but because any bad publicity could get him tossed from the film . . . The [stunt] guy got him back home with Neile in about two minutes flat.'

His friend found the whole thing disquieting. It gave him a faint inkling of what Steve had to put up with all the time.

McQueen later defined his MO on these occasions – there were literally scores of them – to Jay Sebring: 'My job is I keep my head down, but if anyone fucking wants a fight they can have it.' The studio PR machinery was always there to make amends, though, as Sebring said, 'The problem wasn't a few bar brawls. They came with the territory . . . The problem was when Steve went to war with people who weren't fighting with him.'

His neighbour, for instance.

McQueen was in Defcon Two mode that spring while he simultaneously shot *The Sand Pebbles* and planned for *Day of the Champion*. Solar and John Sturges had signed with Warner Brothers to begin principal photography at the Nürburgring Grand Prix in mid summer. On 2 March Sturges arrived in the Orient just in time to be caught up in the earthquake that served as the central metaphor for the whole *Champion* fiasco. Sturges's assistant Bob Relyea remembers how 'it became a life-or-death race to get Steve's film up and running before one being developed by John Frankenheimer and Jim Garner called *Grand Prix*. When *Sand Pebbles* overran, Jack Warner got nervous. He knew about the other picture and he also knew that the market wouldn't support two car films . . . He folded us up.' McQueen went 'totally berserk', says Jim Hoven. 'He hated to lose to anyone, let alone a guy he thought of as a decent actor but a candyass driver . . . Steve was in a virtual coma for a week after that. He went nuts.' One result was that McQueen became, if possible, yet more suspicious of even his closest friends. Another was that, as well as lobbing beer cans, he got in the habit of wandering out to his balcony late at night and pissing down towards Garner's house.

'Like he did on my movie,' Steve explained.

The spectre of Vietnam managed to haunt *The Sand Pebbles*, which duly mixed period drama, romance and some choice notions about *yanqui* imperialism. Bob Wise's slow-simmering direction covered all the bases, though the lavish sets and the story itself were mere garnish for the main course: the casting. McQueen played a cynical, machine-mad sailor, monosyllabic and misunderstood, and that was about right. His real-life love of motors and gadgets would communicate itself to the audience as it did to Wise, who says, 'I've never known someone who slotted into a character like he did. It really hit him where he lived.' The part where he introduced himself with the line, 'Hello, engine, I'm Jake Holman,' satirically dopey in cold print, was given a twist that made the scene warm, human and even tender. Similarly, Steve's arrival on the gunboat (recalling the equivalent shot in *Hell is for Heroes*) well suited the universal perception of him as a moody, tough-minded bastard and added to the general sense of impending rampage. He dominated every scene, but always in his tense, fixated, mute way. *The Sand Pebbles* allowed him to express more of who he was as a man, and as a star, than he could ever have hoped for.

The film opened on 20 December 1966, eliciting a mixture of awe and impatience. The two most frequently heard beefs were that it was too long, and that there were too many clanking Hanoi parallels. Underlying the melodramatic plot was Wise's compulsion to provoke severe queasiness in both cast and audience. For instance, there was the moment when a character was flayed alive, or the various other torment, torture and murder horrors. As a morality tale, *The Sand Pebbles* creaked under its own political obsessions. As an epic, it worked brilliantly and quickly found a mass audience: McQueen's points would translate into a cool $200,000 for him. Uniquely, he agreed to a coast-to-coast promotional tour for the film, mugging his way through *The Ed Sullivan Show*, *The Tonight Show* (where Steve squirmed under Johnny Carson's praise for the bike-jumping climax to *The Great Escape*) and *What's My Line?* He scored the *Photoplay* Gold Medal and was the Foreign Press Association's 'World Favorite Star' for the third year running. *The Sand Pebbles* also brought McQueen his first and only Academy Award nomination. The all-British competition that year came from Paul Scofield, Richard Burton and Michael Caine. Wise, who attended the Oscars with him, remembers 'McQueen just beside himself to be there. The key words would be proud and thrilled . . . The man had a healthy ego.'

Neile herself would always claim that 'I knew if Steve won, he'd be impossible to live with.'

McQueen arrived back from the Far East haggard, fifteen pounds lighter, sick, exhausted and so relieved to be home he literally threw himself to the ground and kissed the airport tarmac. It's not surprising that he desperately needed a break. The family spent much of that summer driving the Condor up the back roads through Nevada, Utah and Wyoming into Montana, where they camped out by Flathead Lake. Mornings there were hard to believe. The primeval freshness, spilled down out of the Rockies above Polson, was held close to the earth by the mist. Outside and in, it was dank, wafting up at them, and smelt like a florist's shop. Bear and possum roamed up to the motor home. Late one afternoon, when the stinging sun had burnt through the cape of moisture that clung to the mountains, Steve sighted and shot a deer. This was a popular local sport, but the moment would prove a turning point. 'I can still see it,' McQueen said years later, 'the look on its face and the bleating noise it made. I asked myself, "Why the hell did you *do* that?" I was sick inside.' From that day on the ex-huntsman took a reverent, almost Buddhist view of all animals. A family friend would remember him 'reading the [Riot Act] to Neile and the kids because one of them had half-killed a bug and left it twitching in a garbage can. That sent Steve into orbit.'

Several new movies were also mooted. McQueen asked everyone he knew in Hollywood not to call him that summer. Most refused the request, so he hung up on them and went about his business.

Steve, of course, was a complete contradiction, and examples of his colossal capacity for doing odd jobs (odder than films) made his life rarely less than entertaining. For instance, he served on the Advisory Council of the Youth Studies Center at the University of Southern California, the only actor so honoured. McQueen personally arranged for a number of juvenile offenders about to be sent to jail to be transferred to Boys Republic instead. He gave generously to the Variety Club, the Kidney Foundation, as well as to schools and orphanages. Some donations were made in his name, many more anonymously. All over California, and now internationally, there were gyms and cafeterias and even well-stocked libraries being built and enjoyed with his money.

Lest all that be taken as evidence of deeper stability, McQueen continued to lead an exotic private life. He still ruthlessly pursued his love of sex, drugs and, increasingly, rock and roll. Nor were his commercial interests ignored. Through the Solar Plastics and Engineering division Steve negotiated a contract to market a motor-bike of his own design. He began to model his trademark turtleneck sweaters and cropped jackets and, less conspicuously, his designer Italian suits. McQueen went to the Metropolitan Opera (which he left again after five minutes) and talked about opening a Mexican restaurant on Sunset Strip. Finally, that September, in keeping with his new-found conservationism, he narrated *The Coming of the Roads*, a TV documentary about the pollution of the American wilderness.

With *The Cincinnati Kid*, *Nevada Smith* and now *The Sand Pebbles*, McQueen was a blue-chip star with a track record, a value stock rather than a junk bond already starting, like a Garner, to flicker. Those spots on *Carson* and *Sullivan* were only one end of a chain reaction widely shared in Hollywood and in a much broader community. There was an ever deeper presentiment of 'cometh th' man' towards Steve in 1967; at a time when domestic screens were increasingly filled with imported talent (witness all three other Best Actor nominees for that year's Oscar), he was the one true American star to emerge since Newman. McQueen was a phenomenon, and was phenomenally rewarded. Solar would soon go on to do a six-picture deal with Warner Brothers, Sturges's assistant Bob Relyea signing up as the company vice-president. Steve's own price more than doubled, to $700,000 per title plus 50 per cent of the profits. Nobody else was getting that kind of money then, not even John Wayne.

'Acting's a good racket,' he now allowed. 'And let's face it, you can't beat the bread.' Steve's arrival at the top was confirmed by the glittering ball he and Neile threw at the Castle – 'the moddest wing-ding of the season', in one trade's strangulated lead – and the equally lavish profile in the *Saturday Evening Post*. The story, headlined A LOSER MAKES IT BIG, presented McQueen as the sentinel safeguarding American values from foreign corruption. He was now playing the role of superpatriot.

On 12 January 1967 Steve accepted an invitation to address a film-school class held on the 20th Century-Fox lot. One student asked him, 'How do you go about picking your movies?' McQueen's answer cut right to the heart of what Hoven calls his 'shrewd, superiority-inferiority complex'. Steve looked up and laughed lightly.

'I do it by instinct . . . good instinct. But I have to be careful because I'm a limited actor. I mean, my range isn't very great. I have to find characters and situations that feel right . . . Even then, it's a fuck of a lot of work.'

Steve then threw off a few remarks about Ibsen and Beckett, posed for photographs, got back in his car, drove to the Castle and finished pouring concrete for his new garage. The blue-collar handyman with a penchant for beer and dirt-bikes, the wide-eyed artist observing the cultural scene; both were McQueen. But within a year or two he grew to detest his 'he-man bit', bringing it out of the closet only when alimony or other crises left him short of funds. As he put it at the end of his life: 'First I was a superstar, then I was an actor.'

Meanwhile, Steve still abased himself to Tinseltown. He told friends that he read 102 scripts that winter of 1966–7. John Huston's *The Kremlin Letter*, and Richard Brooks's *In Cold Blood*, the latter to co-star McQueen and Newman, made it to the Solar boardroom, though Steve ultimately vetoed both. He also toyed with *Two for the Road*. Here some discrepancy exists between the studio's minutes of the meeting ('Mr McQueen . . . expressed full confidence in the artistic integrity of the photoplay') and Steve's own take ('I only woulda done it to bang Audrey Hepburn'). Offers came in daily, literally from all parts, often with quite complicated bribes and inducements from producers for him even to skim their proposals. At one office McQueen was greeted by a specially made documentary of his life and a gold watch engraved with his name; in another the gift was a pouch of high-quality coke. A development company in Paris pleaded with him to allow them to send their corporate jet to fly him across the Atlantic. From London, Lew Grade offered him return tickets on the *Queen Mary* and use of his private Rolls. ('Not bad for a farm boy,' Steve would say of himself.) He passed on them all. Meanwhile, as international telexes and special deliveries rained down on the Castle, exactly two miles away in his home at 313 North Barrington, Norman Jewison was busy preparing a film he then called *The Crown Caper*.

On 21 March 1967 Steve and Neile pulled up in his red Ferrari at the Chinese theatre on Hollywood Boulevard. There he ceremonially pressed his prints and the word THANKS!! into a wet cement slab in the forecourt, the 153rd star over forty years to do so. Of those 153, fans couldn't help but notice, McQueen was the only one whose slab, and message, faced in the wrong direction. (Staring down Sophia Loren's, as it happened.) Steve would remark to the organising committee that he appeared to be screwy, fucked up, quite literally all turned around. 'Ass-backward as usual.'

It seemed to them that he spoke with satisfaction.

6

The King of Cool

A nd the winner was: Paul Scofield.

McQueen, who'd expected to triumph, sat up through that entire night after the Oscars. When friends met him for breakfast around six the next morning he was rat-eyed with fatigue. 'He looked bad,' says one, 'but not as down as you'd think. Most of the time, Steve handled failure a helluva lot better than success.'

In fact, McQueen was in a philosophical mood, attributing his defeat to 'the honchos dig[ging] some Alistair Cooke type, not a grease monkey who grooves on his wheels' (translation: the Academy preferred the costume dramatics of *A Man for All Seasons* to the vivid, blue-collar characterisation of Jake Holman). It was another milestone down the road of Steve and Hollywood's mutual wariness of each other. Wariness and, of course, need: on 4 January 1967 McQueen signed a new, high-powered contract at William Morris, while Solar did their precedent-making deal with Warners. *The Sand Pebbles* turned over a fat profit for the remainder of the year. Twelve months later it was still generating a million dollars a week, making it one of the most successful and admired films in the world. Steve used to chuckle how, at least commercially, it left *Man for All Seasons* in the dust. The figures weren't just a way of poking Scofield in the eye with a burnt stick, though they were that all right; McQueen simply wanted a 'good, American movie' to restore domestic supremacy, reversing a slump that Hollywood thought divinely fixed. 'Brits out' was his artistic credo that spring.

When producers cast around for a native son, they looked no further than the corn-fed Missourian whom one Warner brother called 'not really handsome . . . and not *that* great as an actor. But he's no phoney, either. McQueen projects a certain contemporariness. He's the man of the moment – surly, tough and cynical, yet somehow very innocent and gentle.' Just about the only claim Steve made with any passion for himself was also on behalf of his 'doing the times'. Flamboyant, eager, tense and a little warped, the first ever rock and roll film star.

The full flower of his art, however, came in the reassuringly old-fashioned values. 'Steve is the only guy around,' sighed another tycoon, 'who can do the kind of stuff that made big stars of Gable, Cooper and Wayne.' McQueen's fans admired the laconic action hero, but what the studios admired was the durable symbol of American mores, the wise underdog, the shrewd hick, the cynical plainsman. When Steve came on the screen you could see the Stars and Stripes flapping behind him.

On a routine visit to the Castle that January Stan Kamen finally dropped off the script for *The Crown Caper*. It was one of a dozen projects on the table, and, Kamen thought, the one least likely to interest McQueen: a luxe tale of white-collar crime with frothy romantic potential. He read the outline and told Kamen he wanted it. Badly. By now Steve's agent had come to the conclusion that his client's mind wasn't just unusual, it had the seer's dimensions of foresight and insight. Thomas Crown, Steve shrewdly reasoned, was 'essentially a rebel, like me. Sure, a high-society rebel, but he's *my* kinda cat.' On that note he began to bombard Norman Jewison. Jewison, who'd had in mind a Sean Connery or Jack Lemmon, opposite Brigitte Bardot, remembers 'McQueen [drove] to Barrington and spent two hours talking me into casting him . . . I kept telling him he wasn't right for it. Tommy Crown wore silk shirts and Boston ties, a kind of sardonic, upper-class shit unlike anything Steve had ever done before. "That's exactly why I want it," he said. I think McQueen was probably trying to grow up as an actor . . . Like most of the characters he'd played on screen, he could be stubborn as hell. Let's say he was a hard man to refuse.'

Jewison tried.

'It's not that you weren't great,' he allowed, 'on *Cincinnati*.'

'Aren't you proud of me, Norman?'

'Hell, yes. But, Steve –'

McQueen cut in on him with a sudden flip of tone. 'No. Listen to me. I'm doing the fucking film, so stop twisting my melon.'

Steve signed to star in what was now *The Thomas Crown Affair* on 3 February 1967. His fee was $54,166.66 per week for twelve weeks, $1,000 weekly living expenses, a house, car, driver and first-class return flights to LA from location in Boston. The financial negotiations were simple enough. McQueen got everything he wanted. It was only when he began actually to put the part together that he realised how much work it was going to be. Steve asked his Beverly Hills tailor, Ron Postal, to fit him out in $400 suits; he had his hair pouffed by Jay Sebring and learnt to play polo. Jewison recalls how 'Steve was so competitive . . . he was out there one evening practising until his hands literally bled.' Early the next morning Steve asked Postal to get him a pair of tight-fitting Italian shoes and walked around in them all day until his feet, too, were rubbed raw. Before he went to bed that night, Neile could hear him rehearsing in his den.

Jewison, meanwhile, was spending his days scouting locations, auditioning, fleshing out Alan Trustman's brief, thirty-page script and phoning Paris. He could forget about Bardot, her agent told him. Instead he cast twenty-six-year-old Faye Dunaway, fresh from her breakout role in *Bonnie and Clyde*. The whole crew then transferred to the east coast, where Jewison and Walter Mirisch were handed an official letter from the FBI:

Mr De Loach has received . . . your request to photograph our Boston office in connection with the proposed motion picture *The Crown Caper* [sic]. This screen play has been reviewed in the Crime Research Section. It involves a bank robbery . . . sex both explicit and implied throughout the story . . . ends when the FBI is outwitted by Crown, who flies to Brazil.

This is an outrageous portrayal of the Bureau . . . No doubt the producer foresees this film as a great money-maker at the box office as a result of its great emphasis on titillation and sex.

We will have absolutely nothing to do with the picture [and] be so advised.

(Also in the Bureau's McQueen file, a sorry note on the Whisky à Go Go: 'This unique entertainment phenomenon continues to draw capacity crowds and features live and recorded watusi music and dancing. Among its clientele are well-known legitimate people, as well as entertainment celebrities and in addition, pimps, bums, prostitutes and other notorious characters . . . It is popular with Steve McQueen.')

Steve, Neile, the children and their pets spent that Summer of Love in a fortified compound in Beverly Farms, on the shore just north of Boston. The last night before filming began, McQueen told a friend, 'Both [Kamen] and [Jewison] seem to think – which I think's full of shit – that even if I screw up in *Crown* I can still survive, professionally. I don't have any illusions on that score . . . I got to do it. But if people laugh at me, my ass is gone.' This bleak fatalism, so characteristic of McQueen, was responsible for the biggest gamble of his career. He told Neile, too, that it was 'for keeps' when the cameras rolled the next morning. Steve stayed up all night worrying that it was do or die – 'If I fuck up now, it's over' – road's end, with nowhere to go.

He didn't fuck up. McQueen arrived for work in the morning wearing his jeans and cardigan, butt end clamped to his lip, carrying a cheap thermos of coffee. An hour later he was suited up as a Boston Brahmin, with his own plane and a Back Bay mansion, a role he inhabited just as snugly as a Hilts or Jake Holman. From that moment on Steve became the unlovable banker. 'Call me Tommy,' he kept repeating, with all the joyous fascination and intrigue of a child's make-believe. 'You must be Tommy,' said one grip, supportively. 'Tommy Crown, right?' piped up someone else – before, emboldened by the progress the back-line crew seemed to be making, McQueen duly 'came on all fiscal' to his director.

'I only signed for a week of pre-production. Let's fucking roll 'em!'

At its worst, the shoot provided endless such opportunities for Steve, as the stuffed-shirt Crown, to put Jewison straight. More than a little of the character's ice, in a tart mixture with the actor's own petulance, would surface over the next three months. Jewison remembers it all as the sort of summer work experience it's kindest to call bittersweet. 'There were a few scenes,' he says (Bob Relyea also remembers 'refereeing between Steve and Norman'), 'partly a result of McQueen's paranoia . . . For instance, he had twenty-four-hour surveillance and security on the front gate of his house. But Steve, being Steve, decided he needed it patrolled from the back as well. At the back was a private beach and the Atlantic Ocean. Who the hell did he think was going to get in from there?' But – well, OK, then. More security. The suits jumped to it, which was all he'd wanted in the end.

As to the actual shoot: Jewison fondly recalls the day 'we had everything lined up for a scene on the beach at Magic Hour, just as the sun was going down. Beautiful. We'd waited all day, conditions were perfect, everyone was ready – except Thomas Crown Esq., who was out in the surf in his dune buggy, not answering his radio . . . Eventually Steve came back and said, "I'm ready now, Norman." I told him it was too late, the light was shot. Just as I said it I looked down, saw a gull feather and stuck it in Steve's hair. "You're the big chief," I said. "You wear this." I could see he was angry . . . Weeks later, after we wrapped *Crown*, I was sitting on a plane waiting to take off for Hawaii. No one else, to my knowledge, knew where I was. We were taxiing on the runway and the stewardess came up to me with a box. Inside was an Indian headband with a feather and a note from Steve: "I'm sorry, Norman. *You're* the chief." To this day, I've no idea how he nailed me.'

Steve got to keep the $5000 dune buggy. He also went home with all of Postal's tailor-made suits, the shoes and most of the props, including some stray cash. But the brass ring, the best prize of all, was the deal he signed with Warners that September to resurrect *Day of the Champion*, now renamed *Le Mans*. After the development meeting McQueen dictated his notes to his secretary. 'A great day . . . I never gave up . . . I'm glad we waited to get [*Grand Prix*] out of the way . . . Our movie will be an honest, down-to-earth racing film, and it'll be the best thing I've ever done.'

That was probably the biggest error of judgement McQueen made in his life.

Steve had a great gift for topping himself. After Eustis Clay, each of his roles outdid the last in its intensity, even as the movies themselves varied from the mournful to the actively butch. But something was missing. Steve the laid-back dude wasn't a character who ever seemed to make an appearance in the numerous trade profiles and gossip about McQueen the actor. He'd alienated too many people, spoken too freely of the failings both of those who trusted him and of the whole Hollywood pack. For instance, Jim Garner, a quiet, steady actor and much the same as a driver, who, Steve continued to mutter, elevating a simple race to the level of operatic treachery, had 'butt-fucked', or at least badly buggered up *Champion*. Several other peers would be similarly held guilty of the one unpardonable sin, disloyalty to the Supie. 'The man never forgot, never forgave,' says one. Yet McQueen could, and did, exist vividly as a warm, attractive and sensitive human being to the few who got past his radar, particularly if they happened to own a bike. Anyone seeing him with a Don Gordon or Bud Ekins would have hesitated for an eternity before accepting some of the stereotype labels such as 'McShit', or worse, that enemies gave him over the years. The actor Dean Jones would 'suit up and roar over Palm Desert with him to Steve's favourite bar, the Stein Room. You'd come right up over the sand to the front door, go in and quaff frozen mugs of beer all afternoon. That's how he unwound. What's not to enjoy about a guy like that?'

Around 1967 McQueen found a hobby that was good sport and relieved his long-term tantrums as much as the drinking and biking did. Like them, too, it lasted a lifetime.

Witness the scene in the Hong Kong nightclub. Steve had begun dabbling in the martial arts around the time of *The Sand Pebbles*. The private, ad-lib tomahawkings were soon replicated in formal, public lessons with a man named Bob Wall. He then had a number of kung fu workouts with Burt Ward (Robin in TV's original *Batman*) and later came to know and like Chuck Norris. On the set of *Thomas Crown*, meanwhile, McQueen met one Nikita Knatz, the film's sketch artist, to whom he introduced himself by asking, straight-faced, 'How'd you like to shake hands with a big star?' Despite this unpromising start, things went steadily uphill from there when Steve learnt that Knatz, too, was a master in judo and akido. The two started training together. Knatz soon realised that, for all his swagger, McQueen remained an insecure man who often suffered from endearingly humble doubts about himself and his job prospects. Steve was awed by Knatz's strength of character and aura of competence. All that granite toughness overimpressed him; in the presence of 'together' men McQueen could shed the more vicious and spiky side of his character in his frustrated urge, as glimpsed in the Stein Room, to be one of the guys. For the last seven or eight years of his life Steve's closest friend would again be his karate tutor, Pat Johnson.

In between Knatz and Johnson, Steve met and befriended Bruce Lee. It was a typically troubled McQueen relationship: complicated by his actual *jeet kune do* technique, which Lee described as 'Maximum violence – don't hang around, don't warm up gradually. Go loco. Hit them like a freight train . . . That's what Steve did,' as well as by McQueen's lifelong credo, 'Nobody really trusts anyone – or why do they put "tilt" on a pinball machine?' A perfectly credible story is told of Steve turning down a script Lee submitted to Solar with a curt 'I'm in the business of being a star, not making them.' On the other hand, the Hong Kong child prodigy and future Hollywood cult possessed several qualities that appealed to his new pupil. A self-made man, Lee had a strong, if sometimes satiric, philosophical bent; an absolute discretion when it came to respecting confidences; a warm sense of humour; and an intuitive sixth sense which let him empathise with difficult people. McQueen somehow tuned in to that empathy, and gradually grew more comfortable with Lee. Their sparring moved from the professional to the social.

A mark of Steve's respect for Lee was his unprecedented offer, after declining his script, to both buy him a car and lend him the down payment on his new home. By mid 1968 the two men were spending long days in Brentwood or in Hong's restaurant downtown, where a pet rat shuffled indifferently up and down a ladder in a glass tank – one step ahead of the health inspectors – while pondering Lee's classic, two-word belief system *Know yourself*. Bruce would tell interviewers that Steve was one of the gutsiest, craziest men he'd ever met. In private he also considered McQueen 'very uptight . . .

highly strung, you know?' and, shrewdly, that 'he's still on the level of regarding [martial arts] as an excitement, like his bike and his sports cars – some form of release of his anger, or whatever you call it.' Both craziness and anger would be on hand when the two of them had dinner in Hong's a night or two before Steve began location work on *Bullitt*. He'd been in a bad mood all evening, glowering long and hard at the rodent tank while muttering about the shit-heels he'd be forced to deal with over the next three months. 'I'd like to drop that fucker down Jack Warner's pants.' Lee sympathised. They paid the bill, made a date to meet on the set, and exchanged numbers.

'So long, man,' said Steve. He hugged him.

But then McQueen had a brainwave as he was leaving. The heavy glass lid rattled and gave off a stink when he lifted it.

'What are you *doing*?'

'The rat comes with me,' he said.

The Thomas Crown Affair opened that same summer, the month of race riots, anti-war marches and the second Kennedy assassination. It was, as Pauline Kael wrote, 'pretty good trash', superior escapism that managed to be both of its times and a relief from them; the film's jazzy split screens and Day-Glo colours, in particular, rooting it squarely under the heading 'swinging sixties'. Jewison himself fondly calls it 'a crowd pleaser', a film that could morph into anything, but whose preferred form seemed to be a mildly hep, post-Doris Day thriller.* At worst, *Thomas Crown* was lovely to watch, thanks largely to Jewison's editor and photographer, as well as to the smoochy score by Michel Legrand. As for the plot, its director calls it a genre study of the 'love between two shits', the McQueen and Dunaway characters. But the more interesting relationship was that of Steve to Tommy Crown, the former skilfully giving the latter a world-weary humanity that renders moving what could otherwise be a parody. Imagine what, for instance, Marlon Brando would have made

---

* While a number of critics tried turning *Thomas Crown* into something heavy or even profound, McQueen's own take, as usual, was on the money: 'A lot of people are going to look for some real deep message there, but all it is is good entertainment. There are no moral messages about the Establishment or protests against the System. It's an audience participation film . . . escape.'

202

of the silent, erotic chess match between Crown and his pursuer.

McQueen's achievement was to make the character a uniquely demented individual, but also a very recognisable one. Instead of his stock role as the delinquent who always thought he'd be found out, Steve played his polar opposite – a mogul with a Nietzsche complex – and did it brilliantly. What seemed effortless on screen took unprecedentedly hard work. McQueen's graceful, cool, off-the-cuff mannerisms were rehearsed for weeks. The equestrianism, for example; although he'd ridden professionally for years, McQueen had never sat an English saddle. When he asked for advice, Jewison arranged for him to take lessons at the elite Myopia hunt club a mile or two north of Beverly Farms. 'You come down to location early. We'll get you a polo horse, you'll start in the morning and come back in time for dinner.' Steve proved more than willing. He learnt to ride all over again, using his knees not his arms, perfecting shots, training hour after hour, busting, if not his melon, then several other tender parts. McQueen literally worked his backside off for weeks, and became such a proficient player that the blue-blooded Myopia team gave him a standing ovation. He then learnt to fly a glider and play chess. Finally, McQueen perfected Crown's brisk, self-confident strut, his ability to turn a one-liner on a dime, and the 'suited taciturnity' that often broke Jewison's heart in his attempt to crack both the character's and the actor's moods. 'I can honestly say Steve was the most alone guy I ever worked with.'

McQueen was complex and scrupulous. Behind the scenes he tested, weighed, probed; he was the opposite of laid-back, doing everything necessary, literally whatever it took, for the character. Sometimes he was hot shit, sometimes just shit. With him, it changed by the hour.

Still, Jewison was pleased and proud to see how quickly he took to the part, and was convinced he hadn't made a mistake. As usual, Steve's underplaying was masterly: over the course of 102 minutes he would grin, leer, smirk, sneer, grin again and suddenly close down like the Method actor he once was. And all the time, the same quick-moving mouth hardly spoke. 'Tomorrow. Us. Dinner' – that counted as a soliloquy by his standards. 'Steve was the only actor I've ever taken lines away from who loved it,' says Jewison. That seemingly endless chess scene was played out without either character uttering a word.

The actual game (a replay of a Grand Masters' match in 1899 Vienna) was tediously symbolic sex as sport, just as *Tom Jones* had featured food for sex and, for that matter, *The Cincinnati Kid* a gunfight with cards. But Jewison's money shot was the Kiss, a lingering 'Suggested for Mature Audiences' snog protracted as though McQueen and Dunaway were sucking the life from each other. *Hot shit*, he said, loosening up more than he ever had. Steve would never again, in the eleven films remaining, achieve the same generous raunch quota as he did in those sixty seconds. Like his riding, McQueen's dexterous intimacy with his substar seemed part of a spontaneous, inevitable process. It was in fact due to a happy amalgam of frenzied rewriting, improvisation and Jewison's sympathetic talent; that and exhilarating, insightful acting. Throughout, McQueen's Crown was a vivid case of the self-indulgent – you feel his smugness as he carries off both flesh and fantasy. Morally, the character was a cypher. He and Dunaway circle each other in a quizzical dance; he seems genuinely amused by his weakness for his enemy, an unheard-of dimension for any McQueen film. As Jewison foresaw, Steve was trying for new depths in this, his seventeenth picture. By the end he'd been overtaken not by greed but by – of all things – a need for companionship. *The Thomas Crown Affair* was fashioned as a glitzy pop item but daringly, against type, McQueen single-handedly brought it the human factor. It was another triumph.

Released on 26 June 1968, *The Thomas Crown Affair* was a certified hit by August. It broke house records in LA, Boston and New York, $27,000 at the 86th Street Astor alone in just two days. Queues and ticket touting were everywhere. Long before Christmas it was one of the most talked about and successful movies in the world, eventually reaching down as far as Plains, Georgia, where the future President Carter saw it, rather worryingly, sixteen times.

According to Solar's books, *Thomas Crown* grossed $10,140,000 in a year and went on to top $13 million. After basic production costs of $6 million, Steve's 25 per cent of the action made him $1.75 million. No other film star now enjoyed the same kudos, freedom of choice, circle of disciples, influence and above all power he did.

Not surprisingly, *Thomas Crown* was one of McQueen's own favourite movies. He not only used the name as an alias but, in later years, tended to conduct business negotiations as if he were, in fact, his alter ego. 'He fell for it,' Jim Hoven confirms. Reciprocally, *The Thomas Crown Affair*, even more than *Love with the Proper Stranger*, converted him into a true matinee idol. With his sculptured suits (toned to his deep blue eyes) and newly bleached hair, Steve was now something not even Newman could trump: the 'sexiest male alive', according to the Belles of Memphis, a group of Southern society women. In being both mainstream and undeniably hip, McQueen was just the man for 1968.*

Merely arriving at *Thomas Crown*'s Boston premiere was a gala performance of its own. In early evening a black town car slowed to a stop in front of the Sack Music Hall and, suddenly, flashbulbs lit up the overcast sky and TV reporters with cameras in tow began to push through the crowd towards the action. 'Steve!' a woman screamed as he started out of the limo with Neile. 'Steve! Over here,' a reporter shouted. 'Tommy!' another yelled humorously, waving a microphone under his nose. Amid the orgy of upside down faces mouthing tributes through the windscreen, a teenage girl squeezed out a bare breast at McQueen and begged him to sign it. (He passed.) If Steve and his wife were overwhelmed by the jostling and the madness, they certainly didn't show it. In fact he laughed out loud when two cops assigned to the stage door physically prised him from the car and hoisted him onto their shoulders to get him through the mob and into the theatre.

For once in his life McQueen was at least precariously on top of the world, and seemed to be loving it.

★ ★ ★

* Just as Pierce Brosnan, undeniably suave but with the charisma of a watch fob, was the perfect choice for the 1999 remake. Comparing the two films was to prove easier than even McQueen's greatest fans could have imagined. Says the critic Barry Norman, 'The second, of course, was more obvious. Like most movies today, it was made for people with the concentration span of a gnat, by people with the concentration span of a gnat. The words subtlety and ambiguity aren't the ones that come to mind.'

Although Neile and men like Don Gordon say that the phenomenal success of *Crown* didn't affect Steve personally, he knew he was now king of the heap. He'd made seventeen films in just over a decade, the consummate actor's actor – McCool or plain God to his fans – who still enjoyed being someone else more than being himself. Nineteen sixty-eight was a – or the – high point in Steve's Horatio Alger, rags-to-riches trajectory, and suddenly the 'dorky' school dropout was a cottage industry. McQueen was in demand everywhere. When producers couldn't get to him or Stan Kamen personally, they gambled on virile, muscle-dude clones like Burt Reynolds, whose *Navajo Joe* was a blatant lift from *Nevada Smith*. *Smith* itself spun off a TV adaptation in November 1968 with a McQueen impersonator in the lead role. *Crown*'s receipts, meanwhile, soon surpassed those of any previous UA picture since *The Magnificent Seven*. No further proof was needed: not only had Steve succeeded as the 'sardonic, upper-class shit', he'd triumphed. He'd been right, and everybody else had been wrong. 'When you tell McQueen he can't do something,' Kamen would sigh after the premiere, 'he's going to bite your head off just to make a point.' As far back as he could remember, Steve had wanted to be the biggest, baddest star in Dodge. Now, thanks to a Boston banker, he was.

Fame soon became a more ceremonial business than he would have guessed. For now, he enjoyed it.

Solar's mission statement, at least in those days, followed down the same trail of 'hip conservatism' being blazed, half a world away, by the Beatles' Apple Corps. 'We think of our company as a family, and when it comes to production, we encourage everyone to contribute,' Steve said. 'Often a grip or a juicer will come to us with an idea, and all of us will sit down and discuss it. This isn't a normal attitude in the film industry.' Actually Steve's next and best movie, *Bullitt*, had its origins in something more conventional. It began because McQueen felt that periodic urge to both make money and meet a challenge, specifically that he couldn't play an authority figure. 'Steve,' Kamen remembered, 'loved being told what kind of picture not to make. "Stan," he told me when he read [*Bullitt*], "after that tight-ass Crown, why *not* a cop?"'

The source material was a novel called *Mute Witness*, a confused and confusing Mob yarn which Alan Trustman buffed into an accept-able script. Neile and Kamen himself both lobbied Steve to take the job which, crucially, now included a high-speed car chase. Bob Relyea had sat watching McQueen frowning at his desk.

'We'd been in Solar's nice, upholstered new office for four months, reading and turning down every script in town . . . One night Steve said quietly, with that brilliant instinct of his – instinct was always the key – "Let's do *Mute Witness*. Fuck it, it's really another kind of Western: instead of a gunbelt I'll be wearing a seatbelt, and the shootout is the chase scene." While I was pondering that I went over alone to meet Jack Warner. The dialogue actually did go like this:

'"We're gonna get off our ass at Solar and make a picture."

'"OK – what's the deal?"

'"It's called *Mute Witness* and the lead is a cop."

'"Why does Whatsisname want to play a cop?"

'"Because Whatsisname, who's the biggest box office star in the world, thinks he can do authority a different way."

'"How much?"

'"Four million bucks."

'"When?"

'"By Christmas."

'We shook hands, I drove back across town and went straight in to see Steve.

'"OK," I said. "*Now* we're pregnant."'

McQueen and Relyea quickly hired the Englishman Peter Yates, whose caper film *Robbery* was good enough to have rivalled *Thomas Crown*, to direct what became *Bullitt*. Steve personally vetted everybody to do with the movie. On his say-so, Robert Vaughn reappeared from *The Magnificent Seven* and Simon Oakland from *The Sand Pebbles*. Bud Ekins and Loren Janes returned to do stunts. There was a cameo for Bob Duvall. McQueen's female co-star, or substar, was twenty-three-year-old Jacqueline Bisset, who forgot her antagonism with Steve just long enough to fall into bed with him. McQueen himself appeared on location in San Francisco without Hong's pet rat but with his old friend Don Gordon and their for-bidden bikes.

'Steve never admitted he got me into that part. But I know damn well he did. That was typical of the guy . . . McQueen had a very tender, sweet side to him that came out if he trusted you. Trust was his biggest thing. Very important with Steve. I never met anyone straighter or more real than he was.'

The hardened technicians at the San Francisco city morgue had much the same reaction when, prior to shooting *Bullitt*, they invited McQueen along to watch a particularly grisly autopsy of a homicide victim. No problem, he said. Throughout the procedure Steve stood casually munching an apple. Then he spent that same night happily bouncing around for eight hours in a police cruiser. By the time he was dropped off at his hotel, the transformation was complete. McQueen was no longer a candyass actor who liked to play cops and robbers; he was Frank Bullitt – tough, together, a man on the move.

Steve's eyes twinkled with mirth and firmness. Now he was the honcho around here.

The self-contained world of the film as a whole seemed afire with violence and energy those first few weeks. Steve spent much of his off-duty time, particularly in pre-production while Neile stayed home in Brentwood, roaming about goggle-eyed in a state of priapic excitement. He was appropriately awed by both Bisset and the harem attentiveness of local groupies for whom sleeping with McQueen, whether individually or, it was whispered, in bulk, became a kind of contest. As usual, his total lack of orthodox faithfulness took a predictable form. There were literally dozens of casual pick-ups padding out the time between takes. Later, as dusk fell, after a final battleground conference with Relyea and Yates, Steve would lope off with Don Gordon for a wolfed-down meal and a late-night run on their banned Triumphs. The old friends rode fast up and down the San Francisco streets, or sometimes as far afield as the San Mateo foothills. They honked around there in the rocks and dirt. Once or twice Steve pulled over to swig a beer, look over the city lights, then almost instantly relieve himself. Nobody pissed down from a greater height than he did. But nobody could be better, cooler and more alert than him, either. Nobody.

Don Gordon remembers one particular night when 'Steve bounced off a slope and literally became airborne, then landed again at top speed and carried on to do the same thing again on the next hill.'

First thing in the morning McQueen told Yates he had a great new idea for *Bullitt*'s car chase, and that this time around, he was going to 'do it all myself'.

Not, as it happened, his only asphalt ambitions that spring. On 7 March 1968 Jack Warner formally green-lighted *Le Mans*, with the proviso that it be directed by the same man as *Bullitt*. Actually the film went back into turnaround, the local equivalent of a coma, for a further two years, and would then be made by Lee Katzin, not Sturges or Yates. If the actual shoot was still hazy, the project was now, at least, viable, and sustained Steve through some dark times. (Nor did the money hurt: McQueen's basic fee for *Le Mans* would be $750,000, plus $46,875 a week overtime.) That same month Solar agreed to film a *Life* magazine story called *Man on a Nylon String*, a prototype of the kind of vertiginous romp scaled by Clint Eastwood in *The Eiger Sanction*. For the next year it moved lethargically through development and various scripts on a pre-planned schedule until Steve was available. By the time he was, Warner himself had sold out, the studio had changed hands, and Solar's six-picture contract was torn up. McQueen told Jim Hoven he didn't give a fuck about not going rock-climbing. After *Bullitt*, he added, his phone now rang itself off the hook.

Thus mandated, as he saw it, Steve, says Hoven, 'began to go quietly mad for about a year, at which point he went crazy'. After his spring spent mingling at Bay Area happenings and the herbally scented 'head' shops of Haight-Ashbury, McQueen still retained the glacial cool so characteristic of Hollywood's elite, but with a contemporary edge, both hip and humanising, that marked his singular contribution to Tinseltown and the world's notion of celebrity glitz. Some of his dowdyism was now part-exchanged for dandyism. As well as his trademark roll-neck, Steve sported a collection of fashion rings, bracelets, breathtakingly tight trousers, and shirts, beneath which medallions gleamed and clanked, whose sail-like collars extended earthwards to his nipples. He experimented with incense and joss-sticks. His hair grew frizzily over his ears. When he attended Harry Mirisch's funeral later that year, Sam Goldwyn didn't even recognise McQueen. Jack Warner, for his part, could never decide whether Steve's 'difficultness' ('*Fuck you*' read his tart reply to a formal letter forbidding him to ride his bike on *Bullitt*) was responsible for his new look, or whether it was to dramatise the look that he turned bolshie. Probably the former, the studio boss eventually guessed. A certain bloody-mindedness, after all, had been detectable from the off.

By the time he freaked out around 1968–9, Steve had joined a small fraternity of individuals, including Fuckwit and Sean Connery, who were objects of special attention for some of Hollywood's most powerful actresses. As McQueen told a biking friend, Don Modi: 'Look, a certain type of broad goes to a movie and there's this guy on the screen – it's like seeing a rock at Tiffany's. It's seductive, it's *meant* to be seductive. There's a helluva lot of sex to showbiz. Those women are like men. They go after what they want. It's like I'm the chick. Can you dig it? I'm being chased around town by *them*.' One of these predators was the forty-six-year-old Ava Gardner. There were others, closer to his own age, or younger, all of them an outlet for McQueen's astral sex drive. As one of his Whisky friends relates, 'I'd sit in a chair sometimes and talk to Steve while he was giving it to some snatch. I'd watch TV and sit in a chair, because he wanted somebody to talk to . . . Two, three women at a time. He'd be fucking one, rubbing up another, and we'd be calmly laughing and chatting to each other.' What depressed and surprised McQueen's friends more than the promiscuity was how little happiness it seemed to bring him. As his own daughter put it a few years later, 'My dad hated all women but me.'

One morning, two or three days in, a local model hired to speak a few lines in *Bullitt* suddenly left the set, handing Steve her resignation and smacking him hard across the cheek with it. 'That's what you got comin'. Mess with *me*, mister.'

He watched her, quite calmly, trot into the distance.

'You know,' McQueen said, 'this is a lousy job. You got to sit and tell some dope how she's a great actress, and at the same time you got to keep from being raped.'

One of his male colleagues whistled. 'You mean to say she's a nympho?'

Steve lit a cigarette, sighed and said slowly, 'I guess she would be, man, if she just cooled down a little.'

If it sounds as though McQueen was going a little crazy himself, that's because he was. And it's not unconnected to that reason that he was a great actor.

Bud Ekins, who did some of the stunt driving on *Bullitt*, thought Steve an 'upright, let's say totally loyal guy – always provided he trusted you – who got a bit cranky around [1969] . . . He did too much beer and cocaine.' It was about then, too, that McQueen first began to suffer memory lapses, causing him to freeze once or twice in front of the camera. One afternoon he couldn't recall the simple line, 'He's dead,' or even the title *Bullitt*. 'Holy shit!' he told Yates. He had to give up drinking. He thought of that old principle with which he used to chide Julian, that a lush is never more than one swig from disaster. And then he came up with what he thought was the equivalent of Einstein discovering his theory of relativity: a lush was also never more than one swig from salvation. Instead of stopping for ever and a day, he'd just skip the next drink.

'I think it's wrong for people to be zonked all the time.'

And Steve stood where, exactly, on the broader issues?

Several places, and nowhere in particular, at once. By 1970 the rich, fit, alcoholic pin-up of blue-collar legend also performed a neat balancing act politically. McQueen had a lifelong fear, almost a phobia, of joining things. Particularly causes. For twenty years he stayed well clear of the star system pieties of a man like Newman. According to Bob Relyea, 'He didn't want to sign up for anyone's crusade. Never. Never. Steve's instant reply was always to tell 'em to go march without him.' Because of the way he was brought up, he felt no liberal guilt. According to his FBI file, McQueen had been 'one of a number of Hollywood notables who indicated he intended to participate in the March on DC [in support of Martin Luther King] in August 1963'. Though the mere rumour landed him in the Bureau's black book, he never actually turned up in Washington, nor joined the 'Hollywood for Kennedy' bandwagon four and a half years later. Steve was, if anything, a 'good conservative', whose moral protests were more personal, rather than of the pristine ideological left. He wasn't partisan. There was little political, still less pc about McQueen. One night at Warner's mansion he'd snarled out, 'I thought we were gonna have dinner,' when caviare was first handed round, muttering, 'It's like Biafra,' when later queuing for the buffet. In so far as Steve had an ethical centre it was, like Jefferson's, 'life, liberty and the pursuit of happiness'. He was interested in pushing goals, not agendas. He didn't vote. 'As far as the System goes,' McQueen announced in August 1968, 'I think the one we've got here is about the best one going.'

At the core of Steve's value system there wasn't so much a thesis as a temperament. Essentially, it was the same as his 'fuck you' policy towards the likes of Warner: he wanted hustle, speed, maximum revs, total freedom, anything to convey a sense of self-will and nonconformity. For McQueen, illumination went with tough-mindedness and the oppressed found truth through hard graft. Behind this train of thought lay a broad streak of Toryism, even Thatcherism, but it directed his compassion on to those he saw as fellow-travellers. Later in the seventies he'd mail an annual cheque to an underprivileged school in Nakuru, Kenya, after reading about it in the *LA Times*. In return the schoolchildren thanked McQueen by sending him a special remembrance, delivered on or around his birthday. It was a home-made wooden box, a square crate, knee-high, fashioned from rough boards. Everything inside was densely layered, as if for the afterlife. On top sat hand-drawn greetings cards showing him in character as Hilts or Tommy Crown. Nestling underneath were clay artefacts such as ashtrays, baked in the school's kiln and painted with more film scenes. In the corners there were wampum beads, trinkets with a tooled religious motif and, once or twice, a rosary.

Sometimes all it took were the crude THANK U STEVE headlines on the cards. 'He'd just choke up, just quietly,' Hoven remembers.

McQueen didn't exaggerate his personal conservatism; he was defiantly old school. Among his core values remained patriotism, integrity, personal responsibility. Self-help. He could be, and was, quietly generous. For the most part, however, Steve's views on money, and specifically on giving it away, were violently non-hippie. To thank the mayor of San Francisco for helping with street closures during the filming of *Bullitt*, for instance, McQueen agreed to hire 300 local kids to work as extras, and later donated an Olympic-sized swimming pool to the mainly black Hunter's Point neighbourhood. There's no evidence that either gesture cost him, or his company, a penny. All Steve's gifts and overruns were squeezed into the budget, duly upping it from $4 million to $5 million, that Warners signed off on. When the studio subsequently pulled the plug on the six-movie deal, McQueen told them to go fuck themselves. Fuck the big contract. Fuck the ass-kissing and the brown-nosing. Fuck all that. He'd make a film out of a fucking William Faulkner story, and still the crowds would come.

They actually did, too.

Nevertheless, Steve enjoyed shooting *Bullitt*, the gifted but temperamental kid left in charge while grown-ups were away, and was even more desolate when filming ended. Early every morning he'd become one of the crowd that gathered around the Solar trailers mapping out the day's work. In a sudden shift on *Action!*, he'd plunge again and again up the city streets in his green GT Mustang – now fitted out, for the beating, with heavy-duty shocks and springs, as well as yet more asbestos lining – flinging it downhill at 100 m.p.h., then into traffic, overcooking, panic braking, sometimes uttering exultant cries as Yates crouched in the back seat rolling a hand-held camera.* Steve would spend all day, for two weeks, perfecting that seven-minute scene. Then, at night, he'd cut to the chase with Don Gordon. McQueen had his own apartment in San Francisco, complete with a pool table, telescope and an outsize bed. Altogether, he said, not a bad bunch of fruit and nuts. Later still he'd pace restlessly through the dark rooms, a mute presence, with some new piece of ass there cooing for him, and thirsting to be on the move again, not least to piss off the studio. And with a final scene scripted of Bullitt ducking behind the fanjets of a giant 707 on takeoff it was inevitable that Steve would again tell the Warners safety man to go fuck himself. He did most of the plane stunt all on his own, too.

One morning, Bob Relyea remembers, a 'wild-looking guy in combat fatigues, muttering, bust loose in a crowd scene and started making trouble, scaring the shit out of the security people.'

---

* McQueen, Bud Ekins and the stuntman Carrie Lofton took turns driving the Mustang down the San Francisco hills, several of which, to make it more interesting, remained open to the public.

213

Everything seemed set fair for a confrontation, possibly even gunplay, until McQueen 'glanced over and casually said, "Hey, lemme talk to him," took the guy into his trailer and in two minutes flat calmed him down . . . He had a lot of good qualities like that. Steve understood real people, particularly kids, like nobody else. He had incredible street smarts. It was just the Hollywood brass he loathed.' Particularly the new head of Warners, one Ken Hyman. McQueen physically evicted Hyman, or any of Hyman's people, whenever they showed up on set. Steve flogged himself hard, demanded the best of his crew, and didn't need any loon-panted moguls telling him his business. Warners, for their part, were convinced that *Bullitt* would be an undisciplined, runaway flop.

This wasn't so far off the beam. McQueen was actually the consummate pro once on set, but you could see how the suits might have had their doubts. Part of the problem, for Hyman, anyway, was connected to Steve's love of movement. In a hammock, he was always rocking to and fro; walking, he loped ahead of the pack; on wheels, he left even Don Gordon in the dust; in conversation, he flitted constantly; he was an inveterate twitcher. Above all, he hated to sit down to meetings. Then there was the fact that, as Norman Jewison says, 'quite sane people seriously thought Steve was a warlock. Every full moon, he'd take off on a bike into the desert or go nuts somehow. When McQueen's friends knew a full moon was coming, we'd go a little crazy ourselves. "Shit! What's he going to pull this time?"' Jim Hoven remembers one night, on *Bullitt*, when 'Steve told me he rode off into the San Mateos, made a camp fire, stripped buck naked, threw an old Navajo blanket around himself and smoked dope until the sun came up.' Not the sort of rehearsal scene likely to endear itself to the average studio head.

McQueen, true enough, shunned the kiss-ass inanity and witless shmoozing of most stars. He didn't, however, completely steer clear of the lifestyle. 'Steve,' as Hoven says, 'was as solid as the Missouri hills.' But not quite as green.

The Olympic screwing went on, in his apartment or an anonymous suite at the Huntington Hotel, for at least the first half of the *Bullitt* shoot. 'Call me', the messages on his machine always said. I'll be waiting. Dreaming sweet dreams. *Call me*. The debris of discarded clothes, cigarette butts and daubed phone numbers on the wall was everywhere in that flat. Even Steve's bedroom mirror was cracked, bad evidence of the day – his birthday – Neile had found an unfamiliar woman's hairbrush on the dresser and had gone, he said ruefully, nutso. McQueen's omnisexual days, when he'd soul-kissed James Dean and hustled around New York, were long since over. Even at that sorry pass, he'd never been out and out gay, just voraciously greedy. Whereas then he'd attended bisexual orgies, at least one of them, in the Gramercy Park Hotel, surreptitiously taped by the FBI, nowadays collectivism tended to be in the form of a medieval court and protocol system; the consort usually, though not always, turning a blind eye to the stream of models, starlets and, at worst, 'tail' all dancing around the king, two or three of them on the trot. Low-life pleasures, of course, had been in McQueen's game plan for thirty years. But the posterior yen somehow still jarred in the would-be dispenser of sanity and truth to an industry maddened by crass 'shit'. Steve was a bottom man. At least a man newly appreciative of a woman, fore and aft. 'He loved a nicely shaped ass on a girl – called 'em "bubble asses",' said Elmer Valentine. If he wanted to combine that with a mission of pure American art, he would.

Clearly, things were spiralling out of control.

More accurately, spiralling down on a flood of beer and cocaine, Steve's daily fuel along with the pot, acid and plethoric fuck-flings. He was still going strong but he was thirty-eight, and at the bottom of the day, after cooking it for hours in the Mustang, he looked it. 'Running out of gas,' McQueen sometimes mumbled. 'I'm fucking running out of gas.'

Yates and the crew would smile at him around the trailer. One of the drivers would bring up the car and hold open the door for him. Steve McQueen would sigh deeply. And then once again the strapped muscle would be pumping hard on the juice.

'*Turning!*'

Then there was nothing candyass or uptight, just heat and speed and a rushing wind as Steve barrelled downhill.

Surrounded always by groupies, McQueen would nonetheless tell several of them he felt alone, emotionally bereft. Depression had dogged him from the off, and he sidestepped it only by becoming different people. Just as he'd once swung every which way sexually, now the pendulum went to and fro in the way he acted and spoke. McQueen was the Hollywood god who'd take a tray and stand in line for food with the rest of the crew; the hippie icon who demanded total punctuality and professionalism on set; the strait-laced Mid-westerner who could, after the second beer, be cheerfully crude in male company, telling them one particular girl had a 'cooze like the Holland Tunnel'. There were at least three warring characters making up the McQueenly trio, each pulling violently in a different direction from the others. The first Steve was a family man and good friend, the second a virtual psychopath, and the third a serious and ambitious professional. On set, he who wasn't with the third Steve was against him, including the first and second Steve. Probably only Don Gordon ever fully got to know all the sub-personalities, though McQueen's wife – saintly in just about every account – and martial arts guru saw more than most. Neile and Bruce Lee both visited him towards the end of *Bullitt*.

Steve was a realist – 'There is violence in the streets and I don't think we should hide it,' he said – and always or usually self-aware. In a trade bloated with vulnerable limelight addicts, flitting between ecstatic fame and private clinics, he was a hardworking, sane, if hard-nosed Indianan; the one who'd grown but not swelled. As a rule, too, McQueen had more time for humanity than for individual humans. He was much better at dealing with people as groups, audiences and statistics. Bob Relyea confirms that 'Steve liked you to keep your distance from him, as he did from you.' It's true that literally hundreds of the crew and extras on *Bullitt* would speak of McQueen's very real charm and charisma. They were right to. But if anyone leaned on him as an emotional prop, they made a serious blunder. What Relyea and the rest really got wasn't friendship, but friendliness.

He had an ego. Neile clearly remembers 'the morning after he won a World Film Favorite award, Steve announced himself on the phone as "The biggest guy in Hollywood" – and meant it.' Similarly, McQueen often referred, quite straight-faced, to his alter ego Supie. In later years he liked to stand staring up at the mural of himself painted on the side of a building on Union Avenue in downtown LA. Above all, Steve wasn't so much vain as hypersensitive to the slightest drop in his personal Dow-Jones. Beyond the limited scope of his screen image he was 'almost unbelievably touchy', as even Sebring put it. 'McQueen sizzled like a lit firework.' When a reporter quite innocently stopped off to speak to Robert Vaughn before interviewing Steve one morning in San Francisco, he went berserk. McQueen stormed back to his apartment, splenetic, though not incoherent, with rage. 'Judas!' he shouted. And 'Ben Arnold!' One of the flunkies rolled him a joint while McQueen cried and threw bundles of clothes into the street.

Men like Relyea, Yates and Bud Ekins never underestimated his paranoia. According to Don Gordon, 'Steve changed his home phone number more often than I change my socks.' He only ever opened up to, at most, half a dozen trusted characters. Beneath them, the gofers, groupies and dirt-bikers dutifully rounded out the clan, one that made Sinatra's look like the Algonquin set. This same trend would still be painfully obvious, nearly ten years later, to his second wife. 'If Steve had one glaring defect it was that he needed to have the approval of his small group of "yes men", people who worshipped him . . . In a room of men who were his equals, though not necessarily in his field, he was incredibly insecure.' McQueen told one of the cast on *Bullitt*, ' "Bootlickers – that's what I want" . . . He was just out of the loop. Steve only really tuned in to one or two old cronies, Neile, his kids. They got it all.'

You're proud of me, he asked them, *aren't you?*

Late one night at the Castle McQueen woke up to the noise of someone jemmying open his front door. Incredibly, a prowler by the name of Alfred Pucci had eluded the presidential-level security, shinned up the electric gate, crunched over the moonlit gravel drive and evaded the cameras and guard dogs, all, as he later told police, in a demented search for 'refuge and peace of mind . . . I'm a pretty good judge of character and thought this guy would understand me, as I have seen many of his movies.' Steve's response to this left-field endorsement was electric. He seized his 9mm Mauser, put it in Pucci's ear and offered to blow his brains all over Brentwood. After that there was a loss of interest in refuge or in Pucci's prolonging his stay in the Castle. Don Gordon remembers, 'McQueen told the guy, "Hold still while I call the cops, or I'll fucking kill you." He would've done it, too. Nobody screwed with Steve's family. Never. Never. Never. My sense is that he was really wonderful with his kids. With Neile too, after his fashion.'

The McQueens' back bedroom was breathlessly hot, even at night. However, it was the only room in its wing with a big enough window on the outside; Steve could shut the door to the balcony over the patio where the cruiser had just taken Pucci away, and where by day the help invariably gathered for their work and their gab. He lay awake for hours after that, listening to the barking of dogs in the canyon road below. The main object of contemplation was stardom. Apparently yet more shit, better grade perhaps but no less putrid, went with it. The brass ring. McQueen was already used to the autograph hounds and dumpster-dippers, human scavengers who rooted through his trash, those lunatic entrepreneurs. But this bastard. Jesus! His thin lips seemed to move. *Adios*, he whispered to himself. He lay there trembling, like the fucking Blob, wondering why, after ten-something years of busting his hump, he was still killing himself for nuts like Pucci; wondering why the fuck he bothered taking it up the ass from the studio when he already had plenty in the bank; wondering where the fuck it would all end.

Once again, speed triumphed over paralysis. Early the next morning Steve fired up his Harley and headed off into the hills. He felt wonderfully light and powerful as he manoeuvred the machine with his knees to the centre of the dirt road. There was a small cliff up there, about sixty feet high. When McQueen got to the edge he stood looking down at Brentwood, the red and white roofs mostly hidden behind trees, smoothing his forehead a few times and then squinting into the rising sun, directly above the Hollywood sign. He laughed himself dizzy when he saw that, making a strange animal sound from deep within. Then McQueen rode back into town at top speed.

Back in the Ferrari, those days, he took it fast and hard, using the straight-arm style on the wheel, braced against his seat, now soaring over the brow of a hill, then snapping the brake pedal to the floor, shedding rocks and garbage in his wake. 'Steve trounced me in a race up one of those canyon roads,' says Gordon. ' "You've got a better car," I told him. McQueen's response was to silently get out and hold open his driver's side door for me. Then he got in my car and we raced the same track . . . Needless to say, Steve whipped my ass all over again.' As ever, he only came fully alive purling around the backstreets where McQueen, like Bullitt, could be both silent and totally in control. He not only trusted in the physical laws of momentum – unlike those governing most human relationships – but, it was quickly apparent, understood them too. In December 1969 Steve even designed his own race-car accessory (a moulded Baja Bucket seat, patent number 219,584, for gourmets of such detail). Especially when the likes of Pucci came calling, McQueen found it quite easy and agreeable to tear off at speed, until whatever it was chasing him faded into black.

Me first, everybody else nowhere.

Most of the hacks Foster brought him now treated McQueen like a composite Stirling Moss and channelled James Dean. More was to come: his rebirth as a biker icon, giddily vertical on dirt or cinder where most of his celluloid self was glumly horizontal. This culminated in 1972 in an entire book on the subject by one Bill Nolan, which gave the impression that Steve's whole life took wing in 'race tuned production models . . . and dune buggies, modified jeeps, formula machines, brutal desert specials and on all types of competition cycles'. Sir Stirling himself says that 'McQueen was good, sure enough, but there's a big difference between being good and being a professional.' Bud Ekins adds that 'Steve rode like a bat out of hell, always cornering too fast and hitting things . . . Someone like Don Gordon might be slower, but he'd get there.'

What mattered more, McQueen loved his machines, the way they sounded and smelt and responded to his touch, almost to the point of fixation. Not quite erotomania, but rather more than most weekend warriors would own up to, unless they were a touch obsessed. Steve was on turf far beyond that.

'Man, *there's* a thing of beauty,' he told Biff McGuire one morning when they were shooting *Thomas Crown*, staring intently out the window onto a busy street. 'He was sort of gazing down, bug-eyed, and licking his chops. McQueen seemed to be having a vision, I assumed of some nubile girl – which would have been in character.

It really was like he was suddenly in the grip of a full-blown fantasy.'
It took another moment or two for McGuire to join McQueen at the
window and identify the object of his desire, a red Lamborghini.

'I'd love to take *her* up to speed,' Steve said. 'Wouldn't it be great
if a chick could perform like that?'

For him, the great thing was the immediacy – just the turn of a
key, a small commitment that seemed such a minor deal, and yet
the result was so sudden and thunderous: the first belch of smoke,
the quick rush and fading rasp of the ignition, the roaring busyness
of the throttle that spluttered and caught and sent Mike, the family
dog, scurrying for his basket. It all took a split second. The average
film, by contrast, Steve always said, was like 'throwing a rock at a
window and waiting a year for it to hit'. No wonder he kept rolling
back the date he promised Neile he'd finally quit racing. By now
McQueen had a small stable of corsairs and the kind of modified
jeeps he'd driven in *Crown*, and still entered various bike events. In
1969's *Easy Rider* it seemed that Hollywood, finally, was catching
up with him. But Steve was fucked if he was ever going to cruise
with those tattoo-and-gold-tooth types, 'the high-handlebar guys in
leather jackets with spit flying out of their mouths and I FLIRT WITH
DEATH on their backs – you know, the skull-and-crossbones crowd'.
Just to emphasise the difference between the cartoon cut-outs of the
Hell's Angels and himself, McQueen painted one of his Triumphs
with the slogan THE MILD ONE.

Springtime in northern California: on speedways the Nortons and
Hornets were revving up, as cocky as mosquitoes, racing along
sand washes at 70 or 80 m.p.h. with no apparent effort. Out on
location, as principal photography finally wound down, McQueen
was working a similar startling sleight of hand on a spellbound crew.
In *Bullitt* the same sense of *sangue* – apparently not giving a fuck –
was elevated to an art form which was both the subject and the object
of Steve's act. Privately, he was out of sympathy with the popular
culture that, in his view, was too laid-back. The well-oiled tag
team of Neile and William Morris would keep the first-refusal scripts
and offers ticking over for years to come. By 1969 McQueen's support system included not only his agency and production company
but half a dozen rabidly loyal gofers, like Betsy Cox and one Mario

Iscovich. Nowadays Steve rose early (albeit more slowly than the Sun King) and kept up a steady flow of directions, wisecracks and asides, as well as esoteric stuff about lighting and camera angles, from dawn to dusk seven days a week. Little or nothing was left to risk. Anyone thinking that McQueen's fame was an accident, a kind of listless fluke – or that he met even Yates on equal terms – should have seen him pacing the San Francisco streets, bullhorn in hand, lips pursed, scowling, having his finicky, almost algebraic way with the form of the film. By the time everyone went home he'd managed to make dynamic and suggestive a script that consisted of a farcical cop yarn. As his producer says, what's usually understood as Steve's 'touch' is almost always better understood as his sheer, bloody-minded professionalism.

Anything could happen when he was on form. McQueen had it all, the talent, the charm *and* the mean calculation. There were other stars in whom two of these were evident but no one else in whom all three applied, and applied simultaneously. Soon even the technicians were showing up at the trailer to conduct serious Q & A sessions with him about lenses and turrets, while the book-keeper would regularly stop by with sheaves of bills for him to sign.

McQueen as an actor, that miraculous tool for making a little go far, was equally well organised. 'I never worked with anyone so disarmingly aware of himself,' says Bob Wise. 'A lot of big names will tell you they can handle anything. With Steve it was just the opposite. He knew he had a certain range, deep if not very wide, and that was it. Outside that, he'd ask for script revisions, almost always involving less lines. Inside it, he was brilliant.' According to Don Gordon, 'He bust his ass on *Bullitt*. The hell with him being a movie star, he was an *actor*.' In this sense, too, McQueen made the difficult look absurdly easy. Amidst all the film's gut-wrenching stunts and risible plot, his stillness and command stood out.

They went up to the airport, fifteen or twenty of them, one raw spring morning before dawn. The crew got out and quickly dispersed in different directions, smelling the jet effluent. The place was very quiet. A lone 707 was ready to roll at the end of the runway. A few silent extras milled around the terminal or out on the apron, jumping up and down, half from cold, half with anticipation. Yates and the camera crew quickly set up camp, the lights of which, a kleig pro-fusion, flashed twice for '*Action*'. On cue McQueen sprinted directly towards the plane as it gathered speed, at the last second ducked, kissed the wet tarmac, took a blast of 250-degree heat, calmly rolled and continued his end-run out of shot. '*Cut*,' yelled Yates. He ran up to Steve, awed by the hush that enveloped the crew and – he knew better than to risk a hug – shook him by the hand.

It was ever thus on *Bullitt*. Like its director, most who saw the film would long remember McQueen's stunts, his physicality – how he bundled up Bullitt's whole character and flung it on screen – both underplaying and yet pouring so much into it that he made drama of potential dross. Steve's twinned art and craft brought deservedly warm reviews and the biggest pay cheque of his career to date.

And what he suddenly concluded from it was that he didn't want to, or have to, take any more shit from anyone – which is exactly what happened.

In film after McQueen film the PR people had coined phrases like 'lonely odyssey' and 'searing hell', which made some of them sound more cheery and upbeat than they actually were. Steve, for his part, unceremoniously plunged audiences into a torrent of character and event. In *Bullitt* everything now went up a gear. The acting combined the qualities of the ritual and the thriller. McQueen balanced plausi-bility against the yawning gaps of the plot. Long before those heroics at the airport, Bullitt had become as familiar, if endearingly flawed, as Steve himself. Hoven says, 'He played the part from deep, deep inside. You just can't fake that stuff on people.' Neile, too, remem-bers that her husband 'had all this turmoil churning in his head. Steve always wanted to do right, but he had kind of a mean streak. That conflict translated brilliantly onto film,' particularly *Bullitt*. For three months, and weeks later in the editing, McQueen gave the character everything he had. Pumped up on the steroidal effects of box office points and bonus schemes, as well as on old-fashioned dedication, Steve forged a performance that, even by his standards, was graphically right. He customised it.

McQueen did a good job of personifying macho snake-handling, crashing cars, shrugging and dodging jets. But the very last scene, where he stared himself down in a mirror, then turned away, spent, like Cooper in *High Noon*, showed *Bullitt*'s true sense of conceptual bottle. That shot both stuck to the formula needed to re-moisten hankies still damp from the climax (similarly ambiguous) of *Crown*, and brought Yates and the crew back to their feet once more. It took some time for the applause to die down. It was a simple but brilliant ruse, the 'point of view' camera again securing the all-important audience identification by putting them not only in the room, but inside Bullitt's head. 'That's a motherfucker,' Steve shyly confirmed. And there, a month late and a million dollars over a Warners-imposed budget, it all ended.

Bullitt went public on 17 October 1968 and quickly became a way of life. Within weeks it ceased being a film at all and floated instead into the cultural stratosphere, trading on level terms with that winter's other Events – kaftans, safari jackets, Warhol, race riots and the portly, weighted tread of the Beatles' *White Album*. McQueen now had to accommodate the fact that he was one of the most widely recognised faces, and names, on the planet. No small accolade for a man who still insisted, 'I eat loneliness,' with only two or three longtime cronies, and, says one of them, 'shit in the way of friends'.

The actual movie was that weird mix of fantasy and realism, Steve bringing off the feat of staying astride it throughout its nonstop mood swings. Everything he did in it implicated the viewer. *Bullitt*'s first and last scenes were among its very best, the one echoing McQueen's taut arrival in *The War Lover*, the other a timely link between the what's-it-all-about dissolves of *High Noon* and Clint's *Magnum Force* (a film Steve could have had for his own). In the opening shot he looked fresh and young. At the close, though notionally only a few days older, McQueen was razzled and wormeaten. Heavy make-up played no part in his scheme of things; the before and after Bullitt set the film in a neat frame. But understanding much of the 100 minutes of crossword clues in between was beyond most people. Jacqueline Bisset, for one, played an architect with no apparent design skills or even numeracy, neither British nor American, and somewhere in the no man's land between Bullitt's wife, fiancée and girl-friend, a role never spelt out for the audience. And she was the rock-solid one of the bunch. The Mob characters, for their part, would periodically appear, impose a few grunts on the scene and leave again, half baked and yet not ambiguous enough to be interesting, let alone tragic figures. *Bullitt* was a good film of a bad book, at best nicely unpredictable, at worst almost embarrassingly revealing of its fudged script problems.

The bigger problem of 'doing authority differently', meanwhile, the punch-line of Solar's pitch to Jack Warner, was handled with dispatch by the man who, ten years earlier, had done much the same in *Wanted Dead or Alive*. Nor was portraying a cop that big a stretch for an actor who'd just pulled off *The Thomas Crown Affair*. Steve succeeded in *Bullitt* because he played him as a man, not a mere action dude. In one neatly improvised scene McQueen as Bullitt tries to buy a paper from a vending machine, can't find the right change – typical of Steve not to invest a penny more – looks about shiftily, visibly embarrassed, and prises one out. It was a funny moment, and had the added advantage of being human. This film of a thousand twists and turns offered no greater thrill than those little larks, and no better key with which to both unlock Bullitt's off-centre charm and enjoy McQueen's intuitive genius. The vital, rather than technical intelligence of the picture was what stood out. Above all, McQueen made a connection between manner and matter. Bullitt, like Steve himself, could and did convey whole speeches by a mere look, his power of suggestiveness and menace. Even with a source text as murky as *Mute Witness*, vivid touches could be fished from the narrative mud. As Bob Relyea says, 'McQueen always felt that he, his virility and body language, were better than dialogue. And he was right.' But the set of Steve's mouth or flick of his eyebrow weren't the only things that kept *Bullitt* afloat: there was also, for example, the way he relaxed his ban on ad-libbing, doing a long take opposite Gordon with no script or even rehearsal, and improvising most of the romantic interludes with Bisset. Those one-on-one scenes were buttressed, instead, with all Steve's support systems of irony, scepticism – especially with the sex – paranoia, competence, and, all in all, a lovingly harsh attitude to life. A walking labyrinth of contradiction and self-division, wild, earnest, tense but passive, a tough man on the prowl, yet still adrift in a childhood pool of wonder and bemusement. The two McQueens located two moral realities within one character. Although Bullitt seemed to be a man in a hurry, he was just as famous for his long silences, when his body and face froze and his mind seemed busy elsewhere. But he'd also be silent when staring down an adversary, deciding whether or not to murderously bust his melon. That was why the audience never took their eyes off him.

By now, Steve's disillusionment with scripts and the inky trade generally was complete and absolute. 'Face it,' he wrote Bruce Lee, 'it's impossible to train writers. Janitors, sure, or camera men, or chimps. Each of them has some idea of the Big Picture. But writers . . . are idiots and not only turn on each other at any moment, but fuck up the movie. Who needs 'em?' *Bullitt*'s two most famous sequences, the car chase and the stunt at the airport, were both played out without McQueen speaking a word.*

Bullitt's disastrous success changed both the course of Hollywood history and Steve's life. On a popular and critical level, everything now went overboard. Financially, too: eighteen months post-release, the film had turned $24,950,447 in gross receipts, with a final production cost of $5,435,303, making Solar's 42.5 per cent of the action worth $8.3 million. As well as the money, McQueen walked

---

* For the mechanically minded, the two cars involved in the high-pursuit scene were McQueen's modified 390 GT Mustang, and a 440 Magnum Dodge Charger driven by 'Wild Bill' Hickman, a stunt professional who'd been following James Dean when Dean crashed to his death, and who went on to stage the chase sequence in *The French Connection*. PhD theses have been written on the implausibilities and mad geography of *Bullitt*'s own chase, which began more or less at Enrico's, a nightspot on San Francisco's Broadway, wove a loop through the Marina district, took an improbable lurch down Lombard Street and suddenly re-emerged five miles further south, near McLaren Park, before heading on to the James Lick freeway. The recurrence of the mysterious green Volkswagen (driven by one of Carrie Lofton's stunt team), Steve's restless gear-changing and the unfeasibly large number of hubcaps bouncing about all excite film buffs to this day. McQueen completists will know that he did most of his own driving except for the hill-jumping on and around Chestnut Street (doubled, at Neile's insistence, by Bud Ekins, also seen taking a skidding dive off a motorbike into the Mustang's path), and the final side-swiping climax handled by Lofton. The subsequent fiery crash of Hickman's Dodge into a gas station was slightly mistimed. It's only fair to add, too, that Loren Janes stood in for Steve for some of the airport sequence, including the running scene Yates finally used, though the shot of McQueen lying under the screaming fanjets, and the burn marks to his neck, were real enough. ('Couldn't we have used a dummy?' one of the awed crew had asked. 'We just did,' Steve told him.) Nit-picking aside, *Bullitt*'s main action set pieces quite deservedly became cult classics. Both delicately conceived but fearless stunts remain among the hottest yet, in the McQueenly sense, coolest ever committed to film. Together, they're Steve's most sustained piece of heroics.

225

off with a hatful of *Film Daily* and *Boxoffice* awards, won a Golden Globe and was named Star of the Year by NATO, the National Association of Theater Owners. Overseas, it was the same story. Steve was the biggest draw in Britain, Germany and France, and the officially designated 'Mr Hollywood' in Japan. He wasn't only the right choice for them but, in his unique way, the embodiment of the American samurai spirit. He and Solar had no trouble taking their business elsewhere, initially to CBS, following the split from Warners.

Less successful, in fact near fatal, was the touch of vanity and narcissism, never too far from the surface with McQueen, that soon curdled into megalomania. All that mattered for him now, for months at a time, was the living of his longed-for role as Supie. As well as his price, Relyea couldn't help but notice, McQueen's ego also skyrocketed. 'Steve and I should have guarded against the cockiness that came at the end of the sixties. *Bullitt* led us to the wrong conclusions.' According to this reading, the film wasn't only McQueen's high peak but also the beginning of the end, morbid proof that he'd blown it.

His rather generous self-awareness collapsed.

Steve loved the cash that teemed down for *Bullitt* but he was struck even more, and amused, by the effect it had elsewhere. Hollywood quickly geared up to making more 'gritty' and 'street cred' pictures, with the idea, at least, of establishing audience identification with their dubious, sub-McQueen anti-heroes. There was a gurgling echo of him in countless baby *Bullitts* in the years ahead. As a genre, the film directly spawned the *Dirty Harry* saga – which Steve swiftly turned down – as well as several others that tried and failed to copy its definitive treatment of 'doing authority differently'.* The chase scene itself would be retrodden by everyone from *The French Connection* to *Ronin*. Meanwhile both policemen and men generally began wearing Bullitt's roll-necked sweaters rather than their regulation shirts and ties, an impact as big in its way as the Regency look, all frills and buttoned-up Brummell coats, being wafted from Carnaby Street. Above all, it was one of the first movies to have legs, in the

---

* *The Seven-Ups*, *Die Hard* et al.

peculiarly Hollywood sense of the word, shrewdly tapping a deep lode of both anti-authoritarianism and escapism. *Bullitt* began big, at New York's Radio City Music Hall, and quickly went on from there to become a bull market with queues of fans returning two, three or even a dozen times. For their money they got a scenario infinitely richer and more involving than its source novel, and far and away the best of Steve's great, screwy-yet-dignified macho vehicles. Among those venturing their two dollars that winter was a twenty-nine-year-old model, who, for one of the few times in her life, left the theatre 'with my knees actually knocking' for the star. He had a 'tigerlike quality . . . ready to pounce or attack . . . Steve exuded danger.'

Something new was happening to McQueen, something fraught with the rage and triumph he repressed on screen, something that would cost him his company, his family and friends and, having done that, would make that fan, whose name was Ali MacGraw, his wife.

'My torment seems to be working itself off,' Steve insisted as *Bullitt* was released. 'I seem to be close to the brass ring. What I want, I guess, is to be able to sit back and watch my kids grow fat in the orchards.'

It's true that Steve had plenty of fellow feeling for his children, and some, at least, for his wife, and even today there are dozens of happy photos of them in McQueen's Hollywood archive. Positively proconsular, Steve seems to tower over his mate, who gazes up, humble and deferential. You can see a kind of ruined grandeur there, while not ruling out the possibility of mutual respect. When he arrived at the Oscars eighteen months earlier, McQueen had been asked by a reporter what he attributed his success to. Without a pause he'd looked down at Neile and said, 'Right there.' It was the same story to the *New York Times* in August 1968: 'Yeah, I dig her. She's my lady . . . She's the reason I'm so responsible these days.' Later that year of *Bullitt* he gave Neile a heart-shaped diamond ring on their anniversary and told her, 'If it weren't for you, baby, I'd still be clawing my way out of the jungle.' At that stage, she says, she still thought everything would be all right.

McQueen, Neile adds, could be the sweetest, most charming man in the world when he was in the mood. The problem was that Steve only wanted to be in that mood for a few days a month. For the rest he was, at best, a restless spirit who liked to take off, shirtless, into the desert, quaff beer and dope – including, it was now thought, heroin – or shoot pool, swim and generally, though passively, enjoy the reduced scale of life at his Palm Springs pad. McQueen 'positively loathed doing anything to feather the nest', said Stan Kamen. 'He'd spend all day hauling rocks to build himself a bigger wall, but something like housework or mowing the yard – no way.' At worst, Steve was a thirty-nine-year-old juvenile delinquent, cocky, newly opinionated on a host of topics from Vietnam to race relations, known for impulsive, awesome fits of rage, particularly after that anonymous call warning him he was being outed, and someone even John Sturges called a 'brat'.

'I'm an artist' and 'America needs me' were only the two screwiest of the slogans to materialise at the manic end of McQueen's mood swing, while, at the other extreme, he brooded about the Pucci incident for months. Underlying McQueen's perky engagement of fame, underlying *everything*, ups, downs, cold wars, truces, was the flummoxed boy of nine alone on the cross-country bus. The world had bitten him and he went mad.

For most of the sixties and his own thirties there had never been much 'front' to Steve – only the pure excitement he got from sharing his success. The man had had an ego, Kamen knew, but *Thomas Crown* and *Bullitt*: there was something about them, in particular, that brought out McQueen's psychosis. Like the two title characters, he now had a fuck-you world of his own – his own empire, his own rules, where he 'used you to make sure he got what he needed'. And just as Steve was either all-giving or all-conquering, according to mood, men like Kamen were expected to be all-forgiving, all the time. McQueen's hypersensitivity made him both hell on a short fuse and utterly demanding of others. Particularly his wife.

Steve was a full-bore, proverbial lech who loved what he could do to women, but this hard-living, macho male from off the Indianapolis streets frequently failed the morality tests of Hollywood. His prudish side came out, as well as his sensitivity to the market, whenever

Kamen passed him a script with a nude scene in it. 'Not in a Steve McQueen movie,' was the unvarying reply. It wasn't just his own body he vetoed – he made it clear he didn't want 'tits' or, for that matter, 'cussing', either. By 1969, on the other hand, no such restraint was embraced in Steve's home life. According to Neile, 'The sexual revolution was upon us, and now his mid-life crisis was upon us too. Had [McQueen] not been the age he was, he would have been one of the flower children . . . He then adopted their life-style, which, of course, helped to undermine our marriage.' In fact, the 'sexual revolution', as McQueen saw it, had yet to disturb the age-old ideal of women as ornate and emotionally uncomplex – it merely meant they were more available. In particular, the semi-professional groupie, the kind who 'want[ed] to get laid as quickly and as often as possible', now became, like Steve's air-conditioned trailer, just one of the perks. Screwing them had all the emotional resonance, for him, and he assumed for others, of flossing his teeth.

'Main thing is them bubble-asses,' he once told Hoven.

'Right. But can I say something? It's nice to make a connection *up*stairs, too. Body and mind.'

Bubble-asses, Hoven thought. Can it be?

'Uh-huh,' said McQueen, with his flat, tough-guy mumble.

'It's more fun, trust me. You don't know what you're missing.'

'Uh-huh.'

When Neile started to renovate their new Palm Springs hideout shortly after *Bullitt*, Steve turned to her and said, 'Just think of this as my place, baby, OK? Decorate it as if it belonged to a bachelor.' A weekend or two later she found a strange dress hanging in her closet. By then, McQueen was unzippering himself all over town, shtupping every starlet in Hollywood, promising them, says one, 'he'd leave his wife and die horribly before ever being unfaithful again'.

Most lasted a couple of hours. Then he'd be back line-reading scripts, carefully parsing and turning down parts others would, and did, brawl over: *Ice Station Zebra*, *The Cold War Swap* and *Suddenly Single* all went the way of, more famously, *The Wild Bunch* and *Ryan's Daughter*. Meanwhile McQueen's PR man and now aspirant producer, Dave Foster, tried to interest him in a property then called

The Sundance Kid and Butch Cassidy. Steve was to play the Kid. At some stage Fox's president Richard Zanuck replaced Foster with his, Zanuck's, friend Paul Monash and hired Paul Newman to co-star. McQueen went bazootie. Nature and experience made him absolutely, unwaveringly, flat-out competitive, particularly towards his one true rival. 'Steve wanted top billing in that film, or at the very least to flip a coin for it,' says Neile. 'Paul refused.' After McQueen quit Newman and the studio first thought of goosing the movie with Marlon Brando, then gambled on a thirty-one-year-old under-achiever, name of Redford. Hoven says Steve 'wanted that role, but I guess he wanted it on his own terms . . . He used to tell people he'd told [Zanuck], "Fuck you, motherfucker. I'm Steve McQueen. I walk if I have to." That was part of the kick.'

Fuckwit, he later admitted, was brilliant in *Butch Cassidy*.

As McQueen's power grew and he became a kind of law unto himself, he could have had any shoot-em-up film in town. He chose instead to make a slight William Faulkner novel, *The Reivers*.

'Steve and Stan Kamen should get credit for that,' says Neile. 'By then we were having our problems and I was more marginalised.' Bob Relyea remembers being on a plane with McQueen that winter and 'him turning to me saying, "So now I'm gonna play a hayseed. After this I'll probably never work again." At the time, we happened to be flying to a dinner in Washington, DC, where NATO were giving Steve their Star of the Year award. The insecurity of the man . . . He was totally convinced he was going to lose his public but equally convinced that, as an actor, he shouldn't be too comfortable'; twisting his own melon. Beyond talent, beyond technique, the power of every great star stems from the same willingness to both restate first principles and wing it. It was especially true of McQueen. All the precariousness, doubt and constant mobility that began in Slater were there in spades in his later career. And also the judgement: while the familiar contours of a *Dirty Harry* came and went, he committed to a gentle tale of 1900s Americana and made it into a joyous rediscovery of youth that stood out as nothing less than the *Tom Sawyer* of its own time and place.

A perfect illustration of how Steve could turn a fable into something to be seen, and to be believed.

Part farmboy, part greaser, it was McQueen's lot to be torn evenly down the line between Slater and Indianapolis, schizophrenia that was also the keynote of his movies. Representing the city were *The Cincinnati Kid*, *Thomas Crown*, *Bullitt* and most of the attitudinal Westerns. Then rural America and all its hassles, together with all Steve's hassles, had been anatomised, summarised and brilliantly distorted in *Baby, the Rain Must Fall*. Late in 1968 he nearly committed to another war film, John Sturges's *The Yards at Essendorf*, then backed out and began telling Kamen he wanted to do something his uncle Claude would have dug, dedicating it to the old man, but without excluding the other six or seven million viewers. McQueen's uncontrollable secret urge to play it both ways, to live to a hundred full of years and honour and yet be a neglected genius, led to him doing *The Reivers* around a specially constructed canary yellow Winton Flyer, the period equivalent of the Bullittmobile.

'The car was his safety prop,' says Relyea.

They went down to Mississippi that winter, McQueen, the cast, crew, his friend Bruce Lee and the Faulkner specialists Irving Ravetch and Harriet Frank. Most of *The Reivers* was shot in the tiny hamlet of Carrollton, so far up in the hollows that, as the saying goes, you had to pipe in daylight, and just across the Big Black river from the town of McCool. Steve loved that. Bob Relyea remembers how 'the first day, our little two-storey motel was totally mobbed by kids and the entire local police force struggling together in a chant of "Steeeve" . . . It was pandemonium.' McQueen, 'this supposedly tortured, inarticulate actor', stepped out on to the balcony and began to speak to the crowd baying below.

'"We're gonna get along fine," he said. "I'll come down to your school and groove with you. When we're not working, I'll do anything you want me to. But please remember that we've got a job to do and we've gotta get some rest. So for now everybody go on home."

'At that,' says Relyea, 'two thousand kids nodded and calmly dispersed.'

Steve was then decanted into his own boarded-up suite and snapped open a small briefcase, courtesy of Sebring, containing beauty supplies, hair gels, tonics and half a dozen packets of finest cocaine. Meanwhile, Mario Iscovich acted as a kind of turnstile against the more discreet, all-female siege at McQueen's door. One enterprising local girl, Cheryl Hise, queue-jumped by coiling up under a room-service trolley and, once inside, telling Steve she loved every one of his films, which was good. He, in turn, loved her speedy, romantic pledge to make no demand on him the minute after they parted, which was better. 'McQueen was a voyeur,' says Hise. 'He looked me over, admired my "bubble ass" and invited me to stay – there was nothing erotic about it at all. It was more like a job inter-view, and I knew there were a dozen more right behind me.' Sex was a procession. Steve didn't have affairs, letters, red roses, any of that shit; more like sleepovers. One body after another. Nor was any road trip of his likely to be a stranger to combinations.

The Reivers' director was Mark Rydell, the ex-heartthrob and soap-opera star whom Neile herself had been dating when she met McQueen. 'And, God, Steve made him pay,' she sighs. 'He had an elephant's memory for anything like that.' First McQueen went out stock-car racing at the Carrollton speedway, in breach of contract, airily flipping Rydell the 'fuck you' finger through the windscreen. Next, echoing the events of 1956, there was a brooding rivalry between the two men over a mutual girlfriend on the set. Finally, in yet another familiar twist, Steve demanded to see the rushes of the first week's work, hated them, and instantly placed a person-to-person call to the boss of CBS Films, Bill Paley, demanding Rydell's head. Paley refused. This really irritated McQueen, who replied, typically, by withdrawing the favour of his labour from the movie. Overnight, a frantic posse of CBS and Solar bigwigs talked him back onto location for some long overdue close-ups. Then he really unloaded on Rydell:

'What you've got here is simply a fucking lousy piece of shit, and if you don't want to try and improve it, that's your funeral. Let's get on with it.'

The gauntlet was down, and now Rydell exploded, explaining that he'd been primarily pissed off by McQueen trying to take over the picture. Steve then announced at the top of his lungs, 'There's only room for one boss on this movie.' Rydell cut him off with an angry chop of his hand. 'Yeah, that's me.' Yet again, McQueen recognised true 'mud' when he saw it and backed off. The film got made, a mellow, small-scale epic that concealed the flexed brawn behind it. Steve told a few friends in later years that he dug *The Reivers* but regretted not having bust the candyass's melon. Rydell, for his part, refuses to discuss McQueen, though he made good on his promise not to work with him again. Ever.

For most Steve's notoriously thin skin came as a shock, not a surprise. Friends like Kamen saw the hot fires as both a curse and a blessing: McQueen could erupt any second, 'but that same voice in his ear was what made him a great star and, don't forget, a moneyman. By '69 Steve was on top of the whole heap.' Solar itself had a payroll of twenty-seven, with a well-padded office in Studio City and a new $20 million production deal with CBS's Cinema Center Films. After passing that spring on *Adam at 6 A.M.*, a *Reivers*-like script transplanted to the Midwest, McQueen finally returned to *Le Mans*. Meanwhile, across town in Rancho Park, Paul Newman, Sidney Poitier and Barbra Streisand were formally launching First Artists, a partnership to fund and distribute their own product, the idea being that greater control would make for both better movies and higher profits. The tale of confusion and greed that almost incredibly led to Solar's downfall would, within two years, bring McQueen into the fold.

That was friendship, he said, gritting his teeth, that joint venture.

But where was Newman now? *Harry Frigg*, shit. He, Steve, was top dog, so identified with blockbusters that he looked out of place in lesser fare, even *The Reivers*. As McQueen again flew to the NATO awards in Washington (where he mediated in a row between studios and exhibitors), the industry competed to fawn over him. To them, McQueen was keeper of the flame, a human repository of the kind of hopes and sales projections last stirred by Brando. He was a golden man in an age of lead. When Hollywood came to fix on its favourite son for 1969 there weren't many entries and the verdict was quickly reached. The Oscars aside, Steve was a popular sweep of every glittering prize going, though it was only the rare few he collected in person. For the rest, he begged off with the excuse that he was busy actually making movies. All over the country, in his absence, hard-nosed studio bosses stood on platforms singing McQueen's praises. Each rave rising on the horizon from NATO or the Golden Globes met with another in the media. Both there and in corporate boardrooms, virtues were now discovered that had somehow previously failed to surface. Suits everywhere grovelled to Steve, and not just because, as Paley said, he was 'second in interest only to Niagara' among North American natural wonders. With his cynical yet patriotic *mores*, utter competence, droll, laconic quips on the value of character and the need for good faith, Steve perfectly reflected his home values; on him thudded the shroud of spokesman, not for his generation, but for the American Way.

Son of a fucking bitch, he said. *Mr America.*

It couldn't have got any better or any bigger, and it didn't. What it got, however, was richer: his per-film advance doubled yet again in 1969 and Steve took a childlike delight in his new earning power. 'I made a million bucks today!' he'd blurt out after signing a contract. He did so not cockily but with the glee of one savouring freedom. As ever, McQueen could be tight with his cash or awesomely generous. 'When a friend was down on his luck, Steve was like Gibraltar,' said Kamen. 'He was there.' Some of McQueen's grand gestures may have been an assertion of power – spending money to put people in his pocket – but most were impulsive, unpublicised acts of kindness. Boys Republic and several children's charities, among others, would get a regular, signed blank cheque.

One Friday night Steve got held up as he was leaving a new swinger's pad he'd rented near the CBS studios in West Hollywood. He mildly gave the three muggers all the change he had on him, waited for them to leave, then ran up Fairfax Avenue, ducked down a dark alley and confronted the same gang as they got into their parked car. When, after a polite request, they still declined to reimburse him, McQueen wouldn't take no for an answer. On the cue of '*Fuck you, honky,*' Steve straightened up holding a gun that hadn't been visible a second before and cocked the trigger with the words, 'I'll give you thirty-eight reasons to give me my bread back – now.' They did so. Steve then calmly walked back towards his apartment, stopping off for an Old Milwaukee at Sofi's on Third Street. There the Hollywood superstar made the better acquaintance of a showgirl named Marla Douce, who duly wound up with him in his nearby love nest. The next morning over coffee, recalls Douce, 'McQueen got off the phone shaking like a leaf. He'd just found out that Jay Sebring was murdered the night before.'

It was worse, and a closer call, even than that. Sebring, Sharon Tate, Abigail Folger, Voytek Frykowski and Steve Parent had all been butchered by the Manson family in Cielo Drive, a ten-minute ride up the canyon road from the Castle. Tate, who'd tested for *The Cincinnati Kid* and whom Steve later called 'my girlfriend', had invited Neile and him to her house that night for a small dinner party. But after his mugging and the pick-up McQueen decided to stay in for the evening. Several years later when he was lying in a Mexican clinic he told friends, 'I'd have been offed a long time ago if I'd gone to Sharon's that night.'

For once, the paranoia was justified. He'd escaped being repeatedly stabbed and shot and bludgeoned by Manson's cult, then, like Sebring, trussed and left dying in a pool of blood on the living-room floor. Parent's body was the last to be identified, and for an agonising hour or two friends actually feared it was Steve. He took a few happy pills with his beer that morning, muttering, 'Coulda been,' again and again, something that haunted him the rest of his life. Manson himself, it emerged, had been one of the hundreds of aspirant stars to send in a hastily rejected script to Solar. When it became apparent that the finance and fulfilment he'd been denied by a mercenary, cruel world wouldn't, in fact, be forthcoming, he duly added 'that fucker Bullitt' to his celebrity hit-list. Earlier that summer, while planning his pogrom, Manson had talked his way into a charity screening of *The Great Escape*. At the stage door he got off a shot of Steve with his camera. He later bragged to a girlfriend that he could have done it there and then. Manson's more twisted vision, however, was to start by murdering Doris Day's son, Terry Melcher, a record producer who had likewise snubbed him (and also expected to be at Cielo that night), then move on to the Beach Boy Dennis Wilson and finally the movie colony. McQueen's own fate, in this scenario, was particularly grim. Manson meant to personally menace him at gunpoint into swallowing a fatal overdose.

In Mexico, he used to talk about that often.

Over those next few weeks and months Los Angeles outgrew the boundaries of mere panic. It was like a municipal nervous breakdown. A frenzy of stories, of drug perversions and orgies, of witchcraft and satanism, of devil worship and black magic and the occult, of anal-erotic sex, bondage, bestiality, S&M, ritual mutilations and other, less easily classified debauches shrieked out, in both private gossip and banner headlines, from the Hollywood rooftops. McQueen, all in grey, wearing shades, attended Sebring's funeral that dark August, after first having swept his friend's house of incriminating drugs. (Cocaine, briefly thought to be a motive for the murders, was, however, found in Sebring's car.) Steve, too, felt shocked, he told friends. And relieved, obviously.

The instant result was to make him simultaneously more uptight and yet more sensitive to the inner circle. Don Gordon recalls, 'Steve drove out to my house while I was away in Europe. He wanted to make sure my family was OK . . . McQueen never just blew you off with the usual "Call me" crap. He went over that house inch by inch, explaining about burglar alarms and security and how to deal with an intruder. He didn't leave until everyone was happy. The result was that my wife and little girl went to bed and slept easy that night.' Most of the Manson family were arrested two months later. Among the pre-trial disclosures was that they'd killed with no particular agenda other than 'because the knife feels so good going in', and that McQueen's name was ringed in red at the very head of their list.

As soon as the stores opened the next morning, Steve went out and bought himself and Neile more guns. He now packed one under his jacket, in his trailer, at the office, in the downtown apartment and under the seats of all his cars, as well as several scattered around the Castle. The fucking Alamo, he called it.

Then Steve was away, back on the move, rasping to and fro. When you actually faced death it was sort of a rush.

By the time *The Reivers* came out McQueen was being sucked more and more into a decadent mania of mass celebrity. As well as the autograph hounds, stalkers and obsessed cases there were the cranks and fringe nuts – the ones writing *those* letters, the ones in blood, the Satan ones. It was enough to make Steve even more paranoid, and it did. Nowadays he was like a virtual keyhole on madness. He tried to tell himself there was good reason for his seclusion, if not for his spiritual collapse, but at the same time McQueen was never quite happy when locked up. His periodic need for fun and pure speed was baffled by four walls. Over the next year or two Steve made a luxury jail out of his condition, like living in a designer padded cell, something he fought against all the way. 'People hit on me, I gotta duck or hit back,' he told Hoven. McQueen's nails bit into his palms as he demonstrated.

It was this note of attack, this quality of swinging from retreat to rage, that made an interesting high-wire act out of being Steve's friend. Dean Jones happened to meet him at Bud Ekins's shop not long after McQueen had done *The Reivers*. 'Both of us were on top at the time, Steve for obvious reasons, me because I'd just made *The Love Bug* . . . When McQueen saw me there he ran up, grabbed me to him, pinned my arms and spun me round and round, all the while yelling, "*Big shot . . . Big shot . . . Big shot!*" in a loud, breaking voice. Whatever it all meant, it came over as scary as well as weird. Steve's competitive juices were flowing, because I'd had the temerity, as he saw it, to also have a hit.' Another day, McQueen beheld a fellow actor with a similarly high-pitched 'Hey, superstar! Kiss my ass!' His private impersonations of men like Newman and Warren Beatty could, and did, make his biking friends scream with laughter.

The Reivers was out that last week of the decade, a warm, pastoral film that might have been painfully sappy and obvious in the hands of a lesser lead. McQueen played one Boon Hogganbeck, the man-child on a literal jaunt, and symbolic rite passage, from Mississippi to Memphis. What with an Uncle Possum, Doc Peabody, Sheriff Lovemaiden and sundry Bosses and Butches, the film's own trek was into silly-name country, though without ever coming off as cynical pandering or self-consciously wacky. Or, mercifully, cute. At a time when American screens pulsed with so-rendered homo and lezzy films, as well as newly respectable porn, shlock and skin flicks, Steve had the gall first to do *The Reivers* at all and then to treat the material like good sex. He took his time. Savoured the buildup. Delayed the outcome. Instead of dipping into the Marx Brothers territory of *Honeymoon Machine*, the humour here was nuanced and ironic, building to a genuinely dramatic climax at a horse race, McQueen's crinkly smile, presence and sheer timing making something memorably funny and touching out of moonshine.

By way of context, the gently picaresque story wasn't only something 'Uncle Claude would have dug', but a subtly doffed cap, too, in another direction. The shiftless, gambling, cheating, womanising Hogganbeck was, above all, Steve's tacit homage to his vanished father. Like Bill McQueen, the character was a dreamer and a dead flop. And yet, as Steve played him, Boon was so many other things, and so compellingly, that, the more he admitted to being a louse, the less and less eager audiences were to agree with him. Along with a boy and a black sidekick, McQueen's journey in the Flyer had some of the off-key and whimsical aspects of the shunned *Butch Cassidy*, though without the heroics. The only derring-do in *The Reivers* came in the advertising, which somehow identified it as a 'Steve McQueen actioner' and, at the same time, he griped, 'made [me] look like a village idiot'.

'I wouldn't wipe my ass with it,' he told Paley, feeling cheerful for the first time in weeks.

Almost everyone involved with *The Reivers* had something major at risk. Rydell's only previous film as director had been a neglected lesbian piece called *The Fox*. Solar had its $20 million production deal to justify, as well as offices and staff to maintain. The CBS subsidiary bankrolling *The Reivers*, Cinema Center, spent $6,042,706 (more than the total cost of *Bullitt*) in pre-production and photography. More pertinently, Steve himself was coming off five hit pictures in succession. Just as he'd predicted, his pedestal made a precarious perch and *The Reivers* was never the financial or critical smash of a *Thomas Crown*.* It ultimately did a respectable $20 million worth of business in the US and bombed overseas. Yet while director and studio both survived, it was McQueen who turned commercial dis-

---

* Rupert Crosse, playing the sidekick, was, however, nominated for Best Supporting Actor, which he lost to Gig Young in *They Shoot Horses, Don't They?* According to Bob Relyea, on the day the short-list was announced 'Steve, who wasn't nominated, came into the office, picked up the phone and called Crosse to congratulate him. He didn't sulk. [McQueen] was proud of the picture and proud of what Rupert did in it. That was a hard call for Steve to make, but there was nothing formal or dutiful about it . . . McQueen was the perfect superstar when it came to dealing with most fellow actors. It was just the directors and producers he hated.'

appointment into creative triumph. In playing the story as if it meant more than a fat pay cheque, Steve did some of his best and most human work, refusing to deflate Boon with clichés, run away from his flaws or otherwise smother the plot in fancy effects. He would have laughed and denied it, but McQueen now became a true artist. That the world saw him as a superstar remained his private joke.

McQueen flew to London in June 1969 for a tribute by RADA. After that he ended up in bed in the early hours with some arty British type who was happy, as Neile herself wasn't these days, just to listen. He'd taken some coke. All Steve could babble about was the race he and the Solar crew were going to shoot the next day in France; 30,000 feet of 'workhorse footage' that they'd ship home and splice into their own new picture. *His* picture.

What he found, of course, in London and back *en luxe* in Paris, were rather more fuck-flings than work assignments.

By now, Steve's fascination with the Le Mans 24-Hour was itself an obsessive endurance test. After four years and half a dozen false starts, he'd finally talked Cinema Center into a $7 million budget and John Sturges back into directing. McQueen was going to spend the summer of 1970 in France, then shoot some quickie piece of crap in Mexico called *Yucatan*. The latter got tossed when the race movie ran three months long and $2 million over budget. *Adios*, Steve would say. Plenty of other things got blown off, too, in the backdraft of *Le Mans'* excesses. Losing another picture was the least of it.

McQueen tuned up that autumn by entering the 832-mile Baja 1000, an off-road race for 250 jeeps, trucks, buggies and low-slung muscle cars down the Mexican peninsula. Somewhere out in the high sierras he blew a transmission gear in his Chevy, abandoned the car there and then and chartered a Learjet back to Hollywood. Steve entered a few other heats in California that winter, winning in a Porsche at the annual Sports Car Club gig in Holtville, blowing the gearbox again at Riverside, twisting his melon and breaking his left foot besides in a motorbike shunt at Lake Elsinore, then famously placing second, that March, in the twelve-hour endurance race at – of all poignant places – Sebring, Florida. Steve, with his foot in plaster, and his partner Pete Revson finished twenty-two seconds behind the fastest Indy champion of all time, Mario Andretti, driving at his fastest. Not bad, as he said, for a crippled movie actor.

When the marshals helped McQueen peel off his boot, there were gasps of horror. The plaster had melted into the skin. The sight, though, of Steve's face, at once euphoric and calm, settled the crowd down. They recognised in him the true racer. Compared to McQueen, everyone else was just a driver.

Now all that remained was *Le Mans*, scheduled to begin principal photography on 7 June 1970. People on the film knew there was a hard streak to Steve, an occasional coldness. And every so often a chill wind did blow through McQueen country as he surveyed the horizon. It all made him shiver with power, and with fear too: on this picture he'd be a driver, actor *and* hands-on manager. Particularly the last. Amongst *Le Mans*' logistical joys were 20,000 props, twenty-six high-performance race cars with fifty-two drivers from seven countries, along with 350,000 French-speaking extras. And no finished script. The film's eventual plot would make *Bullitt*'s seem like a paragon of clarity. There were few lines, even for a McQueen film, and no intelligible structure. 'Cars,' he told everyone in stern overview. 'We film the fucking *cars*.' The whole sorry ordeal would grind up Sturges, drive Neile and Bob Relyea to despair and out of Steve's life, and nearly finish him as a bankable star.

McQueen occupied a curious place in the Hollywood firmament in 1970. Witness the NATO 'Star of the Year' award, the people who ran cinemas – and the fans who actually paid to sit in them – bracketed him with or above John Wayne. Unlike their client groups, the studios never quite warmed to the equation in which independence could equal enhanced profitability. For a man like Ken Hyman, Steve was a studio's worst nightmare: the truly gifted, restless Supie who demanded the best. (McQueen had told Hyman to fuck himself when Warners originally wanted *Bullitt* shot on the back lot.) As long as he was still the cash-generator, fine. But the second a *Le Mans*, for instance, tanked, McQueen knew he was finished. He was the star liked by ordinary people, but not by the tycoons who hired him.

If Steve worried the honchos were out to get him, that's because some of them were. And it's not unconnected to that fear that the stakes were so high on *Le Mans*.

On the global scale on which the studio superpowers fought, McQueen was like a land mine, sensitive and indiscriminately explosive. For long periods the rules of engagement, the normal Hollywood scrambling, gouging and backstabbing, would remain civil, with everyone concerned keeping the larger peace. But if those rules were broken – if the scam, as Steve saw it, was abused – there lay the prospect of real havoc. *Go loco. Hit them like a freight train.* Neither Lee nor anyone else who knew him ever doubted it. In his manic phase, McQueen could be high-spirited, optimistic, fun, making his cronies shout with laughter, while others nervously awaited the side of him bursting with grievance and indignation, the shit side.

Schizophrenia. When not passing himself off as a biker, even Steve's dress code was a diagnostic giveaway, dominated as it was by fringe jackets, flares, chambray shirts, literally hundreds of pairs of silk socks, Murray's space shoes, designer suits and beads, flaunting a conflict of styles such as might have been favoured by Elvis in a sartorial pile-up with Sinatra in his 'Ring-a-Ding-Ding' phase. In this age of Aquarius Steve was still squarely planted in the Arian 'me' tradition, the one who operated to his own internal cues. A friend like Lee would see a philosophical McQueen debating civics with Bob Dylan, a physical McQueen leg-wrestling and swinging from trees, and nowadays an aggressive, focused McQueen wrangling extras like Rommel positioning tanks.

Bob Relyea bumped up against the 'real Steve' twice, both times at an airport, neither involving a screaming 707. 'On Sundays when we were shooting *Bullitt*, McQueen and Bill Hickman would go out and rehearse the chase scene on a disused runway. I'd see Steve's face when he got in the car. He'd be beaming. Just shaking with glee . . . screeching off on the tarmac, accelerating, skidding, barrelling towards Hickman, nearly crashing, then swerving at the last second and laughing, giving Bill the high-five through the window . . . He just felt so good. Most people never feel that rush. Ever!

'Some time later Steve and I pulled up for a flight out of LA. We were late and I was worried about having to handle him, taking care of Superstar and missing the plane. Nothing doing. McQueen grabbed the tickets, showed me where to park, told me to meet him and then took off at a run into the terminal. By the time I got inside ten minutes later he'd checked the bags, got the seats, charmed the good-looking girl behind the desk and generally taken care of business. Brilliantly organised. For those ten minutes, he was sincerely more interested in being Steve McQueen than in being Supie . . . Then, once we were safely on the plane, it was a case of "Where's my drink?" and "Please fluff my pillow" again. That's the kind of man he was.'

McQueen still went back to Chino, usually alone, once or twice with Neile or a trusted friend. He'd speak with each one of the boys privately, never coming on as the god or that much different from them, then sit down with them together in a dormitory. The fifteen-year-olds would shift around, kneading their rough, gnarled-looking hands, swinging their legs, while Steve, remembering the noise and the heat and the stench, the sounds and smells that ran through his blood, knowing that he, too, might have gone their way – even Manson's way – cleared his throat and spoke to them, sounding more sincere than he'd ever done:

'Thing is to find some chicks,' he said. They laughed at that, now warming to the stand-up guy who really *was* just like them. 'Ya get pretty horny in here, I remember.'

Lust, rage, fear. Revenge. A man in whom hatred bred genius. Steve remembered, all right. He'd gone from this same stinking basement to the very heights of Candyland. A long way for a single life. He was the extraordinary ordinary man whose concern was always for the weak, the old or the young, now shrugging off the 'movie jazz' when the boys mentioned it, and making the speech that would become his most celebrated legacy.

'I dig you guys,' Steve told them. 'I was a hardnosed tough guy – just like most of you – but I shaped up, and this place helped set me straight . . . The world is as good as you are. You've got to like yourself first. I'm a little screwed up, but I'm beautiful.'

'Turning forty was rough for him,' says Neile. 'Steve's age was gnawing at him and I, suddenly, wasn't getting any younger either. You could say he panicked. "Look, baby, my life's half over – I wanna fly."'

That summer he was fast down the road to Le Mans, headed for his own rendezvous with a nightmare version of his fun hobby. Hitting the male menopause full tilt was the path to ruin for McQueen, but the path to escape, too. It was this journey, partnered with his finally rationalising the 'movie jazz', that showed what true cool could be.

At home McQueen would flop around with his beer and bikes, his guns, his ugly dogs and even uglier minders, and – most of all – his moods. A friend recalls that Steve 'wore shades around the house, sat like a furled umbrella, and left most of the small talk to Neile'. As for dope: wild experimentation had taught McQueen that coke's effect, on him, was of heightened aggression and megalomania. If anything, he needed less of that. What Steve wanted these days was a drug that induced greater timidity and an enhanced sense of mute resignation. Now clinically paranoid, he severed all press relations early in 1970. After doing the cover of *Look* that January, McQueen didn't give another movie-related interview for nine years, and then only to a high-school paper.

Compounding Steve's mental problems and drug problems were, for the first time in ten years, money problems. By mid 1970 there were thirty or more full-time employees in McQueen's care, plus valets, maids, cooks, gardeners. As fast as the cash from *Bullitt* came in it was haemorrhaging out again on salaries, overheads and lunatic design schemes – the ones involving fluorescent moon buggies or amphibious jeeps – from Solar's Plastics and Engineering wing. The parent company was still solvent, operating out of a mock Italian villa, but there was a downside. Solar's internal report made it clear that the chances of it going public, or of even surviving, depended on whether or not *Le Mans* turned a profit.

Nor was Steve, as he admitted, altogether ignorant of the fact.

Just before leaving for France, McQueen hired a new business manager named Bill Maher. Maher audited the books and told Steve he was technically broke, at least 'not fluid'. Suddenly he was a bankrupt tycoon. He was a bankrupt husband. Steve was now bedding two or three different women a day in his apartment or the beach place in Malibu he'd rented from Vincent Price. 'McQueen was stoned all the time there,' said Mario Iscovich. 'That place was a veritable whorehouse. He picked these girls up from anywhere. He even picked up hitchhikers . . . I used to ask him, "Why do you do this? You're gonna blow it all, Steve." His answer was, "Hey, why not? I'm the biggest star in the world. The number one sex symbol! All those women, man . . . I want it all." '

Neile appeared phenomenally tolerant and even generous when the fresh tail kept coming – perhaps she saw that McQueen's fuck-flings, none of which ever lasted, would stabilise her own marriage. To her Steve was still the great man, the roguish but lovable Supie, the glamour boy and model father of their two children. But there was a quid pro quo: Neile rebelled in small ways – letting her hair grow out, contrary to McQueen's orders; and large – demanding that they get about and socialise with people other than his biking cronies. By 1970 so much of her energy was going into countering her marriage, in trying to carve out some minor happiness, that she, too, now began an affair. His name was Maximilian Schell, the dark and teutonically handsome star of, most recently, *The Castle*. A few years earlier Schell had earned rave reviews for his performance as an enigmatic defence lawyer in *Judgment at Nuremberg*. What's more, Neile rationalised, he'd actually *won* the Oscar.

McQueen didn't know about his wife's lost afternoons in a bunga-low at the Beverly Hills Hotel. Yet. But with the booze and the coke and the fuck-flings and the cash-flow crisis, Steve and Neile still had plenty to rattle the Castle roof with. She threw him out once or twice, but always took him back. He drunkenly yet seriously considered hiring a hit man to 'ice' her. McQueen soon snapped out of it, but the story and his babbled threat got around. Steve's rage was indicated by the choice phrase, 'I'll kill the cunt,' which humiliated not only Neile but the man who said it. More and more, their war went public.

McQueen later told of a kind of dreamlike state and desperation which took over when he finally got to make *Le Mans*. Ever since (taking a bead from Kirk Douglas's 1955 romp *The Racers*) he and Sturges had agreed to do the 'definitive car movie' immediately after *Magnificent Seven*, Steve had treated the project as though it were some sort of private circus in which to do acrobatic turns. His own mood swings, along with wholesale script revisions and turnarounds, not to mention all the studio false starts, had themselves become a kind of epic. In the ten years since McQueen had first dreamt of *Le Mans* he'd been overtaken first by one arch rival and now another. Garner's *Grand Prix* was followed by Paul Newman's vehicle *Winning*. Fuckers, both. He'd fix their hash, as well as shake down some much-needed cash as part of his salvage plan. Steve's deal with Cinema Center called for a guarantee of $750,000 as well as heavy points. Meanwhile, McQueen signed a new seven-year deal with Solar, effectively agreeing to pay himself $500,000 a year. After allowing his company to sink like a badly made cake through the very late sixties, he planned to magnificently resurrect it, and more importantly himself, in the first months of the seventies.

That was the plan. The reality was a nightmare of greed and vanity to join the ranks of Hollywood's killer films, later filled to bursting with the likes of *Heaven's Gate* and *Waterworld*. McQueen's combined road trip and ego trip began badly when he prematurely announced his 'actual participation' in the 24-Hour race, partnered by the Formula One champion Jackie Stewart. In fact, Stewart, in keeping with most Grand Prix drivers, had long since learned to leave Le Mans alone. Amateur thrill-seekers, even ones as good as Steve, were all too often followed by the sound of screaming sirens on their way to the scene of a shunt. Stewart walked on him. Stirling Moss, too, chafed at his role as a glorified car wrangler and would say that the finished film 'stank'. By the time McQueen and the Solar crew got to Europe there was still no script or even minimal plot, no schedule and no leading lady. Steve wanted Diana Rigg, who was unavailable. The former model and future Bond girl Maud Adams tested, but was too tall for McQueen even in his Murray's lifts. Much later, he settled on the unknown and Lilliputian Elga Andersen.

Steve finally flew to Europe on 2 June 1970. Neile and the children were to follow by sea three weeks later. After stopping off in London, where he shtupped the night away at Tramp's, McQueen and Bob Relyea took a private jet to Paris, picked up their 908 Porsche Spyder, a gift from the Porsche people, and drove south-west through Normandy. Dusk was already falling over the hills when they came on a bare open space where the road slanted down, flattened and then went into a wood. It was strung with flags and, bizarrely, the red and green neon of a travelling carnival blazed through the trunks of the trees. The two got out and looked around. As they came to the edge of the rise they saw lights and booths and a Ferris wheel ahead, and, away off on the shoulder of the hill, the spark-shedding thump of the bumper-car circuit.

'Let's stay here,' said Steve.

The rest of the night went swimmingly by *Le Mans* standards. McQueen rented the attraction, straight off, corralled some nearby kids, stuck them in the cars and stayed until two in the morning, happy and professionally thrilled, lurching to and fro, around and around, dodging, crashing, laughing wildly at each new shunt. From behind, Relyea could see only Steve's head and shoulders bouncing up and down. Sometimes he'd playfully towsle his own hair, turn and stick his tongue out. 'When he finally came down he was chortling like an excited child.' Relyea had no way of knowing that that was the last fully friendly day he'd spend with McQueen for over six years.

'Steve's big thing on *Le Mans*,' he says, 'was a need for peer approval – for the professional drivers to respect and like him.' Everything was conditioned by this burning fear of appearing candyassed. It was how McQueen wanted to be remembered, and it worked.

Less successful, in fact catastrophic, were Steve's efforts to be a de facto director, producer and screenwriter. Once in Le Mans he was king and undisputed Supie of a 100,000-square foot empire known locally as Solar Village. Along with the 150-strong crew, there were drivers, cars, technicians, marshals, dollies and high cranes all jostling together in a fenced-off camp patrolled by red-shirted 'security experts' who, seen from above, darted like a shoal of tropical fish. The muddy two-lane road leading through the town up to the track where the shoot was looked like Dunkirk. All around, Le Mans was strewn with tents, trailers, lights, Portaloos, hovering agents, *Paris Match* grotesques, ever-swelling legal teams, beer- and burger-shacks; Steve had his own flown in from Hollywood. Faced with the ordeal of imposing order on the chaos, McQueen managed by indirection when he managed at all. Unbelievably passive while not on stage, he spent most of the first two weeks at the fourteenth-century Château Lornay, rented for him thirty miles away amidst the green fields of Vire-en-Champagne. His favourite view there was of a double row of trees along the riverbank, where the mist seeped down like fluid, and a cottage with a working water wheel. Steve loved to slump around, staring for literally hours through the open side of the mill, where a saw rose and fell, or cataloguing the local wildlife. Everything natural now struck him as a sign of fate. McQueen's mind latched obsessively onto the number of times a particular bird cheeped outside his room or the number of times a given song was repeated, or even onto the number of notes audible in each tune. With the help of a tarot deck, he'd work out whether the 'vibes were right' for him to visit the set.

Then he'd be away, trundling on eager feet to go spy on people.

According to the terms of a side deal struck with CBS that May, McQueen was also to have $1000 a week mad-money, a limo and chauffeur, bodyguard, hair stylist and make-up man, plus his Porsche and home gym, as well as approval over everything from the number of parking spaces for the crew to the name of the still photographer. None of these superstar perks, however, mattered as much to him as his customised trailer. When not at the château, Steve spent entire afternoons holed up in the Cortez, unobserved, from the vantage point of a pit-stop in the very heart of the village. It was his personal refuge and tracking station. Above the locked door and tinted windows he had a powerful boom mike strategically positioned out of sight among some cables on the roof. From time to time crew members would wander by, complaining about life, not realising they were being snooped on. Even connoisseurs of paranoia might have been struck by the scene. Inside, Steve McQueen would be listening through headphones, feverishly taking notes.

It was all costing $90,000 a day and as yet there was nothing remotely resembling a script. A full decade's preparation had left star and director still apparently only half aware of what it was they were doing. Sturges, in brief, wanted a human-interest story about auto-racers and their love lives; McQueen, for his part, was lobbying for a 'pure' three-hour film that would be more or less a documentary on Le Mans. The thin, not to say gaunt ten-page treatment he'd worked on in Palm Springs baffled both cast and drivers alike and Steve was even laughed at in a few production meetings. A certain sarcasm abounded.

McQueen responded by arguing that 'the movie tells itself'.

Digging himself further into a hole, he added, 'We whipped this problem on *The Great Escape* and we'll whip it here.' He then finished himself off with the legendary quip that 'the story's all in my head, man'.

Meanwhile at least three teams of writers, each working independently of the others, were trying to translate Steve's mental vision onto paper. Not his only vision, as it happened. While they crouched in their own trailers, McQueen was developing a sort of mysticism to go with his numerology, the mysticism which combined Christianity with useful pagan ritual, such as suppressing lust by means of unlimited screwing. A variation he sometimes favoured was to merely watch several women performing on themselves. Sex. And violence. When Steve took his latest groupie and Mario Iscovich out in the Porsche late one night, predictably ramming a tree and breaking his assistant's arm, he started ranting at the car, the road and then finally at Iscovich himself. Fat fucker. Why hadn't he warned him? Don't try and sue me, pal. 'You'll never work in Hollywood again' – *that* classic assertion. Poor Iscovich went to hospital and duly kept his mouth shut.

McQueen's family and friends all tried hard to remember his many gifts and his humour and the mercurial delight of his company. They reminded each other of his childlike side and his great stories leavened throughout with his sense of the absurd, in which he was quite often the first skittle to be shied at. But, by 1970, Steve's much cherished 'vibes' were mere exercises in nostalgia. More impartial observers now tended to chart McQueen's descent into clinical lunacy, where he unleashed his always fertile suspicions against totally innocent colleagues. His ultimate solution was simply to fire people. When Steve heard through his listening post that one of the hired drivers had told a reporter he was doubling for him, McQueen, the man was sacked on the spot. One of the three writing units was similarly axed. Steve reacted worst of all when Elmer Valentine casually mentioned that he was flying home to look after his club. McQueen retaliated by making melodrama of his friend's defection, distorting it into grand, operatic 'shit'. Another disloyal fucker, he snarled. *Adios.*

At the instant Valentine walked out of the door Neile and the children arrived. McQueen greeted his wife, at the first private moment, by telling her, 'Look, there'll be people coming from all over the world to visit me this summer.'

'People?'

'More like women,' said Steve.

The silence that followed this admission was deafening. Neile retreated into the back seat of a nearby parked car, lay down, and, as she says, cried her heart out. Four or five hours passed before a concerned crew member gently knocked on the window and asked whether he could drive her back to the château. The man dropped her off at the front gate. Still sobbing and stumbling in the dark and rain, Neile made her way upstairs to the master bedroom. She found it quite literally infested by bats; a gory curtain-raiser to what followed.

McQueen came into the room, lay down next to his wife and then, 'quietly and gently, in an almost fatherly way', asked whether she'd ever had an affair. No, said Neile. His response was to go rummaging around, then produce some coke and ask her to take it. No again, Neile said. He kept insisting it would blow her mind, dry her eyes, generally get her in touch with her inner shit. Neile still declined. 'Take it,' Steve said. So she took it, and again there was this arching of eyebrows over whether or not she'd had a fuck-fling – and this time she admitted it. Suddenly McQueen's indifference ended. Excusing himself, he calmly walked out and strolled back a few moments later carrying a gun. Grabbing Neile by the arm and pointing the barrel at her head he asked her, 'Who was the motherfucker?' She told him.

Torture and confession bled off into violence. The full story of Schell, the hotel and the retaliatory affair came out by degrees, McQueen and his wife now sitting there in the dark only inches from each other's faces. And quite objectively, without a bit of apparent rage, coldly, mechanically, 'like the Gestapo', she says, Steve looked at her and reached out and slapped her over and over, varying the routine by yanking her head back by her hair. Tramp. Bitch. Stinking little fucker. She could smell the hot snarl of his breath between his jabbing and hitting her . . . Whore. Was Schell better in bed than he was? Slut. Dirty fucking cunt: and so on. Finally, after an hour of this, McQueen slammed the door with sensational volume, got in the Porsche and took off into the night. 'He terrorised me,' she says, treating her like shit and telling her how she was probably doing it all over town, behind his back, in parked cars, every chance she got. Out on the track from then on, he always made her sit where he could see her. A friend who caught sight of Neile stumbling around there thought she 'looked like a prisoner being led from one jail to another'. A condemned case. Steve also made enquiries about hiring the motherfucker kraut Schell to do some high-speed driving on *Le Mans*. Perhaps wisely, Schell turned him down.

All in all it wasn't a pleasant film to work on. Any project with McQueen could be full of laughter, or it could as easily turn into a nightmare.

As for the actual shoot, he spent a lot of time, sure enough, barrelling around Le Mans and allowing himself to be filmed. Steve had said he thought the idea of doing a 'straight' car movie was plenty dramatic enough, and it might have been; but what's dramatic in concept didn't turn out so on screen. Somehow even the racing scenes were painfully flat. 'All we were really doing,' Relyea says, 'was laboriously moving Car 22 in front of Car 23 and vice versa . . . It was excruciating.' A whole day could be spent shooting a few seconds' film. Steve agonised for hours about the cut of his driving suit or the precise amount of dirt to be applied to his tyres. Entire conferences took place on colour-coordinating the drivers' helmets. The ebb and flow of such minutiae wafted the breath of life to him, even when performing drudge work that might have been best left to gofers. McQueen once even had the flunkies carefully glue dead insects to his windscreen, then walked to and fro looking at the car from every angle, bending down, squinting, and finally shaking his head.

'No – wrong kind of bugs.'

Masterly. Such attention to detail, the crew thought. And typical of the way McQueen micro-managed the tiniest thing to do with the hardware.

Off track, away from the asphalt, it was another story. *Le Mans* – unlike *The Great Escape* – never filled in the hole at the heart of its plot. There was virtually no human interest and the token dialogue, sadly uninvolving even at the level of the phrase, made the 'yep –

nope' riffs of *Hell is for Heroes* seem tediously wordy by comparison. For the first quarter of the film, the only voice heard was the one echoing over the track's Tannoy system.

McQueen still drove out to the château ever night, where he ate with his family, put the kids to bed and then started in on Neile again. The interrogations followed a well-trodden path. Unhappy at not being able to convince everyone, himself included, that he was greater than everyone else, he couldn't help taking revenge on people, on all people, but especially those stinking little cunts who dared remind him he was mortal. Steve sundered a few last friendship delusions that summer. *Le Mans* was a perennial source of conflict. Better, as he'd said, to have bootlickers. When he arrived on set each morning the paid minders cleared a way for McQueen as if they were swimming, doing the breaststroke. Anyone who took an unauthorised snap was likely to get their melon twisted.

By early July Steve had not only lost control of events but had the greatest difficulty in finding out what was happening. Even the previously trusted inner circle had taken to avoiding him out of a sense of self-preservation. Nowadays the *Paris Match* stringers and paparazzi flocked just outside the guarded perimeter could gauge the film's mood by the film-makers' own physical disintegration. Relyea's co-producer Jack Reddish was on his way to losing 20 pounds and breaking out in sores. John Sturges's remaining hair went white. People who had never smoked or quit years before suddenly found themselves lighting up first thing in the morning and going on from there to the Valium. The loyal, sweet-natured Mario Iscovich, still with his arm in plaster, was fired for the offence of giving a fan one of McQueen's pet Fruit of the Loom T-shirts. Relyea, himself the gentlest, most long-suffering of men, wigged out in front of an old friend – who also happened to be a Cinema Center employee – and thus unwittingly triggered the alarm that rang, long and loud, back at the CBS building in Hollywood.

Then things went into turnaround.

'They took the view that we, Solar, were now fighting amongst ourselves and obviously needed disciplining.' The home office reaction was every bit as bad as Relyea feared. 'Cars, cars, cars, who gives a fuck?' was one studio executive's newly considered opinion.

251

Others followed in kind. What's more, when the original outburst, *'The film's outta control,'* was reported back to McQueen, Relyea, too, was soon purged. Finally John Sturges threw in the towel. Neile remembers 'his actual and classic words were, "I'm too old and too rich to put up with this shit."' He flew home, and out of his protégé Steve's life for ever. Sturges's replacement was one Lee H. Katzin, a TV director who hired on at three days' notice, drove to the set, stuck out his hand and made the provocative remark: 'Hello, Steve. Nice to meet you.'

Steve grabbed the man by the tie, lifted him up and told the little fucker it was 'Mr McQueen', and not to forget it.

Star and studio now began to strafe each other in earnest. Steve, of course, had a mind trained for exactly this kind of thing. Confrontations, showdowns. Jets swooping in from Los Angeles. A delegation of beetle-browed CBS, Cinema Center and William Morris agents duly arrived in France to seriously consider whether to replace McQueen with Robert Redford, or even to shut the whole thing down. *Bango!* as one of the suits put it. Pink-slipped.

Round-the-clock negotiations finally produced a grim compromise. Steve would relinquish his $750,000 salary and, more pertinently, his creative control in order to at least get the film made. A new deadline was imposed: and grudgingly agreed. Now in full rant, McQueen gave orders to Bill Maher to begin firing Solar employees and winding the company down to little more than a shell. It was a blood bath. Overnight, long-time staff and cronies would find their presence no longer required: locks were changed, phone calls unanswered, the reasons, if any, never given. Stan Kamen, the man who'd stood loyally by Steve for eight years, was a nice guy. But he, too, was no longer good enough. He hadn't stood up to the Cinema Center brass when they'd come calling. After McQueen told Neile he wanted to change agency, she begged him to at least tell Kamen upfront and direct.

He did. 'DEAR STAN, YOU'RE FIRED. STEVE', ran the overnight cable.

McQueen and his wife then issued a statement announcing their own separation. In the looking-glass world of *Le Mans*, it actually meant the exact opposite of what it said. In reality they spent the next two weeks in Morocco trying to 'patch things up' while something similar went on, in their absence, to the hurriedly revised shooting schedule. Neither repair job really took. McQueen, for the first time in his life, now admitted to the few close friends who remained, 'I think I'm going impudent.' Limp! Him! Steve McQueen, for Christ sake! The same cronies soon noticed how he began slagging off Neile in front of total strangers. The movie, for its part, abandoned the high road and went more for the simple approach – it, too, would be wound down into a shell of itself.

In the end, after the usual shit with Katzin, 106 minutes of acceptable film would be cobbled together. A near mutiny among the crew was averted at the last minute when Cinema Center released their back wages. Police unsealed the village's offices only after local landowners, too, were finally paid for the lease of their property. The manager of the Hôtel Ricordeau in nearby Loué went as far as obtaining a legal seizure of Solar's lights and cameras in lieu of rent. Even the last weeks of the shoot were marked by a disastrous series of bad 'vibes' and mysterious accidents. The driver David Piper hit a guardrail at speed during a routine setup and fractured his leg so badly it had to be amputated. Robert Hauser, *Le Mans*' director of photography, was nearly killed in a separate shunt. McQueen himself had several near misses, including one on the final day of shooting, now incredibly in mid autumn, after he apparently told both his director and his partner he meant to 'end it all'. By then Neile, too, had suffered her own death-in-life crisis. Discovering that she was pregnant with Steve's child, she had an abortion in London.

Nobody thought to celebrate when *Le Mans* finally went to bed that November. Steve and Neile immediately drove to a clinic in Switzerland where they spent two weeks, physically recovering but, in his case, depressingly fixated on his wife, Schell, the whole *Le Mans* fuck-up – he used the term fuck-up. When they got back to California the McQueens first went to a marriage counsellor, then began seeing separate psychiatrists.

Editing *Le Mans* only detracted from relationships already long since strained to breaking-point, with McQueen spending hours adjusting the volume of insect noises on the sound track, or laying out the glories of an eagle swooping symbolically across screen during the final credits. Bob Relyea went home to LA and got a call from Cinema Center 'suggesting I go in and take a look at a cut of the picture, which I did . . . I watched it and gave them a whole ream of notes, which were totally ignored. And that was basically the end of me and Steve.' Sturges would complain that all his own hard-won footage was scrapped, and that what remained 'distorted' the original concept. He made only two more feature films, one of them oddly named *McQ*. By this stage Steve himself wasn't concerned with distortion. His whole life was torn into parts which didn't cohere: his need – a pathological one – for fame; the price he paid for it. His sole connection to the real world now was his children.

Neile was going. Sturges and Relyea and Kamen had gone. Solar was radically restructured – downsized – and then hit with a $2 million back tax bill. Most of the friends Steve didn't desert would desert him. The only thing standing between McQueen and utter ruin was his talent. Armed with a new agent, the cheerfully self-confessed 'barracuda' Freddie Fields, his salvation was already quite literally to hand in the form of two freshly optioned books, *The Getaway* and *Papillon*. Neile encouraged him to read them both, and Steve's second-act comeback would owe as much to her good sense as his whole success had to her support.

McQueen at forty was in a sorry state. Addicted, insolvent, if not broke, a monster of paranoia – something Neile believes had become 'near-possession' ever since that anonymous call and uninvited guest in the Castle – he was now living nocturnally and largely indoors, arming himself against the outside world by buying more and more guns. Back in Brentwood, his wife seriously considered taking out a restraining order against him. She didn't, primarily, she says, to 'protect his reputation – for everyone's sake'. The cycle that had emerged in France still persisted, now under even greater stress. Neile would do or say something that set Steve off on a rant, usually verbal, at other times slapping her across the face; her hurt made her cry; and her crying drove him, mortified, out of the house. That new year McQueen moved from the Castle into a small guest cottage nearby in Pacific Palisades. He promised one day soon afterwards that he'd give up the drink and drugs and other women. Steve told his shrink that he was tossing all three of them out. He never did it. Instead, after a few more fuck-flings (including one with Natalie Wood) it would be McQueen himself who was evicted, first moving from Pacific Palisades to a hotel and then eventually a larger, flower-strewn villa on Coldwater Canyon. Now formally separated, he responded with a spree of gunplay and sex, tooling around, he said, 'greasing every groupie in Hollywood'. Suddenly, Steve had no use for any of the abstention shit any more. The latest objects of his passion, by early 1971, were antique firearms and much younger women – chicks.

I'm a little screwed up. At worst, a self-proclaimed nut whose raging insistence miraculously got him through.

But the monster was also a model of good works and generosity. Most afternoons McQueen still drove himself across town to Brentwood, playing with the kids, charming the staff, paying the bills and taking his wife out on psychiatrist-approved dates. To Neile he spoke movingly about the fact that he no longer, as he once had, thought it 'candyass' to seek professional help. He continued his visits to Boys Republic and made frequent unpublicised cameos in orphanages and pediatric wards. Back in Pacific Palisades, Steve once opened the door to a group of schoolchildren and their teachers out collecting clothes for the needy. They left an hour later, loaded down with shoes, socks, shirts and more Cardin sweaters than they'd ever dreamt of seeing in one day. McQueen was both reclusive and yet warmly available, a presence and an absence: he was both things genuinely, and both to extremes.

The cynical, adrift star indulged his eccentricities. If he was in bed and heard a noise of any kind outside, he immediately got up and shot at it. He rarely read his correspondence, examining incoming padded envelopes with a scanner to determine whether or not they contained 'bad shit', namely explosives. He seldom left the house except for family or charitable visits. Just as Solar went into eclipse, so Steve now did something similar. He continued to live in LA, but increasingly as a cooler king, not as the mythical Supie. That winter, for instance, McQueen told Dave Foster not to bother arranging any more interviews for him. If he could help it, he no longer went near movie openings or public events. Wherever he moved, he tried to arrange it so that he could also rent any next-door property, in order to 'stop people gawping' at him. Autograph hounds would be told to fuck off. Nowadays Steve alternated between dressing up in hip-hugging suits or in sweaty, ragged denim and cowboy boots: the clothes, in one, his ex-power image; in the other, his two-fingered salute to Hollywood. There were one or two surprising, exhilarating moments that demonstrated the old Hemingway-cum-Dylan persona, but, more and more, Howard Hughes won the day.

The dates with Neile always ended with the same questions and aggression, but otherwise went well. There were times when she spent the night at Pacific Palisades and other times when he spent the night at Brentwood. Part of her still wanted it to work. Even now McQueen could flash the wit and sheer *joie de vivre* that often stunned those who knew him as Julian Crawford's son. But it wasn't enough. Both kids were now being caught up in the crossfire, a tension which only increased with time as Chad, particularly, found himself bewildered by a world he didn't accept. Dire, yet on another level, depressingly familiar. He was ten, the age at which Steve had lain in bed listening to Julian pleading and begging through the wall, and then to the sound of her husband punching her. Now dark days were repeating themselves. Along with Neile, McQueen might be screaming at the top of his lungs when the children came in; if Terry and Chad wanted to have friends over, they could never be sure what state their parents would be in. The fighting was incessant and sometimes brutal. One day Terry was upstairs with Neile in her dressing room when Steve slammed open the door, grabbed his wife, yelled at Terry to stay away until he called her, and then started slapping Neile around. After a while, he took off on his motorbike.

Something in him akin to remorse was tripped. He always regretted it.

The genius and the tyrant both came from the same basket. His merely showing up as, for one, Jake in *The Sand Pebbles* put you on notice that the character was tense, fissile, vigilant, together. Mr America. Steve was like that, too, just as sudden, like one of his taut, wound-up yet massively steady roles; possessed of a crooked integrity. He could break off from fighting with Neile to sprint to his children when the Castle was rocked by a violent earthquake, or, equally, spend days nursing a sick friend. As always, his moods lightened and darkened on his own internal cues. McQueen, the man and the actor, was really a miniaturist, and, with that, someone who rarely owned up to much candyass emotion. If any. 'I'm fucked,' for him, counted as almost Shakespearean status. It seems ironic, but not untypical, that Steve chose to crack up and then abruptly put himself back together in a locked house on what was then named Solitary Row.

7

Love Story

McQueen soon learned not to go near the windows or to draw back the double curtains in order to look at the view down the canyon trail. His new house had been built in the shape of an upright slab, so that the rooms were high, with no trees to shade them from the onslaught of fans, reporters, FBI men, nuts like Manson and all the other various parties hassling him. All them. Retreating back up into the craggy fastness, rather than bringing respite, intensified Steve's paranoia. Now he was completely alone. After the housekeeper left for the day at five, everything out there became creepy and forbidding, and by dusk he'd be sitting back with a beer in one hand and a gun in the other. The air-conditioning roared at one end of the den, and still the oven heat from the hills leaked through the windows. A few hours later, now well into the coke, McQueen would light a log fire, without bothering to adjust the cold vent still blasting away, and flop down between the two zonal extremes. Although it was typical of Steve to say less and less as he got more stoned, Hoven, who visited him, felt that his silence wasn't merely failure to respond. It was heavy, pregnant.

Such was McQueen's almost parodically *Sunset Boulevard* existence for several months in 1971. As well as his boozing and brooding he still sometimes drove downhill, heavily disguised, to visit either the Castle or his psychiatrist Dr Goodheart. But those were his only two significant excursions for weeks at a time. A sunset mood truly did run through his new life, that of an ex-party balloon now reduced to a ragged triangle of limp red rubber. Thanks to his trips to the shrink, Steve assured Neile, he no longer needed to use drugs or violence as a means of expressing himself. In fact there was no evidence of any such outbreak of sanity – quite the reverse. His own studio doctor lectured him about, as the file said, his 'growing dependency on prescription and non-medicinal narcotics'. An addict, in other words, McQueen told friends. Him. A fucking junkie.

Nobody had a good answer.

For nearly ten years Steve's career had worked in close connection with an obvious parallel, the Beatles.* And now the whole saga had turned full circle. Like theirs, McQueen's overnight breakthrough, after a mere seven years' precise measuring out of charm and rebellion, came in 1963. Five years later, *Thomas Crown* and *Bullitt* summed up an exact time and place as powerfully as a *Sergeant Pepper*. And, after those dazzling sixties peaks, both empires would start to crash, and keep crashing, in 1970. Now, just as Apple Corps wound itself down in London, Steve's own company moved out of its plush offices on Ventura Boulevard into more modest, pre-*Bullitt* digs in North Hollywood. It was impossible even to reach the new place except by climbing up a stony path over the embankment and continuing down the side street which, no longer kept in repair, was constantly being washed away by mud slides and strangled by tall weeds. McQueen now quite literally walked among the ruins of what he'd destroyed.

He'd still go for meetings there, as well as in Freddie Fields's comfortable office. Steve also accepted an invitation to co-present the Oscars that spring of 1971. After a while he'd come to a VIP suite where Ali MacGraw was sitting, nodded, and walked on past without stopping.

The images that most stuck in the mind that year, long after the last frame of *Le Mans*, were of Steve's clothes and his hair: those cane-cutter shirts, the bare chest just a little too sleek, and the medallions too shiny, the tight-buttoned flares and the high heels. Or

---

* McQueen knew and liked all the band members, especially John and Ringo, although he cheerfully admitted he was tone deaf. *Baby, the Rain Must Fall* and *The Reivers* would seem to confirm this.

plain jeans. He was still feared by some as Big Mac and pitied by others as small fry – a has-been. There were rumours that he was broke, not only 'creatively spent' (*Variety*) but, he griped, fucking homeless too. For a few days, between addresses, McQueen actually moved into the Cortez as his official residence. His sole public appearance in the first half of the year would come at the Oscars. Backstage he'd smoked some weed with a friend he knew there, then complained, in a loud aside, that most of the Academy honchos couldn't find their own asses with both hands. Specifically, they'd given an award to the kraut. Where was *his*, Supie's?

It wasn't enough that he'd been paid millions, feared, coddled, cosseted and generally indulged like a human hand grenade. McQueen needed to be the outsider, too, by making out that he was still an oppressed, disenfranchised loser and the plucky guardian of all that was beautiful, truthful and noble as well. Fuckers. This time he'd make a movie about a washed-up rodeo star, no sex, no violence, and *still* the kids would come. Cutting himself back to size was both inevitable and brilliantly intelligent – Steve walking before they made him run with everything riding on the story. The genius lay in making his mid-life crisis universal, and not just in the beholder's eye.

That was then. For now, everything exploded into fire and madness. McQueen was still on the way down. Fire and madness and just before the latter a final turn of the screw.

Le Mans opened on 23 June 1971. It meant more to McQueen, and his new self-image as an *auteur*, than all the horse operas and shoot-ups he'd done in his life put together. 'I'd like to leave some scratch marks on the history of film-making . . . I could fail, but as long as you fail with your ass hanging out, that's OK. But to fail when you're driving down the middle of the road, that's a sin.' In fact the two hours of *Le Mans* turned out to be a punishing penance. All Steve's gifts for emotion, dramatic ingenuity and threatening, physical presence were sacrificed to the plot's dreary contrivances and lack of the human touch. Crucially, the whole exercise failed to make audiences care about the McQueen character or his fate because they never really got to meet the man, just a cardboard cut-out who drove too fast.

Not that this timely climax to Steve's auto fixation was ever less than technically slick. *Le Mans* had its share of icily tense scenes, like the one where a Porsche windscreen suddenly breaks out in deadly white fracture blooms, thus rendering it blind and a shunt gruesomely inevitable, so that we wind up, horrified, watching the whole wreck from the driver's point of view. Or the various squealing setups of cars sliding, fish-tailing and generally throwing themselves around the oval at 220 m.p.h. Critics rightly praised the camera work by Robert Hauser, whose preference for POV shots – actually putting you in the cockpit – over faked inserts of an instrument panel – to let you know the speed – proved expert both at conveying terror and the broader human involvement sadly lacking away from the asphalt. The staggering 450,000 feet of raw film (bought in for $7,573,797) was, too, brilliantly edited. As a spectacle, *Le Mans* looked gorgeous, uniforms and cars in exquisite taste, everything detailed, capturing both the intoxication and claustrophobia of sitting trapped atop an overcooked 600-hp engine. Finally, there were the few neat, if under-written cameos by the likes of Derek Bell, David Piper and Mike Hailwood. McQueen himself had a weary, though too affected charm, as though he'd somehow strolled onto the set by divine acci-dent to grunt a few reflections on the state of love and death, while Elga Andersen did her best to suggest that somewhere there might be the shreds of a storyline.

There weren't. As a plot summary, Cinema Center's 'cars, cars, cars', either factory new or ultimately with knackered engines and the clichéd wobbly tyres, was about right. However thrilling the docu-mentary footage, *Le Mans'* fictional story never quite got out of first gear. The result was much like a minor Kubrick film, elegant and somehow empty and pedantic, all style and precious little content except that which was tediously precious itself. McQueen's own arrival was megalomaniacal, the camera pirouetting slowly around instead of allowing him, as the greats always do, merely to walk on. He didn't speak his first line of dialogue for forty minutes, and then only a mumbled 'Hello'. Everything from then on was exaggeratedly heavy. For his part, McQueen's substar, the light comedy actor Sieg-fried Rauch, looked uneasily like a badminton champion who'd wan-dered inadvertently into the shot-putting cage. According to Neile, the problem of finding the right cast, specifically a leading lady, along with the problems of Steve's ego and coke addiction, ultimately did for *Le Mans*; McQueen got so bogged down in the car rather than the plot mechanics that all the passion drained away. Rauch and Andersen did their best, showing flashes of joined-up, adult emotion, at least of despair, but only the drivers' silent screams of panic pierced the heart. There's something wrong with any picture where Jacky Ickx gives the best performance. *Le Mans* was one of those over-crowded films in which the actual people just seem to get more and more lost and stylised in all the wrong ways with the passage of time.

A long but bitty, very expensive home movie.

Even critics who applauded *Le Mans*' action sequences would gag at the picture's pretentiousness. Words like 'overblown' and 'leaden' came around like pit-stops. Rants such as the full-page one in *Time*, rather than the few raves, held the field. 'Steve McQueen's style of glacial cool has been perfected close to the point of impenetrable mannerism . . . Hollow . . . Ironic . . . McQueen is still a potentially good movie actor, but he needs someone to loosen him up, make him play a part, not pose for it. He's surrounded himself with the sort of production talent that offers no protest to his rampant self-indulgence.' While rating McQueen with the first rank of amateur racers, even Stirling Moss was disturbed by the film's implausibility: 'I thought it piss poor. I'm very protective of my sport – if you deviate from the truth, or take too much licence with it, I'm not interested. There was no humour or passion to *Le Mans*. Not much cop at all. Frankly, I'm surprised Steve even released it.' 'Shit' was the dim view of *Rolling Stone*. To such personal and professional pans was soon added a bitter self-critique. McQueen blamed both the shadowy 'industry' and himself for the film's failure. According to his friend Pat Johnson, '*Le Mans* was a watershed for Steve. A total turning-point. When it flopped, he shut down even more than before. Terrible isolation. It was the last time he ever halfway trusted anyone in Hollywood, particularly the studios . . . He resented them even more after that.'

The bile was rising. Now it was only a matter of time.

The notoriety and ensuing fallout from *Le Mans* didn't, however, affect McQueen's price. He was still bankable. For one thing, thanks to foreign rights the picture actually grossed a respectable $20 million, not that Steve himself saw a penny of it. Muscular negotiating by Freddie Fields and the residual warm glow of *Cincinnati Kid*, *Nevada Smith*, *Sand Pebbles*, *Thomas Crown* and *Bullitt* meant that, properly chaperoned, he could still make any picture he liked. It meant, further, that McQueen was now represented by a man feared and respected even in the hard-headed world of showbiz agency, where everyday morals would have jerked grunts of recognition among the Manson cult. As for Fields himself, Steve was withholding half of his agreed commission as a way of 'testing' the new relationship. Like so many other McQueen relationships, this one had a shadow existence in his past life. Neile felt that it was a case of 'If I hold this from you, will you still work for me or will you like me as much? Steve never needed an actual reason to act against an imagined grievance.' After she intervened, McQueen paid Fields what he owed him.

He could afford it – that small room in North Hollywood was still banking between half and three-quarters of a million a year merely from *Bullitt*. Steve enjoyed a $500,000 annual salary, as well as his investments, two houses, rental property and $5 million insurance policy placed with his own brokerage firm. Solar itself might have been pared to the bone, but the various agents, accountants and McQueen's old lawyers Mitchell, Silberberg & Knupp flexed brawn not only doing new business but, on Steve's orders, in constantly auditing the old. Naturally, it was an article of faith for McQueen that the studios were screwing him. Always making a movie's 'break even' figure recede further over the horizon. In late 1971 he was still hammering Mirisch-Alpha over his overtime pay for *The Great Escape*, now nearly ten years in the past. He haggled with Allied over access to the books for 1963's *Soldier in the Rain*. Then there was the matter of *Love with the Proper Stranger* right through *Thomas Crown*. Slippery fuckers. Line-reading each and every one of those accounts was Fields's christening act, early proof that he was going to have to earn his keep.

Fields soon also fixed him up with a million-dollar Honda commercial (*Steve McQueen – for a man's ride*) in Japan. But when he told his client the good news he got nothing but a grunt and more shit about commissions, and he soon realised that it was only the beginning of the melon-twisting.

'I don't like it,' Steve said, 'but I guess I'll cough up.'

'That's certainly a load off my mind,' said Fields. 'What about everything else you owe me?'

McQueen gave a small cold smile and laughed.

'So sue me.'

But Steve, in his deeply weird way, wasn't only obsessing over his precious – but actually groundless – past suspicions about being, as he put it, dicked. Second thoughts and 'fuck you's' straightened all that out, allowing him to move on to the future. His basic vision comprised a few key ideas which consistently recurred, and which served him well, rather than any formal wisdom. The McQueen who emerged around his forty-first birthday was comprehensively ignorant. He barely bothered with the papers, let alone books, and tended to a conversational stew-of-consciousness that mangled orthodox English and threw up whole new phrases – 'We're honkin' on pretty good . . . let's groove back on the thirty and punt, y'know' – created in the process. He often had no idea what was being said to him. The pow-wows with Mitchell, Silberberg and the rest were punctuated by Steve's irritation and grief over the fact that their understanding of previous meetings diverged so sharply from his own. He respected his own people so little that they, too, soon fell prey to his latent paranoia. McQueen now audited his auditors.

Unlettered as he was, Steve was, however, that much more valuable thing – natively shrewd. A wit once observed that McQueen's vocabulary contained no more than 300 words, but the remarkable thing about them was that he always used them in the right way, at the right time, and in the right place. He had quite brilliant instincts. And empathy: like his friend John Lennon, Steve believed that if he wanted to understand his audience, he only had to look into his own heart. Like Lennon, he was usually right.

Intellectually McQueen was a stopped clock, but at one or two important junctures – often involving what new part to take – he told the correct time. As his pumped-up underlings had urged him to 'go big' after *Bullitt*, maybe with *Dirty Harry*, Steve had announced plans to film Bill Faulkner. (Bob Relyea confirms that 'McQueen, faster than any of us, immediately recognised *The Reivers*' merits'.) As Fields and others competed to see who could bring him the hottest property immediately following *Le Mans*, Steve selected a gentle, bucolic script called *Junior Bonner*. As the major studios insisted angrily that he steer clear of any more car documentaries, he blithely self-financed one about motorbikes which grossed eighty times its production cost. McQueen may not have known what he was doing, but he did it very well.

For all his occasional bilge about being a new Fellini, he was really devoted to the grail of making superior mass market pictures alternating with fables. In doing both as well as he did, McQueen never fitted the neat ideological stereotype that was presented in respective forms by vacuous 'actioners' and arty junk. He was an American original, both in form and substance. Nobody thought more clearly or more deeply about his films than he did. Thus Steve vetoed *Dirty Harry* and *The French Connection* because, as he was apt to remind Fields, 'I'm only good for doing authority my way,' and that way had been *Bullitt*. At around the same time McQueen read the script of *Play Misty for Me* and told friends, 'It's basically the girl's gig, not the guy's,' a mischievous and stingingly sharp précis. (The movie duly passed down the line to Clint Eastwood.) Next he turned down Don Siegel's *The Beguiled*, on the answerable grounds, 'I ain't gonna play half a movie with my leg sawn off.' Steve similarly torpedoed *The Johnson County War*, the epic Western that warped into *Heaven's Gate*, and blew off the dire but, at that pre-production stage, highly touted remake of *The Long Goodbye*. Conversely, McQueen was always the first to admire young talent like Peter Bogdanovich or Francis Coppola. He picked up in a flash on the then unknown Martin Scorsese and praised Scorsese's first feature, *Who's That Knocking at My Door*, fully five years before the critics did. Instinct was Steve's ozone. In life and on screen, time after time, he wrong-footed the elite with a shrugged-off 'Yep' or a grunted refusal. McQueen was a reflex genius cleverly disguised as a schlub. You never knew quite where you were with him, whether he was way behind you or way ahead, and this tension was part of his baffling charge. Call after good call suggests that he had the rare ability not just to 'see' a finished product from a few lines of text, but actually to *visualise* it something like a hologram. A lowbrow by nature, Steve was a savant when it came to his own business.

And when, only a few years later, he met Lee Katzin again, McQueen didn't seem to remember him at all, something Katzin was relieved about.

Steve's ode to motorbiking, *On Any Sunday*, opened that summer just five weeks after *Le Mans*. It was everything the main feature wasn't: lean, nippy and dramatically gripping purely by virtue of being a documentary and not attempting anything more. (On the few occasions *Sunday*'s director-narrator Bruce Brown strained for 'meaning', he showed as much insight into the human condition as a walnut.) A total cost of $313,000, the sort of budget Steve had blown on amyl nitrate in France, was rewarded by a staggering $26 million worldwide gross. McQueen himself, who raced under the alias Harvey Mushman in several of the motocross scenes, didn't, in the end, see a dime. Most of his appearance fee went to pay off his back tax bill. Not that he gave a shit. His one actual line, 'Every time I start thinking of the world as all bad, I see some people out having a good time on motorcycles – makes me take another look,' was a key suggestive speech. He wrote it himself. For years McQueen had been accused of talking either too much or, rather more often, too little. That particular set-piece said it perfectly.

On 19 May 1971, McQueen agreed to do *Junior Bonner* for $850,000 and points.

Like God, Steve was everywhere that summer: shooting the new movie in Prescott, Arizona, flogging *Le Mans* for all it was worth, watching *Sunday* kiss itself in on awards and undreamt-of profits. And finally achieving biking's highest accolade, the cover of *Sports Illustrated*. Much as it was a coup in itself, it was also a front – a scam. McQueen started putting it around that 'Funny thing about my marriage: all the racing killed it. And I don't compete any more. So after all these years, just when I finally decide to hang up the goggles . . . it's too late.'

Total bullshit, says Neile.

'My marriage to Steve didn't end due to his predisposition for cars and bikes . . . In the end, the machinery didn't come into it.' What did was the madness of McQueen's revenge trip, turning him from a lovable kook into a militant drug addict and, not coincidentally, a paranoid sadist. What followed, for a few wretched months, was the worst study of self-absorption since *Hamlet*. With added violence.

Immediately after signing for *Junior Bonner*, Steve went out with Neile on a shrink-approved date. He drove up to the Castle already high. Neile looked at his face in the evening sunlight, and saw a peculiar intensity there. She knew the expression: it came from coke.

The stash came out straight away, on the way to the Mexican restaurant downtown. Three drinks over dinner. A little more grass in the car on the way home. Then it started: *Fucking bitch. Slut. Cunt.* On and on about the cocksucking asshole kraut until McQueen was driving with one hand on the wheel and the other yanking Neile's hair. As they pulled in the Castle driveway she tried to make a run for it but he grabbed her, his foot slamming in, and as he kicked her he began asking, 'Why? *Why*, you whore?' He slapped her three or four times. Each time she went down on her knees. Each time Neile staggered back up, badly winded but now frantically pleading. Each time he came back at her, a cyclone of speed and viciousness. Hearing the commotion, their butler Ariel first yelled at McQueen, then picked up the closest thing to hand – his Motorola radio – and smashed it against the wall. His sudden intervention seemed to paralyse Steve. For a moment he stood there balling his fists, dazed. Then swiftly he bent down and helped Neile to her feet, upstairs, and into bed. He said he was sorry and kissed her goodnight.

But the evening wasn't over.

Spent and contrite, Steve sat down next to her, shuffling the sides of his feet and apologising again and again. Neile lay there sobbing.

'I'm going to have to leave you,' she finally said. 'I must because if I don't, someday you'll kill me. And my God, Steve, what will happen to the kids? I don't want that for them. Do you?'

McQueen didn't want it, either. Not that. Never that.

He got back from *Junior Bonner* in late August, three months later. Incredibly, he actually started to date Neile again, and they had at least one dinner at the Santa Ynez Inn in Pacific Palisades, near his old guest cottage. According to the actor Jim Geller, who happened to be sitting a few feet away, 'They spent a lot of time drinking beer and, I couldn't help notice, pouting and crying . . . Neile sat there in stony silence while Steve cranked it up. Then she seemed to retaliate and there were a lot of ugly words being thrown around. Over and over, McQueen kept signalling for more brews. Six or seven in a couple of hours.' *Adios.* The very next evening, back there with a companion, Steve started in again until finally he fell asleep. His girlfriend and the manager helped carry him out to the car. 'Oh, this happens all the time,' she said.

Another night Steve came back to the restaurant on his own and started swigging down Mexican beer from the bottle. A few diners recognised him and one or two, at his invitation, joined him at his table. McQueen called for tequila, and even more new friends came over, two of them with a plastic bag of coke – but then one had to lie down on the floor, and the other was rushed to the hospital with chest pains. The mob of people at Steve's booth became a mini-riot, and some of them yelled for everyone who wasn't a 'personal friend of Mr McQueen' to leave, and Steve himself yelled the opposite, as the waiter tried to push through with two more huge trays of drinks. This went on until midnight. By then McQueen was again fast asleep, sprawled out on the tile floor with one arm held grotesquely up in the air. Twelve or fifteen people he didn't know were eating his food and passing around coke and calling for more booze to be added to his bill. The party broke up towards dawn. Steve spent the rest of that short night on a bench in Topanga Park amongst the junkies, early morning joggers and packs of wild dogs.

While he slept, he'd been tapped out like a human cash machine. Steve woke up and found hundreds of bucks gone.

Despite or because of their occasional dates, Neile filed for divorce on 10 September 1971. It was just seven weeks short of fifteen years since the whey-faced couple, the successful dancer and the struggling actor, both of them terrified, had been married on the fly with two cops as witnesses. Then, they'd struck friends like Bob Wise as 'two smart and slightly wilful kids whom everybody loved'. Now, as they will, those same friends formed camps around the warring parties. The gap between how the couple were seen when together and how they were judged once apart wasn't just unusually wide, it was yawningly so. With the factions locked in battle like fighting beetles in a jar, Neile formally cited 'irreconcilable differences', the only causes needed under new California laws, and said her marriage had broken down that May. She asked support for herself and for the children. Steve, who'd evidently seen himself as honking on, still getting his shit together with his wife after she betrayed him, wasn't just surprised – he was shocked.

'I never expected you to file,' McQueen would tell her at regular intervals for the rest of his life. 'Why'd you do it?'

The case, number WED-18882, wound its way through Superior Court on and off throughout the winter of 1971–2. *McQueen v McQueen* was an exhausting, publicly dignified but often privately ugly process, containing whispered claims, never denied, of Steve's shtupping everyone from the babysitter to Natalie Wood, trying to get it off with cheerleaders, maintaining an LSD, grass and coke habit, and – as if there could be anything worse – listening to the Mamas and the Papas at top volume. It was agreed that Terry and Chad, at least, would be placed in Neile's custody, though, as she said, 'that was just a technicality . . . The children are as much Steve's as mine.' This commitment was a welcome reminder that he could be as loving and warmly available as any father.

More protracted was the row about money and, of all things, the couple's furniture. Specifically, the pool table. This treasured link to McQueen's vanished past was where Neile – so she told Steve when the removal van came – had made out with yet another actor, the *Psycho* and *Spartacus* star John Gavin. McQueen later described the scene: how he stomped off without the table, though threatening to blow Gavin's brains out. How, years later, he was on the phone at the Beverly Wilshire and two drunks began giving him shit – 'Hey, McQueen! What d'ya say, superstar? Asshole!' – and in the middle of the inevitable brawl he'd heard a third voice somewhere behind him saying, 'Don't do it, Steve. Think of who you are.' It was Gavin. Immediately the two fights had overlapped and became the same fight, McQueen knocking down one of the drunks, scaring off the other and cocking back his red-knuckled fist at Fuckhead. That was the scene that ended, according to Hoven, with Steve screaming, 'Son of a bitch! You porked my old lady!' and the future

US Ambassador to Mexico running for his life down the street.

'McQueen told me he didn't actually hit John Gavin. But he put the fear of God in him.'*

In March 1972 Neile was duly awarded a $1 million settlement, in addition to alimony and child support set at $7000 a month for the first year, $5000 for the second, and $1500 thereafter up to a total of ten years. Publicly, Steve was stoic. 'She deserves every penny of it – without my old lady, there wouldn't have been any in the first place.' Privately he corked off at Neile for years, complaining to Pat Johnson how 'she tried to bust my balls', and describing her elsewhere as 'a crazy bitch' and 'loony as a tune'. Sixteen months later Steve insisted that Ali MacGraw sign a prenuptial agreement because, she says, 'he told me Neile had taken an enormous amount of money from him when they divorced'. Many good judges would, and did, say that it was actually Steve who lucked in in his first marriage, precisely through Neile's generosity. She'd put up with more than most thought humanly possible because, as she says, 'I loved him, and also for the children.' To their mutual credit, both parties agreed that Terry and Chad were free to come and go between their parents' houses, and that their welfare was paramount. After a final financial hearing the McQueens' divorce was made absolute on 26 April 1972.

The marriage was formally wound up in the bare-walled courtroom in Santa Monica. It never really ended. After four years of civility for the kids' sakes, Steve and Neile began seeing each other again in June 1976. He used to tell her how much he missed her, that the face was her experience and the eyes were her soul. Anything to get her in that hotel room. They were still making love at regular intervals until near the very end of McQueen's life. Not only that, Steve seriously used to propose the odd threesome with his second wife, if not a full-blown ménage à trois. Once or twice he even asked if Neile would take him back. 'All I needed was for you to give me time . . . I needed time until I could clear my melon.' It never happened, but they did achieve something rarer, a true second-act friend-

---

* Gavin says today that he 'didn't know Mr McQueen well enough to make any significant comment' for a biography. Poignantly, his controversial appointment as ambassador to Mexico came in the very week that Steve went there to die.

ship. The bond was now firm because they'd worked through hostilities not by resolving differences, but by mutually agreeing to walk away from them. McQueen's interest in threesomes seemed to pass from the active stage; and they had the shared love of the family. Neile clearly doted on their children. Steve too, though all that brooding and fussy re-fighting of old wars had visibly drained him. He was already dying of acute inwardness, a disease that would spread.

'Most marriages in the industry crack up fast, mainly due to [the] pressure. But me, I'm no party stud. I'm with one woman at a time and she's my lady and that's it . . . No matter what you read in the gossip rags, I'm not a cat who sleeps around when I'm into a heavy relationship . . . I don't do no orgies. That's just not my style.'

Actually, by 1972 Steve didn't just go to orgies, he *was* the orgy. As well as his promiscuous dating of the co-eds and ski bunnies, there was the model Lauren Hutton, the singer Mary Wilson and the starlet Barbara Leigh, twenty-four, who helped prop him through the *Junior Bonner* shoot. (A friend once remarked that he would call McQueen's sex drive bottomless were the adjective not so inappropriate.) Leigh herself says she always felt he missed the 'stable force in his life' that he'd long lacked and now lost, more than he did the actual woman. But that loss lasted less than a year. After giving him the freeze for a few months, Neile herself would remain touchingly close to his life and work, and come out with some remarkably supportive comments on both, no matter how much they were in the grip of a then bitter divorce.

Bonner, meanwhile, took a surprising twist, and not just because it all went smoothly.

Over the course of several weeks Steve became seriously enmeshed with Leigh, a tall, pretty woman, thin, with black hair, and something of a free spirit. The inevitable happened, and, as she says, they enjoyed a 'wonderful, intense' relationship. He asked her to move in with him during the shoot. (This was while McQueen, evidently, still harboured hopes of reconciling with his wife.) But Leigh got pregnant, made a difficult decision, then changed her mind, the plot finally giving way to the depressingly familiar tropes of just a year

271

before: the agonised confession, Steve in this case told, 'The baby isn't yours.' The arrangements.

A stupefied kind of loss would come with that abortion, too. Meanwhile, McQueen and Leigh applied themselves to *Bonner*, a film with a radiant glow.

Into his work there crept a new and more gentle note, a ringing demand for control, and yet for control that would create 'good shit and a family atmosphere'. A true melon-twister. Most people who'd had direct experience of Steve, especially when making a movie, associated him with hot-headedness. *Le Mans* had shown that yet again. But the world associated him with the polar opposite, being cool. McQueen was an example of an actor who did well out of his stereotype. Yet even closer to the man there were sane, intelligent people like Neile and Don Gordon and Bud Ekins who admired him not for his style but because he was a loyal, all-weather friend, a lover of the tired, the poor and the huddled masses, and above all a regular guy who dug ditches with his own hands, ate in diners, wanted to be 'better' and was, in fact, ultimately converted, but still avoided preaching and martyrdom, laughing off the tragic personal myth already gathering round him as he lay dying in the clinic. Gary Combs, who knew Steve for fifteen years and four films, says that for most of that time 'he desperately wanted to be a good guy. The tragedy was that McQueen was able to figure out the problem, but not quite able to figure out what to do about it.'

Barbara Leigh, too, speaks about the 'uptight but childlike' man. Though half-dead from excess, Steve's personal and professional comeback twisted his fumblings into a kind of triumph.

Not that the studios cared about all that redemption. When the bottom-lines were added up, six of Steve's last eight films had been major successes, and even stiffs like *The Reivers* and *Le Mans* shook down $20 million apiece. For more than a month now ABC/Cinerama had been paying Solar a thousand a day in palm-money merely to sweeten the deal for him on *Junior Bonner*.

Although it had its roots in Jeb Rosebrook's script about a greying cowboy's own breakdown with the world, *Bonner* emerged like a walking hangover during and after McQueen's actual mid-life crisis, the tale of a vanishing America, using rodeo as a metaphor – a slice

of death drawn from a larger ruin. Steve 'got' the story immediately.
A tape exists of McQueen in script conferences with Rosebrook and
the film's director in which Steve hammers the historical-figment
over the heroic – 'The guy's kind of a dinosaur, just like me.' It was
all a throwback to the original, doomed hustler theme of *Cincinnati
Kid* envisaged by Sam Peckinpah, which wasn't surprising, since
Peckinpah directed *Junior Bonner*. The tapes reveal that he and
McQueen worked hard on 'keeping it real', with a hero who dared,
literally, to 'fall on his butt', get 'shat on', and generally become a
seminar in 'big-time fuck-up. In short, Steve refound his roots.

As well as the $850,000, McQueen got his usual perks covering
living expenses, security and the like. He had Freddie Fields specifically draft in a clause on transportation:

> In order to maintain the value of Artist's services hereunder, it
> is necessary to maintain his image which is special, unique and
> extraordinary and is associated with but not limited to vehicles
> such as motorcycles and racing cars, and Corporation agrees to
> pay such expenses connected with the maintenance of his 'star'
> image . . .

Special, unique and extraordinary? He was obviously all of that. The
whole subject was very fully covered, as was Steve's agreeing to ride
mechanical bulls, not to 'use automobiles and/or motorcycles in an
unusual manner or race them during the period commencing with
the date hereof' and, as ever, to conduct himself 'with due regard
to public conventions and morals'. Grinning like an imp, McQueen
ripped off a belch and duly signed. Over a third or fourth celebratory
beer he told the suits that at least he wouldn't need much in the way
of wardrobe. Even up there among the brass and marble in the ABC
boardroom he was perfectly groomed for his role as the last cowboy
– he loved dressing in frontier drag.

Thirteen years earlier the actress and pioneering director Ida
Lupino had been one of the original Four Stars who gave McQueen
his break in *Wanted*. He returned the favour by hiring her in *Bonner*'s
supporting cast. She was paid $21,000, at $3500 per week, a fraction
over 2 per cent of his own fee. The two of them then happily sat
around Prescott at all hours, amusing each other with tales of old

Hollywood: sex, violence, certain laughs Lupino had had making *Sierra* with Bogart; guns; horses; Josh Randall. The good days. Steve, who still called her 'Miss Ida', even spoke fondly of the $750 a week, plus endorsements, he'd made in 1958, contending that the studios had been systematically sly-fucking him ever since.

When McQueen, as Bonner, had to buy his father a plane ticket in the film, they gave him a wad of real money. After the scene he handed the cash back to the prop master, who happened to notice it was 300 dollars short. Steve didn't deny it. Instead he insisted that the money fell within *Bonner*'s incidentals budget and was therefore studio responsibility. He knew they would ultimately eat the expense, and so they did. When Lupino ragged him about it McQueen told her he didn't give a shit for ABC's conventions and morals. It was as if each time he went to work he was determined never to work in the industry again: a kind of combined death wish and lifelong need to humiliate the suits.

One shared by Sam Peckinpah. The forty-six-year-old *enfant terrible* of *The Wild Bunch* and *Straw Dogs* first appeared on set swigging from a paper cup of gin, then went on from there to order breakfast: five or six industrial-strength Death cigarettes, tequila, and a vitamin B12 shot delivered neat to the buttock. Perversely, or ironically, Peckinpah spoke in a low, whispering voice, appeared friendly to his leading man and evidently bore no grudge about *Cincinnati Kid*. On location in Arizona, treading the sound stage in his cracked, unlaced sneakers, mumbling through a bullhorn as he choreographed the whole 1940s time warp, controlling not only the rhythm but also the volume of the film, and sculpting the audience's feelings as he went along, Peckinpah was both ringmaster and conductor of a quiet American classic. There were no walkouts or other churlish humiliations; Peckinpah's star had always been prepared to accept firm direction. Nobody would see the self-dramatising Supie as they had during *The Great Escape* or *Thomas Crown* or *Le Mans*. On both set and screen *Junior Bonner* was that seeming contradiction in terms, a tranquil Steve McQueen film.

Once a week, on a Friday, he'd bring in beer and cold cuts for the whole crew. One of the lowliest of gaffers was once standing at the end of the buffet table when he became aware of a presence beside him.

'Mr McQueen.' As he spoke, Peckinpah's words came into his head: Don't hassle him, *don't ask for nothing*. Nervously, the man looked down at the spread and said, 'Nice eats.'

'Yep.'

A moment later: 'And brew.'

'Yep.'

He realised that that was Steve's way of dealing with strangers, a word at a time. Still, within that massive constraint, he seemed nice enough. People found his terseness calming. It was as if he were giving them guidance. He always lowered his head, they noticed, when he was listening, particularly when Peckinpah described some excruciatingly fiddly shot.

'Shit, Sam, just *roll 'em!*'

The inclusive energy of the shoot fed Steve's creativity. At six every morning he was huddled with Peckinpah and Rosebrook in yet more story conferences, dashing off whole notebooks, filled with zigzagging currents of energy, gentle words and sharp ones. *Fucking roll 'em!* McQueen knew not only his own lines but, unprecedentedly, every-body else's, too. To coin a phrase, he was the model professional. And father: Terry and Chad visited the set for three weeks that summer, for once without their mother. Steve would work hard under their gaze all morning, then, when the heat rose off the Weaver mountains to the south, all brown and baked-looking and furrowed in strange shapes, and the sand of the bull pen stung under their feet, he'd call for a wrap and take off in his Porsche with the kids and Barbara Leigh. Before he left, McQueen had a quiet word of encouragement – usually with an added hug or high-five – with each member of the cast and crew. Then he was gone. Fast. Peckinpah once had to shout through the bullhorn to catch him.

Back in the rental home, Steve also worked hard to atone for his gaffes with Neile, and to build up form as a divorced parent. His pivotal obsession now was to flog himself for his children. McQueen had that rich mix, guilt and basically sound instincts – the very feel-ings the old McQueen would have sabotaged, lest the guilt made him think and the instincts led to change. It had; they did.

Over the next month Leigh found herself reflecting that McQueen was a soul with a little boy in him, and rather more excitable than most forty-year-olds. She thought also that just about any woman could fall for him. Many had. She wasn't quite sure enough of her feelings for *that*, but, well, it was up to him to make sense of it all. He always knew best. What a man.

'I just love this,' Leigh said. Her head was on his shoulder. 'I just love this so much.'

'Things look good.'

And *Junior Bonner* was, just as he'd hoped, a major turning point. Not only did Steve begin clawing his way out of the hole, he gave one of his richest performances. The echo of John Wayne in his *True Grit* phase was loud in most of McQueen's remaining seven roles, a cool and clear return to what both men did best: the sort of arch reticence Steve had in mind when he told the young Chuck Norris, 'Let the other actors say what the fuck they want. You only say what's important, and you own the scene.' Simplicity and clarity like that were now once again McQueen's ideals, and in time he'd come to tout the neglected 'character' pictures as the sweetest sugar of them all. There was a completely absorbing integrity to *Baby, the Rain Must Fall* and *The Reivers* as there wasn't to *Le Mans*. Like the very best Hemingway, they eschewed the laziness of unnecessary complexity. *Bonner*'s own mute reconciliation scene between Steve and Bob Preston, playing his father, touching and unusually vulnerable, utterly changed the rules of a Sam Peckinpah movie in its blend of tears instead of blood and sweat. The botched emotions were the film's keynote – it basically retold the familiar 'big-time fuck-up' saga in a way which responded to Steve's own history. What's more, *Bonner* bridged the gap between McQueen's unspeakably gawky and knowledgeably cool personae: quite a coup. It was the cleverest movie he ever made.

That whole year was fucking special. So he told friends when he got home to California: a kick-starting not only of a new career but of his own new life. Out went the old Supie crap. 'I've cut everything down,' Steve said. 'Now I think of Laurence Olivier when he goes to work. He's got a little black bag with a couple of fake noses, his wig, or whatever he's got in there. And that's all I need – a pencil, a script, and a briefcase.' He might have added a calculator. On 31 October 1971 McQueen signed a new forty-two-page internal deal with Solar covering anything from Wardrobe and Image through Fan Mail (read and answered, if at all, by his secretary) up to Compensation – still a guaranteed half-million a year. He had Freddie Fields buy him in to First Artists. By early 1972 Steve was notionally a partner along with Sidney Poitier, Barbra Streisand and Paul Newman. Now he and Fuckwit were kindred spirits in a scheme whereby each would take no upfront salary from a given picture, in exchange for 10 per cent of the gross. It sounded good. And for three or four years it was. But being a company man, for McQueen, sooner or later meant getting neurotic around the suits. It was a kind of addiction.

The scene would be a Hollywood boardroom. Right in the middle of the patter would come the sound of a raised Midwestern voice. Everyone would stop. The Midwesterner would rip off a stick of gum. A man wearing a white suit over a French sailor jersey and heavy mascara would purr, 'Mr McQueen?' All eyes would turn. The Midwesterner would munch slowly and then, with a scowl and a downward sweep of the right forefinger, record his vote:

'The deal stinks, man. Mr McQueen says so. Mr McQueen.'

Steve and First Artists were mutually shaken by their association. Within a year or two he was at war with the company president, Phil Feldman, primarily about the seed money that got the movies made in the first place. McQueen wanting more, Feldman less. To illustrate his point, Steve burst into that same boardroom one morning wielding a chainsaw. After a few preliminary rips of the cord he didn't actually succeed in starting it, but instead grabbed Feldman by the knot in his tie, McQueen later said, 'and yanked him over the table, right on top of the fruit platter . . . I told the little fucker I'd chop him into pieces.' According to Steve, Feldman rose and slunk out.

The vendetta was, by McQueen standards, short lived. Just five years later in the Mexican clinic, he told his last ever interviewer, 'I've had a battle in my business with somebody . . . I think I really want to let go of the pressure.' No small release. Above all else – above pushy broads and press and shyster lawyers – Steve seldom made himself congenial to those corporate suits. But by then it didn't matter much. He privately renounced his few remaining feuds.

McQueen at forty-two was clearly in transition, not yet a full initiate. There was still no moral centre. His friend Pat Johnson remembers him 'always putting you on ... Steve was so smart he'd pick up on different people's perceptions of him and then play out that role. That's why if you ask ten people about him you'll get ten comically different answers.' By now McQueen was, among other things, cocky, shy, egotistical – poring through Neile's scrapbook of his press cuttings – cool, eruptive, fun, gregarious and the still haunted child who told Peckinpah's assistant, Katy Haber, 'Never had a woman as a friend. Don't even think you can,' or asked Hoven, 'Where do I keep screwing up?' Each of these roles had something to say for it, with the exception of being haunted – the only part McQueen ever played with total conviction – and even that, as he often said, gave him a depth Fuckwit could only feebly approximate.

Late one night there was a loud pounding at Don Gordon's door in Hollywood. Steve was there, alone, dressed in his biking leathers. It was pouring with rain. 'C'mon man. Let's go for a ride.'

Gordon suited up.

On McQueen's lead, but without any further explanation, they rode east through the storm up Sunset Boulevard. For a while the all-night movie marquees sent down a pink flush onto the asphalt, soon darkened again by a relentless diet of boarded-up slums. Finally Steve pulled off the road, onto a side street and stopped in front of a stucco row of cheap apartments and fleabag motels. The place reeled with the cheerful din of amplified rock, women crying, dogs growling, TVs blaring and .38 specials snapping off in the distance. It was the very ghetto where McQueen had been terrorised by his stepfather Berri in 1942. The old friends stood there in silence for a long time. Then Gordon in turn showed Steve the nearby house where he, too, had been dumped and abused as a child.

At least for him, the incident was over. It meant nothing. Don wasn't even bitter about it.

Later that same night McQueen and Gordon took shelter from the storm in a neighbourhood coffee house. 'Steve asked me to go in and order, which I did. He knew he would've been mobbed in a public place . . . So the two of us sort of hunch outside there, in the pissing rain and dark, drinking coffee, and sharing our feelings about the past. Very emotional. At some stage much later on a biker dude comes out of the store, ambles over and starts talking away about engines and tyre pressure and all that shit. A friendly enough guy. So Steve brightens up a bit. Then we get on to racing and scrambling and really technical stuff. Steve brightens up even more. Finally the dude stands up to go, squints through all the rain and says, "You know, man, if you weren't all wet and fucked up, you'd look a bit like Steve McQueen." We both had a good laugh about that. Steve loved the fact that the guy related to him as a real biker, not as a candyass movie star.'

From the beginning, then, everything was subordinate to the cause of success and power, combined with an intense awareness of humanity and moral responsibility.

Apart from Gordon himself, not too many friends would match Steve's restless gear changes over the years. For those compelled to keep up, the learning curve soon became an endless spin cycle: men like Bob Relyea, Kamen, Valentine and McQueen's props manager and motorcycling buddy Steve Ferry were all banished in the wake of *Le Mans*. According to Hoven, 'The guys who carried the biggest strut with Steve were those who were the best at their business – the Bud Ekinses of this world – who respected him as an actor without treating him like Zsa Zsa Gabor. Once you grovelled, you were finished.'

After training with Bruce Lee until Lee's Hollywood breakthrough *Fists of Fury*, then with Chuck Norris until he, in turn, opted for *Return of the Dragon*, Steve now found a new martial arts tutor and blood brother in Pat Johnson. No one would see McQueen more often, or know him better during the last eight years of his life than he did. Not only was Johnson, a ninth-degree black belt, the best at his trade; crucially, like Don Gordon and Steve himself, he was a Dickensian child, raised alternately by a single mother and the local Catholic orphanage. Most mornings when not actually on location, McQueen would drive himself from the Palisades or Coldwater Canyon to Johnson's studio in Sherman Oaks, work out and leave.

Not a single word. Then one day, after a dozen lessons, he quietly asked Johnson where he'd grown up. Then it was an invitation to coffee. Then it was coffee and breakfast. Then Steve 'very gradually began talking about his personal life, his feelings about his own parents. Lots of unresolved stuff there . . . For obvious reasons, I had kind of a feeling of where McQueen was coming from, namely always expecting to be left and quite often ensuring that he was. And touchy. Steve was the most aggressive person I ever met. He fought like he behaved generally – fast, furious, with lethal opening moves, intense and incredibly focused. In eight years I never once saw him have a lapse of concentration.'

In fact it was unlike Steve to even speak to an opponent.

The two men not only bonded over karate, but McQueen increasingly came to depend on Johnson's good judgement. 'Steve started from the premise that everyone was bad unless proven good, whereas I study someone to find their flaws, then make damn sure I'm never in a position where those flaws can hurt me. I think Steve appreciated that perspective, and even adopted it . . . It was one of the things we shared together.' In time McQueen would become a virtual uncle to Johnson's four sons, stay at Johnson's house, drive his car and, whenever discretion called, specifically during his second marriage, use him as an alias. 'He must have shacked up in half the motels in LA with different women under the name Pat Johnson. I *still* get funny looks at some of those places.'

Jim Hoven phoned one morning while Steve was staying at the Vagabond Inn to tell him the president of Warner Brothers wanted him to read *The Towering Inferno.* 'He tried calling you direct, but the switchboard told him there was nobody there called McQueen.'

'I'm being followed,' said Steve. 'Registering as Pat is a way of protecting myself.'

From Hoven came a low whistle of homage. 'You're right, Steve. That's exactly the safeguard we should all take to keep against being offered a million bucks a movie. The studio's left messages all over town.'

'What's that to me?'

'Be at Warners at ten, man. Use the employees' entrance.'

But McQueen didn't follow directions. Instead he went shopping at a Hollywood novelty store for a Groucho mask, then turned up at the studio front gate hours late. He was still wearing the fake nose and moustache, and chewing a cigar, when he reached the Warners boardroom. The suits themselves had arrived earlier in the morning as though borne to their destiny on a tide of optimism, eager and erect, then gradually slumped down as more and more of the day ticked by. All their poise had crumbled by the time McQueen showed up. And all of them knew to say nothing, about either his lateness or his get-up, or else risk inciting Steve to growls of disparagement for their own appearance, and to the reiterated charge that plenty of studios had wasted his fucking time, too. So he slouched there, in his cheap party mask, asked a few questions – still in character as Groucho – and scrawled a signature that would eventually earn him $12 million from a single film.

Steve turned his back on the blandishments of the suits and went out to the Vagabond for another night.

'McQueen had that childlike, if you want, childish, sense of humour,' says Johnson. 'He'd get giggling like a kid. One of his favourite expressions [was] he'd eat a carrot and turn to me and say, "Well, you never saw a rabbit wearing glasses, did you?" Every time he'd say it, he'd laugh, I'd laugh, everyone else would laugh ... There was always that young Steve inside the old one, the hungry kid who wolfed down pork chops and pie who also happened to be a millionaire star.' And merry prankster: McQueen retained a lifelong love of clockwork mice, silly walks and upturned pails of water. He could do funny accents. Another feature, says Hoven, was Steve's famed ability to 'pick up on somebody's quirks' – a facial tic, a peculiar laugh – and mimic them into the ground. While Hoven thinks 'it jarred against the loner image', Jim Geller isn't convinced. If anything, it was a put-down. A pie in the face from McQueen said *fuck off*.'

His most incoherent rage was reserved for the studio chiefs and moneymen who, he reasoned, should have been his core supporters. 'Steve openly seethed at all the Hollywood backstabbing and compromises, especially after *Le Mans*,' says Johnson. In particular, anything that reawakened McQueen's old sense of betrayal sent him into his 'shit' moods, though they could be ominously contained. Hoven saw one plaintive example when 'Steve was pissed off at Phil Feldman [but] instead of yelling he sat down in his den whimpering and singing into a tape recorder, in the voice of a small child: "No one can stop me from being me." *Then* he wigged out.'

This wasn't about mere textual-hysterical nitpicking at McQueen's scripts. Or even his budgets. It was more the concrete details of Steve's whole style that represented his true war with Hollywood: specifically, that he drove motorbikes twenty years before they became an industry fetish, swaggered around with dirt under his nails, inclined to torn, tight-fitting denim, turned up late for meetings and didn't reply to official letters. Ever. Then there was the fact that he was a perfectionist, always or usually uptight on set, broodingly suspicious behind the scenes. Any studio who worked with Steve knew that sooner or later they could expect to be audited. McQueen even dared to buck the star system pieties of his fellow First Artists directors Newman and Streisand. He told them he didn't give a fuck about voting for George McGovern, or anybody else, in the 1972 presidential election. His particular causes weren't the candyass ones of McGovern's social-uplift agenda. At a meeting that autumn Steve asked Newman not to make any political donations out of First Artists funds. They were supposed to be partners.

Then, late in December, an earthquake devastated western Nicaragua, killing 7000 people and severing communications with the outside world. Hearing that many of those worst affected were children, McQueen quietly bought $50,000 worth of food, blankets and anti-typhoid serum, then chartered a jet to take it to Managua, again without publicity. No one in Hollywood even knew of his gesture until years after he died.

In all, says Geller, 'Steve was Steve . . . No other star so doggedly fused the brilliant and the foaming mad. That crazy fucker could drive the studio brass nuts – quite literally.' How McQueen's friends laughed to remember when the head of Cinema Center, Gordon Stuhlberg, after swooping in from LA, had changed planes in Paris, then landed at the tiny airstrip outside Le Mans that hot summer night in 1970. Steve was personally there to meet him in his Porsche Spyder. The jet-lagged tycoon was expecting to sit down for crisis talks with his wayward star, to, as he said, 'shake some sense' into him. Instead it was Stuhlberg himself who was jolted as McQueen swiftly took the Porsche up to full chat, honking along the country lanes at 120 m.p.h. until Stuhlberg could only cower, open-mouthed, in his seat. By the time Steve dropped him off at the hotel, his would-be lecturer was speechless: 'literally dumbstruck', said Stan Kamen. McQueen tried variants of the same softening-up technique with a number of his more prominent colleagues. Another evening in France he brought the car – this time with Katzin in the passenger seat – suddenly barrelling to a halt on a busy road, climbed out, faced away and began peeing, calmly talking to the director over his shoulder as he did so.

If you happened to be a Hollywood authority figure in the early 1970s, you simply couldn't go wrong shaking your head and muttering down the table, 'That mad bastard.' Everyone agreed.

Back around the time of *Le Mans*, when he first told the Golden Globe committee he'd accept their award but was fucked if he'd go there in person to collect it, it was McQueen who was the nut. Within five years, after both George Scott and Brando refused their Oscars and the ceremony itself turned into a superior freak show, loomed over by the *National Enquirer*, Cher and low-flying Hueys, the establishment looked a lot nuttier than he did. Steve's snub of the Globes, the theory goes, led directly to his own repeated snubbing by the Academy. (That and the fact that he'd shtupped fully half of the nominating committee's wives.) Even Dustin Hoffman believes that McQueen should have won for *Papillon*. The hard truth is that Steve didn't particularly enjoy his work, let alone all the luvvie sub-culture, notably the awards and ass-kissing. 'I don't think I'm going to be around acting much longer,' he said in 1972. 'I've had it all . . . and I find what's really best is nothing. In the simplest form. Jeans and a shirt.' *Running outta gas.* It was just that, as both public and trade acknowledged, he happened to be the very best in town at what he did. In poll after poll throughout the seventies the same five stars revolved: McQueen, Eastwood, Reynolds, Newman, Redford. That was astronomy according to the people who owned cinemas or actually paid money to sit in them. For most of the decade it was 'Steve über alles', Hoffman said, in that retiring way of his.

McQueen's reputation as one of the Beautiful People, at least around the chi-chi aquarium of the Academy, stood low. Elsewhere it was a different story. Steve's 'realness', if not always his niceness, was Hollywood lore. His second wife, for instance, says he was 'just great with kids. So straight. But he [was] like that, really, with everyone close to him. He dealt on a very straight level. He [said] exactly what he meant to whomever he felt like talking to, and ignored the people he didn't like.' He wasn't even being rude, adds Geller. He was being Steve.

'McQueen wasn't one to sit around with a kiss-ass smile telling you he loved your work. "Fuck you! I already acted enough for one day." He was a complicated straightforward guy.' Both more and less than the myth. That isn't in any sense to belittle McQueen's greatness. No aspect of the legend has been so completely missed as his core normality. The popular stereotype of the icily cool, well-connected Supie ignores the true complexity of the man and puts him on a pedestal. 'My best memories,' says Pat Johnson 'are when he'd amble in, fish around for a beer at the back of my fridge, and slump there, talking and laughing all hours, and generally be Uncle Steve.' No acts of projection, revenge or self-justification. Just that 'ordinary extraordinary guy'.

All the time, however, McQueen *was* growing icily cool towards most of the dozens of scripts Freddie Fields sent him. Almost all of them were formulaic: Steve standing in complete and heroic antithesis to his penny-ante, loser rivals in films like *Dirty Harry*. Most bored him shitless. 'I don't even get a pulse, let alone a rise when I'm reading them.' What did arouse McQueen was an offscreen romp that would constitute one of the most entertaining and enduring human dramas ever staged, certainly in Hollywood. Steve himself loved it, at least at first. By mid 1972 he was like a pig in shit, he confidentially told friends. Loved it! An absolute *wallow* in the stuff.

Thanks to friendly press agentry by Neile, McQueen's friend Dave Foster had duly won the rights to Jim Thompson's *noir* novel *The Getaway*. Now a cult, then largely neglected, it was less a book than a series of dispatches from inside the head of its anti-hero, 'Doc' McCoy. There was a plot, just about, which found a husband-and-wife gang masterminding a bank heist, with added sex, infidelity, speed, violence, betrayal and a break for the Mexican border all shadowing the core elements of Steve's own life. He signed up immediately after *Junior Bonner*. Sam Peckinpah returned to direct. As for *Le Mans*, cattle-calls were held. Various leading ladies, including Angie Dickinson, Dyan Cannon and Farrah Fawcett, among others, were either rejected or proved difficult. Then Bob Evans, head of production at Paramount – a *wunderkind* and walking vanity plate later parodied by Hoffman in *Wag the Dog* – began lobbying for his wife, a thirty-two-year-old actress with a stellar gift for portraying kooky, doe-eyed college girls.

Ali MacGraw.

MacGraw's last two movies – she'd done only three in her life – were small pictures called *Goodbye, Columbus* and *Love Story*. The latter made her world famous: a slim, tooth-white girl who looked like something out of a Scott Fitzgerald novel. In fact, when McQueen drove up to the Evanses' French Regency mansion in Beverly Hills, MacGraw was still hoping to talk him into co-starring with her in *The Great Gatsby*. She was a romantic. He was the fabled Hollywood cocksman. All the rich-girl staples had been fed during MacGraw's leafy, Westchester County youth in a home where her father did most of the housework. McQueen was the Midwestern orphan who grew up assuming that anything domestic was candyass. She was a Wellesley college graduate; he was semi-literate. She loved ballet; he liked to honk off on a souped-up Harley and smoke dope with the Navajos. She ate French cuisine; he loved to binge on burgers and pie, chased down by cans of Old Milwaukee. Given all the differences as measured in age, background and day-to-day 'shit', the practicality of their even working together would have seemed to be nil. Contact.

Several Bentleys were parked in the Evanses' driveway, and when McQueen rang the bell there was a loud tolling of 'Greensleeves' and poodles began to yap inside. The security arrangements were elaborate. An oriental butler turned Steve over to a secretary, who directed him to an oak-panelled library. He was served coffee on a silver tray. Finally Evans himself gambolled in on Cuban heels, his bouffant hair seeming to precede him by a half-second. Behind him was MacGraw. 'Ali in those days was absolutely mesmerising,' Hoven says. 'There was something coltish about her, almost virginal – even though she was on her second husband.' What Steve saw that morning was a creature bred and groomed to be as fey and seductive as any *Gatsby* heroine, from her flowing, centre-parted black hair to her gypsy dress and hand-tooled Indian sandals.

'Let's talk turkey,' said Evans.

Inside a minute MacGraw had forgotten about Scott Fitzgerald. Inside two she was duly signing for *The Getaway*. She had to stop her hand from shaking as she did so, arguably the best bit of acting she ever managed. First locking eyes, then touching knees under the desk with McQueen was 'like a thunderbolt . . . I saw him and almost passed out. It was the strongest electric connection I've ever experienced in my life.' Within days Steve, too, was talking up Ali as 'heavy, well educated, classy, knows the ways of the world' – and, yes, he told Pat Johnson, 'with the greatest ass of all time'.

McQueen's first wife talked him into reading *The Getaway*.

MacGraw's husband, worried at her being typecast by *Love Story*, told her that she, too, would be perfect for the film. It fitted. Even the two stars' names were assonant. In February 1972, while Neile was in divorce court and Evans was editing *The Godfather*, *The Getaway* formally began shooting in Huntsville, Texas.

First, however, MacGraw had a talk with her friend Barbara Leigh about the men in their lives. Then Ali moved the discussion from the abstract to the particular. 'What's McQueen like?' she asked.

'The best. I may as well say it. He is.'

'What's good and bad about him?'

Leigh named the qualities.

MacGraw herself played a kind of good bad girl in *The Getaway*, itself full of such discrepancies, a clanging, whirring film that, in keeping with the fugitive theme, wove through the Texan panhandle, jagged between San Marcos and San Antonio, whistlestopped Ozona and tore to a finish in El Paso, North America's drug mecca and, not coincidentally, one of Steve's favourite hangouts. McQueen's most notorious movie after *Le Mans* moved at wild speed. By the time the shoot wrapped at the Mexican border, only two months had passed since Steve first drove up to the Evanses' mansion, and the restless flitting by cast, crew and extras up and down Highway 10 was, almost incredibly, concentrated into a few weeks in March and early April. Such was the velocity of *The Getaway*.

The movie's backers, by contrast, were more cautious than most people realised. *The Getaway* was costed at $3 million, just over half of *Bullitt* and roughly a third of *Le Mans*. Money was so tight that MacGraw agreed to work for no upfront salary and, in a deal hammered out by Freddie Fields, settled instead for the film's German profits, a half-million dollars' worth as it happened. Steve himself took 10 per cent of the worldwide gross. All in all, it was another time of real truth for him, one of several that year. McQueen hadn't had a commercial hit since 1968 and he still owed the IRS close to $2 million. The economic pressure might have helped create the siege mentality that *The Getaway* evinced right from the start. The one-two punch of tax liens and Neile's alimony demands almost surely impressed on McQueen that he needed a smash; and also that cover-ups and convenient mental lapses could be useful tactics. Right to the end, Steve was known for his elephantine memory – until called on to supply detailed accounts of earnings in divorce court, when his recall sometimes seemed to fail him.

'It made some dough,' McQueen would say a year later, when the film's first month's take was totted up. 'It wasn't a big deal.' Nor, however, was it a small deal, especially when combined with the $2 million and points he got merely for signing to do his next movie, *Papillon*. Steve's decision to finally play an out-and-out thug in *The Getaway* was rewarded by global receipts of $35 million. In sheer box office it was First Artists', if not McQueen's, finest hour. Certainly Sam Peckinpah's. Peckinpah's first rule on *The Getaway* was 'anything for the picture', including long rehearsals, multiple takes, unflinching realism and brilliant use of props, making for a film people admired not so much for the surface plot but for the atmosphere, the gory undercoat to it. In *The Getaway*'s climactic scene all the surviving gang would converge on a flophouse in downtown El Paso for an apocalyptic shoot-out that made *The Wild Bunch* look like *My Fair Lady*: literally *rivers* of blood. There was no second rule. Peckinpah's verisimilitude served the movie well, and it served as Steve's inspiration. McQueen's other sense memory – the recalling of emotions from the past for dramatic purposes – drew heavily on

Neile's fuck-fling with Max Schell, infidelity rumbling as a sub-plot on *The Getaway*. Steve also cleverly reanimated the Bogart role from *High Sierra*.

For the public McQueen's name, like Bogie's, appeared on marquees as a guaranteed sales promotion tool. But blind fan worship was matched, in private, by a mixture of fear and technical respect. It was quickly apparent that he knew his business.

'First day of shooting,' says the actor John Bryson, 'I was supposed to drive up to the prison at Huntsville in a chauffeured Cadillac and lay a message on McQueen, who was playing a convict getting out. By now, I was damned edgy and nervous – for once nobody had said do it this way or that way, nothing. Finally, McQueen, a very strange guy I didn't like too much, he stuck his head in the window of the car and said, "Just relax, man. Remember, in your role you're a rich, influential member of the Establishment, and I'm just a little piss-ant convict that you couldn't care less about. Hang on to that and it'll go great."'

It did. Steve doted on the pleasure of doing the underdog.

Less impressed with the unit publicist, Rick Ingersoll, a man who worked all hours with Dave Foster to build a name for McQueen in the late fifties and early sixties. Ingersoll's crime on *The Getaway* was to set up a series of high-profile interviews for MacGraw. And that was it. Even though Steve didn't want any publicity himself he didn't want *Life* and *Cosmo* drooling over the substars, either. Ingersoll was fired. Steve's stunt double, Gary Combs, narrowly escaped the same fate. 'We were always waiting for McQueen on that set. Always. And the main reason we were waiting was because the instant I was standing there in an outfit that matched Steve's, he'd run off to his trailer to change. Whenever I put my wardrobe on, McQueen would take his off. And vice-versa. The problem, as he saw it, was that there were always hundreds of people milling around watching us film. Steve didn't ever want them to think he had a double. I mean, never.' Exasperated, Combs finally complained to Foster and one of the production assistants, Jim Silke.

McQueen, says Silke, was 'a total asshole' in his opinion.

Frequently Steve paced up and down the sound stage, muttering, the metal tips of his tiny biker boots ringing on the concrete floor. Even Peckinpah would step back.

As time went on they all began to feel that the functions of stardom were crowding out his private personality. McQueen, fulfilling his destiny as the psychotically warped kid, could certainly be brattishly uptight; Ingersoll was proof of that. But the selfsame brat always reached out to those he saw as fellow-orphans. Bo Hopkins, who played one of McCoy's gang in the film, says, 'First time I ever saw Steve he was in the nurse's office getting his chin sewn up. He'd been out biking and got hit by a rock. Not only was the dude sitting there taking the pain, he was the nicest guy in the world, at least once he heard I'd been in reform school. One of the great soft-hard men of all time.' The costume master Kent James remembers, 'Steve pulled this shit where he'd take his shirt off and drop it in the dirt . . . I saw this and told him to get me a plane ticket home right away. If he wanted a valet, I said, try the Yellow Pages. It was the old initiation test . . . you had to stand your ground. McQueen looked startled, then held out his hand and apologised. He realised I didn't give a shit for all that movie-star BS. We got along fine after that.'

The Getaway, shot in the very weeks McQueen's marriage was being wound up, had its share of such BS and roguish laughs alike: the opening setup, where Peckinpah insisted Steve had to shower in the – but of course – 'actual faggot wing' of the cellblock and McQueen raging for days later at the indignity; the time he strayed away from the real chain gang for a smoke and a pack of trained hounds, blissfully ignorant that they were also extras in a movie, chewed away the seat of his pants; the scene with the actress Sally Struthers where 'Steve hit me right smack in the middle of the face and knocked me cold . . . McQueen went straight for my kisser. He didn't do a side-swipe like in the Westerns, where the other actor snaps his head to the side and pretends to be hit. Steve did a shot that hadn't been seen in the movies in a *long* time.' (Some thought it was a case of projection.) The fine details – McQueen's always inventive and frequently inspired use of props, specifically of clothes, guns and cars. And even of money: after a take which called for Steve to lie in bed with $35,000 in real cash, the prop master Bobby Visciglia found $250 on him as he was leaving the stage. 'He had the stuff in his mouth, his armpits, behind his legs . . . I was shaking him down while Ali was laughing her head off over this cheap movie star who was trying to steal money.'

'Well, Jesus, what the fuck,' McQueen told him. 'I mean, if you wanted a kiss-ass, what the fuck did you get me for? Why didn't you go get fucking Pat Boone?'

To cynics, the way he twisted melons, the things he did and said sounded like a put-on; surely, they said, he must be kidding. He wasn't. There may be no such thing as a saturation point in avenging a childhood like his, but Steve was certainly groping for it. He exasperated most of Hollywood; he smoked dope with Indians; he did hundreds of women; he once had the exquisite pleasure of standing on the winners' rostrum at Sebring; he became the biggest star in the world and waved his fist under Fuckwit's nose. If all this was supposed to induce a sense of security, it seemed to have failed badly. 'A château-bottled lunatic,' Hoven calls him.

All the desperate eagerness marked the upswing of the McQueen mood cycle, something they saw often on *The Getaway*. Some random facts: Steve enjoyed his morning beer jags, as well as his hash brownies, amyl nitrate and coke. The backstage hospitality at Rolling Stones and Elton John concerts. Late nights gunning his bike. The time he mashed his rental car through the front hedge of his hotel. And the day Katy Haber remembers, when 'Steve missed his exit on the freeway and, instead of doing the drearily conventional thing – waiting for the next one – left the road at eighty m.p.h. and bounced up a sheer hill where, sure enough, we got stuck, nose pointing to the heavens, rear wheels grinding in the mud.' When a policewoman came McQueen charmed her out of even issuing a ticket. 'That man could coax the birds out of the trees when he was in the mood,' says Geller. McQueen himself demonstrated the avian technique, so irresistible to women the world over, once the tow-truck had hauled him safely back onto the highway. 'So, wanna party?' he asked the cop broad.

Now it only remained to nail down a 'heavy lady', someone who would follow if not replace Neile as Steve's composite lover-mother. McQueen did this in several ways. After Barbara Leigh left, he asked two or three women to move in with him over the winter of 1971– 2. When those glorified fuck-flings drove him mad with their mediocrity, he focused more on revisiting his past, suggesting that Neile herself spend her weekends at Coldwater Canyon. She turned him down. Eventually, and with the self-restraining qualities of a tidal wave, Steve knocked on his co-star's door, said, 'Ali, I need to talk to you,' poured her a drink, tore all her clothes off and instantly shtupped her right there on the floor. MacGraw says it was the very spontaneity of the man that attracted her. 'I thought, Here's fresh air. He doesn't do any of that charm thing. He's just there!

'That's what I wanted in myself, and I went after it in him . . . Being with Steve was like a drug high.'

For the next month the sexual tension was palpable – they were doing it between takes, in the Cortez, every chance they got, even while Ali's one-year-old son, Josh, visited with his nanny – but the veil of illusion prevailed. In mid March MacGraw briefly flew to New York for the opening of *The Godfather*, where she mingled with the likes of Henry Kissinger and waltzed her unknowing husband around the floor of the St Regis roof. It was Evans who'd worked so hard – pimped virtually – to cast her opposite McQueen in the first place. He soon regretted it. 'This was the best time of my life, but it was a fraud . . . My wife was fucking another guy, and I had no idea. She had as much interest in being with me as being with a leper. She was looking at me and thinking of Steve McQueen's cock.'

Back in Texas, McQueen and MacGraw, the rebel and the power wife, began to adopt the mopy love-struck postures, the unmistakable signs of a movie-set romance.

. It was at this point that Peckinpah, and several others, realised that *The Getaway* had problems, and that the whole thing had the potential for disaster. Dave Foster braced himself for the worst – 'Is Bob Evans going to come down here with a shotgun? Is it going to become a scandal and the film won't be taken seriously? Are the press going to descend like they did with Burton and Taylor on *Cleopatra*?' as he put it to the author Marshall Terrill. Compounding the drama was at least one other on-set affair, as well as Peckinpah's increasingly wild behaviour. 'The [studio] thought they'd cure me,' he said, 'but they didn't.' This wildness, the sickness which wasn't cured, was actually a euphemism for wholesale drink and drug addiction. When McQueen once caught the director swigging neat tequila before breakfast, he challenged him by daring him to finish the entire bottle. If you puke, he said, go to your condo, sleep it off and come back – we'll fine you a morning's pay. Peckinpah, who had been belting it down since dinner the night before, smiled and calmly drank his way to the end.

On 26 April, as *The Getaway* folded camp in El Paso, Steve's divorce finally went through in Santa Monica. By then he and Ali were going at it fast and furious. McQueen phoned his ex-wife to tell her that he'd found his heavy lady and described MacGraw as she was then: 'smart, classy and crazy'. Neile always assumed Steve would sleep with his leading ladies. Most star-struck ingénues had lapped up the myth, the cool, confident Supie who'd introduced himself to *The Getaway* crew by totalling yet another car, this time into a river, and sitting there submerged in water, patiently waiting to be rescued. But Ali was different. Now McQueen had found a perpetual audience for his exploits – someone, he told his ex, who gunned his very engine. Big time. *Roll 'em* and *action*, three of the most common words in Steve's professional speech, reflect a persistently low boredom threshold. Perhaps, too, he fell for Evans's wife because he felt that danger was good for an artist, the source of his wisdom.

When *The Getaway* wrapped, McQueen quite seriously asked his producer and old PR man, Dave Foster, to tell Evans the bad news about his marriage. Instead MacGraw chose to take on this 'hellish gig' herself. Exact information on what they may or may not have said privately isn't available to an author, some of it not even to the third party. McQueen himself could only speculate. What happened was that Evans ordered Ali home to LA – Steve crouching behind her on the plane disguised in a hat and sunglasses – and then to 'think it over' at an exclusive spa in Murrieta Springs: his self-restraint a model of what every cuckolded husband might hope to display in the circumstances.

It wasn't enough. When MacGraw left the spa to briefly return to Evans's desert mansion, McQueen phoned their mutual friend Katy Haber. 'He turned up on my doorstep, poured his heart out about Ali and asked me to get a message through to her. Steve was desperate. He told me that he'd never been in such pain in all his life.'

Haber gave him a hug, then drove up to the mansion to tell Mac-Graw that Steve loved her.

A few days later, after returning from a 'second honeymoon' in Venice, Ali left her husband for ever. She took off at midnight, first driving tearfully through the rain to McQueen's in Coldwater Canyon, then renting a place immediately across a field from his. The fugitive dimension to it all was very real. Evans and several of his friends went looking for Ali and black cars followed Steve about all week, before finally giving it up. *The Getaway* co-stars duly became Hollywood's most obvious, if furtive, on-screen/offscreen duo.

Meanwhile, after suffering from laryngitis, on and off, for most of the shoot – stress and a nasty cold, the production nurse told him – Steve finally admitted himself to Cedars-Sinai hospital in LA. There doctors removed a small polyp from his throat. Neile, Freddie Fields and Ali were the only three ever told about this technically simple yet ominous procedure. The first two of them visited, while Mac-Graw, still extracting herself from her husband, sent flowers. She had no idea, at least then, that he'd resent her absence for the rest of his life. 'Steve never forgave that,' says Neile. 'And he never admitted it, either . . . I remember he was out of bed only a day after the surgery, telling everyone he was fine. But he wasn't. He wasn't fine at all. Looking back on it, that was the exact moment when the cancer presented itself.'

Junior Bonner was out that second summer of love, a comedy drama about a fading cowboy. True, it wasn't strictly speaking autobiography; the McQueen character worked with bulls, not bikes and cars, but in its low-key way it had a reverential, gentle, nostalgic feel for 1940s Slater, a thin strip of wilderness still clinging on. For all sense memory purposes, Junior's world was Uncle Claude's.

The result was an off-centre, if faintly derivative classic. (*Bonner* echoed the lyrical, vanished-America plots of *Scandalous John* and Peckinpah's own *Ballad of Cable Hogue*, and preceded the likes of *J. W. Coop* and *Honkers* in a veritable stampede of rodeo yarns.) On a budget several million dollars lower than *Le Mans*, Steve put on a performance which had heart and soul rather than flash and noise. Not that it much mattered. For most McQueen fans, the movie's sepia warmth was an aberration – nothing to trouble his reputation for jet-black, icy, neurotic cool. A blood-spattered heist film, with matching 'Homebreaker' headlines, was a pretty tough act to top.

Bonner's hypnotic simplicity was part technical – Peckinpah's trademark collage of fast cuts, swirling camerawork and slo-mo; and part human – the whole interplay between Preston and Lupino, just odd enough to be a genuinely poetic creation. But too much else was held in, hidden, turned self-consciously wacky. It was, after all, a *vanished* America; the crowds flocking that summer to their screenings of *Dirty Harry* and *Shaft* knew as much about the Prescott Rodeo as they did about Ruritania. But there were consolations. Everything that was missing in *Bonner* became apparent with McQueen's stunning entrance. Tanned and leathery as an old football, he filled the screen with crisp, understated presence. Inert. Near mute. Here, Steve's whole act was weightless and sometimes infuriating, and yet it got to you; no one else could have combined the same impeccable timing, virility and 'What next?' expression, a look that was both witty and oddly right. Those few stray 'yeps' and 'nopes' shouldn't have added up to much of a performance, but that came from the face. Bonner and his world were part of the same peeling exterior – you knew even before McQueen spoke that his character had been around, suffered. 'If you really want to learn about acting,' Peckinpah would say, 'watch Steve's eyes in close-up.' *Junior Bonner* was a true dramatic movie, and one of McQueen's finest moments.

Bonner got scant attention, and remains McQueen's only picture ever to actually lose money. ABC/Cinerama weren't happy with it. In fact there was a lot of griping. Steve, though, 'patently didn't give a fuck', Peckinpah said. 'In any relationship, the one who cares less has more power, and McQueen was willing to walk at any time.' That gave him enormous creative muscle with the studio, who soon watched *Bonner* gradually ascend into an American masterpiece: both critically and even commercially, virtues were discovered in the film in the 1980s that had somehow previously failed to surface. Even Brando would 'dig' *Junior Bonner*, saying 'It might've been worse' – high praise from one so sparing of it. Steve, who thought that ABC both bungled the movie's distribution and over-hyped it to boot, told Pat Johnson it was one of his favourite pieces of work.

There was some mellowing in McQueen in the early seventies, the New Man shocked into life by love rather than rage or insecurity. 'Miss Alice', as he told Geller with a throb in his voice, was everything Neile had been. And more: a working actress who wouldn't quit for him, funny, gaudy, original. Creative. The really impressive thing about MacGraw's creativity was the way she took an adolescent moon-child sensibility and hammered it into something practical; the sort of woman, says Hoven, 'who'd traipse into a dumpy motel room and inside of ten minutes transform it', by way of seashells and poppies and votive candles, shut in by velvet drapes and batik scarves flung over lamps, 'into her own world', the overall feel of a Moorish hash den with submerged *Gatsby* pretensions. When Steve's own personal and professional life had hit a wall with *Le Mans*, there was a strong element of masochism in the way he complained of fucking up on two fronts – never having had a normal, settled home and then apparently pissing away his career. Now, two years later, he stepped forward to reclaim his life, playing it better and with a more ferocious intimacy than any mere movie script. McQueen, he announced, was back: official.

But first there was the troubling conversation in their adjoining field with Miss Alice, who admitted she could do without some of the old Steve. Specifically, his drinking and snorting coke and shtupping every woman in Hollywood. 'You're over forty now, for Christ's sake, and you think you have the rights of a teenager. I hate addicts – of any kind. They're always wanting something.' A long pause followed this, broken by McQueen's quietly promising to cut down on the booze and drugs. He'd already throttled back on his racing. Nowadays Steve only ever went out dirt-biking at weekends, and then usually with his two children. Aside from the sex, his only other known vices were those of ordinary American life: he collected guns, swigged beer, chewed Juicy Fruit gum and was known to drive for hours in order to gorge on Sue Johnson's special thin pork chops, which he shovelled in with his fingers. MacGraw admitted she was both enamoured of and scared by Steve's Supie reputation. 'Everyone knows you're banging women two, three at a time. Cheerleaders, biker chicks, every groupie in town. That's another thing I hate – deceit.' And then disclosed, after a second pregnant silence, that she and Evans had been coming apart at the seams almost from the very start. That crazy house, all those butlers and maids, the twenty-six pink telephones. 'Oh, Steve. I used to live in a Bonnard painting – long black hair, haunted, floating around trying to convince myself I was happy.'

'We gotta make sure that you are.'

'But I want to perform,' said MacGraw. 'I must perform.'

Performance was a kind of vocation with them; their habits died hard. While Ali still saw herself as more than the mere star of an American tetralogy – *A Lovely Way to Die*, *Goodbye, Columbus*, *Love Story* and now *The Getaway* – Steve, too, never entirely renounced his taste for hopped-up bikes and Old Milwaukee. When the kids left him on a Sunday night he'd still drop into the Whisky or casually shtup one of the bubble-ass groupies. But that wasn't the worst of it. Both the old and the new Steve had a penchant for secrecy, a distaste for sharing credit and a romantic view of themselves as loners. Neither had the ability to revel in someone else's success. McQueen's grim ambition was the result, Hoven thought, of 'Steve knowing he had to work, but that Hollywood needed him. He'd chosen an industry starved for style.' Style he had.

In private, he didn't always trouble to remove the barbs. The central core McQueen matured around was selfish. He couldn't help it – it was another chronic addiction. Hurting others just to protect himself was what came naturally. Steve made an important exception in the case of children, as well as most car and bike people. A Bud Ekins would see a 'layer-cake of McQueens': the icing was the public image, cool, confident and self-possessed; the first layer 'a one-on-one guy who didn't trust people in the plural'; just below that 'a well-meaning man who'd had no experience of normal life'. Other layers included 'the rebel', 'the paranoiac', the courageous 'risk-taker', 'the junkie' and 'the loyal friend'.

The mood-swinger. While Ekins did get to glimpse a certain continuity of attitudes, loves, hates, widespread relish for Personality, acceptance or rejection of actual personalities, Steve's throughline was his inconsistency. In May 1972, for example, he pledged to quit drinking and give up on the lost weekends. Exactly a month later, a black Trans Am was seen making circles one morning in a busy street in Anchorage, Alaska. A policeman approached. A few bystanders and the reporter Lawrence Van Gelder gathered to record the scene as a black-clad figure, still nursing a can of beer, emerged from the car.

'Hi, I'm Steve McQueen and I'm having a good time in your little two-bit town.'

'Hi, I'm a sheriff and you're under arrest.'

He'd promised MacGraw, walking there in the field between their houses, that he had every intention of easing up. 'Still cruising but running out of gas' was the general message. Instead – thanks to what seemed a continuation of McQueen's manic high into actual insanity – he suddenly found himself facing a reckless driving charge. It was soon dropped, but Steve in turn caught hell from Miss Alice, whose overwrought emotional state now led her to yell 'Fuck off' and see him do so, roaring off on his Triumph to one of the bubble-asses' houses, mangling a few small trees on the way, early warning that any relationship co-starring McQueen would be something other than tranquil.

As Geller says, 'That was a hard dog to keep on the porch.'

MacGraw had known, of course, that he was a famous star, but not the heroic extent of his fame. By most litmus-test standards, McQueen was still the biggest name in Hollywood. Certainly at ground level. There were literally scores of cranks and fringe nuts, as well as the lovestruck fans who doffed their clothes to him. One seventeen-year-old who kept up a more or less fixed vigil at Steve's door once threw herself at his feet as he trudged out for his mail. She was naked. Another girl left gifts in his post-box: a script and pouty glamour polaroids of herself. Complete strangers wrote and said, 'Steve, I'll do whatever you tell me.' His poster was everywhere, his look copied and his one-liners like 'D'you play?' or 'Bullshit!' tantamount to holy writ. His life and achievements were already being transported into legend. He was the pop-icon movie star. When his friend Mick Jagger needed a rhyme for *screen/obscene/pussy clean* in his ditty 'Starfucker' there weren't many candidates, and the name was quickly reached. After McQueen himself listened to the song, Jagger asked him to sign a disclaimer and told him, 'After this, groupies will be pounding on your door.' Not overly impressed with that prospect, Steve grunted.*

That was the shell. What lay inside McQueen's fame was a brilliant intuitive mind for parsing movies. The best film actor of his generation also happened to be the best script visualiser of his generation, and managed to be both creative and practical at the same time. Steve's motives in walking on projects like *American Flag* and *The Long Goodbye* were, he told Ali, purely artistic; but there was also a hidden wisdom in his job selection. He still had to pay off his tax bill. On 18 July 1972 McQueen duly signed the contract for *Papillon*. As well as his $2 million and points, Steve insisted on a clause specifically involving his co-star:

> Actor hereby consents to the according by Producer of credit on the screen and in paid advertisements issued in connection with the photoplay to Dustin Hoffman ('Hoffman') as follows: Actor's name shall appear in first position of the entire cast . . . Hoffman shall be accorded credit in second position among other members of the cast . . . On the screen, said credit shall appear on the same card as the credit accorded to Actor, but Hoffman's credit shall appear on the right hand side of said card and Actor's credit shall appear on the left hand side of said card . . . In paid advertising, Hoffman's credit shall appear on the same line as the credit accorded to Actor, but Hoffman's credit shall appear to the right of the credit accorded to Actor . . . No likeness of Hoffman or of any other member of the cast shall appear in any advertisement without Actor's consent, except in the case of promotional advertisements (i.e., when Hoffman or such cast member is promoting the Picture) or of congratulations for recognized achievements such as Academy Awards . . . If the likeness of Hoffman or any other member of the cast so appears, in any advertising whatever, then Actor's

---

* Among McQueen's other mentions on vinyl and CD: Deep Purple's 'Highway Star', Prefab Sprout's *Steve McQueen* (retitled *Two Wheels Good* in the USA after a run-in with his estate) and Tori Amos's 1998 epic 'Father Lucifer'.

likeness shall appear in such advertising and in first position
and at least as large and prominent as the likeness of Hoffman
or any other cast member . . .

A month before filming began McQueen and MacGraw were still
keeping their separate addresses on either side of the field. Steve and
Neile were at the lowest ebb of their own long friendship, not even
making love after handing their children back and forth at the weekends. Ali was divorcing Bob Evans. They, too, were at their leaden
nadir. Evans had forbidden her to take their son out of California,
or to in any way let him live under the same roof as McQueen. For
MacGraw there were professional blows as well as personal ones.
The cherished role of Daisy in *The Great Gatsby* now went, on Evans's
orders, to Mia Farrow. 'I'm the scarlet lady,' Ali told the *New York
Times*. 'It's the opposite of the golden girl syndrome, I guess, and I
was the Golden Girl for a long time. I'm hurt by it . . . Everything
inside me is run down – my blood, my hormones, my emotions . . .
The lot.'

Steve nodded his head and promptly told the *Papillon* people, 'I'll
do it. *Roll 'em.*'

The McQueen law of dynamics materialised fully in 1972.

Rejecting the fake modernity of the likes of *Dirty Harry*, he and
Peckinpah demonstrated in *The Getaway*, out that Christmas, that
the old styles are the best. You could imagine a Bogart or a Cagney
having snarled their way through it in the 1940s. As with *Bullitt*, the
actual plot was confused to the point of impenetrability – for a movie
about escape, it seemed desperately trapped in its own convolutions.
If you wanted the Peckinpah who made *Junior Bonner*, with all its
lightness and impassioned fantasia, you'd have to wait for his next
film, *Pat Garrett*. Meanwhile, this one was rescued by McQueen and
the craggy-jawed Al Lettieri as his partner turned stalker. Both were
brilliant, both struggling against a script as ultimately flat and empty
as a crushed beer can.

The mystery about the film was that the actual getaway was accomplished almost entirely without drama, speed or ingenuity. Not that
you'd know it from MacGraw's over-acting. At one stage she and
McQueen would actually flee by calmly boarding a Continental bus,

to which Ali reacts as if they'd just entered the NASA space shuttle. Watching the real-life couple make love was uncomfortably voyeuristic. Also in the debit column was the shamelessly tacked-on dream sequence, as well as the incongruously smoochy close-ups included over Peckinpah's veto. The director hit the roof, quickly followed by the phone to *Variety*, when he saw the final cut. 'McQueen's playing it safe, and that's going to be his downfall ... He chose all these *Playboy* shots of himself.' *The Getaway*'s last few minutes, at least, were salvaged by the presence of Slim Pickens, best known as the pilot riding his nuclear bomb bronco-style all the way down to its target in *Dr Strangelove*, whose largely improvised portrait of folksy, banal humour was a gem. *The Getaway*'s actual ending dared to let the crooks get away. Peckinpah's point appeared to be that 'everybody's at it', and that there was no higher office than exercising the moral imagination necessary to believe, as he did, that 'the only crime nowadays is getting caught'. McQueen and MacGraw blithely drove into the Mexican sunset with the loot in the film's American and British version, but in Spain, at least, the picture carried an 'official' postscript mentioning that the couple were later arrested and jailed. In Franco's regime, you still couldn't get away with it.

McQueen himself brought off a sense of control and tension that made his McCoy – the icily smooth hoodlum in the black suit – seem not only credible, but perfect. Never had his motto, 'I'll give you a look that'll say it all,' been in better context. The accumulated rage behind the scene where he beat MacGraw up for her infidelity wasn't only a fascinating, disturbing character study; it was virtually unwatchable for anyone who knew the full story of Steve and Neile at the Château Lornay. His McCoy was a coiled, terrifying thug who was also, at times, subversively charming. Both exotic and familiar; dangerous and complicated. A practising chameleon. The problem was that MacGraw was just the opposite, an anti-dramatic moll whose forte, as in *Love Story*, remained the ordinariness of life and her inability to change or in any way adapt her depressing destiny. They didn't even look right together: her head and hips were both larger than his.

Release date came, and the flash of lights and the blare of full-colour posters emblazoned MCQUEEN–MACGRAW set up the ritual for another *Cleopatra*-like frenzy. *The Getaway* grossed $18,943,592 domestically in its first year, and more than twice that worldwide. Steve's take was 10 per cent of the action. Commercially, the film was so hot it had to be kept in a Godfather's Pizza carrier, a Lazarus act of self-resurrection by a star, the *Times* wrote approvingly, who was now a 'vulcanized Beckett hero . . . the basically decent man hopelessly in conflict with the world'. McQueen himself didn't know about vulcanic existentialism, or care. He liked the money.

'*Top* dollar,' he beamed.

Steve's fortune was fully restored, with interest, although he and Peckinpah never spoke again, in part because of a farcical row about *The Getaway*'s soundtrack. Peckinpah's alcoholism had affected his low-end hearing, while constant bike-racing had ruined McQueen's high-end hearing – in his one good ear, of course – so the two fought for weeks over the film's mixing board, one sliding up the volume, the other turning it down. Peckinpah stayed up all night laying in a score by Jerry Fielding. Next morning Steve wiped it out. Quincy Jones was hurriedly commissioned to write a new one. Neil Rand, one of the grips on *The Getaway*, says that what he found most difficult was 'Steve's trivialisation of other people. He treated the crew as if they were rats.' When Peckinpah finally saw the finished movie in his home screening room, he stood up, calmly faced the projector and delivered his verdict.

The ovation, to the extent that one occurred, was a standing ovation only because Peckinpah was standing while he pissed, all too literally, over the film. The critics would do something similar on Miss Alice. 'Last time I saw Candice Bergen, I thought she was a worse actress than MacGraw,' Pauline Kael wrote. 'Now I think I slandered Bergen.'

A blow to the groin couldn't have brought Steve closer to tears. By early 1973 the miracle had occurred: he told friends like Don Gordon he wasn't even looking at other women. Something was happening with Ali that, patently, hadn't happened with Neile. For the first time ever, McQueen was deferring to his 'lady'. MacGraw's cultural ambitions for him made his first wife's seem like models of restraint. Steve was, in his unpretentious way, quite sophisticated.

He liked music and American art, and he could be an engaging conversationalist around people who made him feel good. Nevertheless, MacGraw grew somewhat embarrassed by him as they began to move in more glamorous orbits. 'In some ways Steve was the kid in that relationship,' says Jim Geller. 'Very dependent on Ali, very protective of her ... Poignantly, he told me he started a serious exercise regime, outdoors and not just in the gym, because he wanted to live to be a hundred with her.' It was there on the track while running his gruelling five miles seven days a week that many of Steve's best thoughts came to him, and there also that he discharged, for a time, the stewing hostility and cancerous rage that were as much a part of him as flesh and bone. McQueen felt buffed up after he ran. As he said, 'Less dope – more staying power.' A veritable Bob Dole on Viagra. Within a few months, Steve no longer suffered from the early-morning hots for Miss Alice. Now he had them all day long.

With a Byzantine consortium of Franco-American backers – inevitably, the target of a later audit – and a script still being frenziedly drafted, *Papillon* began shooting in Spain that February. Even getting to the Basque coast proved to be pandemonium. Steve and Ali weathered a storm of tabloid abuse in the time-honoured roles of the Shit and the Slut. She couldn't take her son out of the country. Nor could she leave McQueen alone for six months. Without ever quite enshrining it in policy, MacGraw's choice of lover over child brought a note of outrage to what was otherwise the most entertaining movie-romance story in years. The press exploded. (Steve, by contrast, still gave away nothing of what he thought of the paparazzi who now tailed him everywhere he went – 'a pack of shitbag cunts', they found out later.) In staccato terms, the *New York Post* and *People* leads became versions of LOVE STORY, full of sleaze, superlatives and triple exclamation marks. For more than a decade McQueen's headlines had dazzled. Now, they blinded.

Apart from Ali, Steve's two closest friends on location were his bodyguard, one Jimmy Jimenez, and Don Gordon. Gordon was there when McQueen and MacGraw pulled up at their hotel amidst a heaving collection of reporters and photographers. Three muscle-bound bouncers were doing their best to hold back a crowd of several hundred people. The old friends were halted a moment by the sheer hysteria on the steps. Even Burton and Taylor had seen nothing like it. Gordon could tell that a few seconds of sharing a confined space with the mob was already imposing unbearable strain on Steve's fragile PR sense. 'Those fuckers chased up upstairs, down a corridor, right to the doors of the suites. Steve started to go at it with a photographer . . . Everyone's screaming in Spanish, it's fucking chaos . . . After Ali gets safely inside her room I run back, sort of jump in front of McQueen and cock back my fist at the photographer. I actually took a swing and missed him. The guy lost his footing and went down anyway. More loud yelling . . . Then Steve and I started to laugh and we ran back to Ali. Things calmed down a bit after that.'

From Spain, Jamaica. 'Steve and Ali were in this beautiful villa on the beach. In all the time they were there it was like a fantasy, ten people for lunch . . . fifteen for dinner. Warm tropical nights. Musicians would come and play. And all the time we were in this fantasy, none of us were getting paid . . . Oh, it was mad. As I heard it, the suits were taking cans of film, getting on the night flight to Paris, showing the backers the raw footage, and coming back with enough cash to at least keep the cameras rolling. When he found out what was happening McQueen went to the producers and said, "Unless everyone gets paid, I don't work." From then on, after all that shit, the per diems came like *lightning*.'

Still pressed for spending money, Gordon asked Steve to lend him $2000. McQueen did it on the spot. When Gordon paid him back three days later, just as he'd promised, Steve wasn't merely surprised – he was shocked.

'You remembered.'

'I wouldn't ever screw you,' said Gordon.

'What do you mean?'

'I wouldn't ever screw you.'

McQueen's chief emotion was perplexity. 'I still don't get it.'

'Shit, Steve, we're friends.'

McQueen moved his lips to reply but no words came. After Don left, he began crying.

For the eponymous part of Papillon, 'the butterfly' Henri Charrière banged up on Devil's Island, McQueen should have been slim – 160 pounds – but after a month on location, he'd balloon up to 180. His favourite foods in Jamaica were meat loaf, curries and refried beans, accompanied by Red Stripe beer and industrial-strength skank. He was still running and now even kick-boxing every day. But Kent James had to find ever bigger and baggier prison uniforms to give Steve the underfed look. 'McQueen had a puffy face and quite a gut on him in that film. I think it was the first time he'd ever acknowledged he might have a weight problem. He didn't like it one bit.'

James had known Steve to complain before, but never about himself. One or two close friends heard him talk seriously about retiring.

'What's going to happen to us?' Steve had asked Neile after watching a film together one night in late 1967. The movie in question was *The Graduate*, and by 'us' he meant established Supies like Newman and himself. More specifically, McQueen was shaken by Dustin Hoffman's arrival as a bankable star. Many were. 'Good actor, yeah,' he allowed, 'but he sure is homely.' To illustrate the point Steve promptly stripped off his shirt and stood in front of a full-length mirror in the Castle's front hallway. 'Look at that, baby, take a look at that face and that body and tell me the truth – who would you pick, him or me?'

Neile had to laugh at the ridiculousness both of the question and the whole scene, but deep down, she says, 'I knew he was dead serious.'

Six years later Steve was still to reconcile himself to Hoffman's success, since formalised by films like *Midnight Cowboy* and *Straw Dogs*. For one thing, he didn't much care for the pictures themselves. Crap, crap, crap. Dirty movies. Geller, who once mentioned that *Straw Dogs* wasn't in the least the kind of film he associated with picket-lines and protests, discovered the volcanic intensity of a McQueen eruption. 'He just corked off in the worst language you ever heard – "That fucking shit . . . You really think I'm gonna do that? No one flashes her tits in a Steve McQueen movie" – the height of nunnery, and then, offscreen, he swore like the fucking Marines. But only concerning his work.' Steve also had his professional doubts about Hoffman who, in many ways, just like his character in *Papillon*, served as a foil to the older pro. The ex-conservatory pianist wanted to make the 'purest art possible'; the hardened, cynical film star spent weeks fine-tuning his contract before even deigning to step in front of a camera. Hoffman was often flamboyant and histrionic; Steve was boyish, vague, hard to read. Dustin was squat and dark; McQueen stood six feet in his lifts, with bleached hair and electric-blue eyes. Hoffman's whole wardrobe and love of prosthetics shouted 'Method'; Steve more or less turned up, said the lines and went home. To Hoffman, McQueen 'was a wonderful guy. Offscreen, he was the nicest, classiest man ... On the set itself he became very intense.'

And competitive. One morning Hoffman appeared with his teeth dramatically yellowed and sporting thick, Coke-bottle glasses. Steve responded by affecting a theatrical, stuttering walk that nobody had seen before, let alone rehearsed. Dustin began one speech babbling at McQueen at warp speed. Steve stopped him with a curt chop of his hand and the great advice, 'Less, man. Less. Toss that shit out, you don't need it. Keep it simple.' Hoffman invited a few close friends as guests to watch a day's filming. McQueen had them physically thrown off the set.

No superstar incident ever ends there. Hoffman complained, and from then on *Papillon*'s quality was at odds with its harmony. The shoot went well, but, with a few rare exceptions, it wasn't a happy one. According to Geller, 'That was Steve's working-pro approach to film-making. He wouldn't read or role-play or BS all day like some guys ... McQueen would come on, give you a brilliant take, then, if the director grovelled, a second one. *Boom. Boom.* Then back to the trailer. If someone or something got in his way, he'd explode ... Anyone who wasted Steve's time was toast.'

The venom rose; in the years ahead McQueen and Hoffman would both entertain friends with razor-sharp impersonations of one another. Steve got the mannered jabber down to a fine art. Hoffman, in turn, sent up some of McQueen's insecurities, and told Kent James on the set of *Rain Man*, fully fifteen years later, 'That son-of-a-bitch! Some relationship ... Can you believe he threw my guests off *Papillon*?' Hoffman would call that relationship 'friendly rivalry'. Steve wouldn't bother to call it anything at all, and the two men never actually spoke to each other again.

*　　*　　*

Papillon wrapped in late May 1973. Steve and Ali were now keeping house together on Broad Beach Road, Trancas, an exclusive colony near Malibu, cruising around on his antique bikes, quaffing Old Milwaukee – America's Sweetheart slumming it in the world of greasy, bolted-down meals and daytime TV. McQueen took her to her first boxing match. What really matters, he often told her, 'has to be done – not performed'. Meaning, again, that in the surface of things you saw the heart of things. Steve acted in the way Muhammad Ali fought, both minimalists who beat the traffic out of the heavy punchers. After *The Getaway* and *Papillon* McQueen was once again king of a vast hill – and responded with a growing list of principles, causes and ambitions which he no longer believed in; and which, near the top, contained a swelling subdivision of 'shit' that included most film roles. By 1973 friends like Jim Hoven could see the change in Steve. He'd never had much interest in Hollywood ass-kissing. Now he was relinquishing what little he had.

Bizarrely, Steve did somehow get himself bracketed along with Newman, Gregory Peck and Jane Fonda on Richard Nixon's 'Enemies List', leaked that summer. A true melon-twister: McQueen's vaunted radicalism remained as apocryphal and elusive as Nixon's own sane, laid-back personality – no distinctive sign of either existed. He had to laugh. For all Steve's whirlybird self-promotion, he'd never given a fuck about national politics, either. On 27 June, the very day the list was published, McQueen ran up a huge American flag outside his home. 'What's Tricky Dick got against *you*?' Ali asked him. 'You're the most patriotic guy I know.'

McQueen just shook his head.

Steve at forty-three: bemused, laconic, *sangue* – could he care less about Washington? – withdrawn, back to basics. Boots and jeans. Bare chest topped out with a Navajo necklace. Rolex Explorer always worn on the right wrist. His hobbies the all-American ones of sex, guns and junk food; with four or five hours of 'personal time' logged nightly in front of the tube. Nowadays there was a similar simplicity, and intensity, in McQueen's professional life. He was again the bad-dest star in Dodge, commanding eggshell-treading respect as well as the fattest fees: $50,000 merely to *read* a script. Later that summer he rang Neile to tell her he was considering taking a 'small role, not

The 'embarrassment of paradoxes' who gave his last ever performance in front of camera on 28 November 1979. Less than a year later, he was dead.

spite the all-action style
Queen, coughing violently
complaining of his
icago cold', struggled
ugh his twenty-eighth
final film, *The Hunter*.

William Kelley,
McQueen's doctor (seen
at a rare light moment),
who refuses to accept the
conventional version of
his final days.

The unlikely star of Ibsen's *Enemy of the People*, remembered by one of the cast as 'incredible . . . black jeans, black T-shirt, heavily bearded – he looked like a werewolf'

McQueen with his third wife Barbara Minty (*left*), backstage at a Rolling Stones concert. Steve enjoyed 'twisting Mick Jagger's melon' later that night.

Meanwhile, McQueen's long rivalry with Paul Newman embroiled a
small army of lawyers and agents in the haggling over the two men's
exact billing in *The Towering Inferno*.

The Getaway, shot in the very weeks McQueen's marriage was being wound up, partnered him with his second wife Ali MacGraw. 'Being with him was like a drug high,' she says.

eve never admitted he
me into that film,' says
Don Gordon (*right*) of
llitt. 'But I know damn
well he did. That was
typical of the guy . . .
McQueen had a very
tender, sweet side to
im that came out if he
trusted you . . . I never
met anyone straighter
or more real.'

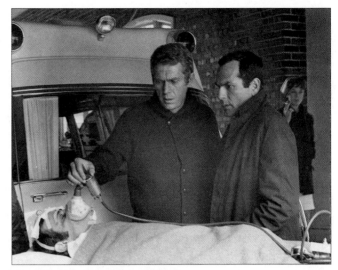

'Steve sprang at me like
an animal,' Karl Malden
says of a scene in *The
Cincinnati Kid*. 'He was
absolutely terrifying . . .
I was in awe of him.'

ngside the professional
ect, McQueen had his
ubts about his *Papillon*
-star Dustin Hoffman.
stopped one speech of
fman's with the advice:
ess, man, less. Toss that
out, you don't need it.
Keep it simple.'

While shooting *The Sand Pebbles* in Taiwan and Hong Kong,
McQueen was also planning his cherished racing picture *Day of the Champion*.
It was eventually released, after numerous false starts, as 1971's *Le Mans*.

Thomas Crown: a film its director fondly calls a study of the 'love affair between two shits'.

much more than a cameo' in *The Towering Inferno*, and what did she think? Steve eventually made $12 million from that one part. Meanwhile, he banked another half-million from his commercial in Japan, where McQueen-mania remained at Shinto level. That job took him exactly four hours.

In time the combined temptations and attractions reached down as far as Steve's friends, like Don Gordon: 'We were out at this Italian bistro . . . Late in the meal some guy at the bar caught my eye and nodded for me to come over. Why not, I thought, maybe he recognises me . . . so I go up. Talking fast, the guy tells me he's a producer, all right, and if I can get this script – he shoves it at me – into McQueen's hands, literally just walk it a few feet, he'll pay me twenty-five grand. "Go fuck yourself," I told him. You should have heard Steve laugh when I got back to the table. "You jerk," he said. "You should've taken the money . . . I'd have told the prick I read it." That sort of shit happened to him all the time in Hollywood.'

Meanwhile he was giving up on the Gospel of Strenuosity, two or three movies a year, tired of the crap. That was his story, anyway. The more they offered him, the less he cared.

Soon, McQueen put out word that Ali would work only on films that he, Steve, starred in. And he wasn't starring in any. Bob Evans's long arm did for their chances in *Gatsby*. Other projects, like *The Betsy*, *Sorcerer* and *Gable and Lombard* would all be dropped when McQueen found something wrong, as he always did, with either the script or the schedule. By mid 1973 his block veto stirred talk of him 'fencing Ali off', of not wanting her to work again – ever – hewing to the same basic agreement he'd made with Neile. He wanted Mac-Graw to spend more time with him and their extended family. He wanted a merger.

The legal proem: on 21 June Ali's divorce from Bob Evans went through. She took pride in the fact that she neither asked for, nor got, a penny in alimony. Three weeks later, over breakfast in Malibu, Steve casually asked MacGraw, 'What was the best thing about getting married in the first place?'

'It gave me security.'

'Don't you think I need that security, too? Don't I deserve that?'

'Of course you do,' said Ali, and read the pre-nuptial contract he calmly slid across the table to her. The document was short, crisp and completely watertight, the first paragraph straight to the bone: '. . . Neither party hereto, by virtue of marriage, shall have or acquire any right, title, interest in or claim to the real or personal estate of the other, in any circumstances whatever . . .'

By virtue of marriage? That was the first Ali had heard of it. Steve's roundabout proposal worked: after phoning her lawyer, she duly signed that afternoon, 10 July. On the 11th McQueen and MacGraw visited Neile, who gave them her blessing and the gift of a plot of land in Palm Springs. The next day Steve, Ali and their three children flew and then drove to Cheyenne, Wyoming. It was as far away from Hollywood as they could manage; a western outpost where the meadows were cut brown and wavy to the line of aspens along the banks of the Crow river, and where bear and elk grazed instead of reporters and paparazzi. Even in this idyllic spot, it was as if McQueen was racing to catch up to his one true peer. Until 1973 Cheyenne's only other twentieth-century claim to fame was when Ernest Hemingway had married his third wife there.

Steve, Ali and the children spent the night of 12 July in a single room in the downtown Holiday Inn. On the 13th, a Friday, McQueen and MacGraw, dressed down for the occasion, wandered across the dusty town square to the courthouse. They were married, outdoors under a shade tree, by a local judge named Arthur Garfield, hurriedly summoned from the golf course. 'They make a lovely couple and are obviously very much in love,' Garfield noted. Ali herself would say she '[didn't] remember the split-second service, only how dazed I felt at being the wife of yet another powerful Hollywood man. It was another moment of unreality.'

Somehow, the fantasy was all part of the crazy charm. Ali was still smiling numbly when, after an all-night keg party in Cheyenne and a weekend camping trip to Yellowstone Park, the couple flew home to Malibu. There was no formal honeymoon.

Bo Hopkins, one of the cast on *The Getaway*, heard his name called out in a costume store a few days later. 'I turned around and there was a bearded McQueen telling me he'd just gotten hitched. Obviously he was a hard guy, if not impossible to get to know, but I'd say he was happy. Shit, he was *beaming*.'

This was a development for which Steve's friends, though ever vigilant, hadn't made that much provision of late. Knowing him, especially around 1970–71, had had its share of lows as well as of giddy highs. Now McQueen was on another upswing. Everything was set to improve. There were no affairs, nor even any fuck-flings for at least the next year. It was 'all wonderful', says Ali: their new beachhouse was full of dogs and children, and the McQueens' neighbours could hear the noise of high-pitched laughter echoing across the water. Steve seemed to blossom amid the informality, the tuna fish and chowder lunches on the porch, the surfing and the biking expeditions when he'd roar up the dirt road to the local honky-tonk or get lost in the Topanga canyons. Birthdays and holidays at the beach were special occasions, days set aside for picnics and feasts and barbeque dinners; a neighbourhood Easter egg hunt was held every year in the McQueens' back yard. They all remained part of the same group of friends and still spent most Saturday evenings together with the rest of their crowd.

It was Ali who rebelled first. By the mid seventies and her own mid thirties she seemed to be doing nothing more, professionally speaking, than killing time during her slow petrification. The movie offers slowed and then stopped altogether. She wanted to work; he wanted her to clean and cook. And work out. As McQueen grew fatter, Ali, to his evident pleasure, grew thinner. He used to have her pose, nude, in front of him so he could appraise her 'great butt', the best one yet. A true bubble ass. Now there's a nice lay, he thought to himself, as he politely complimented her. Almost inexorably, however, the couple were drifting apart. Within eighteen months of marrying, he seemed to have little time for his wife. If you were a star, and neither particularly liberated nor needy but somewhere in the middle, it was hard going being Mrs McQueen. It didn't matter how much you loved him, you had your role cut out. MacGraw couldn't help but notice Steve's habit of slamming down the phone on her friends, or of getting up and walking out of the room if they happened to visit. The whole house was like two worlds violently segregated: hers festooned with candles and lace, his full of biker gear, the stuffed heads of wolves and sheep and a few sticks of furniture made of bones. McQueen also bought a home on Southridge Drive, a private road with a guardhouse at its base, in Palm Springs. From the big living room Steve and Ali looked over the entire Coachella valley, perched between two mountains rising 10,000 feet above the flat desert floor. Nobody bothered them much there, either.

McQueen's son Chad, a pocket version of his father who raced go-karts and wanted to act, chose to live with Steve in Malibu. His daughter Terry stayed with her mother. That she looked and sounded just like McQueen only added an extra dimension of guilt and loss to the bitterness of breaking up his family. MacGraw's son Josh also moved into Broad Beach Road.

McQueen's protégé Bruce Lee died later that same summer, apparently of a brain haemorrhage. Steve, along with Jim Coburn and Chuck Norris, acted as a pallbearer at the funeral in Seattle. The professional rivalry that occasionally disrupted the two men's friendship was swept away by McQueen's obvious sorrow and the support he gave Lee's family for years afterwards. He paid a condolence call on the widow the evening of the burial service, white-faced and wearing his trademark jeans and leather jacket. 'Steve, who had famously strong tear glands, went into this fanatic speech about Bruce and what he'd stood for . . . He told us he was proud to have known him,' says a source close to Lee's family. A fanatical speech, but also a moving one; McQueen went on to speak about Bruce's 'know yourself' philosophy and how he realised, now, that Lee 'was a wonderful guy [because] he also knew himself in everyday life . . . In some ways, he was just the sort of man I'd love to be.'

Closer than ever to attaining the quiet if not the peace he craved, McQueen settled in with his new family. Before he started turning Ali's friends away, he tolerated a few carefully screened guests – Candy Bergen, for one, his co-star from *The Sand Pebbles* and fellow near-victim of the Manson cult.* Meanwhile, Steve's seclusion from Hollywood spelt even greater involvement in the real world, specifi-

---

* Bergen had been living in the Cielo Drive house with Terry Melcher, Manson's intended prey, only weeks before the murders.

cally with children's homes and orphanages. An embarrassment of paradoxes, McQueen still had an unstoppable energy for helping others less lucky than himself. He often took MacGraw to visit Boys Republic. And so far from his being cheap, Don Gordon insists, 'Steve lent money all over town.' The generosity was real, the charity was actual, the fellow-feeling was repeated, and the need for privacy apparently near total. That autumn McQueen and MacGraw were spotted browsing at a flea market in LA, his woollen hat pulled down and collar turned up. Bearded and heavy, McQueen's whole look said: Ignore me.

His relationship with Hollywood had been bad at first, then quite good, and now, not so good again.

Tinseltown, at least in those days, was no place for old men. Movie culture was a paedophile's delight. McQueen's seclusion reflected the dearth of action-hero parts for stars in their mid forties, but it was also a function of his boredom. By now Steve was privately badmouthing mass-market flotsam like *The Great Escape* (while auditing the movie's books for the umpteenth time), and going on from there to trash certain colleagues as 'virtual morons – putting on lipstick and pantyhose like a bunch of pansies'. When he took his next role in 1974, the last true Steve McQueen role he ever did, he mocked and revelled in the idea of his own stardom by writing out his lines on sticky post-it notes and then slapping them on the cast members' foreheads for him to read during close-ups. Real idiot boards, he called them. Banged up at home in Malibu, Steve griped that the 'whole candyass bit' was now out of control, typified by histrionic performers like Hoffman and lovingly recorded in *People*, the new weekly substitute for immortality that Ali herself brought home, along with his smokes and Old Milwaukee, from the Buy-Lo market. Total fucking shit: as far as McQueen went, those honchos in the magazine were all technique and no poke; the disassociation of fame from actual achievement became insanely complete. The culture was finally swallowing its own tail.

Running out of gas.

Of course, having said it was shit, Steve didn't necessarily not want a piece. He still got an introspective kick out of having a media-monitoring service and his lawyer paste up his press cuttings. Or they might be asked to count up all the references, imitations, steals, rip-offs and grand larcenies doing the rounds – everyone from Clint Eastwood down. McQueen's paranoia was a motor that never stopped ticking. MacGraw would drive him to distraction by coming home from the movies raving about Redford or De Niro, treating them as 'serious artists' the way she didn't (and, in his mind, never would) treat Steve. On those nights McQueen would sit up late in his den, pacing around, muttering and railing down the phone at Freddie Fields, among others. The gist of these calls, says Hoven, was the story of McQueen's whole second-act career.

'Steve wanted to be a great actor, as Ali defined it, but he didn't want to do any acting.'

McQueen's professional schizophrenia was the public counterpoint to the stop-and-go romance with Ali and their still happy, quarrelsome extended family. The domestic peace held through 1973–4. Then isolation and coke addiction and the whole post-*Le Mans* scene again caught at Steve's heels. After MacGraw lost the baby she was carrying in mid 1974, McQueen casually resumed his fuck-flings, still rooting around in bed for what he'd lost in childhood. Steve was always belligerent, but now, as if he needed to reinforce his own belief in his sexuality as well as the rest of the world's, he was maniacal. One morning, while shopping with Ali in Malibu, he picked a fight with her.

'Who's the biggest stud in Hollywood?' he asked her.

MacGraw, who was without doubt deeply in love with her husband, was thrown by the question – her attraction to Steve was romantic and spiritual. To her, McQueen was a gentle, insecure soul with no need to prove anything.

'Beatty, Nicholson and someone called McQueen,' she joshed. 'So I've read.'

'Yeah,' Steve said impatiently, 'but who's the *biggest*?'

Ali thought it over. She knew all about Steve's glass ego, the need to constantly reassure him not only that he'd succeeded, but that others had failed. Still, he could take a joke, too, and often sent up his Supie persona, calling himself 'Mr Hollywood – the guy who shits pineapple chunks'. She had enough experience of his funny, self-mocking side to go out on a limb.

'Gee, I don't know,' Ali said teasingly. 'Warren's pretty cute.'

312

McQueen whirled round with blood in his eye. 'Fuck you!' he screamed. Ali stared at him. '*Fuck you!*' Dazed, MacGraw stumbled out into the street and ran back in tears to Broad Beach Road.

That Christmas he bought her a printed silk robe and a construction worker's hard hat. The thinking was that she was both sexy and strong. MacGraw loved that. But she flinched when she finally heard the full and terrible saga of Julian Crawford. 'I reminded [Steve] of his mother in ways that were intolerably painful . . . He acted out his rage and distrust on all the women he met, particularly his wives.'

McQueen's rage and distrust were also, of course, the first source of his inspiration as an actor. That sense-memory of being first dumped and then locked up went into every frame of *Papillon*, a prism for yet another tour of Steve's childhood. His recall, in its laid-back way, was stunning.

Set on Devil's Island off the coast of Venezuela, a spot that made Stalag Luft III look like Butlin's, Franklin Schaffner's epic was an accomplished but uninvolving bit of magical realism: Charrière's true story given a big budget makeover – inappropriate here in jail – into a knotty, serpentine plot with more mishaps and double-crosses than *Bullitt* and *The Getaway* combined. Costed at $4.5 million, the film came in at three times that. Aside from the above-the-line salaries, there were the transatlantic locations and heavy 'commissions' demanded by the Spanish and Jamaican governments. With those sort of overheads, it's not surprising there wasn't much left to actually put on the screen. For all its length, *Papillon* was curiously short on sweep and all too leisurely, instead, in gory detail. Not since Buñuel had anyone striven so tirelessly to show human life sinking – all but wallowing – in the *merde*: we get severed heads, buggery, bestiality, bloated corpses, rotting lepers, open sores, louse-infested soups and rectal safety-deposit boxes. Why would millions of people pay good money to see man and his higher functions dissolve partnership? Because McQueen was worth it.

Always a gifted salesman of his own traumas, Steve got both feet in the doors of perception as the weaselly but wrongly convicted Charrière. His stretch in Chino, and the various hell-holes that followed, made for the most intense performance even he ever gave – a stark contrast to the showy, stylised Hoffman's. 'Me they can kill,'

McQueen would tell his co-star. 'You, they own.' It was true enough. As in *The Great Escape*, the credits rolled with Steve oozing defiance, then the indomitable Cooler King, now the unbreakable Pappy yelling, '*Hey, you bastards. I'm still here!*' towards the sky. In a sense, the whole movie was little more than a two-and-a-half-hour docudrama of McQueen's life. What fired it up, and took it to the brink of greatness, was that lines like that were delivered neat, without an unnecessarily large number of self-conscious actorly tricks.

Rush-released for Christmas, *Papillon* was hammered by the critics and ignored by the Academy, who chose instead to honour the likes of *Save the Tiger* and John Houseman's one-note performance in *The Paper Chase*. Audiences loved it. The film did $60 million worth of business within a year, and enjoyed all the stock accessories of an American blockbuster, including a lawsuit over its 'Parental Guidance' rating (in those satirically quaint days, a few bare breasts were considered controversial) and an unholy row over TV rights, only the top end of a cottage industry churning out homages, clones and spin-offs for years to come.

McQueen himself casually sued for a few million, then relented when the studio, Allied Artists, truthfully pleaded that they were haemorrhaging money and laying off many of their non-union employees. This was followed by a truce; Steve actually made a generous donation to Allied's redundancy fund. He hired some of *Papillon*'s blue-collar crew, mainly carpenters and labourers, to work around his house in Malibu. Several dozen of them. It was the two halves again: the lawyered-up superstar McQueen and the kind, artisan Steve with a talent for projecting ease and empathy, an ability to size up a person or a group of people, grasp their practical need and act on it. And so, like the movie, the man doled out both the pain and the deliverance.

8

Abdication

ornings, after McQueen left the hot tub and kick-started the Triumph, winding down and up through the small canyons, MacGraw would watch the trail of dust that rose in the bike's wake, sometimes breathing it in when the Santa Anas blew from the high desert to the east. The fine powder piled up on every surface which was anywhere near level, notably Ali's prize Moroccan throw rugs and not excluding the wrinkles in the skin, the eyelids and even the mouth. The stuff got in everywhere. MacGraw knew to have the place radiantly bright and tidy by the time Steve wove back, after a day slumped over the buffet at Neptune's Net or downing Old Milwaukee in the Stein Room, for an early dinner with the kids. He needed total order, to live in a place with no mess, no hassle. No noise. Nobody ever heard him laugh, sing or raise his voice, except once when, after telling her she needed to cool off, he tossed Ali over the second-floor balcony into the pool below. For the most part McQueen resolved his marital fights by simply leaving home for a week or two at a time.

'There was plenty of passion,' says Pat Johnson, who knew both parties well. 'Ali was *the* love of Steve's life – I mean until the day he died. The problem was simply in bottling all that lightning and turning it into a working lifestyle.' Most of McQueen's own work took place in the musty chill of the back terrace, sloshing around in the tub where he chewed the cud of his solitude, spinning yarns that spiralled into a mixture of McQueenly cool and resignation; he reckoned he had 'one or two more movies, max' left in him. He could give a shit. He'd been at this racket for twenty years, ten of them as Supie. Let Warren fucking Beatty have a go.

Living at the beach instead of Brentwood or Beverly Hills high-lighted the differences between Steve and Ali. They tried to work out their problems. They spent a few days in New York after McQueen heard of an antique bike auction there. MacGraw liked the high society, but unhappily for her he thought the opera and ballet, and most art generally, candyass. The one time she got him anywhere near the LA Philharmonic, he left during the interval. Sooner or later Steve would always be back in the hot tub, dragging on his fat cigarette and beefing about the noise or the dust in the squat, narrow living room, if not the lateness of his supper. After a year or two of this America's golden girl was suddenly a thirty-five-year-old mother, cooking and scrubbing dishes. 'Never having to say you're sorry' had been Ali's punchline in *Love Story*, and now she reflected on the theme. A housewife, Hollywood's beauty queen, and she'd become a drudge. Waving though not yet drowning, she decided to invite Steve out for lunch to talk things over.

'Off the meter?' he asked.

'Yes,' she assured him. 'My treat.'

Fuck it. A free meal. The main concern, as always, was money, though he could spend it as well as save it. Temperamentally, too, Steve was still the Cincinnati Kid, doggedly committed to the hoard-and-binge cycle, forever counting his chips, well-meaning but with a sliver of ice in his heart. The power lunch in question settled nothing. Ali wanted what her Hollywood friends had – a normal pipeline to the outside world through at least some semblance of social life. He wanted to be home, in bed, by 9 p.m. It took a certain asceticism, not to mention a subdued sense of self, to stay married to McQueen and actually get a kick out of it. The pay was lousy, the hours were long, and if things went right the reward might well be the satisfaction that comes from hearing your mate belch after a good home-cooked dinner. Almost by definition, the lifestyle strained against common decency. Yet there were consolations: Steve's will-ingness to appear sympathetic to 'real folks', along with his desire to charm and please, made it hard to tell whether, deep down, he was really more of a gentle, troubled soul who was struggling to rein in his dark side or a psychopath who truly believed that 'people are shit'. At the time, most of his close friends thought that Steve was the former; MacGraw considered him 'a Star [who] exuded mystery and danger', yet with a marshmallow centre. 'Underneath an almost caricature machismo was a sweet, kind and intelligent man.'

He gave children the gift of taking them seriously, listening to them, responding warmly.

One unusually cold, dank morning in June 1974 MacGraw was sitting with Steve on the set of *The Towering Inferno* when she looked down to see that she was in a pool of blood. McQueen rushed her to the hospital. Ali's miscarriage – she hadn't even known she was pregnant – would be an early, cruel milestone down the road towards divorce. Steve in particular 'always felt that if we had a child, we could save our marriage'. They went back to Malibu that night and cried out their disappointment together. McQueen put his arms around Ali's waist and hugged her closer for warmth. In his few moments of sleep he burrowed with his face flat on her chest; her breathing sometimes woke him, but he preferred the noise to the cold. Steve whispered to her that it would be all right, that he still loved her. He'd always feared 'something going wrong' with Terry or Chad when they were only babies. Now he knew why. The black mood would pass, but something inside both McQueen and Mac-Graw changed for ever. It was a long night.

So keeping himself busy became Steve's main artistic priority, or at least having somewhere to go in the mornings did. He threw himself into *Inferno* like no other movie since *Le Mans*.

A mindless but wildly successful piece of escapist hokum in a line from *The Poseidon Adventure* as 'disaster' yarns, *The Towering Inferno* would trawl the same plot as the all-in champion of the genre, 1997's *Titanic*. In both movies catastrophe strikes on the debut of a new superstructure; in both the builders are blamed, though the real villains are the blockbuster-franchise scripts, with talented actors coming off uncannily like cartoons. Some of them were so clichéd that they seemed to have stepped out of a Harold Robbins script, but with this crucial difference – Robbins knew how to animate his characters and *The Towering Inferno* didn't. Both movies would boast the odd sharp observation, but as human drama barely troubled the evolutionary ladder routinely scaled by the likes of *The Reivers* or *Junior Bonner*. Both earned undreamt-of profits.

The producer Irwin Allen conceived the 1974 epic much like Frankenstein's monster, all nuts, bolts and clanking parts cobbled together from the novels *The Tower* and *The Glass Inferno*, then packaged it as a joint venture between Warners and 20th Century-Fox. McQueen was sounded and told Fields to come up with a 'sweetheart deal'. Fields did: $1 million upfront and a full 10 per cent of the gross. The original plan was for Steve to play the part of the architect, the one later taken by his arch rival – the Fuckwit, Newman. What happened that autumn between McQueen and his ex would repeat itself often over the years ahead, and it would be a bonding for their odd third-act relationship. 'He asked me to read the script and tell him whether I thought he could handle the role of the fire marshal,' says Neile, who did so fulsomely. Steve promptly signed on as Chief O'Hallorhan.

McQueen then counted up the number of words written for each character, discovered that Newman had exactly twelve lines more than he did and exploded. 'Goddamn it, that fucker's always twisting my melon,' he told Hoven. 'Twisting my melon.'

Steve then reiterated his many grievances against Newman, real or imagined, going back to the days of *Somebody Up There Likes Me*. 'Talk about bitter,' says Hoven. 'That mindset came from within, and I'd say stemmed from self-doubt and rank paranoia, McQueen's trademark combination of trust and mistrust . . . No wonder the guy was a riddle to most of his friends.' Steve hurriedly put in a call to the screenwriter Stirling Silliphant and ordered him to come up with a suitably doctored script. Silliphant told him he'd work on it, but that first he and his wife were embarking on a long-planned cruise.

'Fine,' said Steve. 'We'll get another writer.'

Silliphant missed the boat. McQueen got his extra twelve lines.

In between dodging the paparazzi Steve always insisted he enjoyed his time shooting *Papillon* in Navarre and Montego Bay, but now, only a year later, his variant of 'location, location, location' was a stark 'No foreign shit – gotta be right here on the left coast.' Once again, he was treated with the deference and majesty of a latter-day

Sun King. Most of *Inferno*'s interiors would be shot at Fox's Malibu ranch, fully two miles from Steve's front door, with the occasional foray to San Francisco. McQueen then had a passing word with Allen about his, Steve's, interest in plugging the movie. He had none. 'I don't need the juice and I don't want it.' When the studio grovelled, he told them – nothing unsatisfactorily enigmatic here – to go fuck themselves. And the press. Strangely enough, it wasn't McQueen's few bad reviews he most objected to. Just the opposite. Steve's compulsion to convert his critics extended down to the media. Pundits who attacked him (up to a point) were likely to be called, cajoled, stroked and even invited out to dirt-bike with him. What twisted the melon was when they dragged his kids and Ali into it, the way they always did sooner or later. When one of the tabloid hacks had sneaked onto the set of *The Getaway*, Steve protected his family by promptly knocking the man down a flight of stairs.

Thanks to Fields, McQueen got virtually everything he wanted from *The Towering Inferno*. As he was the only watchable thing in the film, which turned an instant $80 million profit worldwide, nobody begrudged him his basic nut; perks like the Cortez, limos, drivers, personal stand-in, valet, make-up man and barber; the private gym and steam room; or the masterful stroke he pulled over billing. The papers were duly signed on 12 April 1974.

'Steve was a genius at micro-managing a movie,' says one of Fox's directors. 'On the day of each [contract] deadline, he'd come in to see me with his lawyer. McQueen would always fight with me and the rest of the board: no to this word, no to that clause.' Steve line-read the deals with a mixture of instinct and mind-numbing pedantry that would query even font sizes and punctuation. More than once he challenged the use of a bracket. Literally nothing was left to chance – exact start and finish dates, working hours and over-time rates (gauged to the minute), all were hammered out with a zeal that would have glazed a shop steward's eye. 'But when McQueen did commit, he gave you everything. The second the cameras rolled, he was on . . . Once his shit with Paul was settled, Steve was a pussycat to work with.'

McQueen's 'shit with Paul' went back eighteen years and only now, post-*Papillon*, was he indisputably the bigger name, the one who got first refusal of parts and scripts – when Steve declined *Fort Apache, the Bronx*, the film went into turnaround before being offered to Newman five years later – with the clout to make Allen Klein, no less, jump.* *Inferno* settled all doubt in McQueen's mind. From here on, he didn't need to prove himself against anyone. He'd done so.

Klein wrote, on 19 July 1974, to Steve's lawyer Kenneth Ziffren.

Dear Ken

We have previously advised you that in accordance with the billing clause, being Article 32 of the agreement between Steve McQueen and Twentieth Century-Fox relating to *The Towering Inferno*, that McQueen (herein called 'Artist') shall be afforded full credit in the following manner:

(A) If Artist's full name appears on one (1) line, and should Paul Newman's name also appear on said line, then the bottom letters of Paul Newman's name shall be no higher than an exact prolongation of a line drawn through the true middle of Artist's name, in the following manner:

~~STEVE McQUEEN~~ PAUL NEWMAN

(B) If Artist's name appears on two (2) lines, and should Paul Newman's name also appear on said lines, then the word 'Newman' will appear on the same line as Artist's first name, in the precise following manner:

PAUL

STEVE   NEWMAN
McQUEEN

– and so on, covering every typographical and stylistic twist of the two men's billing, all on condition that McQueen's name, not Newman's, appear first. That one proviso was revenge superbly controlled. Now Steve was officially on top of the world.

*   *   *

* The legendary ex-manager of the Rolling Stones and the Beatles, by now working for Fox.

On 6 May, a week before *Inferno* began shooting, McQueen and MacGraw were sitting in a briefing room with LA Battalion Chief Peter Lucarelli, the technical adviser on the film. Suddenly an alarm and Lucarelli's phone both rang. He listened for a moment, cupped his hand over the mouthpiece and calmly told Steve, 'The Goldwyn studios are on fire.'

The pattern of McQueen's life always had something of the structure of a drama. Act One would be his childhood and Dickensian youth, Act Two the scuffling years in New York, and so on to the grim dénouement of the Mexican clinic. Such dramatic patterning is rare in real life, and helps add the patina of legend to the true story; a legend, from time to time, Steve himself was keen to polish.

'Let's go,' he said.

'We have rules,' Lucarelli told him. 'No civilians in harm's way. In other words, you can watch. Not fire-fight. I'm talking about standing on the other side of the street, taking notes if you want. *Capice?*'

McQueen nodded.

'Really. No funny stuff.'

McQueen nodded.

'No heroics.'

'I got it, man,' Steve said. 'Rules.'

But when their car pulled up to Goldwyn's sound stage 5, McQueen immediately ran towards the fire, crawled through a ground-floor window, grabbed a hose and trained it on the blaze. He stayed there for a full hour. It was a true raging, if not towering inferno: $7 million of damage done, large parts of the studio (including the director Billy Wilder's office) razed and thirty-five crew and technicians hospitalised. When Steve staggered out, red-eyed and gasping, hardened emergency teams lined up to applaud. This was no candyass actor who wanted to play make-believe, but 'real folks' – a man who more than held his mud, the one whose star Ali and the kids and now scores of others trusted in a life-or-death situation. When Fox and Warners wanted him to recreate the whole scene for PR purposes, dolling him up like O'Hallorhan in a press conference, Steve told them to go fuck themselves. Again.

Actual newsphotos of the Goldwyn fire still made all the major papers. He may not have wanted or needed the juice, but when you were Steve McQueen it was too much to hope for privacy. An awkward moment occurred when a photographer appeared outside the Broad Beach Road house begging Steve and Ali to come out and pose, but it passed off when they set their dog on him.

The Towering Inferno began filming a week later. Other than a pulled ligament and the more serious matter of MacGraw's miscarriage, all went well during the twelve weeks' principal photography. McQueen made no secret of the fact that he despised most of the shit of filmmaking (hence his satirical prank of slapping lines not only on bits of furniture, but on his colleagues' heads), yet he possessed a kind of perfection – a grace, poise and informality both of body and speech that triumphed over the more actorly Newman. He, Steve, was now the quintessential movie star.

'Proud of me?' he asked Ali.

When *Inferno* wrapped that September, McQueen got on his Triumph and rode the short distance down the Pacific Coast highway back to Trancas. As soon as he told Fields 'Fuck it', he readily adjusted to his well-padded early retirement, quickly putting on both ten pounds and a full beard. Now and then he glanced at *People* and the trades, particularly the lies about himself, but mostly Steve sat in the hot tub overlooking the beach, smoking pot, his hair frizzy, unkempt, a can of beer clamped in his hands, to all appearances an old hippie passing the time, each day an exact replica of the one before and the one that would follow. When Irwin Allen came calling to offer him $3 million to star in *The Towering Inferno II*, McQueen barely bothered to tell him, too, to fuck off.

This hunkering down, creating a safe haven with only his wife, kids and stepson, was typical both of McQueen's ambivalence towards Hollywood from the start and of a natural loner who tended to seclusion anyway. As early as December 1959, when he was fighting Four Star over *The Magnificent Seven*, he'd harped on longingly about moving to Australia. Retirement talk, usually involving fantasies about a farm, surfaced regularly over the next fifteen years. As Jim Geller says, 'Steve approached films like someone else would approach the electric chair. I mean, every fucking time. If you go through the movies year by year, there's exactly one he was gung-ho to do [*Le Mans*], and even that backfired . . . McQueen's first reaction was always to say "no" until or unless he needed the dough.' He now had $4 million, and counting, in the bank.

Steve still skimmed a few scripts, for $50,000 and old time's sake. But framing these bleary readings was always the beginning and end of his every exchange with a producer.

Why bother?

Not that McQueen's inward crawl was merely indifference. Not financially. He was still – now more than ever – famously well managed. Solar's books paid lavish tribute to his vigilance. Like a stagnant pond, motionless to the naked eye, Steve's whole empire, though portraying itself as dormant, was inwardly teeming with furious, invisible activity. As well as Bill Maher, McQueen hired fund managers and accountants, and took on a new secretary named Toni Geniella. But the one he leant on most was clearly Ken Ziffren, whose law firm kept up its avalanche of demands and writs on Steve's behalf – week in, week out, the same endless supply of angry letters.

To the *Papillon* producer, Robert Dorfmann:

> Reference is made to that Certain Memorandum of Agreement, dated as of July 18, 1972, as amended July 18, 1972, & December 27, 1973, between you and our client, Steven McQueen . . . Despite repeated requests that you issue statements of account, including a statement of cost of production and distribution reports, as required by the Agreement, our client has not received any such material . . . Demand is hereby made that you forthwith issue full and correct statements of account, [failing] which we have been instructed by Mr McQueen to institute litigation to secure each and every sum due to him thereunder . . .

Some of this epic personal control came across in *The Towering Inferno*, rush-released for Christmas 1974. Only McQueen could have saved it from its all-star idiocy; and did. His O'Hallorhan was the one true role, let alone character, in the whole misbegotten cast. Like its high-rise setting, *Inferno* was a towering, ill-designed folly of monumental tedium. Allen and his director John Guillermin (the genius behind *Tarzan* and *King Kong*) badly undermined the fire-power of even their action scenes; no one could care less if cardboard cut-outs like William Holden lived or died. Between them they created a spluttering Roman candle of a film – plummeting elevators, exploding helicopters and blazing partygoers all crisscross the screen, a whole series of gaudy vignettes that might have been set on an alien planet. There was no heart, no soul, no minimal human factor. No chance of audience involvement. It's not until well into the second half that *Inferno* acquires a dramatic, as opposed to a mechanical, life. Before that the film has all the outward signs of dynamism and speed but, like a man on a running machine, never seems to actually go anywhere.

This was really a good old-fashioned star vehicle, where the lead jump-starts a dull script. The film's sloth getting off the mark – locating the story behind the pyrotechnics – jars with a genuinely thrilling, even moving climax, the epitome of an 'escape' movie but one played with humanity and its nearly forgotten handmaiden, restraint. Only at the very end is some emotion achieved. The explanation is simple: McQueen.

As a rule, *Inferno* took up where the *Airport* formula left off in goosing Jurassic-era plots with *Star Wars*-like special effects. It was as though Allen had combed his *Poseidon Adventure* for something which might count as a gimmick, found one, dragged it home, dried it out, tarted it up, set it on fire, smothered it in sub-*Grand Hotel* clichés and flogged the whole thing to death. With unintentionally disastrous results. Confronted with the novelty of shadow-acting in front of a blue screen, most of the cast, too, came across as oddly synthetic. As just one example: the glittering San Francisco skyline seen from the top floor of the burning tower was in fact added in later, by computer, so if Newman and the rest looked straight through it you could hardly blame them.

Since *Poseidon* Allen had become known as a sure thing, and now the inquests into his films also ran on familiar lines. They followed down one of two tracks. On the one hand, the tabloids and certain trades touted *Inferno*'s scale and enterprise (quoting bizarre statistics like the number of asbestos Nomex underpants worn on the set).

The alternative view was taken by those who measured blockbusters by their own high standards. They judged *The Towering Inferno* alongside *The Godfather* saga and found it wanting. Narratively, the whole thing was as shallow as a mirror. Visually, *Inferno* was just another cold-blooded Hollywood product, a moribund yarn that came alive only when McQueen, with his gift for the swift sketching of character, hove suddenly into view at a point when the audience was in an ugly mood.

Critics loved him. The actual film made 'The Worst Movies of All Time' anthologies.

At least, however, there could be no complaints under the Trades Description Act. Sure enough, it was about a towering inferno. The film's *raison d'être* smouldered in every frame, yet the emotional temperature stubbornly refused to budge. Nearly thirty years later, *Inferno* has some of the seventies retro-chic of *Airport*, but without the wrenching emotions of that movie, and it suffers from a major structural flaw: in the layer-cake of stunt casting – on top, old faithfuls like Newman and Holden; in the middle, designer luggage like Bob Wagner; at the bottom, novelties like O. J. Simpson – the icing comes too late. Before McQueen, *Inferno* has all the requisite effects; it's hyper-frenetic, but about as exciting as watching a hamster in a wheel. The second he appears, everything ignites.

There are 138 storeys in the fictional tower, and almost as many sub-plots. In the place of real people we get a houseful of stock types: there's the lovable rogue (Fred Astaire), the dastardly shit (Dick Chamberlain) and even the token love interest (Steve's old flame Faye Dunaway). Allen was inordinately proud of the swirling storyline, which, like Hitchcock before him, he begged fans to keep to themselves, the better not to 'spoil it all' for second- and third-wave audiences. In truth there wasn't much to report, apart from an obsession with fire, rain and – a less planned element – hot air. *Inferno*'s douse-the-house climax was explosively hectic (technicians dropped a million gallons of water on the set), dramatic yet apt for a movie which was wet through from the start. For completists only.

Steve's performance was as incandescent and ultimately heroic as the tower's. He volunteered for most of his own stunts, including the one down a lift shaft and another dangling from a helicopter, both unhesitatingly tackled by a man who, in real life, suffered from crippling vertigo. Characterisation and pure film sense made up for the plot; as usual, McQueen's instinct of what worked for him was brilliantly on the money. He was terse, sharp, credible – you never saw him acting – eminently 'natural' and yet a master with props. Just as he had with Hoffman, Steve effortlessly scored over the better-trained Newman. Nobody else understood the look and feel of a character like he did.

On the very first day on set McQueen appeared kitted out in regulation fireman's uniform. But something was bothering him. The helmet he had to wear, he felt, made him look like an idiot. Everything seemed set fair for a tantrum.

Allen told Steve not to worry. He'd take full responsibility for the wardrobe. But he dreaded the hassle. On his way out to berate the costume department, Allen heard McQueen say, 'No, wait. Turn around and look, Irwin.'

Allen took one look and his mouth cracked into a grin, even behind the heavy bullhorn he always carried.

'Don't you like me better like this?' Steve asked. Lying on a shelf he'd spotted an ancient tin helmet shaped like a Stetson, and, as Allen approached, McQueen winked at him under the brim, playfully.

'Fucking genius,' said Allen.

Others performed; Steve *became* the man.

Detail like that was the subliminal reason crowds flocked to McQueen and, specifically, *The Towering Inferno*. There was also the sheer, multiplex spectacle of the thing: people burning in front of your eyes in wide-screen Panavision, amplified by state-of-the-art 100-watt speaker systems. Something-for-everyone made it a world-wide hit. *Inferno* reaped $55 million in the US alone and twice that globally, making it the then highest grossing movie of all time. Steve's 'sweetheart deal' translated into an instant $5 million, merely the first wedge of what became a stipend – the books confirm he banked more than $12 million from the film. He was a brilliant success but now he had the 'fuck you' money he'd wanted all along. Steve McQueen was on course to becoming the action hero legendary for doing nothing.

*　　*　　*

'After *The Towering Inferno*, it was as if the effort to catch up to Paul Newman had tired him out,' says Neile.

That's certainly one theory. Most of his friends never bought it. More likely, a towering contempt for the candyass and fuckwits, fuelled by his own soaring drink and drug habit, now led Steve to spend his time 'count[ing] my bread, not making it'. In fact, for most of 1975 his stock portfolio, like many Americans', was regularly tossed by waves of panic selling and panic buying. By his forty-fifth birthday McQueen was valued at $15 million, more or less. At times his net worth slopped around by a million dollars a day, like water going back and forth in a bathtub. Out of chaos – agony for one who hated change, let alone the dreaded 'shit' of life – came this hunkering down: Steve had Bill Maher transfer most of his cash to Treasury bonds, while the lawyers wrung every dime out of McQueen's back catalogue. Financially, Steve retrenched. Personally, he did something similar, turning his beach oasis into a desert refuge fortified by walls, wire and, not infrequently, a bawled threat from the front terrace.

'One of the things I really liked about Steve was that he almost totally lacked tact,' Geller says. 'If you hassled him, he told you so. His way of dealing with paparazzi was to tell them to fuck off, and, if that didn't work, to set the dog on them. Always the direct approach.' During McQueen's lost weekend, the littoral slump widely stigmatised as his 'ageing beach-bum' phase, he still worked out with Pat Johnson most mornings. Johnson denies his friend was ever, like Elvis, committing suicide on the instalment plan. 'I trained and fought with him, and I should know . . . Steve was by nature the most tuned-up, aggressive guy in the world. That never changed.'

The portrait of McQueen's hermit years was captured in a sneaked photo which showed a beer-gut has-been flopped in a lawn chair surrounded by a stack of biker magazines and a pile of empty bottles; the cooler king on his wino's throne. Again, Pat Johnson proves a shrewd judge of McQueen's slump. 'Steve had bad posture. He slouched [and] when he sat down he hunched over like Groucho . . . He put on some weight, sure, but he was never that fat.' More worrying was the mental bloat, which combined vestiges of McQueen's old misfit-belligerence with growing signs of steady, if not heavy, dope addiction. At worst, the man whose career had come back from the dead himself died a bit – the cool gilding completely gone, replaced by a wounded, muttering torpor. At best, Steve still had unfinished business with his parents.

McQueen again began seeing an analyst. He told Ali to keep it quiet, because he didn't want people to think him candyass.

'You still dig me, don't you?'

'Adore you.'

'And you wouldn't twist my melon, would you?'

'Do what?'

'Blab about me seeing a shrink.'

'No, baby.'

'Never?'

'Make the appointment, Steve,' said Ali.

So he went. No stigma there. Enrolling in therapy added up to nothing more worrying than proof that McQueen was living in California, and an actor. Everybody did it. Steve evidently enjoyed the first few sessions at the clinic in Beverly Hills – ideal terrain, apparently, for him to then do what he did best: start role-playing, skipping appointments, having Tony Geniella ring and tell the shrink, 'Mr Crown is unavailable today.' Within a few weeks he quit bothering to go at all.

When Ali confronted him, she asked him when the shit would stop. The constant guilt and rage cycle. When does a forty-five-year-old get over the feeling he's done something wrong?

'It never stops.'

For two years, then, Steve was famous for what he didn't do. He turned down Lew Grade and Francis Ford Coppola, said no to cover stories, passed on premieres (including *Inferno*'s) and failed to sort out his feelings. He didn't become a father again.

His big thing had always been sensation. The adrenalised kick of speed, of sex, of pulling off an exquisite scam. Now McQueen was into just the opposite – inertia. As Ali would say, 'It was easy to count the Old Milwaukee beer cans and joints in the ashtrays and come up with the obvious fact that Steve was somewhat stoned every day of our relationship.' The press became as devoted to frenzied rumour as he did to anaesthetised indifference. To them,

McQueen turned into Hollywood's very own Howard Hughes. Ali couldn't go out to the store without people asking her if he was all right.

As Steve passed his days deep in the hot tub, oblivious to the world at large, the tabloids still covered the McQueen phenomenon, though with a new ghoulish fascination. As the world's highest paid star and – to them – an obvious nut, he was doubly stigmatised. Long used to being fêted in the *Reporter* and *Variety*, seeing himself slagged in the *National Enquirer* ('Man Mountain McQueen Balloons to 240 pounds') was a challenge. The gauntlet was dutifully picked up. Steve responded by telling his press-cutting agency to copy the stuff out for him onto a continuous sheet of 'fluffy paper', suitably rolled – a polite way of saying he knew where to put it.

Even if McQueen hadn't dropped out, even if he'd come out of *Inferno* stronger and sharper than ever, it was a different world now. The Hoffmans and Beattys were the new masters, arch, post-Watergate ironists who marked the true end of the sixties. Within a year or two, the very phrase 'action hero' would be too embarrassed to sneak out alone without its inverted commas. Normally nothing lit up Steve's bullshit meter like a 'busy' actor. Someone who took his own key policy of working hard to achieve effortlessness and turned it upside down. But now he had nothing public to say about the matter. As for the more private acts of lolling in the tub, quaffing beer, yelling at Freddie Fields or Bill Maher, throwing punches in the Beverly Wilshire, cocking his fist back at John Gavin, McQueen remained McQueen: a legendary gutter fighter, brutal, uptight, spring-loaded to do it to you before you did it to him.

A restless, angry man, alone.

He went up to the Castle for the last ever time that winter, punched in the code and started down the winding driveway to the Spanish courtyard, fought with Neile about the furniture; then left again. They sold the place to Zubin Mehta. Steve never lost the snapshot of the house, with both of them there on moving-in day looking young, golden and in good company, he always kept it in his wallet until he died.

They didn't even speak for a while. He went back down to the beach and he didn't know where the fuck Neile went.

By now his self-suffocating fame – a stardom that cut him off from his audience, leaving him in a limbo of enabling groupies and a wack pot habit – also served as Hollywood's latest morality tale. The *Enquirer* was out, and the rumour mill was churning: the king of cool was soon eclipsed by the Prisoner of Trancas, a stoned alter ego whose weirdness seemed to swell with his waistline. Whole forests were sacrificed to the question 'What went wrong?', but the answer was obvious. It's not that friends didn't already know. The fabric that held the McQueen halves together now came apart into Steve and Supie. The former was a skinny kid who grew up disliking noise and hassle and not wanting much to do with the human race; the latter was, and still is, the male version of the American dream. Now McQueen reverted to type. He always thought his Hollywood career had been a glorious scam. Walking, before the honchos made him run, had been in the game plan all along.

In the trench warfare of film-making Steve's name was always the heavy gun, the one to shake down the millions needed to fund a *Bullitt* or a *Papillon*. For twelve years producers had said, 'We need that guy,' and generally got him. Guided by Neile, McQueen had submerged his former lonely-kid persona in a chairman-of-the-board mentality, doing the deals and cranking out product. Fabulous product. But through it all he'd flouted every expectation of how he was supposed to act (gratefully), instead counting the days until he no longer had to flog himself in the one role always beyond and beneath him.

Steve just couldn't do deferential.

Fuckit.

Nowadays, McQueen turned down parts lesser talent sat up and bayed for. He could have been Rambo, Superman and the Jack Nicholson character in *Cuckoo's Nest*. Universal again offered him the lead in *Gable and Lombard*. The actual Rhett Butler role in *Tara: The Continuation of Gone with the Wind* was his for the taking. *The Bodyguard*, *Close Encounters* and *Raise the Titanic!* were all tailored for the star Hollywood still banked on, gross after gross, for a box office score. All vetoed. *The Gauntlet*, *Raid on Entebbe*, *Fancy Hardware* . . . after a while the scripts tended to mingle and merge, each with a $50,000 reading fee he promptly cashed in return for a form refusal slip regretting, 'Steve McQueen can't do as you ask.' He had the plain 3 × 5 cards run off, a dime a dozen, at the local Print King. At any given time there were a couple of hundred of them nestling in Steve's desk drawer.

Early in 1976 Freddie Fields at last sent McQueen a script he liked. The original plan was for him to play the part of Willard in Francis Ford Coppola's *Apocalypse Now*, a sixteen-week commitment for $3 million. Then Steve found he didn't, after all, care to spend four months on location in the Philippine jungle, so Coppola offered him the role of Kurtz. That would have meant only three weeks' actual filming.

'OK,' said McQueen. 'But I still want the bucks.'

'I began to see if this kept up the industry would some day be paying $3 million for eight hours, plus overtime, and have to shoot at the actor's house,' says Coppola. He turned Steve down. 'But I can't blame him for asking.'

The puny kid, by unending persistence, had for years pumped his body to pro-weightlifter class. Anyone who did less was candyass. Anyone who did less was an actor. So came the Gospel of Strenuosity, and with it McQueen's denial of illness and matching dislike of doctors. Specifically, the fact that he didn't want 'malaria shots and shit', the same regimen of *The Sand Pebbles*, weighed heavily against his taking *Apocalypse*. More ominously, Steve now refused to consult specialists or undergo tests once his throat problems returned in 1975–6. All the time he was turning on and dropping out at Trancas, he was also losing his best chance of an early diagnosis.

Soon, he would be coughing himself hoarse most nights.

People began to realise something was wrong. Steve didn't want to do any long shoots. But it went beyond that: Steve didn't want to do much of anything. There were murmurings about a mental breakdown in some quarters, particularly among the honchos who pounded on his door.

McQueen would never make it to the Philippines. He simply refused to go without the cash and the points and the jet and his personal hot tub dismantled in Malibu and air-freighted to Manila. And, critically, without his best friend. 'Steve asked me what I felt about tagging along,' says Pat Johnson. 'I told him I wasn't too keen.

Two of my sons were still kids and I didn't much want to go. So McQueen turned it down.'*

He sent Coppola a fancy, one-off card, decorated with a design of funereal laurel leaves.

One day Katharine Hepburn came calling to interest Steve in *Grace Quigley*, an abysmal misfire of a film – eventually shot in 1985 – about a hit-man shuffling amok in a nursing home. MacGraw remembers that summer morning in Trancas:

> I was very excited and nervous . . . Just before she arrived, Steve said, 'I've got to go for a ride,' and he got on his motorcycle and drove off, leaving me to face the great Hepburn. She arrived, quite annoyed he wasn't there, and announced that she was hungry and would I make her lunch. The only thing I had was a salad, which she didn't want, and some canned soup. I made that, and when Steve came back, she was all charm with him – and he with her – and she complained that I made bad soup.

Improbably, Steve finally began to consider directing and briefly optioned a project called *Deajum's Wife*. Improbably and yet not so improbable: it's unlikely a star could be found who knew more about the mechanics of film than he did. He was a brilliant rewriter of dialogue (usually by lopping it down to a few monosyllables), had great visual sense and understood esoteric stuff like fades and halation and lighting. Bob Relyea remembers McQueen enjoyed the idea of directing in the obvious sense – of peering through a viewfinder and telling actors what to do – but the business of 'actually getting up early to deal with costume-designers and so on was too much of a hassle'. *Deajum's Wife* went into permanent turnaround.

Next Steve told the Rambo people to fuck off.

That same month McQueen heard a familiar, British voice on the phone. 'If you want to do a good film,' it said, 'I'm your man.'

It was him. He recognised the accent. He remembered when the limey had deigned to show up with the rest of them in Geiselgasteig,

---

* After a search mission nearly as protracted as the one on screen, Coppola would eventually cast Martin Sheen and Marlon Brando as Willard and Kurtz, respectively. Brando demanded and got even more for his time than McQueen.

and all the enjoyable shit of that shoot. Then *The Sand Pebbles*, and the gut-eroding BS *that* entailed. Dickie Attenborough. It was him on the line from London. Now he was casting something called *A Bridge Too Far*. The setup would be simple, Attenborough said: three weeks' work with old friends like Sean Connery and Gene Hackman.

'Who else?' yawned McQueen.

'Mike Caine . . . Jimmy Caan . . . Tony Hopkins . . . Larry, dear Larry . . . Eddie Fox . . . Max Schell . . .'

At the last name Steve suddenly came to life.

'Schell?'

'Schell wants to play a cameo.'

McQueen hung up after telling Attenborough his people would get back to him. Fields formally announced Steve's terms a week later: $3 million for eighteen days' work; the usual crap about perks and flunkies; plus $50,000 to house Steve's personal entourage on location. The final demand was the one that caused fits. McQueen wanted Attenborough's studio to buy his Palm Springs home off him for $500,000. 'I don't want to deal with realtors,' Steve explained. 'I hate them. They're all grovelling shits.'

Attenborough quietly signed up Robert Redford.

After that McQueen personally tore up the postbox at his Trancas house. He made arrangements to use the local Gulf station as his own private mail drop. He'd always been quite well looked after there. Steve McQueen walking into a garage was a bit like Oliver Reed walking into a pub, or Elizabeth Taylor into a beauty shop. They were glad to accommodate him, and dozens of scripts and reading fees soon piled up for him on a greasy work bench in the back room. Among the correspondence, Steve could have read – if he read fan mail – letters comparing him to Lionel Barrymore and Spencer Tracy. Even in semi-retirement, he was voted 1975's favourite star in a poll conducted by Quigley Publications, beating out Redford, Eastwood, Nicholson. And Newman.

The garage mailbox consisted of a cleared space between drills, hammers, jacks and banks of disembowelled engines – the kind of scene Steve revelled in. Two or three times a week, after slitting open the envelopes and promptly shredding the ones without cheques, McQueen took the opportunity to tinker with his current car. Of a typical two-hour visit to the station, he spent perhaps ten minutes sorting post and the rest fiddling about under the hood. And talking. All the regulars loved him. It was there, down among the oil stains on the cement floor and the girlie posters on the wall, that Steve liked to kick back and tell Hollywood war stories until the mechanics were holding their sides laughing. After a while even he started to notice how many of them now acted like slightly muted descendants of the Cooler King: 'real folks' with that same roguish squint and way of communicating with a grin – it was like watching an entire audition for *The Steve McQueen Story*. By the mid seventies almost every adult American knew at least the wire-jumping scene or *Bullitt*'s car chase or the 'Hey, you bastards. I'm still here!' riff from *Papillon*. Quite literally millions of would-be impersonators. It wasn't a bad legacy.

Ironically, about the one blue-collar male not overjoyed at the McQueen image was McQueen himself. Those sub-*Towering Inferno* scripts consigned to the bin were proof that he, for one, wasn't interested in self-parody – or much else to do with Tinseltown. Short of having the word NO tattooed across his forehead, it was hard to see how much more clearly Steve could have made his point to the honchos. He'd moved on, they hadn't.

At the same time, he was determined to get what was rightly his in the marketplace. McQueen wasn't Midwestern for nothing and he took no pains to spare people's feelings. Or, for that matter, their debts: the Orearville reject could read a balance sheet like a CPA. True to tradition, Steve now line-audited *Towering Inferno*. Ziffren & Ziffren were already busy suing the *Papillon* producers. Correspondence rumbled on about nearly every picture since *Soldier in the Rain*, thirteen years earlier.

On 17 January 1976 United Artists, as part of a peace offer, sent McQueen a newly restored print of *The Great Escape*. In a time of reduced profits for the studio, and studios generally, his name still meant healthy residuals all round. It would be a strange, often numb year for Steve himself, but even he must have been struck by how it started: there in his darkened projection room overlooking the Pacific, slumped, stroking his frizzy beard and remembering the vanished, golden days when everything still lay in the future.

Behind the scenes Steve was also at chainsaw point with Phil Feldman, the president of First Artists, who forcefully reminded him of his promise to deliver three films to 'the syndicate' (like some fucking Mafia den, McQueen griped), as for his original contract. That was in 1971. In the five years since Steve had signed up with Poitier, Streisand and Newman, only *The Getaway* qualified as a company production. Now McQueen had to pick from a stack of scripts several feet high, or face the prospect of a lawsuit. Steve's difficulties with the front office led him to express his thoughts about Feldman publicly.

'Hitler,' he called him.

Meanwhile, Freddie Fields was in the throes of trading up from being Steve's agent to himself becoming a Paramount mogul. (The man who introduced *American Gigolo* to immortality.) Obviously, McQueen was never going to pander to Feldman or any studio. He never had. But now, suddenly, as a serious artist who hated wasting his time in a medium that debased his best work, he was alone against the system. Again. Around the same time he watched his print of *The Great Escape*, Steve also began plotting a brilliant, surrealistic move ruled by his twin obsessions of love and revenge.

His next film would fuck up Feldman and win back Miss Alice.

That miscarriage had proved a turning point. From then on the McQueens would wear the stigma of a burnt marriage, and face the full brunt of their mutual 'shit'. Steve told Geller he'd dreamt of a mix of party and arty companionship with MacGraw, but got only the latter. All that ballet crap. Both of them being Arians, Ali in turn explained, led to 'tension and sadness', though there didn't seem to be much astrology to it. Friends saw more sublunary stuff: a clash of screwed-down ambition and drab reality. Steve's abhorrence of the fake or candyass was well known, and Ali was deprived of most of her Hollywood friends. She soon wanted to go back to work. Now that MacGraw's phone began ringing again, that was another enemy. Steve liked an unchanging routine and his 'old lady' there to cook and clean for him. Ali wanted what she'd walked away from after *The Getaway* – another chance at the brass ring through, at first, her agent Sue Mengers.

'Steve and I fought over Ali,' Mengers says. 'They only had one line in the house. I'd say to my secretary, "Get Ali MacGraw," and the line would be busy for hours. And then, finally, the phone would ring and Steve would pick up, and my secretary would say, "Miss Mengers calling Ali MacGraw." He'd say, "If she wants to talk to Ali, let her dial the phone herself!" And hang up.'

MacGraw soon parted company with her agent.

But the hangups between Steve and Ali were more intense. He maintained his image of what a wife should be – amenable, classy, someone who didn't drink or do dope, a 'heavy lady' who presented both charm and passivity around the house. He wanted empathy, support and intelligence within what was suitable for a biker's moll – all as part of his fantasy of Ali, rather than what the real woman was or hoped for. Yet his own example was abysmal. McQueen was guzzling ever more beer and pills. Pot had long since gone from being a habit and crossed over into that less recreational zone, addiction. For the first time since Chino, Steve wasn't interested in physical fitness. He treated his body like a precision vehicle – a Harley that he ran at full speed along the verge of the Malibu clifftop.

As to women, the throughline of McQueen's life, Ali knew that she could expect to be hurt at any time. He'd promised in front of the judge and the kids to take MacGraw to his wedded wife, to live together, hold her, comfort her, honour her and, forsaking all other, keep him only unto her. Plighted his troth right there under the shade tree; told her he'd love her, for better for worse, for richer for poorer. Bent knee to her reverently, discreetly, soberly, eternally, and in the fear of God.

It lasted about eighteen months. Steve didn't look at another woman until after *The Towering Inferno*. Then the fuck-flings got worse.

While McQueen played, Ali worked out with her dance class or fixed Steve's favourite fatty-food meals. With trimmings. McQueen now traded down from his cherished Old Milwaukee to a beer known locally as 'swamp oil' that tasted, rather, of brake fluid. Prompt at six every evening the It Girl of her generation was expected to rustle up the burgers and brews, after which Steve took off on his bike or flopped in front of the TV. Ali, too, was now well on her way to becoming a prisoner of Trancas.

Once, in a moment of contrition, he told her he would do anything he could to make her happy. 'Just name it, baby. Jewellery, furs. Shit, we can even make believe we're tourists and take a trip.'

Silence.

'I thought maybe zip up to Frisco.'

Ali gazed at him in utter stupefication. 'Why would I want to do that?'

'You said you dug it. We'll wear wigs, hang around Ashbury and I'll buy you that cute little tattoo you wanted down below.'

'Don't do me any favours, Steve.'

'Just *name* it, baby. Diamonds? Cars? Money? Hell, there must be *something* you want.'

MacGraw concentrated with a pout. 'I'd like to eat out for a change,' she decided. 'I'm tired of offal.'

On that benign level, the McQueens' marriage already consisted of mastering the art of conveying despair with such absolute calm. At its leaden nadir, the whole thing now tipped into violence. She threw crockery; he was known to throw her. MacGraw writes in her memoirs that 'one fight resulted in Steve inadvertently backhanding me on the forehead, breaking open the skin next to my eyebrow'. Like Neile before her, she both loved him and had a healthy fear of his rages.

She was disorientated. It was like finding a phantom room in a house you thought you knew.

After their worst scenes Steve would drive off into the night, by himself, to cool down. Sometimes he ended up in a motel or sleeping in Pat Johnson's spare room. Quite often he took the road east, between the Chino hills, back to Boys Republic. Now more than ever, McQueen's definition of paradise was to sit there with the kids, listening, as he did in special schools and orphanages the length of southern California. It was more than mere do-goodery. As a rule, Steve's causes tended to be unpublicised and practical, not hoked-up and political; adding extra cover where the missing skin ought to be. They were fully human. Up and down the coast, scores of children went to bed happy because he'd taken the trouble to find them. In charity wards and dormitories from Ventura to San Diego, people who never went near the movies had cause to know, and thank, the name McQueen. That was true fame.

Steve no longer saw much of the old gang like Don Gordon, Bud Ekins or Loren James. It was as though he was embarrassed by his Fat Elvis persona. Gone was the boyish face and peerless physique that graced *The Great Escape* and *Bullitt*. In their place, snapped by the paparazzi, was an ageing hippie of flabby aspect, bearded, wearing ill-fitting jeans and a faded lumberjack shirt that strained across his once-vibrant figure.

McQueen did still see Pat Johnson, the wisest and arguably the closest of all the inner circle. Johnson, as he says, combined being 'both an ass-kicker and a Christian' with a deep appreciation for Steve's efforts to 'destroy the dark side' – to rise above himself. He frequently did so. Hell as he was to live with, McQueen's friendship was quite often heavenly, his idea of fun being to anonymously help out. 'I saw him do that dozens of times,' says Johnson. Years after Steve died, old cronies were flabbergasted to learn that he was the one who had paid their children's medical bills or had had presents delivered to their doors on Christmas Eve.

Come August 1976, the day of Johnson's fifth wedding anniversary, he planned to take his wife Sue to dinner, a movie and a local motel for the night.

Just as they were leaving home a white stretch Cadillac pulled up to the door. 'When Sue and I explained to the guy there's some mistake, he tells us, no, get in, the car's ours. We're taken to a fancy restaurant. The place is completely full, but we're waved in; after dinner they won't even take our money. Then it's on to a hotel, where our room is mysteriously awash in flowers and champagne . . . Next morning the driver takes us out to breakfast, then back home. He didn't want anything. None of them did. They'd been taken care of. An incredible gift. Even more so, because Steve always denied he had anything to do with it. Totally disclaimed the whole thing. But I know very well he set it up.'

Sometimes when Steve watched old prints of his films he'd call up the gang, scared, sad and lonely. He worried that in a few years everything he'd done would be forgotten. Mostly he sat out there in Malibu, alone, recalling one of Julian's many maxims for coping. 'Life's shit,' she'd said. He wasn't comforted.

Autumn. In the early morning the light leaned on the Santa Monica mountains. He could see it gilding the ridges westward and slowly burning the fogfall that lay over Topanga Park. The flat sun shone down on the beach and turned McQueen's tanned face to copper, his body temperature almost as high outside the tub as in. The candles along the rim burned with a near invisible flame. A bottle of swamp oil sweated in his hand. Steve flopped in the water at six most mornings, lit a joint and lay under the cottony roll as white as the clouds in a movie. An hour or two passed, the sky now a Hollywood blue. Still with a bottle in hand he lay back, squinting towards the shuttered window. A grey stir of movement was receding up there. He could see a shape defined by the candles that grew brighter as the shadow approached, and then went dim, shrank to swimming points, blowing out as a door slammed shut. A damp, warm wind wafted up from the ocean into his face.

He and Ali barely spoke now. Steve lay in the water all morning, every morning, his world shrunk down to the elements: the sky, the candles and the brew. A few snacks spilled and crumbled, beer sprayed out when he laughed at a sudden memory. The long-suffering maid always spread newspapers around the base of the tub. McQueen would loll about most afternoons, play with the kids, then share their early supper. He still bunked down like a high-school student with biker and car posters plastered on the wall. His domestic arrangements offered few challenges beyond switching channels on his TV. One night as he was lying there, half stoned, *it* came on. He remembered the music. The grainy tune of *The Blob*. McQueen calmly picked up the phone, called his teenage daughter and said, 'If you want a good laugh, your old man's on the tube.' The casual manner was authentic Steve – 'authentic' is a word his friends tend to use even more than 'cool' – but it wasn't without guile. Next morning he rang Terry again to ask her what she'd thought of it. Then McQueen told Ziffren & Ziffren to go back over his original contract and see whether they couldn't sue for some residuals.

His lament for the past was the most wrenching. *Running outta gas*, he'd always tell friends, before showing them yet another of the old movies.

Steve still had his bikes, of course, though he no longer raced. Sometimes Ali rode pillion when they went to visit Pat Johnson or eat out at Malibu's Inn of the Seventh Ray. Another new obsession was with curios and, at worst, junk – vanished Americana, plastic fake-Zippo lighters with a flag painted on them, jackknives, Kewpie dolls, Wurlitzers, antique petrol pumps and, eventually, the world's second largest vintage motorbike collection (after Bud Ekins). Like the other great Hollywood absence, Garbo, McQueen was known to spend an entire day zealously trawling for bargains. For her part, the It Girl was now reduced to wandering the local flea market, hiding beneath a floppy hat and a wig, while her husband haggled over the price of Chevy hubcaps.

Despite it all, they still cared; their breakdown always faltered at the lawyer's door. McQueen now began planning a film that would show his wife he could 'really act' like a Newman or Beatty. A true labour of love. Ali, in turn, asked Pat Johnson to speak to Steve. 'He's smoking dope and drinking the whole time. I don't know what to do.'

Pat told McQueen he had a problem. 'What you're doing isn't good for you at all.'

'I know,' said Steve. And then instantly lit a joint. 'You're right. If you never want to see me again, I'll understand.'

Pat Johnson was the most loyal friend he ever had. A week later, they got Steve into a Schick Center to at least help him quit smoking. (He checked in there under Johnson's name.) Meanwhile, Ali began seeing a therapist every day.

After *The Towering Inferno*, says Neile, 'Steve started getting sick. I mean physically. The disease was beginning to spread until finally the doctors told him he had to get away from the damp sea air.' No one was yet using the word cancer. But McQueen almost certainly knew that something was wrong and that it was unlikely he'd have much time to make the serious films he'd talked about.

Willingly or unwillingly, he began planning a comeback. Perhaps Steve went to work again because he wanted to divert Ali's depression. Quite possibly he was only humouring his own starved need for love.

The Castle had gone. Neile and Julian and most of the sixties crowd had gone. As far as Hollywood went McQueen, too, was already history. Men like De Niro, Hoffman and Pacino had all now risen like rockets over the American sky and would hang there garishly for years to come. Jack Nicholson seized on the brass ring like a hyena lunges for meat. Schwarzenegger and Stallone were both muscling up behind, fast. Steve was too experienced to be suckered by reviews – the one that called *Rocky*, for instance, a twist on the 'old McQueen shtick' about the loser who wins – although he resented some of them because they struck a note that came close to his own preoccupations. 'It's weird,' he told Geller. 'Screw that ambition jazz. I don't have any poke any more. Don't really want to do anything, or one part of me does and the other doesn't . . . I watch these movies about sex and shit and people doing dope, and Bobby De Niro in the cab, it all seems so crap to me. Who cares? I mean, what happened to quality?'

One day Bud Ekins invited Steve onto the set of a sub-*Dukes of Hazzard* romp called *Dixie Dynamite*. Ekins was the bike-wrangler for the film. 'McQueen did a day's work for union scale – $185 – plus a six-pack. No one recognised him, but the producer did see his name on the pay roster. 'Is that *the* Steve McQueen?' the guy asked. I told him, 'Sure, he often works for me.'

Soon, Steve began groping his way back towards the studio film scene. Running, but not quite, out of gas. He still had 2000 names in his shiny office rolodex. He stuck handwritten notes from Ronald Reagan on his refrigerator, photos of himself and Princess Grace with their arms around each other. Life's a scam. McQueen at first went forwards by going back; talking all hours not about Rambo and Superman but Renoir and Von Sternberg. He actually bid for the rights to Samuel Beckett's *Waiting for Godot*. (Beckett, who had never heard of Steve, turned him down.) McQueen finally found a literate script he liked in *Nothing in Common*, a thriller being developed by his old *Soldier in the Rain* co-star Tony Bill. Bill says, 'I called Steve and asked him to read it. He thought it was a great part, everyone was stoked, and we went to pitch it to Phil Feldman at First Artists.' Feldman killed it.

'It would compromise our third-quarter fiscal strategy,' he added with a passing chill.

'Drop dead,' said McQueen.

Nowadays, he, Newman, Streisand and Poitier never fought. They also never saw each other. The other three tried to indulge him, waiting for a fucking film now for years and years, but it made them furious and all parties wanted to get it over with.

McQueen soon began his own litany. In the weeks ahead he vented continually about 'Adolf' Feldman and First Artists; how they were screwing him on script approval and budgets – just $3 million a film; how people all over the world expected the best from him and mostly got it, but that that was fucking *B*-film money, not enough to make a real picture. 'I got to be real,' he said, and illustrated the point one morning by bellying up to the glass-and-marble boardroom with his chainsaw. Then things took a turn for the worse.

Very soon the First Artists president was seen fleeing for his life from his prime corporate asset.

Furious that Feldman would use the three-movie deal to try and force him into under-priced dross, Steve stopped bothering to go to meetings at all, hung up whenever Feldman called, and, the sharpest slap, relieved him of the honour of co-producing *Rambo*. When Irwin Allen came calling with *The Towering Inferno II*, offering to package it as a Fox/First Artists joint venture, McQueen literally slammed the door on him. This would lead to another kung-fu round of recriminations. Feldman sent Steve a lawyer's letter reminding him of his obligations under the 1971 contract. McQueen sent Feldman a flying tomahawk of a fuck-off reply, telling him he planned to shoot a ninety-year-old script that he, Steve, had chosen.

Next, Steve phoned his old manager Hilly Elkins to get his take on the project. Despite all their problems he'd always respected Elkins's critical judgement. (As with *The Blob*, nowadays McQueen could even laugh off *The Honeymoon Machine*.) 'I asked him what the hell he was doing,' says Elkins. 'It was insane . . . On the other hand, Steve was pissed at both the studio and management. The movie in question might have made scant sense as a career move. As a form of artistic revenge, it was brilliant.'

McQueen hired a new agent, Marvin Josephson.

Josephson, a slight, trim, freckle-faced man who combined being both scholarly and blunt, headed the giant International Creative Management, a talent agency whose roster read like a *Who's Who* of showbiz and the media. By late 1976 ICM's stable included Woody Allen, Sean Connery, Tom Jones, Tennessee Williams, Peter Sellers, Barbra Streisand and over 2000 others. Josephson personally handled just two clients – Henry Kissinger and McQueen.

Bill Maher introduced Steve to Josephson on the busy main street in Palm Springs. McQueen's first words to him were arresting. 'Hey, I've got to pee.' Eschewing the short walk to a public bathroom, Steve turned around, unzipped and did it there in the gutter.

'I ignored him,' says Josephson. 'Obviously, it was Steve's idea of an initiation test – "What kind of rise can I get out of this Eastern establishment type?" ... Always putting you on the spot. That's what I mean when I say McQueen taught me a lot about dealing with people. As a lawyer, I was used to thinking my way out of situations; Steve had a much more direct, physical approach. But brilliant with it. The way he reacted to things was to get the other guy off balance, plus make it crystal clear that it was he, not you, who was the big star – the actor. Steve was so street smart, so aware of his audience, you could never quite tell when he was on and when he wasn't.'

McQueen wanted Josephson to lower his agency commission from a standard 10 per cent to 7.5 per cent.

'Do you hate me?' Steve asked softly. 'I'm crazy, you know.'

'No, I don't hate you.' Josephson spoke with his face partly averted from Steve's fascinated gaze.

'Aren't you pissed at me now, Marvin? Not even a little bit?'

'I'm very proud of you.'

McQueen eased off. 'Maybe I'll pay your commission.'

Meanwhile, a TV executive came calling to ask Steve to speak at a live tribute being put together for Loren Janes, his old friend and stunt double. McQueen turned him down. 'Steve hated to do stuff like that,' says Janes. 'Not having much of a vocabulary, he'd sometimes grope for a word and start stuttering . . . No way would he risk blowing it in public. But he did do a voice-over for the show, which was great.' At home McQueen spent hours practising his short speech, sweating it out in the tub, fretting he'd 'dry', suffering a spasm of utter panic, a black, blinding bolt of despair before finally submitting to the – by now – ordeal, a nervousness that bulged his eyes and stammered on his lips at the very thought of oratory.

Steve's lowbrow pose was, however, only one part of the scam.

A non-writer who could barely spell, McQueen now began devouring authors like Chekhov, Beckett and Pinter. 'Great imagery,' he told Ali one day, after finishing *Riders to the Sea*. He'd slapped the play shut and burped. Steve's dualism was well established by the time he met Josephson: seclusion in the 'real world' of drink, dope and chewing the fat with gas-station mechanics; and the intense crash course in classical literature. By mid 1976, when his reading became obsessive, McQueen was talking nonstop about Gogol, Ionesco, Wilde. And his favourite of favourites, Ibsen. What began out of boredom and a sad need to impress MacGraw soon became habitual.

'Everything Steve did, he did to the limit,' says Josephson.

Including parenthood. Since dropping out, McQueen had become a much-studied man. The study had been a confusing one at times, largely because of the contradictions within the man himself; as *Time* said, 'always pushing the razor-fine line between genius and madness'. The only thing to do with such cases is to aim for the heart. Steve loved his kids. It touched even the long list of sworn enemies and ex-lovers to see how this restless, tense man melted around his children and around children generally. McQueen was extraordinarily patient and generous in giving them both friendship and advice on life – everything from 'Watch your back' to 'Just call them the way you see them and the hell with it'. Bedrock stuff he practised himself. As Jim Geller says, 'Steve McQueen was a loner. I don't mean that in a derogatory way. He was a guy who was comfortable being alone. But the two people who were always in his world were his kids. And that was enough. The truth is he didn't need anybody but them.'

The role of a lifetime: around Terry and Chad, Steve had the nerve to be nothing like his screen image, with none of the static violence. Instead he was a tactile, loving father, happily doing the school run or babysitting when Neile was back hoofing it in Vegas. Re-creating an Eden of cosmic merriment – a constant round of teenagers' parties – dotted the wastes when McQueen felt blocked, stale or spent. Nowadays, that was often. More and more, the accent, so central to Steve, was on the world of innocence and youth, of the primitive

emotions, even of regressing to the first flush of life. He wasn't around
Terry much; not, anyway, in the sense of the average commuting
parent. When McQueen rolled up, it might be for hours or days at
a time. But absent or not, his presence was felt, his voice heard.
Neither she nor Chad ever doubted that they had a strong,
demanding, protective father.

Ironically, Terry, who physically mirrored Steve, took after her
mother. Chad had Neile's swarthy looks but a broad streak of his
father – self-absorbed, a pocket Bullitt who raced miniature cars,
poked his head up his teachers' skirts and worked out with Pat
Johnson.

Terry took her parents' divorce harder. As Neile says, 'She loved
Steve but couldn't control her anger towards him. She blamed him
and Ali for having wrecked our home life. Ali didn't always help. At
times, when Terry phoned up to ask if her father was there, she
would just say, "No," and put down the phone.'

McQueen generally lived quietly, by his own defiant standards,
lobbing his little jolts of joy and fury at Ali when the mood struck
him. That particular mood was often family-triggered. Steve 'shot
upright in his seat', according to a witness, when his daughter first
lit a cigarette in front of him. There were other adolescent shocks:
when Terry rebelled and started skipping school, McQueen insisted
she see a shrink. Then, at sixteen, she brought her first boyfriend
home to dinner.

'Kid,' Steve ventured, fixing the boy with the pale-eyed intensity
of someone high on cocaine. 'You're not going to take advantage of
my little girl, are you?'

'No, sir,' the kid responded. 'I'd never do anything like that.'

A wave of relief went around the table. Then all faces fell.

'Why not?' demanded Steve. 'Isn't she good enough?'

The boy's voice, like many others before it, tended to quaver in
argument with Supie. 'I didn't mean that, sir.'

'No?' bellowed McQueen, surging up from his seat and soaring
into full Shakespearean mode. 'Well, I got news for you, son. I don't
want you so much as pawing her. Ever! You cross that line and you
answer to me!' He changed in a second from choleric belligerence
to serene self-confidence and slumped back with a lopsided grin.

345

'Never bullshit a bullshitter,' he said.

That desire for honesty, for cutting the crap, played out in various ways. McQueen made Chad work all summer long in order to pay for his first car (a used Chevy) and, more pertinently, learn the value of a buck. But when Chad grew old enough to have sex, Steve didn't waste time with phoney lectures. As a combined Christmas and birthday gift in December 1976, McQueen escorted his son upstairs to the terrace. Ali was out of town. Steve chuckled, 'Here's your coming-out present. Last one in's a loser,' and promptly applied himself to the tub. After a second's hesitation, Chad, too, virtually dived into the water.

Three naked women were sprawled back there, waiting.

Ultimately, what's so striking about McQueen is the degree to which – no matter how one tries to focus – the twin images persist, resisting alignment, irreducible: the two Steve McQueens. Hollywood's preferred view of him as suave and butch, someone tough as pig iron. But also pliable and sweet, the man who saw life through a child's eyes. Contradictory impulses that pushed and pulled him in restless, frenetic circles. Forever shuttling between these two polar zones.

He had that eager set to his eyes and mouth – picture Bill Clinton – of always wanting to be looked at.

But the disparate parts of McQueen coalesce when seen from the perspective of his overriding identity. In deed and in word, Steve was moved by a fellow-feeling for the lonely and lost – the 'little people'. This was shorthand for strays and waifs. Even his old foes brought low by misfortune: when Paul Newman's son Scott overdosed on drugs, McQueen was the first one to call. Nor was it a case of 'I'm here if you need me'; somehow Steve always managed to find the right words in desperate circumstances. Thereafter a wary respect, and even friendship, broke through the old rivalry.

Quite unpublicised, McQueen cut a wide swath through LA's under-class generally, supporting distressed actors' groups, generously hiring redundant colleagues and donating tens of thousands to his beloved alma mater, Boys Republic. Anything to make some connection.

Loren Janes remembers when the Stuntmen's Association voted

Steve an honorary member, an unheard-of tribute for a mere actor.
McQueen showed up in person to collect the award. There he was,
the tough, granite guy crying tears of joy. He stood up and said,
"This means more to me than winning an Oscar." And he meant it
. . . Steve was just in ecstasy at being accepted by straight, down-to-
earth guys as opposed to Hollywood phoneys. That really made an
impression. Steve bounced off with a big grin. In twenty-two years,
I don't think I ever saw him happier.'

He could still, just about, give a convincing performance as a loving
husband. There was hugging and ass-punching, some exuberant
expressions of desire and affection. He bought Ali and himself a pair
of erotically engraved belt buckles as a third anniversary gift. 'Can
we still make it, baby?'

'It's up to you,' she said.

Bill Friedkin, of *The French Connection* and *Exorcist* fame, came to
Malibu to sell Steve on his film *Sorcerer*, an expensive remake of
Wages of Fear set in the Latin American jungle.

McQueen said, 'This is the best script I've ever read. Better than
Cincinnati, Tommy Crown. Better than *Bullitt*.'

'Will you do it?'

Here Steve's inherent tactical sense surged to the fore. 'There are
other concerns, Bill,' he began his negotiations. 'Can you shoot it in
the US?'

'No, the location's real important. It's got to be Brazil.'

'I'm worried about my marriage to Ali. If I go out of the country
for three months, I won't have shit left when I get back. Can you
write something for her?'

'No.'

'What about making her line-producer so she can be with me?'

'No,' said Friedkin.

Steve passed on *Sorcerer*. Ali never knew anything about it.

'He still loved her and he wanted her to be with him,' says Pat
Johnson. 'Steve was getting incredible grief from First Artists during
this whole period. That's when he most needed Ali.'

A few months later twenty or thirty of them were sitting around
at the wrap party for McQueen's new film, Ibsen's *An Enemy of the
People*. It was a formal affair, but Steve came in his plaid shirt and

jeans, unshaven, swallowed up by a long-billed baseball cap, the only man there not wearing designer gear.

MacGraw leaned over to the film's associate producer, Phil Parslow: 'You know, I gave up a mansion and living like a queen to ride on the back of a motorcycle with that man.'

Parslow laughed, surprised by her directness. 'Obviously you love him.'

'Yes,' she smiled. 'I still do.'

Later, Steve turned to two or three other members of the crew and raised a glass in his own heartfelt toast. The restaurant fell silent. 'I'd like to crawl inside her, man, that crazy, bubble-assed lady, just crawl inside back where it all starts and zip her up and die.'

The silence deepened. Had he gone too far?

McQueen often said he only felt 'truly alive' when he was with Ali. But, by 1976 it seemed he only wanted to be truly alive in that way a few hours a day. The rest of the time passed in a stale crackle of television and bickering. Beyond needing her around, Steve had no real agenda or plans for MacGraw other than culinary ones. Bored but always well-fed: his weight now swept towards 200. Loved fry-ups. Loved to take off on a bike, too, often alone, occasionally with Ali. They spent long weekends at Ventana, the exclusive spa up the California coastline at Big Sur. Or they'd take in a concert at the Hollywood Bowl. Candy Bergen and the actor Charles Durning (co-star of Steve's new film) would go along, sometimes finishing up at Musso & Frank's or even in Beverly Hills. McQueen, though, as evidenced by his squinting glare, hated to vary a routine. Or risk blowing a good thing: he always spoke of his more adventurous colleagues, even old rivals, with genuine awe. 'People think we guys are such old farts but Newman's doing a movie that mixes up Buffalo Bill and PT Barnum, kind of funny and sad both, and low dough, he was telling me, for Paul. That's how much he's pulled up his roots.'

'Paul's not like you, baby,' Ali teased. 'He's not scared of change.'

He could take that fat greasy burger and in one swoop push it into her face. Instead Steve calmly excused himself and went outside to the Porsche, gunned it and took off into the hills. That would be the last Ali saw of him for two or three days. He loved that car, his half-ton truck and, of course, his stable of bikes. Always roaring up Pacific Coast Highway on one or other of them to the latest fuck-fling or, more and more often, events like Melrose Mart day. Los Angeles specifically and California generally had become a minor antique-dealing capital in the seventies. Traditional Americana, which was also Steve's theme, informality, anonymity and plain, old-fashioned money sense were compelling bait. In his last three or four years McQueen would betray a weakness for almost anything, whether movies, books or collectibles, that reminded him of the 1930s.

He tried his hand at writing, too, first notes for an authorised biography and then drafts of a screenplay. It was less a script than that histrionic blend of speed and violence (though never, strangely, sex), inscribed into a text shot through with sub-Joycean monologues. Though most of Steve's fiction lacked unity or logic, it at least had the beauty of pace. Sometimes it had kinetic brilliance.

Literarily, McQueen's tastes tended to the extreme lowbrow or the highbrow. Sartorially, they weren't elevated – the jeans and plaid shirt he wore at the wrap party were typical. It was that same winter that a would-be producer, Mike Fargo, encountered Steve in Malibu and provided this candid snapshot: 'Bearded, pot-bellied, in a rumpled Columbo raincoat . . . He had that whimsical, jaded air, a bit mocking, that we were so ready to recognise in "arty" folk, although he probably wasn't one at the time.' Fargo had been mes-merised by Steve's screen presence and now experienced it first-hand: 'Direct, penetrating, blazingly tuned in to you, but also amused, flip, chock full of sarcasm . . . I'd say a man struggling to take Hollywood, and maybe himself, seriously.'

'Steve was well on his way to becoming Howard Hughes,' says Neile.

So McQueen, the Prisoner of Trancas. There was another McQueen who loved to cruise down to the Whisky à Go Go, but, more and more, the silences deepened into the hermit's chosen emp-tiness. Compared to Steve, even Hughes was just a loner.

This same McQueen still wandered around town, indulging his passion for the great average. The fringe entrepreneurs and undiffer-entiated faces at the flea mart were company enough, and the few stabs Ali made at a more formal social life were almost torture, the hours in a poky seat at the ballet or ass-kissing some fat honcho. One of Steve's Malibu neighbours, the director Robert Altman, only saw him to speak to 'two or three times' in as many years. Fifty yards in the other direction up the private dirt road was the rock drummer Keith 'the loon' Moon. McQueen would stare down from the hot tub and see Moon doing wheelies on his motorbike – apparently in obscure homage to *The Great Escape* – or sloshing around the surf in a full SS uniform. One afternoon he came looking for Steve. Instead Moon encountered the sixteen-year-old Chad, who may or may not (and only after asking Moon to leave) have delivered a well-aimed blow to his chin. There were published reports that a fight broke out, that the McQueens' dog bit Moon and that Moon bit it back.

Moon came back to apologise the next day. For once he declined to wear Nazi regalia. He dressed in drag instead.

'Don't ever,' said Steve, 'fuck with my children.'

'Your children seem pretty safe to me.' Hoarse and slurred, Moon's voice crawled down into a pit from which rescue would be difficult. He shook his laughably sad face, a train-wreck personality then in the throes of losing his family, his group and his best friend, with two years left to live. 'One thing's for sure,' he said, 'things can't get much worse' – and passed out cold.

A week later Moon's new girlfriend, Annette, was sunbathing on the private, fine-grain beach beneath the villas built, like Steve's, of overlapping cedar boards covered with milky whitewash. A shadow fell over her. A man stood there, nearly invisible behind his beard and woollen cap, a sinister, incongruous figure dressed like a cold-weather lumberjack. It was McQueen.

'You're on my sand,' he grunted.

Annette picked up her towel and moved a few feet up the residents' communal beach. When Moon later installed powerful floodlights that shone over his neighbours' property (the better to catch Ali in the buff, he confided) Steve solved the problem by grabbing his Mauser and promptly shooting them out. McQueen then slid back inside, still light as a cat, to enjoy the sudden and total tranquillity. There were no more demarcation disputes with Moon, or anyone else. All up and down Broad Beach Road, nobody ever doubted that, as long as Steve was around, they'd come out of any tiff second best.

The Prisoner of Trancas was in fine form that year, surveying the scene with his legendary detachment and moving through Malibu's pastel world in his sweaty clothes like a summer storm, an exception to all the rules. From the classic McQueen image to a composite of sado-promiscuous-pothead-Elvis, it's tempting to see his journey as that of an American icon into a sad grotesque, the latest victim of the lunacy that inevitably attends pop celebrity.

'You look a bit like Brando,' a friend told him. 'Also you've got those same glittery eyes. Are you on something?'

'Nope, but every day kids run away from me in the street. I've always had the death-ray,' Steve said, and despite his racking cough he laughed.

The friend wasn't able to make anything of these remarks.

McQueen insisted that, when would-be producers came to meet him, they strip off and sit with him in the hot tub, nude as the troglodytes of Stone Age caverns. (The actual house might be bugged, he explained.) The honchos and Steve slumped there together on the wooden slats, four or five bodies covered with beads of sweat, and fairly soon eyes would meet eyes and one of the producers would say they should do lunch one day, and it was a pleasure to have met. They left McQueen in the froth, dripping and hunched, like an animal sitting out a storm in his favourite mud-hole.

He used to tell people, 'My mother died when she was fifty [sic], my father died when he was fifty, and I'm going to die when I'm fifty. Why sweat it?' More numbers. By adding his birthdate (24/3/30) to his Social Security (556-32-8432), he latched on to the same grim arithmetic.

In his avidity to live, to wring every second out of the few years left, Steve betrayed his own body, the gut thickened, the extra weight of the burgers and beer grew like a murderous burden, energy gone. Along with the junk diet came a whole galaxy of uppers and downers; when the pot made him tired, McQueen snorted himself awake again. The sight dizzied old friends. Hadn't he used to work out two or three hours every morning? Him, the Cooler King. The shining blue eyes halfway out of his head and teeth flashing as he ran laughing down-stairs to the Castle gym. Whirling by. Now Steve stood, tottering, on thick pillar legs affected with a sort of Stilton mottling of the ankles. Prematurely stooped. Seeing himself this way only made McQueen more determined to keep his own course, like that final scene in *The War Lover* when he rammed his plane into the cliff.

Pat Johnson loyally insists, 'Steve was only ever fifteen pounds overweight. The combination of a chunky sweater I bought him, the beard and the worst posture in the world made it seem worse.' In the grainy *National Enquirer* photo McQueen looked like a massive sand dune with an overhang of shaggy crab grass. Five million people saw that particular snap. Not only did Steve deteriorate physically (spreading beyond the narrow confines of his office chair, says one guest, like a ripe cheese), his whole act seemed to confirm the *Enquirer*'s rumours of a crackup. His old *Sand Pebbles* co-star Richard Crenna remembers 'Walking down the beach . . . A motorcycle came screaming down the highway, past us, and as it went by I heard this shout . . . I turned around, looked, and I saw this man who was about the size of Dom De Luise – not small, in other words – with a flowing beard, long hair and dark glasses. I looked . . . He turned the bike around, approached me and I realised it was Steve.'

Jim Coburn, a friend for twenty years, likewise failed to 'print the strange-looking guy' standing uncomfortably close to him in the lift of the Beverly Wilshire hotel. An actor? Someone he might choose to go upstairs and have a drink with? It seemed highly improbable. A second later it became inevitable. 'Hey,' the stranger said, in his familiar dried-up mumble. That one syllable was all it took.

Norman Jewison, too, walked past a figure one day on the MGM lot without bothering to look up. From behind him, he heard a voice say, 'Forget me, would you?' The director turned and looked into a pair of blazing blue eyes, hidden beneath a cap, the inimitable McQueen death-ray.

'There was a wildness there that shook me,' says Jewison.

The strange thing was, even with the coke and the grass and the extra ballast, Steve was trying for the first time to put it all in perspec-tive. It was at this physical and creative nadir that he first tentatively asked friends like Pat Johnson and Loren Janes, 'What should I do?'

and admitted 'something [was] missing' from his life. Running out of gas. Conversion was still two years off; but it seems apparent that in his long meditation McQueen felt keen to explore the soul, something that lay deep within him as a man and an artist.

He began seeing Neile again, then sleeping with her. 'Do you suppose we could try over? Come stay with us at Trancas.' The fluent perfection of his apologies and protestations of love almost overwhelmed her.

'But, Steve, what about Ali?'

The two women were friendly, but not that civil.

Robert Relyea got a phone call out of the blue six years after McQueen blew up on the set of *Le Mans*. 'Hi, Bob, it's Steve. I'm not having any trouble with my old lady.' Relyea thought that odd, since nobody had mentioned McQueen's marriage.

They met that night, the last time they ever did, walking around for hours after dinner, passing by the old William Morris office and, for at least a block or two, down El Camino towards Steve's hotel, entertaining common happy memories – of McQueen first upstaging Brynner and then outwitting the krauts, that one shot of him apparently soaring, cool and poised, soaring and falling, hanging there on the bike before falling to earth, defying gravity.

McQueen's life always had its parallel in the films, but only recently had he got around to re-enacting whole chunks of dialogue at home.

Doc McCoy, Steve's character in *The Getaway*, was the part that relaunched him as a post-Bogie anti-hero, the key role model from which popular tough-guy styles of disaffection could be borrowed. Cops, robbers and wives – all were equal when it came to Doc's rages. Ali herself had played the love interest opposite his incandescent lead, proving that anyone, including her, rash enough to get into close contact with the man was likely to catch fire.

DOC: Can't trust a thing nowadays.

CAROL: Tell you something, Doc. One of these days you're going to have to trust somebody.

DOC: I trust . . . [*Peels off banknote*] . . . You wanna see what

I trust? 'In God I trust' – it's the words on the back of
every bill.

CAROL: Just keep that up, Doc, and it won't matter how far we
get away because there won't be anything left between
us. Understand that? Nothing.

As they walked down the beach together now his feet felt heavy, as
if the world had taken on new gravity. The brightest of springs, but
to Steve it was permanent winter. With the exception of his kids, he
shunned anything animate. *In God I trust*. He had MacGraw sign the
pre-nuptial again, three years on when, as she says, 'we were really
rioting'. On the night of her thirty-eighth birthday Ali was celebrating
quietly with a few friends at the ultra-chic Le Bistro in Beverly Hills.
Steve appeared late, atop a vintage Harley. He rode the motorbike
into the restaurant, did a slalom down the wheelchair ramp and
between the tables, holding a mangled cake under one bare arm.
MacGraw could smell the swamp oil on his breath.

'Either get your act together,' she said, 'or I'm taking Josh and
we're leaving. I'm tired of living with a drunken beach bum.'

That was the week he told her he was doing the Ibsen. *Me, him*,
he kept saying there on the beach, remembering the crack about
Newman and all the other bastards, though not Ali, who'd ever
doubted him. He'd fix their hash. Feldman's, too. At that McQueen
grinned. In fact he did an impression, flashed his best Bogart leer,
with that sudden slit mouth and convict's smirk. Fuckers.

Ali followed him back inside, head down, saying nothing.

Nowadays their bedroom was wired up with separate his and her
earphones. She lay listening to classical music while he tuned in the
football. Now that she'd challenged him it was like a door had been
shut in Steve's mind, a vow was broken, the marriage was starting
to show its underside: she was *asking* for it, he reasoned. The fuck-
flings, the little betrayals. That summer Ali flew to Manhattan to do
a Francesco Scavullo photo layout of the 'world's most beautiful
women'. The night before the shoot McQueen rang her there at the
height of a raging thunderstorm, then, an hour later, turned up in
person; he hadn't mentioned that he'd been calling from a New York
airport. Drunk, he began cross-examining MacGraw about who else

had been in her hotel room, on and on, accusing her, like Neile at Le Mans, of doing it all over town, behind his back, every chance she got. (All totally unfounded allegations.) In harsh sweeps the rain clattered on the windows, rumbling like McQueen's voice until gradually he wound down, the only sound MacGraw heard a grunt Steve gave when he passed out on the small bed. Ali then tried to read herself to sleep coiled up on the bathroom floor. Dawn was already breaking over Turtle Bay when she finally dozed off.

The actual glamour spread looked fabulous, McQueen had to admit.

When Ali began remodelling their beach house, Steve rented himself a pied-à-terre suite across town in the Beverly Wilshire. If there's such a thing as a designer asylum, it may have been that soundproofed penthouse, knee-high in motorcycle gear and scripts and beer crates, where Steve read Ibsen every day, trying to come to grips with his life.

Most nights after rehearsing or, later, shooting at MGM, McQueen would wander into the hotel's El Padrino room – the one into which Julia Roberts sashayed in *Pretty Woman* – introduce himself as Fat Joe and enjoy a drink or two in total anonymity. It was the ultimate disguise; even the autograph hounds and paparazzi he'd come to fear over the last decade contrived a sudden disappearance in 1976. Steve's new-found latitude was no fluke. Literally nobody recognised the rough customer slumped over his beer and bar snacks like some biker-dude caricature: that frayed, itinerant look. Even the wild tufts of hair stuck out like weeds from desert asphalt.

But Steve was again the master of two McQueens. Not that many tattoo-and-gold-tooth types could command, as he did, a $1000-a-night hotel suite. Or quite as many old ladies.

Ali would later write that 'Steve's room, right next to the pool, was the scene of a constant parade of models and starlets.' McQueen's old lover Barbara Leigh confirms that 'he went on a big binge of seeing a *lot* of women'. Leigh herself went to the Wilshire to visit him for the first time in five years. 'Steve looked quite different, of course – that Smokey the Bear beard – and even when he flashed his old bad-boy grin it seemed something was missing.

'I could tell he was unhappy.'

The fuck-fling element of his breakdown was, however, a side issue.

After the bubble-asses had been looked over, tape-measured and Pola-roided for McQueen's personal inventory, he soon went back to work. In success or in failure, the essential ethic was always preserved.

The Ibsen in question was his sombre 1882 fable *An Enemy of the People*, a circular elaboration on a theme: human rights and more specifically, women's rights. At first even friends thought it a joke. It was as if John Gielgud, in the twilight of his distinguished stage career, had decided to play Conan the Barbarian. Only a few privi-leged insiders knew of the boardroom spats at First Artists – rampant with 'creative differences' as they were with waste – and rightly guessed that the primary motive behind McQueen's choice was neither his finances, nor his artistic vision, but pure rage. Marvin Josephson agrees that 'Steve was fascinated by the piece and by the character, but it was also to spite the studio. It got to the point where he was backed into a corner and it just became a dare. McQueen wouldn't back down.' Phil Parslow, too, says Steve did the picture because 'he was going to make a film where nobody would make any money [in order to] punish' First Artists. Perhaps because Feldman and the suits had by then fallen darkly out of favour, McQueen seems to have welcomed the chance to count off another film against his slavery contract while simultaneously stretching as an actor.

Katy Haber is one of those who thinks 'Steve did it to prove a point to Ali.' '*Proud of me?*' he'd asked, looking away from her with an apparent indifference utterly at odds with the harshness of his tone. Certainly he wanted to show her he could straddle serious and workaday popular idioms; on one level his respect for MacGraw was almost as great as his contempt for poor Feldman. *Enemy*, all in all, was being given a lot to live up to. Not least by the critics.

The shock, Jesus. McQueen loved that – the incredulity and howls of protest. He wasn't only going against type but against everything he stood for; that way he had of implying action, communicating with a twist of his lips, his jaw, his chin or even that weird birthmark on his cheek (in short, what Peckinpah called his 'live ammo' head) with no verbal eruptions, let alone Ibsenian screeds. Definitely no windbaggery. Remembering the old Broadway days, Neile (who was aghast at *Enemy*) is only the most compelling witness to the hard fact that 'Steve had zero – nil – stage presence'. McQueen's new film wouldn't quite be as theatrical as *Hatful* and the rest, but it was, nonetheless, shot entirely on sound stages amid carefully reconstructed period sets and costumes. Stark nineteenth-century detail, with no muscle cars or hardware, and absolutely nowhere to hide.

For fifteen years McQueen had clung to a formula that worked for him, the screen image first switched on with such voltage in *Never So Few*. Now he was bored with it. He found himself in the unusual position of having his public show more confidence in him than he felt in himself. Steve's concept of self-reliance and violent independence had been taking a beating, and he saw self-parody coming around the corner, fast. '[The studio] want me on the screen with a gun in my hand,' He told William Nolan:

The full macho bit. McQueen the rebel, the cool killer. Same crap I've been into for years ... Sure, [*Enemy*] was written nearly a century ago, but the theme ties right in to the problems we face today with polluted lakes and poisoned air and chemicals in all our food. That's what attracted me to this play, the message it carries – that we need to take personal responsibility for what's happening around us. That's what Ibsen was saying.

And:

All these hard-assed guys [I've] played are about as representative of the real world as a french fry is of a potato. We need to get back to mother earth ... women ... that side, the wives and daughters ... God, when you think how you've treated some of them, you just feel terrible. You feel sick inside.

Steve McQueen, feminist.

The idea of his prize asset doing a Norwegian morality play was obviously a bit rich for Feldman; one account has him threatening a suit – 'folly' was his confidential report on *Enemy* – before gracefully accepting the inevitable. Provided Newman, Poitier and Streisand agreed, and Steve brought it in for under $3 million, he could develop virtually any project he wanted. Sure, there were some mumblings here and there among the other board members, and McQueen's list of props was quixotically extensive, but at least nobody balked at his fee: union scale, $1500 a week, against 10 per cent of the profits.

The film, of course, tanked.

Even so, the lower-key style and plumbing of depths only hinted at in *Baby, the Rain Must Fall* was a revelation. (*Enemy* made that movie look like *Star Wars*.) Doubly so, as there were also scenes that were wry, witty and potent. It was Steve's boldest film, one of his best.

Enemy celebrated one Thomas Stockmann (McQueen), a country doctor who stubbornly campaigns to close down a poisoned spring, which also happens to be both a tourist trap and a major source of income, in a Norwegian coastal spa. The local establishment, including Stockmann's brother, themselves campaign to have him run out of town.

The script by Alexander Jacobs was based on Arthur Miller's freehand translation, one that unsurprisingly stressed the parallels of *Enemy* with McCarthyism. There was also an oblique resemblance to the plot of *Jaws*. The film's director would smile in admiration while Steve circled around that latter point, again and again.

An ornery, bloody-minded, principled loner who can't be bought off or otherwise silenced. Nothing *there* to remind anyone of vintage McQueen.

Steve first met *Enemy*'s director George Schaefer on a hot Sunday afternoon in west Hollywood. The Yale drama school guru and the world's greatest instinctive film actor discussed Ibsen over dinner at the Hamburger Hamlet. Schaefer, then fifty-five, remembered McQueen as a 'strange bearded character' who had just come back from a flea market, where he bought two headlights. 'Fucking great,' Steve kept saying in unaffected pride. 'Ten bucks the pair. Nobody printed me, either.'

Later that night Schaefer called his associate Phil Parslow.

'I'm going to be doing *An Enemy of the People* with Steve McQueen. Come into the office and meet him and, when you do, don't let him scare you. He scares the shit out of me.'

When Parslow walked in, 'Steve sort of jumped into a chair and was squatting down, looking at me face-to-face, and he said, "You know, I deal a lot in vibes, how I feel about people. That's what I do. Instinct. And the vibes between me and you are very, very good."'

This succeeded in getting Parslow's attention. 'But I got to tell you something, and always remember this: I'm crazy. I'm crazy and I'll do crazy things, but hang with me.'

Between the three of them they put together a watermark cast: Bergman's protégé Bibi Andersson, Nicol Williamson and Michael Cristofer. Williamson was fired when he called in, drunk, on the first day of rehearsals. From Hawaii. The role of Stockmann's brother went instead to the character player Charles Durning. Richard Dysart (of *LA Law* fame) went up in the elevator to Schaefer's office one morning to discuss a part. 'I was coming down the corridor and this guy loped by me in the other direction, black jeans, black T-shirt, heavily bearded – he looked like a werewolf. I smiled hello, did the audition, and then the same guy came back into George's office and introduced himself. Incredible . . . I always think I got the job because I was friendly to the weird-looking guy, not to Steve McQueen the big movie actor.'

Now everyone got busy.

Feldman and the First Artists lawyers agreed a minuscule budget of $2.5 million. There was talk until then of filming some exteriors in Norway, or at least around Big Sur; instead they settled on the dreary no man's land of a sound stage at MGM. Steve, meanwhile, issued a handwritten statement to the press:

> We don't have an auto chase to sell in this one. What we do have is dignity and truth. If the people who see it leave the theater feeling enriched, they're going to tell their friends – and an audience will be created. But I'm not doing this picture to make bucks. I'm doing it because I want to have something I can be proud of, a film that's *pure*, that is done with total quality in mind.

Next McQueen settled in to three solid weeks of rehearsals. The first day he assembled the cast and told them, 'This is your world, not mine.' He flushed sheepishly. 'I'm a little out of my depth here, but I can promise you I'll give the best I have in me. If I fuck up I won't blame anybody. The fault will be mine.'

He cleared his throat. Steve's nervous smile betrayed an excitable state. His legs: numb. His face: hot. As the shoot wore on, the difficulties of making high art on a low budget became painfully evident.

The second or third day, one of the junior cast happened to park his car in a spot reserved for MGM bigwigs. Noticing this, a security guard followed him onto the sound stage, interrupted work there and began a loud harangue about issuing fines and/or having the man banned from the lot. Suddenly a third party cut in with a cough, that quick ringing hack of his, like change tossed onto a counter. 'What's it to you?'

'Well, Jesus, I'm just doing my job.'

'Job!' The word spun heads the length of the room. 'You want to talk about jobs? Do you realise this man has to go in front of a camera and *act* now? For a living? All he brings to the part are his emotions, and you've just hassled him with a lot of crap about parking.' Humpbacked and scowling, the character shrugged on a jacket and left.

'Who the fuck?' the guard asked Charles Durning.

Durning told him.

'Well, shit a pickle!' The man sank lower into the depths of his uniform. 'What am I supposed to do now?'

'Just go up to him and say, "Mr McQueen, I'm sorry. I'm an asshole."'

That seemed to work.

'Generally, Steve was a friendly, childlike guy,' Durning says. 'Particularly to other actors. I remember he liked me to come and watch him practise karate with Pat Johnson. He'd say, "Come upstairs and see this." That boyish lilt of enthusiasm. But Steve was mostly cool professionalism, a class performer. What I'd call lucky with talent, as opposed to wasted with talent – men like George C. Scott. McQueen just had that inner flame.'

'Steve was great,' Richard Dysart confirms. 'Always there, first on set in the morning, lining up shots with the DP.' There were also the inescapable glances back into McQueen's home life. 'Something, I could tell, was bothering him. The grim plot was matched by a concern I sensed about what would happen to him when he finished filming.' In fact, most weekday evenings Steve drove off back to Chino or Silver Lake – never Malibu – dismounting there to stare up at his old homes. An analyst would later tell him: 'What you're doing is . . . something went wrong, and you're going back to see if you can fix it, if you can make it right.'

Restless, slithering up and down sheer canyon roads, always heading somewhere in a hurry. It might have been nostalgia, the shrink wasn't sure.

Charles Durning is one of those who thinks Steve already knew something was wrong physically. 'It was impossible for a guy as tuned-up as he was not to . . . McQueen told me a joke one day about someone asking his doctor, "Do I have the Big C? Just tell me, I can take it" – and then passing spark out on the doc's floor. At the time I laughed. But maybe it was more real than I thought.'

The *Enemy* shoot went well, though the actual film was neither the triumph nor the disaster predicted. It was competent. Revived here with a strong cast (especially Durning), the sterile, museum-like sets and Schaefer's preference for the long shot both worked against any real intimacy. Everything was so meticulous, so worthy and so grave that it might as well have been a workshop production on the original Nordic stage. In this leaden atmosphere even the very best film actors were always likely to struggle to find a voice. It wasn't that they were bad; merely that some of them, anyway, had neither the skill nor training for what Schaefer called the 'privileging' (read: talky) screenplay. Many of them seemed to treat the set as a static backdrop with a few stray chairs on which to slump and declaim from. There was also a lot of Bibi Andersson. Would she and the other townspeople conspire to keep their water flowing? It was impossible to care: you always knew you were watching a performance.

McQueen was brilliant.

Abstracted yet never remote, impassioned, alternately wordy and mute, he lent Stockmann a grace and spirit that stayed understated even when the film turned clumsily melodramatic. Steve surfaced beautifully for the final speech, the longest of his career, a tirade in which his own volatile nature irradiated the screen. That verbal showdown alone was worth the price of admission.

As much as McQueen distrusted eggheads and egghead critics, or even the whole idea of criticism, now he hoovered up the word-of-mouth and preview cards more than for any film since *Le Mans*. Not that lightning struck. When *Enemy* was eventually released, escaped anyway, most pundits were hostile, at best royally baffled. A very few, like Barry Norman, got the point about the broadening actor – the rest just sniggered at Steve's physical bulk. Closer to home, too, reviews were mixed. Old friends like Neile and Hilly Elkins and Bob Relyea turned away, embarrassed. Provincial test audiences did the same. Loren Janes remembers sneaking into a preview with McQueen himself, sitting there for two hours of sighs and yawns, then hearing a teenager say as he was leaving the cinema, genuinely flummoxed, 'Well, hell, which one was Steve?' McQueen loved that.

Perhaps the most compelling quote of all, however, came from MacGraw, who said Steve was 'magnificent' in *Enemy*. 'He made me cry. The truth is that behind his tough-guy image he's the most sensitive man I know. I'm very proud of him ... I've tried to tell him that the garage mechanics and electricians won't go to see the movie. And I've also tried to tell him it won't matter, that they'll all go to see the next McQueen spear or gun picture.'

'Well, shit,' Steve said on the last night, 'I tried' – and threw himself into her arms, home at last.

When the preview scores came in, Warners first began desperately flogging *Enemy* as an art film, then changed course and took out an ad reading:

> In a time when people say there are no more heroes – there is still Steve McQueen. You cheered for him in *The Great Escape*, prayed for him in *Cincinnati Kid* and held your breath with him in *Bullitt* ...
>
> Now Steve McQueen portrays the most striking hero of them all – the man they called ... AN ENEMY OF THE PEOPLE!

Next it was 'a classic ADVENTURE, with all its love, loss and heavy drama, starring America's rebel with a cause ... STEVE (*Papillon*) MCQUEEN'.

They billed it, but they didn't come.

After more test runs and a tense preview in the First Artists board-room ('I'm not going to say anything,' Feldman snarled to the *New York Times*. 'I won't talk about *Enemy of the People*'), Warners took the unprecedented decision not to distribute it. 'It's a goddamn embarrassment, a piece of junk' was one executive's bleak, and widely published, assessment. As they say in Hollywood, it died in the can. *Enemy* was shelved for more than three years, surfaced on cable TV in August 1980 and finally opened at New York's Public Theater, an orphanage for lost films, a year later. It has never had a general release.

'What happened with *Enemy* hurt me more than anything I can remember,' Steve told Bill Nolan. 'I put my heart and guts into that film and when it got the reaction it did, I was wiped out.

'Worse than *Le Mans*,' he said in stern conclusion. McQueen didn't forget, and he didn't forgive.

$\boxed{9}$

Restoration

T oday was Feldman day. He might as well have put a gun to Steve's head.

McQueen had to go to First Artists to discuss what, if anything, he meant to do about delivering a third and final film under his contract. Once again he found the bile rising in his gorge. Even the phone call from Feldman's secretary to make the appointment had twisted his melon. 'Some time on Friday,' she'd trilled, treating Steve to a chuckling undertone of scorn and familiarity. 'What shall we say, around nine? Nine thirty?'

'Earlier would be better.'

'Make it ten,' said the woman. 'I like to work with round numbers. He can spare you fifty minutes.'

But when McQueen arrived he was told to take a seat in the lobby. Feldman was running late that morning. For half the allotted meeting time, one of Hollywood's biggest and best-connected stars sat waiting for a man he, in effect, employed. A full thirty minutes passed. Several questions rose simultaneously in Steve's mind and battered against each other in a rush to get out – 'Who the fuck do you think you are?' being the overall gist. Finally McQueen stood up, brushed aside the secretary's protests and punted open the door of the inner office. Feldman was sitting back there, alone, gazing out the window. 'I like the first ten minutes of *Enemy* but not the next ninety,' he said calmly. 'Not that it's a blockbuster to begin with. We'll do our best.'

364

'Gee, thanks,' said Steve.

Feldman no longer veiled his anger. 'You owe this concern a fucking film.'

McQueen could be sure that his wasn't the only craw in which Feldman's words stuck with nauseating effect. Originally set up as a bold experiment, a company designed to free stars of the creative shackles of big studios, First Artists had become a corporate crazy quilt. By 1977 it had interests in TV, music and casino ownership, and soon branched out into the overcrowded designer sportswear racket. Feldman's simultaneous attempts to impose discipline on his star assets – somewhat against the whole freewheeling ideal – became a cautionary tale about what happens when art meets commerce. Both Sidney Poitier and Barbra Streisand balked at Feldman's demands that they turn out saleable 'product' rather than, respectively, ghetto movies and *Yentl*. The newly aboard Dustin Hoffman, meanwhile, would charge Feldman with violating his contract by taking over two films in which he, Hoffman, starred, *Straight Time* and *Agatha*. Before long the actor was suing his own company for $158 million.

But it was the saga of the fucking Norwegian – Ibsen – that nearly tore things apart.

There was plenty to criticise about *Enemy of the People*. McQueen was too cautious about revamping the text and too fixated on period authenticity. But it was no worse than Newman's *Pocket Money* or Streisand's *Up the Sandbox*, two follies that somehow got by Feldman's desk. Those had been mere professional disappointments. With Steve, things got personal.

They loathed each other. Shunning the First Artists board to spite Feldman, McQueen sent out four scripts he liked to a market research company in order for them, in turn, to test them on professional readers. Two came back marked 'non-viable' and two were well received. The board turned puce. What about channels? To teach McQueen his place, First Artists sent a dozen of *their* best scripts to the same market research firm. All twelve came back rejected.

Patently, Steve no longer cared quite as much as before. He still had Marvin Josephson and Ken Ziffren on board, and he still occasionally ran a rule over the books at Solar (now operating out of Josephson's office on Beverly Boulevard). But mostly McQueen was stubbornly fixated on projects that were 'pure ... with total quality in mind' rather than more shootups. Seeing him in the privacy of ICM or at Trancas, it was hard to even imagine him as the Supie of old. Alone or surrounded by family and close friends, McQueen was relaxed and disarming. The drawl, the clothes, the quizzical manner, the slow grin, the china-blue eyes – all imparted informality and charm. He was colloquial, and in private conversation used a fair quota of fucks and cunts and occasionally stronger terms, but only ever witticising at the honchos' expense. Never at real people. To make the distinction, Steve still visited children's wards and schools and above all Boys Republic; once he stayed in Chino an entire weekend, discussing and showing movies, and, of course, satirising most of Hollywood. Total quality was his keynote there, too.

The business has a way of cutting mavericks and rebels down to size, but, in Steve's case, the process was mutual. In the space of nine months the scripts for *Raise the Titanic!*, *The Bodyguard* and *Close Encounters* all landed on Josephson's desk. There were dozens of others. Josephson flagged up the very best of the bunch and sent them on with elaborate cover notes to McQueen.

All of them came back.

Late that winter of 1976–7 Steve did, however, read and enjoy several plays. His most promising find was Harold Pinter's *Old Times*. Soon enough the two men, the great dramatic stylist and the intuitive but defiantly non-cerebral actor, duly met in the Carlyle Hotel, New York. 'I found McQueen charming, funny and totally tuned in to the work,' says Pinter. 'He told me straight away, "This play is about a man drowning between two women" – a brilliant analysis.' The scholar-squirrels who 'parse [Pinter's] stuff down to the syllable' should have been as spot-on in their own rambling theses. Steve had little doubt he could handle the material if once given the chance, as he was a master at that sinking feeling between women.*

In time the reading was over and the two men progressed to a celebratory drink. Even here Steve's technique was concise. Pinter

---

* Faye Dunaway and Audrey Hepburn were under discussion as McQueen's *Old Times* co-stars.

watched him calmly flip the top off a bottle of Old Milwaukee instead of, like himself, using an opener. 'Christ, McQueen, you must be made of iron.'

'I *am* made of iron.' Steve, licking his lips with a look of triumph, reached out to show Pinter the bottle; it was a screw-top.

There was a pause.

Shortly afterwards, McQueen's friend Michael Cristofer flew to London to edit the *Old Times* text with its author, specifically weeding out anything Hollywood might find too English. A few minor cuts were made and Pinter believed the whole project was on track. 'It looks good,' said Steve with an emanation of authority of the kind for which he was justly renowned, and none of the infinite regress for which Hollywood was universally panned. 'I'm going to get some rest, Harold, and I'll call you back.'

But while McQueen slept, a viper crawled into the nest. Someone made a special point of bringing to LA and placing into Feldman's hands a copy of *Old Times*. Feldman erupted. When the shouting had died down, he demanded an immediate 'treatment' – Hollywood-ese for a fully developed narrative close to a final screenplay – of whatever it was the crazy bastard McQueen had in mind. Steve in turn mentioned the problem on the phone to Pinter, who got tetchy. 'Don't shout at me, Harold,' said McQueen. 'I'm not your butler.'

Now it was Pinter who gave a terse laugh. 'I never shout at my butler.'

'OK then, about this –'

'Treatment,' Pinter anticipated despairingly. 'Look, I'll do a screenplay for my normal fee, but nothing else. Agreed?'

'Agreed.'

First Artists, of course, killed the film. McQueen then sued them for $88,000 to recoup the seed money already put into pre-production. The suit was settled in March 1977, when Feldman reimbursed Steve, who in turn promised to do a horse opera for him called *Tom Horn*. That would be the third and final film under the pestilent contract.

Next McQueen paid Pinter for his time, in full, with a personal cheque. Steve made a mental note to call him again once *Horn* was safely done with. Two years later he realised he had forgotten. And he also realised it didn't matter. By then Steve's first artistic goal was to get out of Hollywood so fucking fast there would be no time for meetings, and treatment had only one, more ominous meaning.

McQueen settled with First Artists and agreed to make *Horn* in a contract dated 24 March. This, as it happened, was his forty-seventh birthday. Running ever faster out of gas.

Steve had told Charles Durning on the set of *Enemy* that he only wanted to work with stage actors, in classics to boot, from then on. Less than six months later he signed up to make a Western. McQueen's co-stars in *Tom Horn* were the TV siren Linda Evans, once of *Beach Blanket Bingo* and soon of *Dynasty* fame, and the ex-stuntman Dick Farnsworth. Durning believes 'he almost certainly knew he was sick but wanted to prove he wasn't . . . *Tom Horn* and [*The Hunter*] were his "Hey, you bastards. I'm still here!" movies.' Bob Relyea agrees that 'Steve knew way ahead of time he was ill. For the last couple of years he wasn't concerned about quality so much as keeping busy.' And, in the case of *Horn*, at least, divorcing Phil Feldman.

It was still a perfectly good film. McQueen played yet another anachronism in *Horn*, a real-life Wyoming bounty hunter framed and hung, for the crime of doing his job too well, by his own employers. Where a Frank Bullitt, with his arch, tough-talking hopefulness, had been just right for his moment, so Horn's gentle irony and bittersweet backward glance were perfect for his. But in the latter film, more than a decade later, Steve had seasoned as an actor, the grave, suddenly lined face signalling a different sort of crash, Horn's plunging headfirst into history. Both movies combined bursts of bloodshed with long, contemplative passages of stillness and silence. *Bullitt* was the more explosive of the two; Horn the more rounded, compelling character.

It's not unusual in Hollywood for two or more studios to be working on the same picture at the same time. *The Towering Inferno* had been a classic case, though there Warners and Fox had pooled resources to their mutual profit. Now, on the very day McQueen confirmed he was doing *Tom Horn*, Robert Redford revealed that he, too, was developing the same story. ('Every time I look in the rearview mirror,' said Steve, 'I see ol' Bob.') Redford soon ankled the film, only for David Carradine to announce his own TV movie, *Mr Horn.* Steve came into rehearsal one morning with some news. 'We better snap things up. I heard Disney's doing a musical in modern dress – *Thomas Horn, Esq.*' His deadpan expression turned irony into reality. Stomachs actually plummeted around the room. Either Hollywood finally had flipped or McQueen was enjoying a quiet joke.

Or both.

Steve signed his closing agreement on *Horn,* watched by Feldman, in the First Artists boardroom. Solar was to be paid a flat $1 million, $83,000 for each of twelve weeks' photography, plus points. After that he could have his divorce any time he wanted it.

That summer McQueen drove up to Cheyenne and spent a night under the stars at Tom Horn's gravesite. He stretched out there for an hour, face down, on the actual slab. 'I could feel him move. It was like he said to me, "Please do my story. Please tell my story."'

McQueen was jarred from his reverie by news that a reporter was lingering outside the cemetery in hopes of a scoop.

In the event there was no formal interview, as such. But the local paper did carry a captioned photo of Steve; he was snapped outside the Crazy Horse motel, allegedly 'one of [his] favourite places to stay – They got colour TV and everything.' It's doubtful that McQueen did any slumming. He was back in Hollywood on 9 June, the day of Terry's eighteenth birthday. McQueen attended the party at Neile's new house. There were a few fresh faces there and Steve reached deep inside himself for empathy and patience. When away from his turf, Terry knew, he was often ingenuous in a way strangers might call rude.

'Fuck off,' he invited one autograph-seeker.

Neile thought that Steve 'looked awful – blown up like a giant balloon'. He both came and left alone. Friends knew better than to ask him where Ali was.

For a virile man who chased sensation his whole life, Steve displayed a notably thin skin. He reacted personally – and often petulantly – to disappointment. Distraught over *Enemy* and very probably aware he was ill, McQueen now began to talk more and more openly about his obsession with dying at fifty. 'If not the big C, then some nut,' he reasoned. 'I've had threats.'

In fact that very week the FBI filed a letter promising that thirty celebrities would be murdered if three convicted felons weren't first released. Steve's name was high on the death list. It had been thus for years: McQueen was the target of last resort for stalkers and overadrenalised fans ever since that day, in 1958, when a drunk had called out, '*Hey, fag! C'mere and show me that big gun of yours,*' in a popular Hollywood restaurant. The place fell silent as Steve slowly stood up: the narrowed eyes, the stubble, the bulging forearms and fists all gave the tourists instant visual gratification: this was what they'd come to see. (Steve dropped the man with a single punch – *adios*.) It was enough to make him even more morbid, or paranoid, and it duly did.

Compounding which, McQueen found himself with an immense unwillingness to admit that the more he tried to 'zonk out' and 'take the edge off things', the worse they got. He was no drug-free zone. Thanks to Schick and to sheer willpower, he'd actually kicked ciga-rettes; that left only coke, pot, amyl nitrate, prescription downers and, it was rumoured, the occasional hit of heroin in Steve's chemical locker. He was still bearded, overweight, and seemed to have flu constantly. Not exactly the stuff of which Hollywood legends were made any more.

Charles Durning remembers McQueen telling him to keep in touch after the wrap party for *Enemy*. 'But then he stopped returning calls. The doors closed.'

The reassurance that he 'felt fine' jarred badly with the evidence Neile saw with her own eyes. 'What have you done to my man?' she asked Ali.

MacGraw swore that she did her best.

At forty-seven McQueen was a stooped, mumbling figure, with eroded features, and yet he had a boyish, athletic side, zipping around town on his bike and still diligently working out with Pat Johnson. As usual there were two Steve McQueens: Moody Steve and Happy Steve; Elvis's long-lost, kamikaze big brother and the sharp, percep-tive man who re-entered therapy that summer.

In a rare interview, the last one he ever gave, Steve told a spiritual doctor named Brugh Joy in 1980:

I've had three years of it, so I have some small perception of myself. When a kid doesn't have any love when he's small, he begins to wonder if he's good enough. My mother didn't love me, and I didn't have a father. I thought, 'Well, I must not be very good.' So, then you go out and try to prove yourself, and I always did things that other people wouldn't do. Dangerous things . . . I was always kind of a coward until I had to prove it to myself. I think that's where that came from. Most of it.

McQueen instinctively worked this out, with a little help, and it changed everything for him. Once he 'got' his past, he moved on. Jangling his spurs and blowing the smoke off his six-iron suddenly seemed passé and absurd. Steve, evidently, looked on this as a logical, chronological evolution. But to the old-fashioned corporate honchos, he was way, way outta line – a self-indulgent nut who bit the hand that fed him; another celebrity casualty.

Now Howard Hughes was gone. Elvis, Steve's fellow-traveller in being a karate-suited hulk, went that summer. And while McQueen himself carried on the American-burnout tradition, the archetype fairly screamed Code Blue. Jim Geller saw him for the last time that August. Steve didn't see Geller. McQueen was pasty-faced and bloated, cap pancaked down on his head, hobbling up Malibu's Piuma Road while chewing on a Mars bar. His lunch. Stumbling and swaying, he sat down on the stoop of the small Asian grocery store. At the store there were no all-American film fans. The figure out front catching his breath meant nothing to them. So McQueen slumped there, another derelict.

Now Ali's old agent Sue Mengers called to make a pitch.

'Do you remember a script called *Convoy*?'

'Indeed I do,' was MacGraw's stout response. 'Steve and I read it years ago and hated it. It stank.'

'Honey, your marriage is in trouble, you have no money, and you better take this job before it's too late. You're lucky to get the offer.'

So Ali signed to make *Convoy*, Sam Peckinpah's thirteenth feature film and probably his worst. MacGraw mentioned it to Steve that night. He was sitting in a chair, nursing an Old Milwaukee. 'Fine,' he said calmly. 'In that case we're filing for divorce.'

Still, he couldn't dislike this brown-eyed woman who'd been his hausfrau for four long years that July. Ali duly flew to Albuquerque, cropped her hair and joined in the organised limbo of *Convoy*, awash as it was with sex, drink, drugs and, worse, a script confused to the point of gibberish. Steve and MacGraw's son Josh followed to New Mexico a few days later. McQueen's friend Gary Combs, doubling for Kris Kristofferson in the movie, was in the crew hotel one morning when a 'seedy-looking character wearing wire-rimmed glasses and a patched jacket ambled up to me . . . I thought he must be some crazy fan. Then he smiled and said, "Thank you for looking out for Ali." It was Steve.'

Other cast members saw McQueen hand his wife an empty beer can filled with daisies. 'Miss you,' he told her.

'*Convoy* was torture for Steve,' says Pat Johnson. 'He categorically didn't want Ali to do it, particularly after [not that she knew it] he'd given up *Sorcerer* for her. I remember he'd call her in her hotel room at two a.m., desperate, missing her and certain she was cheating on him.' Often he would put his head on Johnson's shoulder and cry. 'I can never feel the same again,' McQueen said.

'You just have to work it out.'

'I don't think I can.'*

The whole thing, which had begun on the set of one Peckinpah film, ground down in the heat and dust and wholesale futility of another. *Convoy* was a disaster. The very day Ali flew home from filming she learnt that Steve had left that morning to drive up to Idaho and his latest fuck-fling, one Barbara Minty. Another American beauty: in the tilt of Minty's dark-haired head friends were startled to see a touch of MacGraw herself, some fifteen years younger.

The first time Steve himself saw her was on the cover of *Vogue*, where she happened to be wearing a snug T-shirt. Minty was then a twenty-two-year-old model and horse-ranch owner with mild, and

---

* Years later, MacGraw wrote that 'the truth was that I had a kind of druggy affair periodically during that movie, but as it was now common knowledge that Steve had been living a flagrantly free life for some months, I thought that if I didn't go into my escapade, the sheer mess of our lives might blow over and offer us a fresh start.'

unfulfilled, celluloid dreams. (Though never actually making it in Hollywood, she'd nonetheless had that ritual audition, a night with Warren Beatty.) McQueen wasted no time in putting in a call to the magazine. 'That built chick,' he asked, 'what's her number?' Next he was on the line to Minty herself, who not only knew of Steve, but turned out to have had a crush on him for years. Bango. Soon McQueen was roaring up Interstate 15 and then northwest into Ketchum, where he asked his new friend if she'd like to take a ride. According to Pat Johnson, 'She never wore a bra and she was clinging on to him, squeezed up against him on the back of the bike.' Whistling appreciatively, Steve took off down the country road and waited for something to happen. Minty slipped off her shirt and tied it round her waist. Then he knew he had it made.

Friends smiled that McQueen's 'heavy ladies' had become, like Russian dolls, diminishing or at least younger versions of the same basic type. The cynics among them scoffed that Minty, unlike MacGraw, was 'a squaw', the 'Stepford Wife type' and 'didn't give Steve any crap'. The give-and-take of life with both Neile and Ali was shut down completely. But Minty, on the other hand, as Steve often put it, was 'totally there'. She obviously took pride in being seen around town with him, always ravishingly dressed, and simultaneously protecting his privacy, even from old cronies, of which she became the ever-vigilant gatekeeper.

Steve was at lunch in the El Padrino room that autumn with Bill Maher, Phil Parslow and the director John Frankenheimer, discussing a project called *Tiger Ten*. A waiter brought a phone to their table. When McQueen picked it up he said nothing for a minute, merely listened. And then he suddenly jerked up to his feet, mumbling, 'Oh fuck, oh fuck,' pacing around the room and whipping the phone cord over people's heads at the nearby tables. It was Barbara Minty on the line from Idaho, telling him that the *National Enquirer* was banging at her door and threatening to run the story that they were lovers. 'Talk to us! We'll be discreet!' they promised. There was nothing muted about Steve's reply. 'Sh-*iiiitt!*' he began in a flying burst that spun heads as far away as the lobby, and went on from there to get tense. 'She'll freak.' If anything, that underestimated Ali's reaction when she duly read the *Enquirer*'s screaming headline.

McQueen was mortified by his wife's tears and stirred with a tender-ness foreign to him. 'God, baby, I'm sorry.'

They tried one last time, at a retreat in Montana, but then Ali made the mistake of being friendly to a handsome big-game hunter they happened to meet and the inquisition began all over again. He went at her. He'd heard them talking together in French, or some fucking crap, and he could hardly focus with rage. *Dirty. Whoring. Bitch.* Was there violence? MacGraw never said so. But, back in Malibu, there were ugly scenes that would have levelled a house less sturdily built. 'I want a divorce,' Ali soon heard herself bawling. 'Get out of my fucking sight! Now! I'll need a month to find somewhere else – don't try and talk me out of it. You'll be hearing from my lawyer!'

In fact it was MacGraw herself who received papers that Novem-ber, case number WE 0 32363 in the Superior Court. Steve quickly moved Barbara Minty into Trancas and gave his second wife – just as the twice-signed pre-nuptial had promised – nothing. In the immediate days and weeks ahead McQueen's friends all got the impression that he missed six-year-old Josh Evans more than he did his mother.

The day Ali and her son moved into their new house she rang Steve, in a fit of contrition, to tell him she thought they had made a terrible mistake. A minute later she knew better. 'I'm not in love with you any more,' he said. 'I love you, but I'm not in love.'

MacGraw was stung again by how much, borne in on her over the years, he'd hurt her just to protect himself. Feeding blindly and incessantly on itself, McQueen's rage was a motor that rarely stopped. She'd either have to get used to it or forgo any hope of a reconcili-ation, and she knew now it would be the latter.

'I don't get it,' she said. 'How can you turn your back on people when you say you love them?'

'It's a talent,' he replied.

Still, Steve's indifferent act could be deceptive. He not only con-tinued to write and call and send gifts to Josh. That same winter he flew to New York specifically to visit Ali's brother, an artist living in Greenwich Village. Something about both him and his lifestyle touched McQueen deeply and he came back raving to Minty (herself a clergyman's daughter) about leaving Hollywood and finding God.

She took a polite interest in this information. 'Oh Supie, I love you and love you and love you just the way you are.'

In the cold light of morning Steve lingered in the hot tub with his head in both hands, wondering what the fuck he had done.

Minty – soft, warm-hearted and loyal where Ali was bluff and entrepreneurial – not only assumed day-to-day responsibility for Steve's home; in a sort of triptych arrangement with Josephson and Maher she took care of literally everything it wasn't vital he do himself. On the surface, at least, McQueen had what he'd always wanted: unconditional love, admiration and surrender. He told Pat Johnson that Barbara was everything he dug in a woman, except that the passion was missing. Johnson knew Steve had landed on his feet. 'You're her whole life. She worships you.'

'The vibes are good,' McQueen agreed.

'She was slavish to Steve,' says a mutual friend. 'It was like Versailles-cum-Malibu. She looked on McQueen like the Sun King.'

But a strange thing happened. Despite or because of Minty's deference, Steve began to pay attention to her in a way that hadn't always been true with Neile or Ali. Within a few weeks he was back in the gym again. His weight dropped; the beard was stylishly trimmed. Apart from the pot and his cherished Old Milwaukee, McQueen even stopped doing drugs. 'I was destroyed,' he said, 'and she saved me.'

Steve soon purchased a five-acre spread in North Fork, Idaho, in the foothills of the Salmon River mountains. The only access road to the place wound up a steep slope, dipping occasionally, but always climbing. At the summit, as far as McQueen could see, was a pine-tree plain, the trunks baked to the touch, smooth barked, sending down their leaves in a mist of needles and sweet fern. On one side was a range of hills, far off to the other the line of a river. From Steve's log cabin you could catch glints of the water in the sun.

McQueen planned to spend six months a year there with Barbara. Lest anyone miss the point, he named his new home Last Chance.

Steve now plugged himself back in like a neon sign. One of his truly greatest performances was the one he gave at forty-eight, when he turned his hunched back not only on dope but on the truism about Hollywood careers not having a second act. Few had even tried for one. Of those who did, everyone from Bela Lugosi to John Wayne had resurfaced only to fade away again, knock-kneed and laughing, mere parodies of themselves. But not McQueen. The junk food disappeared, the juicer and the skipping rope came out and Steve announced that the vibes were right for a comeback. It was almost as if he still wanted to prove something, as he already had to so many: Julian, Bill, Neile, Ali, Newman. When asked who he was doing it for now, McQueen responded: 'Me. Self-respect.'

Steve's new-found idyll would last about two years. Then, almost inevitably, the bliss began to fray.

He talked seriously to Barbara about having kids, raising them there in the Idaho woods and 'schlepping back to LA to do stuff'. McQueen soon took her to visit Boys Republic. A lifelong ally of the downtrodden, he kept up his almost pathological charity. When he read a news story about an eight-year-old who was dying of a brain tumour, Steve treated the boy and his family to a weekend at Disney-land. (First class, with hotels and limos provided.) The other 'stuff' McQueen now did included: supporting distressed actors, leading the fund-raising drive on behalf of a slum orphanage, collecting nearly $100,000 for a homeless shelter at Hollywood and Vine, donating scripts and costumes and movie memorabilia for auction; and gener-ally giving thousands to float literally dozens of good causes, all without it ever being used or milked for publicity.

And, when he had time left over, reluctantly playing the world's favourite tough guy. The day McQueen signed for *Tom Horn* and shook Feldman's hand, something inside him wanted to scream.

In July 1978 Steve and Barbara were themselves treated to seats at a Rolling Stones show, not one of their best ever, in Anaheim. McQueen's friend Mick Jagger donated the tickets, then happened to run into his guest later that night in the hotel bar, during the course of which Jagger was accused of being even more of a swish and less of a true pilgrim – a fucking drama queen, in fact – than most people suspected. He picked up the bill for their drinks.

The next afternoon, over breakfast before their second Anaheim show, Jagger mentioned the meeting to Keith Richards. 'As soon as we were alone, he started twisting my melon.'

'He did what?'

'He called me an old tart and twisted my melon. That's how McQueen talks. "You guys give off weird vibes," he said, and started giving me crap. Then he asked for more freebies. Twelve fucking seats for tonight. I'm not kidding.'

'I know you're not kidding. But what'd you tell him?'

'I said I'd try.'

'What you mean,' interjected Richards affably, with that flair for graceful and laconic expression people admired so much, 'is the cunt gets his tickets.'

Jagger's shaggy brown eyebrows beetled in resignation. 'Fuck,' he said, 'he's Steve McQueen.'

Later that year, when Minty was out, McQueen invited Ali to visit his new California spread up the coast at Santa Paula. Ali went. Steve drove her around town in his truck, apparently healthy, happy, his eyes sharp as thorns again, then, almost mechanically, suggested they pull off the road and make love in an orange grove. MacGraw declined the offer. 'Just checking,' Steve shrugged. After lunch in a local diner she drove back to Hollywood and never laid eyes on him again.

Barbara was still out when McQueen got home. They were all out, and he walked around the fruit fields in wistful dejection, remembering the very similar look and smell of the Slater landscape. Steve wasn't often nostalgic, but he clearly hankered after the 1930s curios which he was block-buying at that very moment: cars, motorbikes, jukeboxes and every kind of child's knick-knack. Collectomania. McQueen was getting more and more sentimental in middle age. He could suddenly remember, as he walked, the way the Missouri prairie-grass grew, knee-high, and the clumps of elms and cotton-woods; a green swelling country with frequent rises and slopes, warm underfoot and alive with vermin noise. He wished again that he was where Darla More was, still living across the river by the Chicago & Alton railway, rooted, content, not giving a shit about Feldman and Hollywood and never thinking of them again.

Steve's nostalgia didn't, however, extend to visiting Slater during the town's centennial in 1978. Their invitation was turned down flat.

Physically, at least, McQueen owed his genre-bending comeback to exercise, fresh air and relatively clean living; it was to get more of them that he bought into Santa Paula and Idaho in the first place. When old friends saw him now they were positively astounded that the chiselled, ruddy looks had survived the last three-plus years. Those thirty or forty months hadn't blunted Steve's ambition or competitiveness, but they had made him more pensive. Certainly more time- and age-conscious. He did, by now, feel almost old enough to retire, and he felt even older when most of 1978 was pissed away trying to get a script and budget together for *Tom Horn*. Life, he often said, was a scam. It was also too fucking short.

He again began to tell people he had a 'couple of movies, tops' left. When Steve rang the actor Ben Johnson, to ask if he'd work with him in 1979, he used phrases like, 'This is probably the last one I'm gonna do,' and startlingly, 'Are you afraid of dying?' Before Johnson could even reply, McQueen hung up. A man on the move. Steve withstood Feldman's blustering and gesticulating about *Horn* with a series of impatient grunts, the darkened wart of his face like a primed timebomb.

'Let's just fucking *do* it,' he said.

First McQueen seemed to have a cold, then a cough, then finally pneumonia. He wouldn't go in for tests, merely swigged down the linctus and swallowed a few aspirin. Neile happened to see him in Malibu that summer, wrapped in a bathrobe at midday and leaning heavily on a cane. 'My heart went out to him,' she says. Steve's simultaneous revival and gradual, final decline was more pitiable than any film, any *Love Story*, the deep, unearthly howl with which he woke Minty one night vibrating in its own impact for seconds afterward like a seismic shock. 'I feel like I'm on fire,' he gasped.

In public, McQueen never complained. 'The fans don't care if I sleep well,' he said. 'They only care if I act well.'

Tom Horn was dead. That was the basic flaw in his philosophy. Script crises were matched in turn by director crises; Don Siegel (*Dirty Harry*) and Elliot Silverstein (*Cat Ballou*) both came and went, two men with ample IQ but, in Steve's assessment, no brains, whereas he, Steve, was the opposite: an actor who knew immediately and instinctively what worked, but with a predilection for mumbling around all sides of a question and seemingly never coming to the point. 'McQueen gabbled a million words a minute, like a machine gun,' says Silverstein. 'Very hip. Little or no grammar. Even his friends couldn't always tell what he was saying.' Warner Brothers, meanwhile, as keen to be shot of First Artists as Steve was, signed off on a $6 million budget instead of the $10 million McQueen wanted and told him, in effect, to go ahead and make the fucking picture or see them in permanent litigation. Phil Parslow, trapped uncomfortably between the two, soon quit as producer in favour of Warners' Fred Weintraub. Steve muttered about that, too, right up to the day Weintraub reanimated *Horn*, hauled everyone down to Arizona, and told the new director to start cranking. Action. A few years ago McQueen would have erupted, but now he shrugged.

Then Steve did a sad little bit of business, out in a far corner of the set, that only a few people saw. With a quiet, stifled groan, McQueen made a pistol of his thumb and forefinger and blew his own brains out.

There was still no word about *Enemy* by late 1978 and Steve, with commendable nerve if not much hope, went over the studio's head and appealed direct to the public. He began organising small, art-house screenings around LA. Next McQueen sent a print to the renowned critic Charles Champlin, who went to meet him in the lobby of the Beverly Wilshire. 'I remember, bizarrely, he was slumped there in one corner of the room and his PR man was sitting in the other. Like boxers.' The occasion was only slightly marred by a gaffe when Champlin, somehow 'expecting Thomas Crown and not this bearded figure', at first failed to even recognise his host. From that low point things improved. 'Steve was anxious for a good review and I tried to be as positive as I could. The truth is, he was battling against such a powerful pre-image it was an almost impossible sell. That apart, I liked the job he did on *Enemy*.' The next week McQueen went down to Loyola Marymount and did a Q & A session with Champlin's students in the film school.

'Me doing Ibsen is like making a purse out of a sow's ear,' he told them. 'Let's face it. I spent a lot of my life being a coward and spent a lot of time trying to overcome that influence. Ibsen showed me the courage in the common man. That's why I did the film.'

Both Warners and First Artists wanted nothing to do with it. Maybe never had, especially that female executive, whose joy in ball-breaking McQueen was sublime. She had every quality of a dog, he reflected, except loyalty. 'Another bitch,' Steve told Hoven. His life seemed to be full of them. McQueen went back to the El Padrino room that same night and stayed there very late.

End to end, he added, one big dykehouse.

At first light he took a perfunctory shower, then drove up to Burbank and demanded to see Steven Ross, the Warners head honcho, whom Steve confidentially thought candyass. An accurate prognosis. Ross fled in terror; McQueen put it about that he'd entered the witness protection programme and opened a hog farm back in Iowa. But, wherever he was, Ross showed an understandable reluctance to come out and debate marketing strategy with a man toting a can of Old Milwaukee in each hand. Steve's case for releasing *Enemy* was actually a compelling one. The only thing missing was somebody to put it to.

He didn't even bother with Feldman much any more. By late 1978, having gambled away time and cash on a failed casino venture, First Artists was already winding itself down. When word of its corporate implosion got back to him, McQueen admitted he stopped loathing Feldman and even started feeling sorry for him. Almost overnight, it seemed, the whole thing was in pieces, an ex-media conglomerate now reduced to a struggling sports shirt- and pop-based concern with little left to show of its core interests. Feldman himself quit in 1979. The voting trust that ran the firm on behalf of its shareholders expired that December and First Artists was duly out of the movie business. Steve survived the company that had plagued him to the point of dementia by slightly less than a year.

A free agent, McQueen began entertaining new offers even before the first take of the first scene of *Tom Horn*. Walter Hill's *film noir The Driver*, with a car chase sequence straight out of *Bullitt*, was read and rejected. *The Chinese Bandit*, *Blue Collar* and *Quigley Down Under*, among scores of others, all landed on Josephson's desk. He must have particularly enjoyed reading one of those postmodernist larks from Andy Warhol, a manuscript Steve himself picked up, all too briefly, with a pair of tongs. (Something about mutant lesbians.) With McQueen now that contradictory thing, a classical actor who once again wanted the bucks, Josephson began hunting around for an epic adventure, God alone knew what, and, incredibly enough, found it. The whole saga would be good for one of the loudest and very last laughs of McQueen's career.

Meanwhile, while *Horn* was bogged down in interminable script rewrites, Steve signed to do a yarn called *The Hunter*. It was yet another bounty-hunter role, and people wondered whether there wasn't something strangely cyclical about it. After twenty years in front of the camera, McQueen was very nearly back to where he'd begun.

If on a higher budget: Steve took home $3 million 'guaranteed compensation' for *The Hunter*, payable at $250,000 per week for twelve weeks, plus 15 per cent of the gross. No wonder he laughed aloud when he signed, holding in check a deeper, more explosive delight. In all, it turned out to be the most rewarding event in McQueen's career since the day he suited up as O'Hallorhan, and one of the best ever. Those final three months' work would eventually net him and his heirs $8 million. According to the contract, as well as the cash 'Artist [was to] be furnished with first-class transportation . . . first-class residence or the best suite at a hotel . . . car and driver . . . the Cortez . . . portable gym . . . "top star" dressing room at all locations . . . name above the title . . . merchandising, commercial tie-ups, royalties etc.'; the sixteen clauses, full of perks and bonuses and sweeteners, proved yet again how far McQueen had come. He put the money to good use, gave some of it to a church, donated tens of thousands more to charity, and bought an old-fashioned family home deep in farm country. People in Hollywood disliked him because he was such a flagrant nonconformist.

The movie itself wasn't bad, based on another real-life story, though this time in modern dress. Steve played one Papa Thorson, an itinerant gun for hire – like him, no spring chicken – with a fervently 'cute' habit of wearing bifocals and bunny slippers around the house. The self-referential running gag that Thorson can't actually drive was both funny and even endearing when handled

381

by the star of *Bullitt*. It was McQueen's anti-heroic view of life, in which gentleness and sloth meant more than velocity and volume, and all the really best things were antiques. While, in the last resort, characters like Hilts and Thomas Crown had belonged up among the lights – brilliant and dazzling, but no heat – Thorson was the most human, if not the most realistic part Steve ever played.

The Hunter's main problem was McQueen's true-life one of schizophrenia. Drama or comedy? It worked well enough, in patches, as one or the other, but over ninety-seven minutes this frantically plotted Josh Randall pastiche struggled for an identity. The action never seemed organic as it did in *Wanted*. 'Gratuitous' was the fell word used by *Variety*. The jokes, too, were merely dumped in and the dialogue moulded around them, which would have mattered less if the jokes were funnier. Aiming for everything, *The Hunter* turned out to be about not much of anything.

McQueen met Warhol for the first and only time that year in New York; drove downtown to The Factory, rang a bell labelled DO NOT RING, lumbered up in the antique lift and stared at the huge stuffed dog in the reception area. The door to the back room was opened by Warhol's assistant Paul Morrissey. Warhol himself appeared dressed like Erich von Stroheim, wearing a white aviator's scarf, jodhpurs and swishing a riding crop. He shook hands with an icy, reptilian grip.

'Will you star in my new film?' he asked.

'I'm sorry,' Steve said regretfully in a low, courteous, melancholy voice. 'Thanks anyway. But as I said on the phone, I'm getting out of the movie business.'

Warhol's face fell. 'Can I at least take your picture?'

'Go right ahead.'

Warhol snapped away with a Polaroid, chewing his clotted dry lower lip excitedly, and panning down from McQueen's head to his toes. 'Oh Steve,' he said, his tremulous voice suddenly jumping an octave. 'I love your work. Lu*rrrve* it. You almost make your characters seem real.'

'They are real, Andy.'

'You're the best there is,' Warhol cooed. By now he was peeping through the viewfinder and panting slightly from the labour of his art. 'You're sure you won't work for me?'

McQueen shook his head.

A few days later Warhol met up at Xenon with Steve's other new friend Truman Capote. 'What'd he say about me?' he asked excitedly. 'What did McQueen say?'

'He said you posed him.'

'I know that. I know that. But what'd he say about me? What'd he say?'

'You make him puke.'

A changed, gentler man, and yet not so changed. Marvin Josephson advised Steve to do another big film, to prove he was still a player.

'OK,' he said. 'But let's make it *really* big. Get some headlines. I'll be a long time parked, I guess.'

Josephson soon came up with the goods. Meanwhile, McQueen, ever the vigilant due-collector, lobbied with dour impatience for what was his. When other actors had followed his lead and starting auditing their back catalogue, he went one better by auditing *The Towering Inferno* twice, then three, then four times; then he griped about the TV rights, and after that he sued four Japanese companies whom he accused of using his photograph without permission to promote their wares. (Under the cosh, they all paid up.) It was a sign of Steve's new-found tranquillity that he condoned literally dozens of lesser ripoffs where the culprit was an individual, sometimes even a friend, merely trying to turn a buck. To his credit, he rarely went after small fry. Stories of McQueen's niceness to 'little people' were legion, and undoubtedly true. Bad debts would be forgiven, old enemies rung up and invited for a beer at the Beverly Wilshire. By 1978, says Mike Fargo, 'Steve was a guy who put the premium on generosity, humour and trust.' Generosity, that was, of course, *within* the circle; corporate honchos weren't necessarily eligible for the same consideration. Mellow or not, McQueen clearly still saw himself as in a death-struggle with the likes of Warners, thanks to the cumulative frustrations and now cancellation of some of his best work. From LA to Tokyo, the studio bigwigs never doubted that they were dealing with a superstar.

'*I'm* the one they photograph,' Steve told them.

Top of the heap and yet apart from it. Lesser Hollywood draws had their own approved causes; they listened to LPs that emitted only the songs of distressed seals or schmoozed photogenically with the Dalai Lama. Three or four times a year they all climbed into the soup and fish, went down to the Golden Globes or the Oscars and became ecstatic at the sight of one another. Heartwarming. Made the whole industry seem like a family.

McQueen wanted nothing to do with them. Yet his was still the name that twanged the nerve of mass fantasy, the one men wanted to be and women wanted to sleep with. As famous for being as for anything he actually said or did. At forty-eight, Steve was no longer seen merely as an actor or performer. He was a synonym for nostalgia, a pillar appreciated not just for himself but for having survived so long. It was enough that he existed. People came to the films out of residual affection, larded with respect and awe, just as they might visit a listed monument, whatever its current state of ruin. A true American original; having appeared just as the traditional star system was fading, he picked it up and shook it inside out with pictures like *Crown* in which, sensationally, the hero pulled a caper (and got away with it). A long, long time before there was a Nicholson or a De Niro there was McQueen, reinventing the whole ideal of a male lead. Even into the 1970s, while Dustin Hoffman did Italian comedy with a funny voice, Steve was still tearing up all the rules in *The Getaway*. Role after role for nearly twenty years, his name was redolent of titanic risks and achievements, self-loathing, paranoia and redeeming talent – almost an allegory of the times themselves. Life's a scam. A living legend whose lean, tentative smile loomed down from a thousand hoardings. McQueen was Hollywood's acknowledged icon, celebrated in hushed tones even by Billy Wilder (*Fedora*), held generally in something between deference and terror, the one to whom Jagger and Warhol and scores of others bent knee. Part of it was the magic and alchemy of celebrity; much more was the solid achievement of a dozen classic films, the stunts, the one-liners and those closeups where the camera refused to move from him.

Such was fame.

The inner circle saw a very different Steve, or more accurately Steves. When he was with biker people, he was the consummate biker, just as when he was at home he was the consummate father or, with Harold Pinter, the consummate actor. There are several mysteries about McQueen, semi-literate dropout and world authority on Ibsen: the chief one being that he seemed to be several different people. A dozen interviews yield a dozen Steves, each one cannily playing to the house. Loren Janes, for instance, 'never once, in twenty-two years, saw him take anything stronger than an aspirin'. Cliff Coleman calls McQueen 'a lovable Scrooge'; Don Gordon, 'the most generous guy in the world'. Pat Johnson confirms that 'Steve was always on . . . Certain mornings we'd go to meetings together with the suits, and he'd tell me beforehand, "This is what I want from these guys and here's how I'll handle it." I'd sit there watching him playing a role, or two or three different roles, picking up on whatever image people had of him and bouncing it right back to them. Brilliant. Sometimes I'd glance at Steve while the suits weren't and he'd wink at me, like a kid outsmarting all the grownups. The unsaid phrase was *Got 'em.*'

Sometimes he'd drive down Pacific Coast Highway to visit Tony Bill in Venice.

'Better stay off the beach,' said Bill. 'You'll be mobbed.'

McQueen laughed calmly. 'What the fuck do you mean, mobbed?' he asked with a smile, and strolled out into the summer crowd. 'I'm only recognised when I want to be.'

Steve squatted down in the sand and cracked open a beer. No one bothered him.

Bill found his old friend 'bearded and mellow, like the true hippie he was. One day I sold him a pair of vintage cars, a Packard and a Caddy. Both 1930s. Steve was in his collecting phase, apparently for anything that gave him a second shot at childhood.'

Bill never saw him again. McQueen moved with his cars and bikes somewhere out of town, and left no forwarding address.

Steve especially enjoyed a joke, the cornier the better, but almost never for public consumption. He remained a taut, restless, uptight man who was aware of everyone's needs but his own and wanted everyone to be 'real' but himself. It seemed even to friends like Coleman as though he'd hidden the true Steve behind the fictive

Supie. For twenty years. To the root causes of McQueen's accelerating illness, Mike Fargo plausibly adds another: nervous strain.

'He told me he had to get the fuck out of Hollywood or, basically, die.'

Not Steve's only move, as it turned out. Without realising what was behind it, his few close friends in LA gradually found themselves dealing with a new, radically improved McQueen. They were indulged, teased, humoured and kidded about with all day long. Even his karate workouts with Pat Johnson were leavened with a few laughs.* Under the titanic front a fierce and austere self-deprecation, and matching generosity, waved impatiently to get out. Now, in a week of loyal flourishes, McQueen hired Johnson, Coleman and Bud Ekins's daughter Susan to work, in varying capacities, on *Tom Horn*. 'I trust you,' he went so far as to tell Josephson, a key reversal of the long, rumbling spats with certain earlier agents. 'Let's make the next one *huge*.' Steve sat back and smiled distantly in contemplation.

'Check,' said Josephson. 'And the one after that. You're really bringing them running again.'

'I can't believe they're that interested.'

Josephson squinted closely at a pile of scripts on his desk. 'Steve, all of these, and dozens more, could have a McQueen role in them. You're sure you won't even read them?'

Steve shook his head.

He drove up to Neile's house three days after Christmas 1978 to celebrate their son's eighteenth birthday. It was both a curtain-call and introduction, the last time McQueen, his first wife and their children were ever photographed together. Chad, too, was now promptly hired for *Tom Horn*. Barbara Minty was there, sitting quietly in the room full of high-school and college kids, nearly her own age, who ignored her. She wanted nothing to eat or drink. Chad himself stared at her covertly from bulging brown eyes out of his aura of

---

* McQueen still kept up his daily sparring with Johnson, whose other pupils now included Marvin Josephson. Josephson remembers fondly how 'Steve adopted street fighter tactics even in the gym. His idea of a gradual, full-length contest was to go ballistic in the first ten seconds, swinging at you like a threshing machine . . . You could be his best friend in the world, but the instant you squared off with him you were the enemy. Let's just say he didn't pull a punch very well.'

black fuzz, marvelling at the cool, phlegmatic strength with which she handled the mass rejection. His father aside, he was the one McQueen most moved by her heroic self-denial.

Neile and Terry weren't convinced.

Twenty-one years earlier Steve had shuttled forlornly between LA and his wife's rented digs at 108 Koval Lane in Las Vegas. She had a long-term contract to appear at the Tropicana, he was mugging his way through dross like *Never Love a Stranger*. Underemployed and bored, he was 'driving me batty', Neile recalls. 'It was probably our lowest ebb . . . We'd jumped into [marriage] because we were in love and it was new and dramatic, but this was the real world. I'd look at Steve and the word *divorce* would come to mind.'

Now Neile was back in Vegas, starring in a production of *Can-Can*. As soon as Minty was out of town, McQueen was again roaring up I-15 to visit his first and, many thought, greatest love. There was still no end to their finite but expanding relationship, in which even new wives and live-in mates competed for second place. Soon Neile was shuddering with a familiar feeling, midway between excitement and dread, as she read the message. *Mr McQueen called.* The mere sound of that name had made women's hearts pound and their breath come in laboured gasps. They would have to close their eyes and force themselves to inhale deeply. Oh, Esteban. Even Neile felt herself in the presence of the mysterious. But now, too, of the sadly mundane. 'Steve had this big beard and extra weight. He looked like an old bag man. He asked me to pick him up at a nondescript hotel . . . The very last time we made love was in that seedy room.'

It had been an epic, sometimes harrowing affair, but even McQueen must have been struck by how it ended: lying there in a Vegas motel, alone again, staring across the asphalt courtyard to Koval Lane. For a long time after Neile left he lay drifting with his eyes half closed, not daring to admit the throb of pain in his chest or the taste in his mouth because of his uneasy feeling that something unknown was waiting for him in real life.

Steve drove back and began shutting up the Malibu house for good, telling Minty he meant to divide his time between North Fork and Santa Paula. He no longer gave a damn about his image, although he was losing weight and at least brushing his hair again. Burrowing deep into farm country was certainly no career move. McQueen did it either for his health or to put ever more mileage between him and the honchos; it was impossible to say which. In either case it was all part of his lifelong escape plan.

Steve told Fargo the beach place was spooked for him.

'Bad vibes,' he elaborated. Too many memories.

In January 1979 work finally began on *Tom Horn*, the turn-of-the-century tale of one of the West's unsung heroes. After *Enemy* it was a return, more or less, to a full studio-mould production, if not quite to the 'spear or gun' genre gleefully slated by Ali. McQueen discussing in a kind of near-blank verse the various moral aspects of frontiersmanship wasn't ever about to compete with the likes of *Octopussy* or *Life of Brian*, *Horn*'s contemporaneous pop-culture yardsticks. Its main fascination today is the final glimpse it gives of the Steve McQueen legend, Nevada Smith and all the other taut, emotional mutes of his earlier and better films.

The inevitable tendency of movies to get mired down in preproduction was gloriously confirmed by *Horn*. By mid 1978 Steve had a producer, Fred Weintraub, a script of sorts, but no director. On a trip to North Fork that summer he met Jim Guercio, ex-manager of the faintly tedious rock group Chicago and responsible for one of the strangest cop films of all time, *Electra Glide in Blue*. Whatever Guercio said to McQueen, it was enough. Over Weintraub's vocal objection, he was hired. Steve then cast around, signed up his old stuntman Dick Farnsworth and his, McQueen's, alleged lover Linda Evans, before auditioning his co-star on *Baby, the Rain Must Fall*, Don Murray. 'I went into the office . . . McQueen was there, haggard and grey, spewing into a Dixie cup he held in his hand. Obviously a very sick man. Friendly but blunt. Basically he wanted me to read for the part and I told him no, I wasn't going to do it there and then, stone cold, and what the hell, he knew my work anyway. Steve kept pushing the script at me and telling me to read. And I said, "No, I won't do it." He said, "Oh! You're a big star now?" and started needling me, all the while honking into his paper cup. We were looking at each other, and I remember telling him fuck it, I'd already done thirty movies and he could watch them anytime he wanted. And then I left.'

McQueen turned to Guercio. The old days could go fuck themselves, and sentiment could kiss his ass. He had big plans for *Horn*, and no actor who wouldn't do it his way was getting anywhere near it.

After a lot more like this, with various run-throughs and rehearsals, and numerous script re-treads, location work got under way in Arizona. Steve shaved off his beard on the first day of photography. The money shot of him, the camera zooming in on his lean face after completing a slow, reverential pan, instantly established that McQueen, albeit older, still cast a tall shadow. The magic was intact.

A day or two in, Marvin Josephson drove up to the set. He'd lined up the big deal as briefed, the biggest one ever done for an actor: $10 million plus 15 per cent of the gross for Steve to star in the film of James Clavell's *Tai-Pan*.

McQueen immediately looked his agent dead in the eye. 'You realise you'll make a million bucks' commission?'

Josephson's heart bled. 'Oh, how terrible, Steve. That only leaves you nine million.'

'But I thought we were friends.'

'We are,' Josephson said obstinately. 'We are. What's more, I've just cut you the sweetest movie deal in history.'

But McQueen had fastened obsessively onto a different detail. 'I'll pay you the fucking commission, but then I'm not going to use you as my agent any more.'

The meeting was over.

True to his word, Steve gave Josephson the freeze for a full three months, then came back to the fold. He wasn't going to read all the stinking scripts by himself. Plus, he told Josephson, maybe it wasn't such a bad scam after all; *Tai-Pan* fell through when the second of the ten pre-payments was late and the producer defaulted on the contract. Since McQueen had already, quite legally, banked the first instalment, it was he, not his agent, who walked away with a cool million.

Tom Horn broke down almost immediately Josephson drove back to the airport. Without even trying, Steve now accomplished in just two days what had taken him as long as a week on *Le Mans*: chaos.

He was hell in a car, but the vehicle he rode hardest of all was a film crew. *Horn* proved yet again that, no matter how great an actor, McQueen should never have been allowed near a call sheet or a bullhorn.

First, Guercio was fired. Cliff Coleman, first assistant director on the film, remembers 'Steve constantly sidling up to me asking, "What's wrong with the dude?" What was wrong was that he never flattered McQueen. Professionally speaking, I mean. Never a "Well done" or even "That's a take" – just some pop music guy ambling around in leather pants and a beret. Steve couldn't take that kind of negativity.'

On the seventh day of filming McQueen sent Guercio a note asking him to report to him in the Cortez. When Guercio arrived he was greeted by Steve sitting behind a small desk, still dressed up as Tom Horn, cradling a rifle on his lap. Peering at him with slitted eyes from under the brim of his Stetson, McQueen said, 'I really have to make a change and this isn't the movie I want. Thanks. Let's stay in touch.'

Guercio left, striking a note about halfway between a groan and a snarl. That was the last they saw of him in Arizona.

McQueen then actually took over the job for a couple of days, until somebody pointed out that Guild rules wouldn't allow it. So Coleman brought in his friend William Wiard, a veteran of *M*A*S*H* and *The Rockford Files*, to do his first ever feature film. Including McQueen himself, that made a total of five directors on *Horn*.

It wasn't, then, an unerringly calm touch on the tiller that distinguished Steve from the crowd. Rather, it was the grace and resignation that he brought to hand, a nagging professionalism and his intuitive feel for the audience. A great actor, not a film-maker.

On the other hand age was making him more considerate, and the cast on *Horn* saw a less cursory and, at times, altogether warmer McQueen. Whether lending money out of his own pocket or shutting down production for a morning to buy long johns and electric heaters for the crew, the old miserly reserve had matured into an empathy for his fellow troupers. Especially Linda Evans.

Minty herself came and went during *Horn*'s three-month shoot. As soon as she arrived she'd begin telling Steve about her latest modelling coup with the girlish excitement that appeared as natural to her as her chestnut hair or dewy eyes. He seemed to enjoy the company. Pat Johnson remembers how Steve and Barbara lived in their own trailer, with a corral out front, high up on a hill above the shoot, and that he, McQueen, would start every day with a run and then a workout; but then Minty would fly back to the coast and Steve withdrew into the world he automatically chose whenever threatened by desertion. The old habits died hard, although he had, at least, kicked the smokes.

McQueen wasn't aging that well. His skin looked like it was about to peel off in leathery strips.

Cliff Coleman's wife Martha was *Horn*'s unit nurse and before long Steve began asking her about respiratory problems. 'What should I know about bronchitis?' or, 'Tell me about pleurisy.' Coleman believes McQueen knew he was ill, and quite probably that he had cancer.

'Having raced with him, I know for a fact he used to pull an asbestos mask up over his face, breathing in that shit for years, primarily because the studios would have freaked had he burnt himself . . . Then, once he *was* ill, Steve quite truthfully wouldn't go for radical treatment, specifically chemo, because he didn't want his hair to fall out.' On this reading, a combination of paranoia and vanity tragically resulted in McQueen's death.

At the same time, he swaggered, swivelled a gun, ran and rode with all the old flair on *Tom Horn*. Nothing seemed to throw Steve until the climactic hanging scene, which, even after multiple tests and dummy runs, he wanted nothing to do with. His old friend Gary Combs doubled for him. Coleman suggested that they then shoot a close-up of McQueen's face, for verisimilitude's sake, 'with his eyes bulging out and all that stuff. My logic was if the hero's going to die, it should at least look realistic.'

No fucking way, was the curt reply.

Instead, Steve pulled back his cheeks with the sides of his hands to show how he'd looked when he was young. The face: fallen. The body: still gym-honed crumpet. Nobody was about to twist *his* melon, or smear him up like a pantomime dame. His skin, nicked with a few lines, had an embalmed colour, though his china-blue eyes were ageless under their heavy lids. McQueen confronted the camera with the look of an autumnal cowboy.

Much of *Horn* itself was worthy but shapeless, slow and often sullen where a *Getaway* had been shrill and strident, and so moodily lit you needed a miner's helmet to watch it. But there was also that primary-colourful, classic Western feel brought off by everything from *Shane* to *Nevada Smith*. *Horn* featured a generous minimum sunset quota, as well as a predilection for plains and shimmering mountains. The jangling spurs, chaps and floor-length duster coats were all present. For good measure a long rifle was thrown in. All that separated Horn himself from Josh Randall was the passage of two decades; that and the script, which called for Steve to sit squinting into the distance for what seemed longer than the title song of *Paint Your Wagon*. In a world where even the most perfunctory exchanges – 'What's it like in Injun territory?' Long pause. 'Lonely' – take up whole scenes, it's not surprising that nothing much happened in *Horn* until its hero, perversely enough, died.

Once you accepted the glacial pace and reworked history, *Horn* was an insinuatingly well-acted film. In particular, McQueen didn't so much play as inhabit the part, taking the audience with him into the dark and complex heart of the last of the 'enforcers', a journey of constantly unexpected discovery and frequent reappraisal. His Tom Horn was a genuinely original and credible and even occasionally moving creation. The character has the rangy quality of a Nevada, but also a wry gentleness not normally associated with Steve McQueen. Horn was, in short, fully human.

Released in March 1980, the film was a relative flop – doing less trade in a year than *Papillon* had in a month – suffering, like *The Shootist* and *Bronco Billy*, from public apathy towards the genre. A cyclical one: within ten years *Horn* would be rediscovered as a masterpiece of myth-debunking and a powerful starting point for the modern, deglamourised Western – notably Clint Eastwood's *Unforgiven*. McQueen and his various directors were responsible for a cult classic, in which narrative, character and human experience triumphed over blood and guts. A meandering film but an honest one. A less principled star would surely have rewritten the ending.

The second *Tom Horn* shut down Steve was off and running again,

junk-shopping with Minty in a new pickup truck, zigzagging down
I-15 laden with antique phones, lamps, fans, shoeshine stands, spi-
toons, coal scuttles, gum machines, ashtrays, radios, TVs, military
caps, hats, helmets and one fully working German blunderbuss. They
hauled everything west, then looped north again, bypassing Malibu
for Santa Paula. McQueen pulled into a diner right there at the
roadside and picked up the payphone.

'Get Feldman,' he told the First Artists switchboard. 'Don't tell
the bastard who's calling.'

'Who was it?' asked the other honchos, then in the process of
voting themselves out of existence in the boardroom.

'Superstar,' Feldman replied with a definite trace of alarm. 'Who
else?'

'What did he say?'

'"Take my final fee, change it into nickels and shove it up your
ass."'

Roughly fifty miles northwest of LA the road wound through
groves of orange and lemon trees into Santa Paula. Steve pulled over
at the exit and smelt cows and goats grazing in green fields that
reminded him of Slater. Except for the farms – neat, whitewashed
plantations staked out by American flags – there was nothing there
but open country, mile after mile of tall prairie-grass sweltering under
the California sky.

'Home at last,' McQueen sighed, wearing, for a moment, the same
warm, meditating smile as Minty. A full revolution had brought him
in a circle.

They moved there that spring, first camping in a large aircraft
hangar and then a four-bedroom, twenty-acre ranch nestling between
two gently rolling hills in the Santa Clara valley. It was an idyllic
spot. There were wide wooden steps that led up to the porch where
Steve liked to sit all evening, looking out over corrals and chicken
coops onto a small brook running into the river, and snow-capped
mountains beyond. He told a friend, 'I finally feel I'm back where I
belong. I want to die here.'

'McQueen was in seventh heaven,' confirms Bud Ekins. 'Right up
to the end, that last year was the happiest of his life.'

Cliff Coleman had told Steve that if he was serious about moving off the beaten track, then he should buy a plane and learn to fly. It became McQueen's latest obsession. The whole thing might have turned into a millionaire's fad for him, as it had for so many others who bought Learjets, dolled them up with Mylar mirrors and bathtubs and took off for their 'wellness' weekends in Aspen to discuss their next movie. But Steve wasn't interested in the future. He harked back to the past, to an era of barnstorming and air circuses, when pilots moved their dual-wing planes from one county fair to the next, skimming upside down, diving, swooping, miraculously soaring aloft in fragile crates made only of wood, linen and wire. There was a palpable danger to being a flyboy in those pioneer days, a breezy whiff of speed and seat-of-the-pants adrenaline; a true courtship of both life and death.

Bill McQueen's very world.

Steve and Barbara soon wandered into the small Santa Paula airport, leafed through some trade magazines and ordered a bright yellow vintage Stearman, followed, a few weeks later, by a green 1931 Pitcairn Mailwing. While the ranch was being fixed up they moved into the planes' hangar, bedding down there among the fuel drums and spare parts. By day McQueen began wearing oil-stained slacks or coveralls, his hair tucked under goggles and a flying helmet, his hands grimy from tinkering with engines. He loved to sit around with a beer talking to the old stagers, a new variant on the campfire jamboree he'd celebrated in yarns from *The Magnificent Seven* through *Tom Horn*. Steve was too advanced in the school of life to be reborn by a mere change of scenery, but friends like Ekins were left in no doubt that he was a more relaxed, benignly nostalgic man than they'd known before.

When McQueen introduced himself around Santa Paula he would mutter his first name and flip out a cold, limp handshake. His manner was always friendly but cagey, constantly assessing the all-important vibes, watching for the smallest effect of his celebrity. A day or two after buying the hangar, Steve quite deliberately rolled up a twenty-dollar bill and furtively dropped it on the floor whilst talking to a group of pilots. One of them reached down and promptly handed it back to him. McQueen told Mike Fargo that he'd been 'figuring the guy [would] wait till I wasn't looking, then put the loot straight in his pocket'. Real trust soon surfaced in the coinage such unheard of honesty brought.

'Nobody in Hollywood would have done what he did,' Steve told Fargo, with a bashful smile. 'Most of those bastards are like Dillinger.'

Soon he began taking lessons in the Stearman from a retired test pilot, Sammy Mason, significantly both an envelope-pusher and a devout Christian. Like Pat Johnson and Loren Janes, Mason was living proof of the fact that virility and faith weren't mutually exclusive. McQueen spoke glumly about his own chances of salvation, dissecting his whole life so expertly that it read like a film script. He summarised frankly, 'I've been a badass.'

'We all have,' Mason said. 'But there's good news.'

Steve took to the air as though born to it. Within four weeks he soloed for the first time, droning up between the mountains, then, on a flyby, flipping the Stearman over on one wing, waggling it, before climbing higher and higher until he tore finally into a calm, spring-blue sky that was sunny and pure, where he soon began, despite himself, mumbling a prayer somewhere between terror and sheer joy. McQueen made a perfect landing.

But, as always, Steve's sense of detachment held in what might have been best shared with others. His health, for instance.

When friends came to call on him in the hangar, he often received them lying flat on the concrete floor because his back hurt. Above a new beard flecked with grey, McQueen had a wan, pinched smile and a curious glitter to his eyes until they, too, darkened over. Scattered in his talk about flying and religion were hints that he couldn't sleep. 'I spew all night,' he told one friend enthusiastically – it was a point of pride for him to keep going, that he'd cough and sweat for hours on an oily stone floor and then hit the cockpit at a run. Steve treated all doctors, and particularly hospitals, much the way he treated movie studios. No forelock-tugging or due respect; only a wary disinterest and a truculent self-containment. By mid 1979 he was essentially re-staging the climaxes of both *Hell is for Heroes* and *The War Lover*, rewritten for real life. Suicide by combat was out, but suicide through passive, half-chosen fatalism was a final shrug of indifference, the

395

ultimate rebellion, a sort of unanswerable *fuckit*. Even Sammy Mason and the others had no comeback to that.

It was hard, until the very day he moved to Santa Paula, to imagine McQueen growing old and contented. Steve himself could never envisage 'wrinkling up and dying with a martini in my hand'. The prospect of parodying himself to an audience of paunchy, geriatric fans in the twenty-first century was unthinkable to the man who still insisted life ended at fifty. Later that year McQueen even seriously proposed mounting – at least financing – a paramilitary raid, along with his friend Chuck Norris, to rescue the American hostages in Tehran. His recklessness, in fact, almost killed Norris and several others who occasionally clung to him, for dear life, on the back of a motorbike. They didn't understand Steve's apparent death wish; but they were willing to take his word for it. Sure enough, he wrapped at least one Harley into the white birches that grew near his house, along the bank of the Santa Clara.

By midsummer there were only a few weeks left in which McQueen could have been diagnosed and, quite probably, successfully treated. 'I'm not going to a fucking quack!' he shouted at Minty.

'Never?' she asked softly.

'I passed the studio exam, didn't I?' It was true; the Warners doctor had asked his age, noted his height and weight and praised his ability to read off a chart. Then he'd had his nurse come in and take a picture of himself with his superstar patient.

'You're sure you won't go in for tests, Steve?'

He shook his head.

Gossip noted that McQueen, shockingly, now seemed to be at peace with his community. Unlike Malibu, there were few sensitive neighbours who were offended by his rasping late-night passes on the bike. In Santa Paula people were both proud and protective of the town celebrity. True, Steve made generous donations to funds for both the church and the airport. Yet the remarkable solidarity of the local farmers and migrant workers, not ones to be star-struck, wasn't the result of mere charity. McQueen, the practical joker, seemed to take life as a glorious lark. McQueen, the born actor, seemed to regard his open-door evenings as a performance with his guests as audience, and unless he entertained them he was a flop.

McQueen, the pilot, charmed the other fliers with his modesty and professional respect. McQueen, the collector, could get lost in contemplation of a fifty-year-old child's toy. McQueen, the new man, liked to throw open the door of his hangar and announce to the world, 'Welcome to another day in paradise.' Steve was the star of any occasion. He was tough, capable, kind, never Supie yet always his own man, not only a famous figure but a popular one.

His quiet enthusiasm and energy were infectious. There was an intriguing sense of suspense whenever he appeared at the airport, since no one knew what would happen next. Mr Steve, as he was coming to be called, was a shrewd judge of men and had a lively appreciation for loyalty. He was quick to muck in. And he was sentimental enough to do literally anything within his power for a child. When a local woman named Crystal Endicott mentioned that she desperately needed a week off with her gravely ill husband, but wondered who would watch their seven kids, McQueen's reply was instant. 'Me.' With that he moved in, played on his hands and knees all day, ate pizza, read bedtime stories, slept on a sofa in the living room. Seven children, seven nights. When Crystal Endicott got home she was met with an ear-bashing din at the front door. It was her young family begging that Uncle Steve be persuaded to live with them permanently.

Noise of another growing stir rose from McQueen's ranch that night. He built a towering bonfire and incinerated his entire drug stash on it. Now Steve's only chemical vices were beer and chewing tobacco.

Certain friends were inclined to wonder about the latest of McQueen's performances, particularly about his latest lover. Minty was the least competitive or professionally minded of his live-in mates, the most willing to be submissive to the Great Man. Many cronies didn't even know of her existence, although they would hear her scurrying into hiding when they called, or catch a glimpse of her hands nimbly passing a beer through the serving-hatch. Her first job, in fact, was to completely remodel the new house for him. Barbara remained, some churlish souls sniffed, more like a composite PA and geisha than a true partner, though others gave her credit for nagging Steve to kick drugs once she discovered that Steve would let her get away with it. A rare exception to the protocol of previous affairs, or of Santa Paula's Old Gang restaurant – where the all-female staff fairly fell over themselves to serve McQueen. Most women still only had identity for him as sexual quantities. Bubble asses.

By and large, Minty was happy to float about the house, smiling, with a mild, placid expression as glassy as water. Her mind was open on almost every subject.

One reason remodelling proved difficult and expensive was that the new home wasn't just a living space but a mosaic of Steve's memories, daydreams and possessions. He had to have old-fashioned fixtures and appliances, antique lighting, hardwood floors, anything that conveyed period authenticity. Builders added a warehouse for McQueen's growing collection of vintage bikes and other Americana. Then a customised garage. More corrals. The whole thing wasn't only a vast construction project but also a complicated assembly job that kept Barbara, a carpenter named John Daly and Daly's crew in repeated sessions around the clock. Meanwhile, Steve continued to operate out of a corner of his plane hangar, with just a thin mattress and a few sticks of office furniture, for five months.

As to movies: it seemed as though McQueen had wanted to quit them for years. He told Bud Ekins he planned to do *The Hunter* while he still could, his throat already raw, his voice gruff from the strangling intensity of all the coughing jags. (Ekins also believes that 'Steve didn't have enough money to retire. He damn near got wiped out by his first divorce, and don't forget, he was collecting like the Smithsonian.') McQueen was impatient to roll them. He met *The Hunter*'s producer, Mort Engleberg, there in the hangar, stuffed the script in his pocket and walked around with it for weeks trying his lines out on the dog. Padding through the shadows, mumbling, like the ubiquitous ghost said to haunt the ranch. A final, though not magnificent, obsession. There would be no more glory days. No more career moves.

Steve hired his old friend Eli Wallach for *The Hunter*, their first meeting in fifteen years. McQueen struck him as 'consciously looking for a way out; retirement, maybe, or something like Paul Newman achieved with his Foundation and his charities – whatever. I can tell you, though, Steve was tired of the treadmill.' Wallach had no idea that he was also mortally ill.

McQueen, Josephson and Solar's new secretary Holly McDermott read a few scripts and turned them all down. *Superman*, *Hang Tough* and *The Manhattan Project* duly joined the long list of teasingly unconsummated deals. Some mediocre directors had their reputations enhanced merely by the rumour that Steve was talking to them, or more accurately that they were listening to him ramble affably about their projects without the slightest hint of a commitment. Still role-playing, as if the only alternative were indeed the death he feared.

There was one exception. Loren Janes gave McQueen the screenplay of *Pale Blue Ribbon*, an unfashionable tale about two decorated American heroes of the Vietnam War. It wasn't a script for those who like their fighting men to be tinged with angst and bitterness and self-doubt and all the joys of an *Apocalypse Now*; this was a Vietnam shot in red, white and blue instead of the usual dour black and white. McQueen signed up immediately.

Six months later, on the very day pre-production was due to start, Janes got a call from Barbara Minty. 'Steve's ill,' she told him in a businesslike manner. 'We have to sit tight.'

'When can we re-schedule?'

Minty answered bluntly. 'Maybe never.'

Along with Janes himself, Pat Johnson and Sammy Mason, McQueen's lover formed a quartet of fiercely loyal *consiglieri*, the first three of whom he fondly called 'ass-kickers' who paradoxically launched his interest in religion. Minty's predecessors, meanwhile, faded from view. Neile now bought a new family home in Beverly Hills and asked Steve if he could lend her $40,000 towards its remodelling. He duly wrote the cheque, then called back the next day to tell her he was cancelling it. 'I'm broke,' he added.

'Sure, baby. I understand.'

McQueen lowered his voice. 'What does that mean?'

'It doesn't mean anything. I believe you.'

'No, you don't.'

Neile managed to speak without sarcasm. 'You can't afford to lend me the forty thousand. That's fine. Don't worry about it.'

'*Thousand?*' Steve rasped with gargantuan scorn. 'I gave you millions!'

399

He hung up. Later that same month Neile met Al Toffel, an ex-fighter pilot and distinguished president of the Norton Simon Museum, a man, she proudly says, 'who does in real life what actors do on-screen'. That was the last time she ever approached her ex-husband for a loan.

Then there was MacGraw, whose bizarre sex comedy *Just Tell Me What You Want* took the glitter off even her other post-McQueen romp, *Players*, in which she appeared as Maximilian Schell's wife. From there it would be downhill to the 'epic' TV mini-series *The Winds of War*, itself a Reithian public-service broadcast compared to Ali's role as Lady Ashley in *Dynasty*. That was the end to her screen career for a decade. MacGraw still occasionally phoned Chad McQueen in 1978–9, but could only wait for the day Chad's father would call her.

He never did.

Steve, meanwhile, was beating a remarkably optimistic path, almost to the brink of ecstasy, back in Santa Paula. Never had his prospects seemed better. He looked out of the cockpit at the clouds and the high sierras and caught a glimpse of heaven. Soon he began talking to Johnson and Janes, and then particularly to Sammy Mason, about what made them different, at least significantly calmer than himself. Mason invited McQueen to attend church with him. Ten years earlier 'on any Sunday' had famously meant revving up a dirt-bike followed by some vintage after-hours stuff involving, at minimum, beer and women; now it meant Steve shaving, putting on clean jeans and a jacket and driving the fifteen miles back to the coast, to Ventura Missionary Church, where he stood anonymously in the congregation every week for three straight months.

Not once that anyone knew of was he recognised, let alone hassled, that whole summer.

Shortly afterward, McQueen introduced himself to the pastor, Leonard De Witt, and asked if they could get together. The next day at lunch he told De Witt he was 'sick and tired' of Hollywood, had 'led a godless life' and – typically for one who did his research on every new face, let alone commitment – 'asked me repeated questions about Christ and the Christian walk'.

De Witt, in turn, had only one question of Steve.

'Are you willing to be born again?'
'Yes,' said McQueen.

Some of the old gang had a cynical interpretation of what they were
seeing. Steve already knew he was dying; he'd never have set foot in
a church except as a kind of insurance policy. But that was to woefully
neglect McQueen's famous sense of pity and compassion, self-evident
in all the donations and, more to the point, his lifelong empathy with
the underdog. De Witt himself, no soft touch when it comes to
character judgement, insists, 'Steve made a genuine conversion.
Christianity was all of a piece with his leaving Hollywood and search-
ing for new values. That's what we talked about for literally days on
end.' Soon enough McQueen wasn't only attending Sunday service
but a Baptist Bible Study group every Thursday morning at seven,
an hour at which he'd been known to be rolling his first joint. That
second half of 1979, shuttling between the church and his planes
and his prized antiques at the ranch, was the first time in his life that
Steve seemed like a whole man, instead of somebody trying hard to
play one.

That only left *The Hunter*. McQueen and his producer hired Buzz
Kulik* to direct, then joined the crew on location in Chicago. Steve
took and passed his studio physical. He rehearsed. He worked on
the script, blue-pencilling whole pages in favour of a looser, freer feel
– that brilliant grasp of his, as arduous as it was intuitive, for 'how
folks really talk'. Still, he wasn't fooling anyone. Even as he suited
up to become 'Steve McQueen' for the last time, he had Marvin
Josephson announce that his non-negotiable fee would now soar
from $3 to $5 million, plus 15 per cent of both the domestic and
overseas gross: unheard-of figures. Most friends agree that this was
McQueen's way of coolly pricing himself out of the market.

They'd never imagined his disdain had any use to it, but this time
it did.

The Hunter itself was another urban Western, although, like *Tom*

---

* Kulik had worked with Steve once before, in February 1958, on a live TV episode of
Climax called 'Four Hours In White'. The director had thought him 'a royal pain in the
ass . . . talented but undisciplined and totally insecure'. They kept in touch.

Horn, it hardly followed the conventional contours of a 'spear or gun' yarn. There were several spry, off-centre characters, notably Steve himself, who chose to play Thorson both laid-back and drolly against type. It was the same sort of self-parody John Wayne perfected in *True Grit*. With a few rare exceptions, the McQueen of this picture was resolutely uncool: anachronistic, low on gas, and romantically flummoxed. Above all, he was getting old. Older and better. But Steve's measured touch of humanity did little to redeem the shoddiness of the plot, terminally holed below the water line by a weakness for melodrama and farce, almost every scene either self-consciously jokey or stuffed with disturbing 'dark' ironies. McQueen did win the day, but uncertainly and unheroically, and most fans came out of *The Hunter* more perplexed than moved.

There were compensations. The tones and sub-plots were tethered tightly to character, Steve's own as well as Thorson's. Uncomfortable facts tricked up as fiction: the hunter as prey and maybe endangered himself, warily circling his younger, pregnant girlfriend amid the tribal savagery of the American health-care system. (McQueen's leading lady, Kathryn Harrold, was a ringer for Minty.) Most of the antique toys, the bifocals and the yellow Chevy were from Steve's own collection. The final scene of him lying spark out on the hospital floor, his eyes closed, was guaranteed (and probably designed) to jolt audiences just a few months later. As a film, *The Hunter* was untroubled by much atmosphere, let alone emotion; as a snapshot of McQueen's whole career it was a masterpiece of ruefulness. Who but him could have woven Josh Randall, a byword for youthful cool, into Papa Thorson? He couldn't have dreamed of a more perfect cycle, or shown up any better what it's like to actually live a life. It's left to *The Hunter* to remind us time and again not only of Steve's genius but also of how the man, too, like his characters, is a vanished breed.

By 1979 McQueen had begun to back off from the monstrous figure that he knew he'd cut on earlier films. There were no tantrums on *The Hunter*. Chad was again on location, as was Sue Ekins. Gary Combs thought Steve 'the warmest I ever saw him, particularly around children. He just couldn't help himself with kids.' Breaking a ten-year press embargo, McQueen now granted a front-page exclusive not to *Time* or *Rolling Stone* but to the *Federalist*, a local high-school newspaper. He told his teenage interviewer, 'I think the press is full of shit, but I do have a certain respect for youth.'

When the crew first arrived in Chicago, the supporting cast were shown to the midtown Holiday Inn while Steve and Barbara bunked down in a suite at the Drake Hotel. Engelberg waited in vain for a fractious call from Supie, quite possibly touching on the need for deeper jacuzzis or a private elevator. Instead, McQueen asked his producer, 'Where's everybody else?' then calmly insisted that he, too, be moved downmarket. Thereafter, Steve would sit up all hours in his room at the motel, playing poker with the grips and electricians and cheerfully ordering in pizza. While the guys laughed huskily over the cards Barbara sat hunched with her needlepoint, turning out one chunky sweater after another to ward off McQueen's – now perennial – 'cold'.

Seeing the change in mood, some of the crew weighed the merits of consulting Steve on previously taboo technical matters.

Within the week Loren Janes felt the moment had come to approach McQueen discreetly. 'Do you mind if I take this trenchcoat off? Or would you rather people still don't know I'm doubling you?'

'Oh, shit,' said Steve in a long sigh of amusement. 'Toss it. I don't mind *who* knows any more.'

From most insiders' point of view, McQueen's film sense was still intact; a talent Kulik called a cocktail of rattiness, humour and exquisite timing, and Wallach equates to a Rorschach test – 'He didn't seem to be doing anything much when you were actually acting with him, but then you step back to watch and whole pictures loom up out of the dots.' Yet something was badly awry. Steve wasn't interested in doing even the simplest of stunts any more. He often sounded short of breath. Janes felt 'McQueen was at his best and worst on *The Hunter*. It was one of his braver films, in my opinion, he couldn't have been sweeter, but it just seemed something was gnawing away at him. At the time everyone guessed pneumonia.' Pat Johnson, also on location, would sometimes rescue his friend from a crew party and gently suggest it was time for bed. None of his old gang had ever seen Steve tired.

Bob Relyea watched *The Hunter* the following summer and

immediately thought, *He's gone.* 'I knew him well enough to pick up on it. There was something tentative, almost laboured about the way he moved, not quite limping but hiding pain. It was one of the saddest things I ever saw.'

One day between setups in Chicago Eli Wallach happened to join McQueen at a window. They looked down and there in the street saw a young man loading up a truck before driving off with his girl. 'My God,' said Steve. His eyes narrowed mistily and he fell silent, swallowing. Wallach waited for him. 'God,' he muttered with a deep breath when he was able to continue, 'I'd love to do that – get rid of the office, the company, the agent, the manager and the lawyers and just take off into the hills with a good woman.'

Religion, meanwhile, had stealthily receded from McQueen's day-to-day priorities. But not quite. He still felt moved to give a cheque to the local Catholic church, specifically asking that it never be mentioned to the press. Steve and Pat Johnson occasionally went to mass together while in Chicago. Johnson was touched to see that McQueen would sing and affirm enthusiastically, but declined to kneel or join in most of the other ritual.

'I dig the serenity.' Outside, Steve bobbed his head again several times with a thoughtful air. 'Being in the house of God is wonderful. The greatest. It's the mumbo-jumbo I can't take.'

His ability for practical Christianity remained unmatched. McQueen's bent was for the grass roots, not for gourmets of religious arcana. With an unerring radar for the worst-off, Steve strolled over to a teenage girl working as an extra on *The Hunter*, gently introduced himself and asked how she planned to spend her per diem money. Nursing her dying mother, was the stark reply. McQueen made enquiries, confirmed the girl's tale and quietly arranged both to pay the mother's final medical bills and also to enrol her daughter in a private school. Steve's success in then keeping the unit publicist from hyping the story was itself a major achievement. A reticence at right angles to standard superstar behaviour. One night, again quite anonymously, McQueen and Loren Janes visited a recreation ground in a slum neighbourhood and left hundreds of baseball uniforms and bats and balls in the fieldhouse there. It wasn't a complex about his own wealth, Janes says; more that 'Steve had nothing growing up . . . His thinking was, he was going to give kids what he never had.'

Janes himself was lying alone in his room in the Holiday Inn on his birthday. A bleak, bare-walled cell that took on a life when Steve himself happened to be in it and a dearth when he wasn't. The house phone rang. A familiar voice asked Janes to be downstairs in five minutes, they were going for a ride.

'Where to?'

But McQueen just giggled and wouldn't say another word. He and Janes roared off onto the freeway.

It was actually a beautiful bit of road north of Chicago, with the lake below them on the right, and then sweeping fields on either side with the last wash of summer on them, and whether sitting, walking or driving, it was always a thrill to be with Steve when he was in the mood. An hour over the Wisconsin line he silently turned off the main road and cruised downhill towards a group of low-slung houses, junk shops and an old-fashioned diner. It was only a little farm town but they spent the rest of the day there, the two of them, browsing and eating, and when Janes looked up at a signpost he was so astonished that he burst out laughing.

The name of the town was Janesville, and McQueen gave his friend the personalised gift of a lifetime.

They finished shooting *The Hunter* back on a sound stage in LA, where Steve, now coughing violently, would complain of his 'Chicago cold'. Still, the wrap party put him in better humour, as it always did, and when he and Barbara drove up the dirt track to their ranch and watched the sun setting over the Santa Clara, he was in high spirits. It was Thanksgiving, 28 November 1979, the day Steve McQueen last performed in front of a camera.

He took his past to the bank in *The Hunter*, out the following July, which netted him an instant $5 million. But the larger public and particularly the press both turned away, embarrassed. It was as if the critics had been waiting for him. *The Hunter* did get a rave on 'Good Morning America', but others said it was trite, vapid, with no sense of the way a Thorson actually works, just an old actor's parody. A few years ago McQueen would have countered with a blockbuster, just as he'd followed a *Junior Bonner* with *The Getaway*; each new

405

work seemed to be a reaction to the criticism of the work that came before it. But not now. *Adios*. A reporter named Dave Wolf actually managed to call him at the ranch to commiserate. 'People genuinely want the best for you, Steve,' he said, when he came on the line. 'It's like they're personally bound up with who you are, so they're apt to be disappointed . . . That's the price for being real to them, Steve,' he added gravely when he heard his deep sigh.

'I dare say you're right, Dave,' McQueen agreed.

Steve had first worked with Eli Wallach in 1960. 'See you in another twenty years,' he told him hospitably, roaring with laughter, when *The Hunter* wrapped. But, all the same, Wallach couldn't help feeling something was wrong. He remembered what McQueen had said about wanting to take off into the hills, and he wondered where and when they might actually meet again. To his surprise, Wallach found he was shaking all over.

'That was the last time I ever saw him.'

Steve spent two weeks finally able to enjoy his new house, fully refurbished by John Daly into a combined period home and museum for the antique accumulation of years – entire fleets of vintage cars and bikes, Western memorabilia, furniture, kitsch, guns, knives and several hundred model planes – which McQueen insisted be moved from his hangar. He flew. He went back to church. Two or three times a day the shooting pain began, and Steve had to lie on the floor, but after a while it eased off, and he sat up and chewed some tobacco. Then one winter evening, in the bedroom, McQueen keeled over as if he'd been shot. He could barely catch his breath again. Overnight, Minty's deference ended. Steve, who had never taken orders in his life, had orders now that he'd take if he wanted to keep her. Tests. No more bullshit. A full diagnosis and treatment. Resigned, McQueen nodded groggily. His doctor in Santa Paula took X-rays on a small, portable machine but couldn't find anything much wrong. Still muttering that he was being shanghaied, but now racked with pain, Steve allowed himself to be admitted to Cedars-Sinai hospital in LA. He checked in there, under the name Don Schoonover, exactly a week before Christmas.

It was the very place where Terry and Chad had been born, where he'd been sewn up time and again after his latest shunt, and where he used to sit, quite alone, reading for hours to the patients in the pediatric ward. That night he lay there in the dark, struggling with the thought that the children of the world were all suffering terribly, sick and hungry, until, gradually, the phobia was replaced by a real one. Minty came back at a run when the results were in four days later. Even down the corridor she could hear him coughing and then start wheezing and laughing it up with the nurses. No doubt about it, he was an operator, but at least he was her operator; he didn't divide his loyalties, and in the last year McQueen had been kind, considerate and even faithful beyond her wildest dreams. He loved her, she remembered, knocking quickly with the code on Room 8501, look at how he'd given up dope. A big deal like that, all for her. But Minty had also changed him in matters of more importance to himself. What she'd given Steve, though she didn't recognise it, was precisely the thing he'd been chasing his whole life, and whose consequences would have stunned even Neile or Ali: the desire to truly live and be happy.

Barbara went into the room and listened to the diagnosis. She stood at the window but didn't hear or even notice the Christmas parade go past on the street. It was all lit up. Darkness had already fallen over Hollywood, blank grey to its farthest reaches.

The Role of a Lifetime

'We'll fight it,' said Barbara. 'We won't give up.'

'Do I ever?' said Steve, and he laughed.

That was all they said, but it stuck in Minty's mind as a counterpoint to the doctors' clinically impassive verdict: a large pleural tumour on the right, already metastatic, evidence of a rare form of cancer called mesothelioma. The prognosis was terminal.

McQueen spent his last ever Christmas in hospital, in that dreary green room with photos of his children and his planes taped to the wall nearest his bed. After chemotherapy (soon discontinued at his request) and several painkilling drug cocktails, he was able to discharge himself on 29 December. When all the nurses leaned out of the window to wave goodbye, they noticed he stood there like a statue, his face grim and set, while his blue eyes shone with extraordinary brilliance. The doctors warned Barbara that Steve would gradually begin to lose his faculties, and that with a high-grade malignancy like his, spreading wildly through his body, surgery was useless. They gave him three months to live.

McQueen put it about that he had a 'fungus infection on one of my lungs – nothing serious' and actually asked Marvin Josephson to keep sending him scripts. He kept the news to a tight circle: Barbara, Sammy Mason, one or two other friends in Santa Paula. Neile heard, and then the children. Two months later, on 1 March, Pat Johnson got back from working on a new film in Texas. There was a phone message from Steve. Johnson drove out to the ranch the next morning. After a few minutes' small talk the pair of them went up the winding farm road for a walk. When they reached the top of the hill McQueen turned round and put both his hands lightly on Johnson's shoulders. It was a bright, early spring day, and from the hilltop they could see the far-off Rafael mountains, with islands of dark pine rising out of the plain. Oil drills bobbed in the distance and the dust they raised coated the leaves of the trees. Steve stared at him with his wide, friendly eyes and, speaking in a level voice, told him the whole story, promising to fight and keep fighting, until Johnson felt his heart hammering and his own eyes filling with tears. They walked back downhill in silence to the ranch. As he went inside McQueen was smiling again, and, smelling his beloved pork chops, almost found himself giving Barbara a wink.

Brave was no word for it. It was as if he were consoling *them*.

Steve said nothing to his other close friends. But he did drive back to the Missionary church in Ventura. Leonard De Witt remembers, 'He brought me up to speed . . . The exact phrase I recall is, "Now I've become a Christian, I have a greater reason than ever to live. I *want* to live. But, if I don't, I know where I'm going."'

'I mean to cure the cancer as naturally as possible,' McQueen added. He'd already had his fill of chemotherapy and radiation; the side effects were everything he'd feared and, as he told De Witt, 'I don't want shit messing with my mind.'

'And have you settled on an alternative?'

'I haven't. Not yet.'

In fact, Steve was in and out of Cedars-Sinai regularly during those first weeks of the new decade. Further X-rays only confirmed that the cancer was spreading. All the doctors could reasonably hope for was a holding action – a stay. New, experimental drugs, particularly one called interferon, made McQueen's face swell up and left him with a palsy so that his hands often shook uncontrollably. But on his better days he felt indomitably that he'd win through by sheer willpower. He always had. Steve's main ire was directed not at the disease itself but at the so-called specialists, his latest models of that towering ego endemic to the breeds of condescending, uppity bastards he'd long fought in the film business. After a day or two in hospital McQueen would have himself driven back to the ranch again, just the spark needed to trigger another explosion about 'those fuckers downtown'. To a skewed imagination like his, the spectre of Cedars-Sinai conjured up a miasma of both greed and cravenness, and the realisation that the 'medical establishment' had all the vertebral qualities of the Blob.

Steve didn't like being told he couldn't do something. Especially when that something was to carry on living. So he finally checked himself out and decided to explore other options; also hellish enough, although the spectrum of pain was infinitely wider.

His independence was unimpaired.

McQueen, in his last ever interview, would say the mesothelioma had 'two causes . . . One is asbestos poisoning in my lungs, which is very rare. Two is, I think there were times when I was under pressure – I had a battle in my business with somebody for about five years.' In the search for culprits, Steve's casual stripping of ships' engine rooms and his later use of a padded driving mask both tended to be cited along with the other risk factors like stress and cigarettes. Then again, both his parents had died in middle age. There were those, too, who remembered how he'd often stayed in and around the desert town of St George, Utah, on his way to drop peyote with the Navajos. St George was an atomic test site as well as the location for a film called *The Conqueror*, almost all of whose cast (including John Wayne and McQueen's old friend Dick Powell) were later stricken by cancer. Some credulous fans even felt that, by vanishing at the peak of his power, Steve was somehow fulfilling the plot-line of *The Thomas Crown Affair*. In other words, that he faked the whole thing simply to fade away.

McQueen didn't dwell on it much, himself. Speculation was an idle luxury. Seeing that he'd been handed a death sentence, the great thing was to beat it, or, failing that, to live the best possible life with the largest possible range of options. If that meant twisting a few final melons down the way, he would.

'We'll fight it,' she'd said.

'We'll fight it,' he replied, gently pulling her down into the hospital bed. As the minutes ticked away, he stared at Barbara's small body and waited for a dog, a car, another Christmas float, anything, to break the silence that hung over the room.

It was quiet on the ranch too back in January, the month Steve brooded on his future, except for the night sounds of insects. You could hear their embroidering movements in the weeds outside, which somehow gave the effect of some grating voice in the night, needling him. Or you could listen to the fat thudding of the light bugs and the batting of their big wings against the wooden porch behind McQueen's bedroom. Some of the bugs were clinging heavily to the dozens of hanging baskets, like idiot killer bees in *The Swarm*. One fucking disaster he hadn't made, Steve thought, as his face worked into a strained, chesty laugh. They'd actually asked him, too.

Under this droning canopy two people sat in silence, tilting back and forth in wooden rockers, violently so, the woman almost sprawling into the man's knees. Crowded, he swung around and faced the dark ground below. Down a flight of steps a dirt track rose and fell straight ahead with antique gas pumps, barber's poles, chairs, benches and a big kerosene stove all strewn around a clearing, sliced cleanly away, between two steep hills. It was late and he liked to sit in the shadow the hanging baskets made against the house light. In the grass and the glade, and on the track itself, he could see whole rows of vintage bikes, some with sidecars, a green pickup truck, spare parts scattered about, tyres, mechanics' tools and, around them, in the clearing, more ancient rocking chairs.

'How many have we got?' he muttered.

'Rockers? Exactly a hundred and one.'

'I may need one soon for the plane,' McQueen said. 'I'll bet there's a law against it, but my back kills me when I'm up there. It's crazy to bust my hump flying.'

'For you, baby, nothing but the best.'

Steve started with mistrust. 'What do you mean by that?'

'Oh, sweetheart.' She laughed aloud. 'I mean it. It's so thrilling to be in love with a man who's the best on the ground *and* in the air. I can't tell you how happy I'll be when we're married.'

Barbara had actually begun this campaign nearly a year earlier, when she put their friend Crystal Endicott up to asking McQueen what his intentions were. He'd told Endicott, 'I'm not interested if she's after my money.' Steve did, however, acknowledge Minty's own

411

good qualities, like his, both horizontal and vertical. She continued to lobby throughout 1979, gradually impressing even seasoned McQueen-watchers like Loren Janes as 'yet another one-in-a-million woman'. Janes had told his friend on the set of *The Hunter*, 'Introducing someone as "my lady" may be your idea of class, but it isn't mine. It isn't classy at all. What you're really saying is, "This is my shack-up."' He pinned Steve with a deep stare. 'Neile was a saint. Ali was a saint. And Barbara's a saint, too. You ought to marry the girl. You'll both be much happier.'

That kind of horse sense got McQueen thinking. When the news came in that Christmas, he told the Endicotts, 'If I'm a goner, then I want to make sure Barbara's provided for.' Another, less charitable view is that it was precisely Steve's own welfare, not hers, he was most concerned with. As a friend says, 'He was sick and he needed her to be there.' It's inconceivable that McQueen didn't already know, in his mind's eye, about the horrors to come, the many nights drugged or in pain, with the prospect of increasingly tortured breathing, sunken cheeks, withered arms and legs, stomach swollen like a pregnant woman's, all freedom, all joy and all life drowned out by the reek of wastes and disinfectant, and the inevitable final submission to strangers looming down at him, now kept going only by sheer willpower, wearing their hideous, institutional uniforms. He certainly knew.

In the end, however, Steve's thinking may have been neither compassionate nor self-pitying. It was competitive.

Neile and her partner Al Toffel planned to marry on 19 January 1980. She told McQueen over the phone that he wouldn't be invited. 'I love you, Steve, but *I'm* going to be the star of my own show.'

That same night McQueen phoned the county clerk, contacted Leonard De Witt and told Barbara to go shopping for an outfit. He beat Neile to the altar by exactly seventy-two hours. Steve's third wedding, like his second, was informal, held right where he sat in the living room of the ranch. The groom wore a sports shirt, blue jeans and tennis shoes. Minty chose all-white, with a small wreath of baby's breath in her dark hair. De Witt not wanting to condone a previous divorce, the service was conducted by his assistant Leslie Miller. Sammy Mason and his wife Wanda were the only witnesses.

Also invited, though outside, were two farm workers, brandishing rifles, who blocked all access to South Mountain Road. In the end, there was no problem – the tabloids were as taken aback as Neile was.

Among his biker friends, at least, it was a running gag that McQueen still wanted to get all three of his wives together in bed. Instead, he soon made a friend of Neile's husband and even apologised to them for having upstaged their own wedding. He didn't want people to think he'd been jilted, he said.

The first morning Steve headed back to Cedars-Sinai after the ceremony, Minty was waiting at the door, his travelling case packed and ready. Then, head lowered, lugging her own bag, she followed him into the car.

Once they exchanged vows, Steve approvingly noticed a resilience begin to flower in Barbara's personality, at least as expressed around himself. The thought that she wore a ring on her finger (even if, as friends noticed, he didn't) seemed to give her a new lease of life, and she stuck with him through all the agony and reproach to come. Meanwhile, she organised the ranch for him, served up his favourite burnt pork chops and pie, even, in time, learned to fly. But she had enough respect for her late father to realise that Christianity meant more than mere empathy, and that first Sunday morning after leaving hospital she had the truck revved up to drive her new husband to Ventura. Thereafter they were regulars at the eleven o'clock service, until McQueen's health broke down and they resorted to their own 'intercessory sessions' at home. Steve, she noticed, prayed in a low voice, but with the emphasising effect of a piledriver.

One of the other Ventura parishioners was lighting a fire in the grate before early morning Bible class when she heard a step behind her. She paused, a bundle of saplings on her knee.

A man's shadow fell across the patch of dusty light thrown over the cherry-wood floor.

'Am I early?' asked an apologetic voice.

Steve came in, a bit thinner than before, helped the woman with the kindling and then sat down, half in firelight, half in shadow, to talk. For nearly an hour he spoke about his personal commitment to the church, his admiration for that 'together cat' Leonard De Witt,

413

his deep respect for the Bible. McQueen told her he was reading John 14, and indeed he quoted the verse, 'Let not your heart be troubled, ye believe in God, believe also in me,' as 'real sparky . . . I wish somebody'd hit me over the melon with that twenty years ago.'

That gospel made a big change in Steve. For the first time in his life, he said, he was 'grooved together'. Finally, at the last, at peace with himself.

All the same, some of the old beer and biker clan just couldn't credit it. To them, the views he held, the things he said (particularly about being born again) sounded like a scam; but meanwhile, McQueen carried on in much the same way on the ranch, with only Minty and a few friends. The verse he'd memorised was matted and framed, and hung over his bed. He still loved to fly and to collect ever more period junk, but the highlights of his week now fell on Thursday and Sunday, respectively kneeling in the Fireside Room, or standing in his favourite place in the church balcony.

Steve's serenity was tested severely just a few days later. Yet another demoralising trip to the hospital: the interferon and all the other drugs he'd been taking since Christmas had done nothing. By now the tumour had spread to both sides of McQueen's chest and was attacking his liver, stomach and pelvis. To compound matters, word about his condition was beginning to get out. This put half Hollywood in a flutter, because everyone who had ever even heard of him had a theory, usually to do with dope, some post-Manson juju, or, at the very least, an exotic killer like syphilis. Terminal cancer, apparently, was insufficiently hip.

Pity had taken the place of anger in him. Steve not only never complained – not once – about the worsening physical pain. He now felt that the tabloids, like the doctors, were 'just doing their gig', however badly, and he began praying for them.

McQueen also quietly told Marvin Josephson not to bother sending him any more scripts. *Tell 'em I've retired*, he said. *Tell 'em I'm a flying rancher*. The scam was over. How could he be satisfied by the cartoon cut-out of a *Superman* when real life stared him in the face, and his prayers howled to be answered? Steve was losing his taste for play-acting. There was much more he was good at, namely guts, grit, poise and sheer stoicism, all of them, in the end, cool and above all more rawly heroic than any film. Even the biker gang were struck to the heart by his combination of courage and good grace.

There was a reason that fate had brought him to the top of the heap. It would be up to fate now to lead him somewhere else.

Where some stars have trouble retiring, McQueen had been counting the days. Had he lived, it's quite probable he could have had a long second career as a character actor, much like his old friend Paul Newman. It's debatable, however, whether Steve would have wanted to still be in the saddle at seventy-five. For the very life of him he could never take the candyass side of the job seriously. Particularly as a Christian, McQueen saw the strangest contrasts between the ridiculous aura of fame and glamour that surrounded Hollywood and the legacy of trash and mild depravity it left in its wake. He now claimed to enjoy 'only a handful' of movies, tops, most notably *High Sierra*. Of his own twenty-eight pictures, Steve's vaunted coolness took second place in his personal hit parade to the quiet resonance of *Junior Bonner*.

Twenty-nine years earlier, McQueen's friend Mark Rydell had immediately seen how he had talent but wanted to avoid giving even the faintest hue of any moral commitment to his craft. 'He got into acting because he didn't want to bust his ass. Plus, there were more chicks in the profession.' It was one of the paradoxes of Steve's superstardom that, like most things he really wanted, it soon turned to dust on the getting. He went about acting in much the same way Nixon went about politics: shrewdly but always warily, paranoid, hate-filled, stress spots dotting his mouth like dollops of blood. McQueen never recovered fully from *Le Mans*, and took but spiritless notice when the critics panned his last few films. He told a friend and employee, Grady Ragsdale, 'Let's face it, pal, I'm out of the picture business. I've done my last movie. Good riddance.'

Meanwhile, life on the ranch was strictly casual within certain set rules. Steve liked to spend his mornings out at the airport, either aloft, or, in bad weather, holding court in the hangar. A few friends would be invited to lunch at the house, where McQueen sat indolently, often feeding scraps to two or three dogs who swarmed around him at the table. Nowadays his schedule called for a mid-afternoon siesta. He'd then reappear to tinker with his antique toys or canter out with his wife until dinner. Steve had no real appetite any more, or it came and went, but he liked to linger over dessert on the back porch, sometimes picking at his pie for an hour or more. On his better days he and Barbara might eat out at the nearby Old Gang or Las Quince Letras restaurants. But the good days were fast drawing to an end; more and more, life became one long series of visits to the hospital and the church until they, too, ended.

Three months after diagnosis, the full time he'd been given to live, McQueen now stayed close to home, both he and it watched over by Minty, Ragsdale and a housekeeper named Wilma, all of whom knew that, for Steve, period detail, antiquity, anything that conveyed tradition and nostalgia scored heavily over 'modern shit'. They probably also realised that what they were seeing was one man's revolt against history, a kingdom that was hermetically sealed against the republic that surrounded it, an oasis of vintage Americana in a desert world of *Polyester* and punk rock. McQueen was fast losing both weight and interest in that spring of 1980. 'Did you read the piece in the *Times*?' Ragsdale asked.

'What piece?'

He took a calculated risk. 'The review panning *Tom Horn*.' Steve barely looked up from his workbench. 'Why not write back and tell the guy he's full of it and you're still the best-loved actor in the world?'

McQueen shrugged. 'What's my motivation?'

He truly didn't give a shit any more. What mattered nowadays was church and the airport and the Rose Bowl flea mart, where he still went every weekend chasing both kitsch and antiques, a collectomaniac who bought Zippo lighters as well as Old Masters. By the time Steve died he owned fifty-five cars, 210 motorbikes and more than 10,000 pocket knives, toys, appliances, gizmos, gas pumps, cash registers, jukeboxes, safes, ashtrays and telephones. Between times he'd drive in to see Pat Johnson or fly the Stearman down to Sand Canyon, park it and eat lunch with Loren Janes right there under the wing. Janes, who was one of the first to hear of the cancer, found 'he was ready to try anything, be a guinea pig . . . His feeling was even if he died, maybe the doctors could learn from it and help somebody else.' But the opportunity for a cure, both men surely knew, had gone. The late-afternoon sun shone through the struts and gave both McQueen's plane and skin an orange cast; towards dusk the old friends hugged, and then Steve took off again between the mountains. Janes stood watching the yellow biplane soaring with increasing speed over the horizon.

Most of the inner circle could scarcely believe their eyes. Men like Janes and Bud Ekins had never seen McQueen so calm before. Whether through religion, remarriage or illness, he was at his very best in the year before he died. This conciliatory, sober man reminded them of the young actor because the two were nothing at all alike. The young actor was titanically ambitious and pushy; this man was docile. The young actor was promiscuous; this man was a model spouse. The young actor had believed in nothing and trusted nobody; this man believed in God and his own redemption. 'A lot of stuff's been written about me over the years,' McQueen would tell Ragsdale. 'Some of it's true and some of it's not. Good or bad, it don't matter. Things are different now, and I have Barbara to thank for that. Now I only want to be happy.'

They were two of a kind when it came to this. He'd caught on. He was caught in. From now on he and Minty were only in a race against life.

Steve did, however, suit up, climb on a Triumph and meet Dean Jones one last time in their favourite watering-hole. They came in across the desert for miles until they reached a chaotic shack ringing with laughter, blazing with red and yellow lights and echoing with the snarling thud from the jukebox. The place had no pretension to elegance. To the beautiful people from Palm Springs, the Stein Room wasn't good enough: hopelessly downmarket, smoky, naff, urinous and catering to greasy bikers. It was the best bar in which McQueen had ever set foot. He couldn't think of a runner-up. 'Home, sweet home,' he smiled. A gum-chewing waitress loomed up from behind a pile of sprockets and asked him what he wanted.

'Frogs' legs Provençale,' he said, winking at Jones.

Ten minutes later she served them up, as fresh as if they were dining at Maxim's. Simple as that. (The Stein's new cook, it miraculously emerged, had been the chef at a five-star restaurant in Chicago.) To Jones, the whole scene was freighted with both humour and a sense of destiny, as if Steve automatically expected to be served frogs' legs at a desert pitstop. He was witnessing an example of how strongly McQueen wanted things and, not infrequently, still got them. The old friends parted with a hug.

Sammy and Wanda Mason happened to call in at the hangar one morning that spring and found Steve slugging an Old Milwaukee. He looked up at them with that piercing, icy-blue gaze. 'I suppose you disapprove.'

'Not at all. But, you know, you may find the Lord takes that particular desire away.'

It was true. Within a week or two McQueen couldn't bear to touch a beer. With a quizzical shrug, he went out behind the hangar and emptied his entire stock down the drain.

That 24 March Steve turned fifty, the age at which he'd always said 'the guy on the bike [would] hit the broken glass' and die. In fact, McQueen's breakneck crash-and-burn scenario took nearly eight more months to play itself out. With his reputation for contrariness fully intact, the endgame began.

He spent that same afternoon sitting on an office chair outside his hangar, speaking to Ragsdale with that incandescent nostalgia that often moved him on birthdays. 'I sure don't feel any older,' Steve said. 'Hard to imagine all the stuff I've crowded into my years. Thank the Good Lord some of it's been good . . . real good.'

Ragsdale nodded, and McQueen gazed up at the mountains, gradually laughing harder and harder until his lungs ached and his mouth was full of the taste of bile. He remembered the good times with Neile and the family, racing, and then all the shit. You could count on the shit. But he'd felt himself change, not just physically, although he'd swollen up and shrunken down, but spiritually too. Deep down. He'd felt it and he'd watched it, and he wanted to make a film about it, shout it from the mountain tops, bawl it out: *Let not your heart be troubled, believe in God.* But now he never would. Slowly he panned back, studying his audience through the corner of his eye, hesitating tactfully.

'I want to ask you something,' he said at last. 'You know, I've done everything there is to do. Freaked out in the drug area and the women area, and all that. I don't want to go into details, but I just need to know. Can someone like me enter the kingdom of heaven?'

'Yes, Steve,' said Ragsdale.

McQueen nodded slowly. 'Seems like I've spent half my life getting into trouble and the other half trying to get out of it.' He pulled a face and turned away. 'I've wasted so much time.'

'But you've been a huge success,' Ragsdale reminded him loyally. 'Aren't you proud of what you achieved?'

'No.'

By now people noticed how thin he was looking under all the padded clothing. Most of his friends knew something was badly wrong, and finally even the most quarter-witted Hollywood media, the ones Steve had shunned for their glib dramatics, got behind the story. One of the nurses at Cedars-Sinai told an agent, who told somebody's manicurist, who duly told a reporter. That same week of his birthday the *National Enquirer* led with the scoop: STAR'S HEROIC BATTLE AGAINST CANCER. The article spoke of a 'vicious and inoperable' disease and informed the world, for the first time, that Steve McQueen was a dead man.

Publicly, he threatened to sue.

Privately, he used the word 'terminal' and told old friends to pray, though not to worry about him.

In a show of defiance, he and Barbara drove in to the press review of *Tom Horn*, held down the road in Oxnard. The small Mann Theater was refurbished for the occasion. Towards dusk the local police began putting up barricades to accommodate both the overflow audience and hundreds of curious bystanders. The lobby was turned into an art gallery, festooned with original posters from *The Great Escape*, *Thomas Crown*, *Bullitt*, *Papillon* and enlarged stills showing Josh Randall in an array of tough-guy poses. Two huge klieg lights picked out the marquee – STEVE MCQUEEN IN TOM HORN. As the curtain went up, the man himself was still nowhere to be seen.

'Now, folks,' the theatre manager said, 'I know this is a big night. But if everyone will just remain calm and –'

The man's walkie-talkie had started to crackle. It was the Warner Brothers publicist stationed at the corner of Highway 1. 'McQueen party on the way!' the lookout squawked. Soon enough, the old green pickup slowed to a stop on Main Street. Wearing jeans and a leather jacket, ten pounds lighter than he appeared in the film, Steve jumped out with Barbara at his side. They were mobbed by fans and reporters alike, both wanting to know if the *Enquirer* story was true.

'Do I look like I have lung cancer?' he smiled.

McQueen got through the night with a mixture of skill, grace, actor's training and sheer *chutzpah*. Once back at the ranch he collapsed with exhaustion. While the red carpet was being rolled up at Mann's, Steve was heavily sedated and returned to his room.

McQueen, it was pretty widely acknowledged, was a tough customer. For most of his life he'd gone out of his way to be different, but he was never merely perverse: the likes and dislikes were always functional, building up an apparatus of self-containment, what Jackie Bisset calls his fugitive side, 'glad to be there, glad to be gone'. High on Steve's list of pet peeves were institutions in general and hospitals in particular. Over the years he'd done everything possible to self-medicate rather than submit to treatment – for his deafness, for instance – let alone to surgery. He swore he couldn't understand why anyone but a professional masochist would want to be sawn open by strangers, or why anyone but a sap would follow doctors' orders; while if everyone just chugged two aspirin with an Old Milwaukee, as he had, the world would be a better place.

In April the specialists told him, yet again, that there was no hope. McQueen's chest now wheezed like the mew of a cat and the sweat-soaked nights were torture to both him and his wife. When Cedars-Sinai suggested that he check in there and, in effect, wait around to die, Steve rapidly began sifting his options: homeopaths, nutritionists, Mexican-licensed endocrinologists, anyone at war, as he now was, with the American Medical Association. Later that spring he spent six weeks flat on his back in a camper parked behind a squat, rundown clinic in the San Fernando Valley, being fed an intravenous diet of vitamins, minerals, antioxidants and more exotic substances. McQueen had to rent the camper since legally the clinic couldn't provide the treatment on its own premises, or at any other business address in the United States. When Cedars-Sinai then took more tests, including a lung tap, Steve found his condition the same, if anything worse, the surgeons' platitudes unchanged. 'We can make you comfortable,' they said.

He wanted to kill them.

Aloud, McQueen said nothing, but that night he told Barbara to start buying up health magazines, journals, self-published alternative rants, anything she could lay hands on. Later that week he took her on a belated and, as it turned out, truncated honeymoon, cruising down to Acapulco on the SS *Pacific Princess*. It was a disaster. Barbara herself bounded up the gangway on the first morning smiling and waving. Steve, tottering behind, gave no stronger sign of pleasure than a thin, ambiguous smirk. People noticed how painfully thin he looked. The couple kept to their cabin (number 348; McQueen had its own chart done) for three days, then rushed home by jet. Steve had spent the whole time heaving in grim rhythm to each wave, unable to eat, drink, walk about or sleep. He lost nearly twenty pounds. As soon as they drove up to the ranch, Barbara rang Loren Janes to tell him what he already guessed, that *Pale Blue Ribbon* was in turnaround.

Clearly, McQueen reacted to his diagnosis both as a challenge and as an opportunity to accept the inevitable gracefully. Soon he began phoning most of the old friends he'd jettisoned down the years: Elmer Valentine, Yul Brynner, Stan Kamen, Mark Rydell, Mario Iscovich, Richard Attenborough. One morning that summer Hilly Elkins got a call. 'Come to lunch,' said a raspy but familiar voice. 'My treat.'

Elkins succeeded in not actually gasping. 'Where?'

'Ma Maison.'

Now he was seriously rattled. 'The old Steve, the Steve I knew, wouldn't have gone near the place,' Elkins says. 'More likely a burger joint downtown.'

They duly met in the celebrated restaurant, McQueen almost concave around the cheeks, brandishing a foot-long Veracruz cigar, his new treat to himself, and waving happily when the other customers cheered him. 'He wanted people to see him functioning,' says Elkins. 'To remember him as the man he once was.'

And so Steve settled back with an air of victory, finished every last scrap on his plate, hugged Elkins and finally strode out to the pickup with Barbara on his arm. People were still clapping when he started his truck. Applause and ignition: the last two sounds McQueen ever heard in Hollywood.

Meanwhile, Ali kept leaving messages, wanting to visit. As some friends see it, Steve's refusal wasn't so much a moral stand as an act of revenge against MacGraw for unspecified offences committed during the marriage. It's more likely he simply didn't want her to see him in his humbled state. Physically bowed, but mentally charged. Already the twilight zone of Malibu seemed to belong to an unrecoverable past.

'Not now,' McQueen told her on the phone. He cleared his throat quietly. 'Best leave it alone.'

'But we needn't.' Ali pursued the point doggedly. 'I could be there in an hour.'

'Best not,' said Steve softly. 'I never wanted to disappoint you. I don't want to now.'*

The drawbridge clanged shut. But McQueen had, through Barbara's persistence, already read an article in the *Journal of Health Science* that caught his eye. It was about nontoxic treatment for cancer and, specifically, one William D. Kelley, the former Texas dentist now running the International Health Institute out of his farm in Winthrop, Washington. Steve and his wife drove there. The place was an outpost at the fork of two rivers, where the grey early light seemed to linger between the hills and ancient tractors worked in the blowing dust, all of them decorated by small American flags snapping in the wind. The end of the line, long since fixing a frontier legend on the world: the first ever Western novel, *The Virginian*, Gary Cooper's breakthrough, was written in Winthrop.

McQueen introduced himself to Kelley as Don Schoonover. Kelley, a lean, rangy man – like some wrangler in *The Virginian* – looked grim, and Kelley grim was as joyless as an upright corpse in cowboy shirt, jeans and boots. He looked Schoonover over and told him he

---

* McQueen did, however, later call to ask Ali to bring Josh Evans to visit him, and presumably to say goodbye, in Santa Paula. Unfortunately she wasn't free on the suggested date, so the meeting never took place.

needed to start a 'body-cleansing diet' without delay. Schoonover, as Kelley still thought of him, duly took away the literature and promised to stay in touch.

Steve actually knew much more about Kelley than Kelley knew about Schoonover. As usual before entering into a relationship, he'd hired a detective to do a background check into the other party. The man's report was a mixed one.

Kelley was then fifty-five and fighting a guerrilla war against what he calls the 'vast cancer industry' in America, with its terrifying and expensive preference for radiation, surgery and chemotherapy over the kind of holistic regimen he set McQueen. Kelley himself had apparently cured his own cancer some years earlier by way of vitamins, large quantities of enzymes, shampoos and massages. He was also something of a pioneer in the use of coffee enemas to detoxify the body. To help the process along, he even marketed a particularly strong roast called Kelley Koffee. What Kelley claimed to be 'ecological therapy' was dismissed elsewhere (and still is) as rank quackery. His book, *One Answer to Cancer*, was temporarily banned by a court order. At the time Steve met him in Winthrop, Kelley was being investigated by more than a dozen federal agencies, notably the Internal Revenue Service and the Food and Drug Administration. He and his wife were selling wholesale vitamins and busily developing his 'theory of metabolic subtypes', by which patients were given a custom-tailored programme designed to bolster their own immune systems against the disease. There are perhaps two or three dozen people alive today who credit their survival to the Kelley method. Most mainstream cancer specialists, on the other hand, tend to see him as nothing more than a cocky charlatan with a permanent place on the Cancer Society's unproven-methods blacklist, and a nasty sideline in anti-semitism.* Kelley today describes himself as a

---

* As just two examples, the startling charge that 'the great Tuberculosis, Polio, AIDS, and Cancer epidemics of this [twentieth] century have been proven to be caused by the biological agents used by *the enemy within* – the Establishment – the Jews and their Whores' and '. . . They, the Jews, Satan's literal children, cannot help stealing, lying, cheating, deceiving, plundering and murdering. They are evil and lawless Luciferian animal beings.' (Sources, respectively: *Cancer Ignorance* by William D. Kelley and Carol Morrison-Kelley; and *Gene Pools* by William Kelley.)

'medical missionary.' By general consensus he's kicked against the establishment for thirty-five years, haranguing, in particular, the American Cancer Society with contrary views and a relentless flow of articles and speeches. The establishment, for its part, has learned to yield Kelley a wide berth rather than enter the briar patch of a row with him. His attraction to a man like Steve McQueen seems obvious.

Kelley was just then moving his home base to Mexico, as all medical missionaries must, because that's where the 'controversial' and 'sinister' clinics are, squat red-roofed bunkers baking in the dust, well out of reach of American law.

McQueen, ironically, was then considering his own move in just the opposite direction. For at least a week or two he managed to convince himself that his cancer had been brought on by the pesticides the local farmers sprayed onto the fruit groves around his ranch. He resurrected his idea of retiring to Idaho. Ernest Hemingway and Gary Cooper, Steve's two great American role models, had done exactly that in the late 1950s. Men like Clint Eastwood and Arnold Schwarzenegger would buy homes in the state in the 1980s. Idaho was McQueen's Great Escape, and it was easy to see the connection he must have made between North Fork and the good earth of Geiselgasteig, the square green and gold fields and the brown, sunbaked mountains on the horizon. The land was cut by streams and the white of a river showed through the trunks of the tree plain. 'I wish we already had a family and we could all live there,' said Minty.

'I wish I could fucking breathe and I could live there,' Steve snapped. His wife took the brunt of his frustration. 'I can hardly cross the street now, let alone the country.'

'But you're doing so much better.'

'My ass is gone,' said McQueen.

A decision was deferred. With his legendary cussedness Steve kept going and even kept denying he was ill. Bud Ekins rode up to Santa Paula one Sunday afternoon and found McQueen sitting on his back porch drinking coffee. 'What's this shit going round? You got cancer?'

'Fuck, no,' said Steve, pulling off his shirt and happily cocking his head. 'Does it look like it?'

Ekins echoed him with a laugh. 'Fuck, no.'

McQueen carefully kept his hands by his side, which is why his friend couldn't see the fresh biopsy scar in his armpit.

Soon afterwards, Steve and Barbara had dinner with Don Gordon at Gordon's beach house. They hadn't met for months and Gordon instantly knew something was wrong. 'You sound kind of rough. What's up?'

McQueen was guarded in his reply. 'Just a cough,' he said and hesitated. 'I can't seem to shake it.'

Again, no mention of cancer. But by now Steve was desperately ill, kept bolt upright only by brute willpower. He told his last ever interviewer how he'd considered going out not with a whimper but with a bang heard round the world, flying one of his vintage planes into the ground. The tumour might have so hollowed him out that at night it was all he could do to stop from screaming, but McQueen's mind was miraculously clear. His hoarse aside to Terry as he went in for yet more futile therapy had a pathos and raw integrity worthy of a Jake Holman.

'I'll take any pain they can throw at me and maybe it'll help somebody else. Killing myself won't.'

'Promise me, Dad.'

'I promise.'

Gradually, Steve stopped going first to the church and then to the airport. He only barely had the strength to drive without help. Now gaunt but with a distended belly, heavily bearded, McQueen would see only Barbara, Neile, the children, along with one or two intimate friends. He was bedridden most of the time he was at home and he received visitors sitting in a wheelchair. But he was alert, and he was feisty, as only Steve McQueen could be feisty, angrily zapping the doctors downtown for 'stiffing' him. Each day he lived was another day that Cedars-Sinai had told him he wouldn't. *Adios.* He'd already proved the candyass specialists wrong by four months.

He went in for more tests that last week in July, the same week *The Hunter* was released to decidedly mixed reviews. The head doctor pulled Barbara aside and told her, 'It's incurable, it's inoperable. All I can suggest is that Steve gets his affairs in order.'

'Bullshit,' McQueen snapped when he came round from the sedative. 'Get the truck, gas it up. Pack. We're heading out of here.'

'Where?'
'Mexico.'

Life's a scam.

Apart from the odd lunch, the habit of not paying for anything
was deeply ingrained in McQueen, in part sustained by some
unusually good friends. Stan Kamen's own last present to him was
a prototype mobile phone. It weighed five pounds and sported an
aerial, but for the next few days scores of people around the country
– Yul Brynner was one – picked up their own phones and heard
Steve calling from his truck 'just to say hi'. He loved the new toy so
much that, stricken with guilt, he finally rang Kamen himself and
offered to pay him for it. Kamen told him no way, let bygones be
bygones, it was his.

McQueen responded to the gift by also letting Kamen pay off his
first month's phone bill.

Even with his new plaything and a large on-board cooler stocked
with chocolate, cakes and pie, the journey south was a sorry descent
for Steve. He'd spent twenty years with a loyal entourage who rode
with him, tabbed him, drank and smoked with him and, above all,
came when he whistled for their company. Now he was a lonely, sick
man, with only Barbara beside him, stealing over the Mexican border.
At least it was terra cognita for McQueen; from his first honeymoon
through *The Magnificent Seven* and dozens of dirt-races, safaris and
lost weekends since, Mexico had long been a second home. He revelled in the simpler life south of the border and would wander happily
around Tijuana, loosening his tight springs and lubricating himself
generally over a round of tequilas. Steve was mild as the night air
down there, and his heart felt as light. Even fucking Brynner brought
back fond memories.

The battered truck crossed through Customs early on 31 July, a
Thursday, and continued down dusty, one-lane roads twenty miles
to the seaside town of Rosarito. There, on a hill, Steve saw a compound of red and white Spanish bungalows surrounded by trees
and fences. A pool, tennis courts and freshly manicured lawns all
confirmed the impression of a well-heeled resort. McQueen pulled
up and stared across the bluff at the sheer white beach below. It was

perfectly quiet. Slowly Steve got out and stood for a moment on the clifftop, breathing hard, almost ready to run down to the water and jump in, but paralysed in the hot morning sun, finally turning back towards the gate as a deep murmuring rose around him.

'Mr Schoonover?' He grunted yes with his hands stuffed in his pockets.

Two massive guards in dark suits waved him in. The place, which was called Plaza Santa Maria, had actually been a spa until only a few months earlier. William Kelley, among others, was now running it as a clinic. Kelley's numerous critics would claim that, with no lab and no X-ray equipment, Plaza Santa Maria still seemed more like a composite club-asylum than a medical facility, though there were nurses, therapists and young American doctors – many of them completing their qualifications – on hand. Barbara kept assuring Steve that she was with him and that he was doing the right thing.

Kelley himself was there to greet the gaunt, stooped figure who checked in, pulling nervously on a cigar and only now revealing himself, for the very first time, as Steve McQueen. When Kelley re-examined his patient he found a blood clot in his arm, a tumour in his neck and fluid in his abdomen. One lung had collapsed. McQueen was immediately put on painkillers and shown to a two-room cabana with Barbara and a nurse called Teena Valentino. It would be his last real home. Steve spent many of his remaining nights there, alternately praying with the women or berating them, strangling with rage and bellowing in pain simultaneously with each agonising gasp for air.

Kelley's core philosophy involved detoxifying and strengthening the patient's own metabolism. He went about it by developing a complicated computer program of treatment for each case, specifically prescribing high-fibre diets, large doses of vitamins and minerals, baccilli Z extract, laetrile, sheep embryo shots, enzyme implants, saunas, massages, shampoos, chiropractic adjustments and twice-daily coffee enemas. This last indignity particularly grated with Neile and many of Steve's old friends when they heard about it. Men like Don Gordon and Dave Foster could only look balefully on the whole Mexican circus.

One morning six weeks later McQueen woke up euphoric and a

believer in miracles. He actually felt halfway well and appeared to be hungry again. Kelley insists that his patient was, at this point, in dramatically better health, although sceptics like Neile counter that what the clinic offered Steve (for which he was paying $10,000 a month) wasn't so much a cure as hope.*

McQueen began taking short walks along the clifftop and even watching some of his old films on video. Barbara, saintly in just about, if not quite every account, sat up with him and, on his good days, fed him his favourite ice cream. On Steve's bad days she played every role imaginable beyond simply that of wife – gofer, nurse, someone for him to rant at in pain. Even then, he always told her he'd make it. His entire confinement, until the very end, McQueen betrayed the stubbornness of someone who still loved to twist melons. With mesothelioma, sadly, further relapse was inevitable and fatality the rule.

Before he could prepare himself, the improvement abruptly ended.

Meanwhile, the decadent lunacy began. Tipped off by a nurse, the *Enquirer* and the rest began staking out the clinic, generally pandering to the unstable affections of fandom, and specifically offering $50,000 for a picture of Steve shuffling around. Pending that, more gaudy voyeurism: Kelley himself flew to LA, arranged a press conference and appeared on the chat show *Tomorrow*. He took the opportunity to raise not only hackles but public awareness of his war with the American Medical Association. '[Those] doctors gave [McQueen] no hope. But his chances are excellent . . . I believe with all my heart that this approach represents the future of cancer therapy. It took Winston Churchill to popularise antibiotic medicine. Steve McQueen will do the same for metabolic therapy.'

From that day on, McQueen had only to set foot outside his bed for the media frenzy to begin.

The hysterical doorstepping soon revved up with local and European paparazzi, stringers for *Time* and *People* and a satellite-uplink truck from CBS (with its corporate logo of a leering eye) all jostling together on the bluff overlooking Plaza Santa Maria. Before long the

---

* 'His chances are excellent if he has the discipline to follow the programme,' Kelley now announced.

whole place was a shrill, seething crowd of klieg lamps and bazooka-barrelled lenses. Several of the trade writers arrived from Hollywood. One bard announced he was there in order to prove to the world 'the bastard is really croaking'. The fights began at once, raging not only over turf but soon ploughing down ideological lines: two journalists began rolling about on the ground debating Kelley's methods, then two others. Four more columnists lurched by in a rowdy group, and joined in the conversation; three were yelling, and one whimpered brokenly about suing should anyone touch him. One more hack appeared, bellowing querulously about an exclusive, bringing the total congregating there in just a few minutes to nine, all but one of them screaming at the top of their lungs. The guards at the gate cast a cold eye, alternately watching the fracas and the lazy meanderings of the pet iguanas that had long ago fallen into the habit of living off scraps from the clinic kitchen. The wind blew dust along the ground into their mouths as they gorged.

McQueen woke up the morning after the *Tomorrow* interview with an acid stomach and exactly the same excruciating lung symptoms he'd had when he checked in. He realised at once what it meant, frenetic optimism giving way to pitiable melancholy. Then other-worldly calm. Steve himself was never drawn to the full-bore riot thundering just a few hundred feet outside his bungalow door. 'My only job,' he said with genuine conviction, 'is to turn people's heads around a little bit. Prove that I'm into the Lord, and that [Kelley] is cool. He's got this whole gig going for a dying movie actor.'

'What are you talking about?' Barbara asked suspiciously. 'You're not dying.'

'Of course I'm dying. We're all dying. Do you think I'm afraid of it?'

That same evening he showed a print of *Le Mans* to some of the other resident patients in the clinic's common room. Many of them stood to applaud him. Steve was wheeled up to the screen, where he acknowledged the tribute with a smile and a wave of his baseball cap. His extreme weakness was obvious, and brought tears to everyone's eyes.

He was, however, controlled and collected. McQueen told Barbara that his mind was grooved because of a new verse he'd found in the Bible, 'For God so loved the world, that he gave his only begotten

Son, that whosoever believeth in him should not perish but have everlasting life.' He quoted it incessantly as he submitted to the dire boom-bust cycle of the therapy and of the cancer generally: moments of mild progress followed by inevitable relapse. The end was coming, and he knew it. He was a man who'd spent his lifetime honing a remorseless honesty, selling reality (an escapologist, never an escapist), facing unpalatable facts. But there were consolations. For all Kelley's competing claims, the true presiding God, for Steve, remained the one he had first discovered in the blue skies above Santa Paula. Quotations from the Bible were plastered everywhere in his room, many of them illustrated by candles flickering alongside white stucco busts of Jesus and the Virgin Mary.

It was hot and humid inside the cabin, and McQueen was either too weak or too paralysed by the various treatments to do much moving around. He listened like an unwilling eavesdropper to the muffled, often rising drone of the voices at the gate. As he lay sweating in the shuttered bedroom, his breathing shallow, his eyes blank, he sometimes made or even took calls on his field phone. Stirling Moss remembers speaking to him, and Steve 'not complaining about or even mentioning his illness'. Kent James heard from him sounding 'quite calm, and wondering if he could visit Montana'. Much closer friends like Bud Ekins and Loren Janes agree that McQueen didn't seem particularly enamoured of the new confessional culture. The last time he ever saw Ekins, he'd yawned and said casually, 'If anything ever happens to me, I want you to have the best two bikes in my collection. No fucking arguments.'

'That,' says Ekins, 'was Steve's way of telling me he was going to die.'

A few weeks after their last dinner McQueen had invited Don Gordon to Santa Paula. They sat out in the sun at the airport, talking and laughing and bullshitting about the old days, until, towards dusk, Gordon remembered that he still had to pack for a night flight to London. 'I'll see you,' he smiled, deeply impressed with how well Steve was.

McQueen turned towards him with a faint glimmer of mischief. 'Yeah, see you.'

For the first time in twenty-two years, the two men hugged. That, too, had been Steve's way of saying goodbye.

Back in the clinic, McQueen was more forthcoming about his condition, which he didn't downplay. 'He said to me, "I have cancer. I don't know what to do,"' says Norman Jewison. 'But, knowing the guy, I still felt he'd beat it.' Hilly Elkins, James Garner and Buzz Kulik all offered encouragement. Ali MacGraw wrote, but never got a reply. Dozens of letters from ordinary well-wishers also found their way to Rosarito. Dean Jones called on the same day he learnt that Steve was ill. They spoke innocuously for a while, and then Jones asked if he could visit.

'I don't think so,' Steve replied in a faraway voice. 'I look so bad, I wouldn't wish myself on my worst enemy.'

McQueen's answer didn't upset Jones so much as the funereal tone in which it was spoken.

'How do you feel, Steve?'

Jones sat down. He was surprised to find that he was almost weeping.

'You've heard, have you?'

'Just generally.'

'It's not that I'm afraid to die,' McQueen said quietly. 'I'd just like to live long enough to show Christians I'm not a flash in the pan. That I'm born again.'

Steve gave orders for almost everyone to stay away, Ali included. He wouldn't have them see him that way.

'*Never*,' he'd say, as he tried to chew some tobacco, just before the Mexican orderly came in the bungalow. He and the nurse gathered around McQueen's bed for another galling round of treatments.

Of those who did make the journey to Rosarito, most remember it as a looking-glass world suspended between the sea and the mountains, where scraps of bird-song mingled with the sad little church bell tolling below them in the plaza. The few friends McQueen allowed came up the dusty beach road, at the top of which a lavender tree swayed in the breeze; as into a cave, they entered into the field of its shadow. Once through the mob, they gave their names to the guards, passed through the wrought-iron gate and turned down a cobblestone lane to Steve's simple white bungalow. Barbara or Teena

431

Valentino would peer through the curtains and open the door. The place was deathly quiet. Candles blazed in front of the scriptural quotations and a few Polaroids of cars and planes. Privileged visitors like Chad and Terry were shown into the back bedroom, awed by the hush that enveloped the whole house. Although McQueen was desperately ill, his upper face was still that of a mischievous child; his pouchy dark eyes widening at the sight of a Mars bar. He still talked like a kid, too, in breathless arpeggios, but he coughed agonisingly in old man register, and his mouth looked grey and worn as a burnt tyre. It was difficult for him even to swallow.

Grady Ragsdale appeared at the clinic in mid September, bringing with him Steve's flying helmet, goggles and other treasured possessions. 'I can only sit up for about twenty minutes at a time,' McQueen told him. 'But the doctors are really encouraged. They say my tumours are definitely shrinking.' Bill Maher came a few days later and Steve began to cry. A nurse wanted to work on him right there, even while his business manager was with them in the room.

'Beat it,' McQueen growled, rising with as much dignity as the pain permitted. 'What kind of way's that to treat someone? To treat *me*?' he added in a gruff whisper, as though the truth had only dawned on him in that moment. Him. Supie, the man who had had everything.

The scene upset Maher, but that was nothing compared to Neile's reaction. Steve's first wife visited Rosarito on 26 September and was appalled to find him in a 'sham' clinic, being treated by a man certified in dentistry. Neile's misgivings intensified as she watched, numb with shock, while yet another of McQueen's nurses filmed him even as he spluttered and winced over a vitamin cocktail, on the grounds that 'he looks so cute'. The debate between Steve's family and friends soon reflected the growing controversy about Kelley in the media generally. When Don Gordon, back from London, heard about Plaza Santa Maria, he seriously considered putting together a rescue mission.

'We'll hire a helicopter,' he told Neile. 'Land the fucker right there in the grounds, grab Steve and bring him the hell home.'

'We'd never pull it off,' she told him.

'I can raise the money,' he persisted with a rush of blood, imagining his old friend being simultaneously abused and neglected. 'It'd be dangerous, but what the hell – he's *dying*.'

'Don, please don't. There's nothing we can do.'

So McQueen lay there as the southern nights drew in, watching his old films, praying and reading the Bible. The gateway outside was full of small noises: the whining of photographers, the falling to the ground of bits of lavender, ever more voices pleading their claims on Steve and how to cure him. A very few of them made it to the bungalow. McQueen spent much of his last month on the fringe of unconsciousness, listlessly agreeing to the odd suggestion, usually involving a combination of religion and left-field holistics. At one stage he sent for a faith healer. Towards the end, Steve asked for Neile and her husband to visit again and made them promise to look after Terry and Chad after he died. Al Toffel, Neile's real-life hero, agreed immediately and would never once waver from his commitment in years ahead.

Bill Maher returned early the next day along with McQueen's lawyer Ken Ziffren. 'Let's roll 'em,' Steve said. There was no time left.

Ziffren snapped open his briefcase. At various moments over the last year McQueen had made certain promises about bequeathing gifts, mainly cars and bikes, to old friends like Loren Janes. Relatively few of these promises would be incorporated into the will he signed from his bed that morning. Some of those same old friends could, and did, wonder about the balance of McQueen's mind. Shortly afterwards Steve found himself negotiating with Televisa, Mexico's national radio and TV network, about his broadcasting a message of thanks to Plaza Santa Maria. Neile, on hearing this, suffered a further plummeting feeling as she realised 'the charlatans were winning', her once-proud Esteban just a tool in someone else's propaganda war.

Certainly too, in these final weeks, McQueen was nearly maddened with pain. At all events, the solace of a devoted wife, his ex, his son and his promise to his daughter wasn't enough to deter the possibility of suicide. Boiling blood, a drowning feeling in the lungs, weight loss and nausea; it's not surprising anyone would have taken a hard look at his options and wondered if the game was worth the candle.

433

Mesothelioma tends to be an idle cancer. It rouses itself to killing only when the patient is demoralised and it can give the *coup de grâce*. By early autumn Steve was in abject shape. Mouth and throat were inflamed, he found eating near-impossible, with little appetite anyway, and his nights were hellish. Only a man of his mettle would have refused, as he ultimately did, to crack under the stress.

On 2 October McQueen had his press agent, Warren Cowan, issue a statement confirming what the world had known for two months: 'The reason why I denied that I had cancer was to save my family and friends from personal hurt and to retain my sense of dignity, as, for sure, I thought I was going to die.'

Steve's ambivalent feelings about going public were only escalated when yet more journalists gathered at the gate, men and women whose concern about personal hurt and sense of dignity were quickly matched by the consideration of a hefty bonus. The deathwatch now began. The Hunter had become the prey, holing up (just as he had in *The Getaway*) south of the border, down Mexico way; the fugitive-bounty theme extended by a new going price of $80,000 for a shot of McQueen in extremis. According to one reporter who says he was seized by remorse and shame each time the press cracked a new joke about the coffee enemas, 'We were only doing our job. Steve would have understood.'

McQueen was ill. McQueen was dying. And what really mattered, he was also sensationally good copy. After that first public statement William Kelley found himself being flown, first class, to network television studios to prop heated debates more reminiscent of professional sports coverage than of the previously staid world of tumour therapy. Speaking on NBC's *Today* show, one California surgeon accused Kelley of 'total quackery', bringing the retort: 'We have a good, scientific programme, based on years of medical research. Steve McQueen has upset the establishment by coming forward to challenge the chaotic medical care system in our country. When he came to us, Steve had been sent home to die. We have already extended his life beyond maximum predictions.'

With politicians like Orrin Hatch (broadly sympathetic to Kelley) jigging along, the American Medical Association, *New Age* magazine and Plaza Santa Maria all now began a *danse macabre*, with Neile and Don Gordon watching, distraught, from the wings. 'I firmly believe [McQueen's] chances are excellent,' Kelley announced. He spoke rapidly, in a low modulation like Steve's, the words all run together. There was something about him many in the McQueen camp didn't like, a faintly ghoulish manner and an ego not wholly averse to publicity. Even on television, they noticed, Kelley remained a bony, hollow-cheeked man with the look of a prematurely hatched bird, whose Adam's apple danced up and down his narrow neck. They disliked him perhaps out of plain jealousy over his having staked a claim on Steve, or perhaps because they hated the idea of all his vitamins and enemas and shampoos, the image therapy by which, to them, Kelley conned his desperate marks. Either he appealed to McQueen on some gut level or a giant hoax was in the offing.

Or both.

On 6 October Steve's negotiations with Televisa bore fruit in a brief speech he read (though only an old photo of him appeared on screen), aired between two prime-time programmes:

> To the President of Mexico, and to the people of Mexico. Congratulations to your wonderful country on the magnificent work that the Mexican doctors, assisted by the American doctors, are doing at the Plaza Santa Maria hospital in helping in my recovery from cancer. Mexico is showing the world this new way of fighting cancer through nonspecific metabolic therapy. Again, congratulations – and thank you for saving my life. God bless you all . . . Steve McQueen.

His voice husked over the last few words. To friends like Bud Ekins it was a gutsy final act of rebellion, while others, notably Don Gordon, could only wince as Steve was paraded, something like the glazed-eyed POWs in Hanoi, in support of Kelley's magnificent treatment of him.

Ali MacGraw happened to tune in to the speech on her car radio as she was driving up Pacific Coast Highway to Malibu. Hearing that familiar but strange voice, she pulled off the road and wept.

★   ★   ★

435

Kelley insists that McQueen was actually recovering and 'could have returned to a normal lifestyle . . . Steve's tumours were dead or dying. As a doctor, I saw some hope.'

In contrast, Neile and many of the other non-medical visitors were extremely pessimistic. They didn't regard Steve's withered limbs and swollen belly as evidence of the miraculous triumph of radical over conventional therapy. They regarded the sight of a weak, barely conscious McQueen as a sad commentary on what happens when a dying man and his young, well-meaning wife hook up with a plausible operator like Kelley.

In fact, the real miracle-worker was Steve himself.

He never once complained, protested or broke down in public. Despite telling his last ever interviewer, 'It's pretty tough . . . they [the doctors] won't let me have anything to ease the pain,' McQueen remained typically or mainly cheerful, and always up for a good prank. He was in a predicament: ravenously hungry in his dreams, but nauseous in his waking hours. McQueen's solution was to dictate a long list of forbidden foods, burgers, fries, shakes, brownies, fudge and lashings of ice cream, which he charmed the orderlies into smuggling in for him. Little or none of this junk would actually be eaten. It was enough that he had it there just to gaze on.

Steve's pastor Leonard De Witt was one of the few friends invited to Plaza Santa Maria. He remembers McQueen as 'very weak though very coherent, and at peace with God'. The two men discussed plans to have the evangelist Billy Graham visit either the clinic or Santa Paula. After De Witt left, Steve turned to his nurse. 'The thing is,' he said in a quietly choking voice, 'I used to be a badass. Neile left me because she couldn't take it any more. Now I want people to know I've accepted Christ, turned my life around. I'm not afraid to die.'

'You're not?'

'No.' McQueen spoke softly, leaving no room for misunderstanding.

Pat Johnson and Marvin Josephson followed to Mexico a few days later. They happened to coincide with one of the cancer's false remissions, when Steve actually looked and felt better for a day. Relief from pain flooded through him, raising a flush in his cheeks. 'Pat,' McQueen ventured, winking at him from out of a gaunt but ruddy face. 'I'm going to get well, move up to Idaho with Barb, kick back and sit around a potbellied stove all day. Will you come with me?'

Johnson said that he would.

The next day Steve was worse again. 'I used to be more macho,' he told his final interviewer, Brugh Joy. 'And now my ass is gone, my body is gone, is broken, but my spirit isn't broken. My heart isn't broken.' He reaffirmed his Christianity. McQueen's final recorded words were, 'It's not that I'm falling apart, but I'm running out of gas.'

On 24 October, against Kelley's advice, he discharged himself from Plaza Santa Maria, insisting on 'a vacation' at home in Santa Paula. The McQueens' truck was brought to the back of the bungalow and loaded up under cover of night. Steve was in excruciating pain. He himself took the wheel for the entire 200-mile journey.

Meanwhile, in scenes out of *Mission: Impossible*, decoy cars with smoked windows took off up the Ensenada highway, then fanned out in a diversionary movement south and east down Baja California. McQueen was safely back on his ranch before the pursuing media pack realised its mistake. When they doubled back up to Tijuana, the press were stopped at the border by American immigration authorities who kept them waiting for hours before letting them into the country. The delay was because of an anonymous tip-off someone had phoned in about drugs.

Steve and Barbara spent the next ten days in Santa Paula. It was a change but not a vacation, not quite that. McQueen was now visibly sinking, as evidenced by his slate-grey eyes, grizzled skin and freakishly swollen stomach. He could barely chew, and the challenge was further complicated by the fact that, now that he could, he binged openly on junk food and cigars, chased down by a few tasteless but nostalgic nips of beer. According to Kelley, Steve was, in fact, quite 'cancer-free' and the bulbous tumour on his abdomen already dead, although he was, admittedly, suffering from associated problems like backache and urinary blockage. McQueen himself revealed no more emotion at this apparent miracle than a faint, knowing smile. Most of his friends, as opposed to the doctors, believe he had no illusions about his health. Visitors to the ranch had an uncanny conviction that Steve could see the future with altogether too much clarity. He said little, yet knew everything.

McQueen's old biking friend Cliff Coleman talked his way past the flacks and drove up to Santa Paula. He hadn't seen Steve since *Tom Horn*. 'I got there and saw the house with all the vintage cars and antique gas pumps outside in the yard. It was strangely, almost spookily quiet. Eerily so. From somewhere behind a tree I could smell smoke . . . I walked over and there was this skinny old man, no more than a skeleton with dark eyes and a matted beard, sitting swallowed up in an armchair, nipping on a cigar. I did a double-take and it was Steve.'

The sight shocked him; McQueen looked like a corpse and in a dry, rasping voice began asking Coleman about painkillers. 'I can't take it anymore,' he told him.

Coleman couldn't find the right words for a moment. 'Morphine,' he mumbled at last. 'What's that do for you?'

'Nothing.' Steve bowed his head in mute frustration and began to weep.

Coleman felt close to tears himself. 'I don't know what to tell you, kid, except to go back to Mexico and give it a try.'

McQueen flung down his cigar. 'Shit, they're doing their best,' he granted philosophically. 'But I don't know how much more I can take.'

'If anyone can beat it, Steve, you can.'

'I don't know.'

Halloween came and McQueen rang Kelley at Plaza Santa Maria. He wanted his stomach tumour, whether dead or alive, surgically removed. Kelley and a Mexican heart specialist named Cesar Santos Vargas flew to Santa Paula to examine Steve and warn him of the risk – some say fully 50 per cent – of his not surviving. Kelley knew that complications could arise from even a simple tooth extraction, and so advised his patient. McQueen, now constipated, nauseous, insomniac and breathing from an oxygen tank, was in no mood to worry. Arrangements were duly made for Dr Vargas to operate on him at the Santa Rosa clinic in Juarez, immediately across the border from El Paso, the town where Steve and Ali had famously bolted at the end of *The Getaway*.

Pat Johnson came the next day and found McQueen in bed, desperately thin, barely conscious, and with a loaded .45 pistol on the night stand next to him. Steve saw Johnson notice it. 'I've thought about it,' he whispered, stabbing a bony finger towards the gun. 'But I promised . . . I'm gonna fight it, Pat. See it through to the end.' Johnson kissed him gently on the head. The deterioration was so terrible that for a while, like Coleman before him, he felt as if he were trapped in a nightmarish film. Johnson had never seen McQueen so weak before, nothing like the hale man he'd just visited in Mexico. For the first time he wondered what was going to happen. He was less sure of himself than before when he continued, and his voice wavered.

'I love you, Steve.'

There was no more to be said. Everything was clear and McQueen nodded his head. The only unknown factor, the future, suddenly seemed the most obvious of all.

Neile soon followed with the children. Twenty-four years of laughter and tears had prepared McQueen's first wife for anything. But the silence was so deathly, the room so still and the old man in the bed so pitiable that they heard her suck in her breath. When Steve woke up he told the family he planned to spend that Christmas with Barbara and Al Toffel and them in Idaho. With incredible fortitude he smiled and even cracked jokes, his face winking up at them in a fold between the muted light and the shadows. It was his last performance. Later, when Terry and Chad left for a minute, McQueen took Neile's hand, looked her in the eye and said, 'I'm not going to make it.' He apologised for all the years of philandering. As Neile, now also blinking back tears, left the ranch she realised that it was 2 November, the day that could and should have been their own wedding anniversary.

Steve's final visitor in Santa Paula was Billy Graham, who prayed and read the Bible with him for several hours. Graham recalls that 'I'd planned to minister to [McQueen], but as it turned out, he ministered to me . . . I saw once again the reality of what Jesus Christ can do for a man in his last days.' Steve's parting words to him, still beaming broadly, were, 'I'll see you in heaven!' There spread through even the hired nurses wheeling McQueen out to the car a sense of awe that a man could smile so easily at such a time, with such things ahead.

Then everyone made for the airport.

McQueen was flown by Learjet to El Paso, where a scan done at the Eastwood Medical Center showed a large tumour on the right, as well as metastatic disease around both lungs, the liver and pelvis. Steve himself knew it was effectively a death sentence – had known, most friends agree, for two years. But now the degeneration had passed beyond any therapy, and his last, perhaps most truly cool line was uttered when he agreed to go under the knife.

'I got nothing to lose. Roll 'em.'

Those tests in El Paso, so far from proving McQueen's tumours to be dead, the patient not only in recovery but cured, showed instead that, after three months of metabolic therapy, his right lung, liver and entire intestine remained covered with cancer. There was no noticeable remission. Steve was being kept alive by bloody-mindedness. Billy Graham had sat there on his bed and looked right into him, catching a glimpse of the strength that, even as he wasted away, kept up everyone's spirits.

All of them still trusted in McQueen's star.

Plaza Santa Maria not being equipped for major surgery, Steve was once again driven across the Mexican border, this time to Dr Vargas's clinic in Juarez. It was a curious town, half Sodom and Gomorrah, half Disneyland, where Americans came not only to vacation but to buy drugs. In recent years it had followed that certain of the locals suddenly found themselves rich. They could scarcely believe it themselves, but there was the money, and still the *yanquis* kept coming and leaving more and more of it under the counters of their shops. Many of the dope-dealers had bought huge Cadillacs which they raced up and down the grimy streets, their radios tuned to the Texas rock music stations. Others engaged in their native love of explosive firecrackers and gunplay. The local sunsets always seemed to be blood-red, the skies heavy and arterial – an apt image for Juarez, which was and is teeming with violence. Here, to a flat, stone building nicked with bullet holes, in a suburb surrounded by graveyards, Steve McQueen came to die.

As usual, he revealed the quality of true greatness under maximum stress. In the face of his multiplying crises, McQueen's nerve never failed. He was a rock of reassurance to Barbara, Terry and Chad, as well as to the doctors and nurses. It moved Vargas and his surgical team to see how calmly Steve submitted to yet more tests and answered their questions with a smile or a small quip. They were astonished at the hour-to-hour change in him. His whole bony, sunken face seemed to go soft and to be lit up from within. That first evening McQueen lay down on a table in a dark backroom. He was scheduled for a blood transfusion from Chad, and Steve could hear him grunt slightly as they inserted the needle. He propped himself up and spoke quietly through the gloom.

'Does it hurt, son?'

On 4 November, a Tuesday, it was decided to operate on Thursday morning. McQueen heard later that night that his friend Ronald Reagan had been elected President, enough for him to smile and flash Barbara the thumbs-up sign. It was twenty years since *The Magnificent Seven* had wrapped, ten since *Le Mans*. On the 5th he was given a cardiac exam and told that his heart was quite strong enough to survive radical surgery. Just seven since *Papillon*. Steve assured Vargas and the other doctors he was ready. Less than one since *The Hunter*. The next morning he was bathed, shaved and prepped by a Mexican orderly. Barbara, Chad and Terry, as well as Grady Ragsdale, were all in the clinic. Many of McQueen's friends sat throughout the day waiting for the ring of a phone. Ali MacGraw was at her new home in Malibu.

Neile, meanwhile, spent that very evening in the Castle as a guest of Zubin and Nancy Mehta. It was just as she remembered it, the red-carpeted staircase spiralling up to the den with its sweeping view of the Hollywood hills. She breathed in and closed her eyes. The feel of the place was still in her blood, Steve's face in her mind, and as if from far away she heard his drowsy voice with its long-perfected mumble, making you listen intently to every word he said, even flung down in a telegram:

I ADORE YOU I ADORE YOU I ADORE YOU I ADORE YOU I
ADORE YOU I ADORE YOU I ADORE YOU I ADORE YOU I
ADORE YOU I ADORE YOU WHEN WE START MAKING LITTLE
ONES WE WILL GET A FAT LITTLE ONE FOR YOU AND A THIN
LITTLE ONE FOR ME AND WE WILL MAKE THEM GO OUT AND

SUPPORT US SO WE CAN BE TOGETHER MY LOVE IS WITH
YOU DARLING NEXT TO ME YOU ARE THE MOST TALENTED
PERSON IN THE WORLD AND NO MATTER WHAT THE BAND
PLAYS WE WILL ALWAYS HEAR OUR OWN MUSIC I LOVE YOU
AND I LOVE YOU

ESTEBAN

McQueen made it through the five-hour operation, performed by Dr
Vargas with William Kelley and Dwight McKee, both of Plaza Santa
Maria, in attendance. Kelley recalls graphically that 'when Steve's
skin was pulled back over his liver, his large tumor literally fell out
onto the table. A procedure was also done on [McQueen's] left
collarbone . . . Everything went off without complication.' Immediately after the surgery Vargas came to the waiting room to tell Barbara
that Steve was 'fine' and, specifically, that his heart was 'going strong'.

As McQueen himself regained consciousness, his first words were,
'Is my stomach flat now?' He was able to smile and speak hoarsely
to his wife and doctors. Kelley remembers him 'giving the "OK"
sign and talk[ing] affably'. Then the sedation began, and Steve drifted
off, but after a while he half opened his eyes and muttered a few
sentences. By common agreement his last coherent line, spoken in
Spanish, was '*Lo hice* – I did it.'

While Barbara and the children went back to the Las Fuentes
motel, McQueen was wheeled into his small, bare-walled room with
the barred window. Dr McKee and two nurses supervised his
immediate recovery, checking on his vital signs every few minutes.
By seven that evening the room was a deep red, reflecting the crimson
sky, and Steve tossed feverishly, sleeping now and then, and during
the periods of wakefulness complaining of the heat. His temperature
was low but his pulse fast. It soon grew dark inside but they could
see his look; they knew it only too well. He was fading, his face
flushed, with a voice that was barely audible. It was another brig;
Boys Republic; laundry; 3188; scrub those up, Ma. Sleep. What
struck them most were the long red slightly freckled hands, now
curved in like talons, pressing ice cubes to his cheeks.

That night became a final ordeal to McQueen. What he said to

McKee and the nurses in that anguished pant of his consisted mostly of numbers, and a few broken words about Chino. Soon, a full moon sent down chopped-up light onto the narrow bed. Now and then, a blood-coloured firefly would float silently through the lifting gloom. For a moment Steve's great grey eyes started from his head. Then they closed. His face was suddenly like the face of a sleeping child. His mouth opened and his chest quickly tilted upwards. There was a sigh, a sigh which rose when McQueen's whole body, now bathed in moonlight, shuddered as though thick with moving water. Then silence.

He died at 3.50 a.m. on 7 November 1980 of a massive heart attack.

When Barbara and the children came back to the clinic they found him with a smile on his lips and his eyes bright blue again. The Bible that Billy Graham had given him was open on his chest. Barbara began to sob, repeating the words, 'He belongs to God now . . . Steve belongs to God.'

The press thought he still belonged to them, and in the days and weeks ahead the debate about his treatment and death outlived him. On the morning of 8 November a front-page story appeared in the *LA Times* under the headline DOCTORS WARN AGAINST UNORTHODOX TREATMENT. *Newsweek* ran a long feature. The *Globe* and the *Enquirer* both plied their shrill trade. Neile felt moved to write a letter to *People*, diplomatically allowing, 'Steve was offered a glimmer of hope . . . but I feel it would be a tragedy if people who are being medically treated under a doctor's care and who have average resources were to flock to similar programs.' And so on. The thought that he couldn't even die without creating a stir would have given McQueen's shade some wry amusement.

One story that never surfaced even in the tabloids was that Steve McQueen, as Kelley now insists, was murdered.

According to this reading, immediately after the operation one of McQueen's doctors was asked to take the excised tumour to a pathology lab in Mexico City for analysis. However, perhaps the arrangements were changed as he never arrived at Santa Rosa and finally, as the time for the Mexico City flight neared, Kelley was prevailed upon to take the tumour to the lab himself. Clutching the

443

jar containing the five-pound mass, and with a faintly uneasy feeling, 'I left the clinic where, as far as I was concerned, Steve was recovering successfully.'

The implication being, someone – again not named – wanted Kelley out of town.

At eight o'clock the next morning, 7 November, Kelley was duly speaking with the city pathologist. The latter examined the tumour incredulously. 'I've never see anything like this,' he said. 'It's completely dead.' At that very moment of vindication, the phone rang and a nurse at Santa Rosa told Kelley that McQueen had died of a cardiac four hours earlier. By the time Kelley got back to Juarez, Steve's body had been flown to Ventura and was, in fact, cremated later that same day.

To Kelley, there was only one scenario that fully explained McQueen's death. Someone with access to his room during the night of 6–7 November had deliberately injected him with a blood-clotting solution. It was no mere clinical error: not only weren't anticoagulants administered. Coagulants were. Under the restless moonlight that swept in the window this individual had quietly shot Steve full of a fibrinogen extract, swiftly triggering a fatal embolism. By then the whole clinic was silent, the corridors dark, the silvery fireworks exploding in the hills acting as a strobe. An execution took place. The official 'complications from surgery' was a criminal sham. Seeing that McQueen would likely have got better and spoken (as he had in Plaza Santa Maria) of the 'mainstream cancer-treatment racket', the only thing was to ensure that he said nothing at all. Not another word.

Kelley realised that he'd seen Steve as he really was, a plain-spoken man with a vast audience, as sudden and mysterious as those flares that lit up Juarez, and just as visible. He realised that McQueen's survival would have been living proof that the 'racket', as opposed to his, Kelley's, treatment, was a swamp of fear and greed. And he knew that Steve, ultimately, had died as he'd lived, his deepest wishes unfulfilled.

It would be a long, long time before another man would emerge and force people to question their own treatment at the hands of the mainstream. A long, long time - perhaps for ever.

★   ★   ★

They came, meanwhile, for the simplest of reasons: there was nowhere else to go.

There would be no funeral and no public service of any kind, no memorial, no gravesite, not even special showings of McQueen's work. So hundreds of anonymous mourners began pouring across the border to stand silently outside Santa Rosa, many of them clutching candles or stills from their favourite films. On they came, all through that Friday and into the weekend, even after the body itself was removed in late afternoon. For one last time, as the makeshift coffin was wheeled by, the fans' cries and even a few screams rang out. Light rain pattered on the dusty side street. Hanging back from the clinic door, they watched the plain, unmarked car grow invisible in the gathering night. Gradually, it disappeared around a bend. The corpse was taken briefly to a mortuary, then brought back across the border and flown by chartered Learjet to Ventura. Steve's plane took a northerly route over the town of Truth or Consequences, banked hard over Prescott, scene of *Junior Bonner*, came in low over his beloved desert and landed in California in dense fog.

Every so often the public surprises an established class by a spontaneous display of grief for a figure who has died. In this case the vigil also took on the quality of a mini-riot as fist-fights broke out between fans, Steve's entourage and the press. The last hounded him to the very end. In all the siege lasted nine months, from mid February to mid November, with the media's finest hour coming that same Friday evening. An agency photographer located the Prado Funerales home, bribed or talked his way inside and calmly got off a shot of McQueen's body. That particular picture would appear in full colour on the covers of *Paris Match* and the *New York Post*. When Ali MacGraw saw it she publicly broke down and wept.

For a long time after he died, it seemed as if he were still around. As if, Barbara herself said, he'd been on the porch with her a minute ago and had just taken off on a Harley.

Steve's widow organised a private service at the ranch on Remembrance Sunday, the ninth of November. All the wives were there, Barbara and Ali meeting for the first time. Surveying these very different but physically similar types – self-styled graduates of McQueen University – Neile turned to the other two and said wryly,

'Blondes he fucked – but brunettes he married.' During a tour of the house that same afternoon, a long-time biking friend marked the precise moment when grief fully turned to affectionate humour. Chuckling, he looked up and saw the three of them, Neile, Ali and Barbara, all huddled together in Steve's bedroom. *You cool bastard,* he thought.

'The old fucker may not have lived to see it, but his big fantasy came true in the end.'

In fact McQueen's presence was so pervasive that the day didn't even require much formal structure. Family and friends simply knew their roles and went to work. For the most part they drank beer, ate steaks, admired the cars and bikes and told war stories. Leonard De Witt presided, but even his brief was more celebratory than strictly clerical. 'I stood there, outside by the corral, and tried to offer encouragement: that Steve had not only lived, but quite clearly wasn't afraid to die. I told them that his one regret, as he often admitted, was that he wouldn't have enough time to prove his new faith, although he certainly did so to me. He went out like a star.'

As De Witt finished speaking, which he could just barely do without emotion, there was a growing drone overhead. Eight small planes appeared in a cross formation directly above the ranch, dipped their wings and then disappeared slowly over the western horizon.

After that the crowd stayed where they were for the late afternoon and most of the evening, on a day miraculously free from the week-long rain. As befitted such surroundings, everything was indeed kept simple; there were some mumblings, however, about the guest list, which had raised knotty problems about who was 'in' or 'out' at the time of McQueen's death. Pat Johnson, Bud Ekins and Sammy Mason were all there; Loren Janes was busy on location in Texas; Don Gordon, quite inexplicably, wasn't invited.

None of the actors were.

On his deathbed Steve had asked to be cremated and 'dumped anywhere – no big performance'. They were surprised, knowing him to be a man who loved plans, craved order and rarely if ever left anything to chance, but they promised just the same.

They also broke the promise, but McQueen would hardly have held that against them, since he knew how much they wanted to give him a proper send-off. So five days later Sammy Mason and his son Pete took the urn up in Steve's favourite big bug, the yellow Stearman. They flew it south along the line of the Santa Clara, then out over the vast ocean, where they dropped down and scattered the ashes. McQueen's large and troubled spirit was released into a clear sky tinged with red. The time was near sunset, the place about seventy miles due west of Hollywood – as Steve would doubtless have laughed, a symptom of his refusal to ever fully belong there.

Just as he'd wanted, there would be no marker or memorial. All fans had to remember him by were the twenty-eight films, many of which were swiftly re-released. McQueen always insisted that people should worship the work, not necessarily the man, and, fortunately, for once, the studio bosses completely agreed with him.

None of the honchos were invited to the service, either, and most cordially returned the contempt. In stark contrast to the usual outpourings of grief for a departed son, there was exactly one industry tribute – from United Artists – printed in *Variety*. A number of the rich, famous and revered men who run Hollywood remain convinced that Steve actually looked down on them. This was true, but it was nothing personal. Some of the suits' feelings, in comparison, were and are downright ugly: such as the well-known producer, still in the saddle today, who remarks, 'I'd like to have gone to his funeral, just to make sure the cunt was really dead.' Five months after McQueen's final rites the Academy Awards staged a woeful, tap-dancing production number 'honouring' both him and three other film personalities who had died that year, Alfred Hitchcock, Peter Sellers and Mae West. One or two other TV profiles followed with equal merriment.

The theatre owners' organisation commissioned a special bust of Steve. Perhaps the box office perceived immediately what the boardroom missed. Around 1967–8 McQueen had virtually saved the American movie industry.

The obituaries, by and large, were better in the nationals than the trades, longer in Europe than in America. Somehow, in London and Paris virtues were discovered that failed to surface in Los Angeles and New York. The gap between McQueen's press at home and abroad wasn't just unusually wide, it was freakishly so; his whole career had marked a new high in cultural export. It was obvious now that style gurus in Britain, at least, took to this deceptively casual, cool but tortured man in a way which he'd never suspected. Imperiously, *The Times* drew a line. 'None of the many pretenders can hope to portray America better.'

Early death is often like a kind of martyrdom. Much of the home media treated Steve's that way, as though he were a victim, and when *Life* came to mourn its 'late greats' in 1980, there was McQueen's name alongside those of American servicemen killed in the Iranian desert. In *Time* his photograph was between that of Tito and a Kennedy. Some of his legend drew strength, too, from its apparent similarity to John Lennon's. Here was a drama in which a great man emerged, hit a peak, paused, stumbled and regrouped, only to be destroyed at the very moment of comeback. Lennon survived his old friend by just thirty days.

Like Yoko Ono, Steve's widow caught her fair share of flak in the days ahead. Minty was said to have begun packing up the ranch on the very night McQueen died, and would reportedly leave for Idaho with most of the furniture (including several paintings of Neile's) immediately after the memorial service. Sceptics wondered whether Barbara's ten-month marriage in fact qualified her for a chunk, if not the bulk, of Steve's estate, particularly when Ali, among others, got nothing. Nobody said so in public. Behind the thick walls of Beverly Hills, however, there was an abundance of evidence as to the true depth of feeling. The effect on Terry McQueen, for one, was stupendous – and immediate. First a glass fell from her hand and she gaped at the removal van, parked in plain view during her father's wake, as though thunderstruck. Next a plate went down with another shrill crash. The sarcastic phrase 'the bereaved widow' was heard, though none of the family broke rank or had much to say to the press. They knew that was the way that Steve would have wanted it.

When Terry went to clean out her father's strong box, she had a sudden and surprising jolt of insight into his true values. Instead of gold or diamonds she found a St Christopher medal, a certificate of thanks from the LA Fire Department, his award from the Stuntmen's Association, and several letters from small children around the world. There was also Bill McQueen's engraved Zippo lighter, the same one Steve claimed to have flung down the gutter.

No Oscars, no Golden Globes, no Hollywood memorabilia.

As well as Barbara, McQueen's two children were both provided for in the will, reportedly with $3 million apiece.* Pat Johnson was left a car, Bud Ekins two vintage bikes, Sammy Mason a plane. Steve also gave $200,000 to Boys Republic. Loren Janes is one of those who insists, 'McQueen promised a lot of things to a lot of people, me included – then went and signed a new will while he was out of his mind with pain in Mexico. It was bad enough for us to have fought it, but that wasn't any way to honour Steve . . . We grinned and bore it.' Further mystery surrounds the relatively small amount of cash found in McQueen's bank accounts. Cliff Coleman, who long admired Steve's legendary tightness with a buck – once or twice to Coleman's own cost – believes that he hid much of his money under an alias. 'The guy had slush funds all over the world. No way would Steve declare everything.'

Strangest of all was the rumour, denied by Barbara, that McQueen had left her not only cash and real estate but a small phial of something more precious, his frozen sperm. It was said that he'd wanted her to one day bear his child. This tale became Hollywood lore in the years following Steve's death, as well as a parallel one – not implausible, given his erotic track record – about there being two, three or as many as a dozen bastard heirs. Not once that the scandal-sheets knew of had any blond, blue-eyed love child actually come forward, but it all added to McQueen's tabloid immortality.

There was more.

According to Cliff Coleman, 'A lot of us were shocked by what went down in the last few weeks. Jesus, it was so *sudden*. What happened? Nobody really saw the body . . . We'll probably never know if Steve was killed by the cancer or something else. Did he really die? I *still* have dreams where he'll sneak up from behind, tap me on the shoulder and whisper, "It's OK. I'm alive. Don't tell anyone." Somewhere inside, I just don't believe he's gone.' McQueen was a famous prankster, and people wondered whether he wasn't still, somehow, twisting their melons. And they also wondered why,

---

* Three years later Solar was formally liquidated and the McQueen Children's Trust – Terry and Chad's nominee fund – became the beneficiary of most of Steve's film rights.

for a whole week after 7 November 1980, their phones rang at the same time every night. When they answered them, there was no one there. Some of Steve's friends and enemies were numb with fear that it was him, calling from the beyond.

Still, their legs took them to the requiem and the various other rituals.

McQueen left over 200 cars, trucks, buggies, vans, jeeps, trailers and bikes, most of which Chad and Terry auctioned off in November 1984 at the Imperial Palace in Las Vegas. Steve's favourite dark-green Jaguar, which he'd once bought for $4000, sold for $148,000. A 1934 Packard went for $70,000, the yellow Winton Flyer (mysteriously purloined from the set of *The Reivers*) for $20,000. Anything McQueen had driven, sat in or merely stored brought five or six times its official estimate. All told, the sale raised more than $2 million for the Children's Trust and the IRS.

That was the authentic Steve speaking from the grave, in a way that doubtless found echoes in the hearts of many who would prefer to sell at top dollar rather than, say, open a museum. A few years later Neile did, at Karl Malden's invitation, donate several boxes of McQueen's papers, mainly contracts and the like, to the Academy.

A dark corner of a room on Olympic Boulevard: not much to show for a man who defined a school of film acting. Talented old sweats like Malden are almost always struck by the breathtaking quality of Steve's work, and confirm wryly that the good pro and the star, despite superficial similarities, are very different beasts. But some of McQueen's best scenes are almost as different from an average star's as an average star's are from a ham's. They belong in a category of their own. The snappy, insubordinate wit in *Never So Few* and the war films; that last, puzzled shot of *Bullitt*; the moment he emerged in *Papillon*, grizzled and blinking, from years of solitary; all classics, based on McQueen's startling, fresh talent, free from the infernal dross of so much Hollywood spectacle. Even the worst hokum, like *The Towering Inferno*, contains his pitch-perfect performance – a triumph over the longest odds. Mumbling in a punch-drunk monotone, barely 'acting' at all, Steve instinctively filled the emotional centre of every story.

Most icons who live long enough tend to settle for self-parody as gradually they have only the old act itself to act out. McQueen's too-early death at least spared him the fate of a Connery or an Eastwood. His juggling ability to feel the past and trumpet the present perfected a new legend for the future: eternal youth.

Of those who remained, Neile published a memoir revealing several things about Steve his fans might have preferred not to know, wanting to be 'frank' while 'not capital[ising] on [McQueen's] reputation'. The only problem, of course, was that not everyone made the distinction. Bud Ekins is one of those who thinks *My Husband, My Friend* a 'crap' book. Despite the brickbats, Neile's remarkable fighting spirit and sense of humour both resurfaced in her one-woman cabaret show, which she brought to London in 2000. Naturally sensitive about trading on Steve's name, she referred to him only as 'Arthur' in her performance.

MacGraw, too, produced a book, after several doomed affairs and a weakness for tequila had led her to the Betty Ford Clinic. There she stood in a roomful of people and said, 'My name is Ali, and I'm an alcoholic/male-dependent.' From this sorry low, things gradually improved in the 1990s, even while cynics remarked how MacGraw appeared to go from Hot New Star overnight, as it were, to Has-Been. In 2000 she was introducing love films on American cable television.

Minty moved back to Idaho where, for a time in 1988–9, her name was linked with Clint Eastwood's. As the McQueen legend polarised, Barbara began to take a more active role in shaping it. She, too, spoke about him, not in a book but in a filmed profile.

'When I want a thing,' Minty once said, 'I want it dreadfully.' It might have been the motto of all Steve's wives who wanted things dreadfully, and rarely took them.

Perhaps the real achievement of these three women wasn't their long history with McQueen, which collectively stretched from 1956–80, or even that they mostly sacrificed their careers for him. It was the sheer resilience friends most admired. Life with Steve was, in the end, a life of frenetic passion and monklike catatonia, unhinged attacks and quick compliments. Merely surviving it was a coup.

In December 2000 Chad McQueen turned forty, the age at which his father made *Le Mans*. He too has a son, himself named Steve. (At about the same time Minty was dating Clint Eastwood, Chad, in a neat twist, was seeing Eastwood's daughter Alison – not, how-ever, the mother of his three children.) Chad also acts. Except for another John Kennedy, it's hard to think of a name freighted with such large and unnerving expectations.

And such impossible and spurious ones. Chad's run-of-the-mill action romps, with titles like *Death Ray* and *New York Cop*, were no worse in their relentless banality than most. Some bore a passing resemblance, in plot if not audience involvement, to a *Bullitt* or *Get-away*. Each was the bruised yet marketable fruit of a Hollywood adolescence. Chad then began producing his own films, notably one called *Red Line*, turning out about two a year through the late 1990s. He also looks after his father's estate, policing the use of the Steve McQueen name, deciding who can and who can't use it. It was Chad who gave Ford permission to so brilliantly recycle that same *Bullitt* into a TV commercial.

Terry McQueen married and divorced, producing a daughter named Molly. Her own stratagem for keeping Steve's memory alive was to become a spokeswoman for the American Cancer Society. 'His courage made me proud,' she said.

In her thirties Terry was diagnosed with haemochromatosis, an iron imbalance that attacks the liver and other organs. Steve and Neile were both carriers of the gene, but didn't suffer from the disease. In November 1997 Terry was rushed to hospital from her home in Los Angeles. Despite heavy doses of anti-coagulant, she suffered a heart attack and actually stopped breathing. Doctors brought her back from the brink of death and then performed emergency surgery. The McQueens' fighting spirit surfaced again that winter, but the day came when, tragically, Terry's liver failed. She lapsed into a coma and died on 19 March 1998. She was thirty-eight.

Long nourished on triumph and grief, the family grew harder, more resolute, and more private.

William Kelley retired, though he continues to tilt at the American Medical Association and the US government generally. Unlike many such freedom-lovers who pay lip service to racial inclusiveness, Kelley conspicuously has his differences with 'the enemy within', namely the Jews. Neither he nor Dr McKee is any longer associated with Plaza Santa Maria. Rosarito itself soon became a lurid ghetto of plastic-lettered, overlit casinos and American burger bars, *Thomas Crown*-like buggies churning up the white beach. Much of 1997's *Titanic* would be assembled and shot there. With its fame thus secure north of the border, Rosarito began to trade on its Hollywood connection and, belatedly, to interpret Steve's death as its mandate for growth. It relaunched itself as a tourist resort. Overall, the town's new feel was of post-oil Beirut, flowering weeds and dives named Pussy Galore or Rock & Roll Taco set off by a strand of glowing pink neon: HERE MCQUEEN SOUVENIRS.

The British, American and particularly Japanese media, meanwhile, kick-started the second act of Steve's fame with a slew of profiles, analyses, tributes and explanations. One word ran throughout the copy, and that word was 'cool'. Steve's art, the press insisted – in the colour stories in the Sundays, in the waves of retrospectives, in every TV documentary – was, above all, the art of the knack. In particular, his baleful yet smoochy voice and animal dexterity, mainly atop a bike. This latter aspect of McQueen's work found its most public salute in the endless reruns, themselves lovingly freeze-framed, of the Jump. Steve's wider talent was soon seized on, dolled up, colourised and done to death by a few fanatically loyal directors and writers. Several far-sighted critics allied themselves with John Sturges, who spoke about his old friend's 'winning cross of the thug and the underdog'. For years a McQueen Appreciation Society used to meet on the 24th of every month, the date of his birthday, at a table in the El Padrino. Even after these few trailblazers became the majority, they continued to tout Steve as 'aloof', 'a loner', 'the anti-star'. This reflected not only their admiration of McQueen but a longtime reluctance to share him with the world.

The world took him back.

By the early 1990s everything from *Premiere* to *Hot Rod* buffed the legend anew. As well as his core fan base, addicts and archivists spread from the grass roots to George W. Bush, with everyone (including Tony Blair) in between. Clubs, websites and conventions all spoke to a McQueen sect. As for the books: they weren't much, but as models of the pathology of stargazing, they stood alone. Steve deserved more.

He touched people – that's the thing. First, McQueen was

453

spellbinding to look at. He appeared to be both tough and vulnerably naïve. Like a whey-faced urchin he seemed to exist outside the drab confines of adult life. Time and again, audiences found themselves ready to indulge him. There was enough of a spark in McQueen, yet enough of the orphan, to make people care. It's the same general reaction, part concern, part exasperation – and part pity – parents might have towards their wayward offspring. Particularly the mothers. Steve's talent to melt the women in his life, quite often despite themselves, was at least half his charm.

The other part was the realisation that even for this legendary king of cool, perhaps especially for him, hot fires burned barely below the ice. Anything could happen, and it frequently did.

Eventually the pioneering critics and groupies were joined by a 'McQueen school', somehow both chillier and more charismatic than mainstream Hollywood – names like Mickey Rourke, Kevin Spacey, Mel Gibson, Michael Madsen, Sean Penn, Kevin Costner. (Rourke even ground out a 1996 movie called *Bullet*.) The influence soon extended beyond the mere technicalities of acting. In particular, anyone who ever tore up a script, snubbed an award, went head-to-head with a suit or rode to work on a 'hog' (in which for daily life Steve was something of a missionary) might be said to be using the privilege, the licence, the perks McQueen helped win them. Then there was the revolution he inspired in the whole way studios would treat their stars. The basic vision Steve proclaimed was that people of good will working together could make 'better stuff'. And if people like himself were to play a part in this process, it would be because they were compensated for their labours. More fruit and nuts. When the honchos were duly reeling from the pay explosion of the 1970s, Steve retorted that it was Supies like himself, not them, who put fans in the seats. That's a principle that Tom Cruise applies today, every time he gets $25 million to appear on screen.

It was usually around Steve's own contract time that the suits were apt to mention that his brains, in their opinion, were twisted, or that a screw, somewhere, was loose. McQueen, they said, had balls. Add the sex and booze and it's not surprising he's become, at best, the human counterpoint of men's magazines like *Loaded* and *FHM*; at worst, the ring-pull of the lager louts' canned sadism. Around the mid seventies a quite serious debate broke out, echoing the 'Paul Is Dead' saga, over whether the Prisoner of Trancas was even alive. After *The Towering Inferno* people weren't sure whether Steve actually existed or not. But twenty-five years on, and more than twenty since that night in Juarez, he felt more real – a greater influence, both good and bad – than ever before.

Almost every line he spoke seems gilded, sharp as a dagger.

The great solitary – McQueen's phrase – is remembered more tolerantly today. Like Sinatra, he's a synonym for a kind of American male, the kind who says what he thinks, pays the price and doesn't live in regret. What's more, Steve still sets the standard for contained, remorselessly honest acting, and a vast public has come to think of him as a true original: bluff to a fault, yet oddly gentle; humorously aware that 'life's a scam' – a marvellous and rewarding scam, at best, requiring a level of cunning, endurance and native wit which few others could match, but still a scam – with bad vibes just ahead.

Then again, in his last two years the legendary 'Steve McQueen' didn't really exist. Even his wife and friends barely felt his dark presence any more, only its absence. With some of the old gang watching askance, Steve faithfully went to church, pored over his Bible and generally turned the whole ugly, painful ordeal of his cancer into something quietly heroic. Not a shred of self-pity. Even so, he fought it to the end, delighting in twisting a few final melons, but going out calmly and fully reconciled, leaving no doubt that for him, by then, life wasn't a scam at all but an ecstatic pre-paradise. Nobody has said the man was without contradictions.

The visionary McQueen all but invented the notion of 'less is more' successfully applied to film. When he wanted to tell you all about himself he might grunt or allow that brief leer to cross his features that, with Steve, passed for emotion. The traditionalist, meanwhile, was a skilful entertainer with a knack for seamless entrances and exits and the slickest use of props – often the kind with wheels or triggers – anyone could remember. In his fierce and vivid infantile fury, McQueen moved effortlessly from near catatonia to breathtaking rage and back again, quite often in the space of a single scene. The action always blazed with his own private mood. Nobody, before or since, has done volatility like he did. It's no wonder Steve has the Hollywood acolytes or the global sect. In Japan, which boasts a *Towering Inferno* museum, he's still worshipped with Shinto-like awe. Unlike most stars whose work is rooted in deft, sometimes brilliant play-acting, McQueen's blooms out of something rarer – humanity.

By 2001 the cult had not only depth but also astonishing breadth: Steve's name appeared on the covers of *Rolling Stone, Time, Spin, People, Playboy*. He was anatomised in medical journals and written up in Christian quarterlies. The Honda Rider's Club magazine featured him atop a SuperHawk bike. The influence extended down to several films. More and more of his fellow actors allowed themselves free parodic rein. Apart from the likes of Costner and Rourke, one Donald Logue would win a Sundance award for his role in *The Tao of Steve*, in which he played a womaniser whose pickup artistry is based on McQueen's.

Most of the portrayals weren't stirring, but at least they were affectionate.

The Blob, The Getaway and *Thomas Crown* were all officially redone. There were TV spinoffs, actionable cribs and adaptations, as well as *Chicken Run*, which substituted a flock of poultry for the cast of *The Great Escape*. This Vesuvius of junk, presumably meant to make fans genuflect to an Alec Baldwin or Pierce Brosnan, had the curious effect of making Steve seem even better. They acted; he did something that remained alive and actual. Unlike Baldwin in *The Getaway*, McQueen didn't have to pretend to be dangerous; he merely raged around doing what he did best, completely in synch with his character, a mild-mannered psychopath, clenched and bony, dressed in funereal black. Unlike Brosnan, he didn't turn Crown into a virtuoso tailor's dummy. In Steve's hands the nervous intelligence gave depth to the polished surface. His performance spoke for anyone who dreamed, and the audience loved it.

He made all of the 'Century's Greatest Entertainers' lists.

At the precise moment McQueen slouched on for the first episode of *Wanted Dead or Alive*, a new paradigm ratcheted into high gear. It would spread. Fast. Steve may not have had a worthy successor but he left a legacy, an exuberantly hip, or at least male, way of doing business, both on-screen and off. Ironically, one of the few target-age men who didn't conspicuously take after McQueen was McQueen himself. He was well aware of the chemistry that first makes a super-star, then transforms him from what he is to what his reputation is. For years, his own act wasn't so much cool as self-centred, cruel, even sadistic, although with emerging sympathies – first for a few, eventually for all. Steve's devotion to 'giving something back' was kindled early on and later voiced by his religion. It went well beyond the normal trite, over-publicised gestures. McQueen may have aged little in front of the camera, but behind it he grew into a figure of extraordinary compassion, concern and vision, as well as rare cour-age. What possible connection could this soft-spoken man have to the violent madness that his Hollywood successors peddle today? The answer is every connection, and none at all. Steve McQueen began something, but ultimately he rose far above it.

Appendix 1

CHRONOLOGY

24 March 1930	Terrence Steven McQueen born in the Indianapolis suburb of Beech Grove.
1937	His first clash with formal education, at Orearville school in Slater, Missouri.
1940	Back in Indianapolis, Steve learns how to shoot pool, rip off hubcaps and engage in welfare fraud. His mother ships him back to Slater.
1942	Steve rejoins his mother, now married to a man named Berri, in Los Angeles. Berri beats him up.
1944	Sent back to Slater, Steve joins a travelling circus and eventually grubs his way west to California.
6 February 1945	Steve's mother and stepfather sign a court order confirming him to be 'incorrigible'. That same night he's sent to Junior Boys Republic, a reform school in nearby Chino.
April 1946	Free again, Steve takes the bus to New York where his mother, now living with another man, has moved. The reunion lasts one day.
28 April 1947	He signs on for the Marines. McQueen

leaves the service exactly three years later with the same rank of Private First Class.

1950–51   Variously supports himself as a card-sharp, gigolo, cab-driver, tile-layer, cobbler and runner in a brothel.

25 June 1951   Encouraged by a girlfriend, he enrols in acting school in New York.

1955   After appearing in three off-Broadway plays, McQueen begins to land better parts on stage and TV.

1956   Bob Wise casts him as a bit player in *Somebody Up There Likes Me*, starring Paul Newman. Steve vows to be bigger than Newman.
McQueen also appears briefly on Broadway as the lead in *A Hatful of Rain*.
On 2 November he marries a talented showgirl called Neile Adams.

20 December 1957   Steve signs a first contract to make what becomes his breakthrough, the CBS series *Wanted Dead or Alive*.

1958   After yet more TV work, he appears in Harold Robbins's *Never Love a Stranger*. Thanks largely to Neile and her manager Hilly Elkins, Steve lands his first ever above-the-title billing in *The Great St Louis Bank Robbery* and *The Blob*.
That September *Wanted* begins its three-year, 117-episode run.

1959   The McQueens' daughter, Terry Leslie,

born on 5 June. (A boy, Chadwick Steven, follows in December 1960.)

In *Never So Few* Steve earns Frank Sinatra's eternal admiration and a growing reputation as Hollywood's next big thing.

1960	McQueen appears in *The Magnificent Seven*, coolly upstaging the nominal star Yul Brynner.

Steve moves to a house at 2419 Solar Drive in Hollywood. The street sign gives him the name for his long-running production company.

29 March 1961   *Wanted Dead or Alive* goes off the air.
McQueen stars in the woeful *The Honeymoon Machine*.

26 June 1962   *Hell is for Heroes* released. The *New York Times* praises McQueen as a new kind of actor 'with presence and a keen sense of timing'. Steve then makes his first and only film in Britain, Philip Leacock's *The War Lover*.
Between roles, he indulges a taste for sex, drugs and most forms of racing.

12 July 1963   McQueen makes the cover of *Life*.
Meanwhile, following *The Great Escape*, out that summer, he becomes a worldwide icon. The family moves to 'The Castle', in the exclusive LA hamlet of Brentwood.
That November, Steve co-stars with Jackie Gleason in *Soldier in the Rain*.
His third film of the year, *Love with the Proper Stranger*, is one of his best. Starring opposite Natalie Wood, he becomes a

461

romantic lead. Among his new female fans is Wood herself.

September 1964   Steve is selected as part of the American team for the international six-day motorcycle trials in East Germany.

12 January 1965   *Baby, the Rain Must Fall* released. It flops at the box office but proves for all time that McQueen can act.

October 1965   *The Cincinnati Kid* becomes the first of five back-to-back smashes that make him a household name.
McQueen's mother dies on the day of the premiere.

29 June 1966   *Nevada Smith*.

December 1966   Bob Wise's epic *The Sand Pebbles* wins McQueen some of the best notices, and the sole Oscar nomination of his career.
He begins plans to make *Day of the Champion*, eventually released in June 1971 as *Le Mans*.

21 March 1967   He ceremonially presses his prints and the word THANKS!! into a wet cement slab outside the Chinese theatre on Hollywood Boulevard.

26 June 1968   Playing against type, Steve scores another success in *The Thomas Crown Affair*.
McQueen follows it with *Bullitt*. As well as the money, he walks off with a hatful of *Film Daily* and *Boxoffice* awards, wins a Golden Globe and makes Man of the Year at

NATO. Overseas, he's the biggest American
star since John Wayne.

August 1969   McQueen narrowly avoids being butchered
by the Manson gang.

25 December 1969   *The Reivers*, a commercial disappointment
and creative triumph, released.

7 June 1970   Photography finally begins on *Le Mans*. In
the film's aftermath Steve fires his agent and
winds down his company. Neile leaves him.

1971   McQueen pockets $1 million by doing a
discreet TV commercial for Honda. He
needs the money, at least in part, to pay for
his divorce.
Steve's homage to motorcycling, *On Any
Sunday*, opens that summer.
He starts an affair with the starlet Barbara
Leigh. Unbeknown to McQueen, Leigh gets
pregnant by him and has an abortion. His
estranged wife has just done the same thing.

February 1972   Sam Peckinpah's *The Getaway* begins filming
in Texas. McQueen starts an affair with Ali
MacGraw. On 26 April Steve's marriage
formally ends.

2 August 1972   McQueen's brilliant rodeo film, *Junior
Bonner*, released.

19 December 1972   *The Getaway*. In sheer box office, it's his
finest hour.

13 July 1973   McQueen and MacGraw marry in
Cheyenne, Wyoming.

16 December 1973   *Papillon* released.

12 April 1974   Steve signs to make *The Towering Inferno*, which eventually nets him $12 million.
For the next two years, McQueen steers clear of Hollywood and spends most of his time at home in Malibu.

1975   Even in semi-retirement, he's voted America's favourite star, beating the likes of Redford, Eastwood, Nicholson and his arch-rival Paul Newman. By now Steve resembles an ageing, bearded hippie of flabby aspect.

April 1976   McQueen emerges to announce plans to star in Ibsen's *An Enemy of the People*. The film, predictably, bombs. Its non-release is the worst blow of his career.

March 1977   Largely to extricate himself from a three-picture contract, McQueen agrees to make the Western *Tom Horn*.

November 1977   He sues MacGraw for divorce and swiftly takes up with a model named Barbara Minty.

January 1979   *Tom Horn* finally begins shooting. He asks the unit nurse about respiratory problems. Some believe he already knows he's ill.

Spring 1979   McQueen and Minty leave Malibu and settle in Santa Paula.
He begins flying antique planes and attending church.

10 September 1979	Work begins in Chicago on his twenty-eighty and final film, *The Hunter*.
28 November 1979	McQueen performs in front of a camera for the last time.
22 December 1979	The cancer is diagnosed.
16 January 1980	Steve marries Barbara Minty, beating his ex-wife Neile to the altar by 72 hours.
28 March 1980	Steve and Barbara attend the *Tom Horn* press preview, his last full public appearance.
April 1980	McQueen meets William Kelley, who pioneers 'nonspecific metabolic therapy' to fight cancer.
28 July 1980	*The Hunter* released. That same week, Steve checks himself into Plaza Santa Maria, a Mexican clinic under Kelley's and others' supervision.
2 October 1980	McQueen publicly confirms that he has cancer. The media circus begins.
6 November 1980	A surgeon removes tumours from Steve's abdomen and collarbone. Coming round from the anaesthetic he mutters his final words, '*Lo hice* – I did it.'
7 November 1980	McQueen dies at 3.50 a.m. of a heart attack.

Appendix 2

FILMOGRAPHY

1. *Somebody Up There Likes Me* (MGM), 1956. Screenplay by Ernest Lehman, based on the autobiography of Rocky Graziano. Directed by Robert Wise. With Paul Newman, Pier Angeli, Everett Sloane, Sal Mineo and Steve McQueen (uncredited).

2. *Never Love a Stranger* (Allied Artists), 1958. Screenplay by Harold Robbins and Richard Day, based on a novel by Robbins. Directed by Robert Stevens. With John Drew Barrymore, Lita Milan, Robert Bray and Steve McQueen (as Martin Cabell).

3. *The Great St Louis Bank Robbery* (United Artists), 1958–9. Screenplay by Richard T. Heffron. Directed by Charles Guggenheim and John Stix. With Steve McQueen (as George Fowler), David Clarke, Graham Denton, Molly McCarthy and James Dukas.

4. *The Blob* (Paramount), 1958. Screenplay by Theodore Simonson and Kate Phillips, based on a story by Irvine H. Millgate. Directed by Irvin S. Yeaworth Jr. With Steve McQueen (as Steve Andrews), Aneta Corseaut, Earl Rowe, Olin Howlin and Steven Chase.

5. *Never So Few* (MGM), 1959. Screenplay by Millard Kaufman, based on a novel by Tom T. Chamales. Directed by John Sturges. With Frank Sinatra, Gina Lollobrigida, Peter Lawford, Steve McQueen (as Sgt Bill Ringa), Richard Johnson, Paul Henreid, Dean Jones, Brian Donlevy and Charles Bronson.

6. *The Magnificent Seven* (United Artists), 1960. Screenplay by

William Roberts, based on Akira Kurosawa's *The Seven Samurai*. Directed by John Sturges. With Yul Brynner, Horst Buchholz, Steve McQueen (as Vin), Eli Wallach, James Coburn, Charles Bronson, Robert Vaughn and Brad Dexter.

7. *The Honeymoon Machine* (MGM), 1961. Screenplay by George Wells, based on Lorenzo Semple's play *The Golden Fleecing*. Directed by Richard Thorpe. With Steve McQueen (as Lt Fergie Howard), Brigid Bazlen, Jim Hutton, Paula Prentiss and Dean Jagger.

8. *Hell is for Heroes* (Paramount), 1962. Screenplay by Robert Pirosh and Richard Carr, from a story by Pirosh. Directed by Don Siegel. With Steve McQueen (as Reese), Bobby Darin, Fess Parker, Bob Newhart, Nick Adams, Harry Guardino, James Coburn and Mike Kellin.

9. *The War Lover* (Columbia), 1962. Screenplay by Howard Koch, based on the novel by John Hersey. Directed by Philip Leacock. With Steve McQueen (as Capt. Buzz Rickson), Robert Wagner, Shirley Anne Field, Gary Cockrell and Michael Crawford.

10. *The Great Escape* (United Artists), 1963. Screenplay by James Clavell and W. R. Burnett, based on the book by Paul Brickhill. Directed by John Sturges. With Steve McQueen (as Virgil Hilts), James Garner, Richard Attenborough, Charles Bronson, Donald Pleasence, James Donald, James Coburn, John Leyton, David McCallum and Nigel Stock.

11. *Soldier in the Rain* (Allied Artists), 1963. Screenplay by Maurice Richlin and Blake Edwards, based on the novel by William Goldman. Directed by Ralph Nelson. With Jackie Gleason, Steve McQueen (as Sgt Eustis Clay), Tony Bill, Tuesday Weld, Tom Poston, Ed Nelson, Lew Gallo, Paul Hartman, Chris Noel, Lewis Charles and Adam West.

12. *Love with the Proper Stranger* (Paramount), 1963. Screenplay by

Arnold Schulman. Directed by Robert Mulligan. With Steve McQueen (as Rocky Papasano), Natalie Wood, Edie Adams, Herschel Bernardi, Tom Bosley, Harvey Lembeck, Penny Santon, Arlene Golonka, Richard Dysart and Vic Tayback.

13. *Baby, the Rain Must Fall* (Columbia), 1965. Screenplay by Horton Foote, based on his play *The Traveling Lady*. Directed by Robert Mulligan. With Steve McQueen (as Henry Thomas), Lee Remick, Don Murray, Paul Fix, Josephine Hutchinson and Ruth White.

14. *The Cincinnati Kid* (MGM), 1965. Screenplay by Ring Lardner Jr and Terry Southern, based on the novel by Richard Jessup. Directed by Norman Jewison. With Steve McQueen (as Eric Stoner/the Cincinnati Kid), Edward G. Robinson, Ann-Margret, Karl Malden, Tuesday Weld, Joan Blondell, Rip Torn, Jack Weston and Cab Calloway.

15. *Nevada Smith* (Paramount), 1966. Screenplay by John Michael Hayes, based on a character in *The Carpetbaggers* by Harold Robbins. Directed by Henry Hathaway. With Steve McQueen (as Max Sand/Nevada Smith), Karl Malden, Brian Keith, Suzanne Pleshette, Arthur Kennedy, Janet Margolin, Howard da Silva, Raf Vallone, Martin Landau and Paul Fix.

16. *The Sand Pebbles* (20th Century-Fox), 1966. Screenplay by Richard Anderson, based on the novel by Richard McKenna. Directed by Robert Wise. With Steve McQueen (as Jake Holman), Richard Crenna, Richard Attenborough, Candice Bergen, Marayat Andriane, Mako, Larry Gates, Simon Oakland, Gavin McLeod and Loren Janes.

17. *The Thomas Crown Affair* (United Artists), 1968. Screenplay by Alan R. Trustman. Directed by Norman Jewison. With Steve McQueen (as Thomas Crown), Faye Dunaway, Paul Burke, Yaphet Kotto, Jack Weston, Todd Martin, Biff McGuire, Sam Melville and Addison Powell.

19. *Bullitt* (Warner Bros), 1968. Screenplay by Alan R. Trustman and Harry Kleiner, based on the novel *Mute Witness* by Robert L. Pike. Directed by Peter Yates. With Steve McQueen (as Lt Frank Bullitt), Robert Vaughn, Jacqueline Bisset, Don Gordon, Simon Oakland, Norman Fell and Robert Duvall.

19. *The Reivers* (National General), 1969. Screenplay by Irving Ravetch and Harriet Frank Jr, based on the novel by William Faulkner. Directed by Mark Rydell. With Steve McQueen (as Boon Hogganbeck), Sharon Farrell, Will Geer, Rupert Crosse, Mitch Vogel and Lonny Chapman.

20. *Le Mans* (National General), 1971. Screenplay by Harry Kleiner. Directed by Lee H. Katzin. With Steve McQueen (as Michael Delaney), Siegfried Rauch, Elga Andersen, Ronald Leigh-Hunt, Fred Haltiner and some forty Grand Prix drivers.

21. *On Any Sunday* (Cinema 5), 1971. Screenplay and directed by Bruce Brown. Motorcycling documentary in which McQueen appears as a racer.

22. *Junior Bonner* (ABC-Cinerama), 1972. Screenplay by Jeb Rosebrook. Directed by Sam Peckinpah. With Steve McQueen (as Junior Bonner), Robert Preston, Ida Lupino, Barbara Leigh, Joe Don Baker, Mary Murphy and Ben Johnson.

23. *The Getaway* (National General), 1972. Screenplay by Walter Hill, based on the novel by Jim Thompson. Directed by Sam Peckinpah. With Steve McQueen (as 'Doc' McCoy), Ali MacGraw, Ben Johnson, Sally Struthers, Al Lettieri, Slim Pickens, Bo Hopkins and John Bryson.

24. *Papillon* (Allied Artists), 1973. Screenplay by Dalton Trumbo and Lorenzo Semple, based on the book by Henri Charrière. Directed by Franklin Schaffner. With Steve McQueen (as Papillon), Dustin Hoffman, Don Gordon, Victor Jory, Anthony Zerbe, Robert Deman, Bill Mumy and George Coulouris.

25. *The Towering Inferno* (20th Century-Fox & Warner Bros), 1974. Screenplay by Stirling Silliphant, based on the novels *The Tower* by Richard Martin Stern and *The Glass Inferno* by Frank M. Robinson and Thomas Scortia. Directed by John Guillermin (with action sequences by Irwin Allen). With Steve McQueen (as Michael O'Hallorhan), Paul Newman, William Holden, Fred Astaire, Susan Blakely, Don Gordon, Richard Chamberlain, Jennifer Jones, O. J. Simpson, Robert Vaughn, Maureen McGovern and Susan Flannery.

26. *An Enemy of the People* (Warner Bros), 1978. Screenplay by Alexander Jacobs, based on Arthur Miller's adaption of Ibsen's play. Directed by George Schaefer. With Steve McQueen (as Thomas Stockmann), Charles Durning, Bibi Andersson, Michael Cristofer and Richard Dysart.

27. *Tom Horn* (Warner Bros), 1980. Screenplay by Thomas McGuane and Bud Shrake, based on the book *Life of Tom Horn, Government Scout and Interpreter, written by Himself.* Directed by William Wiard. With Steve McQueen (as Tom Horn), Linda Evans, Richard Farnsworth, Billy Green Bush, Slim Pickens, Peter Canon and Roy Jenson.

28. *The Hunter* (Paramount), 1980. Screenplay by Ted Leighton and Peter Hyams, from the book by Christopher Keane and the life of Ralph 'Papa' Thorson. Directed by Buzz Kulik. With Steve McQueen (as Thorson), Eli Wallach, Kathryn Harrold, LeVar Burton, Ben Johnson, Richard Venture and Taurean Blacque.

Appendix 3

BIBLIOGRAPHY

Beck, Marilyn, *Marilyn Beck's Hollywood*, Hawthorn Books, 1973

Bergen, Candice, *Knock Wood*, Linden Press/Simon & Schuster, 1984

Charrière, Henri, *Papillon*, William Morrow, 1970

MacGraw, Ali, *Moving Pictures*, Bantam Books, 1991

McCoy, Malachy, *Steve McQueen: The Unauthorized Biography*, Henry Regnery Company, 1974

McKinney, Doug, *Sam Peckinpah*, Twayne Publishers, 1979

McQueen Toffel, Neile, *My Husband, My Friend*, Atheneum Books, 1986

Nolan, William, *Steve McQueen: Star on Wheels*, Berkley Publishing, 1972

—, *McQueen*, Berkley Publishing, 1985

Norman, Barry, *The Film Greats*, Futura Publications, 1986

Ragsdale, Grady Jr, *Steve McQueen: The Final Chapter*, Vision House, 1983

Robbins, Jhan, *Yul Brynner: The Inscrutable King*, Dodd, Mead, 1987

St Charnez, Casey, *The Complete Films of Steve McQueen*, Citadel Press, 1984

Spiegel, Penina, *McQueen: The Untold Story of a Bad Boy in Hollywood*, Doubleday & Co., 1986

Terrill, Marshall, *Steve McQueen: Portrait of an American Rebel*, Donald I. Fine, Inc., 1993

Van Doren, Mamie, *Playing the Field*, Berkley Publishing, 1987

SOURCES AND CHAPTER NOTES

Source one for the life of Steve McQueen are the twenty-eight films and various TV roles performed in the course of exactly twenty-five years in front of the camera.

The following notes show at least the formal interviews, conversations and/or other material mined from around the world. I should particularly thank the Margaret Herrick Library of the Academy of Motion Picture Arts and Sciences, which houses many of McQueen's papers quoted here for the first time. As well as the various names listed, I also spoke to a number of people who prefer not to be named. Where sources asked for anonymity – usually citing intense like or intense dislike of McQueen – every effort was made to persuade them to go on the record. Where this wasn't possible, I've used the words 'a friend' or 'an actor', as usual. Once or twice, I've resorted to the formula of an alias. No acknowledgement thus appears of the help, encouragement and kindness I received from a number of quarters, some of them, as they say, household names.

In the course of two years' research and over 200 audiences in and around London, New York, Los Angeles and Seattle, exactly one person I approached threw a fit – McQueen's *Nevada Smith* co-star Pat Hingle, who seemed not to care much for the author's subject, not to mention for the author. I may have got Mr Hingle on a bad day, but, whatever the problem, I still regret not being able to interview the man responsible for the classic torture scene in *The Grifters*. It's a serious shame.

For better flow, please note that a few phrases and words have been anglicised in the text – for example, 'rushes' instead of 'dailies'.

Chapter 1

For the events immediately surrounding Steve McQueen's death, I'm grateful to his doctor William Kelley, whom I interviewed on 3 December 1999. I should also thank Karl Malden, Biff McGuire and especially Don Gordon for allowing themselves to be quoted. McQueen's obituary appeared in nearly every daily paper in the UK and US; I particularly sifted the *Guardian*, *The Times*, the *New York Times*, the *Los Angeles Times*, the *Seattle Post-Intelligencer* and *Variety*. The late Grady Ragsdale Jr's *Steve McQueen: The Final Chapter*, albeit labouring under its author's infatuation with its subject, is as good a first-hand account as any. I should also acknowledge William Nolan's *McQueen*, Penina Spiegel's *McQueen: The Untold Story of a Bad Boy in Hollywood* and Marshall Terrill's excellent *Steve McQueen: Portrait of an American Rebel*.

Chapter 2

Institutional help in recalling the Dickensian years came from the City of Slater, Columbia School District, IDS, Indiana Birth and Death Records, Indiana Chamber of Commerce, Miller Management Services, National Personnel Records Center, Orearville School, State Bank of Slater and the US Marine Corps. Secondary research went on in the British Library, British Newspaper Library and Seattle Public Library. My own travels took me to Missouri, New York and Los Angeles.

Among individuals who helped: Dale Crowe, Harold Eddy, Toni Gahl, Gene Griffith, Kent James, Sam Jones, Darla More, Jules Mowrer, Gene Neff, McQueen's longtime friend and partner Robert Relyea, Jim Stanfield, Bud Summers and Dora Yanni. My thanks, too, to Neile McQueen Toffel, whom I interviewed on 18 January 2000.

It's a pleasure to again acknowledge, as any McQueen author should, Penina Spiegel's *The Untold Story of a Bad Boy in Hollywood*, with its twist on Steve's Missouri family.

Chapter 3

Interviews and/or taped conversations took place with Mimi Benning, Paul Darlow, Emily Hurt, Dean Jones, Frank Knox, the late Buzz Kulik, Wayne Rogers, Eli Wallach, Robert Wise and, again, Dora Yanni. McQueen's long-running stunt double and friend Loren Janes, his first manager Hillard ('Hilly') Elkins, his one-time colleague Bob Relyea and his ex-wife Neile all patiently answered my questions.

McQueen's FBI file opened as early as 1959 – I'm grateful to John Kelso at the US Department of Justice for supplying it.

Somebody Up There Likes Me, Never Love a Stranger, The Blob and, at a pinch, *The Great St Louis Bank Robbery* are all out on video. McQueen's watermark series *Wanted Dead or Alive* still gets its regular airings, most recently on the Western cable channel.

Chapter 4

McQueen's breakthrough years were well recalled by, among others, Cliff Coleman, Hilly Elkins, Natalie Hawn, Jim Hoven, Loren Janes, Dean Jones,

473

the late Stan Kamen, Stirling Moss, Bob Newhart, Fess Parker, the late Donald Pleasence, Bob Relyea and Eli Wallach. A mutual friend put some of Jay Sebring's thoughts at my disposal. I should particularly mention and thank McQueen's close friends Bud Ekins and Don Gordon, whom I interviewed on 3 January 2000 and 19 November 1999 as well as 5 February 2000, respectively. It was a thrill to be driven around town by the latter.

Neile McQueen Toffel and her memoir *My Husband, My Friend* were invaluable; as was William Nolan's semi-official biography *McQueen*; semi-official because it was written in cooperation with McQueen and reflects his points of view on certain matters. Various brief, selected quotes from this otherwise fine work appear throughout.

Life ('The Bad Boy's Breakout' – 12 July 1963) and McQueen's FBI file were consulted, as were his various contracts and letters on file at the Academy of Motion Picture Arts and Sciences – my thanks to Howard Prouty for arranging access to them.

I visited Klump Avenue, Skyline Drive and Solar Drive, as well as Musso & Frank's in Hollywood.

Never So Few, *The Magnificent Seven*, *The Honeymoon Machine*, *Hell is for Heroes*, *The War Lover* and *The Great Escape* are all currently on video – as is Humphrey Bogart's *High Sierra* (1941), the classic perspective on McQueen's own style twenty years later.

Chapter 5

Comment on McQueen's post-*Great Escape* fame came from Tony Bill, Cliff Coleman, Gary Combs, Bud Ekins, Don Gordon, Jim Hoven, Loren Janes, the late Stan Kamen, Neile McQueen Toffel, Karl Malden, Don Murray, Bob Relyea, Eli Wallach, Robert Wise and a source then working at Mount Zion hospital in San Francisco. I'm grateful to the director Norman Jewison for the lengthy interview he gave me on 7 March 2000.

Steve McQueen's private papers in the Margaret Herrick library were an invaluable field guide to his twinned worlds of art and commerce.

Brief, specific quotes first appeared in Candice Bergen's *Knock Wood*, William Nolan's *McQueen*, Penina Spiegel's *McQueen: The Untold Story of a Bad Boy in Hollywood* and Mamie Van Doren's *Playing the Field*, as well as in the *E!* television profile of McQueen.

Soldier in the Rain, *Love with the Proper Stranger*, *Baby, the Rain Must Fall*, *The Cincinnati Kid*, *Nevada Smith*, *The Sand Pebbles* and *The Thomas Crown Affair* are all still on video.

Casey St Charnez's *The Complete Films of Steve McQueen* provides a useful role-by-role summary of dates and figures.

Marshall Terrill's *Steve McQueen: Portrait of an American Rebel*, meanwhile, skilfully culls some or many of the roles McQueen turned down.

Chapter 6

McQueen's personal and creative highs – and the nadir of *Le Mans* – were crisply brought home by Marla Douce, Bud Ekins, Cheryl Hise, Jim Hoven, Loren Janes, Norman Jewison, Dean Jones, Biff McGuire, Stirling Moss, Barry Norman and Bob Relyea. For first-hand comment on *Bullitt*, I'm again grateful to Don Gordon and a source at NATO, the National Association of Theater Owners. McQueen's FBI file provided colour.

Neile McQueen Toffel's *My Husband, My Friend* remains, by far, the best insider's account of the nightmarish years 1970–71. Recommended.

John Little, meanwhile, enlightened me on McQueen's relationship with Bruce Lee.

Other published sources are the previously named books, most notably Marshall Terrill's *Portrait of an American Rebel*, and articles in *Cinema, Esquire, Photoplay, Playboy* and *Variety*. I should acknowledge the Academy of Motion Picture Arts and Sciences, Hollywood Legends and the Maltese Falcon.

Bullitt, The Reivers and *Le Mans* are on video.

Chapter 7

Sources for McQueen's final 'Supie' phase included Gary Combs, Bud Ekins, John Gavin, Jim Geller, Don Gordon, Katy Haber, Bo Hopkins, Jim Hoven, Kent James, Loren Janes, Norman Jewison, Neile McQueen Toffel and Stirling Moss.

I'm particularly grateful to Barbara Leigh, McQueen's lover at the time of *Junior Bonner*, and to Pat Johnson, probably his closest friend, who both put their views on record.

I again trawled the files at the Margaret Herrick library, as well as the *New York Times, People, Photoplay, Rolling Stone* and *Sports Illustrated*.

Selected quotes came from William Nolan's *McQueen*; the line from Bobby Visciglia first appeared in Marshall Terrill's *Portrait of an American Rebel*.

Junior Bonner, The Getaway and *Papillon* are all on video; *On Any Sunday* (Cinema 5, 1971) seems to be the hardest of all McQueen's films to track down. I'm indebted to Hollywood Legends.

Chapter 8

McQueen's seclusion and eventual comeback were vividly recalled by, among others, Tony Bill, Charles Durning, Richard Dysart, Bud Ekins, Mike Fargo, Jim Geller, Don Gordon, Katy Haber, Loren Janes, Norman Jewison, Dean Jones, Neile McQueen Toffel and Robert Relyea. I'm grateful to McQueen's last agent and friend Marvin Josephson for the interview he gave me on 5 November 1999.

Brief, selected quotes in this chapter first appeared in Ali MacGraw's *Moving Pictures*, in Neile McQueen Toffel's *My Husband, My Friend* and in William Nolan's *McQueen*. Neile's comment on her divorce is from the *Daily Mail* of 15 April 2000; Sue Mengers's quote from *Vanity Fair* of April 2000. Richard Crenna's memory of McQueen is from the *E!* documentary, Ali MacGraw's of Katharine Hepburn from *Moving Pictures*.

I'm grateful again to Howard Prouty at the Academy, and to the source at the Beverly Wilshire.

The Towering Inferno, widely, and *An Enemy of the People*, less so, are on video. The poster for the former enjoyed a brief comeback as a party political parody in the 2001 UK general election.

Chapter 9

It was among the greatest pleasures of the book to interview Harold Pinter (22 November 1999). I'm grateful to him for his dry insights into McQueen, First Artists and the non-making of *Old Times*.

Other sources included Tony Bill, Charles Champlin, Cliff Coleman, Gary Combs, Rev. Leonard De Witt, Charles Durning, Bud Ekins, Susan Ekins, Mike Fargo, the late Lew Grade, Kent James, Loren Janes, Pat Johnson, Marvin Josephson, Neile McQueen Toffel, Sammy Mason, Darla More, Don Murray, Bob Relyea, Eli Wallach and Dave Wolfe.

The late Andy Warhol, whom I met in 1983, gave me his views on McQueen.

It's again a pleasure to acknowledge Ali MacGraw's *Moving Pictures* and Neile McQueen Toffel's *My Husband, My Friend*; as well as the FBI and the Academy of Motion Picture Arts and Sciences.

Tom Horn and *The Hunter* are both on video and, periodically, television.

Chapter 10

Parting comment came from Cliff Coleman, Rev. Leonard De Witt, Bud Ekins, Hilly Elkins, Don Gordon, Loren Janes, Norman Jewison, Pat Johnson, Dean Jones, Marvin Josephson, Neile McQueen Toffel, Sammy Mason, Don Modi, Robert Relyea, Eli Wallach and Bill Wilcott.

The above-named secondary sources, most notably Grady Ragsdale Jr's *Steve McQueen: The Final Chapter*, were all used. I both interviewed William Kelley and read the material he sent me. All the usual papers, broadsheets, redtops and trades alike, were combed for McQueen's obituary.

Finally, I should mention the various McQueen websites, an inexhaustible mine of data over the last two years; and my wife Karen, who stood it all.

Index